MAJOR PLAYS OF CHIKAMATSU

NUMBER LXVI OF THE RECORDS OF CIVILIZATION:
SOURCES AND STUDIES

MAJOR PLAYS OF CHIKAMATSU

Translated by DONALD KEENE

COLUMBIA UNIVERSITY PRESS

New York

Columbia University Press
New York   Oxford
Copyright © 1961, 1990 Columbia University Press
All rights reserved

The addition to the "Records of Civilization:
Sources and Studies" of a group of translations
of Oriental historical materials, of which this
volume is one, was made possible by funds granted
by Carnegie Corporation of New York. That Corporation
is not, however, the author, owner, publisher, or
proprietor of this publication, and is not to be
understood as approving by virtue of its grant
any of the statements made or views expressed therein.

UNESCO COLLECTION OF REPRESENTATIVE WORKS—
JAPANESE SERIES
This work has been accepted in the Japanese Translations
Series of the UNESCO Collection of Representative Works,
jointly sponsored by the United Nations Educational,
Scientific and Cultural Organization (UNESCO) and the
Government of Japan.

ISBN 0-231-07414-X
ISBN 0-231-07415-8 (pbk.)

Printed in the United States of America

c 10 9 8 7 6 5
p 10 9 8 7 6 5 4 3 2 1

RECORDS OF CIVILIZATION
SOURCES AND STUDIES

EDITED UNDER THE AUSPICES OF THE
DEPARTMENT OF HISTORY, COLUMBIA UNIVERSITY

These translations are dedicated to

TSUNEARI FUKUDA

translator of Shakespeare

CONTENTS

ILLUSTRATIONS

FOREWORD

Major Plays of Chikamatsu is one of a group of publications, the Translations from the Oriental Classics, through which the Committee on Oriental Studies has sought to transmit to Western readers representative works of the Oriental traditions in thought and literature. In its volumes of source readings forming the "Introduction to Oriental Civilizations," the Committee has provided a broad selection of excerpts from influential thinkers in India, China, and Japan, discussing the great problems of their times in historical sequence. Insofar as a reading of what Asian peoples have written for their own delight and edification may give us a sympathetic insight into their alien traditions, the present series fulfills the same purpose. Where it differs from any survey, however—and differs also from drugstore anthologies which present the East always in aphorism or epigram—is that it makes major works or authors available in something more substantial than excerpts, and in accurate, readable translations prepared for the general reader as well as the scholar.

There are good reasons why these writings have not been accessible before: they are often formidable works for both translator and reader. But if we have thought them worth presenting here in spite of such difficulties, it is because the admiration in which they have been held for centuries, by both popular and sophisticated audiences in the East, compels our own attention. It is time for more of us to learn why they should have enjoyed such esteem; it is time to face the challenge and gain the rewards of conquering—or being conquered by—these imposing masters.

In Chikamatsu's case there is no single work which reveals all of his genius. His total production, however, as well as his high reputation, leave no doubt of the playwright's stature as the great master of the classical puppet and Kabuki theater in Japan. Here Professor Keene has given enough of Chikamatsu's major plays so that one need no longer draw conclusions from isolated examples. From these eleven plays one may form his own judgment of Chikamatsu's greatness, or perhaps find new criteria for doing justice to a writer who often confounds the classical Western canons of thought and art.

WM. THEODORE DE BARY

PREFACE

Chikamatsu Monzaemon (1653–1725), generally ranked as the greatest Japanese dramatist, by some estimates wrote 160 plays for the puppet and Kabuki theaters. There are doubtful attributions, and other works of slight literary importance, but no matter how we pare the list, we are left with at least thirty or forty plays of exceptional interest. I have been guided in making the present selection both by established opinion in Japan and by my own preferences. I hope that the choice is fair, though I anticipate that some admirers of Chikamatsu will not be satisfied. The severest objection may be that I have included only one history play (*jidaimono*), though plays in this category make up the bulk of Chikamatsu's literary production. Unfortunately, however, the history plays are hardest to render successfully into English, in part because they assume a knowledge of Japanese history which non-Japanese readers might be obliged to glean from lengthy footnotes. They are also much longer than Chikamatsu's domestic plays (*sewamono*), and if given greater emphasis might swell this volume to unmanageable lengths. In any case, I feel sure that the domestic plays are literarily superior to the histories.

Of the eleven plays given here, five have previously been translated into English (including two by myself). The collection by Asataro Miyamori entitled *Masterpieces of Chikamatsu* was published in 1926. For many years it afforded the only decent introduction to Chikamatsu available in a Western language, but today Miyamori's translations are no longer acceptable. The difficult passages in the texts, including Chikamatsu's most beautiful descriptions, are generally omitted or mutilated, and the translations bristle with such old-fashioned locutions as "Fair words butter no parsnips!" or "Oh, for a bare bodkin!" Nevertheless, I should emphasize the size of the debt which all Western students of the Japanese theater owe to Miyamori. Donald H.

Shively's translation of *The Love Suicide at Amijima* (1953) marked
a great step forward in our scholarly understanding of Chikamatsu. I
have chosen to make a new version of this play, because the literal
rendering favored by Mr. Shively differs so greatly from the style I
have adopted that it might not fit in with the other plays here.
As for *The Battles of Coxinga* and *The Love Suicides at Sonezaki,*
translations which I published several years ago, I am glad to have
had the opportunity to prepare entirely new versions of both. The translations in this volume are complete except as noted.

A few words are necessary concerning the rendering of names, places,
dates, and ages. I have followed throughout the Japanese order of
names, giving surname first, followed by personal name. Commoners
in Chikamatsu's day did not have surnames. Instead they used a "shop
name." Thus, the paper dealer Jihei was known as "Kamiya" (Paper
shop) Jihei, and Tokubei, the proprietor of the Kawachi-ya (Kawachi
Shop) as "Kawachiya" Tokubei. I have adopted the modern pronunciations for all names. Thus I call the city Osaka rather than Ozaka,
its pronunciation in the eighteenth century. I have also uniformly
rendered such names as Tokubei, Chūbei, and so on with a final -bei,
though at times, for special emphasis, they were given their original
pronunciation of Tokubyōe, etc. I have rendered women's names as
Ofuji, Otane, etc., though the initial *o,* a detachable honorific prefix, was
sometimes omitted.

In general I have contented myself with transcribing place names
into romanized form, but on occasion, when the meaning of the name
is important to the sense of a passage, I have translated it. For example,
the translation, "We shall bury our fame in Sunken Fields" suggests
more of the flavor of the original than, "We shall bury our fame in
Kubota." My choice of which place names to translate was necessarily
somewhat arbitrary, but I hope that readers will not be confused.

The rendering of dates is a difficult problem. In Chikamatsu's time
the Japanese observed the lunar calendar. An event which occurred in
the "first moon" should therefore probably be ascribed to February or
March rather than to January. Whenever a date is precisely given
(Chikamatsu is surprisingly exact), I have converted it to the Western
calendar. When the only indication is by the lunar month ("first
moon") I have used the following solar month (February) as the near-
est equivalent.

In the case of the ages of characters, however, I have followed the Japanese calculation, though it invariably adds at least a year to the Western reckoning. A Japanese baby, according to the traditional calculation, is one year old at birth, and a year is added to the infant's age at the next New Year, even if it was born late in the year. It is impossible to tell exactly a character's age by Western standards unless the birth date is given, but here Chikamatsu is silent. The translator might merely subtract a year from the age as given, but I have preferred to follow the Japanese numbers in order to preserve the word plays which Chikamatsu sometimes makes on the ages of his characters.

The above are relatively minor problems posed by all translations from Japanese literature of the Tokugawa period. In the case of Chikamatsu there are more fundamental difficulties. The plays in this volume were puppet plays, in which the lines for a whole scene might be recited by a single chanter. Chikamatsu was therefore not obliged to indicate which character delivered which lines. Usually the expression and the context indicate the speaker, but not always. For example, in the climactic last scene of *The Love Suicides at Amijima,* when Jihei is about to kill Koharu, two lines occur which may have been uttered either entirely by Koharu or partly by her and partly by Jihei. I have enlisted the aid of Japanese commentaries in such doubtful cases, but they sometimes disagree.

The texts of the plays, for reasons enumerated in the introduction, offer in places extreme problems of interpretation. I could not have deciphered them without the help of the existing commentaries (listed in the bibliography), but even these were often inadequate. I was fortunate to have learned Japanese friends who patiently went over the thorny spots with me, sometimes spending an hour or more over a single phrase. I am especially indebted to Professor Mori Shū of Osaka Municipal University for his careful and unselfish assistance during several blazing Kyoto summers, and to Mr. Shinoda Jun'ichi, that rarity among Japanese scholars, a prompt correspondent; to Professor Noma Kōshin of Kyoto University, the master of Tokugawa literature; to Mr. Ryusaku Tsunoda, who first initiated me into the study of Chikamatsu; to Mrs. Okumura Ayako for her wonderful hospitality in the Muhinju-an, Kyoto; and to Mr. Aoki Toshiyuki for help in infinite ways.

I wish to acknowledge also my gratitude for assistance in collecting the illustrative photographs which, I feel sure, add much to the text. I owe thanks to Mr. Takano Masami and to Chūō Kōron Sha for the frontispiece; to Professor Gunji Masakatsu for the portrait of Ganjirō in the role of Chūbei; to Mr. Yoshinaga Takao for illustrations of puppet performances; and to the Makuai Publishers for the Kabuki photographs.

My travels to Japan to obtain the help I needed were made possible by a grant from the Carnegie Corporation to the Columbia College Oriental Studies Committee. I wish here to express my gratitude for this precious support.

MAJOR PLAYS OF CHIKAMATSU

MAJOR PLAYS OF CHIKAMATSU

INTRODUCTION

In the late nineteenth century, when Japanese first became aware of the glories of Western literature, they felt impelled to discover a "Japanese Shakespeare." Their unanimous choice for this honor was Chikamatsu Monzaemon (1653–1725), an unfortunate identification from which Chikamatsu's reputation in the West has suffered since. Western readers who hope that Chikamatsu will prove a second Shakespeare are bound to be disappointed: there never lived a second Shakespeare. Chikamatsu's plays offer instead a vivid picture of a unique age in Japan, and have a special importance among the dramas of the world in that they constitute the first mature tragedies written about the common man.

One reason why comparisons between Chikamatsu and the dramatists of Europe are meaningful only intermittently is that he lived in a society virtually sealed off from the rest of the world. During the period of his career Japanese subjects were forbidden by law to journey abroad, and the only visitors to Japan were a handful of Chinese and Dutch traders carefully isolated at the port of Nagasaki. Chikamatsu never read a foreign play, and he knew nothing of the theater outside his country. Because, unlike most European dramatists, he shared no traditions with writers abroad, his plays sometimes astonish us by a modernity not encountered in the West for another century or more, and sometimes equally by a violence or an uncontrolled fantasy which we associate with a more primitive theater. But this seeming modernity or primitivity is misleading, and really means only that Chikamatsu's development in isolation did not follow the course of the drama in Europe.

Another important difference dividing Chikamatsu from European playwrights was that he wrote his major works for the puppet theater. The special demands of this theater obliged Chikamatsu to conceive his plays in a manner which sometimes weakens their literary value: spectacular scenes of mayhem or superhuman feats may be intensely exciting when seen in a puppet performance, but when read as one reads a Western play they often seem absurdly exaggerated.

Chikamatsu, however, was not merely a skillful craftsman of the puppet theater. In his domestic tragedies especially he proved that he was an artist of subtlety and imagination. But here again we are faced with a difficulty in attempting to compare his characters with those of Shakespeare, Racine, or other European dramatists. Unlike classic tragedy with its princes and princesses, Chikamatsu's domestic plays have for their heroes merchants or petty samurai whose sweethearts are apt to be prostitutes. The griefs of Jihei, the paper dealer, lack the dignity of Hamlet's; he is inevitably less a hero determining his own fate than a creature of circumstances. Though we cannot doubt the sincerity and strength of his emotions, their range is limited. Jihei's closest counterparts in the Western theater are probably found in the twentieth-century dramas of the little man whose dreams and aspirations are doomed to frustration.

The expression of Chikamatsu's plays offers similar problems. The dialogue is usually straightforward and marked by the flavor of actual speech. We might conclude from it that Chikamatsu belonged to an age of prose, but his descriptive passages, particularly the accounts of the suicide journeys of the unhappy lovers, have a complexity and intricacy of texture which equal the achievement of any Western age of poetry.

Finally, the morality in Chikamatsu's plays is often disconcertingly unlike that of Shakespeare (though perhaps not so dissimilar to certain French and Spanish dramatists). Considerations of honor may override all other sentiments; when one husband decides to kill his wife as a punishment for adultery he is encouraged by her father and brother. We may even be expected to sympathize with a man who deserts his loving wife and children to commit suicide with a prostitute.

The differences between Chikamatsu's society and that of Shakespeare's (or modern) Europe account for many features of his plays puzzling to readers hitherto familiar only with Western drama. The usages of the puppet theater, where a narrator recites not only lines for the mute puppets but also connecting descriptions, and where a certain exaggeration is necessary to impart the sentiments of living people to wooden creatures, may also be unfamiliar. I have attempted in the following pages to sketch some of the background of the plays, in the hope of clarifying points which may be troublesome to Western readers. At the same time, however, I do not wish to suggest that the plays require elaborate explanation. They should be immediately intelligible despite their occasional unfamiliarities. The matters I hope to elucidate in this introduction are of less importance to an understanding of Chikamatsu than a sensitivity to the themes of love and death which are the heart of his writings.

Chikamatsu's Career

Chikamatsu Monzaemon was born in 1653 in the province of Echizen, the second son of a minor samurai family named Sugimori.[1] In a brief account of himself written shortly before his death Chikamatsu stated, "I was born into a hereditary family of samurai but left the martial profession. I served in personal attendance on the nobility but never obtained the least court rank. I drifted in the market place but learned nothing of trade." This modest confession of failure as a samurai, noble, and merchant does not suggest how important a knowledge of these three classes was to prove in the composition of his plays.

We know little about Chikamatsu's youth. Apparently his family moved to Kyoto when he was still in his teens, and the boy served some years as a page to a noble family. At the time the nobility included patrons of the puppet theater, and Chikamatsu may have had a first meeting with some celebrated chanter in a princely mansion. His own family had literary talents, as we know from a family collection of *haiku* compiled in 1671 in which Chikamatsu's first published work appears:

Shirakumo ya   White clouds
Hana naki yama no   Cover the shame
Haji kakushi   Of the flowerless mountain.

Soon afterwards he left the household where he had been serving, and apparently stayed for a while at the Chikamatsu Temple in Ōmi

[1] See Mori Shū, *Chikamatsu Monzaemon*, pp. 12–15. Genealogical tables are reproduced in *Chikamatsu no Kenkyū to Shiryō*, pp. 57–72. Some scholars read Chikamatsu's surname as Suginomori.

Province. The sojourn may have led young Sugimori Nobumori (as he was then called) to take the stage name Chikamatsu, but this remains conjectural.[2]

Chikamatsu's career as a dramatist probably began in 1683 when, at the age of thirty, he wrote the puppet play *The Soga Successors* for the chanter Uji Kaga-no-jō. Some scholars, however, credit more than fifteen earlier, unsigned works to Chikamatsu. *The Soga Successors* was highly acclaimed, and the great chanter Takemoto Gidayū (1651–1714) used it to open his theater in Osaka in 1684. Two years later Chikamatsu wrote for Gidayū *Kagekiyo Victorious*,[3] so important a work that it is considered the first "new" puppet play.

Puppet plays of a sort go back in Japan at least as far as the twelfth century. The puppeteers, a gypsy-like people, wandered about the country, performing at festivals and wherever else there was a demand. The plays put on were probably elementary skits, perhaps incorporating legends of the shrines where they were performed. By the seventeenth century, when the puppet theater assumed much of its modern form, moralistic plays on Buddhist themes constituted the bulk of the repertory. Most puppet plays (or *jōruri*, as they were called) before *Kagekiyo Victorious* were crudely constructed and filled with stereotyped expressions. *Kagekiyo Victorious*, from its first unconventional phrases, proclaimed the appearance of a new star in the puppet theater.

Between 1684 and 1695 Chikamatsu also wrote many Kabuki plays, chiefly for Sakata Tōjūrō (1647–1709), the outstanding actor of the day. This collaboration proved so fruitful that in the next decade (1695–1705) Chikamatsu devoted his major efforts to Kabuki. From 1705 until his death in 1725, however, he wrote almost exclusively for the puppet theater. Various reasons have been suggested for Chikamatsu's final preference for the *jōruri*. In 1705 Sakata Tōjūrō was fifty-eight years old and soon to retire from Kabuki; Chikamatsu may have felt that Tōjūrō's successors were unlikely to interpret his plays as

[2] Shuzui Kenji (*Chikamatsu*, p. 29) seems disposed to accept this theory, but Mori (*Chikamatsu Monzaemon*, pp. 53–55) offers evidence that Chikamatsu's pen name was derived from his real name by plays on the Chinese characters.
[3] Translated into German by Johannes Barth in *Jubiläumsband* (Deutsche Gesellschaft für Natur- und Völkerkunde Ostasiens, 1933). *Shusse Kagekiyo* is generally believed to have been written in 1686, but Shinoda Jun'ichi argues (in "Shusse Kagekiyo no Seiritsu ni tsuite") that 1685 is correct.

skillfully. Or he may have decided that the puppet theater under Gidayū promised to be more popular in the growing city of Osaka than the Kabuki was in Kyoto. Or, as frequently has been stated, Chikamatsu may have felt dissatisfied with the liberties taken with his texts by temperamental actors and may therefore have decided to write instead for the more obedient puppets. In any case, the huge success of the puppet play *The Love Suicides at Sonezaki* in 1703 determined his future career. The announcement of his *jōruri The Mirror of Craftsmen of the Emperor Yōmei* (1705) bears the inscription "By Our Staff Playwright, Chikamatsu Monzaemon," indicating his new status. Chikamatsu moved early in 1706 from Kyoto to Osaka, the stronghold of the puppet theater.[4]

During the remainder of his career Chikamatsu devoted himself to writing two kinds of puppet plays, those treating the heroes of the distant or recent past, known as history plays (*jidaimono*), and those about the ordinary people of his own day, known as domestic plays (*sewamono*).

Chikamatsu's most successful work, the history play *The Battles of Coxinga* (1715) demonstrates his mastery of the unique possibilities of a theater of puppets. In the first act occur two moments which would be intolerable if performed realistically by actors: the first when the villain Ri Tōten gouges out his eye and offers it on a ceremonial baton to the Tartar envoy as a pledge of fealty, the second when Go Sankei performs a Caesarean operation on the dead empress in order to deliver the heir to the throne. The stylization of puppets, by making such scenes endurable, touches springs of pity and terror forbidden to actors. The second act of the same play presents a desperate encounter between the hero and a tiger. The scene when performed by actors is inevitably amusing, as the audience detects the movements of the man inside the tiger skin, but on the puppet stage a tiger is no less real than a human being, and the combat produces real excitement. The fourth act of *The Battles of Coxinga* affords a series of fantastic scenes which exploit the resources of the puppets. There are distant battles seen in visions; characters who age seven years before one's eyes; ghostly figures who vanish deliberately; and, finally, a rainbow bridge which mysteriously spans a gorge only to evaporate suddenly, sending those on it plummetting down into the abyss. These dramatic

---

[4] Mori, pp. 36–37.

effects do not necessarily contribute to the literary value of *The Battles of Coxinga,* but they account for its stunning success as entertainment. The puppet theater under the guidance of Takeda Izumo (d. 1747), who became the director of Gidayū's Takemoto Theater in 1705, was to feature in the history plays a marked increase in stage machinery (*karakuri*). Takeda Izumo's influence in this direction is so noticeable at times that many of Chikamatsu's plays must be considered as collaborative efforts.

Yet, despite their craving for spectacle, Chikamatsu's audiences responded with enthusiasm to his domestic plays. *The Love Suicides at Sonezaki,* in fact, set Gidayū's theater on its feet after a shaky financial start. This play marked Chikamatsu's first attempt to use themes from daily life as the subject of a play, though other men had occasionally experimented with such materials in Kabuki. The greetings to the public by Tatsumatsu Hachirobei (d. 1734), chief puppet operator at the first performance of *The Love Suicides at Sonezaki,* explained the circumstances of composition. "The play we are about to present, *The Love Suicides at Sonezaki,* was written as the result of a chance visit by Chikamatsu Monzaemon of Kyoto to this city. Learning of the events described in the play, and thinking that they might prove entertaining on the stage, he composed a *jōruri* on the subject for your approval. The story has already been performed in Kabuki at various theaters and has lost its novelty, but this is the first time that it is offered as a *jōruri.*" [5]

The hero of *The Love Suicides at Sonezaki* is a clerk in an oil shop, and its heroine is a prostitute. Aristotle clearly would not have considered persons of such humble station to be fit subjects for tragedy, and not for some years in Europe was a work written in which "for the first time, everyday commercial life is made the theme of a tragedy." [6] But the beauty of Chikamatsu's writing lifted his account of the love suicide of these little people from the gossip of a scandal sheet to the level of tragedy. Chikamatsu showed that their unhappy love was as worthy of our tears as the griefs of mighty princes. His audiences, given to applauding the superhuman feats celebrated in the

---

[5] *Ibid.,* p. 89.

[6] *The Oxford Companion to English Literature,* p. 316. The work referred to is *The History of George Barnwell, or The London Merchant,* a domestic tragedy in prose by George Lillo, produced in 1731.

history plays, responded to this new work because its closeness to their own lives gave the events special poignancy.

Chikamatsu continued to write both history plays and domestic plays until his death. Sections of certain history plays have remained popular favorites and are still presented as written. His domestic plays, on the other hand, have survived on the stage only in the adaptations of later men. The contemporaneity which attracted audiences to *The Love Suicides at Sonezaki* and to Chikamatsu's subsequent domestic plays lost its appeal for audiences of a later day, and the taste for the spectacular scene and the bold dramatic gesture grew ever more pronounced. Chikamatsu's domestic plays seemed pallid beside the works of such men as the second Takeda Izumo (1691–1756), each containing a scene in which a child or an adult is put to death as a substitute for another person. The audience apparently delighted especially in this moving but often inhuman theatrical device.[7]

The declining fortunes of Chikamatsu's plays on the puppet stage should not, however, be attributed solely to their overly literary qualities. Because the texts and music were coordinated with the movements of puppets operated by one man, the adoption of the three-man puppet in 1734, nine years after Chikamatsu's death, produced a disequilibrium. Chikamatsu's lines did not leave the cumbersome new puppets sufficient time to manoeuvre. Moreover, the invention of the three-man puppet whetted the appetite of the audiences for spectacular demonstrations of technique, and they were bored by plays which failed to show in a virtuoso manner the capabilities of the new puppets for both delicate and bold movements.

The same preference for the overstated and florid spread to the style of chanting. Chikamatsu had adapted his style to the demands of the successive chanters for whom he wrote, but he could not anticipate the changes after his death. The ability to utter a hysterical burst of laughter or a prolonged bout of sobbing came to be prized more highly than any subtlety of delivery. The chanters themselves neglected Chikamatsu's plays in favor of showier vehicles for their talents. As a result the music for virtually all the plays was lost and revivals today are at best an approximation of Chikamatsu's intent.

After Chikamatsu's death the distinction between history play and

[7] See Shuzui Kenji, *Giri*, p. 56. For a discussion of later adaptations of Chikamatsu's works, see Wakatsuki, *Chikamatsu Ningyō Jōruri no Kenkyū*, pp. 816–26.

domestic play tended to disappear. Combined historico-domestic works, in which scenes of martial action alternate with quieter moments in the home or brothel, became the typical form. The loose structure discernible behind a history play by Chikamatsu broke down into two or three virtually unconnected stories joined under one title. Many later puppet plays were the product of several men's efforts not always controlled by a single guiding hand. The puppet theater lost rapidly in popularity to the Kabuki at the end of the eighteenth century, and has continued to dwindle since. Puppet plays, including some by Chikamatsu, were adapted for the Kabuki stage, but here too the preference for exaggerated action was so strong that only drastically altered versions which afford moments of bravura display have remained in the repertory. Despite his high reputation, Chikamatsu's works are imperfectly known to theatergoers today.

Chikamatsu's Age

The name Genroku strictly applies only to the years between 1688 and 1703, but it is commonly used today to designate the period stretching roughly from 1680 to 1730, the most brilliant flowering of Japanese culture during the Tokugawa period. The age could boast of Ihara Saikaku (1642–93), the first great novelist since the eleventh-century Lady Murasaki; Matsuo Bashō (1644–94), the master of *haiku* poetry; and Chikamatsu Monzaemon. It was also the age of the painter Ogata Kōrin (1658–1716), of the mathematician Seki Kōwa (1642–1708), of the philosopher and statesman Arai Hakuseki (1657–1725), and of the Kabuki actor the first Ichikawa Danjūrō (1660–1704), all outstanding figures in their respective fields. The ruler of Japan through most of this period was Tsunayoshi (1646–1709), the fifth Tokugawa shogun, a man of culture and learning who turned late in life to extravagance and eccentricity. Tsunayoshi's prodigality resulted in mounting indebtedness which he attempted to relieve by devaluing the currency. After four devaluations between 1704 and 1711, silver coins were 80 percent copper. Something of the confusion and grief that such economic measures caused among the common people is reflected in the domestic plays of Chikamatsu.

The political structure of Japan during the Genroku period was a military dictatorship, the shogunate established by Tokugawa Ieyasu at the beginning of the seventeenth century. The nominal ruler of Japan, the emperor, was a recluse in Kyoto occupied chiefly with ceremonials and poetry. Chikamatsu wrote a number of history plays about ancient and medieval emperors, but apart from one mysterious reference to an amnesty in honor of the accession of a new sovereign, he never alludes to the reigning emperor in his domestic plays.[8] The real ruler of Japan was the shogun in Edo. His government, despite its military structure, was devoted to peaceful pursuits and the maintenance of the existing order.

Society was divided into four classes: the samurai, the farmers, the artisans, and the merchants. The samurai princes (or daimyo) were in absolute control of the political life in the parts of the country they held in fief from the shogun, but their subservience to the central authority was assured by compulsory residence in Edo during alternate years. Several of Chikamatsu's plays tell of the loneliness of wives left behind in their provinces while their samurai husbands are serving in Edo. Chikamatsu depicted mainly the lesser ranks of samurai who suffered the cramping restrictions of a feudalistic society without sufficient income to enjoy their privileged status as samurai.

The farmers, as the sustainers of the nation, officially ranked next below the samurai. In fact, however, their living conditions were by far the worst of the four classes, and any material improvement in their lives was frowned on by the samurai. Many left the land for work in the cities, though this practice was not sanctioned. Farmers figure rather infrequently in Chikamatsu's plays. Chūbei's father in *The Courier for Hell* is a farmer, but nothing distinguishes his sentiments from those of Chikamatsu's benevolent old men of other classes. Chūbei remarks somewhat condescendingly of an old friend that he "has an unusually chivalrous nature for a farmer." Actually, however, the morality expressed in Chikamatsu's plays is essentially that expected of the farmer class.[9] Though Chikamatsu treated mainly the merchant class in his domestic plays, he is far less interested than, say, Saikaku in describing ways of amassing a fortune or business ethics. Nor does he glorify prudence and calculation, the merchant virtues. Instead, his plays accept the unquestioning obedience and selflessness

[8] See Kitani Hōgin, *Chikamatsu no Tennō Geki*, pp. 168–72.
[9] See the stimulating article by Seo Fukiko, "Chikamatsu ni okeru Nōminteki naru mono," in *Bungaku*, June, 1951.

demanded of the farmers no less than of the samurai. One book of maxims for farmers published in 1721 declared, "Cleverness and resourcefulness are aberrations of the intellect," [10] a sentiment in which Chikamatsu, though not Saikaku, would concur. Chikamatsu's heroes are not notable for their cleverness, but in their purity of heart unencumbered by thought they closely resemble the ideal farmer.

The artisans and merchants, though officially distinguished, were usually lumped together as townsmen (*chōnin*). Their status was low, but they set the tone of Genroku culture. Some merchants amassed huge fortunes and even had daimyo for their debtors. They lived in opulence quite unlike the hard-pressed samurai or the downtrodden farmers. But the samurai on occasion demonstrated that political power remained in their hands: in 1705 the richest and most respected of the Osaka merchants, the house of Yodoya, accused of ostentatious luxury not befitting the merchant class, had its entire fortune confiscated. The apparent reason behind this action was to free certain daimyo of western Japan from their hopeless indebtedness to Yodoya, but the central government at the same time received a windfall from the fabled Yodoya wealth. The action emphasized that despite the merchants' prosperity they would be kept in their place.[11]

Nevertheless, Genroku culture belonged to the merchants. Saikaku's best novels were written about and for merchants; the *haiku* of Bashō found widest favor among the merchants; Chikamatsu's domestic plays are mainly concerned with their lives. The gay quarters, the center of town culture at the time, were intended for the merchants' pleasure, and samurai visiting them forfeited their special privileges. The rich merchants could buy the favors of the most beautiful women of the day, and a host of lesser courtesans awaited the call of less affluent men.

The theaters, associated directly or indirectly with the licensed quarters since the birth of Kabuki early in the seventeenth century, were similarly swayed by the tastes of the merchants. Though samurai and even nobles attended the theater, the chief source of income was derived from the merchant class, and ultimately their preferences prevailed. *Ukiyoe* paintings of both gay quarters and the theaters are still another example of the dominance of the arts by the townsmen.

[10] Seo, p. 61. The sentence is quoted from *Hyakushō Bunryōki*, a work of 1721.
[11] See Sheldon, *The Rise of the Merchant Class in Tokugawa Japan*, pp. 102-4.

The classes, though distinct in their functions and pleasures, were not castes. The daughters of rich merchants attracted samurai husbands, and prosperous merchants might themselves become samurai through adoption. On the other hand, samurai and farmers not infrequently became merchants, and there was a good deal more mixing of the classes than the government thought desirable. In *The Uprooted Pine* Okiku, a samurai's daughter, has married the merchant Yojibei. The failure of the marriage is blamed on the difference in class by Okiku's mother. Her father says, "My wife tried to stop the marriage when they were first engaged. She insisted that Okiku would do better to marry a samurai, even a poor one, and that if she married a businessman, no matter how rich he might be, they would never get along together." She now sees her fears justified. To this Jōkan, Yojibei's father, answers, "A samurai's child is reared by samurai parents and becomes a samurai himself because they teach him the warriors' code. A merchant's child is reared by merchant parents and becomes a merchant because they teach him the ways of commerce. A samurai seeks a fair name in disregard of profit, but a merchant, with no thought to his reputation, gathers profits and amasses a fortune. This is the way of life proper for each." In *The Love Suicides in the Women's Temple* a merchant father is against marrying his daughter to a samurai. "A horse goes with a horse, an ox with an ox, a merchant's daughter with a merchant."

Chikamatsu in these and other examples seems to be supporting the class divisions. His lack of criticism of the social hierarchy has exposed him to condemnation as "feudal" by certain modern critics, but they miss Chikamatsu's intent. He was absorbed with the problems of different kinds of men and women within each class; their particular griefs, rather than a class struggle, became the subjects of his plays.[12] This does not mean that Chikamatsu was incapable of criticism; his thinly disguised satire of the excesses of the shogun Tsunayoshi must have found a ready response in his audiences.[13] However, he chose to write in terms of both arrogant and benevolent rulers, noble and depraved samurai, rather than to deal in black-and-white characterizations of an entire class. He describes with compassion the

[12] Mori, p. 205.
[13] See Shively, "Chikamatsu's Satire on the Dog Shogun," *Harvard Journal of Asian Studies*, XVIII, 159–80.

sufferings of his ill-starred heroes and heroines, but he traces the causes to their own mistakes rather than to the ills of the age.

The Plays

Chikamatsu's first important work, *Kagekiyo Victorious* (1686), was the direct descendant of earlier plays on the same theme and is not typical of the mature Chikamatsu. It nevertheless affords a tantalizing glimpse of the kind of dramatist he might have become if he had been writing for a different theater.

Kagekiyo Victorious opens unpromisingly (save for the language) with a disjointed and ineptly written first act, hardly superior to the discredited old *jōruri*. The defeated warrior Kagekiyo first appears as he takes leave of his new wife, Lady Ono. In the next scene he attempts in the guise of a workman to kill his mortal enemy Minamoto no Yoritomo at the Tōdaiji in Nara. His plot is foiled by Yoritomo's omniscient adviser Shigetada, and the act concludes as Kagekiyo, pursued by innumerable soldiers, escapes by flying off (literally!), taking advantage of his supernatural powers. So far little suggests the dramatist that Chikamatsu was to become. In the second act, however, we are suddenly confronted with a genuine human being, Kagekiyo's rejected mistress Akoya. Kagekiyo, retreating from Nara, visits Akoya in Kyoto and asks her to shelter him. She upbraids him for his alliance with Lady Ono, but Kagekiyo, lying, swears that Lady Ono means nothing to him. "How could you suppose that I would love anyone else in the world but you?" he asks. Akoya, at length convinced, answers in womanly tones, "I love you too much. That's why we have these quarrels. At least this one has been harmless." Her flare-up of jealousy, her quick assent to what she wants to believe, and the naturalness of her speech after so much bombast, create a startling impression of reality.

The following day Kagekiyo leaves for the Kiyomizu Temple, intending to spend a week in prayer before the statue of Kwannon, a deity he has always worshiped with special devotion. During Kagekiyo's absence Akoya's brother Jūzō arrives and attempts to persuade her to disclose Kagekiyo's whereabouts. Jūzō hopes for a reward if he can turn in Kagekiyo. Akoya spurns him, declaring that betrayal would be dishonorable. Jūzō counters sarcastically, "Such concern over your reputation! Such a high-minded refusal to take profit! You sound like an old-fashioned samurai! But those ways have gone quite out of fashion these days." [14] He insinuates that Kagekiyo is in love with Lady Ono. Akoya refuses to listen, but at that moment a courier delivers a tender note from Lady Ono for Kakekiyo. Akoya is stung into fury. She betrays Kagekiyo, though she regrets it the next instant. Kagekiyo's enemies at once attack him at Kiyomizu Temple, but he repulses them and escapes, again over the treetops.

In the third act Lady Ono travels to Kyoto in search of her husband. She is captured by the enemy and subjected to terrible tortures in the hope of forcing her to reveal her husband's whereabouts. But Ono, unlike the courtesan Akoya, cannot be coerced into betrayal. The cruel soldiers, having dangled her in vain from a tree, now propose to torture her by fire, when Kagekiyo appears. He allows himself to be bound, rather than cause Ono further pain.

The fourth act shows us Kagekiyo's prison. He is kept under extraordinarily severe bonds in his stoutly built cell. His hair is braided in seven strands fastened down in seven directions. His legs are pinioned by huge logs dragged down from the mountains by seventy-five men, his knees are clamped in iron chains. Kagekiyo, unperturbed, prays to Kwannon. Akoya appears with their two children and begs his forgiveness. Kagekiyo, scorning her, asserts that he would kill her if he had even a single finger free. Akoya tries to explain how jealousy drove her to her act, but Kagekiyo will not hear her. He announces that he no longer recognizes the two little boys as his own children. Akoya in an amazing speech declares that she intends to kill her sons and herself before Kagekiyo's eyes. She quickly stabs one boy, but the other one, terrified, runs to Kagekiyo and begs to be saved. Akoya urges the boy to let her kill him, and he reluctantly consents. Akoya stabs her son and then herself.

Soon afterwards Jūzō returns to taunt the captive, but Kagekiyo with a mighty effort bursts his bonds and slays his tormentor. He starts off, only to remember that Lady Ono and her father will suffer if he escapes. He returns to his cell and takes up his chains.

In the fifth act we are informed that Kagekiyo has been beheaded by his enemies. Shigetada, however, insists that Kagekiyo is still alive.

[14] This passage is of course anachronistic; for someone in Chikamatsu's day these virtues might be "old-fashioned," but in Kagekiyo's day the samurai code had hardly yet evolved.

The others investigate and discover that the severed head of Kagekiyo, publicly displayed at a Kyoto street corner, has been mysteriously replaced by a head of the goddess Kwannon. Priests from the Kiyomizu Temple rush up to report that the head of the statue of Kwannon is missing and the body covered with blood. Kagekiyo's enemies realize that a miracle has occurred: the deity Kwannon, whom Kagekiyo so faithfully worshiped, has substituted her head for his. Yoritomo, impressed by the miracle, spares Kagekiyo's life and grants him a province. Kagekiyo gracefully accepts. The play ends with rejoicing over the reconciliation of the two enemies, praise for Kagekiyo, and prayers for the prosperity of the country.

Kagekiyo Victorious contains many elements inherited by Chikamatsu from his predecessors, but also shows the germs of the future development of his art. The crudities are all too obvious. A concession to popular tastes or a desire to demonstrate the superhuman talents of the puppets may have inspired the scenes of Kagekiyo flying or the horrible tortures of Lady Ono. The miraculous substitution of Kwannon for the condemned man is a variation on a familiar theme of the old *jōruri* which survived long after Chikamatsu. The happy ending (in complete disregard of history) again reflects old *jōruri* traditions. *Kagekiyo Victorious* outstrips its predecessors, however, in the character of Akoya. She figures only briefly in the play, but her actions have a tragic intensity. The scene in which she betrays Kagekiyo is crudely set: it is highly improbable that Kagekiyo would have informed his present wife of plans to stay in Kyoto with his old mistress, and the arrival of the fatal message at the critical moment strains credulity. But Akoya's fury has genuine accents, and the weakness which led to betrayal is entirely plausible.[15] In her next encounter with Kagekiyo she rises to Medea-like emotions. The moment when her second son tries to escape his mother's knife is almost unbearably moving. After this superb scene the rest of the play is anticlimax.

If Chikamatsu had been writing for a different theater and audience *Kagekiyo Victorious* might have served as the first sketch for a true *Medea,* the study of a woman driven by jealous love to betray her husband and kill her children. But though *Kagekiyo Victorious* estab-

[15] In earlier plays on the subject Akoya betrays Kagekiyo in the hope of advancing the fortunes of her sons, and Kagekiyo kills the children. (See Watsuji Tetsurō, *Nihon Geijutsu Shi Kenkyū,* I, 511–18.)

lished Chikamatsu's reputation, it did not accord with prevalent tastes. The puppet theater was not intended to represent characters with life-blood in their veins. The various personages on the stage and their sentiments were normally no more than instruments of the plot and the stage machinery.[16] Akoya killing her children gives vent to individual passions; she might have been more easily intelligible to Chikamatsu's audiences if her actions had been inspired by feudal loyalty rather than by a desire to expiate her guilt. Chikamatsu created many figures who died for love, but none asserts individuality as strikingly as Akoya in her few short scenes. Her violence has a Western intensity which was out of place in the puppet theater.

The oldest play by Chikamatsu still read and performed today is *The Love Suicides at Sonezaki* (1703). The story is simple. A shop clerk, Tokubei, in love with a prostitute, Ohatsu, refuses to marry the girl chosen for him by his uncle. He must therefore return to his uncle the dowry money which his mother has already accepted. He obtains it with difficulty, but is at once persuaded by his friend Kuheiji to lend it for a few days. Kuheiji tricks Tokubei out of the money. In despair over the consequences Tokubei and Ohatsu commit suicide.

The Love Suicides at Sonezaki, at first so acclaimed, came to seem insufficiently engrossing to audiences accustomed to Chikamatsu's later domestic plays; when it was revived in 1717 Chikamatsu was obliged to add a few scenes to increase the complexity. The characters at first blush also seem to lack distinction. Tokubei is an ineffectual, excessively naïve young man, as little like a hero as Kagekiyo is like a human being. Ohatsu, unlike the passionate Akoya, seems little more than a warm-hearted prostitute. Kuheiji is a paper-thin villain. What is most striking in these characters is the contrast with their predecessors. Chikamatsu deliberately created a weakling hero, an insignificant young man who foolishly trusts a wicked acquaintance. Even Tokubei's decision to share in a lovers' suicide is guided by the stronger will of his sweetheart. Ohatsu too is by no means the stereotyped courtesan of earlier plays. A more normal treatment of the prostitute—the faithless woman who sells her favors to any man—was the heroine of Saikaku's *The Woman Who Spent Her Life in Love* (1686).[17] Sai-

[16] Katō Junzō, *Chikamatsu Shishō no Kenkyū,* p. 36.
[17] Partial translation by Howard Hibbett in *The Floating World in Japanese Fiction,* pp. 154–217.

kaku's heroine, devoted to her career, would never have dreamt of committing a lover's suicide with one of her customers. Ohatsu is not only loyal to Tokubei but urges him to the death in which she joins him. Chikamatsu showed in *The Love Suicides at Sonezaki* that a courtesan, even one of low rank, is capable of true feelings. By the magic of his poetry, particularly in the *michiyuki* (or lovers' journey), he managed to transform most unpromising figures into the hero and heroine of tragedy.

Most of Chikamatsu's subsequent love-suicide plays conformed to the general scheme of this early work. Lesser characters were strengthened; the motivation of the suicides (so inadequate at Sonezaki) was made more compelling, particularly for the women; and the role of the villain was given greater depth by lending ambiguity to his motives or imparting a comic interest. But the general outline of the story—the young man of the townsman class who falls in love with a prostitute, is unable to "ransom" her (buy her contract from the owner), and eventually joins her in death—remained the same.

This similarity in plot structure of the love-suicide plays, though modified by the enrichments of Chikamatsu as his art matured, inevitably makes his literary production seem less varied than that of other important dramatists. In general, variety in the Japanese drama is more likely to occur in details—minor twists of the plot—than in over-all structure. Chikamatsu did not expect to surprise his audiences; the titles "The Love Suicides at—" if nothing else give away the conclusions. The developments in the plots of his play were often known in advance from the scandal sheets sold in the wake of interesting double suicides, and Chikamatsu was not even averse to borrowing his material from another man's play.[18] His desire was to create affecting characters from the scraps of information gleanable in the accounts of their suicides, and to transform the pathetic or sometimes sordid details into literature. We know from more factual descriptions of the love suicides treated in his plays that Chikamatsu invented characters and motivations, made fickle courtesans into paragons of fidelity, and otherwise altered at will his materials. His audiences, for whom the love-suicide plays were merely an interlude in a full day's entertainment at the theater, did not demand that they be

---

[18] His last domestic play, *Shinjū Yoigōshin* (1722), is generally believed to have been much influenced by a rival work by Ki no Kaion, produced a few weeks earlier.

of entirely new conception, but welcomed such changes as Chikamatsu imparted to the familiar stories. Within the established framework of his suicide-plays Chikamatsu was able to achieve the kind of variety he sought, as a reading of *The Love Suicides at Sonezaki* and *The Love Suicides at Amijima,* works of roughly similar plots, will show.

The Love Suicides at Sonezaki not only reflected its time but actually started a vogue for love suicides, as we may gather from a publication of the following year, *The Great Mirror of Love Suicides.* In the succeeding years the number of such suicides, both in life and on the stage, rapidly multiplied, until in 1722 the government banned plays with the word *shinjū* (love suicides) in the title. It has been suggested that the unsettling effect of the devaluation of the currency in 1706 contributed to this grim craze, and various natural disasters during the next few years (earthquakes, volcanic eruptions, conflagrations) undoubtedly drove many people to despair.[19] The brilliance of the gay quarters did not flicker, and the theater was better attended than ever, but society could poorly afford these luxuries. The inadequate motivation of the suicides of Tokubei and Ohatsu becomes more convincing in the later love-suicide plays, where financial difficulties play the largest part.

The Love Suicides at Sonezaki was so popular that Chikamatsu refers back to this success in four later domestic plays. *Two Picture-Books of Love Suicides* (1706) bears the subtitle "The Third Anniversary of Sonezaki: Another Dream at the Temma House," and otherwise assumes a knowledge of the earlier work. *Two Picture-Books* is interesting also because of its first paragraphs, a description of the opening of the 1706 season at the Takemoto Theater in Osaka with Chikamatsu's play *The Mirror of Craftsmen of the Emperor Yōmei.*

The Year of the Bird, 1705, will soon be a memory—the 1706 season is about to begin. Long before dawn today the wooden portals were thrown open, and while lamplight still glittered on the first frost, lively shouts of "The show is about to start!" drew eager customers young and old into the theatre. The morning sun has peeped out now, and soon the puppet show, sprung from the seeds of poetry, the age-old art of the ageless Land of the Rising Sun, will move Heaven and Earth, stir the gods and demons, and make the ties between husband and wife or the heart of the fierce

[19] See Yokoyama Tadashi, "Chikamatsu Shinjū Jōruri no Tenkai," *Kokugo to Kokubungaku,* May, 1958, pp. 58–59.

warrior soft as—"Jam buns!" "Cakes!" "Matches!" "Programs!": even the vendors' cries have a lilt at the puppet theatre. "Get your authorized libretto!" "Check your hats and umbrellas!" "Cushions! Cushions!" [20]

The Mirror of Craftsmen, a history play with spectacular effects, marked the first collaboration of Chikamatsu (the staff playwright), Takeda Izumo (the director of the company), and the chanter Gidayū. It has been called the dividing line between Chikamatsu's early and mature work.[21]

Chikamatsu's next important domestic play, *The Drum of the Waves at Horikawa,* introduced new themes. Here he deals not with merchants but with members of the samurai class. Otane, the wife of a samurai serving in Edo with his master, consoles her loneliness with drink. One night, under the influence of liquor (and provoked by another man), she has an affair with her stepson's teacher. The guilty pair, once sober again, are thoroughly ashamed of their transgression, but powerless to change what has happened. When Otane's husband returns from Edo he learns that his wife is pregnant. He forces her to commit suicide. Later the husband and members of the family track down the teacher and kill him.

In the background of this play and two others which Chikamatsu wrote on similar themes was the law that a wife guilty of adultery was to be executed. The severity of this law reflected the double standard which permitted men openly to indulge in the pleasures of the licensed quarters while relegating their wives to neglected homes. The wife was helpless: jealousy itself was grounds for divorce, and the divorced woman was disgraced. The wife who endured without complaint the indignities inflicted by her husband was generally praised. Yet, as Chikamatsu realized, the wife who like Otane was left for a year at a time while her husband served in Edo, or who like Osan in *The Love Suicides at Amijima* waited in a lonely house for her husband to return from nights in the gay quarters, could not be satisfied merely with people's praises for her chastity. She missed her husband sexually, as Chikamatsu tells us with a directness unusual in Western tragedies.

---

[20] The play in which this passage appears was produced in the third moon of 1706. It describes the opening of a play in the eleventh moon of 1705, which marked the first performances of the 1706 season, as it was considered.

[21] Takano Masami, "Chikamatsu Sakuhin no Bunruihō," *Kokugo to Kokubungaku,* March, 1948, p. 21.

The wife in all three plays dealing with adultery is portrayed as an unwitting victim of circumstances. Otane is horrified to discover what she has done while intoxicated; Osai in *Gonza the Lancer* is unjustly accused of improper relations with her intended son-in-law; Osan in *The Almanac of Love*[22] sleeps with Mohei because she thinks he is her husband. Nevertheless, a twentieth-century reader may wonder if Chikamatsu has not drawn these characters in such a manner as to suggest that the three wives subconsciously desired the guilty relations in which they became so unhappily embroiled. Otane, so lonely that she plays games with herself pretending that her husband has returned, is attracted to the polite drum teacher from the capital. She yields to her weakness for saké, perhaps dimly aware that drunkenness will permit a lapse in conduct. Or so it would seem, though it may be dangerous to attempt to analyze Chikamatsu's characters in such terms.

The case of Osai is even more intriguing. Her extravagant praise for Gonza's qualities, her joking remark that she would take him if her daughter did not (an incredible joke, considering the penalties if anything improper were suspected of her!), her impatience at Gonza's hesitation, and her excessive jealousy at the news of Gonza's engagement to another woman, all indicate an interest in the young man which goes beyond a mother-in-law's solicitude. Then, when the two are falsely accused by the villainous Bannojō, Osai proposes to Gonza that they become lovers in fact, ostensibly so that her husband Ichinoshin will have grounds for killing them. Her reasoning is so tortuous that we can only suspect that she is the prey of emotions not fully understood even by herself: she wants to sleep with Gonza before she dies. The complexity of Otane and Osai makes the "adultery plays" among Chikamatsu's most affecting works.

Chikamatsu's other domestic plays have been divided by Japanese scholars into various categories. In some the hero (Chūbei in *The Courier for Hell* or Sōshichi in *The Girl from Hakata*) commits a crime for which he and his sweetheart will be punished; in some the leading character (like Yojibei in *The Uprooted Pine*) is driven out of his mind by grief. Chikamatsu wrote only one murder play (*The Woman-Killer*), fewer than we would expect, considering the popularity of this subject in the Kabuki of the time.

[22] Translated by Asataro Miyamori in *Masterpieces of Chikamatsu*, pp. 65–106.

The later history plays treat events ranging in time from the legendary Age of the Gods to a year-old rebellion in Formosa. The characters include gods, emperors, generals, priests, and commoners. They would thus seem to possess a wider range than the domestic plays, but our enjoyment of them is marred by their extravagances and the inconsistent characterization of the different personages.

Subjects, Characters, and Performances of the Domestic Plays

The domestic plays all share one feature, their contemporary setting. Most of them depict incidents which occurred only a month or two before, and they are made vivid by the use of the actual names of persons involved. Sometimes delicacy obliged Chikamatsu to alter slightly the names and occupations of the chief figures in the different tragedies, a practice to which he openly alludes ("I hear that Kōzaemon's done a play on the murder of the oil merchant's wife, except he's changed it to a saké merchant").[23] Few in the audience can have been deceived by such thin disguises. References are frequently made also to well-known entertainers of the day, to theaters, teahouses, and brothels. Chikamatsu quotes snatches from popular songs, and even inserts what appear to be advertisements for familiar products.[24] In contrast to the improbable activities of the history plays, the allusions in these dramas must have brought smiles of recognition to the spectators.

Chikamatsu's domestic plays have been called "living newspapers." Like newspapers they reflect society,[25] but only a small part of it. There were happy and prosperous merchants in the Genroku era, as we know from other sources, but in Chikamatsu's plays they do not figure prominently. On the other hand, he did not choose to depict hard-working men, devotedly pursuing their trades, who go bankrupt nevertheless because of economic conditions which they are

[23] From *The Woman-Killer;* see below, p. 466.

[24] In *The Girl from Hakata,* for example, he mentions the brand name of a kind of *geta* which Kojorō was especially requested to buy.

[25] In *Ikudama Shinjū,* the hero goes to see Chikamatsu's earlier work, *The Love Suicides at Sonezaki,* performed on the Kabuki stage, and remarks, "Kabuki plays and *jōruri* are the mirrors of good and evil men" (Tadami Keizō, *Chikamatsu Jōruri-Shū* [*Yūhōdō Bunko* edition], III, 70).

powerless to control. Jihei (in *The Love Suicides at Amijima*) has trouble meeting his monthly bills because he neglects his business in order to frequent the gay quarters. Yojibei (in *The Uprooted Pine*) is equally remiss in his affairs. Presumably they would have both been prosperous if they had applied themselves to their work. Chikamatsu does not moralistically hold these men up as dreadful examples. They were the men he chose for his "headlines," and the virtuous, prudent merchants of the day were dismissed with scant mention.

The heroes of the domestic plays are mainly young men of undiluted emotions but weak characters. Tokubei in *The Love Suicides at Sonezaki* is the model for the rest. We can only marvel at his guilelessness in trusting so obvious a villain as Kuheiji. He cuts a pathetic figure when, battered by Kuheiji and his henchmen, he tearfully assures the bystanders of his innocence or when he furtively creeps up to Ohatsu for comfort. Only at the end of the play does he acquire the stature of a tragic figure.

Jihei, the hero of *The Love Suicides at Amijima,* is another Tokubei, but with two women in his life, one of the first tragic heroes to be caught in this predicament. He loves and needs both the prostitute Koharu and his wife Osan. Desperate at the thought of losing either, he can think of no solution. The tragedy develops in terms of the relations between the two women while Jihei lies in a stupor of self-pity. His problem is hopeless. Even if he somehow managed to ransom Koharu, how could he keep her and Osan under one roof? Threatened with the loss of Osan, he implores his father-in-law not to take her away. He promises to reform. But his assurances, though sincere, do not convince us; he lacks the moral courage to renounce his past and become a worthy husband and father. Only in death can the purity and strength of his emotions find adequate expression.

Chūbei in *The Courier for Hell,* like Tokubei a young man in love with a courtesan, is more striking if only for his foolishness. He breaks the seal on a packet of three hundred pieces of gold, though he knows that it will bring disaster to everyone involved. His only justification is the necessity he feels to assert his honor before half a dozen prostitutes. In this total disregard of reason he may stir us more than either Tokubei or Jihei. The audience sympathizes with Chūbei because his emotions are untainted by considerations of personal advantage: this is the indispensable characteristic of a hero of one of Chikamatsu's do-

mestic plays. Hachiemon, Chūbei's friend, though reasonable and
solicitous for his friend's welfare, exerts little appeal on the audience
if only because his emotions are less direct than Chūbei's. Characters
in other domestic plays are redeemed by emotional purity even if
guilty of contemptible actions (like Yosaku in *Yosaku from Tamba*).
Excessively powerful and conflicting emotions drive Yojibei in *The
Uprooted Pine* to madness, without his forfeiting the audience's
admiration and respect.

Chikamatsu neither praises nor condemns his heroes for their hopeless involvement with prostitutes (even when they have wives and
children), nor for the other follies of which they are guilty. The
deplorable circumstances he describes are necessary for the flower
within them—an expression of emotional purity—to bloom.[26] If Jihei
had never met Koharu, if he had remained a devoted husband and
hard-working businessman, the world would never have known of
his capacity for deep emotion, nor of the nobility of spirit that Osan and
Koharu display out of love for him. The failings of Jihei not only
move us to tears, but enable us to see that these humble people—a
paper dealer, his wife, and a prostitute—possess true grandeur. Jihei
is clearly no Aristotelian hero inspiring our pity and terror by a flaw
in his otherwise superior nature; he is weakness itself, but his emotional intensity, which leads him to abandon his wife and children,
kill his beloved, and finally commit suicide himself, somehow wins
our hearts if not our minds.

The heroes of some other domestic plays are so ambivalent that we
may even dislike them until their final display of emotional integrity.
Yosaku is a samurai reduced to working as a horse driver because of
his offenses in the past. He has betrayed his wife, failed to repay his
master's kindness, and abandoned his child. We learn that he gambles
and has recently lost at a game in which the stake was a horse belonging to another man. In order to raise some money, Yosaku persuades
the boy Sankichi to steal. When Koman, the courtesan who is Yosaku's
sweetheart, protests, Yosaku answers, "You're too timid. If the kid
is caught, the worst he'll get is a spanking." Sankichi is in fact caught,
and eventually condemned to be executed. Yosaku and Koman, overcome with remorse, decide they must kill themselves. On their journey

---

[26] Compare the remarks by Motoori Norinaga on *The Tale of Genji* (in Tsunoda, *et al.*,
Sources of the Japanese Tradition, pp. 532–35).

to death Yosaku emerges as a tragic figure, and his transgressions, though not forgiven, seem to have made possible at last the flowering of his true nature.

Gonza (of *Gonza the Lancer*) is an even less likely hero. In the opening scene we learn of his affair with the girl Oyuki and his promise to marry her. He swears that he will live up to this obligation: "If ever I am untrue to what I say, may I fall that instant head-first from my horse and be trampled to death!" But in the very next scene Gonza, discovering that the secret traditions of the True Table tea ceremony can only be transmitted within the tea master's family, agrees to marry his master's daughter. Again he swears: "If I should violate this oath, may I never again wear armor on my back, may I be slashed to bits by Ichinoshin's sword, and may my dead body be exposed on the public highway!" This time his vow is to be granted. Later in the play, much against his desires, he becomes involved in an adulterous relationship with Osai. He has no reason to die with her, but he generously sacrifices himself, and in the end is slashed to bits by the sword of her husband, Ichinoshin. The calculating, deceitful Gonza, more like the villains of *The Love Suicides at Sonezaki* or *The Love Suicides at Amijima* than like Tokubei or Jihei, is redeemed by his most wicked act.

One of Chikamatsu's most unusual heroes is Kumenosuke in *The Love Suicides at the Women's Temple*. At the outset of the play he is a novice at the Buddhist monastery on Mount Kōya. His love affair with Oume, a girl who lives in a nearby town, is accidentally discovered, bringing the violent rebuke of the High Priest and Yūben, a senior priest with whom Kumenosuke has apparently had intimate relations. Kumenosuke, appalled by their censure, asks Yūben, "If I break with Oume, will you be as kind and loving as before?" "Of course," answers Yūben. Kumenosuke shows himself—for the moment at least—willing to give up his sweetheart in favor of his "brother," but on second thought he bursts into tears. "What's the matter now?" Yūben asks. "What shall I do if Oume refuses to break with me?" Surely there could be no less heroic figure.

Kumenosuke is driven from Mount Kōya. In the second act he joins Oume at her father's house. Oume, unlike her lover, is high-spirited and sharp-tongued. In a movingly erotic scene the two beautiful, foolish young people express their physical longing for each other. The act

ends in farce as they escape under cover of darkness, thwarting the
suitor Oume was supposed to marry. In the third act the same young
man who was so abjectly willing to yield his sweetheart and the same
harum-scarum girl who nearly got caught in bed with her lover while
her fiancé grumbled downstairs develop mysteriously but convincingly
into the hero and heroine of tragedy. They journey together to the
Women's Temple, where Kumenosuke kills Oume and soon afterwards commits suicide. The action of the entire play occurs in about
ten hours, but there is infinitely more character development than,
say, in *The Battles of Coxinga,* which extends over seven years. As we
read *The Love Suicides in the Women's Temple* we are persuaded
that the miracle of their transformation is possible. We are even prepared to believe that heroes compounded of such fragile materials are
more affecting than the Aristotelian hero with a solitary tragic flaw.

Chikamatsu's style enabled him to arouse our sympathy for heroes
whose faults he did not conceal. One literary device he employed in
this process was the *michiyuki,* or lovers' journey, a typical feature
of puppet plays (and, in briefer form, of Nō plays before them). The
michiyuki has often been dismissed as mere ornamentation, a pretext
afforded Chikamatsu to demonstrate his virtuosity in elaborating
puns on the names of places passed by the lovers on their journey. The
michiyuki certainly displays Chikamatsu's verbal dexterity, but it
was also indispensable in creating the tragic atmosphere of his final
scenes. Tokubei and Ohatsu, a shop clerk and a prostitute when they
creep out from the Temma House, acquire in the *michiyuki* the
dignity of a man and woman about to meet death. As they travel,
the narrator magically describes their emotions in one of the loveliest
passages of Japanese literature. "Farewell to this world, and to the
night farewell. We who walk the road to death, to what should we
be likened? To the frost by the road that leads to the graveyard,
vanishing with each step we take ahead: how sad is this dream of a
dream!" Any lovers described in such language must command our
sympathy.

Yosaku, the dissolute samurai, stirs us when he tells Koman during
their *michiyuki,* "Three years ago, companions on a secret journey
to Ise, we first exchanged vows. In the middle of Kushida Town I
confessed my deep love—I can still see the purple hat you wore. I
won your heart and we swore by the Jizō of Seki to be true. Though

I bore the heavy burden of love, my feet went lightly as I drove my horse; my heart was buoyant, expansive as Toyoku Plain. How heart-breaking that now, while yet I delight in you, have not had my fill, this autumn frost has overtaken us. Tonight will be our last. We shall bury our fame in Sunken Fields." This passage, true to the traditions of the *michiyuki,* is imbedded with puns on the places passed (some of which are translated above), but it was obviously not meant merely to satisfy a craving for fancy language. It transmits to us the belief that despite Yosaku's failings the strength of his love is worthy of our sympathy and respect.

Our understanding of the characters, then, at times results less from their words or actions than from the manner in which Chikamatsu describes them in the *michiyuki.* Tokubei, hitherto portrayed as a weakling, has found the strength to kill his beloved by the time he reaches the wood of Sonezaki. Kumenosuke becomes an adult on his journey and is ready for the man's business awaiting him at the end. Yosaku, remembering his past, recovers his lost dignity.

Chikamatsu's ability to create complex, evolving characters was no asset in the puppet theater, and the domestic plays, though popular at their first showings, did not long remain in the repertory. In the puppet theater only a limited number of heads was available to represent the different parts. There was a definite head for a male, middle-aged, good character and another for a male, middle-aged, bad character. As soon as the puppet came on stage the audience knew (as clearly as from the mustache on the villain in an old-fashioned Western) whether he was a good or a bad man. One may imagine the audience's uneasiness, then, when despite the handsome features of a "male, young, good" puppet head, Gonza acts in a decidedly am-biguous manner. Yosaku and Hachiemon must also have puzzled Chikamatsu's audiences, as we can gather from the revised versions of the plays (the work of later men). In these versions, the ones still performed today, the ambiguous characters are made clearly bad or clearly good, or else they are omitted altogether. Neither the puppet theater with its fixed categories of heads, nor the Kabuki with its traditional stylized gestures allowed for subtlety. It was possible for good characters to pretend to be wicked and later to reveal their true natures, or for evil characters to repent at the end, but there was no room for characters whose natures were not immediately apparent.

The present repertory of the puppet theater is largely from the century after Chikamatsu's death. With the exception of *The Battles of Coxinga*, a work whose swift action and varied stage effects have always been popular, no play by Chikamatsu is regularly performed as written, though there is a movement to return to the original texts.

The Plays as Literature

Chikamatsu did not intend his plays as armchair dramas, but each of them was printed in many different editions during his lifetime, both for amateur chanters who wished to practice the parts and for readers who enjoyed Chikamatsu as a poet.[27] Chikamatsu's valedictory verse, written just before his death, seems to anticipate that his future fame will rest with these printed texts rather than with stage performances of his works.

Sore zo jisei	This will be my valediction:
Saru hodo ni sate mo	"In the meanwhile . . . Well, then,
Sono nochi ni	Afterwards . . ."
Nokoru sakura ga	If on the cherry tree left behind
Hana shi niowaba	The blossoms are fragrant.

This cryptic verse, which incorporates some of the stereotyped phrases of the old *jōruri* ("In the meanwhile . . . Well, then, afterwards . . ."), has been interpreted as meaning, "If my works, marked by the phrases of the old theatre, surviving in books printed from blocks of cherry wood, are praised by later men [are fragrant], they will be my valediction." [28] If this interpretation is correct, Chikamatsu hoped that his plays, living on in books after his death, would express his message to the world.

Chikamatsu clearly took great pains with his texts, not only to ensure their success on the stage, but to give them literary distinction. He told a friend, "From the time that I began to write *jōruri* . . . I have used care in my writing, which was not true of the old *jōruri*. As a result the medium has been raised one level." [29] Chikamatsu's care shows

[27] In *Shinjū Yoigōshin* one character offers another this choice of reading matter: *Essays in Idleness*, *The Love Suicides at Amijima*, or *The Tale of the Heike* (Tadami, *Chikamatsu Jōruri-Shū*, III, 542). See also the article by Yokoyama Tadashi "Chikamatsu no Maruhon," *Kaishaku to Kanshō*, January, 1957.

[28] Watsuji, pp. 447–49.

[29] Tsunoda, *et al.*, *Sources of the Japanese Tradition*, p. 447.

itself in the extraordinarily varied language of the plays, which ranges from pungent colloquialisms to flights of obscure allusion. The dialogue is often close to the language that was actually spoken, but it is nevertheless a stage language marked by artificial and sometimes difficult constructions. The most beautiful passages, however, are not those of the dialogue but the descriptions narrated by the chanter. A narrator was needed in the puppet theater to supplement the circumstances of a speech or action for the puppets whose facial and bodily expression was necessarily limited, but he was otherwise called upon to announce the setting of an act, often a marvelously vivid evocation of the gay quarters or a festival; to race through such virtuoso passages as the *tsukushi*, a kind of catalogue (of plants, place names, shells, textiles, bridges, and even love suicides) in which puns on the items in the catalogue make up an independent meaning; and to intone the fantastically complicated tissues of puns, allusions, and half-finished phrases of the *michiyuki* and descriptive interludes. The spectators in Chikamatsu's day, though poorly educated, were able to grasp the general meaning of Chikamatsu's intricate passages. Familiarity with earlier plays and with the songs and stories of the day was assumed, and if the audience could not analyze precisely all the word plays in the *michiyuki*, they could at least relax in the stream of beautiful language, carried along by the musical accompaniment.

Chikamatsu's style is almost endlessly complex. We can only marvel that he could produce such astonishing textures of language in the few weeks that normally sufficed for writing an entire play. Perhaps the most characteristic feature of his style is the *engo*, or related word. Chikamatsu seems never to have chosen a word without considering its overtones and pursuing them. For example, the opening description of Tokubei in *The Love Suicides at Sonezaki* runs literally, "A handsome man who has piled up spring after spring can drink one cupful of peach wine and his willow hair is also loosened." In English this does not sound like much, but the original, a chain of *engo*, produces a delightful effect. Chikamatsu, having said "piled up spring after spring" (meaning, to spend a number of years), chooses for "handsome man" an *engo*, the word *hinaotoko*, "doll man," referring to a doll at the spring festival. This festival is known also as the peach-blossom festival, thus occasioning the next *engo*, "peach wine". Willow twigs with fresh young leaves also decorate this festival; hence, the *engo* "willow" as an adjective for Tokubei's hair, long and elegant as willow shoots. Finally, the verb *toku,* used for "to loosen", is at the same time the shortened form of Tokubei's name. A translation obviously cannot do justice to this richness of language; one can merely suggest the central ideas.

Another verbal device employed by Chikamatsu was the *kakekotoba,* or "pivot word". The *kakekotoba* changes in meaning depending on the preceding and following words. Thus, *toku* with the preceding word "hair" means to "loosen the hair", but with the following verb "to be called" it means Toku, the hero's name. Chikamatsu's best pivot words (this is not one) add a complexity to the lines, as if a word set the author thinking of ideas related by sound rather than meaning.

Chikamatsu delighted also in head rhymes and end rhymes. Sometimes these are merely repetitions of the same syllables in successive phrases, as in *asamashiya asagizome.* Sometimes they are more extended, as in *fūfu ni furumino furugasa ya,* with its repetitions of the initial *fu.* End rhyme, though usually avoided in Japanese poetry, also contributes to the music of Chikamatsu's texts. *Kussame, kussame, murazame, murazame to* is a simple example; a more complicated one is *oyakata no mokkyaku ari, waga shinjō no mekkyaku ari, ikyaku mo majiri* (Some have parents or masters to pay for their pleasures, others destroy their own fortunes, and bankrupts mingle among them), where the repetition of the rhyme in *kyaku* heightens the rhythm and sense.

The basic rhythm of the plays is the alternating line of seven syllables and five syllables. Chikamatsu heaped scorn on playwrights who stretched their lines to fit exactly into this pattern, resorting to meaningless particles to fill out the syllable-count.[30] Chikamatsu's dialogue is usually in prose, and he reserves the regular seven-five, seven-five beat for the descriptive passages.

The following excerpt from *Gonza the Lancer* illustrates many of Chikamatsu's stylistic devices:

Shinki shinki no/ sorarinki/ tsui ni wa ga mi no/ adashigusa/ yo no soshirigusa/ ukikusa ni/ Asaka no mizu no/ moresomete/ Sasano no tsuyu to/ okimadoi/ nemadoi ayumi/ madoite wa . . . (Her mind gave itself to the tortured, pointless jealousy that finally became the seed of her undoing and the slander of the world. The water of Asaka

[30] Keene, *The Battles of Coxinga,* p. 94.

trickled away from this rootless plant, to mingle confusedly with the dew of bamboo fields. Awake or in dreams or in aimless wandering . . .).

This excerpt is cast exactly in alternating lines of seven and five syllables. Internal rhyme is used extensively (*shinki* . . . *rinki;* adashi-*gusa,* soshiri*gusa,* uki*kusa;* oki*madoi,* ne*madoi,* mado*i*te). The words in *kusa* (plant) suggest a brief *tsukushi,* or catalogue. *Ukikusa* (a rootless plant) leads to the *engo* of *mizu* (water), and this in turn to its *engo, tsuyu* (dew). The name Asaka (that of Osai's husband) refers also to the famous marsh of Asaka, another watery *engo,* while the dew settles on Sasano (bamboo field), which is Gonza's surname. *Okimadoi* (rising uncertainly) contains the pivot word *oki,* used with the preceding word "dew" to mean "to settle".

These complexities (and there are more) occur in about one line of printed text. Chikamatsu's virtuosity in such passages dazzles us. His dialogue, on the other hand, can be absolutely unadorned. The bareness of the dialogue reflects Chikamatsu's conviction that the social stations of characters must be revealed in their speech. He seems to have felt that a shop assistant would converse in straightforward prose, rather than in poetry, and we have such lines as these by Chūbei to his beloved: "You look a mess. Here, tighten your sash." Shakespeare was apparently less convinced of this point; the sergeant in *Macbeth,* presumably not an eloquent or cultured man, declares, "As whence the sun 'gins his reflection/ Shipwracking storms and direful thunders break . . .". We accept this language from a sergeant as a convention of Shakespeare's theater, but Chikamatsu, writing for a theater in which far greater demands were otherwise made of the audience's imaginative powers, preferred realism in the dialogue of his domestic plays. His sergeants, if any appeared, would have talked like sergeants.

Chikamatsu gave great care to the subtle differences in speech depending on the speaker's class in society and the person addressed.[31] He uses no less than thirteen different levels of politeness for the female characters. Because his plays have no stage directions, it is sometimes necessary to rely on the degree of honorifics to determine who is speaking to whom. In the following brief excerpt three levels of politeness reveal the person addressed: *To lady:* "I'm honored that you have

[31] See the article by Mashimo Saburō, "Chikamatsu no Sakuhin ni mirareru Joseigo," *Kokugo to Kokubungaku,* October, 1959.

come. Would you perchance be from Osaka?" *To lady's servant:* "Please come in and fan madame." *To her own servant:* "Bring some tea." [32]

Chikamatsu did not make much use of individual or regional peculiarities of speech. Almost all his characters use the same stage language of the Osaka-Kyoto area. Occasionally a man is marked by his localisms; the samurai Honda Yasazaemon in *Yosaku from Tamba* uses the familiar Edo exclamation *saa,* and Kezori in *The Girl from Hakata* introduces Nagasaki words into his long monologues. Chikamatsu, though familiar with all classes of society in Osaka and Kyoto, seems not to have known much else of Japan, and he failed to create local color for Matsue, Hamamatsu, or other parts of the country he treated. Chikamatsu's interest in relations tended to be vertical rather than horizontal; though he was at pains to distinguish the speech of a shop assistant from an owner, or a second rank courtesan from a great courtesan, his various Tokubeis, Jiheis and Yoheis talk much alike.[33]

Structure of the Plays

Most of Chikamatsu's history plays are in five acts, probably in keeping with the number of plays presented in a Nō program.[34] The history plays generally lack a sense of unity of time, scene, or even plot. Thirty or forty years may elapse in the course of a work; even a relatively well-knit play like *The Battles of Coxinga* extends over six or more years and requires nineteen different settings. The looseness of the times and places of the action favored diffuseness and complexity; subplots are almost independent of the main story, and each act tends to stand on its own. In *The Battles of Coxinga* only one character who appears in the first act is seen again until the fourth act. In *The Snow Maiden* (1705) several unrelated stories are arbitrarily joined; though the play contains only three acts, no character in the first act reappears in the second.

Each act of a history play was normally built around a familiar

---

[32] *Uzuki no Momiji* (Tadami, *Chikamatsu Jōruri-Shū,* II, 180).

[33] Compare what Gerald Brenan says of Lope de Vega: "It was typical of the popular nature of his genius that he showed little interest in the moral qualities that differentiate people: his characters are built on the way of life or profession" (*The Literature of the Spanish People,* p. 207).

[34] See Keene, *The Battles of Coxinga,* pp. 27, 86.

situation.[35] A self-sacrificing suicide, the killing by a father of his own child in place of his master's child, the inspection of the severed head of an enemy general, the separation of a mother and child, the appearance of a vengeful spirit or a madwoman—any one of these afforded the puppets or the Kabuki actors with superb moments. The audience, relaxed for a whole day at the theater, looked up from its food and drink for the highlights. Because unity of plot was not important, plays after Chikamatsu's death tended to be sprawling affairs in many acts, any one of which could be presented separately. Today at the puppet or Kabuki theater a program often consists of five acts from five different plays.

The spectacular *karakuri* effects in the puppet theater, or the magnificent posturing and resounding delivery in the Kabuki theater are provided by history plays rather than by the more sophisticated domestic tragedies. This may explain why Chikamatsu continued, even after his artistic triumphs with his domestic plays, to devote the major part of his efforts to the composition of implausible, disjointed histories. It is true that some of the later works in this form show insights that we recognize from the domestic plays, but their structure remains flawed, and the scenes of artistic merit are lost in a farrago of disparate elements. Presumably the history plays were what Chikamatsu's audiences really wanted despite the popularity of some of his domestic plays. Rather than marvel at Chikamatsu's attachment to the former, we might better admire his success with the somber themes of his true tragedies.

Credit for the development of the domestic play should probably be shared by Chikamatsu with Gidayū. Between 1703 and 1714 (the year of Gidayū's death) Chikamatsu wrote sixteen of his twenty-four tragedies. In the following decade, at the height of his powers, he wrote only half as many. We might like perhaps to imagine that Chikamatsu wrote the history plays only in order to give himself the leisure to compose works which meant more to him, but little evidence supports such a view. During 1716, while *The Battles of Coxinga* was enjoying its record-breaking run of seventeen months, he did not feel moved to write a single play. In 1718, a more normal year, he wrote four, including *The Uprooted Pine, The Girl from Hakata,* and two of his best

[35] Utsumi Shigetarō (in *Ningyō Jōruri to Bunraku,* p. 151) distinguishes twenty such situations.

history plays. Probably Chikamatsu did not consider one type of play more elevated than the other.

Nevertheless, as readers two hundred and fifty years later, we cannot fail to be impressed by the superior craftsmanship of the domestic plays. Unlike the amorphous histories, these tragedies approach unity in time, place, and action. Both *The Love Suicides at Sonezaki* and *The Love Suicides in the Women's Temple* take place in less than twenty-four hours. Usually only one setting is needed for each act in a domestic play. Above all, the action in the domestic plays is unified. If there is a subplot, as in *Yosaku from Tamba,* it is carefully joined to the main story. Unlike the all but independent acts of the history plays, those in the domestic plays are so closely linked that sometimes Chika-matsu seems to have intended them to be played without interruption. The last words of one act frequently tie directly to the opening words of the following act. Of course, we need not insist that all tragedies be fitted to the Procrustean bed of the three classical unities, but in a work so closely derived from daily life as the domestic play these unities in-crease the tension and the sense of tragedy.

The formal structure of the domestic play is simpler and more orderly than that of the history play. The first act presents a problem, the second sees its crisis, and the final act shows us the resolution in the death of the characters or their miraculous deliverance. The *michiyuki,* a purely ornamental feature of the history plays, acquires in the domes-tic plays a structural function. Not only does it lend tragic stature to the characters, in the manner already described, but its dreamlike atmos-phere provides a welcome contrast to the realism of the other scenes.

Unlike that of the history plays, the conclusion of a domestic play is generally reached logically, perhaps because Chikamatsu worked back-wards from the conclusions in writing these plays. When he learned, say, of a smuggler who committed suicide on apprehension by the po-lice, it may have set him wondering, "But why did he become a smug-gler in the first place?" and so on. In the history plays the requirement of a happy ending could easily lead the whole play into blatantly un-historical conclusions; in the domestic plays the occasional implausible ending seems hastily tacked on in order to make the work per-formable at New Year or some other felicitous occasion. The fact that we find some endings in the domestic plays unconvincing is in itself a sign of their superior merit; in the history plays no ending is more or less convincing than another.

Chikamatsu's success in evolving the tight dramatic structure of such a work as *The Love Suicides at Amijima* was not to be matched in Japan for another two hundred and fifty years.

Morality of the Plays

The greatest obstacle to the enjoyment of Chikamatsu by a Western reader is undoubtedly his morality. The chief elements of this morality were *giri* (obligation) and *ninjō* (human feelings), generally depicted as warring with each other. The meanings of *giri* varied considerably according to the circumstances. It might mean obligation to members of one's own family, to fellow townsmen, to one's class, or to society at large, or refer to something closer to the abstract concept of honor. *Ninjō* represented the human sentiments balancing the austere ideals of *giri*.

In *The Love Suicides at Amijima* Koharu is obliged by her *giri* to Osan as a woman to give up Osan's husband. Later, Osan in turn is moved by *giri* to Koharu, and urges her husband to ransom Koharu, though she knows it can only lead to her own unhappiness. Jihei and Koharu in their final moments together talk not of their love but of their *giri* to Osan, and they make elaborate arrangements to die in separate places so as not to offend her.

These examples of *giri* may seem strained; other examples are positively exasperating. In the last scene of *The Courier for Hell,* for instance, Magoemon yearns for a glimpse of his son's face, but he decides that it is not possible. To look at his son, a criminal, would be shirking his *giri* to society. He starts away, only to turn back and ask Umegawa, "What do you think? Would there be any harm in my seeing him?" She answers, "Who will ever know? Please go to him." But Magoemon decides this time that *giri* to Chūbei's adopted family in Osaka does not permit him to look at a son with whom he has formally severed all ties.[36]

Giri among samurai takes even stronger forms. Shigenoi (in *Yosaku from Tamba*) must reject her long-lost son because of her *giri* to the

---

[36] See Shuzui Kenji, *Giri,* pp. 18–19.

princess she serves; if it is known that the princess's governess has a son who is a horse driver, the princess will be disgraced. A sense of *giri* leads Yura in *The Drum of the Waves of Horikawa* to taunt her brother for his failure to fulfill his obligations as a samurai by killing his wife. Her brother eventually meets the requirements of *giri* only to break down and reproach his family, "If you think so much of your mother, sister, or sister-in-law, why didn't you beg me to spare her life? Why didn't you suggest that she put on Buddhist robes and become a nun?"

In the history plays *giri* assumes its most extravagant forms. In the first act of *The Battles of Coxinga* Ri Tōten gouges out his eye, apparently out of *giri* to the Tartar benefactors of China. Go Sankei, though abused and trampled on by the foolish Ming emperor, retains such a strong sense of *giri* that he kills his own infant son and substitutes it for the imperial child whom he has safely delivered. In the third act Kanki is torn by conflicting kinds of *giri*, which are resolved only when his wife, equally sensitive to *giri*, commits suicide. *Giri* then compels Coxinga's mother to vindicate the honor of Japan by killing herself.

Even more extreme instances of *giri* occur in plays by Chikamatsu's successors. In Takeda Izumo's *Prince of the Great Pagoda* (1723), Saitō Tarozaemon causes the deaths of his son-in-law and his daughter, beheads his grandchild, and finally cuts off his own head, all out of *giri* to the Prince of the Great Pagoda.[37]

Giri, however, is frequently softened by *ninjō*, the tenderer feelings. In *The Woman-Killer* Yohei's mother, a woman of samurai origin, follows the dictates of *giri* in disinheriting her son, but we soon discover that *ninjō* has made her steal money to give her wayward child. Sōshichi's father in *The Girl from Hakata* is prevented by *giri* from looking at his son, a smuggler, but he breaks a hole in the wall big enough for his hand to pass through, and offers Kojorō a cup of water. In *The Almanac of Love* Osan's parents, happily unlike the parents of Osai in *Gonza the Lancer*, trust in their daughter's chastity, and with *ninjō* help her to escape.

Giri untouched by *ninjō* may seem inhuman. It suggests at times the sense of *gloire* in Racinian tragedies with its stern insistence on reason

[37] *Ibid.*, pp. 26-27.

and duty.[38] *Giri* denies the individual's right to be happy at the expense of society. In so doing it preserves society, as *ninjō* unchecked by *giri* must eventually destroy it.

Many Western readers find the manifestations of *ninjō* even harder to take than those of *giri*. Killing one's child to save the child of one's master makes a kind of sense, unspeakable though the act is, but abandoning one's children in order to commit suicide with the woman one loves somehow seems contemptible. Koharu abandons her old mother, doing piece work in a back alley, in order to die with Jihei; Koman gives Yosaku her money and runs away with him, though she knows this means the return of her father to a terrible dungeon. The human feelings which dictate such actions seem reprehensibly self-indulgent, and make us appreciate better the selflessness of *giri*.

But of course we are not meant to consider the actions of the characters in coldly rational terms. "All for Love, or the World Well Lost" might be the title of most of Chikamatsu's domestic plays, and his audiences agreed to this principle, though it meant shutting their eyes to the unfortunate consequences. The sniveling Jihei is, objectively, unmanly, yet we are expected to sympathize with this unfortunate creature, the prey of an overpowering love. Chikamatsu wanted us to feel that despite Jihei's sense of *giri*, which gives dimension to this display of *ninjō*, he is no match for his love. In the end, the strength of this love, which brings him to suicide, will assure him of salvation and Buddhahood.

Religion

Buddhism provides the religious background to the plays as Confucianism, with its insistence on *giri*, provides the ethical basis. The characters in most of the plays are believers in Amida Buddhism, the chief tenet of which is that faith in the bodhisattva Amida's saving grace will enable the believer to be reborn in paradise. The invocation *Namu Amida Butsu* is frequently on the lips of the characters, especially when faced with death. Other Buddhist doctrines which figure in the plays include the notion that causes from a previous existence have their effects in the present existence. Brief passages from the holy writings of

[38] See Francis Fergusson, *The Idea of a Theater*, p. 74.

Buddhism are quoted, and there are descriptions of such popular religious practices of the day as mass excursions to the temples of
Kwannon. However, Chikamatsu's characters evince surprisingly little
real piety. It does not occur to Tokubei and Ohatsu (or the other unfortunate lovers) to spend their lives in prayer instead of committing
suicide. Organized religion is sometimes harshly portrayed, as in the
account of the priests on Mount Kōya in *The Love Suicides in the
Women's Temple*. In *The Courier for Hell* old Magoemon says,
"Some people go to the temples for the sermons, but if they are cruel
here, in their hearts, they might just as well not go." At the end of
the play, when he thinks that his son has escaped, he cries out in joy,
"I owe this to Amida's grace. I must go to the temple again immediately and offer my thanks to the Founder. How happy and grateful
I am!" The next instant, however, a voice proclaims the news of the
arrest of Chūbei and Umegawa, as if in denial of Magoemon's faith in
prayer.

Only rarely is reference made to the specific religious beliefs of the
characters. In *Kasane-izutsu* Tokubei and Ofusa are about to depart on
their suicide journey. Ofusa suggests that they commit suicide before
the gate of a temple belonging to the Lotus (Nichiren) sect. Tokubei
agrees, but on reflection realizes that there is a difficulty.

TOKUBEI: You belong to the Lotus sect, and I to the Pure Land. I'm
not sure that we'll be together after we die if our prayers are different.
I'll change my sect so that we can stay together. Recite the Invocation of
the Sutra Name for me. Hurry.

NARRATOR: He joins his hands in prayer. Ofusa is lost in tears that well
up despite her.

OFUSA: Instead of asking me to join the Pure Land sect, you have been
converted to the Lotus! How happy you make me! Forgive me for having
forced you to it. Your conversion must have been brought about by my
recitation of the Sutra Name a thousand times each day for the past five
years.

The above passage makes clear that doctrinal differences did not un-
duly sway the characters. Regardless of the sect, the lovers who committed suicide hoped to be reunited after death. The present world, as
texts of the Pure Land sect in particular insist, is a place of suffering, and
only the future life—rebirth in Amida's paradise, the Pure Land—affords
the possibility of happiness. Suicide was not condoned, but no canon

against self-slaughter made the lovers hesitate on their final journey. Though their deaths are pathetic they are also filled with joy and confidence in eternal life together on one lotus in the garden of Amida.

Shintō, the Way of the Gods, the native Japanese religion, also figures in the plays, chiefly in the numerous mentions of the sacred dignity of the Grand Shrine of Ise. In *The Battles of Coxinga* the Shintō gods vouchsafe miracles to help the restoration of the Ming. Their importance in the play, however, is patriotic—emphasizing the mysterious strength of Japan—rather than religious.[39] Mediums, faith healers, and other persons connected with Shintō appear in some of the plays. Chikamatsu accepts their powers as he accepts ghosts, will-o'-the-wisps, and other evidences of the supernatural, though he paints some individuals in unflattering terms. Superstitions in Chikamatsu almost invariably turn out to be true, and bad luck is often presaged by violations of superstitious taboos.

Conclusion

A detailed examination of Chikamatsu's time, his language, his religious beliefs, and any other aspect of his work one might choose unfortunately tends to make his plays seem more remote and difficult than when approached without preparation. This, however, is largely true also of Shakespeare, or any other dramatist of the past. We accept the witches in *Macbeth* without worrying too much about Elizabethan demonology, but if we pursued this subject seriously we might become aware of a greater gap between our society and Shakespeare's than we had first supposed. Without research we may sometimes interpret words or sentiments incorrectly, lending them an excessively modern meaning, but in the end such mistakes may become our final truths. Careful study of the text seems to show that Hamlet should be portrayed by a portly, bearded gentleman, rather a dandy, but we no doubt will cling to the image of a thin, beardless, disheveled hero. In the case of Chikamatsu the danger is grave that some readers may be turned away from him by the fear that his society was too remote, his language untranslatable, and his morality alien. Years devoted to a

[39] In the sequel, *The Latter Days of Coxinga*, Kanki denounces Coxinga for his excessive fondness for Japanese ways (including Shintō), and Coxinga is finally obliged to leave the mainland of China for Formosa.

study of these problems would, of course, make Chikamatsu easier. Yet anyone who approaches his masterpieces with an open mind will discover that something important comes through the difficulties, a voice which speaks with human accents about human problems. Across the centuries and the barriers of language and custom we recognize our brothers and ourselves.

THE LOVE SUICIDES
AT SONEZAKI

First performed on June 20, 1703. The suicides described in this play took place on May 22, 1703. Chikamatsu was stirred by them to compose his first domestic tragedy. *The Love Suicides at Sonezaki* has sometimes been criticized for the excessive simplicity of its plot, but it remains one of Chikamatsu's finest works, if only for the poetry in the love journey. Chikamatsu in 1717 added a few scenes to lend the play greater complexity, and perhaps to satisfy a demand that the villain be punished, but the directness of the earlier version appeals more to modern readers and spectators. In the present translation the 1703 text has been used, except that the opening scene, consisting chiefly of an enumeration of the thirty-three temples of Kwannon in the Osaka area (with a pun on each name), is omitted. The scene, virtually unrelated to the remainder of the play, contains no dialogue.

The play, perhaps because Chikamatsu had not yet determined the form of the domestic tragedy, is not divided into acts.

Cast of Characters
TOKUBEI, aged 25, employee of a dealer in soy sauce
KUHEIJI, an oil merchant
HOST of Temma House
CHŌZŌ, an apprentice
CUSTOMER of Ohatsu
TOWNSMEN
OHATSU, aged 19, a courtesan
HOSTESS
COURTESANS
SERVANTS

*Scene One: The grounds of the Ikudama Shrine in Osaka.
Time: May 21, 1703.*

NARRATOR:

This graceful young man has served many springs
With the firm of Hirano in Uchihon Street;
He hides the passion that burns in his breast
Lest word escape and the scandal spread.
He drinks peach wine, a cup at a time,
And combs with care his elegant locks.
"Toku" he is called, and famed for his taste,
But now, his talents buried underground,
He works as a clerk, his sleeves stained with oil,
A slave to his sweet remembrances of love.
Today he makes the rounds of his clients
With a lad who carries a cask of soy:
They have reached the shrine of Ikudama.

A woman's voice calls from a bench inside a refreshment stand.

OHATSU: Tokubei—that's you, isn't it?[1]

NARRATOR: She claps her hands, and Tokubei[2] nods in recognition.

TOKUBEI: Chōzō, I'll be following later. Make the rounds of the
temples in Tera Street and the uptown mansions, and then return to
the shop. Tell them that I'll be back soon. Don't forget to call on the
dyer's in Azuchi Street and collect the money he owes us. And stay
away from Dōtombori.[3]

NARRATOR: He watches as long as the boy remains in sight, then lifts
the bamboo blinds.

TOKUBEI: Ohatsu—what's the matter?

NARRATOR: He starts to remove his bamboo hat.

OHATSU: Please keep your hat on just now. I have a customer from
the country today who's making a pilgrimage to all thirty-three temples of Kwannon. He's been boasting that he intends to spend the
whole day drinking. At the moment he's gone off to hear the imper-

---

[1] His face is covered by a deep wicker hat, commonly worn by visitors to the gay
quarters.
[2] The pronunciation of the name given in the text is Tokubyōe, but I have followed the
more normal modern pronunciation.
[3] A street in Osaka famed for its theaters and houses of pleasure.

sonators' show,[4] but if he returns and finds us together, there might be trouble. All the chair-bearers know you. It's best you keep your face covered.

But to come back to us. Lately you haven't written me a word. I've been terribly worried but, not knowing what the situation might be in your shop, I couldn't very well write you. I must have called a hundred times at the Tamba House, but they hadn't any news of you either. Somebody—yes, it was Taichi, the blind musician—asked his friends, and they said you'd gone back to the country. I couldn't believe it was true. You've really been too cruel. Didn't you even want to ask about me? Perhaps you hoped things would end that way, but I've been sick with worry. If you think I'm lying, feel this swelling!

NARRATOR: She takes his hand and presses it to her breast, weeping reproachful and entreating tears, exactly as if they were husband and wife. Man though he is, he also weeps.

TOKUBEI: You're right, entirely right, but what good would it have done to tell you and make you suffer? I've been going through such misery that I couldn't be more distracted if Bon, New Year, the Ten Nights, and every other feast in the calendar came all at once. My mind's been in a turmoil, and my finances in chaos. To tell the truth, I went up to Kyoto to raise some money, among other things. It's a miracle I'm still alive. If they make my story into a three-act play, I'm sure the audiences will weep.

NARRATOR: Words fail and he can only sigh.

OHATSU: And is this the comic relief of your tragedy? Why couldn't you have trusted me with your worries when you tell me even trivial little things? You must've had some reason for hiding. Why don't you take me into your confidence?

NARRATOR: She leans over his knee. Bitter tears soak her handkerchief.

TOKUBEI: Please don't cry or be angry with me. I wasn't hiding anything, but it wouldn't have helped to involve you. At any rate, my troubles have largely been settled, and I can tell you the whole story now.

My master has always treated me with particular kindness because

---

[4] Within the precincts of the Ikudama Shrine were booths where various types of entertainment were presented. The impersonators mimicked the speech and posture of popular actors.

I'm his nephew. For my part, I've served him with absolute honesty. There's never been a penny's discrepancy in the accounts. It's true that recently I used his name when I bought on credit a bolt of Kaga silk to make into a summer kimono, but that's the one and only time, and if I have to raise the money on the spot, I can always sell back the kimono without taking a loss. My master has been so impressed by my honesty that he proposed I marry his wife's niece with a dowry of two *kamme*,[5] and promised to set me up in business. That happened last year, but how could I shift my affections when I have you? I didn't give his suggestion a second thought, but in the meantime my mother —she's really my stepmother—conferred with my master, keeping it a secret from me. She went back to the country with the two *kamme* in her clutches. Fool that I am, I never dreamt what had happened.

The trouble began last month when they tried to force me to marry. I got angry and said, "Master, you surprise me. You know how unwilling I am to get married, and yet you've inveigled my old mother into giving her consent. You've gone too far, master. I can't understand the mistress's attitude either. If I took as my wife this young lady whom I've always treated with the utmost deference and accepted her dowry in the bargain, I'd spend my whole life dancing attendance on my wife. How could I ever assert myself? I've refused once, and even if my father were to return from his grave, the answer would still be no."

The master was furious that I should have answered so bluntly. His voice shook with rage. "I know your real reasons. You've involved with Ohatsu, or whatever her name is, from the Temma House in Dōjima. That's why you seem so averse to my wife's niece. Very well—after what's been said, I'm no longer willing to give you the girl, and since there's to be no wedding, return the money. Settle without fail by the twenty-second of the month and clear your business accounts. I'll chase you from Osaka and never let you set foot here again!"

I too have my pride as a man. "Right you are!" I answered, and rushed off to my village. But my so-called mother wouldn't let the money from her grip, not if this world turned into the next. I went to Kyoto, hoping to borrow the money from the wholesale soy sauce dealers in the Fifth Ward. I've always been on good terms with them. But, as ill luck would have it, they had no money to spare. I retraced

[5] A measure of silver, worth about one thousand dollars.

Ohatsu rebukes Kuheiji (smoking to the right); at the same time she uses her foot to ask Tokubei (below the porch) if he wishes to die with her.

(OHATSU: *Yoshida Eiza II, operator;* TOKUBEI: *Yoshida Tamao, operator;* KUHEIJI: *Yoshida Tamaichi II, operator*)

Tokubei presses Ohatsu's foot to his throat as a sign that he is resolved to die.

(OHATSU: *Nakamura Senjaku;* TOKUBEI: *Nakamura Ganjirō II*)

my steps to the country, and this time, with the intercession of the whole village, I managed to extract the money from my mother. I intended to return the dowry immediately and settle things for once and for all. But if I can't remain in Osaka, how shall I be able to meet you?

My bones may be crushed to powder, my flesh be torn away, and I may sink, an empty shell, in the slime of Shijimi River. Let that happen if it must, but if I am parted from you, what shall I do?

NARRATOR: He weeps, suffocated by his grief. Ohatsu, holding back the welling tears of sympathy, strengthens and comforts him.

OHATSU: How you've suffered! And when I think that it's been because of me, I feel happy, sad, and most grateful all at once. But please, show more courage. Pull yourself together. Your uncle may have forbidden you to set foot in Osaka again, but you haven't committed robbery or arson. I'll think of some way to keep you here. And if a time should come when we can no longer meet, did our promises of love hold only for this world? Others before us have chosen reunion through death. To die is simple enough—none will hinder and none be hindered on the journey to the Mountain of Death and the River of Three Ways.[6]

NARRATOR: Ohatsu falters among these words of encouragement, choked by tears. She resumes.

OHATSU: The twenty-second is tomorrow. Return the money early, since you must return it anyway. Try to get in your master's good graces again.

TOKUBEI: I want to, and I'm impatient to return the money, but on the thirteenth of the month Kuheiji the oil merchant—I think you know him—begged me desperately for the money. He said he needed it only for one day, and promised to return it by the morning of the eighteenth. I decided to lend him the money since I didn't need it until the twenty-second, and it was for a friend close as a brother. He didn't get in touch with me on the eighteenth or nineteenth. Yesterday he was out and I couldn't see him. I intended to call on him this morning, but I've spent it making the rounds of my customers in order to wind up my business by tomorrow. I'll go to him this evening and settle everything. He's a man of honor and he knows my predicament. I'm sure nothing will go wrong. Don't worry. Oh—look there, Ohatsu!

[6] Places in the Japanese afterworld.

NARRATOR:

"Hatsuse is far away,
Far too is Naniwa-dera:
So many temples are renowned
For the sound of their bells,
Voices of the Eternal Law.
If, on an evening in spring,
You visit a mountain temple
You will see . . ." [7]

At the head of a band of revelers

TOKUBEI: Kuheiji! That's a poor performance! [8] You've no business running off on excursions when you haven't cleared up your debt with me. Today we'll settle our account.

NARRATOR: He grasps Kuheiji's arm and restrains him. Kuheiji's expression is dubious.

KUHEIJI: What are you talking about, Tokubei? These people with me are all residents of the ward. We've had a meeting in Ueshio Street to raise funds for a pilgrimage to Ise. We've drunk a little saké, but we're on our way home now. What do you mean by grabbing my arm? Don't be rowdy!

NARRATOR: He removes his wicker hat and glares at Tokubei.

TOKUBEI: I'm not being rowdy. All I ask is that you return the two *kamme* of silver I lent you on the thirteenth, which you were supposed to repay on the eighteenth.

NARRATOR: Before he can finish speaking, Kuheiji bursts out laughing.

KUHEIJI: Are you out of your mind, Tokubei? I can't remember having borrowed a penny from you in all the years I've known you. Don't make any accusations which you'll regret.

NARRATOR: He shakes himself free. His companions also remove their hats.[9] Tokubei pales with astonishment.

TOKUBEI: Don't say that, Kuheiji! You came to me in tears, saying

---

[7] A passage from the Nō play *Miidera*, here quoted mainly because the first word, "Hatsuse," echoes the name Ohatsu in the preceding line. The last words similarly point to the arrival of Kuheiji. Most of this passage would be sung not by a single chanter but by a chorus, as in a Nō play.

[8] Tokubei, relieved to see Kuheiji, at first teases him about his singing of the Nō passage, but his words have an undertone of criticism of Kuheiji's past behavior.

[9] Readying themselves to come to Kuheiji's defense.

that you couldn't survive your monthly bills,[10] and I thought that this was the kind of emergency for which we'd been friends all these years. I lent you the money as an act of generosity, though I needed it desperately myself. I told you that I didn't even require a receipt, but you insisted on putting your seal to one, for form's sake. You made me write out a promissory note and you sealed it. Don't try to deny it, Kuheiji!

NARRATOR: Tokubei rebukes him heatedly.

KUHEIJI: What's that? I'd like to see the seal.

TOKUBEI: Do you think I'm afraid to show you?

NARRATOR: He produces the paper from his wallet.

TOKUBEI: If these gentlemen are from the ward, I am sure that they will recognize your seal. Will you still dispute it?

NARRATOR: When he unfolds the paper and displays it, Kuheiji claps his hands in recollection.

KUHEIJI: Yes, it's my seal all right. Oh, Tokubei, I never thought you'd do such a thing, not even if you were starving and forced to eat dirt. On the tenth of the month I lost a wallet containing the seal. I advertised for it everywhere, but without success, so as of the sixteenth of this month, as I've informed these gentlemen, I've changed my seal. Could I have affixed the seal I lost on the tenth to a document on the thirteenth? No—what happened was that you found my wallet, wrote the promissory note, and affixed my seal. Now you're trying to extort money from me—that makes you a worse criminal than a forger. You'd do better, Tokubei, to commit out-and-out robbery. You deserve to have your head cut off, but for old times' sake, I'll forgive you. Let's see if you can make any money out of this!

NARRATOR: He throws the note in Tokubei's face and glares at him fiercely in an extraordinary display of feigned innocence. Tokubei, furious, cries aloud.

TOKUBEI: You've been damned clever. You've put one over on me. I'm dishonored. What am I to do? Must I let you take my money brazenly from me? You've planned everything so cleverly that even if I go to court, I'm sure to lose. I'll take back my money with my fists! See

[10] I have converted all dates to the Western calendar, but the dates in the lunar calendar correspond to the end of the third moon. Kuheiji needs the money to pay end-of-the-month bills.

here! I'm Tokubei of the Hirano-ya, a man of honor. Do you follow me? I'm not a man to trick a friend out of his money the way you have. Come on!

NARRATOR: He falls on Kuheiji.

KUHEIJI: You impudent little apprentice! I'll knock the insolence out of you!

NARRATOR: He seizes the front of Tokubei's kimono and they grapple, trading blows and shoves. Ohatsu rushes barefoot [11] to them.

OHATSU (to townsmen): Please everybody, stop the fight! He's a friend of mine. Where are the chair-bearers? Why don't they do something? Tokubei's being beaten!

NARRATOR: She writhes in anguish, but is helpless. Her customer, country bumpkin that he is, bundles her forcibly into a palanquin.

CUSTOMER: It won't do for you to get hurt.

OHATSU: Please wait just a moment! Oh, I'm so unhappy!

NARRATOR: The palanquin is rushed off, leaving only the echoes of her weeping voice.

Tokubei is alone; Kuheiji has five companions. Men rush out from the nearby booths and drive them all with sticks to the lotus pond.[12] Who tramples Tokubei? Who beats him? There is no way to tell. His hair is disheveled, his sash undone. He stumbles and falls to this side and that.

TOKUBEI: Kuheiji, you swine! Do you think I'll let you escape alive?

NARRATOR: He staggers about searching for Kuheiji, but he has fled and vanished. Tokubei falls heavily in his tracks and, weeping bitterly, he cries aloud.

TOKUBEI (to bystanders): I feel humiliated and ashamed that you've seen me this way. There was not a false word in my accusation. I've always treated Kuheiji like a brother, and when he begged me for the money, saying he'd never forget it as long as he lived, I lent it to him, sure that he'd do the same for me, though the money was precious as life, and I knew that without it tomorrow, the twenty-first, I'd have to kill myself. He made me write the note in my own hand, then put his seal to it. But it was a seal which he had already reported as lost, and now he's turned the accusations against me! It's mortifying, in-

---

[11] In her agitation she fails to slip on her *geta*. We must suppose that her country customer has returned during the dialogue between Tokubei and Kuheiji.

[12] This pond may still be seen today at the Ikudama Shrine.

furiating—to be kicked and beaten this way, dishonored and forced to my knees. It would've been better if I had died while smashing and biting him!

NARRATOR: He strikes the ground and gnashes his teeth, clenches his fists and moans, a sight to stir compassion.

TOKUBEI: There's no point in my talking this way. Before three days have passed I, Tokubei, will make amends by showing all Osaka the purity at the bottom of my heart.

NARRATOR: The meaning of these words is later known.

TOKUBEI: I'm sorry to have bothered you all. Please forgive me.

NARRATOR: He speaks his apologies, picks up his battered hat and puts it on. His face, downcast in the sinking rays of the sun, is clouded by tears that engulf him. Dejectedly he leaves, a sight too pitiful to behold.

Scene Two: Inside the Temma House.
Time: Evening of the same day.

NARRATOR:
>The breezes of love are all-pervasive
>By Shijimi River,[13] where love-drowned guests
>Like empty shells, bereft of their senses,
>Wander the dark ways of love
>Lit each night by burning lanterns,
>Fireflies that glow in the four seasons,
>Stars that shine on rainy nights.
>By Plum Bridge,[14] blossoms show even in summer.
>Rustics on a visit, city connoisseurs,
>All journey the varied roads of love,
>Where adepts wander and novices play:
>What a lively place this New Quarter is! [15]

But alas for Ohatsu of the Temma House—even after she returns the day's events still weigh on her. She cannot swallow her saké, she feels on edge. As she sits weeping, some courtesans from the neighboring houses and other friends come for a little chat.

[13] The word *shijimi* means the corbicula, a kind of small shellfish, and the name of the river thus occasions mention of shells.

[14] Umeda Bridge, the name of which means literally "plum field".

[15] The Dōjima New Quarter in Osaka was opened about 1700.

FIRST COURTESAN: Have you heard, Ohatsu? They say that Toku was given a thrashing for something bad he did. Is it true?

SECOND COURTESAN: No, my customer told me that Toku was trampled to death.

NARRATOR: They say he was fettered for fraud or trussed for counterfeiting a seal. Not one decent thing have they to report: every expression of sympathy makes their visit the more painful.

OHATSU: No, please, not another word. The more I hear, the worse my breast pains me. I'm sure I'll be the first to die. I wish I were dead already.

NARRATOR: She can only weep. But amidst her tears she happens to look outside and catches a glimpse of Tokubei, a pathetic figure wearing a wicker hat, even at night.[16] Her heart leaps, and she wants to run to him, but in the sitting room are the master and his wife, and by the entrance stands the cook, while in the kitchen a maid is hovering: with so many sharp eyes watching, she cannot do as she pleases.

OHATSU: I feel terribly depressed. I think I'll step outside for a moment.

NARRATOR: She slips out softly.

OHATSU: What happened? I've heard rumors of every sort about you. They've driven me out of my mind with worry.

NARRATOR: She thrusts her face under the brim of his wicker hat and weeps in secret, soundless, painful tears. He too is lost in tears.

TOKUBEI: I've been made the victim of a clever plot, as no doubt you've heard, and the more I struggle, the worse off I am. Everything has turned against me now. I can't survive this night. I've made up my mind to it.

NARRATOR: As he whispers, voices are heard from within.

VOICES: Come inside, Ohatsu. There's enough gossip about you as it is.[17]

OHATSU: There—did you hear? We can't go on talking. Do as I show you.

NARRATOR: She hides him under the train of her mantle. He crawls behind her to the garden door, where he slips beneath the porch at the

[16] The wicker hat was worn for concealment, but at night this precaution was normally unnecessary.

[17] Standing in the street outside the teahouse was likely to occasion gossip about secret lovers.

step. Ohatsu sits by the entrance and, pulling the tobacco tray to her, lights her pipe. She assumes an air of unconcern.

At this moment Kuheiji and a couple of his loudmouthed friends burst in, accompanied by a blind musician.

KUHEIJI: Hello, girls. You're looking lonesome. Would you like me for a customer? Hello there, host. I haven't seen you in ages.

NARRATOR: He strides arrogantly into the room.

HOST: Bring a tobacco tray and some saké cups.

NARRATOR: He makes the customary fuss over the guests.

KUHEIJI: No, don't bother about saké. We were drinking before we came. I have something to tell you. Tokubei, the number one customer of your Ohatsu, found a seal I'd lost and tried to cheat me out of two *kamme* in silver with a forged note. The facts were too much for him, and he finally met with some unpleasantness from which he was lucky to escape alive. His reputation has been ruined. Be on your guard if he comes here again. Everybody will tell you that I speak the truth, so even if Tokubei tells you the exact opposite, don't believe him for a moment. You'd do best not to let him in at all. Sooner or later he's bound to end up on the gallows.[18]

NARRATOR: He pours out his words convincingly. Tokubei, underneath the porch, gnashes his teeth and trembles with rage. Ohatsu, afraid that he may reveal himself, calms him with her foot, calms him gently. The host is loath to answer yes or no, for Tokubei's a customer of long standing.

HOST: Well, then, how about some soup?

NARRATOR: Covering his confusion, he leaves the room. Ohatsu, weeping bitterly, exclaims.

OHATSU: You needn't try your clever words on me. Tokubei and I have been intimate for years. We've told each other our inmost secrets. He hasn't a particle of deceit in him, the poor boy. His generosity has been his undoing. He's been tricked, but he hasn't the evidence to prove it. After what has happened Tokubei has no choice but to kill himself. I wish I knew whether or not he was resolved to die.

NARRATOR: She pretends to be talking to herself, but with her foot she questions him. He nods, and taking her ankle, passes it across his throat, to let her know that he is bent on suicide.

[18] Literally, "he's bound to end up at Noe or Tobita." Noe and Tobita were execution grounds on the outskirts of Osaka.

OHATSU: I knew it. I knew it. No matter how long one lives, it comes to the same thing. Only death can wipe out the disgrace.

NARRATOR: Kuheiji is startled by her words.

KUHEIJI: What is Ohatsu talking about? Why should Tokubei kill himself? Well, if he kills himself, I'll take good care of you after he's gone! I think you've fallen for me too!

OHATSU: That's most generous of you, I'm sure. But would you object if, by way of thanks for your kindness, I killed you? Could I go on living even a moment if separated from Toku? Kuheiji, you dirty thief! Anyone hearing your silly lies can only suspect you. I'm sure that Toku intends to die with me, as I with him.

NARRATOR: She taps with her foot, and Tokubei, weeping, takes it in his hands and reverently touches it to his forehead. He embraces her knees and sheds tears of love. She too can hardly conceal her emotions. Though no word is spoken, answering each other heart to heart, they silently weep. That no one knows makes it sadder still.

Kuheiji feels uncomfortable.

KUHEIJI: The wind's against us today. Let's get out of here. The whores in this place are certainly peculiar—they seem to have an aversion for customers like ourselves with plenty of money to spend. Let's stop at the Asa House and have a drink there. We'll rattle around a couple of gold pieces, then go home to bed. Oh—my wallet is so heavy I can hardly walk.

NARRATOR: Spewing forth all manner of abuse, they noisily depart. The host and his wife call to the servants.

HOST: It's time to put out the lights for the night. Lay out beds for the guests who are staying on. Ohatsu, you sleep upstairs. Get to bed early.

OHATSU (to herself): Master, mistress, I shall probably never see you again. Farewell. Farewell to all the servants too.

NARRATOR: Thus inwardly taking leave, she goes to her bedchamber. Later they will learn that this was a parting for life; how pitiful the foolish hearts of men who do not realize the truth in time!

HOST: See that the fire is out under the kettle. Don't let the mice get at the relishes.

NARRATOR: They shut the place and bar the gate. Hardly have their heads touched their pillows than all are snoring merrily. So short is the night that before they've had a chance to dream, two o'clock in the morning has come. Ohatsu is dressed for death, a black cloak dark as the ways of love thrown over her kimono of spotless white. She tiptoes to the staircase and looks down. Tokubei shows his face from under the porch. He beckons, nods, points, communicating his intent without a word. Below the stairs a servant girl is sleeping. A hanging lantern brightly shines. Ohatsu in desperation attaches her fan to a palm-leaf broom, and from the second step of the staircase attempts in vain to extinguish the flame. At last, by stretching every inch, she puts it out, only to tumble suddenly down the stairs. The lamp is out, and in the darkness the servant girl turns in her sleep. Trembling, the lovers grope for each other—a fearful moment. The host awakens in his room to the back.

HOST: What was that noise just now? Servants! The night lamp has gone out. Get up and light it!

NARRATOR: The servant girl, aroused, sleepily rubs her eyes and gets up from bed stark naked.

SERVANT: I can't find the flint box.

NARRATOR: She wanders about the room searching, and Ohatsu, faint with terror, dodges this way and that to avoid her. At last she catches Tokubei's hand, and softly they creep to the entranceway. They unfasten the latch, but the hinges creak, and frightened by the noise, they hesitate. Just then the maid begins to strike the flints; they time their actions to the rasping sound, and with each rasp open the door farther until, huddled together and their sleeves twisted round them, they pass through the door one after the other, feeling as though they tread on a tiger's tail. They exchange glances and cry out for joy, happy that they are to die—a painful, heart-rending sight. The life left them now is as brief as sparks that fly from blocks of flint.

*Scene Three: The journey from Dōjima
to the Sonezaki Shrine.*

NARRATOR:
    Farewell to this world, and to the night farewell.
    We who walk the road to death, to what should we be likened?
    To the frost by the road that leads to the graveyard,
    Vanishing with each step we take ahead:
    How sad is this dream of a dream!

TOKUBEI:

Ah, did you count the bell? Of the seven strokes
That mark the dawn, six have sounded.
The remaining one will be the last echo
We shall hear in this life.

OHATSU:

It will echo the bliss of nirvana.

NARRATOR:

Farewell, and not to the bell alone—
They look a last time on the grass, the trees, the sky.
The clouds, the river go by unmindful of them;
The Dipper's bright reflection shines in the water.

TOKUBEI:

Let's pretend that Umeda Bridge
Is the bridge the magpies built [19]
Across the Milky Way, and make a vow
To be husband and wife stars for eternity.

OHATSU:

I promise. I'll be your wife forever.

NARRATOR:

They cling together—the river waters
Will surely swell with the tears they shed.
Across the river, in a teahouse upstairs,
Some revelers, still not gone to bed,
Are loudly talking under blazing lamps—
No doubt gossiping about the good or bad
Of this year's crop of lovers' suicides;
Their hearts sink to hear these voices.

TOKUBEI:

How strange! but yesterday, even today,
We spoke as if such things did not concern us.
Tomorrow we shall figure in their gossip.
If the world will sing about us, let it sing.

NARRATOR:

This is the song that now they hear.
    "I'm sure you'll never have me for your wife,

[19] Allusion to the Chinese legend, familiar also in Japan, which tells of two stars (known as the Herd Boy and the Weaver Girl) that meet once a year, crossing over a bridge in the sky built by magpies.

I know my love means nothing to you . . ."
Yes, for all our love, for all our grieving,
Our lives, our lots, have not been as we wished.
Never, until this very day, have we known
A single night of heart's relaxation—
Instead, the tortures of an ill-starred love.
"What is this bond between us?
I cannot forget you.
But you would shake me off and go—
I'll never let you!
Kill me with your hands, then go.
I'll never release you!"
So she said in tears.[20]

OHATSU:

Of all the many songs, that one, tonight!

TOKUBEI:

Who is it singing? We who listen

BOTH:

Suffer the ordeal of those before us.

NARRATOR:

They cling to each other, weeping bitterly.
Any other night would not matter
If tonight were only a little longer,
But the heartless summer night, as is its wont,
Breaks as cockcrows hasten their last hour.

TOKUBEI:

It will be worse if we wait for dawn.
Let us die in the wood of Tenjin.[21]

NARRATOR:

He leads her by the hand.
At Umeda Embankment, the night ravens.

TOKUBEI:

Tomorrow our bodies may be their meal.

OHATSU:

It's strange, this is your unlucky year [22]

[20] The song overheard by Ohatsu and Tokubei is derived from a popular ballad of the time which describes a love suicide.

[21] The shrine of Sonezaki, sacred to Tenjin (Sugawara no Michizane).

[22] According to yin-yang divination, a man's twenty-fifth, forty-second, and sixtieth years were dangerous; for a woman her nineteenth and thirty-third years.

Of twenty-five, and mine of nineteen.
It's surely proof how deep are our ties
That we who love each other are cursed alike.
All the prayers I have made for this world
To the gods and to the Buddha, I here and now
Direct to the future: in the world to come
May we be reborn on the same lotus!

NARRATOR:
One hundred eight the beads her fingers tell
On her rosary; [23] tears increase the sum.
No end to her grief, but the road has an end:
Their minds are numbed, the sky is dark, the wind still,
They have reached the thick wood of Sonezaki.

Shall it be here, shall it be there? When they brush the grass, the falling dew vanishes even quicker than their lives, in this uncertain world a lightning flash—or was it something else?

OHATSU: I'm afraid. What was that now?

TOKUBEI: That was a human spirit.[24] I thought we alone would die tonight, but someone else has preceded us. Whoever it may be, we'll have a companion on the journey to the Mountain of Death. *Namu Amida Butsu. Namu Amida Butsu.*[25]

NARRATOR: She weeps helplessly.

OHATSU: To think that others are dying tonight too! How heartbreaking!

NARRATOR: Man though he is, his tears fall freely.

TOKUBEI: Those two spirits flying together—do you suppose they belong to anyone else? They must be yours and mine!

OHATSU: Those two spirits? Then, are we dead already?

TOKUBEI: Normally, if we saw a spirit, we'd knot our clothes and murmur prayers to keep our souls with us,[26] but now we hurry towards our end, hoping instead our two souls will find the same dwelling. Do not mistake the way, do not lose me!

NARRATOR: They embrace, flesh to flesh, then fall to the ground and weep—how pitiful they are! Their strings of tears unite like en-

[23] The Buddhist rosary has 108 beads, one for each of the sufferings occasioned by the passions.
[24] *Hitodama,* a kind of will-o'-the-wisp believed to be a human soul.
[25] The invocation to Amida Buddha used in Pure Land Buddhism.
[26] Exorcism practiced to prevent the soul from leaving the body.

twining branches, or the pine and palm that grow from a single trunk,[27] a symbol of eternal love. Here the dew of their unhappy lives will at last settle.

TOKUBEI: Let this be the spot.

NARRATOR: He unfastens the sash of his cloak. Ohatsu removes her tear-stained outer robe, and throws it on the palm tree; the fronds might now serve as a broom to sweep away the sad world's dust. Ohatsu takes a razor from her sleeve.

OHATSU: I had this razor prepared in case we were overtaken on the way and separated. I was determined not to forfeit our name as lovers. How happy I am that we are to die together as we hoped!

TOKUBEI: How wonderful of you to have thought of that! I am so confident in our love that I have no fears even about death. And yet it would be unfortunate if because of the pain we are to suffer people said that we looked ugly in death. Let us secure our bodies to this twin-trunked tree and die immaculately! We will become an unparalleled example of a lovers' suicide.

OHATSU: Yes, let us do that.

NARRATOR: Alas! She little thought she thus would use her light blue undersash! She draws it taut, and with her razor slashes it through.

OHATSU: The sash is cut, but you and I will never be torn apart.

NARRATOR: She sits, and he binds her twice, thrice to the tree, firmly so that she will not stir.

TOKUBEI: Is it tight?

OHATSU: Very tight.

NARRATOR: She looks at her husband, and he at her—they burst into tears.

BOTH: This is the end of our unhappy lives!

TOKUBEI: No I mustn't give way to grief.

NARRATOR: He lifts his head and joins his hands in prayer.

TOKUBEI: My parents died when I was a boy, and I grew up thanks to the efforts of my uncle, who was my master. It disgraces me to die without repaying his kindness. Instead I shall cause him trouble which will last even after my death. Please forgive my sins.

Soon I shall see my parents in the other world. Father, Mother, welcome me there!

NARRATOR: He weeps. Ohatsu also joins her hands.

[27] Such a tree actually existed, as contemporary accounts of the Sonezaki Shrine show.

OHATSU: I envy you. You say you will meet your parents in the world of the dead. My father and mother are in this world and in good health. I wonder when I shall see them again. I heard from them this spring, but I haven't seen them since the beginning of last autumn. Tomorrow, when word reaches the village of our suicides, how unhappy they will be! Now I must bid farewell for this life to my parents, my brothers and sisters. If at least my thoughts can reach you, please appear before me, if only in dreams. Dear Mother, beloved Father!

NARRATOR: She sobs and wails aloud. Her husband also cries out and sheds incessant tears in all too understandable emotion.

OHATSU: We could talk forever, but it serves no purpose. Kill me, kill me quickly!

NARRATOR: She hastens the moment of death.

TOKUBEI: I'm ready.

NARRATOR: He swiftly draws his dagger.

TOKUBEI: The moment has come. *Namu Amida. Namu Amida.*

NARRATOR: But when he tries to bring the blade against the skin of the woman he's loved, and held and slept with so many months and years, his eyes cloud over, his hand shakes. He tries to steady his weakening resolve, but still he trembles, and when he thrusts, the point misses. Twice or thrice the flashing blade deflects this way and that until a cry tells it has struck her throat.

TOKUBEI: *Namu Amida. Namu Amida. Namu Amida Butsu.*

NARRATOR: He twists the blade deeper and deeper, but the strength has left his arm. When he sees her weaken, he stretches forth his hands. The last agonies of death are indescribable.

TOKUBEI: Must I lag behind you? Let's draw our last breaths together.

NARRATOR: He thrusts and twists the razor in his throat, until it seems the handle or the blade must snap. His eyes grow dim, and his last painful breath is drawn away at its appointed hour.[28] No one is there to tell the tale, but the wind that blows through Sonezaki Wood transmits it, and high and low alike gather to pray for these lovers who beyond a doubt will in the future attain Buddhahood. They have become models of true love.

[28] It was believed by practitioners of yin-yang divination that a person's hour of death was determined at his birth and could be foretold by an examination of the celestial stems governing his birth. Death normally occurred with the receding of the tide.

THE DRUM OF THE
WAVES OF HORIKAWA

First performed on March 18, 1706. This play is closely derived from actual events of the preceding year. Chikamatsu changed the names of the chief figures only slightly: the historical Ōkura Hikohachirō became Ogura Hikokurō, the drum teacher Miyai Den'emon became Miyaji Gen'emon, and so on. Chikamatsu's chief addition was the villain Isobe Yukaemon, invented to satisfy the necessities of plot.

Throughout the play (and in the title itself) drum images are frequently employed, in keeping with Gen'emon's profession.

Except for the Nō passages sung in the first act, the narrator's part is curiously lacking in Chikamatsu's usual ornamentation of style, and seldom rises above stage directions.

Cast of Characters

OGURA HIKOKURŌ, a samurai
MIYAJI GEN'EMON, a drum teacher from Kyoto
BUNROKU, Hikokurō's adopted son
ISOBE YUKAEMON, a samurai enamored of Otane
A PRIEST
SENIOR NEIGHBOR of Gen'emon
SOLDIERS, PASSERSBY, SERVANTS, MESSENGERS
OTANE, wife of Hikokurō
OFUJI, younger sister of Otane
YURA, younger sister of Hikokurō
ORIN, maid of Otane
MAIDS, PASSERSBY

ACT ONE

*Scene One: The courtyard of a house in Tottori, the seat of the
daimyo of Inaba. The house belongs to Chūdayū, the father of
Otane and Ofuji. The sisters are hanging out the laundry while
a lesson in the music of the Nō play* Matsukaze *progresses inside the house.*
Time: An afternoon in the spring of 1705.

NARRATOR (*chants in Nō style*):
    And so three years of weary exile
    Yukihira whiled away aboard his boat,
    His heart illumined by the moon of Suma Bay.
    He chose two sisters as his maids in waiting,
    Fisher-girls who dipped the evening tide,
    And named one Pine-Breeze and one Spring-Shower,[1]
    Names he thought well suited to the time of year.
    The sisters changed the clothes they wore,
    Fisher-girls of Suma, familiars of the moon,
    When burning salt along the shore,
    For robes of damask burnt with faint perfumes.

Those were fisher-girls' clothes, but here a matron is fulling her
robes, her occupation during her husband's absence, in service at
Edo. Her younger sister Ofuji fortunately happens to be at home today
and offers to help, tying back her sleeves with a cotton cord. The sisters
apply starch and wring out the clothes with dripping sleeves, so
lovely a sight it is clear why their charms are celebrated throughout
the fief.

    OTANE: It'd be best for you, Ofuji, to stay in service permanently.
Remember always to keep your master pleased, and don't get married.
I know that only too well from my own experience. Hikokurō and
I were childhood sweethearts before our marriage, and I can't tell you
how happy I was to become his bride. But it's sad being of low rank.
Every other year Hikokurō must spend in Edo. Even when he's here,
he must report every day at the castle, and ten nights each month it's
his turn to stand guard duty. We've never spent a single relaxed night

---

[1] Pine-Breeze (Matsukaze) and Spring-Shower (Murasame) are two sisters who fall in
love wth the nobleman Yukihira in the Nō play *Matsukaze*.

in conversation together like other couples. Hikokurō has the samurai spirit, and he encourages me by saying that unless he exerts himself as he does he'll never be able to make his mark in his profession. All the same, I can just see the expression on his face when he left for Edo last July. "I won't be seeing you again till I come back with his lordship next July," he said. "Take care of yourself and watch after the house." Yes, I've never for a moment forgotten that look. It's as if I could see him now before my eyes. I wait here as though we were lovers who met every day, wondering when, when he'll return.

NARRATOR: She stretches the silk with clothespins and ties it with cords to the pines; talking this way has helped dispel her grief.[2]

Her sister Ofuji bursts out laughing.

OFUJI: You're asking for too much, Otane! Look at the marvelous powers of endurance I display, with no husband whatsoever! And they're so strict about discipline at his lordship's mansion. It's forbidden for me to spend one single night away, even here, in my own family's house. I'm sure you'd die in such a place! Anyone hearing you complain would laugh!

OTANE: Listen—there's drum practice going on inside. You mustn't talk so loud. Hush!

NARRATOR: She stretches the cloth on tenterhooks and peers through a crack in the fence. Vague yearnings for her husband are stirred by the beat of the drum. As she hangs his robes on the pine to dry, the piece ends with a final cry.

(Chants.)
    "This keepsake
    Now is my enemy.
    Without it
    There might be a chance to forget."
    The poet was right—
    Keepsakes only deepen one's longing.[3]

OTANE: Oh I'm so happy! Look, my husband's returned! I must go welcome him!

[2] Mention of the pines is dictated by the customary pun on *matsu* (to wait) and *matsu* (the pine). Similarly, *yūte* is at once "tying" and "talking". Numerous other puns dot this section.
[3] "This keepsake . . . to forget" derives from an anonymous poem in the *Kokinshū* (no. 746).

NARRATOR: She runs up to the tree.

OFUJI: Are you out of your mind, Otane? That's just a garden pine tree. Hikokurō's in Edo. Are you mad?

NARRATOR: She reproaches her sister.

OTANE: Silly Ofuji! What makes you think I'm mad? The only solace for my boredom while Hikokurō's away is to pretend he's returned. Here we are in Inaba, just as in that piece they're playing. Listen to the words—"When I hear you're waiting, I'll come back again." Oh, that song and the beat of the drum give me hope again!

NARRATOR (*chants*):

> His song fills me with hope—
> "Though I leave now I will return
> If I hear you pine like the pines
> Growing on Inaba Mountain's peak." [4]
> He spoke of the pines of far-off Inaba,
> But these are the pines of Suma's curving bay
> Where once he lived, that dear prince.
> If Yukihira returns I will approach
> The shade of that pine tree, tenderly.
> Oh, that familiar pine on the beach, I love it!
>
> The wind blows wild in the pines.
> Now, when her loneliness is most intense
> For the husband who is far away,
> The drum has comforted her heart:
> The drum brings rumors that her husband
> Will presently return from the East.
> The wind is cool as she washes and stretches
> The thin raw silk of her husband's *hakama;* [5]
> The mild spring sun will dry it soon.

OTANE: I'm glad I've accomplished something useful. And now I shall wait for my husband's return from Edo and listen to the wind in the pines.

[4] The poem is by Yukihira, found in the *Kokinshū* (no. 365) and in the play *Matsukaze.* In the play Inaba, a distant place, is contrasted with Suma where the fisher-girls live, but here Inaba is the scene of the action.

[5] The trousers of a formal Japanese costume.

NARRATOR: She speaks in high spirits. Bunroku calls from inside.

BUNROKU: Mother! I've finished my drum practice. I'm sure you've heard me talk about my teacher, Miyaji Gen'emon. Wouldn't you like to come in and meet him?

OTANE: I would indeed. I was thinking of it a while ago, but I was so busy hanging up the clothes that the time went by before I knew it.

NARRATOR: She unties the cords tucking up her sleeves and smoothes her clothes. When she enters the sitting room Gen'emon at once changes to a formal sitting posture.

GEN'EMON: I live in Kyoto, at Horikawa near Shimotachiuri. I have the honor to teach the drum to the gentlemen of this fief, and I come here quite frequently now that my pupils are about to be permitted to serve in the palace. Sometimes I stay for three or four months or even a whole year at a time, but I have never had the pleasure of meeting your husband, Hikokurō. Recently your son Bunroku expressed a desire to learn the drum, and I agreed to take him as my pupil. He's quite exceptionally talented, and I can imagine how proud of him his mother must be.

NARRATOR: He speaks very politely. Otane acknowledges his compliments with a bow of the head and a smile.

OTANE: Calling me Bunroku's mother makes Hikokurō and myself sound like old people. Actually, Bunroku is my younger brother. My husband adopted him as his son. We're people of very modest means, and for the time being we've put Bunroku under the protection of a certain gentleman in his lordship's household. His grandfather was anxious for Bunroku to learn—with your kind help—at least one drum piece well enough to appear personally before his lordship. That was why he decided, even though my husband's away, to ask you to teach him. I expect my husband to be returning with his lordship in July, and I'll be very grateful if Bunroku is able to perform a piece for his father then.

NARRATOR: She has a graceful manner of receiving him. So gentle yet dignified are her appearance and actions that no one would object if she were introduced as the greatest lady of Kyoto. Who could guess that she was reared in the mountains of Inaba?

Ofuji enters.

 OFUJI: I'm Ofuji, Otane's younger sister. I'm in service in one of the households of the fief. Your kindness to Bunroku is very gratifying to us all. My sister's husband is away, and he draws only a small stipend. His house is so cramped that we must do the wash and everything else here, at my father's place. That's why we even have to ask you to give Bunroku his drum practice here, though I can imagine how inconvenient everything must be. I'm sure that Hikokurō will invite you to his house as soon as he returns. (*To maid.*) Bring some saké cups, please. (*Calls.*) Father, are you at home? (*To Gen'emon.*) We've just the one maid, fresh out of the country, and even with only a single guest everything is in complete chaos, as you can see. (*Laughs.*) Really, it's quite embarrassing.

NARRATOR: She bows in greeting. Her eyes are as lovely as Otane's.

GEN'EMON: Please don't go to any trouble on my account.

NARRATOR: But even while they exchange these compliments the maid, realizing what is needed, produces saké and relishes.

OTANE: Oh, what a good idea! (*To Gen'emon.*) My father's only a *rōnin,* and we can't offer you anything to eat with the drinks, but have a cup—it'll cheer you.

GEN'EMON: I'm sure you must be busy, but I most appreciate your kindness. Please, you drink first.

OTANE: No, please, guests first. There's no need to stand on ceremony.

GEN'EMON: In that case, what about starting with Bunroku?

NARRATOR: He offers the cup to Bunroku but, tippler that she is, Otane's hand intercepts the cup.

OTANE: I'll play the part of a good mother, and make sure first the saké's properly heated.

NARRATOR: She accepts some saké and drains the cup. She offers it to Bunroku.[6]

BUNROKU: I've never drunk any saké before.

NARRATOR: He swallows a little.

BUNROKU: Excuse me, master, for drinking first.

NARRATOR: He bows. Gen'emon politely accepts the cup. He comes from a family of heavy drinkers, and his lips smack like a drum.

GEN'EMON: Ahhh, what marvelous saké! I don't drink very much as

[6] It is a mark of friendship or intimacy in Japan to drink saké from the same cup as another person.

a rule, but I like a little saké now and then, and I've tried it all over the country. But not even the Kyoto saké can touch this. It has a good color, a fine bouquet, and the taste is excellent. I'm quite impressed by your husband's palate!

NARRATOR: His praise of the saké and his company manners are a trifle too glib; how unfortunate that nobody recognizes this portent of later calamity!

GEN'EMON: Here, I'm returning the cup immediately to Bunroku.

OTANE: Let me, his mother, intervene here, and keep you company in drink!

NARRATOR: She accepts some saké and again empties the cup.

OTANE: Please show you like the saké by having another drink.

NARRATOR: He takes the cup from her hand without even letting her put it down.

GEN'EMON: I'll be delighted, of course.

NARRATOR: He accepts the brimming cupful and swallows it in one gulp. He returns the cup to Bunroku, who again merely touches it to his lips.

BUNROKU: Excuse me, but I'd like to offer my aunt some saké.

NARRATOR: He is about to hand Ofuji the cup.

OTANE: You can't be so unsociable, no matter how unaccustomed you may be to drinking. Here, have a cup. I'll keep you company.

NARRATOR: She lifts the flowing cup and empties it.

OTANE: It's a happy occasion when a mother drinks with her child. To make it all the happier, let's have an extra drink now for your father in Edo. Here, please join us.

NARRATOR: She proffers the cup once again to Gen'emon.

GEN'EMON: I see, madam, that you're partial to a little saké. Excuse my familiarity, but I'd like to see just how proficient a toper you are!

NARRATOR: He returns the cup. Ofuji is dismayed.

OFUJI: No, Otane can't drink so much. Lately especially she's been under the weather and hasn't been feeling too well. Otane, I think you've had enough.

NARRATOR: She stands beside Otane and tries to restrain her, but Otane, as is a drinker's wont, becomes obstinate.

OTANE: What are you trying to tell me? We've nothing to eat with the saké, and the best entertainment I can offer our guest is to drink with him.

NARRATOR: She speaks in haughty tones. Another bottle is brought from the kitchen. Her guest, beating a drum accompaniment with his hands, sings out.

GEN'EMON: Well, then, another for me too.

NARRATOR: They pass the saké back and forth. Here indeed is a splendid (*Chants.*)

Gathering of champions,

A drinking party of bosom friends.[7]

They tilt their cups a number of times, and soon the sun is slanting in the evening sky. A servant comes from the mansion where Ofuji serves.

SERVANT: Miss Ofuji, I've come to escort you back. Please return with me. The gate will be closing soon.

OFUJI: Oh, is that you, Kakuzō? Sorry to have bothered you. Otane, I'll be leaving now. I must apologize to you, sir, for my rudeness, but a woman in service can't do as she pleases. I hope that I'll be seeing you again.

NARRATOR: She takes her leave with these words and departs. Bunroku quietly speaks.

BUNROKU: I think I'll be going too. Tonight they're expecting guests at the house of the gentleman I wait on. Master, would you kindly remain here a bit longer, until my grandfather returns?

GEN'EMON: Well, if you say so. But how will it look if I'm found here with your mother, just the two of us? I'll go to the next room.

NARRATOR: He leaves his seat in some embarrassment. Otane shows Bunroku to the door.

OTANE: Please stop by our house for a minute and ask your grandfather to return. I'm anxious to go home. Ask him to send Rin to fetch me.

BUNROKU: Yes, I will.

NARRATOR: He departs for his master's house.

This is the hour when gates are shut, here on the outskirts of town. The youthful mistress of the house, whose husband has been absent long months in Edo, is a trifle too fond of liquor—she thinks it will bolster her spirits. Her face has not lost its composure, but it is burning hot. In the mirror, when she combs her hair and strokes her heavy

[7] Quoted from the Nō play *Rashōmon*.

head, an indefinable seductiveness glows in her reflection. Tonight she seems to be awaiting her husband.

Isobe Yukaemon, though a fellow retainer of the same fief, was excused from accompanying his lordship to Edo, and remained in the country, claiming to be sick. Now he suddenly bursts into the house through the side door, all alone, without even a servant.

YUKAEMON: I've come to see how you're getting along.

NARRATOR: Otane pushes away her mirror in alarm.

OTANE: Chūdayū isn't here. He's been out ever since morning.

NARRATOR: She intends these words as a dismissal, and starts to withdraw inside when Yukaemon catches her in his arms.

YUKAEMON: I knew he was out. That's why I came. I haven't any business with your father. It's you I've been longing to see. I've felt like a boat, trapped by the shoals of other people's eyes, with the breakers pounding in on me.[8] I knew for a fact that if I spent this year serving in Edo my stipend would be increased, but I gave up all thoughts of advancement as a samurai. I pretended to be sick and I begged permission to remain here in the country. I want you to know that it's all been on account of you. My sickness was a ruse and yet not entirely so—I was suffering from the malady called love, and you were the cause, Otane. Please, I beg you, give me just one small dose of the medicine of your love. I implore you.

NARRATOR: He holds her tightly in his arms. Otane is a little drunk from the saké.

OTANE: Stop it! You're acting outrageously. I can't bear it!

NARRATOR: She shakes him off and evades him, but her hair bristles in terror, and she trembles all over.

OTANE: Dog of a samurai! To think you're a close friend of Hikokurō! It goes against all the rules of human decency. The whole fief'll point at you with scorn, and if his lordship hears about it, you'll be ruined. Don't you realize that? I'm Ogura Hikokurō's wife, a samurai wife! Don't do anything contemptible which will only make you hate me later on. I won't tell anyone what has happened. Now leave!

NARRATOR: She forces out the words.

YUKAEMON: I've thought about how people would criticize me and

[8] The various sea images have for justification the name Isobe, which means literally "shore area".

the disgrace I would suffer. I've taken all that into account. I came here resolved that if by any chance you refused me, I would stab you first and then myself. Rumors would soon be flying throughout the province that we'd committed a lovers' suicide, the kind so popular in Osaka, and we would share a common disgrace.

NARRATOR: He draws his sword and catches her by the front of the kimono.

YUKAEMON: What is your answer to that?

NARRATOR: He menaces her. Otane supposes in her woman's heart that he speaks the truth, and she is mortified to think that she may die like a dog and be branded for a crime of which she is guiltless. She decides that she will trick him.

OTANE: Are you really in love with me as you say?

YUKAEMON: If I'm not telling the truth, may I be dismissed by his lordship and have my head cut off by a common soldier!

OTANE: You delight me. Why should I treat you unkindly? But this is my father's house. Just supposing he were to return now! What would we do then? If you will come secretly to my house tomorrow night, I'll throw off my reserve and chase away all your cares.

NARRATOR: She taps him gently, with artful deceit. The ignorant, illiterate Yukaemon is tricked by one word and turns sentimental.

YUKAEMON: Oh, I'm so grateful for your kindness! I know that it's shameless to ask anything more, but I'd much rather if now, here, we might just—

NARRATOR: He clutches her.

OTANE: You're unreasonable!

NARRATOR: She runs from place to place trying to elude him. On the other side of the partition Gen'emon beats his drum and raises his voice.

GEN'EMON (chants):
 The evil demon of lust
 Will attack and attack your flesh.
 Your beloved one will appear
 Over the Mountain of Swords.
 You'll cry in delight
 And grope your way up,
 Only for swords to pierce your flesh

And great rocks crush your bones.

What does this mean? What horror is this? [9]

OTANE: Somebody's heard! What am I to do?

NARRATOR: She is terrified.

YUKAEMON: Everything I've been saying has all been a joke—not a word of truth in it.

NARRATOR: With these parting words he dashes out and makes his escape. Otane, poor creature, is distraught with shame. Undoubtedly her guest from Kyoto has overheard the conversation without realizing that it was all a trick. Now he will despise her in his heart, and more than that, being a man with a wide acquaintance throughout the fief, he will soon spread the scandal. Then what will she do? Unable to control the agitation in her breast, she rouses the maid and orders her to heat some saké.

OTANE: You can shut the front gate while you're at it. It's time you went to bed.

NARRATOR: She pours some saké and, drinking alone, forgets her grief and bitterness. The one thing she cannot forget is her husband in Edo. Her tears make the moonlight seem the mistier as it bathes the verandah where footsteps now are heard.

OTANE: Oh, it's you, Gen'emon.—Where are you going, sir?

GEN'EMON: I feel rather awkward being here in a house with only women. I'm leaving.

NARRATOR: He starts to go, but she catches his sleeve.

OTANE: Did you hear what happened just now? It was a perfect disgrace, a horrible experience. I'm sure you don't suppose for a moment that a woman with a husband like Hikokurō could actually have meant what I said. I talked to him that way only to deceive him, so that I might escape my predicament. Please don't tell anyone. I beg you most earnestly.

NARRATOR: She joins her hands in supplication and weeps. Gen'emon is at a loss for words.

GEN'EMON: I wasn't listening—or not listening, for that matter. The conversation was exceedingly unpleasant for an outsider to overhear. I sang that piece to distract myself. What happened seems trivial enough, though it's quite a serious matter. I don't intend to tell any-

[9] This description of a Buddhist hell is adapted from the Nō play *Ominameshi*.

one but, as they say, you can hide a gimlet in a bag but it'll soon show itself. I don't know what rumors other people may start.

NARRATOR: He shakes himself loose, but she clings to him again.

OTANE: What a cruel thing to say! You are a young man and I am a young woman—even if what you heard was really true, it would be normal human kindness to hide it as best you could. I won't have any peace of mind if I let you go as things stand. Please exchange a cup with me as a promise that you won't tell.

NARRATOR: She takes the saké jar and fills a large tea bowl to the brim. She empties the cup and filling it again drinks half, then offers the rest to him.

GEN'EMON (*to himself*): This is very strange, giving me the remains of the cup she drank from.

NARRATOR: He accepts it politely and drinks. Otane by now is quite intoxicated. She presses Gen'emon's hand tightly.

OTANE: Now that you've shared a cup of saké with a married woman, your guilt is the same as mine. You mustn't ever tell anything.

NARRATOR: She forces him into a hopeless dilemma.

GEN'EMON: Damn it! What a difficulty to put a man in!

NARRATOR: He rushes for the door, but she throws her arms around him.

OTANE: You don't know anything about love, do you? What an infuriating man you are!

NARRATOR: Her arms still around him, she undoes his obi, undoing his heart as well, for his mind is befuddled with drink and desire. Embracing and embraced, their love has become real before they knew it.

OTANE: Now do you agree never to tell what happened?

GEN'EMON: I thought it didn't concern me, but now that I'm involved, how could I fail to hide what's happened?

NARRATOR: He opens the shōji and they go into the next room. They share momentary dreams on one pillow, the beginning of a short-lived union, an evil alliance, a connection doomed from the start.

Scene Two: Later that night.

NARRATOR: The night is far advanced. Otane's father, Naruyama Chūdayū, returns alone, without a servant, and beats furiously at the gate.[10] Otane, sober now, is awakened by the noise. She looks at herself. Her sash is undone, and the bed where she slept with a man is disordered.

OTANE: Good heavens! How unspeakable! I remember now deliberately enticing him, hoping to stop him from telling about Yukaemon's advances. Yes, I remember that. But afterwards—I was so drunk I can't be sure what was only a dream and what really happened. My sister always warned me about my drinking, but I wouldn't listen to her. Now I have disgraced myself by touching another man's body —a perfect stranger! How depraved of me! I'm guilty of the worst sin a woman can commit, and I'll suffer for it, not only the torments of hell but dishonor in this life. What shall I do, now that I've destroyed the reputations even of my father and brother? I feel utterly wretched. If only this would turn out to be a dream!

NARRATOR: She chokes in tears. Gen'emon, wakened by the sound of her sobbing, rises from bed. Drunkenness had so stupefied him too that he violated the code of a man of honor. Their eyes meet for an instant, then they look down in tears and embarrassment, ashamed to stand before each other. Chūdayū, his patience exhausted, pounds all the more violently at the gate.

OTANE: If my father discovers me, I'll have to kill myself. What am I to do?

NARRATOR: She wanders around the room looking for somewhere to hide. By mischance she stumbles onto the sleeping place of the maid, who jumps up, stark naked.

MAID: Something awful's happened! A burglar's crawled into my bosom while I was sleeping, and now he's ravaging my snow-white skin!

NARRATOR: Carried away by her own shrieks and gyrations, she kicks over the standing lantern. "The darkness of the ways of love" they sing about—how could it be compared to this? Delusion springs even from inconsequential acts. At the gate someone shouts insistently, "Open up! Open up!" and pounds. Otane and the man, trembling with fear, whisper a plan: with her hand held behind her, she pulls his sleeve, shielding him with her body. She unfastens the latch and

[10] Chikamatsu, seemingly carried away by a pun on the name Naruyama, falsely identifies the person at the gate. Perhaps he intended to suggest that this was Otane's misapprehension.

calls, "Is that you, Father?" But it is not her father. Yukaemon, his face averted, stretches out his hands, and tightly clasps their sleeves together.

YUKAEMON: Now, you adulteress, I've got proof of your crime!

NARRATOR: At his shout she slams the gate shut with a cry of dismay, but Yukaemon does not let the sleeves out of his grasp. Gen'emon, in desperation, unsheathes the dagger at his side, and slits off the ends of the sleeves. Opening a side door, he flees precipitously for home. Yukaemon stuffs the sleeves into the fold of his kimono. He forces his way in through the gate.

YUKAEMON: Well, madam, you've been unkind! Why were you so cold to me when you let someone else untie your girdle strings? If you want me to keep this a secret, I expect you'll show me some love tonight in return.

NARRATOR: In the darkness he gropes for Otane, his arms spread wide, an object inspiring terror. As he wanders here and there, he bumps into the naked maid.

YUKAEMON: Now I have you! So this is where you were!

NARRATOR: He throws his arms around her. The maid, knowing her way even in the dark, slips off to her bed.

YUKAEMON: This is wonderful! Thank you!

NARRATOR: He pulls the bedclothes over him and flops down beside her. The maid dislikes his advances, and as she is fending him off, a voice calls from outside.

SERVANT: It's Rin. I've come to take Madam Otane home.

NARRATOR: She enters with a lighted lantern. Yukaemon carefully examines the face caught in the light and sees that it is the maid.

YUKAEMON: How demeaning, and how disgusting! I was about to break my fast to eat a sardine! [11]

NARRATOR: Without so much as looking back, he runs outside. The illusion in the dark was lovely.

ACT TWO

Scene One: The road from Edo to Tottori.
Time: Four months later, July 17, 1705.

[11] Meaning that after having remained continent in hopes of making love to Otane, he has almost lost his virtue for an unworthy object.

SONG:

"See the splendid horse
With a daimyo's wicker trunk,
Seven layers of cushions
And a riding seat above.
First we'll lay the cushions on,
Then we'll put the young lord on top."

NARRATOR: This is the song the drivers cheerfully hum, leading their horses the hundred leagues of the Tōkaidō. The cherries are in blossom and the soldiers in the van of the brilliant procession carry lances—plain, single-pronged, and cross-pointed; their helmets sport crimson-dyed yak tails from China; their robes are magenta; the fish that they eat is sea bream; [12] needless to say, these lancers are samurai. The lackeys carry spears with sheaths cylindrical as the bowls from which they drank their saké this morning, or round as a girl's braided head,[13] shaking, shaking, shaking white snow over Fuji and Asama that now they leave behind. The road is long as the shafts of their many lances; the sheaths are festooned with rooster plumes.[14] Men lead Mochizuki horses famous west of the Barrier.[15] The horses' bits jingle, jingle, jangle, and now there come riding on pack steeds to the beat of the same rhythm the night-guards,[16] the inspectors, the samurai commanders, and the master of ceremonies. Streams of pennants flap on their staffs before and behind the chief of the ensigns. The world is at peace, the waves calm in the seas all around, the wind in the sky has abated.

—"Look, there by the halberds you can see the doctors and philos-

---

[12] From a poem attributed to the priest Ikkyū in the miscellany *Mottomo no Sōshi* (anonymous, published 1634): "Among men the samurai [is best], among pillars cypress wood, among fish the sea bream, among robes magenta, and among cherry blossoms those of Yoshino." The passage incorporates most of the "desirable things" cited by Ikkyū even when essentially irrelevant (*Kinsei Bungei Sōsho*, VII, 290).

[13] The *kaburo* (or *kamuro*) was a prostitute's maid. The word suggests *kaburu* (to put on top), suggesting in turn that the lackeys have had one cup of saké on top of another.

[14] Mention of "rooster plumes" is dictated by the word "barrier" (*seki*) following. According to ancient custom, rites were carried out in Kyoto during times of disturbance which involved tying a rooster at the barriers around the city.

[15] Mention of the "barrier" (Ōsaka Barrier, between Kyoto and Lake Biwa) leads to an allusion to a poem by Ki no Tsurayuki about horses from Mochizuki (*Shūishū*, no. 170).

[16] This and the following are English approximations of three samurai offices.

ophers!" Everybody, pundit and ignoramus alike, gapes at the endless procession of tent pegs, lacquered boxes on poles, rattan-wound bows and black-varnished bows, in numbers beyond reckoning, unpainted bows and half-blackened bows, quivers, arrow cases and arrow holders, cases of the commander's armor covered with double lids, and stands for his helmets.

It seems just yesterday they took the road to the East, but over a year has passed since they left their province. All has gone smoothly; they have safely returned with the Seven Ceremonial Articles: [17] a wicker hat borne aloft on a pole, a long-handled umbrella in its case, an emblem to mark the general's horse (a ball of falcon feathers, true to the name of the clan, Tottori).[18] The horse the daimyo rides and the spare horse too neigh in high spirits at the northern wind of their native heaths. The rear of the procession is brought up by a pair of lancers.

His lordship has been long away from his province, and his return brings joy to his deputy. When a prince acts in princely fashion, his subjects will be true subjects. New casks of saké are opened and singing greets his lordship as he enters his province, where not even needles from the beach pines scatter,[19] in a land which will last ten thousand generations, a land which will last forever.

Men of the household, high and low alike, meet again their parents, wives, and children after a year's separation, and the happy tidings fly here and there. For everyone, down to the lowliest spear carriers, lackeys, and menials, this is a time of exchanging presents and souvenirs, and of noisy celebration.

Among those returning is Ogura Hikokurō. At the moment of the departure from Edo he was singled out for his service and achievements of the past few years, and granted a special increase in stipend as well as a larger retinue of attendants and grooms. He and his family—his son Bunroku, Otane, and Ofuji—are overjoyed to be together again.

Masayama Sangohei, the daimyo's equerry and husband of Hikokurō's sister, is another in the returning party. He has sent a messenger to Otane.

[17] Articles borne in a daimyo's procession, three of which are enumerated here.
[18] The name Tottori is written with ideographs meaning "bird-take"—hence the design of feathers.
[19] An allusion to the preface to the *Kokinshū*.

   Scene Two: Hikokurō's house.

MESSENGER (*speaking for Sangohei*): I am sure you must be delighted to see your husband again after the long separation, and to learn that he has safely escorted his lordship here. I share these feelings. I had planned to offer you a souvenir from Edo, but nothing struck me as really unusual. For want of anything better, I am sending with this messenger some hemp thread.[20] It's a specialty of Edo—they call it Kantō hemp. I realize that it is not much of a gift, but while we were on the road a rumor spread among his lordship's staff that during his absence you had taken to spinning hemp thread. I find, now that I'm back, that the rumor is in circulation here too. I am therefore taking the liberty of offering you this humble present.

NARRATOR: Hardly has he finished speaking than other messengers arrive.

MAN A: Who sent you with this present?

MAN B: It's from a Mr. Something-or-other, a souvenir for Madam Otane.

NARRATOR: Each present arriving strikes terror into Otane's heart. She wonders whether her husband too may not have heard the rumors but, looking at his face, she can detect no sign of suspicion.

HIKOKURŌ: Please help unpack the baggage. We must choose suitable presents for everybody and distribute them accordingly. Oh, I forgot—I should go immediately to pay my respects to my father-in-law. Bring me my *hakama*.

NARRATOR: His wife answers, "Yes," and at once goes inside. Her sister Ofuji brushes past entering the room. Ofuji catches Hikokurō's sleeve.

OFUJI: Hikokurō. You are certainly the most ungallant man. Why didn't you ever answer the two letters I sent you in Edo? Here, I've thought over everything very carefully, and I've written down exactly what I feel in this letter. I ask you please to take some notice of the contents, whether or not you welcome them.

NARRATOR: She pushes a sealed letter into the fold of her brother-in-law's kimono. Hikokurō recoils with an expression of distaste.

HIKOKURŌ: Have you gone out of your mind? Yes, I know, when I was first considering marriage to your sister there was some talk of

[20] A pun. *Ma-o* means at once "hemp thread" and "paramour".

marrying you instead, but nothing ever came of it, and your sister and I are now husband and wife. All that took place over ten years ago, and we're now rearing a son. I can't possibly divorce Otane to marry you, no matter how much you may care for me. I refuse even to hold such a letter in my hand.

NARRATOR: He throws down the letter and goes to the gate. Otane, observing from the inside room what has happened, boldly marches out, snatches up the letter, and thrusts it into her kimono.

OFUJI: Wait! That letter is very important. I don't want anybody else to see it.

NARRATOR: Ofuji clings fast to her sister, but Otane kicks her fiercely to the ground. She picks up a palm-leaf broom and beats her sister until Ofuji's shrieks of pain bring Bunroku and the maids running up.

BUNROKU: I don't know what this is about, but please excuse me.

NARRATOR: He grasps Otane's arm and wrenches away the broom. Otane snatches up a horsewhip tied to the baggage and lashes Ofuji again and again, as if determined to split her head and face. Ofuji's voice rises in a howl of pain.

OFUJI: You're hurting me! You'll kill me! Help!

NARRATOR: She screams, in tears. Bunroku grabs the whip.

BUNROKU: Mother, I don't understand what's going on. If you have a quarrel with Aunt Ofuji, please let it be with words. She may lose consciousness if you continue beating her in that savage way. Then what excuse will you have?

NARRATOR: He speaks harshly.

OTANE: I don't care if I kill her. With my own ears I've heard her say that she was in love with her sister's husband. She admitted sending him letters to Edo. Here, look what I've found.

NARRATOR: She tears open the seal and unfolds the letter.

OTANE: Do you still think I'm lying? Or do you think it doesn't matter even if it's the truth? Here is what she writes in her letter: "Divorce my sister. Send her away and then we'll be married!" Look! She's even torn off her fingernail to the quick and enclosed it in the letter! [21] Read it for yourself. See whether or not I'm making it up. How I loathe her! She infuriates me!

[21] Fingernails torn to the quick were sent as pledges of love.

*Otane accepts a cup of saké from the drum teacher Gen'emon.
"I'll play the part of a good mother, and make sure first the
saké's properly warmed."*
(OFUJI: *Bandō Tsurunosuke IV;* BUNROKU: *Onoe Ushinosuke
V;* OTANE: *Onoe Baikō VII;* GEN'EMON: *Ichikawa Sadanji III*)

NARRATOR: She flies at her sister. Seizing her hair, she twists it round and round in her hands, and pins the tresses under her knee.

OTANE: You hateful woman! I've been waiting for my husband an eternity, the whole year he's been away, counting the months, watching the stars—my husband, my childhood sweetheart, for whom I wouldn't change my parents or a child. At last this morning I saw his face, and just when I was rejoicing that we'd be sleeping together until next year, you had the audacity to order him to send me away! You animal! It infuriates me to let you live!

NARRATOR: Otane strikes Ofuji, indifferent whether her blows land on her sister's eyes or nose.

OFUJI: I have all the excuses in the world. Please, everybody, take her off me. I'm at my last gasp.

BUNROKU: First let's hear your excuses.

NARRATOR: He restrains Otane forcibly.

OTANE: If your excuses don't hold water, this time I'll kill you. Let's hear them, if you have any.

NARRATOR: She pulls Ofuji to her feet and pushes her away with under-standable distaste. Her sister, breathing painfully, smoothes her disheveled locks, holding back her tears.

OFUJI: I can reveal my reasons, Otane, only when the two of us are alone together. Please leave the room, everybody.

NARRATOR: At her request the others all rise and withdraw.

OTANE: Now, no more innuendoes—come out with your reasons plainly.

NARRATOR: Ofuji sheds copious tears.

OFUJI: Otane. It was out of sisterly duty that I sent the letter to Hikokurō asking him to divorce you. I wanted to save your life. I'm sure you know what I mean without my having to say it. You've been rather friendly with that drum teacher Gen'emon, haven't you?

NARRATOR: Otane flies at Ofuji and covers her mouth.

OTANE: Be still! You speak so casually, but it's no laughing matter. What have you seen that makes you say such a thing? Show me your proof!

OFUJI: I don't need any proof. You're four months pregnant. Whose child is it? And who's been taking that abortion medicine that your maid Orin's bought for you? You never guessed anybody knew, but the whole fief is gossiping about nothing else. I saw a minute ago how all those people brought you the same souvenir from Edo—hemp thread! I knew that they'd be coming to Hikokurō to tell him what was going on, to call his attention, as his friends, to the situation. You and you alone are responsible for destroying your family's honor and your husband's reputation as a samurai.

NARRATOR: She weeps aloud. Otane is at a loss for words.

OTANE: I never listened when you urged me not to drink. The liquor was my enemy.

NARRATOR: These are her only words; she can do nothing now but weep. Ofuji brushes away the welling tears.

OFUJI: Your repentance comes months too late. Now you know what I was worrying about. You are disgraced beyond redemption. I've wanted at least to save your life, and I've considered every possible scheme. I thought that if I could persuade Hikokurō to break with you and give you divorce papers, you could give birth to your baby in the middle of a public highway, and it still wouldn't be a crime. You couldn't be killed for it. So I tried, in my poor, feminine way, to help you. I made advances to my brother-in-law and acted like a loose woman. It wasn't only out of sisterly duty to you, however. I thought it was my duty to Mother. Poor Mother! I'm sure you can't have forgotten her last injunctions when, just two days before she died, she called us to her pillow, one on either side. "I've taught you, ever since you were children, the proper conduct for women. You've learned to read, to sew, to spin thread and to stretch cotton wool.[22] Any girl who knows that much has nothing to be ashamed of. But the most important test of a woman's training comes after she's married. You must treat your parents-in-law with the same devotion you have shown to your own parents, and your husband's brothers and sisters as if they were your own. When you are alone together with any other man you are not so much as to lift your head and look at him. It doesn't matter who the man may be—a servant, a member of the household, a stranger, an old man, or a boy—when your husband's away, you must observe the proprieties. A woman who's faulty in this may know the Four Books and the Five Classics by heart, but she'll be of no use to anybody.

[22] Used in padding cotton garments. An ability to stretch cotton wool or silk wool evenly was accounted a household art.

Remember these dying words of your mother. Let them be your Analects and never forget them."

Those words have sunk into my bones and are graven in my heart. I can't forget them. Then Mother went on, this time speaking to me, "Your sister has inherited her father's disposition. She's enjoyed drinking ever since she was in pinafores. Ofuji, you must act as a mother and admonish her in my place." These were her last words. Every day, morning and night, I repeat those last injunctions before her memorial tablet, just as if they were some holy writing. Have you forgotten them so soon? To think that you could wish to bring grief to your sister in this world and suffering on Mother's dead body in the world of the hereafter!

NARRATOR: She utters words of bitter reproach and weeps aloud in her misery. Otane is speechless, choked by tears.

OTANE: I see now that the saké I enjoyed so much was a poisonous brew compounded of the sins of a previous existence. As soon as the drunkenness from the benighting liquor had worn off I decided to kill myself, but I wanted so badly to see my husband's face once again that I put off my suicide from one day to the next. And now I have exposed my shame to the world. I wonder if I have been bewitched by some horrible demon.

NARRATOR: At these repeated words of vain regret the sisters, embracing, weep aloud with unrestrained voices, a pitiful sight in their utter helplessness. Just then a loud uproar is heard by the gate.

OTANE: It must be a fight. Let's leave for a while, until it quiets down.

NARRATOR: After they depart, Hikokurō's sister Yura enters, pursuing her brother with an outstretched lance.

YURA: I know I'm only your younger sister, Hikokurō, but I'm the wife of a samurai, Masayama Sangohei. Something has happened that violates all decency, and I can't condone it, though it involves my own brother. What do you say to that?

NARRATOR: Hikokurō glares at her.

HIKOKURŌ: You impudent little hussy! What effrontery to talk to me, your older brother, about decency or indecency! This is the height of impertinence! Out with your accusations! Out with them, or I'll twist your arms and that lance of yours, and break them both together!

NARRATOR: The words are spoken in fury. Yura laughs at him mockingly.

YURA: Admirably said, Mr. Weak-kneed! I'll tell you what's happened. Your wife has had a secret affair with Miyaji Gen'emon, a drum teacher from Kyoto, and the whole fief is buzzing with it now. That's why everybody gave her souvenirs of hemp thread—to call your attention to what was going on. But you pretend not to have heard anything, because you're unable to avenge yourself on your wife's lover. My husband has ordered me out of his house. He said he couldn't go on living with the sister of Weak-kneed Hikokurō. "You can return," he told me, "when your brother shows a little backbone. Then and only then will we be husband and wife again." We're separated now, and I've come to you. Well, my weak-kneed brother, are you going to reunite me with my husband or aren't you? It's up to you.

NARRATOR: She holds out the lance and brandishes it, seemingly ready to run him through if he flinches. Hikokurō claps his hands in amazement.

HIKOKURŌ: This is incredible—I suspected nothing! I've heard people talk of that Gen'emon, or whatever his name is, but I've never actually laid eyes on him. He's never set foot inside this house. What proof have you got?

YURA: Do you suppose that a man like Sangohei would make accusations without evidence? Your friend Isobe Yukaemon, suspecting that something was going on, used to come here, pretending it was merely to visit. He caught them one night in a secret rendezvous and cut off their sleeves. The affair has become a public scandal throughout the fief. It's impossible to hide it any longer, with the best will in the world. But there are some things that even a close friend can't tell a man to his face, and Yukaemon decided to inform my husband instead of going to you. Look!

NARRATOR: She produces from her kimono the sleeves of the guilty pair, and throws them before Hikokurō.

YURA: Have you any doubts left now?

NARRATOR: Her face is livid. Hikokurō picks up the sleeves and examines them.

HIKOKURŌ: I've never seen this man's sleeve before, but I remember the woman's costume very well. Yura, I promise you I shall lose no time in vindicating your honor. Come with me.

NARRATOR: He leads her into the sitting room. Everyone in the house has heard their conversation, and a breathless silence has fallen. Hikokurō speaks quite calmly.

HIKOKURŌ: Otane, you and the other women come here. Bunroku, I want you too.

NARRATOR: They all know that so curt a summons portends some disaster. They slowly come before Hikokurō and bow their heads. Their bodies are chilled, their spirits faint, they can scarcely breathe. Among them, wretched creature, is Otane, fated on account of an evil deed, none of her intent or desire, yet blamable only on herself, to be impaled on a blade wielded by her husband, as she fully expects. All her long, patient waiting for her husband's return has been in vain. Never, to this very moment when she is about to be killed, has she imagined that the pillow she shared with her husband on the night of his departure in the previous year would be their last together. At the thought she would like to look once more on her husband's face, but her eyes are too blinded with tears to see him. She weeps, her head hanging. Her husband throws the sleeves before her.

HIKOKURŌ: I'm sure you've all heard Yura's accusations. Well, woman, have you no excuse? No, I thought not—you can't answer. Ofuji, I presume you know who was their pander. In crimes of immorality the go-between shares the lovers' guilt.

OFUJI: You foolish man, Hikokurō! Had I known who pandered for them, do you suppose such a disgraceful thing would have happened?

NARRATOR: She weeps bitterly again.

HUKOKURŌ: The servant must have been the go-between. Send for the wench.

NARRATOR: At his summons the girl appears, trembling all over.

ORIN: Begging your pardon, sir, but I don't know anything about it. The other day Madam Otane asked me to buy some abortion medicine. She told me not to let anybody know. I bought three doses at seven *fun* a dose, which made two *momme* one *fun* altogether. That's all I ever did. Even so, I was afraid, master, if you heard about it you might scold me for buying such an expensive medicine. So I paid for it with bad coins.[23]

---

[23] Literally, paying with the debased coinage of 1706 a debt which should have been paid in good Genroku money.

NARRATOR: She prattles on in this inane fashion. Hikokurō is flabbergasted.

HIKOKURŌ: You say she's pregnant? Bunroku, I know you're still a boy, but why, when the whole fief's bursting with the scandal, didn't you kill Gen'emon and get rid of him long ago?

BUNROKU: I heard about it only this morning. I informed the household retainers, and they sent some men to Gen'emon's lodgings to kill him. But they discovered that he'd returned to Kyoto a couple of days ago.

HIKOKURŌ: It can't be helped then. Somebody light a fire in front of the Buddhist altar. Stand up, woman. Come here before the altar.

NARRATOR: His wife wipes away the tears.

OTANE: I expected you to hate me until the end of time. But I know now, when you tell me to stand before the Buddha, that something still remains of your old affection. How shall I forget it, even after death? My dear husband, I did not betray you intentionally, after knowing your goodness all those many months and years. My crime took place in a kind of nightmare. While I dreamt a horrible man—but if I go on it will only make my death mean and shameful. It may be wrong of me, I know, to kill myself before my husband's sword can strike, but let me vindicate myself in this way. Forgive me, please. This is my atonement.

NARRATOR: She pulls open the front of her kimono and plunges the dagger to the hilt into her breast, a moving display of her resolve.

Ofuji and Bunroku cry out in horror. The tears well in their hearts, but abashed by Hikokurō's impassive expression, they clench their teeth in silent grief. Hikokurō unsheathes his sword and, jerking up Otane's body, deals her the death blow with a final thrust. He pushes away the corpse, wipes his sword, and deliberately sheathes it. He rises to his feet: this is the stern behavior expected of a samurai.

Hikokurō takes up the traveling costume he had removed only this morning—his wicker hat, straw sandals, and sword.

HIKOKURŌ: Bunroku, I'm going now to report what has happened to my superiors. I shall ask for leave, though I can't wait until it is granted. I intend to proceed as quickly as possible to Kyoto. While I am busy disposing of my wife's paramour, I want you to escort these women to a safe place with our relatives.

NARRATOR: He starts to leave after these parting words. Ofuji, Bunroku, and Yura, all wishing to follow, vie in their eagerness to join him. Fury blazes in Hikokurō's dilated eyes.

HIKOKURŌ: Do you expect me to take the lot of you along just to kill one man, like some shopkeeper's vengeance? Are you trying to bring even more disgrace on me? If even one of you follows me, I'll never speak to you again.

NARRATOR: He is outraged. The others burst into tears.

OFUJI: You are being too unkind. The man, as far as I am concerned, is my sister's enemy.

BUNROKU: For me he's my mother's enemy.

YURA: And for me my sister-in-law's enemy.

ALL THREE: Can we allow this villain to go unpunished? Please let us go with you.

NARRATOR: The three together join their hands in supplication, weeping aloud. Hikokurō is unable to hide his grief any longer. His resolute expression gives way to despair.

HIKOKURŌ: If you think so much of your mother, sister, or sister-in-law, why didn't you beg me to spare her life? Why didn't you suggest that she put on Buddhist robes and become a nun?

NARRATOR: Lifting the lifeless body in his arms, he shouts his grief, and the others are carried away by tears of sympathy. The misery of it! This is the heartbreaking conduct demanded of those born to be samurai.

ACT THREE

Scene: The intersection of Horikawa (a street bordered by a canal) and Shimotachiuri Street in Kyoto. The action takes place inside and outside the house of Miyaji Gen'emon, which stands at this intersection.
Time: July 27, 1705.

NARRATOR: These are the streets of Kyoto—Temple, Procession, Doughcake, Wealth, Willow, and Border; and to the east of Midway Street, the jewel-like palace fence encloses the five-tasseled Imperial Carriage. Next come Karasuma, Money-changers, Muromachi, Wardrobe, New, Kettle, West Temple, Little River, Oil, Samegai, and Horikawa, the street of the moated river.[24] The level sand of the banks of Horikawa is reflected in the white waves, frost of a summer's night: even now the day breaks faintly at Shimotachiuri, this twenty-seventh day of July, the morning of the Gion Festival.

The four avengers set off at the hour of the Cockcrow Float,[25] with prayers for their success, eager to raise a shout of triumph as soon as the villain's head is severed by the Halberd Float. They wander at the crossroads, their fists clenched in readiness.

The Upper Town, a busy place even on ordinary days, today is noisy with visitors, here for the festival, streaming downtown. People are busy sweeping and sprinkling their gates before the morning mists rise and the crowds grow thick, and the four strangers, fearful lest their appearance arouse suspicions, decide to separate, to the east and west sides of the street. As they hesitate a moment, a peddler of lacquer bowls[26] goes by shouting loudly, "Never scratch! Never scratch!"— a prediction of failure that falls gloomily on their ears, enough indeed to dishearten them. "Heaven help us!" they cry. Just as each nears the bridge, some wretched old crones approach, driving pack horses laden with their wares, ornamental garden stones. One calls the other a familiar name.

WOMAN A: Ofuji! I was in such a hurry to get through my business today so I could go to the festival that I forgot to nail my horse's shoe.[27]

WOMAN B: That's funny. The same thing happened to me. This morning I overslept a little, and I left the house without nailing mine. Neither of us seems to have been able to nail a horseshoe today. Why don't we forget about nailing for the day and hurry back home instead?

NARRATOR: The women burst out laughing as they pass.

The children of Kyoto have a song they sing:

[24] The north-south streets of Kyoto are listed in order, going from east to west. They begin with Teramachi, Gokōmachi, Fuyachō, Tominokōji, Yanaginobambadōri, and Sakaimachi. I have translated the street names which yield a meaning.

[25] Huge floats are drawn through the streets during the Gion Festival. The names of two of them, *Naginata-boko* (Halberd Float) and *Niwatori-boko* (Cock Float, called Cockcrow here to suggest the hour) are incorporated in this passage.

[26] A free translation. The peddler is actually selling *kirazu*, which means at once the name of a kind of bean curd and "won't cut", referring here to a prediction that they won't "cut" Gen'emon's head.

[27] The verb *utsu* (to hit, kill, cut, "nail") suggests to Hikokurō and the others that they will not kill Gen'emon this day.

You can hear it all the way
Up to the top of Mount Hiei,
The noise in every house.
It's breakfast time in Kyoto!
Hear the chopping of the pickles
And the slurping of the soup!

What a noisy place Kyoto is in the morning! Each sound transfixes the strangers. Ofuji, most distressed of the four, speaks in a whisper.

OFUJI: What do the rest of you think? First there was the peddler shouting, "Never scratch! Never scratch!" That was upsetting enough, but on top of that, the old woman just now advised her friend to go home without nailing the horseshoes because they couldn't be nailed today. Everything seems to refer to us in the most depressing way. Worst of all—I know it happens often enough that people have the same name, but can you imagine such an unlucky coincidence? One of the women was called Ofuji! The hesitation we all feel must be a warning from Heaven that we'll surely fail if we insist on going through with our plan today. Tomorrow's another day. What do you say to postponing our revenge one day?

NARRATOR: Their courage falters. At that moment a young man, his hair disheveled and a toothpick in his mouth, emerges from the barber's at the west end of the bridge. He bumps into someone, presumably a friend.

FRIEND: Where are you going so early in the morning without even combing your hair?

YOUNG MAN: That's just it! I went to the barber's to get my forehead shaved so I could attend the festival in style today. But he slashed me— he slashed me! That new razor he used was nothing less than a sword! He slashed my whole head to ribbons! Heaven knows how many people that barber has hacked to death! Look what he did to me!

FRIEND: He certainly did cut you! With a head like that you'd do better as the sacrificial victim at some festival for the God of War than as a sightseer at Gion!

NARRATOR: They separate laughing. The four companions are delighted at the happy omen.

HIKOKURŌ: Did you hear that now?

OFUJI: I certainly did.

YURA: Our luck has turned.

BUNROKU: Everything will be all right now.

NARRATOR: A smile rises unconsciously to their lips; it is easy to imagine how much their spirits have been bolstered.

HIKOKURŌ: Well, then, let's strike without delay, while the good luck lasts. Get ready now!

NARRATOR: He tightens his sash in preparation for quick action.

HIKOKURŌ: It's useless to make plans here. We don't know anything about the inside of his house. You two women enter the little shop by the Horikawa entrance. Once you're inside, kick through the *shōji* and slip into the house. Bunroku and I will break through the courtyard gate at the Shimotachiuri entrance and force our way in. Don't let me mistake my man—I don't know him by sight. Once I find him, I'll tell him plainly my grievances, then dispatch him in a fitting manner. I don't want anyone to say that in our rash haste we resorted to foul play or cowardly tricks. Are you agreed?

OTHERS: We are.

HIKOKURŌ: Are you ready then?

OTHERS: Yes.

HIKOKURŌ: Then let's break our way in!

NARRATOR: They are bracing themselves for the attack when—look!— a samurai and his entourage approach along Oil Lane. He is a young man of twenty or so, dressed in pantaloons of imported silk and a hempen jacket. His men bear lances marked by candle-shaped scabbards. This samurai clearly has an income of more than 300 *koku* a year.

Three young retainers pass bearing lacquered boxes on poles, then a pair of servants, the samurai's sandal bearers, hurry along with a presentation stand labeled, "Ten pieces of silver." At Gen'emon's gate they call in provincial accents, "Visitors have come!"

A servant answers from inside, "Who is it?" Emerging, he crouches respectfully before the samurai at the moat's edge. Hikokurō and the others cannot hear what is said, but a little while later they see the samurai shake his head. He pronounces a message and offers the stand to the servant, who accepts it with a deep reverence and immediately goes inside. Bunroku scratches his head in perplexity.

BUNROKU: I thought we were all ready, but somebody's spoiled our plans. What are we going to do?

NARRATOR: He writhes in impatience.

HIKOKURŌ: Don't let it upset you. I'm sure that's a present to Gen'emon for having played the drum before some daimyo or nobleman. The samurai's just waiting for an answer, and then he'll leave. It won't take long. Wait a while.

NARRATOR: Even as he speaks the servant reappears, seemingly to invite the samurai within. After their master has entered the house the young retainers, servants, and sandal bearers stand their lances against the projecting eaves of the house, and slowly follow him inside.

Hikokurō and the others approach the house, intending to peep inside, but the inner door is bolted, and they can hear only voices. At that moment a priest with a begging bowl comes to the gate crying, "Alms! Alms!" A maid's voice calls, unpleasantly harsh and loud, "We're busy here. Move on." Hikokurō beckons to the priest dejectedly leaving.

HIKOKURŌ: Excuse me, priest, but you really look unsightly in such a tattered robe. Here, I present this money as a contribution. Please buy yourself a new robe. But leave the old one here. I'll give it to some beggar and make him happy.

NARRATOR: He offers the priest a gold coin. The priest's expression shows he thinks it may be a dream.

PRIEST: Thank you, Amida!

NARRATOR: He lifts the coin reverently again and again, and falls on his knees before Hikokurō.

PRIEST: I'll do what you asked.

NARRATOR: He slips off his old robe and leaves. Hikokurō, shaking out the robe, takes it to a dark corner under the crossroad gate. He slides his cloth cap to the back of his head and clamps a wicker hat on top in Amida-style.[28] He throws the priest's robe over his clothes. His disguise completed, he lifts the edge of the gate curtains and looks inside. He begins to intone the Kwannon Sutra, memorized long ago, at once a prayer for success in his undertaking and a ruse for examining the interior. "Trust yourself entirely to me; I will lend my strength." [29]

HIKOKURŌ: "Sutra of the Lotus of the Wonderful Law. The Bodhisattva Kanzeon, the Savior of Souls. Chapter Twenty-five. Thereupon the bodhisattva of inexhaustible thought left his seat, and baring his right shoulder, joined his hands in prayer. Facing the Buddha he rev-

[28] On the back of his head, as Amida wears a halo.
[29] From a poem in the *Shinkokinshū* (no. 1917), attributed to the Kwannon of the Kiyomizu Temple in Kyoto.

erently spoke. 'Your Worship, whence comes it that the Bodhisattva Kanzeon is called the Bodhisattva Kwannon?' " [30]

MAID: What a racket! Shut up, and I'll give you something.

NARRATOR: She runs outside. Accepting the alms from the maid's hand, he casually inquires.

HIKOKURŌ: Excuse me, miss, but could you tell me who that samurai was who came here a minute ago? He's certainly an early guest.

NARRATOR: The maid, like all servants, is a chatterbox.

MAID: Oh, he's a samurai from the country. He's been studying the drum with my master. It seems that he got promoted by the daimyo back home for his drum playing, and he says that it was all thanks to his teacher. He brought my master ten plaques of silver and the mistress five gold pieces, to show his appreciation. The rest of us have all been warmed by a present of 300 coppers apiece. You could recite the Kwannon Sutra all day long from morning to night, till you were sore in the throat, and you still wouldn't get 300 coppers for it. You'd be better off if you forgot all about your sutras and beat a hand drum instead. You'd do well to beat it now.

NARRATOR: She runs inside, still rattling out this unsolicited monologue. Hikokurō nods.

HIKOKURŌ: I see what's going on. That was a good sign—to be told to beat the drum now.[31]

NARRATOR: They all whisper words of encouragement. Before long the visitor, now without his hempen jacket and armed only with a dirk,[32] emerges by himself, his face covered with a wicker hat. He glances around, as if anxious not to be seen. He heads east along Shimotachiuri to East Temple Street, where he turns south. The others gather together and whisper their thoughts.

HIKOKURŌ: I'm sure that samurai has left his servants behind.

BUNROKU: Yes, those lances leaning on the gate will make people think that he's still inside, while actually he's off watching the festival.

YURA: He must have seven or eight servants in there. It won't be easy to kill Gen'emon with them around.

OFUJI: What are we going to do?

NARRATOR: Bunroku is an impetuous young man.

---

[30] The opening words of the so-called Kwannon Sutra, a part of the Lotus Sutra.

[31] Again, beating the drum (*utsu*) suggests *utsu* (to kill).

[32] The samurai is leaving the house incognito, having first removed his hempen jacket (*kamishimo*) and his swords.

BUNROKU: If we keep talking this way we'll never get the chance to carry out our plans. If he's got servants in there, that's all right with us. There's just one man we're after. Let the servants try to help him— we'll slaughter the lot of them. The rest is as our luck goes. Come on, let's break our way in swinging.

NARRATOR: He jumps from his hiding place.

HIKOKURŌ: Wait. I have an idea.

NARRATOR: Restraining the boy, Hikokurō approaches the gate again and lifts the curtain.

HIKOKURŌ: Excuse me, please. The gentleman in the wicker hat who came out of here a while ago has got himself into a fight on Muromachi Street north of Sanjō. He must have gone to see the procession. There's a mob surrounding him. I thought I'd let you know.

NARRATOR: The samurai's men dash out at once in wild alarm.

MAN A: Which way is Sanjō?

MAN B: How do we get to Muromachi?

MAN C: Is it north or west of here?

NARRATOR: They rush off, swords in hand, each determined not to be outdone.

HIKOKURŌ: My plan has worked perfectly. Now is our best possible chance. The hour of victory has come.

NARRATOR: Discarding his priest's robe, he drops it lightly to the ground. Hikokurō and Bunroku pass their dirks to the women, who thrust them into their sashes with a rattle of the scabbards. They knot headbands around their locks and hitch up their robes with under-sashes, so high that their knees can be seen, all white. Their steps are delicate, but their bearing is worthy of heroes.

They pray in their hearts, "We call on thee, Shō-Hachiman, Great Bodhisattva, bestow thy divine strength and authority on us." The two women go to the entrance on Horikawa, the father and son to Shimo-tachiuri. For a moment they are separated, but the next instant they are battering their way into the house, one after another, through the courtyard gate and the *shōji* in the shop. The maids and menservants inside are taken by surprise and flee through the back gate with terri-fied shrieks.

OFUJI: There—that's Miyaji Gen'emon!

NARRATOR: Gen'emon has been idly relaxing until this moment, but at Ofuji's cry he springs to his feet and dashes halfway up the stairs to the second floor. He sits on a step and stares around him with clenched fists, awaiting their attack. The two women, not allowing him a moment's respite, close in from both sides. Hikokurō emits a great shout.

HIKOKURŌ: I'm Ogura Hikokurō! I discovered your immoral relations with my wife Otane, and I killed her on the seventeenth of this month. You're not going to escape either, seducer!

NARRATOR: He charges at Gen'emon, drawing his sword and striking with one motion.

GEN'EMON: Right!

NARRATOR: He lifts his foot and, putting his hand on the step, starts for the second floor. The two women, closely pursuing, try to follow him up, but Gen'emon's wife, snatching a halberd from the wall, engages the women with the weapon and keeps them from climbing upstairs. The servants in the meanwhile burst in with clubs, canes, and brooms, and block the attackers. As Hikokurō and the others hesitate, Gen'emon thrusts his hand through the latticework window and grabs one of the lances leaning against the eaves. He holds it with the point directed down the stairs, ready to pinion anyone who attempts to mount. Hikokurō mocks him.

HIKOKURŌ: What are you trying to do with that lance—stick a rat? You can hold a drum, I suppose, but I see you've never learned how to hold the shaft of a lance! Your defense is full of holes! I'll show you what I can do against your puny little lance!

NARRATOR: He slashes at Gen'emon's lance and splits it near the haft with a crackling sound.

GEN'EMON: You insolent cur!

NARRATOR: He picks up a gaming-table[33] in one hand, a display of main force, and brandishes it.

GEN'EMON: I'm no samurai, and I've never learned to hold a lance. But I know all about beating, thanks to my drums! Here, have a taste of this table!

NARRATOR: Taking careful aim, he slams it down on Hikokurō and follows it with a backgammon board, a shōgi board, a brazier, a tobacco tray, a kettle, teacups, and a box of pillows[34] that he rips

[33] Actually, a go board. Unlike Western chessboards, the go board is a considerable piece of furniture, not easily lifted in one hand. I have therefore used the word "gaming-table".

[34] Small Japanese pillows packed in two layers of five each.

open. He throws anything that comes to hand, so furiously that it is exactly like a driving rainstorm. There seems no way to approach him, but Yura, slipping out the front door, climbs up the corner gate hand over hand, until she stands on the door bar. She crawls up over an overhanging ledge, then, drawing her dirk, slashes at Gen'emon from behind. In desperation he overturns a four-foot screen on her. They struggle, he pressing down while she squirms to be free. He finally twists the dirk from her hand, but at this moment Hikokurō races up the stairs in pursuit. He closes on Gen'emon with his sword, shouting, "You won't get away!" The swordplay reaches a wild climax. Gen'emon, seeing that he is no match for his attacker, leaps from the window to the street. Hikokurō nimbly jumps after him, and chases Gen'emon onto the bridge, slashing all the while. The neighbors from all around slam their gates in alarm, shrieking, "It's a fight!" "Hit him," they cry, "Kill him!" They cluster round the combatants.

The two women call to the crowd.

WOMEN: This is an official vengeance.[35] It does not concern any of you. Don't do anything foolish!

NARRATOR: They station themselves right and left of the gate. The two men, knowing this is the decisive moment, draw deep breaths, then fall on each other. Gen'emon slashes away in life-and-death fury, scattering confused showers of sparks, but Hikokurō, apparently feeling that it degrades a samurai to fight with a townsman, scarcely moves. When Gen'emon attacks, Hikokurō merely repels him, but after two or three exchanges he thinks, "Now is my chance!" He charges, swift as a shot arrow. He slashes diagonally downwards from Gen'emon's left shoulder to his right hand. His enemy falls on all fours like a dog. Bunroku leaps on him at once.

BUNROKU: My mother's enemy!

NARRATOR: He drives his sword into Gen'emon's body.

OFUJI: My sister's enemy! Take this from Ofuji!

NARRATOR: She strikes him hard.

YURA: Here is a sword of fury for my sister-in-law's enemy!

NARRATOR: She rips him with the blade. The four of them lean over Gen'emon and with one accord deal the final thrust, a deed unparalleled in all history.

[35] That is, they have reported to the authorities their intention of seeking vengeance, and this is therefore not a case of murder.

The neighbors gather round with sticks in their hands.

SENIOR NEIGHBOR: This may be an official vengeance as you say, but for our protection in the neighborhood we'll take charge of your weapons. You are not to leave until an official order one way or another is issued. (*To associates.*) Take them to the ward office and lock them up.

NARRATOR: The crowd surrounds the four avengers, who walk calmly off, a splendid, noble, heartening sight. Word quickly spreads everywhere that they have struck their adversary. They have killed him to the jingle and the jangle of the celebrated floats.[36]

The story of the vengeance of the wronged husband has been told in this play by the tongues of the chanters exactly as it happened, and we thank you for your kind favor.

---

[36] The musicians riding aboard the floats play percussion instruments and flutes in a characteristic jingling rhythm. The onomatopoeic sounds of this rhythm blend into other words meaning to kill with a sword.

YOSAKU FROM TAMBA

First performed in 1708. Yosaku and Koman were names familiar to Chikamatsu's audiences from a well-known ballad of the late seventeenth century. The rather improbable ending of the play was apparently dictated by the lines of the ballad, "Yosaku from Tamba was a horse driver, but now he's a sworded samurai in Edo." The ballad places the action of the play about 1665, but essentially it deals with events of 1708.

A congratulatory dance at the end of the play is omitted in this translation; it has no connection with the rest of the work.

Cast of Characters

YOSAKU, aged 31, formerly a samurai, but now a packhorse driver

SANKICHI, aged 11, his son, also a driver

HACHIZŌ, a driver

HONDA YASAZAEMON, the chief retainer of a daimyo

SAGISAKA SANAI, a samurai

INNKEEPER, WATCHMAN, INSPECTOR, HEADMAN, OFFICERS, SOLDIERS, and COURIERS

PRINCESS SHIRABE, aged 10

SHIGENOI, governess to the princess and wife of Yosaku

WAKANA, a maid

KOMAN, aged 21, a prostitute

KOJORŌ and KOYOSHI, prostitutes

PROCURESS, SERVANTS, WIFE of the innkeeper

ACT ONE

Scene: A daimyo's palace in the province of Tamba.

NARRATOR: A single seed born of a daimyo swells to tens of thousands of measures of rice; [1] even in its mother's womb countless vassals pay it homage and sound the drums of their praise.

Yurugi, the lord of a castle in Tamba, has a daughter Shirabe, born to a serving maid while he was home from Edo in his province.[2] Her hair is ceremonially bound with a golden fillet, and though not yet ten, a girl of slender build, she wears a woman's robes. She is promised as a foster child to Iruma, a noble lord from the East, plucked in the bud to be his son's bride. Twenty mounted samurai, headed by one of the highest rank, will escort her to the East, and a children's doctor accompanies her palanquin. Ladies in waiting of high and middle rank, nurses, governesses, and gentlewomen of every quality ride in her train. Their chairs and those of the servants, 480 in all, must be numbered to avoid confusion. The bridal gifts—gold, silver, agate, and coral in branches, long-handled parasols of polished lacquer flecked with gold, halberds and umbrellas in silken cases—are borne aloft in boxes covered with antique gold brocades worked in figured and floral patterns,[3] some with the royal paulownia crest, and tied on top with heavy crimson knots that make one think they are peonies in bloom. The kitchen baggage will be sent by relays, and the valuables on pack horses accompanying the train. The drivers of the thirty horses are accomplished ballad singers, chosen, with no expenses spared, for their good looks and fine voices.

At the appointed hour of nine in the morning, Honda Yasazaemon, the senior member of the escort,[4] appears, his legs unsteady from too much toasting, gallantly attired in damask breeches and a traveling mantle of scarlet silk, his shining bald head and face inflamed—only his fringe of hair is white.

---

[1] A daimyo's income was calculated in terms of *koku*, a measure of about 5.1 bushels of rice. "A single seed" also means "a beloved only child". The sentence as a whole means that a daimyo's child from birth is marked as the heir to a great fortune.
[2] The daimyo were required to spend alternate years in Edo, where they left their wives. Concubines took the place of wives while the daimyo were back in their provinces.
[3] The original text lists the patterns, which include a crest of a crane with outspread wings flying within a diamond, a rabbit with a flower in its mouth, and melon slices.
[4] Literally, a senior retainer serving within the women's quarters.

HONDA: Well, now. If the whole retinue is assembled, those of you in the lead start moving out. You, Bunza and Gengoza, bring up the rear. You are to follow exactly my orders of last night. Junior samurai, lackeys, coolies, and errand boys are not to indulge in heavy drinking. Any rowdiness at relay stations, ferry crossings or elsewhere will be punished. And let there be no flirting with waitresses at inns along the way. For one thing, it's unbecoming in the company of the princess. I daresay, however, that the lower ranks will get bored on such a long journey. If any of you are contemplating lovemaking, please do it quickly and inconspicuously in a dark place. This, after all, is a joyous occasion, and since it's a lady we're escorting, I'm sure a peccadillo or two will be overlooked.

NARRATOR: "Yes, sir" is the reply, and the baggagemasters cry, "Let's be off!" At that moment women's voices are heard from the house.

VOICES: Wait! Please wait! What are we to do? The princess is having a tantrum and insists that she won't go to Edo. Her mother and his lordship have been coaxing and scolding her, but the princess is sulky. She says she hates going so much that nothing can change her mind. Lady Shigenoi, her governess, has tried every argument, but the princess says, "If you want to go to Edo so much, nanny, go by yourself." She struck the governess's back! She's in a dreadful mood.

NARRATOR: Just then the princess, her painted eyebrows washed away by her tears,[5] cries out.

PRINCESS: I don't like Edo or anywhere in the East. I won't go.

NARRATOR: She runs outside in tears. The samurai in attendance and the servants flee in consternation to the gate.[6] Not a single man remains apart from the senior escort. The governess colors.

SHIGENOI: Your ladyship. Even children of the lower classes by the time they are nine or ten will listen to reason. Look now, that white-haired old gentleman and all those splendid samurai have traveled hundreds of miles over mountains and rivers to welcome you. Once you reach Edo you'll be waited on respectfully as the bride-to-be of Lord Iruma's eldest son. But if you won't go, people will blame it on

[5] Japanese girls when sent in marriage formerly shaved off their eyebrows and painted on false ones. The princess, going to Edo to be married, is treated like a bride. Her tears have presumably been smeared by her sleeve onto her brow, and have washed off the false eyebrows.

[6] Only Honda, on service in the women's quarters, would be permitted to appear before the princess; other men run away in embarrassment.

the training I gave you and I'll have to commit hara-kiri, even though I'm a woman. Come, be a good child. Get into your palanquin.

NARRATOR: Threaten and cajole as she may—

PRINCESS: No, no! You're all trying to deceive me. What's so good about the East? Listen to what my maids sing! Come here, everyone. Sing that song of yours.

MAIDS:

> "If you go all the way to Edo,
> Even for a little while,
> You can't see any mountains.
> When will you return?
> Kill me now, before you go,
> For I'll never let you leave."
> So said the girl in tears . . .[7]

SHIGENOI: Stop! Stop! Don't you know that children serving in a daimyo's palace are supposed to sing refined songs to *koto* accompaniment? Wherever did you learn that disreputable piece? You're not to teach it to the princess. I want you to stop this instant.

NARRATOR: What a rage the governess is in! Honda is at his wits' end.

HONDA (*to the princess*): Your ladyship. That song about Edo is just a joke. Edo's the City of Flowers, a much nicer place than Kyoto. I'll show you the cherry blossoms at Asakusa and Ueno in their full glory, and the puppet theater in Sakai and Kobiki Streets, where the drums bang thumpety-thump, and Benkei and Kimpira slash at each other, take-this, take-that. And on the way you'll see a wonderful sight, the mountain called Fuji, that reaches all the way up to Heaven. Come, please, into your palanquin.

NARRATOR: He exhausts all his powers of persuasion.

PRINCESS: No, I won't go to Edo. I hate the thought.

NARRATOR: Her governess is at a loss what to do, and the senior escort is utterly dismayed. Wakana, a maidservant, carrying a wicker hat for the journey, runs inside from the gate.

WAKANA: Excuse me, madam governess. The most interesting thing is happening. A little horse driver, a shaven-headed boy of ten, has spread out a picture of the road between here and Edo, and he's playing an exciting game. Please let the princess see it. I'm sure it'll cheer her.

---

[7] A popular ballad, also quoted in "The Love Suicides at Sonezaki." Used here to suggest the princess's unwillingness to go to Edo.

SHIGENOI: I'm glad you noticed. I've heard about this map game. Yes, please show it to the princess—it may distract her. It doesn't matter even if he's a packhorse driver. He's only a child, after all. You have my permission. Call the boy and tell him to bring his game.

WAKANA: Yes, madam.

NARRATOR: She goes to the gate and returns with the horse driver, a boy with one shoulder bared and a mop of unruly hair. Unabashed in the presence of a princess, he sits on the edge of the verandah, one foot on his other knee.

SANKICHI: Well, now. You folks have really ruined my day. Me and my pals were betting on the map game, and I was about to make me the price of a new pair of shoes, when somebody came after me. What can I do for you, ladies? You'd better hurry. On your horses! We're moving out the horses!

NARRATOR: His tongue is sharp.

SHIGENOI: You're a clever rascal. Boatmen, horse drivers, and nurses are three of a kind, they say—ill-natured the lot of them.[8] That makes you and me the same, doesn't it? Tell me, how old are you? And what's your name?

SANKICHI: I'm eleven. I've been driving horses ever since I was five. I'm a born leader, I am—never was and never will be anybody's fag.[9] My name's Sankichi, the Wild One.

SHIGENOI: That's a fine name. I'm told you have a map game. (*To maids.*) Why don't you try your hands at it, girls? Princess, please play too. Come here, Sankichi. There's nothing to be afraid of.

NARRATOR: She calls, and Sankichi, with an answering shout, unhesitantly joins the ladies, still puffing on his little pipe. That no one finds his behavior amiss shows the advantage of being a child. Sankichi takes out his map and soon all are playing the game together.

Watch the board and shake the dice! Here's the way to travel the fifty-three stages of the Edo Road[10] without leaving your home,

[8] A proverb, sometimes interpreted as meaning that all three were fond of gossip.

[9] Sankichi says literally that he is a born "elder brother" and would never be the "younger brother" in a pederastic relationship. His determination to be the "elder" despite his youth is shown also by his having shaven off his front lock, the mark of a "younger brother."

[10] The Tōkaidō, the highway between Kyoto and Edo, had fifty-three stages, celebrated in Hiroshige's prints. In the map game each of the fifty-three stages has a box with its name and a picture of some local curiosity. The players move their pieces along from box to box until they reach Edo, their progress being determined by the roll of the

giddyap. The dice are of cherry wood,[11] and the cherry blossoms of
Kyoto are at the center of the board, the starting point for each one's
marker. "I'll go first!" The first stage is Departure Beach in Ōtsu, three
leagues away. Pay your passage here for Yabase, all aboard, all aboard!
What an uproar the travelers make, afraid to miss the boat for Grass-
ford! The nurse arrives before the princess gobbles down the nurse
cakes [12] one, two, three. At Threegulps they dance by a dancing bowl of
mudfish soup. Then to Under-the-Hill, the next stage, if so the dice decree. Shake the dice, make them ring at Belling Deer. A lucky throw
leaves the pass behind.[13] Eager to win, each hurries, not wasting a second at Seki on the way. From there to Kameyama; they light their pipes
with flints at Stone Buddha. "Oh, there's the Kuwana ferry!" [14] Landing
by the Atsuta Shrine, it's four leagues more to Chiryū, where again the
dice roll like "the whores of Okazaki, the whores of Okazaki." Oh,
twine yourselves round them, at Wisteria River you'll find them waiting, one for every taste! At Red Hill the hostesses untie their red aprons.
The travelers hurry past Yoshida, Futakawa, and Shirasuka. "Has the
lady a barrier permit?" [15] "Yes, in my sleeve. At Rough Well my sleeves
New Rip." [16] "Here's your boat! And here are clams for sale!" Clams,
clams, all the way to Beach Pines by way of Dancing Hill, three leagues
farther on. When they hear their inn this night is at Fuji View, where
they'll find the girls say "I love you," no one hesitates to empty his
purse. Bag Well, Pack River, on they fly, dismounting in high spirits and
with smiling faces at Chuckle Hill for fern-shoot cakes. What have you

---

dice. For a description of the Tōkaidō see Statler, *Japanese Inn,* or Jippensha Ikku,
Hizakurige.

[11] The dice are apparently not cubes but hexagonal teetotums marked with Chinese
characters on each face in place of numbers. Dice with numbers are, however, mentioned later in the passage.

[12] Most of the place names in this passage, the names of the stages of the Tōkaidō,
occasion puns or plays on words. I have translated these names when necessary to
preserve the pun. Local products are also woven into the plays on words. Here the
name of "nurse cakes" (*ubagamochi*), a delicacy sold at Grass-ford (Kusatsu) refers
also to the progress of the nurse (Shigenoi) in the game.

[13] Suzuka-tōge. They are traveling eastwards from Minakuchi (Threegulps), past
Tsuchiyama (Earth Mountain).

[14] At Kuwana, they save time by cutting across the Bay of Ise to Atsuta.

[15] At the barrier of Arai (Rough Well), a particularly severe examination was made of
travelers, to make sure that no women or weapons were being moved illegally.

[16] I have chosen one possible pun for the name Imagire (New Rip); it might also
mean "new cloth", in which case Arai might be a pun for a word meaning "wash".
Or perhaps no pun is intended at all.

at your side?[17] In all Japan the biggest river, Ōikawa. Now you've thrown snake-eyes,[18] the river's in flood, and you're stuck for two days at Shimada and Kanaya, where eighty streams converge. You've made a lucky throw now—you jump six, seven, eight leagues in one step, forward, ever forward, to Wisteria Branch, where blossoms are opening, to Okabe and to Seto for colored rice. To Utsu Mountain next for strings of dumplings: buying the noted products here and there, we empty our pockets of jack, and playing jacks we go by Jackville,[19] onesey, twosey, threesey, four, through Fuchū, Ejiri, one after the other, and watch the dice roll through Breaking Wave. At Clear View Temple let us draw out the moon over the swelling pine groves by buying the local salve.[20] Past Yui, Kambara, and then Yoshiwara, famous for the fragrant skins of its broiled eels,[21] to Slippery Ford and over Mishima, three leagues more to Hakone. We cross the Barrier, thanks to the dice, but a bad throw would have sent us back to Kyoto, the starting point, to pick up our permits.[22] "Have you understood the rules?" "I've digested them"—the sweet rice pills of Odawara. Past Ōiso, Hiratsuka, Fujisawa, all without hindrance—the dice are lucky, the pace is good, and we hurry on our way to Rush Hill and Quickvale, past Kanagawa, Kawasaki, and Shinagawa. Leading them all, the winner is the winsome princess, first in Edo, city of flowers. Six is the other side of one on the dice, bringing luck, joy, and comfort: the princess laughs in delight with the map game.

Cheered for her victory by the onlookers, the princess, child that she is, speaks in elation.

[17] The line suggests the story of Momotarō. Asked what he has at his side, he replies, "The finest millet cakes in Japan (*Nippon ichi no kibidango*)." But here we are told of the finest (or biggest) river in Japan.

[18] The poorest throw of the dice.

[19] I have tried by a related series of plays on words to approximate the original.

[20] Various puns and plays on names are imbedded here. *Haruru* has two meanings, "to swell" and "to clear". By using the famous salve made at Seikenji (Clear View Temple), one can draw out the moon from the swelling clouds and cause the sky to clear over the pines. For an account of the salve's history and popularity, see Statler, *Japanese Inn*, pp. 153–64.

[21] Mention of Yoshiwara suggests the gay quarters in Edo. The listener, hearing the words "fragrant skin," imagines that this is a reference to the prostitutes, only to be brought up short by mention of broiled eels, the famous product of the other Yoshiwara. The slipperiness of eels leads to the next place name, Numazu (Marsh Ford).

[22] A permit was needed to pass through the barriers. Landing on an unlucky spot in the map game would send the player back "home".

PRINCESS: How exciting the East is! I never realized it before. Let's be on our way. I can't wait to leave.

HONDA: You'll go, did you say? That's wonderful! Form a procession, men, before the princess changes her mind again!

NARRATOR: He bustles about, and the governess is cheerful again.

SHIGENOI (*to princess*): Very well, then. Go drink one final parting cup with your parents. (*To Sankichi.*) It's all thanks to you, Mr. Horse Driver. Well done. Well done, my lad. You have my thanks and I'll give you a reward too. Wait there, please.

NARRATOR: She goes inside with the princess as the place stirs with activity.

Sankichi, the packhorse driver, walks around the room, peeping curiously at the golden panels, quite unlike anything he has seen be-fore. His feet, accustomed only to straw mats, hesitate on the smoothly woven flooring.

SANKICHI: Hey! This room is so damned slippery I can't walk. My own place is a lot nicer than any daimyo's house.

NARRATOR: He mutters to himself. The governess returns with sweets piled high on the lid of a writing box lined with crinkly paper.

SHIGENOI: Sankichi, are you still here?—What a fine young man you are! The princess says now that she'll go to Edo, and it's because you showed her your map game. Her parents are delighted. These cakes are from her ladyship. You should accept them gratefully. And here are three strings of copper coins for you to buy a present for yourself. I'm told that you'll be with us all the way to Edo. Remember, if you need anything, just say you'd like to see Shigenoi, the governess.— The more I look at you, the more taken I am. Your parents must have been desperately poor to have made you drive horses.

NARRATOR: Sankichi listens attentively through this kind speech.

SANKICHI: Are you Shigenoi, the governess who works for Lord Yurugi? If you are, then you must be my mother!

NARRATOR: He throws his arms around her.

SHIGENOI: Ugh, what shocking manners! Your mother! I have no son who's a horse driver!

NARRATOR: She wrenches herself free, only for Sankichi to clutch at her frantically. She shakes him off; he clings to her again.

SANKICHI: What reason would I have to lie to you? My father, Date no Yosaku, used to be your husband, a long time ago when he was a samurai commander here. I'm his son, and I came from your belly. Yonosuke—that's my real name. I was only three when Father made his lordship angry. He had to leave the province, but I can remember him faintly. I learned from the old woman who looked after me in Kutsukake [23] that my parents had separated and my mother was in his lordship's service. She explained everything very patiently. "I've brought you up in the hopes that some day I might unite you with your father. There's no chance of that now. Your best plan would be to look for Shigenoi. She works as a governess for Lord Yurugi. Show her this charm bag she made for you. It will prove she's your mother."

When I was five the old woman went to the festival at Toba. She'd been troubled by the croup for a long time, and some rice cakes stuck in her throat. Before you knew it, she was dead. The people in the village looked after me, but soon I was learning to drive horses. Now I'm working for a horse-lender at Ishibe in Ōmi.

Here, look at this charm bag, please. Why should I lie to you? There's no doubt about it. I'm your son. Let's find Father and stay together in one place, even if it's just for a day. That's the only thing I wish for. I make wonderful horseshoes, and I wove these straw sandals myself. I'll take care of you and Father. I'll drive horses by day and make horseshoes and sandals by night. Please stay with Father. I beg you, Mother.

NARRATOR: He clings to her and weeps.

Shigenoi is almost out of her mind with excitement. The more she looks, the more he seems her son, Yonosuke. She remembers the charm bag, and yearns to hold the boy to her breast. But she thinks

SHIGENOI (*to herself*): My duty is more important. It would be a blot on the princess's name if this were discovered. Shall I lie and send him away with a reproof? No—I can't. I feel too much pity for him. Oh, I wish I could take him in my arms, even for a few moments. What shall I do?

NARRATOR: Her tears of grief for a hundred, thousand woes are too much for two eyes to hold. She sobs.

SHIGENOI: No, no. He's a clever boy, even if he is my own son. He

[23] A village near Suzuka in Ise Province.

won't believe me if I lie. It would be heartbreaking if he despised his mother as a corrupt woman. I'll tell him the truth and make him understand. I'll make him feel ashamed, then I'll send him away.

NARRATOR: She wipes away the tears and steadies herself.

SHIGENOI: Come here, Yonosuke.

NARRATOR: She draws him to her and takes his hands.

SHIGENOI: What a big boy you've become! But why, while you were about growing up, didn't you turn out more impressive, more like a samurai? Those aren't the features, those aren't even the hands and feet I gave you when you were born. Your beautiful black hair has been hacked off, and your arms and legs look as if they belong to some filthy, wild monkey. Yes, a child's upbringing is really more important than his birth.

NARRATOR: She weeps again bitterly.

SHIGENOI: Now listen carefully to what I say. It is quite true that you were born from my flesh, but you're not my child any longer, nor am I your mother. I don't say this, believe me, because I dislike you for having become so coarse. Try to understand my reasons.

When I was first in her ladyship's service, your father was a page in her quarters. The breezes of young love caressed and drew us together, and one night's meeting became two nights, then many nights. I had the misfortune to lose a letter he sent me, and it was picked up in an antechamber by the supervisor of the pages. Discipline for us in the samurai class is severe, particularly so in this household, and the elder retainers decided that your father and I must die at his lordship's hands. Her ladyship pleaded for my life, offering to take the punishment on herself. His lordship was moved in his mercy not only to forgive us our crime, but to make us man and wife in the sight of the world. Yosaku gradually rose to be chief aide to his lordship, with a stipend of 1,300 *koku*. We were so indebted to his lordship that we should have had to kill ourselves if he died. In the meantime I gave birth to you, and a princess was born to her ladyship. As a mark of her ladyship's friendship, I was allowed to offer my milk to the princess.

If things had continued going so well, you would now rank as high as a senior retainer's son and not be obliged to defer to anyone. But unfortunately your father, who was on duty in Edo at the time, began frequenting the prostitutes of Yoshiwara. He bungled his duties so badly that once again he was sentenced to commit hara-kiri.

But if he were obliged to kill himself, his wife could not remain in the mansion. People said that it might bring on some sickness if the princess were deprived of my milk. Your father's life was therefore spared again, in order that I might stay on in the palace, but he was deprived of his rank and stipend as a samurai. It would have been normal for me as his wife to leave with him, but if I had made the princess suffer by denying her my milk, how could I ever have repaid the excessive generosity of his lordship's family? Your father urged that I remain behind and satisfy our obligations. And so, for my husband's sake above all, I chose loyalty to her ladyship in place of wifely duties. Much against our desires, we separated.

Now here you are. You're only a child, I know, but you're the heir of a disgraced father, and I'm worried what may happen if they find you out. Never tell anyone that you're Yosaku's child. Hurry outside now.—Ahhh, what did I ever do to deserve such a fate? To have my own child become a horse driver, and not to know where my husband is. What use is it to wear fine clothes, to be addressed respectfully as madam governess, milady in waiting, or to ride in a splendid palanquin?

NARRATOR: She weeps softly.

The boy is naturally intelligent. His brightness makes him weep all the more.

SANKICHI: What a sad story! But the old woman used to tell me that the princess and I were suckled at the same breast, so if I could only find my mother it would also help Father to get on his feet again. Please, I beg you, appeal to his lordship.

NARRATOR: Shigenoi instantly covers his mouth.

SHIGENOI: Hush! You must never say that you and she were suckled at the same breast. The princess is leaving for the East to be adopted and married. Any girl about to be married, whether she's of a great or humble family, must be very careful. She's going among strangers, and she has to worry about what they may think. It's bound to interfere with her marriage if people learn that she has a foster brother named Sankichi who's a horse driver. A dyke may be breached by the burrowing of a single ant, they say,[24] and though this may seem a small matter, it's very serious. But if we go on whispering, someone is sure to hear. Hurry off now.

[24] A proverb, ultimately derived from the Chinese philosopher Han Fei Tzu.

SANKICHI: Mother, you worry too much about what people will think. Please try and talk to her.

SHIGENOI: Are you still harassing me? You don't understand. How could a mother fail to know her duty, when it concerns her own husband and child? Why are you so obtuse and unreasonable?

NARRATOR: As she attempts to quiet him, a voice is heard from inside.

VOICE: Where is Shigenoi? Her ladyship is calling.

SHIGENOI: Did you hear that? Someone is coming. Leave me now.

NARRATOR: She leads him out by the hand. Poor Sankichi—he is in tears and sobbing, but he covers his face and eyes. He collects his shoes and, tucking them into his belt, goes off, an utterly dejected figure.

SHIGENOI: Boy! Turn this way again. Don't hurt yourself on the journey. If it's stormy or snowy or you must travel at night, pretend you have a stomach ache and rest for a couple of days. Take care not to get sick. Don't eat anything that disagrees with you. Be careful of stomach aches, and watch out for the measles. Poor boy, you look so pathetic, my heart goes out to you. What crime did you commit that you, who should have inherited 1,300 *koku,* have been punished this way?

NARRATOR: She throws herself on the entrance step, where she lies sobbing. Then she takes all the money she has—thirteen *bu* of gold— and wraps the coins in a silk cloth.[25]

SHIGENOI: Here, take this for an emergency.

NARRATOR: Sankichi turns back with bitterness.

SANKICHI: If you're not my mother and I'm not your son, you needn't worry whether I get sick or die. I don't want your money. I'm a horse driver, that's what I am, and I'm the son of Date no Yosaku. You don't suppose I'd accept money from a stranger who's not my mother? You're a cruel woman, and you'll regret this!

NARRATOR: He bursts into tears and his mother, seeing him, is faint with grief.

SHIGENOI: Would I let my only child leave me if I didn't have to think of the princess and the debt I owe her family? Oh, the misery of being in service!

NARRATOR: She weeps in anguish and longing.

[25] Thirteen *bu* would be worth about one hundred dollars. One *bu* was the equivalent of one quarter of a *ryō* of gold.

The entrance to the women's quarters is suddenly noisy with shouts of "We're leaving!" The bearers, lifting the princess's palanquin, stream out in procession. The governess's chair is placed directly before them. Shigenoi speaks in a casual tone.

SHIGENOI: I'd like that little horse driver who was here a minute ago to stay with my chair as a companion for the princess. Ask him to cheer us with a song.

NARRATOR: "Yes, madam," says the leader of the train. He barks out a harsh command. "Hey, wild boy, you over there, sing something!— Look, he's crying! That's a bad sign, just when we're leaving." The boy, taking two or three blows of the leader's fists, sings in a tearful voice.

SANKICHI:

> At Hillside it's shining, shining,
> At Belling Deer it's cloudy,
> At Earth Mountain,
> Earth Mountain in between,
> The rain is falling.[26]

NARRATOR: Thicker than any rain fall the tears of mother and child, hers hidden within her heart.

ACT TWO

Scene: Outside the Shiroko House, an inn in the town of Seki, on the Edo road.
Time: A few days later.

PROCURESS (*to passersby*): Stopping for the night, aren't you? If you're going to stop, here's the place. Stop here, stop here! The rooms are cheap; we'll put you up. We have luxury suites and modest apartments, whatever you're looking for, whatever you like. The dishes are clean, the mats in the rooms were changed this summer. The bedding is good, the saké is good, the tea is the best. Stop just for the cost of your firewood. The bath has its own boiler, there's plenty of hot water; dip a little from the soaking-tub and test it yourself, wash away the dust of the journey. Will you be leaving at the crack of

[26] Part of a well-known ballad. Saka (Hillside), Suzuka (Belling Deer), and Tsuchiyama (Earth Mountain) were places along the Tōkaidō.

dawn or at seven? If you need some diversion in bed, we have what you want, whether a blushing girl or an experienced woman. She'll rub your legs and massage your back, she'll offer you a pipe with a lighted bowl, she'll bowl you over, she'll send shivers down your spine.—Say, aren't you Rokuzō from Shōno? Those are fine ladies you have riding with you. It must make your step lighter.

ROKUZŌ: None of your lip, you hussy.

PROCURESS: Sansuke and Sanzō from Kusatsu! Kinkichi from Ishibe! If your customers are spending the night, put them down here. (*To customers.*) No matter how far you go, the inns are all the same. They sing one note like the birds in spring.[27] You there, with the salty look in your eyes, are you drumming up trade for Ise?[28] Visit the Shrine in the spring! And you, my reverend priest, wearing a paper cloak on a warm day like this—you must be a Sendai man.[29] There's a traveler who looks as if he was born at Yawata—his legs are hairy as a burdock![30] And you, sir, in the straw hat, I can tell you're from Broomland[31]—everything's swept clean around your feet, your waist, your whole body. And you, young gentleman with the crinkly locks, are you from Echigo or Akashi?[32] Look, there's a daimyo, a fine gentleman with a long face like a melon seed—he must be from Tōji.[33] Is the young man in bangs coming behind him from Yoshino? What a splendid nose![34] Those messengers plodding over there are surely from Sticky River.[35] You can tell Hitachi men by their sashes.[36] Oh, look at the footman! You're from Etchū, I see. How do I know? From your loincloth! Untie the strings and spend a night here!

NARRATOR: In the evening dusk she hails the hurrying travelers. Lust

[27] Meaning the prices are the same everywhere. A pun on *ne* (price) and *ne* (sound).
[28] "Salty" because Ise is on the coast. The word "salty" had the meaning of "seductive" at the time. Visits to Ise were most frequently made in spring.
[29] Cloaks made of thick paper stained with persimmon juice were a famous product of Sendai.
[30] Yawata, a town near Kyoto, was famous for *gobō* (the burdock).
[31] Hōki was the name of a province; it also means "a broom".
[32] Both Echigo and Akashi were famous for crinkly silks.
[33] A long face was believed to be aristocratic. The Tōji (or Eastern Temple) is in a part of Kyoto famous for melons.
[34] A pun on *hana* (nose) and *hana* (cherry blossoms). Yoshino was famous for cherry blossoms.
[35] A pun on the province of Mikawa and *mikawa*, a variant of *nikawa* (glue).
[36] Alludes to a custom at the Kashima Shrine in Hitachi of lovers leaving sashes with their names written on them before the shrine. A priestess would then divine whether or not their marriage would be successful.

is a barrier on any journey, and in the town of Seki,[37] known for its statue of Jizō, live Koman, Kojorō, and Koyoshi, women famed the 120 leagues of the Edo road. They beckon passing men with one hand; they hold under the other, hidden by the sleeve, the mark of their spare-time employment—the lid of a hemp threading basket.[38] At bottom, their hearts are twisted hemplike for love; what will become of these unhappy creatures, emotions confused as hemp on a reel?

KOMAN: I've been thinking of the differences among women of our profession, ranging from the great courtesans, the queens of the trade, all the way down to tavern girls like ourselves, accosting strangers. What has our kind to hope for? Up before the break of day to air the place, chattering away like so many sparrows from lunch to bedtime, at long as our breath holds out—and even so, have we any guests? I don't know why, but lately not even lunchtime customers drop in. Next door a daimyo's daughter and her train of 160 people are staying —this makes the third day. Our neighbors are frantically busy with all the guests, but tonight—let's face it—we won't even have the footmen and lackeys stopping here. What's wrong with this house? The master looks so sour I'm afraid his devil's horns will sprout branches. You'd think, wouldn't you, that the horse drivers—they've always been steady customers—would bring guests when we're so short of them.—Which reminds me. Kojorō, why hasn't your sweetheart Shichini been around? Have you had a lovers' quarrel? Or is he exhausted from an overdose of rustling under the stairs? Too much rustling and he won't be able to drive horses! He'll barely be able to shoo flies with his chin!

KOJORŌ: Shichini? Do you mean Kurosuke? That was ages ago. We're completely finished now. I never even hear his voice shouting at the horses any more. At first he was very affectionate. He bought me hair ribbons and stockings, pomade, sashes, one thing after another. He even gave me money to buy shoes for my horse. But behind my back he was having affairs, not merely with one or two women, but with a whole pack—Ogen, the lighter maker's daughter from Minakuchi,[39] the widow of the comb maker of Earth Mountain, and Fatty

---

[37] The name Seki means a barrier.
[38] The reeling of hemp thread was at the time a popular way for women to earn extra money.
[39] Minakuchi was famous for tobacco pipes, leading to mention of the rope matches used to light them.

Oyone of Shōno, the one with hips like a sack of rice. He deceived
me, his old love, with all of them. I suppose he might give up the
women if I asked him, but gambling has made a regular god of
poverty out of him. He's squandered every penny he owns, until he's
down now to one cotton gown and his underwear. He had the bad
luck to draw a thirteen at cards,[40] and it looks as if he won't be able
to pay what he owes his boss in pack horse charges. But from what
I hear, Koman, your dear Yosaku is one of his gambling pals. If
Yosaku means anything to you, you'd better warn him against it.
Koyoshi, you've heard the gossip too, haven't you?

NARRATOR: Koyoshi answers in a low voice.

KOYOSHI: Well, our master had it from a commission agent in
Kameyama, and I heard him whispering to his wife. "That horse driver
Yosaku, the one Koman's so fond of, has become a ringleader of the
gamblers. The next step is robbery. If he comes here again, he's not
to be entertained. He owes me a lot on credit, and I intend to get it
back if I have to strip him naked. Once I do, he'll never cross this
threshold again." The mistress agreed, and then the master went off
to an appointment.

NARRATOR: Koman is in tears before Koyoshi finishes.

KOMAN: That's what I meant by saying that, among prostitutes,
tavern girls are the lowest of the low. I've never told even my closest
friends, but my father at the age of sixty-six was thrown into a water
dungeon for failure to pay his back taxes. He hasn't any other sons
or daughters—I'm an only child. I'm a tavern girl and nothing more,
but even daimyos have heard of Koman from Seki—I couldn't let my
father die in a water dungeon. I got leave. I pretended I was going
on a pilgrimage to Ise, but went instead to the magistrate's office. I
guaranteed to pay my father's back taxes by harvest time, a heavy
undertaking for a woman. I succeeded in getting my father released
from prison, but what am I to do now? I no longer work as I used
to for guests.[41] My only income is from the piecework hemp reeling
I do on the side, and from the tips I beg from ladies stopping here
by telling them I'm the famous Koman. I feel like a crane reduced to
scavenging for grains of millet.[42] It's a miserable, degrading life. The

[40] Cards were introduced by the Dutch in the seventeenth century. In this game the
worst combination to draw was two cards which totaled thirteen.
[41] Koman is being faithful to Yosaku.
[42] A proverb, indicating an unworthy and time-consuming occupation for a noble bird.

*The governess Shigenoi, bound by duty to her mistress, rejects her
own son. "It is quite true that you were born of my flesh, but
you're not my child any longer, nor am I your mother."*
(SHIGENOI: *Nakamura Tokizō III*)

day of the guarantee is approaching, and I've grown thin with worry.
And how I suffer to hear Yosaku abused by everyone when I'm trying
with all my efforts to protect him! What a depressing place the world
is!

NARRATOR: She collapses in tears over her hemp-throwing basket.

KOMAN (*looking up*): Yosaku is coming! I hear his voice! Nobody
else sings the real Komoro song with such flair. Yosaku!

NARRATOR: She waves to him.

YOSAKU (*sings*):
>There's a splendid horse,
>With a daimyo's wicker trunk,
>Seven layers of quilting,
>And a riding seat above.

NARRATOR: Once Yosaku used to ride such a horse, though nobody
here suspects it. He leads the horse to the front of the Shiroko House.

YOSAKU: Hello there, Koman. Give this gentleman a good dinner
and a room for the night. There are three in his party. Here you are,
sir. Step down, please.

NARRATOR: He unties the luggage. Kojorō and Koyoshi flutter around
the gentleman.

KOJORŌ: Here's some hot water, sir, to wash your feet.

KOYOSHI: Please come inside.

KOJORŌ: There aren't any other guests. Please take all the room you
need to make yourselves comfortable.

NARRATOR: They accompany him within.
Yosaku quickly unloads the baggage and the sword box.

YOSAKU: It's been quite a while since I saw you, Koman. I'm glad
you're looking so well. I'll see you again soon.

NARRATOR: He takes the bridle and hurriedly starts away. Koman
clutches the reins.

KOMAN: How can you act that way? I have so much to tell you. I
should think you'd want to talk to me too. Don't be so impatient.
Wait a moment.

NARRATOR: She pulls him back.

YOSAKU: What a nuisance! Your story can keep. I have urgent business now. Let me go.

NARRATOR: He shakes her off, but she throws her arms around him.

KOMAN: What is it? Why are you in such a hurry? Something must
be burdening your mind. I won't let you go unless you tell me.

YOSAKU: Why should my mind be burdened when I've already unburdened my horse?[43] But, since you seem so worried, I'll tell you
in brief what's happened. Listen to my bad luck.

I was envious because my pals were all making money at the fist
game.[44] Kyūza from Seta had the bank, and I thought I'd risk 100
coppers and no more. I kept winning time after time until I ran it
up to 700 coppers. This was a fine start, and I set out with the money
in my belt and my horse bell tinkling for Belling Deer, where everybody was playing the game. I thought I'd try my luck again. I won
600 coppers more. If only I had left things at that! But greed is blind.
Eye River was the next town. I got the horse drivers together and took
the bank myself. I played from two in the afternoon until four, without winning a round. I never so much as glimpsed a winning combination. I dropped over 500 coppers on top of my previous earnings. Somehow, somewhere I had to make up the loss. When I got to Zesai's
pharmacy in Umenoki,[45] I was ready to pound my body into a powder,
but even Zesai's mixture didn't help. By now I had run up a debt of
one and a half *bu* in gold, and it was more than I could stand. I persuaded Hachizō from Ishibe to guarantee me. That was my first bout.

I went next to Eighth Street in Ōtsu, where I dropped 800 coppers.
I was done in for ninety-nine coppers at Komachi's grave in Ono.[46]
I decided, going through Needle Pass, that I had been stuck because
I was too timid. I made up my mind at Settle Village to change my
system. At the Kwannon Hall in Moriyama I pawned some things
for thirty-three *momme*.[47] I felt bold as a devil, but at Tamura Hall
in Earth Mountain I was soon subdued.[48] On a through trip to Ise I
gambled from dusk until dawn at the Morning Star House, and they

---

[43] Yosaku asks literally why he should have "one thing" (*ichimotsu*) on his mind when
he had unburdened his horse of "two things" (*nimotsu*). "Two things" is a homophone
for *nimotsu* (baggage). A bad play on words.

[44] In this game the opponents hold coins in their hands. Each man tries to guess the total
number of coins held by both. In the game described below Yosaku holds six and
Hachizō two, for a total of eight.

[45] Umenoki is a popular name for the village of Rokujizō. The name contains the verb
umeru (to make up a loss).

[46] An allusion to the poetess Ono no Komachi. Her lover was to pay her court
one hundred nights in succession; on the ninety-ninth night he died.

[47] Thirty-three suggests the thirty-three forms Kwannon assumed in order to save men,
also the thirty-three temples of Kwannon at various places. *Momme* was a silver coin;
sixty *momme* made one *ryō* in gold, worth about thirty dollars.

[48] Tamura (Sakanoe no Tamuramaro) was reputed in legends to have conquered demons.

drained me dry. I passed by Matsuzaka, where you pay two months'
interest every month on your loans. I calculated my debts at Kumozu
Ford, and discovered that I owed Hachizō eight *kan*—four loans of
two *kan* each.

I was pondering my predicament when somebody came towards me
driving a horse. It was Hachizō himself, buzzing as usual.[49] He
grabbed me by the front of my kimono and demanded, "What do you
intend to do about the money I lent you? Have you forgotten me?
I'm Hachizō, that's who I am." He spoke in stinging tones.

I couldn't humiliate myself by making long-winded apologies, so
I told him, "I haven't got the money now. Anyway, the money wasn't
borrowed in cash. It was just a debt on paper from gambling. Let's
settle it by a bout between us. Either I'll clear myself of the eight *kan*
or I'll owe you sixteen. Come on, how about it?"

Hachi, an old hand at the game, answered, "I've already given you
eight *kan*. If I lose this time you won't owe me anything, but if I
win you'll have to pay double, sixteen *kan*—agreed? But how do you
propose paying? I won't do it without some collateral."

I couldn't back out once I'd made the offer. "Here, do you know
this horse? It cost nine *ryō* one *bu* at the market in Chiryū. It belongs
to my boss, but I'll stake the horse against my debt.[50] Come on and
play." We went under a tree with our coins in our hands. I asked,
"What's the total?"

"You're on. Seven, I say."

He was holding two coins. "Open up!" We showed our hands. Between us, just as he said, were seven coins. I was done for.

My original guess had been six. I held five myself, and when he
said seven I thought that he must be holding one coin. So I hid one
of my coins in order to reduce the total to six. But when I saw what
he held I realized to my despair that originally there had been eight
coins between us. By hiding one coin I had made the total seven and
played directly into his hands. My bad luck had touched bottom. I

[49] The name Hachizō contains the word *hachi* (bee); hence, the mention of "buzzing"
and "stinging."

[50] Sixteen *kan* in copper equaled four *ryō*, in gold, or about one hundred twenty dollars.
Yosaku stakes a horse worth twice his debt. I have omitted here the sentence, "You
can't complain if you're offered a horse worth 500 *me* in exchange for sixteen *kamme*."
Sixty *me* (or *momme*) were worth one *ryō*. Thus he is getting for 240 *me* a horse
worth 500 *me*.

went limp, which only made Hachi the livelier. He grabbed the horse saying, "It's mine now." But my customer today—with the helping hand of the gods—insisted that I take him to the post station as I had promised. Hachi's customer, another samurai, screamed at Hachi till his eyes looked as if they'd pop from his head for not driving the horses. Hachi said, "I'll collect my horse as soon as I leave this gentleman at Kubota." With that he dashed off like an express courier.

If my boss's horse is taken away I'll never be able to step on the Kiso Road or the Nakasen Road again, much less this one. But I must get inside quickly, before Hachizō comes.

NARRATOR: He finishes his recitation with a sigh. Koman's heart is heavy with darkness.

KOMAN: It's true, then, what people have been saying. I suppose you can't help being affected by your surroundings, but you've become sordid. You were once a distinguished gentleman. I'm sure you'd never have used anyone like myself even as your lowliest servant. But fate willed it that our skins should touch, that we should embrace, and now we are bound inseparably. I don't know whether to feel happy or sad. My love for you keeps growing all the time, but you have this terrible sickness on you. You're behaving like a coolie! I realize that some social obligations to your friends are unavoidable, but you never consider my feelings. Unless I pay my father's back taxes by the sixth of the month when the collector's notice is issued, he'll go back to the water dungeon. I'll be throwing him down from this world into that hell of freezing cold. I'm not telling you this to make you suffer, but I can't help crying when I see you utterly indifferent to me. You're so absorbed with your gambling, that evil pleasure of yours, that you've become heartless.

NARRATOR: She sobs convulsively. Yosaku bursts into tears.

YOSAKU: That's unkind of you. I wasn't gambling for pleasure nor for greed. What is the two *koku* two *to* that your father owes in taxes? The salary I used in former days to give my sandal bearer or my groom! The gambling came as a sudden impulse, after I had strained my wits to the breaking point trying, because I love you so, to find some way to save your father. I was foolish not to have realized that nothing good was likely to befall a man so unlucky that he's sunk to being a horse driver after once he enjoyed a samurai's stipend of 1,300 *koku*. I accept this as the punishment of Heaven for my crime against my master. But it's cruel of you, Koman, to talk of my evil pleasure, my wanton gambling, and the rest. Everything has been for your father's sake. I'd rip open my heart and show it to you if my thoughts were only written inside!

NARRATOR: He beats on his chest protector already soaked with bitter tears. Koman claps her hands in surprise.

KOMAN: I'm most grateful. If you had told me this earlier, I'd never have rebuked you. Please forgive me. I've sold all my summer clothes and borrowed from the other girls in order to raise funds for my father's case. I've scraped together most of the 130 *momme* that way, and I've made up the little remaining with my hemp reeling. Look.

NARRATOR: She takes the money from her hemp basket.

KOMAN: This is the price of my father's life. Please don't worry any more.—It's been quite a while since sunset. I can't believe that Hachi will still come. We haven't any other guests and I'm free. Hitch your horse over there and lie down inside. We'll chase away each other's cares.

NARRATOR: As she unties the cords of his straw sandals, Hachizō from Ishibe appears, his eyes burning with fury.

HACHIZŌ: Yosaku? What right have you to remove my horse without permission? Don't you know that Rough-grained Hachizō is famous all the way to the Mino Road for never letting anything get past his eyes? Do you expect to settle your debt of sixteen *kamme* for nothing? Dirty pickpocket!

NARRATOR: He starts to unhitch the horse, but Yosaku twists his arm.

YOSAKU: What are you doing? If you're Rough-grained Hachizō, I'm Yosaku from Tamba! Do you expect a horse worth 500 *me* in exchange for a pledge of 200 *me*? Yes, I'm sure you'd be happy with that bargain, but first bring me 300 *me* in change! I'm Yosaku, lord and master of the fifty-three stages of the Tōkaidō! Don't start any trouble, you shameless thief!

NARRATOR: He shakes Hachizō, then pushes him away.

HACHIZŌ: Stop playing the hero. Better still, pay me my money and then talk as big as you please. If you want to fight it out, come on!

NARRATOR: He swings at Yosaku, but Koman catches him.

KOMAN: Hachizō! You're not acting very intelligently. You have a master, just as Yosaku has. Do you think he can give away his master's horse? Or that anyone will praise you for accepting it? There's no need to shout that way. You should show a little patience. Heartless wretch!

HACHIZŌ: Slut! Save your tears for Yosaku. Don't waste them on me. I've shown my patience by taking a horse instead of the money.

KOMAN: No, I won't let you. You can't have the horse. I'm Koman from Seki and I won't give you the horse.

HACHIZŌ: Stinking whore! I'll give you a taste of my bamboo whip!

KOMAN: Go on, fight with a woman!

HACHIZŌ: You think I won't?

NARRATOR: He picks up his whip and lashes at her. Yosaku pushes Koman aside.

YOSAKU: She belongs to somebody else. What do you mean by hitting her?

HACHIZŌ: I hit her because she's your woman.

YOSAKU: Very kind of you. Here's thanks from my woman!

NARRATOR: Clenching his fists, he smacks Hachizō squarely between the eyes, so hard he all but leaves a hole.

HACHIZŌ: Come on! If it's a fight you want, I'll give you one.

NARRATOR: They snatch each other's topknots and push back and forth, grappling and battering. A fight between horse drivers is like the trampling of wild horses. Hachizō has only his brute strength; Yosaku, skillfully using judo, grips Hachizō's forearm as he lunges, kicks his shins, and hurls him back with a shout. Hachizō's hip bone smacks against a gatepost. Staggering under the blow, he glares at Yosaku.

HACHIZŌ: Dirty thief! You'll pay for this! I'll tell every inspector, foreman, and horse owner about you! I'll knock the rice out of your bowl along the highways! I'll see you in rags!

NARRATOR: With this final display of bravado, he starts to leave. Koman clutches him.

KOMAN: Hachizō! How can a public horse driver ever make a living again if he's denounced to the foremen and inspectors? I'm begging you—now that you've had your fight, show your generosity. Please forgive him.

NARRATOR: The more she pleads, the more insolent Hachizō becomes.

HACHIZŌ: Forgive him? After lending him sixteen *kamme* and getting beaten on top of that! That'd be fine for you, but not for me.

I'm going out now and I'll shout to everybody in the streets that Yosaku the gambler is a crook.

KOMAN: Look. Here are 130 *me*. This money is needed to save somebody's life, but I don't begrudge it for my man. Please use it to settle your account.

NARRATOR: He snatches the money she holds out.

HACHIZŌ: Make sure you settle the balance. What price shall I put on copper coins? [51]

KOMAN: It doesn't make any difference. Whatever you like.

HACHIZŌ: In that case this makes ten *kamme*. The market rate is thirteen *momme*.

NARRATOR: He goes off, slipping the money into his pouch. Koman inclines her head pensively and with a sigh returns to Yosaku.

KOMAN: I gave him the money and he finally left. I hope you'll never have anything more to do with his kind.

NARRATOR: She murmurs the words. Yosaku is astonished.

YOSAKU: How could you give him that money? I'll take it back!

KOMAN: Wait. You've borrowed his money—how can you escape paying him? Times are different now. They keep the highways under strict control. Once you're reported to the foremen and inspectors and get a bad name, nobody'll employ you. The doors will be shut wherever you go, and naturally we'll never be able to meet. And if by some chance word gets back to your old home, you'll never be able to live down the disgrace. I'll postpone paying my father's taxes as long as I can. If in the end I can't find the money, I'm resolved to take his place in the water dungeon. My only desire now is to help you out of your trouble.

NARRATOR: Yosaku will not listen.

YOSAKU: What disgrace could there be for a horse driver? Think of all you've suffered to save your father. How could you give Hachizō the money?

NARRATOR: He starts off impatiently.

YOSAKU: Good heavens! I'm lost—Saji, the innkeeper, is returning with a crowd of officials. I don't know what's come up, but they're sure to ask bothersome questions. I'll hide for a while. I don't want to meet them. Take the horse somewhere.

[51] Conversion rates between copper and silver or gold currency fluctuated. It was sometimes possible to make a profit by double changing.

NARRATOR: He notices a palanquin, luckily left by the entrance of the neighboring house. He opens the door and puts one foot inside.

SANKICHI: Ow! Ow! Who's stepping on my side?

NARRATOR: The little horse driver pops his head from the door. He gives a great yawn.

YOSAKU: Why, it's the Wild Boy of Ishibe!

SANKICHI: You're Mr. Yosaku, aren't you?

YOSAKU: What are you doing here?

SANKICHI: I'm driving horses through to Edo. I'm staying with the rest of the party at the hostel, but I felt so sleepy after dinner that I've had me a good nap here. Now, what are you up to?

YOSAKU: Nothing to worry you. I don't want the innkeeper next door to see me. Hide me in here.

NARRATOR: Sankichi peeps through the curtains [52] and glances around.

SANKICHI: Is that Koman over there? Quite a dish! Quite a dish! I've known about you two for a long time. I wouldn't do it for anybody else, but the name Yosaku means a lot to me. I won't object, as long as it's for somebody named Yosaku. I'll hide you. Come on in.

NARRATOR: They squeeze together. How moving that the boy should feel filial affection, though unaware that Yosaku is his father! Soon the innkeeper shouts from the gate.

INNKEEPER: Get up, everybody! Get up! The inspector, the village headman, and the members of the neighborhood association are all here. Wife, get up and come here!

NARRATOR: Aroused by his bellowing, the tavern girls and the innkeeper's wife rush out together. The headman and inspector address them.

HEADMAN: Hear the message from the magistrate! At our meeting today we received a summons for Koman of this house. "Koman's father, Hikobei from Yokota, was confined in a water dungeon for failure to pay taxes amounting to two *koku* two *to* over the past four years. He was released on Koman's plea and guarantee. You officials at this post station are responsible for collecting the money from her and paying the taxes." Such was the message, and now we charge you to keep Koman in your custody. Heed these words!

NARRATOR: Koman looks down and sobs. The mistress of the house is surprised.

[52] Hanging at the entrance of the inn. The palanquin is behind the curtains.

MISTRESS (*to Koman*): You've done a disgraceful thing! Are you trying to make trouble for the master?

NARRATOR: The master interrupts harshly.

INNKEEPER: What do you mean, make trouble for the master? I'm not responsible for a penny of her debts. The travelers on their way to and from the capital always give her a hundred or even two hundred coppers in tips, out of deference to her name—the great Koman of Seki. Why, she collects as much as a full *momme* at a time! She could save a hundred *me* or two *ryō* in six months, if she chose. Instead she gives every last penny to that gambler, that thief Yosaku. I'm told she hasn't a stitch of summer clothes—not even an underrobe—left in her wardrobe. Yosaku has received a lot of credit here, and it's all been guaranteed by her. The account book doesn't forget—six nights' lodging with one meal each, two and a half gallons of saké, seventy side dishes at ten coppers each, eighty-five dishes of whale and potato stew, and 150 sticks of dumplings.[53]

Koman, if you throw good money after a bad man, your problems don't concern me. Yosaku could strip the skin from his body, and it still wouldn't be worth the money you owe. Get him to pawn his horse and pay up.—Somebody take Koman inside and keep her there. Sorry to have bothered you all.

NARRATOR: After this curt apology he shuts the door with the sound of a snapping lock. The village headman, the inspector, and the chief of the association joke among themselves. "Well, well, who would have thought that Yosaku had such a big appetite? Regular meals, side dishes, dumplings, plates of stew—and, in between, Koman for a bedtime snack." They leave, each for his own house.

Yosaku crawls out at last, bathed in a cold sweat. He peeps through the keyhole in the gate bar, through the chinks in the shutters, but can see nothing. He presses his head against the projecting latticework of a window. A face suddenly appears. He jumps back in surprise.

KOMAN: Don't be afraid. It's only me.

YOSAKU: Koman?

KOMAN: Yosaku—you heard what they were saying, didn't you?

---

[53] "Dumplings" is a rough translation of *konnyaku,* a paste made from the arum root. I have omitted here the sentence, "Does he think he can pay with sand because it's for *konnyaku?*" This is a complicated play on words, depending for effect on the current belief that *konnyaku* purged "sand" from the stomach.

What a sad thing to happen! I'm cooped up now like a bird in a cage. But at least with me shut up this way they won't cause my father any more trouble. I don't know whether or not I'll be able to see you again. This may be our last farewell. You can't guess from below what our betters will do.

NARRATOR: She clings to his hand and weeps.

YOSAKU: No—the clouds seem to have a silver lining.[54] I don't know why it is, but that imp Sankichi is in love with the name Yosaku. He always treats me with such respect. While we were together inside the palanquin I played on his sympathies. I asked him to steal some money for me from the daimyo staying next door. I told him I was counting on him as a man. The monkey got all excited, and said of course he'd steal for me. If he pulls it off, everything's perfect. If he doesn't, we're where we started.

NARRATOR: Koman interrupts.

KOMAN: No, no, no! Please don't lead a stranger into crime.

YOSAKU: You're too timid. If the kid is caught, the worst he'll get is a spanking. (*Calls to Sankichi.*) Sankichi, I'm really counting on you! You can't back out now.

SANKICHI: Heigh-ho! Fiddle-dee-dee! You do drag on. If you don't need me any more after I steal for you, just throw me away. The Wild Boy doesn't back out when somebody asks him a favor. I've got no father or family, and my head's not worth a five-copper dumpling. Anyone who wants it badly enough is welcome. If I get caught stealing the money, I won't be surprised to have my head cut off.

NARRATOR: His devotion to samurai principles is as incorruptible as the gold he is about to steal. How shameful that one so worthy of his birth is abused!

YOSAKU: I knew I could depend on you. It's a matter of life and death.

NARRATOR: He uses all his wiles to spur the boy on.

SANKICHI: It's funny, but having a friend near me is enough to make me lose my nerve. Go away somewhere, quick. Koman, I'd like to leave this charm with you.

KOMAN: You should wear it yourself.

---

[54] The Japanese is literally "Liquid has formed in the clouds," a proverb which has come to mean that a situation over which one has worried has changed, and there is room for hope.

SANKICHI: I don't want to. My real name's written on the charm. I'd be ashamed if they caught me and found out my name.

NARRATOR: What manliness in his gesture as he unfastens the charm and entrusts it to Koman! He tucks up the hem of his kimono and softly approaches the house.

YOSAKU: I'm going to take cover at Yaroku's, down at the foot of the hill. I'll be back about midnight. Koman, get back inside.

KOMAN: I'm so frightened—I'm shivering all over. Jizō, help me! [55]

YOSAKU: Do you think prayer will do any good now? You're talking too loud. Keep your voice low.

NARRATOR: Stealthily, with pounding heart, he leaves her and goes down the bumpy hill.

Every hour, as is the rule when samurai are traveling, a watchman makes the rounds with his clappers. As he is beating ten, Sankichi dashes out the gate, a gold brocade purse in his hand, in his childish simplicity so elated with his successful theft that he makes no attempt to avoid the man with the clappers. The watchman catches sight of the boy and pursues him. Sankichi in confusion jumps into the palanquin and locks the door from inside. The watchman rushes after him, and pushing hard against the door, raises the blind.

WATCHMAN: So it's you! And you've got the princess's purse! (*Shouts.*) Wake up, everybody! Sankichi the horse driver has stolen a gold purse!

NARRATOR: The boy is like a rat in a trap which will drop him from this world into hell. The guests at the hostel, high and low alike, the samurai stopping in nearby inns, and even people from taverns in the vicinity rush out with sticks in their hands. They drag the palanquin to the middle of the highway and with lanterns borne aloft on poles carefully surround the area. The officer on duty gives orders.

OFFICER: What's all this commotion over one boy? Drag him out!

NARRATOR: The men force open the door and pull Sankichi out by the wrists.

SANKICHI: Sir, here's the money I stole. You can have it back.

NARRATOR: He looks around in bewilderment.

OFFICER: He's just a child. He couldn't have planned this by himself. Let's find his accomplices. Are there any foremen around? Call together all the horse drivers stopping in the town.

[55] The temple dedicated to Jizō in Seki was famous.

NARRATOR: They fan out at once and round up all the drivers. Hachizō has also been spending the night in Seki, drinking heavily.

HACHIZŌ: Who the devil's been up to robbery? Well, what do you know—it's the infant prodigy, the Wild Boy! It doesn't surprise me. I've always said you'd come to a bad end, and was I wrong? You're a disgrace to the whole profession of horse drivers. You should be nailed to a stake!

NARRATOR: He kicks the boy in the back and sends him sprawling on his face. Sankichi's forehead hits a stone and the blood runs crimson over his cheeks.

SANKICHI: Damn you! Trample on me, will you? I'll tear off your hands and feet!

NARRATOR: He jumps up, but the officials restrain him.

OFFICER (*to Hachizō*): You low horse driver! You insolent cur! What do you mean by kicking like a madman in the presence of a samurai?

NARRATOR: He reprimands Hachizō severely.

SANKICHI: Yes! Do I have to stand being kicked by that dog? I never expected anyone from the lower classes would ever scratch me, even with a sword, but to be kicked and bruised in the face this way! If my head flies, I'll fasten my teeth in your ugly face!

NARRATOR: Tears of mortification well up in his glaring eyes. The fury in his young heart is intense enough to make the hair of the others stand on end with horror. His mother, the governess, hearing the disturbance, rushes to the scene. The sight of her child surrounded by a mob drains the strength from her; she can only weep in despair. But if she allows people to discover her secret now, all her efforts to conceal it will come to naught. Supposing it were whispered that the princess has for her foster brother a horse driver and a thief—how distressing that would be! She is torn by pity, resentment, and wrath.

SHIGENOI (*to Sankichi*): I've been keeping my eye on you ever since we started on this journey, but I see that my kindness has been wasted. You've done a dreadful thing. You looked somehow as if you came from decent stock, but there's no escaping a bad upbringing. It's a shame. I'm sure it's thanks to your evil disposition that your parents pretend not to know you, or even to see you, and you've become a horse driver. I know myself what it means to have a child, and all parents' hearts are the same. If your mother heard what has happened, do you suppose that she would come forward now to help you, even if she were ready to dive through fire and water to save her child? You may think she has abandoned you, but in her heart she must be praying in agony to the gods and Buddha to spare your life. It doesn't seem possible that a child of your age could have planned such a dreadful crime. Is your father so poor that he ordered you to steal? Or did a stranger ask you? If you have any excuse, please tell us. I can imagine what your mother would feel. Besides, we've been friends these past days, and I would like to save your life. If I weren't obliged to think of the princess's reputation, I might even say, to save your life, that you were my own child, suckled at the same breast as the princess. Tell us your excuses, whatever they may be.

NARRATOR: The sad tears flow from the depths of her heart, from the depths of her soul, from her very entrails. Her anxiety, her glances, invite those investigating the crime to guess the cause but, not surprisingly, they suspect nothing. Sankichi looks up at his mother's face, then averts his eyes. His voice is choked with tears.

SANKICHI: It's true, ma'am. I committed a terrible crime. But after all, what do you expect of a horse driver? I don't feel ashamed before anybody except you. What an unkind thing to ask—whether I did it for my father! If I had a father, I wouldn't be a horse driver. I don't know where my father is. I've never even seen his face. I've got a mother, all right, but she's timid like all women, and she's tied down by being in service. She treats me like a stranger. What use would it be, even if I had some excuse? I'm known as a thief. I'm dishonored. I'll never be able to look my father in the face. I hope they'll kill me quickly. When you talk to me that way and act so affectionate, I get all confused. The next thing, I might stop wanting to die. Please go inside. I don't want to see your face any more.

NARRATOR: He presses both sleeves to his eyes. The intelligence shining in his face as he yields to tears discomposes his mother.

SHIGENOI: Grant me his life. Spare him, please, samurai.

NARRATOR: She sobs convulsively and falls to the ground in tears, utterly oblivious to what people might suspect. Honda, the chief retainer, emerges from the house.

HONDA: I've had a full report on the matter. I have decided, in view of the recovery of the stolen object, and especially because we're traveling and the culprit belongs to another fief, that so trivial an offense will not require further investigation. (*To Sankichi.*) Your life is spared. Get up and leave at once.

NARRATOR: He raises Sankichi from the ground.

SANKICHI: What good is it to be pardoned after being disgraced? How can I go on living? Do me a favor, if there's any kindness in you, and cut off my head.

NARRATOR: He crouches on the ground, refusing to stand.

HONDA: You insolent little whippersnapper! No law, ancient or modern, prescribes death for such a petty crime. On your feet, and be off with you!

NARRATOR: He is furious.

SANKICHI: It can't be helped then. My life will be spared. Oh, I know what I'll do!

NARRATOR: He jumps to his feet.

SANKICHI: Hachizō, you dirty villain! Step on me, will you, and bruise my face? I'm a samurai's son, you know, and I can't go on living once anybody tramples me. I'll teach you a lesson!

NARRATOR: Even as he speaks he whips out his dirk. Flying at Hachizō, he slashes off his head, swift as a lightning flash. "Murderer!" they cry, seizing him. "You won't be pardoned now!" Sankichi is bound with stout ropes.

HONDA: We'll put him in the custody of the village headman. Send him from here under guard to the magistrate's office. (*To Sankichi.*) Get up!

NARRATOR: They pull the boy to his feet. His mother, bereft of her senses, can only weep, so distraught that she no longer knows what is happening.

SHIGENOI: I've never heard of anybody being tied up like a criminal on a wedding journey.

NARRATOR: Led off by the others, she gazes back helplessly again and again before she goes inside. The boy's glances follow his mother; then, drooping his head, he shuts his eyes and stands a moment in silent grief.

SANKICHI: Everything's turned out as I hoped. I couldn't have gone on living even if my life was spared, not after I got a bad name and was trampled on. I'm lucky, since I had to die anyway, that I could take Hachizō along with me for the same effort. It's better than dying alone. Everybody, my father and mother included, has to die some day. In the next world we'll have all the time we want together. We come from that other world and we return to it. Come on, horse, we're going back to the stable. Fat old brute!

NARRATOR: His unwavering courage excels a samurai's.

HONDA: What a shame he has to die!

NARRATOR: He speaks in tears. The samurai lead Sankichi away; afterwards only the cries of the fire watchmen break the stillness of the daimyo's hostel.

When Yosaku learns what has happened, he rushes to the hostel, intending to shoulder the blame, but he arrives too late. Everything has calmed down and the place is deserted. The gates are shut at the hostel, and not a sound is heard. Koman impatiently taps on the lattice window. Yosaku runs to her.

YOSAKU: What's happened? I hear he got caught.

KOMAN: Got caught? It's much worse than that. I saw what he did from here. Everything, even to killing Hachizō, was for our sake. It looks as if they'll behead him tomorrow. It's heartbreaking.

NARRATOR: She whispers, in tears.

YOSAKU: *Namu Amida, Namu Amida.* We're responsible for killing him! What horrible criminals we are!

NARRATOR: They exchange glances and weep.

KOMAN: I don't think we ought to live even one hour longer than Sankichi. Do you agree?

YOSAKU: If that's your decision, I have no more worries. I'm satisfied. I'd been thinking the same thing since early this evening, but I kept it to myself. I was sure you wouldn't wish to die and leave your father alone in his troubles. Aren't you worried what will happen to him?

KOMAN: Nothing I can do will help my father, now that my every wish is being thwarted. But if we keep prattling this way, our resolution is sure to be blunted. Let us put everything else from our minds and leave at once.

YOSAKU: That's wonderful. I'll go get my horse. He's tied up in back. I'd be neglecting my duty towards the owner if I let the horse fall into anyone else's hands. I'll take him along to wherever we kill ourselves. While I'm fetching the horse try to loosen the latticework on the windows.

KOMAN: That won't be necessary. Thanks to Koyoshi—her lover used to come in through this window—I have only to push the latticework for it to drop off.

YOSAKU: For Koyoshi the window was the passage to nights of pleasure; for us who are about to die it is the iron gate of hell.

NARRATOR: Still murmuring unhappily, he leads out his horse.

YOSAKU: What happened to the dagger I left with you?

KOMAN: Don't worry. I haven't lost it. I have it here at my side.

YOSAKU: Good. Well then, step down gently onto the saddle. Be careful. Don't hurt yourself.

NARRATOR: In the light of the waning moon he who protects and she who is protected seem also to wane: the matted tail of their moon-colored [56] horse is as soaked with dew as their sleeves with tears—which is the wetter? She springs lightly down, and they run quickly a few hundred feet.

YOSAKU: People are constantly passing on the highway. Wouldn't the Ise Road be a better place to kill ourselves?

KOMAN: Ise? That reminds me. Just a moment, please. Sankichi left a charm with me. I want to see from which shrine it comes. I myself carry a charm and an amulet from the Great Shrine at Ise. If we defile them by our deaths, it will prove an obstacle to salvation. I'll leave them in the Jizō Hall.

YOSAKU: I'm glad you thought of that.

NARRATOR: He opens the brocaded, crimson-lined bag she hands him, and reads by the light of the moon.

YOSAKU: "Grand Shrine of the Sun Goddess at Obara. Health and Long Life for Yonosuke, the son of Date no Yosaku, a native of Tamba Province." Good heavens! Was that my son Yonosuke, the child I abandoned when he was three? I remember how he always honored the name Yosaku and followed me about, even though he had no idea I was his father. I never suspected anything! Instead, I forced him to steal, and now he's to be executed. It is as if I had stretched out my hand to behead my own child.

NARRATOR: He slumps down. His feet kick the ground as he raises his voice in lament. Koman too is overcome by tears.

[56] "Moon-colored" meant a reddish dappled horse; probably this color is given for the horse because of the association with the words "waning moon" (literally, "moon of the twentieth day") which it follows.

KOMAN: We have compounded crime on crime, like accursed souls or hardened sinners. Our decision to kill ourselves is our one act in keeping with the will of Heaven. Every moment, however brief, that we linger in this world will make our sins the heavier. Let us go.

YOSAKU: Yes, you're right.

NARRATOR: He tries to stand, but his legs do not support him.

YOSAKU: I'm ashamed of myself. My strength is gone.

KOMAN: How weak you are!

NARRATOR: She pulls him to his feet, but his knees buckle. She lifts him in her arms, but he sags. The end of thirty-one years of sorrow will be on the Ise Road. Yosaku was bred in Ōmi and born in Tamba, famous for chestnuts; Koman helps her husband now to mount a chestnut horse.[57] The wife, taking the bridle, calls, "Giddiyap!" Now they will travel the Six Ways [58] with a relay of horses; they will cross the River of Three Roads; and the mountain ahead is not "Earth Mountain in between" of the old song, but the mountain of death. They journey by through-horse to hell, oh world of dreams!

ACT THREE

Scene: The Journey of Yosaku and Koman on the Road of Dreams.[59]

NARRATOR (*sings*):
Yosaku's a horse driver from Tamba,
But now on the edge of the meadows
He's a runaway colt—
Drive boldly on, Yosaku.
When she thinks of you, Yosaku,
The shining sun clouds over—
Is that shower of tears
From Koman of Seki?
Drive boldly on, Yosaku.

[57] Tamba was famous for chestnuts; the horse previously called "moon-colored" becomes chestnut here because of this new association.

[58] Six Ways and River of Three Roads were landmarks in the Buddhist afterworld. Mention of different types of horses was dictated by Yosaku's profession.

[59] The journey is so entitled in the original text. The lovers take the Ise Road from Seki.

Yosaku, Yosaku,
Your name was called everywhere,
But now even the wagtail bird is still.[60]
We cut *kaya* grass from the field,
And reeds from the eaves of a wayside hut:
These will be fodder for our horse
When we can no longer feed it.
At break of day this grass and we ourselves
Will wither in fields of chirping crickets.

Yosaku has always carried others on his horse, but today he is carried on this fatal journey down the hill at Sakanoshita.[61]

YOSAKU: Look, do you see that man hurrying on his pack horse through the late night? He'll surely stop at Yokkaichi. But we, the sheep for the slaughter, must wander through limbo seven times seven days with no stopping place.[62] Come, horse, trot on.

NARRATOR: He tugs the bridle, he urges the unwilling horse, but it refuses to stir. Brute beast though it is, the horse has feelings—perhaps regret for their end makes it ignore the reins.

KOMAN: At twelve I first began to beckon customers. This year I am twenty-one—nine full years have passed. How many tens of thousands of travelers have stopped in that time in Seki! It's a small town, but I had many friends, men and women both. But their friendship, like seasonal flowers, bloomed quickly only to be scattered by the winds of mortality. When I die no one but this horse will know about me, no one will weep. How sweet of him to neigh for me!

NARRATOR: Yosaku collapses over the saddle. The tears coursing from his eyes splash his sleeve; at Oak Village the acorns spill from the branches.

YOSAKU: Three years ago, companions on a secret journey to Ise Shrine,[63] we first exchanged vows. In the middle of Kushida Town I confessed my deep love. I can still see the purple hat you wore. I won

[60] The wagtail bird taught the secrets of love to the gods Izanagi and Izanami, but it is now silent for these lovers about to die.
[61] Sakanoshita means "under the hill".
[62] For forty-nine days after death the soul wanders in limbo, according to popular Buddhist belief. "Sheep for the slaughter" is a Buddhist image.
[63] Secret pilgrimages to the Ise Shrine, though popular throughout the Tokugawa Period, enjoyed a special vogue in 1705, a fact which (had we no other evidence) would help establish the date of the play as 1708.

your heart, and we swore by the Jizō of Seki to be true. Though I bore the heavy burden of love my feet went lightly as I drove my horse; my heart was buoyant, expansive as Toyoku Plain. How heartbreaking that now, while yet I delight in you, have not had my fill, this autumn frost has overtaken us! Tonight will be our last. We shall bury our fame in Sunken Fields.

NARRATOR: Koman speaks, in tears.

KOMAN: Love is strange. At the time we did not write a single vow, but we hooked fingers by the rapids of Kumozu to pledge love through two or three lives to come. On that pilgrimage where we could not share the same pillow, rather than lie alone and burn with longing we would walk slowly hand in hand, enjoying that happiness. In the evenings we smoked from the same pipe, lighted by one match. But remembering those days does us no good. Yosaku and Koman are fated, like the summer cicada that knows neither spring nor autumn, to weep over the vanished past, and to taste bitter grief in the present, bringing tears thick as the wintry rain that sweeps the pine groves of Ano when we pass. I rehearse the past, insistent as the fishermen of Akogi pulling in their nets. The Two Stones of the Bay of Two Views [64] will serve as a last memento for us who will die, not purified by the shrine, but with bodies defiled by a sword; they suggest the tombstones marking our graves. We transgressed the sacred laws by our crime of love, and our tour of the shrines was a portent of the circles of hell. No, we must not think of the past, never to return. Do not weep, do not weep. I heard once that the cawing of crows foretells a man's last hours, and now I know it is true. Tomorrow morning, on Mount Asaguma, think of the hideous spectacle—our corpses exposed, blocking the road, an offense in the sight of the Shrine of the Vestal, so horrid even to pilgrims that none will vouchsafe a prayer! The past and future are both told by the present.

NARRATOR: Her eyes look at him through tears.—What was that? The eight beats of the drum sounding high at High Field Temple to mark the dawn. "Many, many are the inns we have stayed in, but our journey to the Pure Land in the West will be traveled without change of horse; when we reach the Inn of a Hundred Delights, Kwannon and

[64] Futamigaura (The Bay of Two Views) is a scenic spot near Ise. Two boulders standing in the sea are known as "husband and wife" rocks. They should have purified themselves here before going on to the shrine.

Seishi will take our hands to welcome us aboard a lotus leaf, an inn where you and I are the only guests." [65] *Namu Amida Butsu. Namu Amida Butsu.* They implore the protection of the Amida of Kō. With the words of his Vow on their lips, they reach the Pine of a Thousand *Kan.*[66]

Yosaku, true son of a famous family of archers, is steeled for death. Leaping down onto the bank, he ties his horse to the base of a small pine. He brushes away the dew on the low bamboos, and calls Koman. He takes her hands and looks into her face.

YOSAKU: Twenty-one and thirty-one. Together we make only fifty-two years, not a long life even for one person. I am going to kill you now, my dear one. Is there anything on your mind that you'd like to tell me?

KOMAN: Could a woman about to die with the man she loves feel any regret to leave this world? Yet there is one thing, though it's too late—

NARRATOR: Yosaku interrupts.

YOSAKU: No, it's useless. Human desires are limitless, and we are torn by the cravings of the senses as long as breath is left in our bodies. The more we think, the more we talk, the more there is to think and talk, and all our acts serve but to hinder salvation. To banish these delusions we must free ourselves of the cycle of birth and death and pass into Nirvana. I too have a thousand, a million things to tell you, but I shall put them from my mind. Yet I wince at one blunder. In the pillow stand I left with you there was a scroll listing my ancestors, their glorious deeds in far-flung battles, and the lands they held. It mortifies me that after I am dead other men, discovering the scroll, will mock my family and besmirch its name. Well, what must be, must be.—But how pitiful, how heartbreaking that Yonosuke will be killed for love of his parents—for love of his father—without knowing to the end that I am his father! His sufferings are all my doing. I am not his father but his enemy.

NARRATOR: He falls on the ground prostrate with weeping.

[65] Kwannon and Seishi are the two attendant bodhisattvas of Amida, in whose paradise they hope to be reborn.

[66] A pine where copper coins hung on the branches by pilgrims to the Ise Shrine had accumulated until they amounted to one *kan.*

KOMAN: You tell me I mustn't talk, but see how you've talked, and now you're crying. Let me speak too. I pity my father who in his old age will lose his only child and be left helpless.

YOSAKU: Lingering attachments may keep us from salvation. But how can we help but think and talk about your father and my son, though we sink into hell for it?

KOMAN: Yes, you are right.

YOSAKU: I am sure of it.

KOMAN: Let us say what is in our hearts, though it be a sin, and then, for my father's sake, for your son's sake, let us plunge into hell!

NARRATOR: They cling tightly to each other and cry out with full voices. The wind of Toyoku Plain adds its note of pathos.

YOSAKU: Look! Over there! People running this way with lanterns. They must be fast couriers. We're too close to the road. Let's choose some other place for our death, shall we?

NARRATOR: They push fifty paces farther into the brush. The couriers run by bathed in sweat.

COURIER: We've got to hurry. The governess's prayer depends on it. She's offering sacred dances to pray for somebody's life, and they must be given by ten tomorrow morning. I'm sure we'll get a fine reward if her prayers are answered. Hurry!

NARRATOR: They run past.

YOSAKU: Did you hear that? I wonder whose governess it is. I suppose some child in her care is sick, and she's asking the gods to save his life. There are two useless lives here—if only we could exchange them!

NARRATOR: His tone is bitter. Koman answers in tears.

KOMAN: If we could make a substitution, I'd prefer to die in place of your child, rather than some stranger's. I intend to die anyway—I wouldn't mind being hacked to pieces from head to toe if it would save him.

NARRATOR: How could a sincere heart's grieving not prove more potent than a million words of prayer?

Stealthy footsteps—forty or fifty men's—creep towards them.

SOLDIER A: It's very suspicious. A riderless horse tied to a tree, in the middle of the night.

SOLDIER B: Raise the lanterns!

NARRATOR: The cry is passed along. The men uncover masked lanterns, shedding a brilliance like a festival of ten thousand lights.

SOLDIER A: They can't be far away. Search the fields a couple of hundred paces around.

NARRATOR: A crowd of men shouting, "Yosaku! Koman!" surrounds the couple, blocking all escape.

YOSAKU: They've discovered us! We're disgraced a second time. Let's kill ourselves quickly.

NARRATOR: He unsheathes his sword. At the glint of the blade a cry goes up, "There they are!" The soldiers seize the lovers and pull them apart.

YOSAKU: If you men are samurai, show your sympathy. I was formerly a samurai, Date no Yosaku by name. The supreme moment of my life has come—will you make me botch my suicide? This is humiliating!

NARRATOR: He writhes in desperation. At a command from the princess seated in her palanquin some distance away, a young samurai runs up to Yosaku.

SANAI: It's been a long time since last we met, Yosaku. I suppose you still remember me, your old friend Sagisaka Sanai. This journey to the East should be a joyous occasion for the princess, but the evening's events have profoundly distressed her. She ordered us to investigate and we discovered your real name in Koman's pillow stand. We further identified Sankichi as your son Yonosuke. The princess, moved particularly by the noble devotion of your wife, her governess, decided to spare Sankichi's life. She has graciously brought your wife and son here in her palanquins in order to save you two. She has provisionally granted you an allowance of fifty people,[67] subject to the daimyo's approval. She will also take Koman into her household and consider how best to help her. Such are her commands. I trust that you are grateful. And now, join her in the palanquin and return.

NARRATOR: Yosaku bows his head to the ground.

YOSAKU: I did nothing to repay His Excellency, though I was treated with unexampled kindness from the time I entered his service. Heaven has punished my disloyalty by reducing me to this miserable state, by keeping me from knowing my own son, and finally by driving me to expose a corpse of shame. I can never—not in this life nor in all those

[67] That is, a stipend which would permit him to support fifty retainers.

to come—forget the princess's compassion, but when my wife and son have displayed such magnificent determination, how dare I show my living face to men? As a mark of kindness to an old friend, tell them that you found me already dead. I take my last leave of you, Sanai. Please look after Koman.

NARRATOR: Koman interrupts.

KOMAN: Do you intend that I stay behind? What of your wife's kindness to me? Must I alone be shameless? Must I weep and grieve alone? —But mere talk makes me sound as if I were trying to win sympathy. I'll die before you and settle things my way.

NARRATOR: She clutches her dagger. Yosaku stays her hand.

YOSAKU: You're right. Gratitude, courtesy, loyalty, all the other virtues, are meaningless to a dying man. Come closer. *Namu Amida!*

NARRATOR: They are about to stab each other when Sanai runs up, twists away their daggers, and knocks the lovers to the ground. He glares at Yosaku and gnashes his teeth.

SANAI: You ingrate! You monster! In former days His Excellency granted you a captain's baton to wield over his troops, and whenever you traveled two lancers escorted you. But now you've become a horse driver through and through. I've had many comrades in service, but you in particular I've thought of as a brother. My father Sakon'emon, after all, was your godfather [68] and gave you the name Yosaku. What a fool I was! You make such a fuss about killing yourself. Do you think that suicide is such a remarkable feat? Remember, death for a samurai should mean that he was first in storming a castle, or first to aim his lance in open fighting, or that he was slain after taking the head of a worthy enemy. It is not easy to die like a samurai. Nowhere in the whole body of sacred literature will you find it written that a lovers' suicide with Koman will bring you glory. Don't you realize that failure to requite a master's kindness is a much greater disgrace to a samurai than the petty humiliation which so upsets you? How contemptible you are! A samurai with a sense of honor would ignore personal affronts, even the finger of scorn pointed at him, even being called a vile cur, in order to serve loyally a generous master. That is what being a worthy samurai means. If you can't understand what I am saying and still prefer to die, I won't interfere. Do as you please.

[68] At the *gembuku* ceremony of a samurai, a superior would present him with the ceremonial hat and also give him his name as a man.

But you're a horse driver and not a samurai—you don't deserve to be allowed to kill yourself with a sword. Bite off your tongue, jump from a cliff, or—this would be most appropriate—hang yourself with a pack-horse rope. I'll show my friendship by watching.—Oh, it's exhausting trying to argue with someone who's not a samurai!

NARRATOR: He gives a great yawn. Yosaku bursts into tears.

YOSAKU: I was wrong, Sanai. Misfortune has clouded my mind. I leave everything to your discretion.

NARRATOR: He joins his hands in supplication. Sanai rises.

SANAI: You agree then? Excellent! You are Yosaku once more. I shall intercede for you with her highness.

NARRATOR: He raises his voice.

SANAI: Ladies, report to her highness that, in deference to her wishes, Yosaku has given up all thought of suicide.

NARRATOR: The bearers lift the palanquins to their shoulders and with lively cries carry them closer. The governess and Yonosuke politely bow, in a manner befitting the wife and son of a samurai in the presence of a princess. The four [69] exchange glances, but can only say, "We owe everything to the kindness of the princess." They choke with tears of joy. The princess calls from within her palanquin.

PRINCESS: Is that man Yosaku the Gallant from Tamba they sing about in ballads? Koman from Seki is prettier than the pictures in my story book. I'm told you're a wonderful dancer, Koman. We'll stop here all day tomorrow, and I'd like you to show me your dances. I'll tell the senior samurai to reward you generously.

NARRATOR: Her words are pronounced in a manner worthy of her birth. One word from her and Yosaku receives a thousand *koku,* a thousand *ryō,* to last the thousand ages of the Thousand *Kan* pine, rewards for ten thousand generations. Koman's love is fulfilled, and Yosaku, fortunate man, will soon be a sworded samurai in Edo with a sealed commission.

Make way for the horses! And when flutes and drums summon the dancers, the horses will stamp their hooves in content, and the lovely dancing costumes, matched above and below, will lend joyous color to this scene of merriment.

[69] Yosaku, Koman, Shigenoi, and Sankichi.

THE LOVE SUICIDES
IN THE WOMEN'S TEMPLE

First performed on June 4, 1708. The literal translation of the title is "The Love Suicides of the Stonecrop," stonecrop (*mannengusa*) being the name of a plant which grows on Mount Kōya. It was believed that by immersing the dried plant in water and observing whether the leaves swelled out or remained withered one could tell whether a person was alive or dead. This form of divination is presented in the last scene.

The play is unusual in its treatment of Shingon Buddhism. Most of Chikamatsu's other plays have for their religious background the Pure Land sects which invoked the name of Amida Buddha, but here he treated instead the more aristocratic Buddhism introduced to Japan by Kūkai in the ninth century. Mount Kōya, the scene of most of the action, is the chief sanctuary of Shingon Buddhism.

Cast of Characters

NARITA KUMENOSUKE, aged 19, a page at the Kichijō Temple

YOJIEMON, proprietor of the Saigaya; father of Oume

SAKUEMON, a rich merchant from Kyoto

HANANOJŌ, aged 19, a fellow page of Kumenosuke; brother of Oume

KYŪBEI, a porter

SEN'EMON, a samurai of Kumenosuke's clan

HIGH PRIEST

YŪBEN, the senior disciple of the High Priest

CHŌSUKE, KANSUKE, servants

SHUZEN, HACHIYA, UMON, pages

PAGES, SERVANTS, PRIESTS

OUME, aged 18, daughter of Yojiemon

MOTHER of Oume

SATSU, elder sister of Kumenosuke

MAIDS

ACT ONE

Scene: The Kichijō Temple on Mount Kōya.
Time: March 27, 1708.

NARRATOR:

> On Kōya the mountain
> Where women are hated
> Why does the maiden-pine grow?
> Yet even if the maiden-pines
> Were all rooted out,
> Would not the stars of love
> Still shoot through the night? [1]

More fitting than pine, than plum or willow is the minion cherry, the temple page, for his is the way of Monju the Minion spread by the Great Teacher, the love of fair youths respected even by the laity: this is the home of the secrets of pederasty.[2]

Word has come that an envoy from the Lord of Harima will visit the Kichijō Temple of Southern Valley. The menservants clean the garden while the pages are busy hanging scrolls in the alcoves of the guest rooms, sweeping and dusting the cabinets.

PRIEST: You there, Chōsuke and Kansuke, if you are well along with your cleaning, run over to Fudō Hill and see if the envoy's appeared. Hurry now.

CHŌSUKE: Please send someone else. We've got to arrange everybody's hair.

KANSUKE: Yes, a page in a temple is just like a wife in the lay world. How can we neglect to dress the hair of the High Priest's wives?

NARRATOR: Hananojō takes their joking seriously. His face looks solemn enough, but he is not very bright.

HANA: Does that mean that the High Priest and I are man and wife? Then my father and mother back home must be liars. They told me that on the mountain I'd have to pretend when I ate bean curd that it was sea bream, and that parsnips were lamprey, because priests

[1] Women are prohibited on Mount Kōya; therefore, the argument runs, the "maiden-pine" (*mematsu*) should not be allowed to grow there either. But it does, and even if it were rooted out, fleshly indulgence ("night-crawling stars") would continue.

[2] Popular belief of Chikamatsu's day had it that Monju (Mañjusri) was the patron deity of pederasty, and that Kūkai, the Great Teacher who founded the temples of Mount Kōya, was an adherent of this vice.

aren't allowed to eat fish. They said I should make believe that yams were eels and that the High Priest was my father. That was all they told me. I never heard anything about being the High Priest's wife. But come to think of it, at the festival the day before yesterday I sat next to the High Priest at dinner and I ate thirteen bowls of rice dumpling soup. I wonder if that made me pregnant. Look how swollen my stomach is!

NARRATOR: He rubs his abdomen. His companions, the other young pages, blush and do not answer. Kumenosuke is the senior among them.

KUME: You say the most idiotic things, Hana. The other boys here —Shuzen, Hachiya, and Umon—are three or four years younger than you, but you're so stupid that they're always making fun of you. I'm from another part of the country, and while here I've been dependent on your family. I think of you as my own brother, and it goes against me to see them laughing at you. As long as I am around I don't suppose they'll cause you any real humiliation, but before long I'll be returning home. Then, if you're not careful, you'll become the laughing stock of the whole Mount Kōya. Please try to control yourself a little.

NARRATOR: Hananojō is offended.

HANA: Don't talk such nonsense. Why should it be so funny if the High Priest's wife became pregnant after eating rice dumpling soup by his side? My sainted father Yojiemon owns the Saigaya, the most famous store in Kamiya, and he always eats with my mother. That's how I was born, and that's what brought my beautiful sister Oume into the world. Whenever you come to my house you and my sister always go together, just the two of you, into the storehouse. I suppose you must be eating rice dumpling soup. I've heard Oume's voice saying how delicious it was.

NARRATOR: Kumenosuke blushes. The other pages comment variously, "You mustn't get upset by what this 'wise man' says." "But be careful. If the High Priest finds out, he's so straitlaced you'd never be able to excuse yourself." "That would disgrace all us pages. Don't let anybody know." But even as they caution him the servants, ignoring their words, remark, "You can't be careless, even with idiots." With a knowing wink they go inside.

Soon afterwards a young lackey rushes in, a letter pouch attached to the point of his sword.

MESSENGER: I'm looking for Narita Kumenosuke. I'm a messenger from his father Buemon in the country.

KUME: I'm Kumenosuke. A messenger from home—this worries me.

MESSENGER: There's nothing to worry about. The fact is, your family has decided to recall you, now that your aging father would like to retire. I've brought a letter for the High Priest, and there's a message with your father's instructions for you. Anyway, he says you should ask the other pages to help you get permission to leave.

NARRATOR: He holds out the letters.

KUME: This is most unexpected. I can't disregard the wish of my father's old age. At the same time, I can't go to the High Priest myself. (*To the pages.*) I ask you please to discuss this among yourselves and to do what you can so that permission will be granted. I leave it to you to present this letter to the High Priest in the most effective way.

NARRATOR: He joins his hands in supplication. The others depart together saying, "We'll do our best." But Hananojō turns back.

HANA: Kume, if you get permission and you go away, please give me your bran bag.[3] I'll make it into a pouch and use it for marbles.

NARRATOR: At last he is dragged off by the others. The messenger steals up softly to Kumenosuke.

MESSENGER: Sir, I was lying when I said I came here from your province. I'm Kyūbei from Kishiwada, a chair bearer, and I often do odd jobs for Mr. Yojiemon. Miss Oume requested me to speak with you privately. That paper dealer from Kyoto has come down from the capital and he's been staying nearby. In a couple of days they're supposed to get married. He says that he'll be taking Miss Oume to Kyoto the day after the wedding. Everybody at home is busy making preparations. Anyway, she says that you should leave the mountain without a moment's delay. Then you'll be able to plan some way for the two of you to escape. Miss Oume implored me in tears, her hands joined in prayer, to persuade you to use the forged note from your father as you promised. The poor young lady is desperately anxious that I take you away before the day is out, and considering she's asked this specially of me, I'd like somehow to help. The details are in her letter.

NARRATOR: He takes Oume's letter from the fold of his kimono and hands it to Kumenosuke.

[3] The bran bag (*nukabukuro*) was used in the bath to keep the skin beautiful.

KUME: Of course. I should have guessed. You know so much already, there's nothing to hide. Oume and I can't go on living if she's to be given to another man. As long as people think I'm acting under my father's commands, I can easily slip away, even without the High Priest's consent, providing, of course, I go through the motions of requesting leave. But first, let me see the letter.

NARRATOR: He breaks the seal and starts to read, when he discovers to his horror that, although the envelope is in Oume's hand and addressed to Kume, the letter inside, signed with his father's name, is addressed to the High Priest of the Kichijō Temple.

KUME: I see what has happened. Oume has always been clever at imitating a man's hand. She must have decided to write the forged letter from my father herself, without asking anyone's help. I wrote out a rough draft for her, but she probably copied the whole thing in a dark corner somewhere and put the letters in the wrong envelopes. I wonder if that means the letter for me has gone to the High Priest instead? This is dreadful!

NARRATOR: He turns pale, but nothing he can do—whether he sits or stands—is to any avail. As he wanders about dazedly, Shuzen appears.

SHUZEN: You, messenger. The High Priest would presently like to have a word with you. But first, he says that you should rest.

NARRATOR: Kumenosuke interrupts.

KUME: Shuzen. Has the High Priest already read that letter? If he hasn't broken the seal yet, please remove it quietly and bring it to me. I ask this as the great favor of my life.

SHUZEN: The High Priest read through the letter several times, then he put it in the cupboard and locked the door. He said that his hands had been defiled by a profanation and he went off to wash them. What was in that letter?

NARRATOR: Kume cannot explain, but his heart beats wildly as he wonders what to do if examined. Kyūbei, the messenger, prays in his heart that the letter will return "over the log bridge of Narrow Valley Stream." [4]

Just then the foot of the mountain resounds with a logger's chant,

[4] From a poem by Taira no Michimori (d. 1183) (in *Kozaisho* chapter, Book IX, *Heike Monogatari*): "My love was tripped on the log bridge over Narrow Valley Stream; behold my tear-soaked sleeve." Here *fumikaesarete* (to be tripped) is interpreted as *fumi kaesarete* (the letter is returned).

the voices of men hauling up a tombstone from the Daimyo of Harima, a splendid sight. The priests of the Kichijō Temple, the residence on Mount Kōya of the Harima clan, come forward to accept the monument, and the envoy is seated in the reception room. The High Priest presently appears to welcome him.

HIGH PRIEST: Sir, you have come a great distance. You must be tired by the journey. Come, sit by me, please. (*To servants.*) Bring wine cups and some tea.

NARRATOR: The samurai who has come as envoy politely replies.

ENVOY: This is the seventh anniversary of the death of my master's mother. He wishes therefore to erect on this mountain a stone monument to her memory and to offer daily services in her name. For this purpose he is making a donation of 500 pieces of silver. He requests that you accept the gift and that memorial services be held at this temple in perpetuity.

NARRATOR: He gives the priest the packet of silver together with a list of the contents.

HIGH PRIEST: I am deeply impressed at such piety and such devotion to his mother's memory on the part of a military man. Doubt not but that the Great Teacher will fulfill his vow of uniting with Maitreya[5] all those whose memorial tablets are preserved on this mountain when Maitreya appears in the world 5,670 millions of years from now. But let me write a receipt.

NARRATOR: The High Priest goes inside, and the feast prepared for the envoy is brought from the kitchen—bottles of saké, cups, tiered lacquer trays, then the beautiful bowls, dishes, and salvers of the splendid repast. The priests of the monastery office and of the Kichijō Temple, headed by the High Priest's appointed successor, the Master of the Discipline Yūben, appear by turns to wait on the envoy.

YŪBEN: We're off in the mountains here, and we can't offer any delicacies, but it happens to be time for dinner. If nothing else pleases you, I hope that you will at least have a bowl or two of soup. (*To pages.*) Pages! Come serve his excellency with saké. . . . Please don't hurry with your dinner.

NARRATOR: Charming pages answer, "Yes, sir," and lend gaiety to the scene. The envoy quickly drains several cups of saké.

[5] The Buddha of the future, whose coming to the world was prophesied by the historical Buddha.

ENVOY: What handsome lads you are! I want you each to tell me your name and where you come from.

SHUZEN: My name is Arimura Shuzen, and I come from Tanabe in this province.

HACHIYA: My name is Yotsugi Hachiya, and I'm from Yamato.

UMON: I was born at Ueno in Iga, and my name is Oguri Umon.

HANA: I come from the town of Kamiya at the foot of this mountain, and my name is Saigaya Hananojō. I'm nineteen years old and I'm the wife of the High Priest. I have a sister named Oume who's really pretty. It's too bad she's a girl and she's not for a priest's tastes. I'm called Hananojō because my face is just like a flower.[6] I don't know why my sister is called Oume,[7] but have you ever split open a plum? There's a flat thing inside. I'm sorry to say I've never split open my sister Oume to see whether she's got one inside her too.

NARRATOR: His expression is quite serious. The envoy is embarrassed for an answer, and the other priests, sorry for Hananojō, drag him off. Kumenosuke at the mention of Oume's name is tortured by the fear that he may soon be questioned, now that the letter is in the High Priest's hands. It is as if an eight-inch nail were driven in his heart. He cannot hold the serving tray steady in his hands, and his eyes are blurred with tears. The envoy resumes.

ENVOY: You seem to be the oldest. What is your name, and where were you born?

KUME: I come from Shikama in Harima, and I am Kumenosuke, the son of Narita Buemon.

ENVOY: Indeed! I heard that Buemon's son was on Mount Kōya— is that you?

NARRATOR: He looks up and the tears come to his eyes; he looks down and his eyes mist over. He seems overcome. Kumenosuke, who has no one else he can turn to in his grief, is drawn by his countryman's warm tears. He moves to his side.

KUME: I know that I am being presumptuous, considering that we have barely met, but I am hoping that you will show me the friendship of a fellow countryman. The kindness of your heart, which I infer from your tears, emboldens me to ask a great favor. Some difficulties have arisen which make it impossible for me to remain another night

[6] *Hana*, the first part of his name, means "flower".
[7] *Ume* (with the initial *o* an honorific) means "plum".

on this mountain. Fortunately, someone has come for me from home. I will tell you the details when once we are at the foot of the mountain. If you would be so kind as to add your recommendation to my request for leave and take me with you today, I will consider it the greatest kindness of this life and all those to come, and I will look up to you as my savior.

NARRATOR: At a loss where else to turn, he makes this rash request, helplessly driven because of love, because of youthful ardor. The envoy raises himself in his seat.

ENVOY: Kumenosuke! When you came to this mountain, it was expected that you would one day become a priest. Now you say that you want to leave. That seems to mean that you intend to return to the laity, doesn't it? Have you forgotten the reasons why you were to become a priest? You should be ashamed of yourself. When you were twelve years old you had a quarrel over a cockfight with your friend Unosuke, a boy of eleven, the second son of Ibuki Jūdayū. The boy died tragically at your hands. I am that Unosuke's elder brother, Sen'emon. At the time I had been spending several years on duty in Edo, and only later did I hear that his lordship had decreed that you commit suicide. My parents, however, felt that you were no less dear than the child who had been killed, and that it would do him no good to kill you and bring grief on your parents. Instead it was decided that you should become a priest to pray for the future happiness of the dead boy. My parents saved your life and you came here. Isn't that what happened? I felt such a longing for my only brother—I never even saw his dead body—that I wanted at least to look once at you, the only remembrance left of him. That was why I offered to come as envoy on this occasion. I asked the pages their names. As soon as I heard "Kumenosuke" I thought, "If my brother were alive, he'd be eighteen this year, a budding youth. Is this the man who so cruelly killed him?" But there was no point in voicing afresh my resentment. I realized that you, my enemy, would one day become a priest and earn my gratitude by praying for my brother's repose. I even felt as if you had something of him about you. I shed tears of longing, hating and loving you at the same time.

But now I am furious, Kumenosuke. Even if you were my parents' murderer, as a priest you would be beyond my revenge, but once you return to the world of ordinary men, you become my brother's enemy,

Sakuemon makes advances to his bride Oume who in turn is fondling her lover. "Through the sleeve of the bedclothes lying against her, she rubs Kumenosuke's leg, squeezes his hand, and lends him strength." The room is supposedly so dark that Kumenosuke is invisible to Sakuemon.
(SAKUEMON: *Bandō Minosuke VI*; OUME: *Ichikawa Shōchō IV*; KUMENOSUKE: *Iwai Hanshirō X*)

and I cannot let you escape. You say that you would like to leave the mountain. That is exactly what I hope you will do. We will go down to the foot of the mountain together, and there I will satisfy the accumulated bitterness of eight years. I shall see the High Priest to apologize and to obtain his consent.

NARRATOR: As he rises to leave, the High Priest hurries in.

HIGH PRIEST: I have heard everything. You disgraceful young man! You haven't shaved your head yet, it's true, but you're no different from a priest. You've learned the exorcisms in Nine Words [8] and the forms of worship, and you've had preliminary training in the discipline. You must surely have been told that this holy mountain has been sacred and pure ever since the Great Teacher's day. If ever anyone pollutes it by committing adultery, the whole mountain will shake violently and the adulterer's body will be torn apart by demons and hung on the branches of the trees. Knowing this, you have dared to profane the temple!

I have received a most unusual letter from your father in the country. Today is the first time in all my long years that I have ever touched such a document. "I send you my love. I swear again that my love will last unchanged through two worlds, through three worlds to come. May my body rot away if I speak untruth." A love letter from a woman, sealed in blood! "From Ume" [9] it says. Who is that? From this moment on, no longer think of me as your teacher. You are no disciple of mine. It makes no difference to me whether you die at this envoy's hands or go on living. Drag him away! Beat him! To think that he should have forsaken the sutras and the True Words I've taught him ever since he was a boy of twelve in order to follow the paths of sin! It's a crime against Heaven!

NARRATOR: He weeps bitter tears of wrath. Kumenosuke is sunk in gloom, and the pages and other priests of the temple can do nothing. Sen'emon is thoroughly dismayed. The Master of the Discipline Yūben runs up to Kumenosuke and kicks him so furiously that he all but splits the seat of Kumenosuke's *hakama*. He gnashes his teeth and sheds tears of rage.

---

[8] A Shingon spell used to ward off all manner of disasters. The magic formula is recited, and the priest simultaneously draws with his finger four lines, then five lines, in the air.

[9] I have omitted a line: "When she writes Ume is she likening my wrinkled face to a pickled plum?" This pun on the name Ume (plum) seems a crude lapse on Chikamatsu's part.

YŪBEN: I misjudged you, you little monster. I never dreamt you had such an evil character. What did you mean when you swore the intimacy of brothers with me? Have you forgotten how I always told you that you were to be extremely careful of your behavior when you visited the Saigaya because of Oume? And how I insisted that the most important part of a minion's [10] behavior was to refrain from creating a scandal and bringing disgrace on his brother?

Sen'emon! I had always supposed that if this wretch had some mortal enemy, and that enemy attacked him, I would throw my body on the naked sword. I was ready to give up my life for him. But now I have broken off all relations, and I swear by the Central Divinity of the Two Mandalas [11] that I feel no pity for him. Here is your brother's murderer! Let him perish at your hands!

NARRATOR: He lifts Kumenosuke and throws him from the porch to the ground.

YŪBEN: It would have been a thousand times better for you to have become a priest and given your affection to a handsome boy rather than yearn after some girl. You showed no consideration for me, your sworn brother. You ignored my wishes. How hateful of you! How unworthy! How degrading!

NARRATOR: Tears fall from his eyes, which are as ice. Sen'emon jumps to the ground after Kumenosuke.

SEN'EMON: I may seem cold-blooded, but now that you have left the temple you are my brother's enemy. I will not be fulfilling the samurai's code unless I kill you.

NARRATOR: He unsheathes his sword in an instant, and strikes Kumenosuke smartly four or five times with the back of his sword.

SEN'EMON: He's dead, as far as I'm concerned. My grudge is satisfied. Now I would like to do what I can to reconcile him to his master.

NARRATOR: His is the noble attitude one expects of a samurai. Kumenosuke utters a loud wail.

KUME: I don't consider that beating just now any disgrace. It's only what I deserved for having beaten someone else. But it breaks my heart that now, when I am about to leave the mountain, I have incurred the High Priest's displeasure, and the brother I swore to serve

[10] The "younger brother" in a homosexual relationship.
[11] Dainichi or Vairocana, the central figure in Shingon Buddhism. The two mandalas are representations of the indestructible (Diamond) and creative (Womb) aspects of the cosmos.

through two lifetimes has accused me of betraying him. I am so unhappy. Even if I kill myself I shall never find salvation. If only I had shaved my head long ago,[12] this unpleasantness would never have arisen. But I felt so dejected at the thought of appearing before my brother with a priest's ugly shaven head. I decided to wear my locks long and powder my face, at least until I was over twenty. The care I devoted to my looks has proved my undoing, for it led to Oume's falling in love with me. That too must have been decreed from a former life. If I go to Oume and break with her, refusing to meet again, and come back to you, will you be as kind and loving as you used to be?

YŪBEN: That goes without saying. If only you break with the woman, I myself will apologize to the High Priest on your behalf, and I'll be as affectionate as ever. But if you don't really mean it, the Great Teacher's punishment will afflict you. Can you take an oath, knowing the penalty?

KUME: Yes. I swear.

YŪBEN: Very well, stand up.—Now what is it?

KUME: What shall I do if Oume won't listen? How unhappy I am!

NARRATOR: He falls over with weeping.

YŪBEN: That such a possibility should occur to you is a sign that the punishment is already taking effect. Leave at once.

NARRATOR: He falls prostrate and they weep together. In the meanwhile the High Priest has taken out the letter from Oume.

HIGH PRIEST: It would be a defilement to leave it on the mountain. Take it and go.

NARRATOR: He throws the letter at Kumenosuke who creeps up shamefacedly, takes it, and thrusts it into his kimono next to the skin. Then, his punishment for breaking the vow of chastity, a sudden whirlwind is sent by the winged demons. Rocks and withered trees shake, lightning flashes, rain and hail spatter down. Heaven and earth are obscured by black clouds, and the world is shrouded in the darkness of endless night.

A PRIEST: Disaster has struck the mountain! Chase the villain as far as Fudō Hill!

NARRATOR: Some of the lower ranks of priests and servants drag him

[12] Priests normally shaved their heads completely. Most young men of Kumenosuke's class, even if not in the priesthood, would have shaved their front locks by the age of nineteen.

off by the arms, shouting for sticks and weapons. But Hananojō is still Kumenosuke's friend.

HANA: Don't worry about my sister. As soon as I find out where you are, I'll bring her to you as your wife.

NARRATOR: The words, though well meant, are painful to hear. Kumenosuke slowly leaves the mountain of so many memories. His side locks and topknot have been disarranged; his eyes are blinded by uncontrollable tears. He turns back to call a final farewell, his voice hoarse with weeping like the cries of the early thrush.[13] Pity poor Kume who has forfeited his holy calling for love of Oume!

ACT TWO

Scene: The Saigaya, a prosperous draper's shop in the town of Kamiya, not far from Mount Kōya.
Time: Evening of the same day.

NARRATOR: Long ago, before they met, she was spotless as a sheet of blank paper, but then his secret visits grew thick as cardboard, only for others perversely to rip across the grained paper, and her sleeves were all too often soaked with tear paper. Many-tongued rumor quickly laid her waste paper; weak before its storms as tissue paper, this tenderly protected child is only seventeen, exquisite even in her name, Oume, the plum blossom.[14]

Her father Yojiemon returns home in high spirits.

YOJIEMON: We've finally settled on tonight for Oume's wedding. Ichisuke and Denkurō, prepare the fish salad as I ordered this morning. Natsu, get the dumpling soup ready. Také, be sure to lay the table attractively. My future son-in-law lives in Karasuma in Kyoto, so I suppose black bowls would be best.[15] We won't need any lacquer saké cups—just put some unglazed cups on a serving stand, my daughter's so young.[16] Sliced abalone and kelp will do for the relishes. The

[13] The song thrush (*uguisu*) sings rather hoarsely early in the spring. Here mentioned also because of the mention of Oume (the plum) which blossoms in early spring.
[14] Again, the pun on Oume's name (the plum).
[15] The street name Karasuma contains the word *karasu*, meaning "crow". Black would therefore be appropriate.
[16] One of Chikamatsu's most frequently employed indecent jokes: the unglazed pottery refers to the girl's lack of pubic hair.

fish course will be dried cuttlefish and prawns, and there are those salted shellfish I received from Kumano. Speaking of salted shellfish, where's my wife?

NARRATOR: Fatherly love inspires his gaiety.

MAID: The mistress is upstairs combing Miss Oume's hair.

NARRATOR: Yojiemon runs to the head of the stairs.

YOJIEMON: Listen. I've gone to the town elders and had a talk with them. They've all agreed that, since it's going to be a private ceremony, the announcement can be made the next time he comes here from Kyoto. Once they finish drinking the wedding saké this evening she belongs to her husband. They say we can turn her over to him completely and send the couple off to Kyoto tomorrow morning as man and wife.

NARRATOR: Just to look at her father's face brimming with energy makes Oume choke with tears.

OUME: You talk as if there were some great urgency. I wanted to postpone the wedding, but out of deference to your parental authority I agreed to do whatever you wished. But at least let me wait a while longer before I go to Kyoto. I want to visit our family shrine. And there's my brother—he's an idiot, but he's still my brother. We ought to tell Hana. And there's Yūben, who's always been so kind and given me amulets and charms. And there's someone else on the mountain . . .

NARRATOR: She cannot pronounce his name, but can only hint at her thought, perhaps because she loves him too much. Her mother nods understandingly.

MOTHER: Yes, that's true, but if we told everybody who's been kind about the wedding, we'd only cause trouble and expense, what with wedding and good-by presents. The best thing is to do as the groom wishes. Come now.

NARRATOR: She is about to go into the linen room.

YOJIEMON: By the way, wife. We'll have to give wedding gratuities to the people in the bridegroom's party and to our own servants. Three hundred *mon* each was the figure I had in mind. We can pretend that the money tubes got broken, and slip nine or ten *mon* out of each stick of a hundred.[17]

[17] A money tube of 100 *mon* normally contained 96 copper coins. However, if the tube was broken some of the coins would have been lost.

MOTHER: That's going too far. Why do you begrudge a little money for the great event of Oume's life? Give them ninety-six for a hundred in the usual way.

NARRATOR: With these words she goes with Oume into the linen room. Oume, no doubt because she has been pampered ever since she was a child, is accustomed to speak willfully to her parents, but feeling ashamed of her dereliction, she is incapable now of grumbling or sulking.

OUME (*to herself*): What's keeping Kyūbei? And what's become of Kume's answer?

NARRATOR: She walks slowly towards the front gate. Her women and the apprentices call out to her: "Miss Oume, we've overheard that it's to be tonight." "You're going to be a Kyoto lady."

Even their teasing does not rouse her spirits.

OUME: What are you saying? Are you so sure that I'll be going to Kyoto and not to my death?

NARRATOR: She stands by the gate. As she looks up the hill Kumenosuke, his face muffled, and Kyūbei, with drooping head, come into sight at the crossroads. She runs up to them.

OUME: I'm so glad you've come! It's as I've told you in the letter— tonight I'm supposed to get married to that horrid man from Kyoto. I've felt completely dead ever since this morning.

NARRATOR: She clings to Kumenosuke and weeps.

KUME: You've felt dead! I've been beaten and dragged about until I'm dead in body and mind both. If you think I'm lying, look at this!

NARRATOR: He takes her hand and passes it through his sleeve.

OUME: Oh, how swollen your back is! Your hair is all undone, and your face looks as if you've been crying. What has happened?

NARRATOR: She weeps, without knowing why. Kyūbei answers in doleful tones.

KYŪBEI: You were careless, Miss Oume. You put the letters in the wrong envelopes, and the love letter for Mr. Kume landed in the High Priest's hands. Well, then, when his eyes—they're more accustomed to reading Shingon spells—fell on, "I'll tell you all about it when I see you, dear," he got so angry it was as if he'd seen a devil, and his face turned red as the fires of hell.[18] Then Mr. Yūben, Mr.

[18] Kyūbei uses scraps of Buddhist sutras and spells whose pronunciations suggest "anger", "red", and so on.

Kume's brother, became jealous and threatened to trample him to death. One calamity led to another. There was a quarrelsome samurai from Harima who said that Mr. Kume was his brother's murderer or something like that, and beat Mr. Kume with the back of his sword. It was the biggest rumpus on the mountain since the Great Teacher passed into Nirvana eight hundred years ago. I was sure that next they'd investigate the fake messenger and I hid, without even touching the food they put before me. In the meantime the whole mountain went on a rampage. The winged devils must have been angry—there was a terrible rain and wind and lightning. The priests said it was because Mr. Kumenosuke had defiled the sacred mountain, and he was beaten away. And that's the sad state of affairs. Thanks to you two I've lost my tobacco case. There was a ticket inside for the 74 *mon* I'd put in a lottery. I'm sure the ticket's been stolen by some devil. That's what's meant by a devil of a lottery.[19]

NARRATOR: His grumbling is only to be expected.

OUME: Oh, please don't tell anybody at home! The mountain may be in an uproar, it may have crumbled to pieces for all I know, but I'm together with Kume again, and I'm very happy. Aren't you happy too, Kume? Try to smile a little, please.

NARRATOR: Despite her words, he remembers all that has happened, and his tear-stained face is a pitiful sight to behold.

Her father calls, "Oume!", then notices her at the gate.

YOJIEMON: Who's there? Oh, is that you, Kume? Kyūbei, what are you doing there? (*To Kume.*) I was just about to send you an invitation, Kume. Welcome here. Come right in. Wife! Kume's here! It's dark—why haven't the lamps been lit? This is no ordinary day, it's Oume's wedding! Light candles upstairs. Pull up the wicks in the garden lamps and in the mistress's quarters, and make them blaze!

NARRATOR: He exudes high spirits, but Oume's mother seems puzzled by what is happening.

MOTHER (*to herself*): I wonder if Kyūbei has been up the mountain without telling us. Kume must have heard from him about Oume's wedding—is that why he's come?

NARRATOR: Kyūbei, noticing the suspicious look on her face, at once steps into the breach.

---

[19] *Tengu tanomoshi* was a kind of lottery; its name contains the word *tengu,* a sprightly, winged goblin.

KYŪBEI: Haven't you heard yet about Mr. Kume's good luck? His father in the country has decided to retire, and he's going to name Mr. Kume his successor. They hired me as a fast messenger, and I went all the way to the mountain from his place in the country without stopping. Mr. Kume asked me to drop by with him when he thanked you for all your kindnesses and said good-by. Mr. Yūben should be coming here soon himself. Today's the day Mr. Kume is to inherit an income of 700 *koku!* Sir, this merits further discussion. As long as Oume's wedding hasn't taken place yet, why don't you break your agreement with the other gentleman and let Mr. Kume have her? I'm saying this for your own sake, and I gather that Mr. Yūben in general is of the same opinion. After all, even if a businessman has a fortune of a thousand *kamme,* he may lose it all in one stroke. But a man with an income of 700 *koku,* rain or shine—if you pick a man like that it'll be a real feather in your cap. Your son-in-law will come riding up on a snorting, prancing steed, and your daughter will ride in a gilt palanquin. Come, let's strike hands on it.[20]

NARRATOR: He spreads open his hands.

YOJIEMON: No, I'm not striking hands.

KYŪBEI: You're a hard man to please. You and your lady can ride a wild horse, for all I care.

NARRATOR: All his efforts are to no avail; they refuse to ride along with his schemes.

YOJIEMON: A horse goes with a horse, an ox with an ox, a merchant's daughter with a merchant. The gentleman whose wedding we're to celebrate today is Sakuemon, the owner of the Minoya at Third Street and Karasuma in Kyoto. He's so anxious to have Oume that he gave me 9 *ryō* 600 *me* to settle an unpaid balance of 9 *ryō* 500 *me.* And this autumn when he made his purchases he paid in advance, dropping 250 pieces of gold before me as if they were buttercups. He wouldn't let me pay a penny for this evening's entertainment or for Oume's bridal clothes. You won't find many men who'll accept a girl naked. What do you say to that, Kyūbei?

KYŪBEI: Mr. Kumenosuke can't promise any gold pieces, but if he can have Oume naked, what more could he want?

YOJIEMON: Enough of your nonsense. Go outside and see if the groom has come. Oume, take Kume upstairs and show him your bed-

[20] A bargain was regularly concluded by each party's clapping his hands.

clothes. They've just been finished. Maids, see that the mice don't get the food!

NARRATOR: To think that a man who takes precautions over mice could calmly send the two of them upstairs together! This is what is meant by setting a cat to guard a fish! Upstairs the bedding is laid out —old imported satins embossed with large crests. Kumenosuke looks enviously at the two tasseled pillows.

KUME: I suppose you'll soon be sleeping cosily with that man from Kyoto on these pillows and under these quilts. What an insane thing to show me! Do you want to make me weep again?

NARRATOR: The tears stream from his eyes.

OUME: I don't want to hear any more disagreeable talk like that. What makes you suppose I'll sleep with that horrible man from Kyoto? To-night you and I are going to run off together. Please make up your mind to that! These are the quilts for him to wallow in—how revolting! And how infuriating!

NARRATOR: She kicks and throws the bedding in all directions.

OUME: And these are *my* bedclothes. I'd like to inaugurate them by sleeping with you in them for the first time, but I'm afraid somebody might come. Oh, it's provoking.

NARRATOR: They cling to each other on the folded bedclothes, their hearts beating fast, fearful lest someone should come: imagine the boundless hatred the song thrush sporting among the plum blossoms feels for people who interfere!

Just then Sakuemon of the Minoya bursts in the house with his servant. He grabs Yojiemon by the topknot and pulls him. Yojiemon's wife and the others restrain Sakuemon with cries of "Are you out of your senses?" but he brushes them off, shouting, "Stand back!" He plants the old man before him.

SAKUEMON: Well, Yojiemon, when you try to put one over on some-one from Kyoto, you'd best be prepared for his revenge. You pocketed the change from nine *kamme,* mere dust when you consider that for twenty years—ever since my father's time—we've been steady cus-tomers and done a business close to 2,000 *kamme.* Then you took a pre-payment of fifteen *kamme* for autumn purchases, without my even see-ing the goods. And on top of that you took four *kamme* for wedding preparations. In return for all this, you saddle me with a daughter who's got a lover. I suppose you think that you can separate us later and it'll be perfectly all right. Is that kind of skullduggery still in fashion here? It's long since disappeared in Kyoto and Osaka. Well, which will you do—hand over your daughter's head or return the twenty-eight *kamme*? I'm waiting for your answer, one way or the other. Wake up to your limitations—a one-pint pot holds one pint even if you pour a river or the whole ocean in it.[21] You're up against a truly lucky man. Just think, in the nick of time before the wedding I've managed to save myself twenty-eight *kamme!* Do you suppose that you can get the better of Sakuemon, a man inspired by Ebisu and Daikoku [22] themselves? No more of your trickery, I say!

NARRATOR: At these words of abuse Yojiemon, an utterly honest man, becomes intensely excited.

YOJIEMON: You certainly make a big fuss about Kyoto this and Kyoto that, but I've had more than enough of your jaw. You're much mistaken if you think that a resident of a 700,000 *koku* domain [23] will accept your petty-minded insults. Returning the money would be simple enough, but I'd hate to have people say that I was bullied into it. Besides, it would reflect on my daughter's character. Show me some proof that she has a lover. Have somebody's insinuations made you start regretting your money? My daughter's name can never be freed of this slur unless I make you apologize and retract your dastardly accusation. Come, show me your proof!

NARRATOR: While he argues in this fashion, those upstairs and downstairs alike are frozen with grief. The couple upstairs, having no way to escape, weep and tremble with fear, too confused to consider any solution but death. Sakuemon calms his rage.

SAKUEMON: You'll wish you hadn't insisted on proof with those airs of a man of integrity! I went up Mount Kōya this morning, thinking that it would be my last chance before I leave tomorrow, when suddenly—it must have been about two in the afternoon—the mountain was swept by a storm. There was tremendous wind, lightning, and rain. I can't remember anything so frightening in my whole life. I rushed for shelter into a temple building, and asked what had caused

[21] Meaning that Yojiemon, who aspires to marry his daughter to Sakuemon and enrich himself too, is attempting more than his limited talents permit.

[22] Two gods of prosperity.

[23] The stipends of samurai were paid in *koku*, a unit of measure about 5.1 bushels (of rice). Yojiemon is saying that Mount Kōya, the fief in which he lives, has an income of 700,000 *koku*, a gross exaggeration.

the storm. The priests told me that a page named Kumenosuke at the Kichijō Temple in Southern Valley had been carrying on a secret love affair for several years with Oume of the Saigaya, and the storm was his punishment for defiling the mountain. That was why, they said, he was at that moment being driven away. Everybody went out to look, and I saw him myself. He was disappearing down the hill with a rogue who looked like a courier.

NARRATOR: Hardly are the words out of his mouth than Kyūbei begins to edge furtively towards the back gate. The master of the house glances upstairs in alarm. His wife is more astute.

MOTHER: That's not very convincing proof. Husband, you must remove this stain on our daughter's honor. Please don't destroy her in your confusion. Brace up, now.

NARRATOR: She prods his knee, and he nods.

YOJIEMON: You're right. (*To Sakuemon.*) Look here, you. Just because there was some lightning, as you say, doesn't prove that my daughter did anything improper. I intend to make sure that tonight, come what may, your marriage is celebrated. I won't be able to show my face in the street if I can't send you off to Kyoto hitched together. It'll be a real achievement making you my son-in-law.

SAKUEMON: Yes, I'm sure you'd like me for your son-in-law, now that you've got your eyes on my money. But for twenty-eight *kamme* I can have an unblemished, untouched wife. I'm going to take back the bed-clothes and the rest of the things made with my money.

NARRATOR: He starts up the stairs to the second floor, but Yojiemon pulls him back with a shout.

YOJIEMON: I'll twist off your arm!

NARRATOR: The two men grapple, now one, now the other on top. Kumenosuke draws his dagger, ready at any moment to stab himself, but Oume clings to his arm and bursts into wails. Downstairs, however, they are too busy fighting to hear her. Oume's mother pushes between the two men.

MOTHER: Husband, don't say a word. And, dear son-in-law, please wait.

NARRATOR: She bows first to one and then to the other. Gradually she calms them both, only herself to collapse in tears.

MOTHER: I can't believe that anybody from the capital would behave in such a heartless way. You've gone so far with the arrangements—

everything is set for the wedding. If you break your promise now, how can my husband and I show ourselves before people or maintain our standing? After all, it's hard to say for certain about an unmarried girl that she's never had any relations with a man. Oume's only a frightened child, you know, and that page you mentioned can't stand much punishment either. If they learn how my husband and I are suffering for what they did, I'm sure that they'll try to commit suicide. It's almost too late to stop them now. Supposing I tried to dissuade them, saying something like, "Don't kill yourselves, you mustn't kill yourselves, this is no time to die. You'd make your parents unhappy and expose yourselves to the worst criticism. Consider it's your duty to your parents. Please don't kill yourselves." It's almost unthinkable, I know, that they'd go through with it anyway, but, in the simple-minded way of young people, they might worry only about the disgrace to themselves. And how tragic it would be if they died!

NARRATOR: Each word she utters travels in two directions, upstairs and downstairs. Kumenosuke, hearing her words, returns his dagger to its sheath; they cannot kill themselves now. Silently embracing, they weep.

MOTHER: It's true of every mother that what makes or destroys her reputation is whether her daughter has been well or badly reared. If Oume is stained for life, I won't even be able to remain with this man I have lived with for thirty years, no matter how hard I try to wipe away the shame. Please at least go through with the formalities of the wedding. A man always has the privilege of leaving or divorcing his wife later on—that's the way of the world. Our only wish is for our daughter's name to be cleared. Once that happens it's inconceivable that my husband would fail to redeem his debts, even if it meant selling the house and everything he owns. Perhaps Oume, when she learns her mother's griefs, will decide to show herself here. Let that serve as an opportunity for making up with her, and distribute the wedding gratuities to the servants. I'm sure that, even if Oume herself stubbornly refuses to appear in this room, the page—after all, he's not made of wood or bamboo—will urge her. If she still refuses, it'll prove she lacks all feeling for her parents. They say that before a mother can raise a child she must pass seven times through an ordeal of life and death, but that refers only to when the child is small. Should a child go on keeping her parents from sleeping at night even after she's grown to be seventeen or eighteen? Oh, I wouldn't make such a fuss if I didn't love her so. She'll understand that some day when she has children of her own. What a hard world this is!

NARRATOR: She raises her voice, attempting to persuade them. Kumenosuke heeds her words.

KUME: Whatever may happen later on—dry your tears now and please go downstairs to comfort your parents. I beg you.

NARRATOR: At his urging Oume, tears of resentment flashing in her eyes, hurries downstairs, unceremoniously thumping on the steps.

OUME: Look, Mother. Don't you think you're being a little too concerned about me? After all, if I've been naughty or even dissolute, that's my affair—I'm not married yet. You can forget about anybody who complains about my behavior. The fact that I've appeared before you is apology enough from me, and if Sakuemon still won't see things that way, it means he doesn't really care for me. How could a country-bred girl like myself ever hope to please a man from the capital?

NARRATOR: Her gestures also betray her annoyance. The would-be groom, overcome by Oume's charms, smiles.

SAKUEMON: Father, Mother, please don't say another word. Now that Oume has shown herself and said what she has, I'm completely satisfied. She could do a dance on top of my head and I still wouldn't let her go. Well, to bed, to bed.

NARRATOR: He takes Oume's hand, and a warm glow spreads over her parents and the whole room.

YOJIEMON: Congratulations! Wonderful! But first exchange wine cups here. We'll take care of everything else in the meanwhile.

NARRATOR: Remembering that Kumenosuke is in the bedroom, he writhes in pain.

SAKUEMON: No. It's already after ten. It'll soon be midnight. There won't be any time for sleeping. I'll drink a congratulatory cup in the bedroom.

YOJIEMON: I beg you, drink it here. Then offer a cup to the servants too. Come, pour the wine.

NARRATOR: He desperately stalls for time. Kumenosuke, having nowhere to escape, pulls the bedclothes over him and cringes inside, feeling more dead than alive. The groom sprawls out on the bedding.

SAKUEMON: Who's been sleeping here? The covers are warm. Well, let's creep in the bedding and have our drink.

NARRATOR: He tries to pull away the covers in which Kumenosuke is lying.

OUME: Well, well! Do you intend to sleep there all by yourself? I won't let you touch the bedclothes until we both lie down properly and you finish exchanging cups with me.

NARRATOR: Through the sleeve of the bed kimono lying against her she rubs Kumenosuke's leg, squeezes his hand, and lends her lover strength.

SAKUEMON: I'm delighted that you want to sleep with me! Hurry up with the saké bottle!

NARRATOR: Even while he shouts the midnight bell is sounding. Downstairs the husband and wife are in a panic. Kyūbei and the others have retired to a corner and are serving drinks for Sakuemon's men.

YOJIEMON (*to wife*): As soon as they get drunk, put out the kitchen lamps and make sure that the place is absolutely dark. Then, when they've finished drinking upstairs, I'll start everybody throwing pebbles at the windows.[24] While we're making an uproar, you kick over the candles upstairs. Take advantage of the confusion to lead Kume out to the gate. If you slip up, Oume will pay for it. No mistakes now.

NARRATOR: So they conspire. Oume's mother carries up the food and drink. Downstairs Sakuemon's men are carousing, while upstairs the mother fills the cups, anxious that no one get hurt. Sakuemon, without so much as a nod to the mother, exchanges cup after cup with Oume in the customary manner. This accomplished, he gulps down four or five additional cups.

SAKUEMON: Well, Mother, I hardly need tell you this, now that I've let you pour the wedding saké, but you've done a wise thing getting me for your son-in-law. Yes, you'd have a hard time finding another groom the likes of Sakuemon, if I may say so myself. I know Kumenosuke is quite a handsome fellow with his full head of hair,[25] but I doubt if he's seen hide or hair of any money, the way I have. You'll find rascals like him—the kind of man who seduces young girls—in Kyoto and Osaka too. Most of them end up in double suicides, a sorry

---

[24] Even today in remote parts of Japan villagers conclude wedding festivities by heaping such indignities on a newly married couple as throwing stones at the walls and windows of the nuptial chamber.

[25] Sakuemon's front lock has been shaved, but Kumenosuke still preserves his youthful appearance.

business. But thanks to me, Oume's life is saved, your daughter's saved, and now I'll savor some saké.[26]

NARRATOR: So saying he downs three more cups in a row.

SAKUEMON: Well, to bed. Mother, it's time you were leaving.

NARRATOR: He is about to pull up the bedclothes when suddenly a big stone strikes him. He looks up with a cry of astonishment as a wild volley of stones big and small smash in rapid succession against the windows and shutters above his head. "Now is my chance," Oume thinks, throwing her arms around Kumenosuke. Sakuemon staggers around groping for her.

SAKUEMON: Oume! It's dangerous! Get inside the covers!

NARRATOR: The mother kicks over the candle stand and Sakuemon cries out.

SAKUEMON: It's dark! Somebody light the lamps!

NARRATOR: Yojiemon, for an answer, extinguishes every last light downstairs; the house is engulfed in a night of eternal dark. The mother creeps in, takes Kumenosuke's hand, and guides him out. Kume, astonished, feels he must be dreaming. Oume follows him, clutching his sash, concealed by the darkness from her mother. Sakuemon loses his composure.

SAKUEMON: Oume, where are you?

OUME: Here I am.

SAKUEMON: Don't hurt yourself in the dark. Where's Mother?

OUME: She's gone to get a light. Stay where you are. You don't know where the kitchen is. I'm here with you.

NARRATOR: Her voice lingers behind even as she departs; her mother supposes she is guiding outside only one person. Oume, afraid of what Sakuemon may do, tiptoes out as though over burning fire, fearful lest her mother should hear her footfalls. Trembling all over, she steals to the front step. Her mother whispers to Kumenosuke.

MOTHER: By all rights you should be dead, but my husband and I feel sorry for Oume. Knowing how she'd weep for you, we decided to save your life tonight. But now that Oume's marriage has been settled, you must give up all thought of her. Here is the cup she drank from. Take it as a keepsake and the end of your connection.

[26] The pun in Japanese between *hirou* (to save [a life]) and *hirou* (to pick up [a saké cup]) has been approximated here with "saved" and "savor".

NARRATOR: She puts it into his kimono. Oume and Kume, resolved to die, bid farewell in their hearts to the mother. For a moment Kume hesitates, uncertain in the dark where he cannot see Oume's face.

KUME: I'd like to say just one more word to Oume.

MOTHER: It's late. It's too late.

NARRATOR: She hurries him out impatiently, not realizing that she hastens her own daughter's death. Her mother brought her into the world, her mother now causes her death. The couple open the gate between life and death and disappear into the darkness before them, leaving behind her parents, condemned by love of their child to wander like her in the obscurity of night.[27]

ACT THREE

Scene One: The lovers' journey: the road between Kamiya and the Women's Temple on Mount Kōya.
Time: Late the same night.

NARRATOR:

Life is an illusion,
The pains of birth and death
Prescribed before our coming.
What a world of dust,
What a shambles! [28]

OUME: To what should we compare the life we have led? Three years have already passed since first we met. Our ties of love have been lost in shadows while you, my husband, lived solitary as the lone well of the fields. When once we are dead, will later men remember us as husband and wife, I wonder? Let us leave these keepsakes of our union for our parents. Through the long worlds to come I will see you always in your long front locks, and show you my maiden tresses. The paths are many at the crossing of Six Ways,[29] but we will not lose sight of each

[27] Reference is made to a poem in *Gosenshū*, no. 1103: "Even though a parent's heart is not in darkness, he will wander lost for love of his child."

[28] A statement of the familiar Buddhist theme of *karma*—the actions of a previous existence determining one's fortunes in the present one.

[29] After death a person follows one of the Six Ways—to hell, the world of hungry demons, the world of beasts, the world of nature demons, the world of mortals, or heaven, depending on actions in the present life.

other. Even as I speak the evening moon has set and darkness deepens. Spring has barely come, but how thick the mists lie—good for hiding ourselves, but how hard to see your face this hazy night! Two good things never come at once, they say. Here at Jewel River [30] if storm winds shake the poisoned dews under the trees, I will drink and die without blemishing my body.

NARRATOR: Face brushes face; the tears they shed flow into each other's mouths, like water to moisten the lips of the dying.

OUME: We whose fate is to hasten the final dagger must envy the frost of this short spring night, for it may last unmelted till morning. Outside Kamiya, the town where I was born, the night work must now be over, and the drying paper is spread frost-white on the ground. But even such remembrances stir thoughts less of my parents than of you.

KUME: I can never forget your parents' kindness. Gratitude to them, no less than my love for you, binds me in chains of affection like Fudō's avenging noose; [31] now we have reached Fudō Hill. Next will we traverse the mountain road that leads to death?

Oh, heartbreaking sight, the Vale of Tombstones! Once I stopped a man to ask whose was this grave, and he told me that here lay Karukaya [32] of old; these rank spring grasses are his monument. Sad the question, sad the reply. Karukaya, fierce-hearted man with his bow, one spring night, the moon in the sky, sat under cherry trees, and a blossom, not opened but a bud, fell in his cup, at which he abandoned the world, a night tale of human frailty that fits us well. Nineteen for me, eighteen for you, a short glory, blossoms of the early cherry, scattering tonight by Child's Fall. [33]

NARRATOR: His eyes swim with tears.

OUME: Over there, when we cross, is the Amano ascent of the mountain. I can't forget how I came with my mother last year and prayed

---

[30] It was popularly believed that the waters of Jewel River (Tamagawa) were poisonous. The river flows down Mount Kōya. It is the first of the sites named on the lovers' journey to the Women's Temple.

[31] Fudō, the Guardian King, carries a noose for punishing sinners in his left hand. Here mentioned because of the place name Fudō Hill (Fudōzaka).

[32] Karukaya was the hero of a number of older plays. One day when he was drinking in a garden cherry blossoms fell in his cup, stirring a realization of the impermanence of worldly things. He became a monk on Mount Kōya.

[33] Another famous spot on Mount Kōya, Chigogataki. Used here because the early cherry was sometimes called *Chigozakura*.

at the shrine. Alas, that is the rock which the Great Teacher's mother twisted by her wrath. Her only crime was being a woman, but what must mine be? [34]

> Your love came thick and strong
> As the rains of June,
> But in the end it dried away,
> Like water from autumn fields.

The mountains are asleep and will say nothing. River in the valley, do not raise your voice and tell others how we looked. I keep nothing hidden from you, but when I ask the name of the Buddha you worship, you say the Secret Fudō, [35] as if you are rejecting me.

My brother Hana—it's harder to leave him than even my parents—must surely be heaping bitter reproaches on me. The wind blowing down India Mountain [36] is his punishment on us; it cuts our flesh as we embrace. How pitiful, how pitiful these moments haunted by the terrors of hell! Hated even while in this world, heavily afflicted, we shall be kept by our sins from crossing the sacred bridge; we shall not reach the Inner Shrine. [37] The danger is a presage of worlds to come; by Snake Willow [38] a thousand demons may assail us, but however tormented or afflicted, we shall not part, I shall not let you go.

NARRATOR: They clutch each other's sleeves wet with tears; in their hands are rosaries. "Trust in him, trust in him," each urges, praying with undivided heart, offering deepest reverence to Shaka Buddha of full and perfect powers, and to the sacred relics of his True Body. [39] "Whether we are to become Buddhas or wander by the Three Ways of Hell, pray for us both, offer us water and sprays of plum blossom." [40] As they struggle up Flower-Offering Hill the dawn moon is buried in

---

[34] Women's hearts (even that of Kūkai's mother) were considered by Buddhists to be twisted; that was one reason why they were not allowed on Mount Kōya. When Kūkai's mother learned she could not ascend the mountain, her wrath twisted the rock.

[35] Literally, the "Fudō Outside," referring to a temple consecrated to Fudō which stood outside the main compound of buildings; here the name suggests to Oume that Kumeno-suke is keeping her outside his confidence.

[36] *Tenjiku,* an old Japanese name for India, is here the name of the mountain to the west of Kūkai's tomb.

[37] Where Kūkai, the Great Teacher, passed into Nirvana in A.D. 835.

[38] Name of a place on the way to the Inner Shrine. Legend has it that some poisonous snakes at sight of Kūkai turned into willows.

[39] A section of a Shingon spell; the original is in Chinese.

[40] The expression *mizu kume ya* (offer [dip] water) contains Kume's name, and mention of plum blossoms of course recalls Oume's name.

the clouds of Five Hindrances: they have reached the Women's Temple.

Scene Two: The Women's Temple.

NARRATOR: Their young hearts, strained to thoughts of the world beyond death, relax at sight of the temple.

OUME: I'm happy we're here at last.

NARRATOR: Her joy before long will give way to grief. In the temple, arrived before them, a woman is staying. She wakens at their approach and calls out.

WOMAN: Excuse me, please.

NARRATOR: They cling to each other in terror, afraid to utter a word of reply.

SATSU: Oh, I'm no one to be afraid of. My name is Satsu. I'm from Shikama in Harima, and I'm the daughter of Narita Buemon. I've come to visit my younger brother Kumenosuke, a page at the Kichijō Temple in Southern Valley. This evening I sent my servants up the mountain to inquire about him, but they couldn't even discover whether or not such a person was there. Someone suggested that we ask at the town of Kamiya by the foot of the mountain. Are you perhaps from this neighborhood? I wonder if you wouldn't happen to know my brother.

NARRATOR: A sister treats her brother as a stranger—foretaste of the dark roads of the afterworld. The brother, choking with tears of love for his flesh and blood, pauses a moment, unable to answer.

KUME: Yes, I've heard of Kumenosuke. Somebody was saying that he was suddenly seized by a terrible illness yesterday afternoon, and that he wouldn't last out tonight. We'll know for sure at daybreak whether he's to live or die.

NARRATOR: His sister still does not recognize Kume's voice, muffled by his attempt to hide the tears.

SATSU: I feared as much! People say that if you soak stonecrop picked on this holy mountain the leaves will tell whether a person lives or is dead. The reports I heard about Kumenosuke frightened me, and I thought I would steep in water from that stream in the valley some dried stonecrop I keep in my charm bag. I concentrated my thoughts on Kumenosuke. But even after I'd soaked the plant for half an hour, it was still withered, and gradually it shriveled up. Was this a sign from the Great Teacher that my brother was dead? After having come all this way to find him, if I only had arrived one day sooner I would at least have been in time for his last moments. Oh, if I were a man I would seek him out, even if it meant running all over the whole mountain, but for my sins I was born a woman. What a heartbreaking fate!

NARRATOR: She raises her voice and weeps. The couple is also lost in tears. Oume speaks between her sobs.

OUME: Have you come with your parents? Or are you alone?

SATSU: That is why I am here. My father had been ailing ever since last winter, and he passed away on the twenty-second of March at the age of sixty-nine. He was cremated on the following day. Today is the seventh day of mourning. I've brought Father's ashes with me, hoping that my brother and I might pray together before them. But I discover now that my brother is also dead. I must go back with a heavy heart, and what shall I tell my mother? What unforeseen disasters the world holds in store for us!

NARRATOR: She weeps bitterly. Kumenosuke is distraught to learn that these are his father's ashes. Before Oume now, by what twist of fate or ancient connection, is the father-in-law she has never seen: at the thought grief swells in her heart, and her sleeves are too soaked to hold the tears, hide them though she tries.

Satsu's maidservant, lying on the floor beside them, speaks.

MAID: Listen, that's the bell sounding four o'clock. We'll know when dawn comes whether he's all right or not. Oh, I'm exhausted from this talk!

NARRATOR: She yawns—in her sleepy daze she is unaware of the tragedy around her.

SATSU: Yes, that's right. Forgive me for having detained you with such a long story when you must have business of your own. Some connection between us from a former life has surely brought us together. If you should hear anything about Kume, I beg you to let me know. I feel unusually sorry to leave you both. It is as if we had been sitting together at Kumenosuke's deathbed and were now saying good-by. It's a terrible, helpless feeling.

NARRATOR: The ties of blood mysteriously make themselves known, a source of only more tears. Saying nothing, telling each other nothing, they part—and this too is heart-rending.

Kume and Oume hide in the shadows of the temple.

KUME: Each additional moment we remain in this world of dust, the things we see and hear will increase the obstacles to our salvation. The dawn approaches. Why should we taste yet more suffering and shame? Let us die now.

OUME: Yes, I want to die quickly. I envy your having met your sister, even as a stranger, and being able to die near your father's ashes. I am worried that my father and mother, even in the midst of their grieving, will revile me as a wicked daughter. That would lead to future suffering.

KUME: Look, here's the wine cup your mother gave me last evening. It was touched by her hands, a keepsake into which she put her heart. Here it is.

NARRATOR: He offers the cup.

OUME: Thank you. My mother has always thought of me as a child even now that I'm grown up, and she holds me in her arms while I sleep. Remembering that, I shall die with this cup she touched by my breast.

NARRATOR: She places the cup next to her skin and joins her hands in prayer. Kumenosuke looks at her face as she awaits the blade.

KUME: How lovely you are! And how well everything has turned out! You have your mother's keepsake, and I will die by my father's ashes. We shall be reborn on one lotus with our parents. The appointed time has come. I cannot put it off. Now is the moment!

NARRATOR: He draws his dagger and presses it against her breast.

KUME: May we bathe in the light of the Buddha and be delivered from all our sins! [41]

NARRATOR: A moan as he drives in the blade; when the point reaches her liver Oume's body falls backwards. Murmuring another prayer, he twists the blade until her breath dies away. Kume's sister and her servant run up, startled by the sound of Oume's body falling and her cries of pain. They shout in horror, "Murder! Murder!" But here in the middle of the mountains, in the middle of the night, no one hears their voices. Weeping, they run down towards the foot of the mountain. Kumenosuke hides until they have gone, then returns with a spray of anise in his hand. He places the leaves on the box with his father's ashes. He lifts the box reverently and bows three times.

[41] This Shingon spell is uttered in a Japanese approximation of Sanskrit.

KUME: I return the flesh and bones you gave me. We are one again. All creation is eternal, and this is the stroke that brings eternity.

NARRATOR: He plunges the knife into his throat and falls over Oume's dead body. They lie in death side by side, covered by the flowers of the truth of the Law. Now they return to earth, water, fire, and wind: wind is in the mountains, water in the valley stream, and earth in the sand sprinkled on their bodies in the Shingon rite which brings salvation.[42]

This is the tale told of the suicides of a good man and a good woman in the Women's Temple.

[42] Part of the Shingon burial ritual involves sprinkling sand on a corpse. Earth, water, fire, and wind are, in Buddhist belief, the four primordial elements. The fourth element, fire, is omitted here, perhaps for stylistic reasons, perhaps because implied in the cremation of the bodies.

THE COURIER
FOR HELL

First performed on April 22, 1711. No source for this play has been discovered, though it is presumed that Chikamatsu, following his usual procedure, based the work on actual events. The play was so successful that
it was often imitated and revised. The version at present used in most
Kabuki performances dates from 1830.

Cast of Characters

CHŪBEI, aged 24, proprietor of the Kame-ya, a courier service
HACHIEMON, his friend
KATSUGI MAGOEMON, Chūbei's father
CHŪZABURŌ, a friend of Chūbei in Ninokuchi Village
JINNAI, a samurai
IHEI, a clerk
GOHEI, a servant
CLERKS, MESSENGERS, APPRENTICES, POLICE
UMEGAWA, aged 22, a courtesan of low rank
MYŌKAN, Chūbei's foster mother
KIYO, proprietress of the Echigo House
WIFE of Chūzaburō
MAN, a maid
TOYOKAWA, a prostitute
TAKASE, a prostitute
PROSTITUTES, MAIDS

ACT ONE

Scene: The shop of the Kame-ya, a courier service in Osaka.
Time: Late in the eleventh moon (of 1710?).

NARRATOR: In Naniwa of water-markers, in Naniwa where bloom these flowers,[1] three are the streets in the Quarter of Flowers, Sado and Echigo and Hyōtan in between.[2] To them from Awaji Street "visited by shore birds"[3] comes Chūbei, a frequent visitor, heir to the Kame-ya, a youth barely turned four and twenty, arrived from Yamato four years ago as an adopted son with a dowry. He is clever in business, at assigning packloads, and at managing the thrice-monthly couriers to Edo. Adept in the tea ceremony, poetry, chess, and backgammon, he writes an elegant hand. When it comes to saké, he can manage three, four, or at most five cups, and he wears with the proper assurance a heavy silk cloak with five crests. His plain sword guard, so cunningly inlaid one would never suspect it was of country workmanship, is rare as Chūbei among country lads. Knowing in the ways of love, familiar of the Quarter, he does not wait for evening to race thither on flying feet.

In his absence the courier shop, busy with packing and unpacking, is crowded front and back with clerks scratching in the ledgers and clicking their abacuses. The ease with which they handle tens of thousands of *ryō* and transact business with distant Kyushu and Edo without stirring from the shop makes you think the gold and silver pieces came with wings.

The collector has returned from his rounds of the city and begins to enter the commissions in the register, when a voice is heard at the door.

JINNAI: Could you tell me, is Chūbei at home?

NARRATOR: The visitor is a samurai from a daimyo household, a regular customer of the shop. The clerk answers politely.

IHEI: Ah, it's you, sir, Mr. Jinnai. Chūbei is out, but if you have

[1] The water-marker (*miotsukushi*) was used as an epithet for Naniwa (Osaka). It is today the emblem of the city. "Where bloom these flowers" is a quotation from an old song about Naniwa; the flower in question is the plum blossom, and may be an allusion to Umegawa, whose name contains the word "plum" (*ume*).
[2] Three streets in the Shimmachi licensed quarter of Osaka.
[3] Allusion to the poem by Minamoto no Kanemasa, no. 288 of *Kinyōshū* (A.D. 1128): "Guardian of the barrier of Suma, how many nights have you awakened to the crying of the shore birds that visit the Isle of Awaji?"

anything to send to Edo, I am at your service. Boy, bring some tea!

NARRATOR: He speaks deferentially.

JINNAI: No, I have no commissions for you. A letter has come from the young master in Edo. Listen to what he writes.

NARRATOR: He unfolds a letter.

JINNAI: "I shall send you 300 *ryō* in gold with the courier leaving on the second of next month. Please collect this sum on the ninth or the tenth from Chūbei of the Kame-ya in Osaka, and settle the business which I have discussed with you. I enclose herewith the receipt from the courier service. Surrender it to Chūbei on delivery of the remittance."

These are his orders. Important business arrangements have been disrupted by the failure of the remittance to arrive by today. What is the explanation for this disgraceful negligence?

NARRATOR: He utters the words with a scowl.

IHEI: I don't wonder that you're upset, sir, but with all the rain we've been having lately, the rivers are swollen and it takes longer than usual to make the journey. The slowness of your remittance hasn't been our only problem. We've sustained considerable losses. But there's nothing for you to worry about. Even supposing the courier were set upon by robbers or cutthroats, or himself yielded to sudden temptation on the way, the eighteen courier houses would compensate you in full, regardless of the sum of money. You wouldn't suffer the loss of so much as a mustard seed.

NARRATOR: Jinnai interrupts.

JINNAI: That goes without saying. Chūbei's head would fly if my master suffered any loss. Any further delay with the remittance will seriously hamper my master's business. That is why I've come here today to investigate. Send a courier to meet the one from Edo, and see to it that the money is brought immediately.

NARRATOR: Foot soldier and stripling that he is, he brandishes with authority his sword, silvery-looking, though probably leaden as his heavy dialect. He departs, only to be followed by another visitor.

MESSENGER: Excuse me, please. I've been sent by Hachiemon of the Tamba-ya in Nakanoshima. He says that he's received notice of a remittance from a rice wholesaler in Kofuna Street in Edo, and he'd like to know why the money hasn't reached him yet. He wrote you a letter about it the other day, but hasn't had any answer, and when he sent a messenger, you gave him the runaround. He wonders when you intend to deliver the money. Anyway, my master says that you should turn over the money to me and send me back with an escort. I'll return your receipt. Well, I'm ready to collect the money now.

NARRATOR: He stands legs astraddle in the doorway, making a clamor. The clerk, Ihei, devoted to his master, answers in unruffled tones.

IHEI: Indeed? I can't believe that a gentleman like Hachiemon would order us around in such a high-handed manner. Your company's business is not the only concern of the Kame-ya. This house is entrusted with five or even seven thousand *ryō* of people's money at a time, and our couriers range at will the 130 leagues between Edo and Osaka. It would be strange if deliveries weren't delayed once in a while. The master is expected back at any moment. When he returns, I'm sure he'll send a reply. I'll thank you not to make such a commotion over what, after all, is less than fifty *ryō*.

NARRATOR: The messenger, taken aback by his asperity, leaves quietly.

Chūbei's mother, Myōkan, who scarcely ever quits the *kotatsu*,[4] emerges from the back room.

MYŌKAN: What was the meaning of that? I'm sure that the money for the Tamba-ya arrived at least ten days ago. Why hasn't Chūbei delivered it? All morning long I've been hearing customer after customer demanding his money. Never since the days of my husband has the house received a demand for even a single piece of silver. We've yet to cause the guild the least trouble. In fact, the Kame-ya has always been considered the model among the eighteen courier houses. But haven't you noticed? Lately Chūbei's behavior has been very peculiar. Those of you who are recent employees may not know it, but Chūbei is actually not my son. He was the only son of a prosperous farmer from Ninokuchi Village in Yamato named Katsugi Magoemon. His mother died, and his father, afraid that desperation at being under a stepmother might make Chūbei turn to vicious pleasures, suggested that I take him here as successor to the business. I've had no fault to find with Chūbei's running of the household and the business, but of late he's seemed restless and unable to keep his mind on his work. I've wanted to admonish him about his behavior, but I was afraid that he might think that his foster mother is just as bad as a stepmother.

4 A low table covered with a quilt which reaches the floor; underneath the table is a small charcoal fire. A normal type of heating even today in a Japanese house.

Rather than complain, I've preferred to shame him by my silence. I've pretended not to notice, but I've followed everything deserving of my attention. He's become so extravagant. Why, he uses two or three sheets of fine quality tissue, whatever he happens to lay his hand on, just to blow his nose! My late husband always used to say, "Never trust a man who uses one paper handkerchief after another!" Chūbei takes three packs with him whenever he leaves the house. I wonder how he can blow his nose so often—he never has a single sheet left when he returns. He's young and healthy, but if he goes on blowing his nose that way, he's sure to come down with some sickness.

NARRATOR: Still murmuring complaints, she leaves. The apprentices and errand boys feel sorry for her.

APPRENTICE: I wish he would please hurry home.

NARRATOR: While they have been waiting, the sun has journeyed back to the west, and it is time to shut the shop gates.

Love for Umegawa, a bird in a cage, has turned Chūbei into a swallow,[5] ever winging to the Quarter, but now he trudges the streets, his thoughts tangled like a spider's web with schemes for raising money and fears of what may happen at home. He sees the ten-penny harlots emerging at the street corners, and realizes in dismay that day has drawn to a close. He hurries home now, so precipitously that his feet barely touch the ground. He arrives at the shop entrance, but hesitates, worried about what may have happened during his absence. Perhaps there have been dunning messengers from his customers, and Myōkan has heard their complaints. If only someone would come out, so that he could learn the situation before he entered! This is his own house, but the threshold seems too high for him to cross. He peeps inside and sees the cook, Man, apparently preparing to visit the saké shop. She is a sullen, sharp-tongued[6] creature, unlikely to reveal anything free of charge. "I'll pretend I'm in love and trick her into talking," he thinks, when suddenly she appears. He firmly grips her hand that holds a saké cask. She cries out.

MAN: Master, is that you?

CHŪBEI: Don't make such an uproar! You know too much about love for that!—I'm head over heels in love with you. They say that when

---

[5] The cry of the swallow "*chū, chū*" leads into mention of Chūbei.

[6] The expression *ki de hana mogu* means "to treat disagreeably", but literally is "to wipe one's nose with a piece of wood".

there's love inside, it's bound to show on the outside. Have you seen the look in my eyes? Why do you torture me so with that adorable face of yours? You'd be kinder if you killed me.

NARRATOR: He takes her in his arms.

MAN: I can tell you're fibbing. I've seen how you go off every single day to Shimmachi, and how you use two or three packs of tissue at a time. When you have such a lovely nose to blow, why should you want to wipe it on the likes of me? You're lying!

NARRATOR: She shakes herself free, but he takes her in his arms again.

CHŪBEI: What purpose could I have in lying? It's the truth!

MAN: If you really mean it, will you come to my bed tonight?

CHŪBEI: Of course. How happy you've made me! But there's something I'd like to ask while I'm at it.

MAN: Ask me when we're snug in bed together! You won't fool me, will you? Promise, and I'll take a hot bath before you come!

NARRATOR: She breaks off the conversation and, freeing herself, runs off. Chūbei is irritated, though he is not sure at whom. He looks up.

CHŪBEI: I wonder who's that swaggering this way from the north block? Oh—it's Hachiemon. It'd be a nuisance meeting him.

NARRATOR: He starts off to the east, hoping to dodge Hachiemon.

HACHIEMON: Chūbei! Don't try to avoid me!

CHŪBEI: Hachiemon—you're a stranger in these parts! Yesterday, then today too, and come to think of it, the day before yesterday, I planned to send somebody to your place, but what with one thing and another, I put it off.—It's turned decidedly cold. How's your father's rheumatism and your mother's toothache? Oh—you positively reek of saké! You shouldn't overdo it, you know. I'll send someone tomorrow morning first thing. Oh yes, ee-shay [7] sent a message. She says she'd like to see you one of these days.

NARRATOR: He chatters on, hoping to humor Hachiemon.

HACHIEMON: Drop it. I'm not a man to dance to your tune. Am I mistaken in thinking you run a courier service? Why hasn't the remittance of fifty *ryō* from Edo reached me yet? I wouldn't mind waiting four or five days, but it's been over ten days and you still haven't delivered my money. Friendship and business are two different matters. After all, you charge me high enough rates, and the business must be valuable to you. Today I sent a messenger to your shop and your

---

[7] The word *sore* for "she" is given as *reso,* reversing the syllables as in pig Latin.

damned clerk gave him a surly answer. I can't believe you treat other customers that way. Are you amusing yourself at my expense? Remember, in Kitahama, Utsubo, Nakanoshima and even in the Temma greengrocers' market they call Hachiemon "The Boss." [8] Make fun of me all you like, but today I get my money. Or must I report you to the messenger guild? First, I'll have a word with your mother.

NARRATOR: Chūbei stops him from going inside. He whispers.

CHŪBEI: I'm sorry. I've bungled things. Here, I'm begging you on bended knees—please listen to just one word. I beseech you.

HACHIEMON: What, again! You seem to think you can settle anything with your clever tongue. If you try the same tricks on me you've used on Umegawa, you'll find that a man's quite a different proposition. You've something to tell me? Very well, I'm listening.

NARRATOR: He rebukes him bitterly.

CHŪBEI: If my mother should hear you, nothing, not even my death, would restore my reputation. I beg you, as the supreme act of kindness of a lifetime, keep your voice down.—Ah, I feel so disgusted with myself!

NARRATOR: He weeps bitterly.

CHŪBEI: Why should I hide the truth from you? Your money arrived from Edo two weeks ago. As you know, Umegawa's customer from the country has been using his money to outbid me. I've been at a complete disadvantage with only the miserable sums, two or three hundred *me,* that I've managed to pilfer when my mother and the clerks weren't looking. I was feeling bad enough—more dead than alive—when I learned that her ransom had been decided on, and all that was left was the final striking of hands. Umegawa was heartbroken, and my honor at stake. We should have killed ourselves already. One night we even went so far as to touch the cold steel of our daggers to each other's throats but—perhaps it wasn't yet time for us to die—obstacles of one sort and another interfered, and that night we parted in tears. The following morning—it was the twelfth of this month—the money for you from Edo arrived unexpectedly. I slipped it into my kimono, hardly realizing what I did, and fairly flew to Shimmachi, I have no recollection how. Then, with much effort, I persuaded the owner of the house to break the contract with Umegawa's

---

[8] Kitahama was a section of rich merchants, Utsubo of fish markets, Nakanoshima of samurai residences and storehouses—all in Osaka.

country customer. He agreed to ransom her to me. I managed to save Umegawa by turning over your fifty *ryō* as earnest money. Every morning and night since then I've faced north [9] and worshiped you, telling myself that saving her was possible only because I have a friend in Hachiemon. Yet I knew that no matter how close we are, it is one thing using the money after first getting your permission—that's the same as borrowing—but quite another asking for it later on. While I was wondering what to do, you began to demand your money. One lie led to another, and now that my earlier excuses have proven false, I don't suppose that anything I can say will seem true to you. But other money ought to be coming from Edo in the next four or five days at the latest. Somehow I'll manage to send it to you. I promise you won't lose a penny. It will only make you angry if you think of me as a human being. Consider instead that you've saved a dog's life and forgive me, I beg you.—I see now why there are always people being executed for crimes. I have no choice from now on but to steal. Do you think it's easy for a man to confess such things? Try to imagine what it's like! Nothing could be as painful as this, not even if I had to cough up a sword from my throat.

NARRATOR: He weeps tears of anguish. Hachiemon, a man ready to tackle even demons, also sheds tears.

HACHIEMON: I admire you for making such a painful confession. I'm a man—I forgive you and I'll wait. Work out your problem as best you can.

NARRATOR: Chūbei touches his forehead to the ground.

CHŪBEI: Thank you. I've had five parents—two fathers and three mothers [10]—but it'd be harder to forget your kindness, Hachiemon, than theirs.

NARRATOR: Tears interrupt his words.

HACHIEMON: I am satisfied, if those are your feelings. Well—somebody may be watching. I'll see you soon.

NARRATOR: He is about to leave when Chūbei's mother calls from inside.

MYŌKAN: Is that Hachiemon? Chūbei, invite him in.

NARRATOR: Chūbei has no choice; hesitantly he leads Hachiemon inside. The mother is incorruptible honesty itself.

[9] Hachiemon's house in Nakanoshima was north of Chūbei's place in Awaji-machi.
[10] His real parents, his stepmother, and his foster parents.

MYŌKAN: You sent a messenger a while ago and now you've come yourself. I can see why you'd be impatient. Chūbei, you know his money arrived ten days ago. Why have you delayed delivering it? Stop and think for a moment. What use is a courier service if money is delivered late? Remember the nature of your business. Give Hachiemon the money at once.

NARRATOR: But Chūbei has no money to give him. Hachiemon guesses Chūbei's thoughts.

HACHIEMON: It may sound as if I'm boasting, ma'am, but I'm not in any desperate need for fifty or seventy *ryō*.—I must leave now for Nagabori. Tomorrow will do just as well.

NARRATOR: He is about to go.

MYŌKAN: No, no. I won't be able to sleep at night for worry as long as we are holding your precious money. Chūbei, give Hachiemon the money immediately.

NARRATOR: Thus urged, Chūbei answers "Yes" and goes into the back room. He looks round blankly, but there is no sign of money. He goes through with the pretense of unlocking the cupboard, though he knows it is empty; even the squeaking of the key embarrasses him. Wild with anxiety, he prays in his heart that the gods will grant their help.

CHŪBEI: Thank heavens! There's a pomade jar [11] in this hairdressing kit. Thank you, god of my ancestors!

NARRATOR: He lifts the jar thrice to his brow in gratitude, then wraps it in paper as though it were a packet of gold pieces, and quickly inscribes in bold black characters "Fifty *Ryō* in Gold." How shameless his deceit—passing off a worthless pot for fifty *ryō* and tricking his mother too!

CHŪBEI: Here you are, Hachiemon. As you know, I'm under no obligation to deliver this money now, but I'm giving it to you anyway, to relieve my mother's worries and to show my respect for you as a gentleman. Please accept it without further ado and reassure my mother. I'm sure you won't need to undo the packet. You can tell merely by the feel that it contains fifty *ryō*. Have you any objections?

NARRATOR: He offers the packet. Hachiemon takes it in his hand.

---

[11] *Bimmizuire* is a jar used in dressing the sidelocks (*bin*) in a man's coiffure. It was of an oval shape, about an inch thick, and therefore was roughly the dimensions of a packet of gold coins (*koban*).

HACHIEMON: Why, who do you take me for? I'm Hachiemon of the Tamba-ya, and as long as I get my money, I certainly won't raise any objections. There you are, ma'am. I acknowledge receipt of the remittance from Edo. I'll be expecting you on your visit to the Fudō Temple.[12]

NARRATOR: He is about to leave when Myōkan, apparently convinced by their deception, calls out.

MYŌKAN: Chūbei, it's customary when a remittance has been paid to claim the receipt for it. If Hachiemon hasn't his receipt with him, you should ask him please to write a few words. One has to be careful about everything.

CHŪBEI (*whispers to Hachiemon*): Mother is illiterate—she can't read a word. Please write something, for form's sake.

NARRATOR: He holds out a writing set and winks.

HACHIEMON: That's no problem. I'll be delighted. Here, Chūbei, see what I write!

NARRATOR: He scrawls a note as his fancy dictates: "Item. I am not in receipt of fifty *ryō* in gold. The above is positive guarantee that this evening, as previously promised, I will go drinking in the Quarter, and will accompany you as your clown. I engage always to be present whenever there is merrymaking. In witness whereof, I accept this pomade jar as token of my intention to appear on all festive days." [13]

He dashes off this stream of nonsense.

HACHIEMON: I'll be leaving now.

NARRATOR: As soon as he steps outside Myōkan speaks.

MYŌKAN: Get everything in writing—a written document always carries weight.

NARRATOR: Chūbei's mother, deceived again, is honest-hearted as the Buddha, but like the Buddha, she will grow angry if rubbed the wrong way once too often.[14]

The night spent waiting for word of the thrice-monthly courier from Edo has deepened when outside there is a jingling of horse bells and the loud cry, "The pack horses have come! Open the inside gates!"

[12] A temple in the north of Osaka; to go there from Chūbei's house would normally take one by way of Nakanoshima, Hachiemon's place.

[13] The terminology of this note is a parody of stereotyped phrases normally found in pledges.

[14] From an old proverb, "Even Buddha will get angry if you rub his face three times."

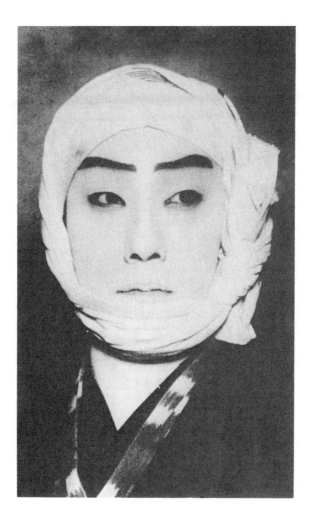

Nakamura Ganjirō I (1869–1935) was considered to be ideally suited to the parts of Chūbei and other young heroes of Chikamatsu's plays.

*Chūbei shows himself above the screen, suggesting to Umegawa
a decapitated head exposed on the execution ground. "Ugh—
how terrible! Please don't do that—you look too much like
something I can't bear."*
(CHŪBEI: *Nakamura Ganjirō II;* UMEGAWA: *Nakamura Tomi-
jūrō IV*)

Men swarm in, shouldering wicker trunks. Chūbei and his mother are overjoyed.

CHŪBEI: Good luck has returned, and next year will be lucky too! [15] Saké and tobacco for the drivers!

NARRATOR: The shop is in a turmoil as the clerks, inkstones at their elbows, frantically jot entries in the ledger. Ihei, the chief clerk, still wears a sour expression.

IHEI: Mr. Jinnai, a samurai, was here a while ago from the mansion in Dōjima. He said that notice of the expected arrival of three hundred *ryō* of gold on the ninth had reached him, and he couldn't understand why it was so late. He left in a huff. What was the trouble?

NARRATOR: The supervisor empties his money belt.

SUPERVISOR: Yes, I know about his three hundred *ryō*. The money's urgently needed. Please deliver it tonight.

NARRATOR: Eight hundred *ryō* in gold, remittances for various clients, are plopped down. Chūbei grows all the more elated.

CHŪBEI: Put the silver in the inner storehouse, and the gold in the safe. Mother, I'll take these three hundred *ryō* to the daimyo's mansion at once. (*To servants.*) Remember, we're entrusted with other people's money. Keep watch on the gate and shut the doors soon. Be particularly careful about fire. I may be a little late returning, but I'll be traveling in a palanquin, so there's nothing to worry about. Finish your dinners and get to bed early.

NARRATOR: He puts the money into his kimono and ties the strings of his cloak. Frost is gathering this night on the gate as he steps outside. Though he fully intends to go north, his feet follow their accustomed path to the south.[16] Absent-mindedly he crosses West Yoko Canal, so absorbed in thoughts of the prostitute that he reaches Rice Merchants' Street before he realizes it.

CHŪBEI: What's this? I'm supposed to be on my way to the mansion in Dōjima. Have I been bewitched by a fox? Good heavens!

NARRATOR: He retraces a few steps, only to stop.

CHŪBEI: Perhaps the reason why I've come here without meaning

---

[15] Chūbei thinks of next year because it is already the end of the eleventh moon. The phrase *shiawaseuma* (good-luck horse) refers to the fact that it was customary to write the words "good luck" on the horse's saddle girth.

[16] North would take him to Dōjima, south to the Shimmachi Quarter.

to is that Umegawa needs me, and my protecting god is guiding me
to her. I'll stop by her place a moment and look in on her.

NARRATOR: He turns back again.

CHŪBEI: No, this is disastrous. With this money on me, I'll surely
want to spend it. Shall I stop while I can? Shall I go to her?—I'll go
and have done with it!

NARRATOR: His first thought was sensible, his second insensate, his
third sends him as a courier back and forth six times a month on the
Six Roads, a courier for hell.[17]

ACT TWO

Scene: The Echigo House in the Shimmachi Quarter.
Time: Later the same evening.

NARRATOR:

> "*Ei-ei!*" cry the crows, the crows,
> The wanton crows,
> On moonlit nights and in the dark,
> Looking for their chance;
> "Let's meet!" they cry, "let's meet!" [18]

Green customers are ripened each day, till evening comes and charcoal fires glow, by the love of courtesans of their choice: the love and
sympathy these women give, regardless of rank, is in essence one.[19]
The Plum blossoms are fragrant and the Pines are lofty, but leaving
rank aside,[20] teahouse girls have the deepest affections. Here comes
one now, guided by a maid in a cotton print kimono to Echigo House
in Sadoya Street—"Oh for a bridge between Echigo and Sado!" the
song goes. The owner here is a woman; no doubt this is the reason why

[17] The courier service went three times a month in both directions between Osaka and
Edo, for a total of six trips. The Six Roads refer to the six ways before the soul when
it reaches the afterworld.

[18] The cry of the crows, "*aō, aō*," is interpreted as the future of the verb *au* (to meet).

[19] Literally, "green wicker hats turn [the color of] scarlet leaves. . . ." Men visiting
the Quarter concealed their faces with basket-like wicker hats. Some commentators take
the passage to mean that the men stay on until their green hats are reddened by the
glow of charcoal fires.

[20] Pines (*matsu*) were the highest rank of courtesan, and Plum blossoms (*ume*) came
next. Umegawa belongs to the humble class of *mise jorō*, prostitutes who call to customers
from their shops. See Appendix 1.

the girls who call feel so at home and open their hearts' deepest secrets of love. Umegawa thinks of the Echigo House as her refuge in sorrow, and neglects her duties elsewhere to come here, hiding a while from the Island House—"island hiding," as Kakinomoto said.[21]

UMEGAWA (*to proprietress*): Kiyo, that blockhead of a country bumpkin has been bothering me all day and my head is splitting. Hasn't Chūbei showed up yet? I sneaked away from my customer, hoping at least to see you, my only connection with Chūbei.

NARRATOR: She slides open the *shōji* door as she enters, even as she will slide it tomorrow at dawning.

KIYO: I'm glad you've come. There's a crowd of girls upstairs relaxing. They're drinking and playing *ken*[22] to pass the time until their customers call. Why don't you join them in a game of *ken* and have a cup of saké? It'll cheer you up. Some of your friends are there.

NARRATOR: Umegawa goes upstairs. The room is draughty and the women—no men are present—are drinking saké warmed over a *hibachi*, their hands tired from the gestures of the game. "*Romase!*" "*Sai!*" "*Torai!*"[23] "A tie!" Takase of the high-pitched voice takes on Toyokawa, and her fingers flash. "*Hama!*" "*San!*" "*Kyū!*" "*Gō!*" "*Ryū!*" "*Sumui!*"

TOYOKAWA: I win! You must drink another cup! You can manage one, can't you, Narutose?

TAKASE: Look, Umegawa's here. (*To Umegawa.*) You couldn't have come at a better time. You're so good at *ken*. Chiyotose's been beating us all evening long, and we're furious. Do take her on. Oh, I'll get another bottle of saké for you.

UMEGAWA: I hate saké and I'm in no mood for *ken*. What I would like from you is a few tears of sympathy. My customer from the country intends to ransom me. Why, just today at the Island House he was trying to badger me into consent. I lost my temper, I hate him so. All the same, he spoke first. Chūbei asked later on, and it took all the master's efforts to get Chūbei permission to put down the earnest

[21] Kakinomoto no Hitomaro, the great poet of the early eighth century. The phrase occurs in poem no. 409 of the *Kokinshū*.
[22] A game of Chinese origin. Each player holds out none to five fingers; the one who guesses the total held out by both wins.
[23] Approximations of the Chinese pronunciations with various suffixes: *romase* is "six", *sai*, "seven", and *tōrai*, "ten". The numbers later in the passage are, respectively, eight, three, nine, five, six, and four.

money. The master even extended the deadline when Chūbei failed to pay the balance as he promised. We've managed to stay together so far but, after all, Chūbei has responsibilities. He must think of his foster mother, and he runs an important business between here and Edo, with commissions from the daimyo granaries and all the leading merchants. Anything at all might ruin our plans.

If I allow myself to be redeemed by that oaf, I could kill myself afterwards and still people would say, since I'm not a high-class courtesan, "Her head was turned by filthy lucre. What contemptible creatures those teahouse girls are!" I must think of my reputation and the feelings of my friend Kamon and the other girls of my class. Oh, I wish I could be together with Chūbei, as we've always planned, and free myself from this endless gossip!

NARRATOR: Her sleeve is soaked with tears as she speaks. Her listeners, the other prostitutes, compare their lot to hers, and nodding, share in her tears.

PROSTITUTE: I feel terribly depressed. Why don't we cheer ourselves with a little music? Will one of you maids run down and ask Takemoto Tanomo to come here? [24]

UMEGAWA: Don't bother—I was buying some hair oil at his shop a few minutes ago and I happened to hear that he went directly from the theater to the Fan House in Echigo Street.[25] But I am a pupil of Tanomo's. I'll show you how well I can imitate him! A samisen, please.

NARRATOR: She begins to play a piece about Yūgiri, using this old example to tell of the courtesan's fate today.

UMEGAWA: There's no truth in courtesans, people say, but they are deceived, and their words but confessions of ignorance in love. Truth and falsehood are essentially one. Consider the courtesan, so faithful to her lover that she is ready to throw away her life for him—when no word comes from the man and he steadily grows more distant, brood over it as she may, a woman of this profession cannot control her fate. She may be ransomed instead by a man she does not love, and the vows she has pledged become falsehoods. But sometimes it happens that a man favored by a courtesan from the start with merely

[24] A leading *jōruri* chanter of his day. He owned a hair oil shop in the Shimmachi Quarter.
[25] The Fan House (Ōgi-ya) was famous as the scene of the loves of Yūgiri, the great courtesan, and Izaemon. The selection about Yūgiri which Umegawa sings is quoted from an early work by Chikamatsu, *Sanzesō* (1686).

the false smiles of her trade may, when constant meetings have deepened their love, become her lifelong partner; then all her first falsehoods have proved to be truth. In short, there is neither falsehood nor truth in love. All that we can say for certain is that fate brings people together. The very courtesan who lies awake, sleepless at night with longing for the lover she cannot meet, may be cursed by him for her cruelty, if he knows not her grief.

If that country fellow curses me, let him. I can't help loving Chūbei, that's my sickness. I wonder if all women of our profession have the same chronic complaint?

NARRATOR: The story of one who all for love abandoned the world induces melancholy reveries, and even the effects of the saké wear off. Hachiemon of Nakanoshima, approaching from Nine House Street, hears the singing.

HACHIEMON: Ah-ha! I recognize the voices of those whores! Is the madam there?

NARRATOR: He charges in. He picks up a long-handled broom and, holding it by the sweeping end, bangs loudly on the ceiling with the handle.

HACHIEMON: You give yourselves away, girls! I've been listening to you down here. What kind of man do you miss so much? If it makes you lonely being without a man, there's one available here, though I don't suppose he's to your taste. How would you like him?

NARRATOR: He shouts up through the floor. Umegawa does not recognize him.

UMEGAWA: Of course I want to see my sweetheart! If it's wrong for me to say so, come up and beat me! (*To Kiyo.*) Who is that downstairs, Kiyo?

KIYO: Nobody to worry about. It's Hachi from Nakanoshima.

NARRATOR: Umegawa is alarmed.

UMEGAWA: Oh, dear, I don't want to see him. Please, all of you, go downstairs and don't let on, whatever you do, that I'm here.

PROSTITUTE: We'll be the souls of discretion.

NARRATOR: They nod and file downstairs.

HACHIEMON: Well, well—Chiyotose, Narutose, quite a distinguished gathering! They told me at the Island House that Umegawa left her room early this evening and went off somewhere, but Chūbei doesn't seem to have showed up here yet. Madam, come closer. You too, girls, and the maids also. I have something to tell about Chūbei, for your ears only. Gather round.

NARRATOR: He whispers confidentially.

PROSTITUTE: What can it be? You have us worried.

NARRATOR: They are all anxious lest Umegawa upstairs hear some unfortunate rumor. Just at this moment Chūbei furtively runs up to the Echigo House, his body chilled by the night and the icy weight of the three hundred *ryō* on his heart. He peeps inside and sees Hachiemon sitting in the place of honor, spreading rumors about himself. Astonished, Chūbei eavesdrops, while upstairs Umegawa is listening with rapt attention. The walls have ears: Hachiemon's words heard through them are the source of the disasters that follow, though he does not suspect it.

HACHIEMON: You may imagine from what I am going to say that I'm jealous of Chūbei, but—Heaven strike me down if I lie!—I feel sorry when I think of how he's going to end his days. Yes, it's true that he sometimes shelters under his roof for a time a thousand or even two thousand *ryō* of other people's money, but his own fortune, throwing in his house, property, and furniture, doesn't amount to fifteen or twenty *kamme* [26] at most. They say his father in Yamato is a rich man but, after all, he's a farmer, and you can imagine the size of his fortune if he had to send Chūbei as an adopted son to the Kame-ya. I'm a young man myself, and like any other young man, I have to visit the teahouses every so often, though it costs me ten or twenty *ryō* a year. But Chūbei is so mad about Umegawa that he's bought her for himself most of the time since last June in competition with another customer at the Island House, though he can ill afford it. I gather that her ransom was recently arranged and Chūbei gave as his deposit fifty of the 160 *ryō* required. That's why the money he should have delivered to various customers hasn't been paid, and he's had to resort to outright lies in order to stave them off. He's caught in a terrible fix. Just supposing he decided to ransom Umegawa as of this minute—she must have her debts, and he could weep his head off, and the bill would still come to 250 *ryō*. Does he think the money will fall from heaven or gush up out of the ground? His only way to raise it is to steal. Where do you suppose the fifty *ryō* he gave for the

[26] Fifteen *kamme* would make about 250 *ryō* and twenty *kamme* over 333 *ryō*. Twenty *kamme* would be worth about $10,000 U.S.

deposit came from? He intercepted a remittance of mine from Edo and that's what he used. I suspected nothing of this, and when I went to claim my money, there was his foster mother, poor woman. She knew that the money had arrived from Edo and she urged Chūbei to deliver it immediately. Shall I show you the gold pieces Chūbei paid me?

NARRATOR: He takes out a packet.

HACHIEMON: See—it looks like fifty *ryō* on the outside, but I'll reveal what's actually inside. This is why Chūbei will end up on the block!

NARRATOR: He cuts open the packet and empties it: out drops a pottery pomade jar. The proprietress and all the prostitutes shrink back with cries of alarm. Upstairs, Umegawa, her face pressed against the *tatami,* weeps, stifling her sobs. Chūbei, whose short temper is his undoing, fumes.

CHŪBEI: Telling something to a prostitute is proclaiming it to the world. Such arrogance and insults on my manhood, all because he advanced me a paltry fifty *ryō!* I'm sure that if Umegawa hears of this she'll want to kill herself. I'll draw fifty *ryō* from the 300 in my wallet, throw them in his face, and tell him exactly what I think of him. It'll save my honor and wipe out the insult to Umegawa.—But this money belongs to a samurai, and besides, it's urgently needed. I must be patient.

NARRATOR: His hand goes to his wallet again and again as he disconsolately debates which way to turn, at cross purposes with himself like the crossbill's beak. Inevitably he fails to understand Hachiemon's intent.

Hachiemon holds up the pomade jar.

HACHIEMON: You can buy one one of these for eighteen coppers. Gold may be cheap, but never since the days of Jimmu [27] has fifty *ryō* in gold gone for eighteen coppers. If this is the way he treats even a friend, you can imagine how he must cheat strangers. From now on you'll see how he goes step by step from cutpurse to cutthroat and finally to the block where his own head gets cut off. It's a shame. When a man is that corrupted, nothing can cure him—not the threat of disinheritance by his parents or master, nor the admonitions of Shaka or Daruma, nor even a personal lecture delivered by Prince

---

[27] The legendary first emperor of Japan.

Shōtoku himself.[28] I'd like you to spread this story throughout the Quarter and see to it that Chūbei isn't permitted here again. I wish you'd also persuade Umegawa to break with him and gracefully allow herself to be ransomed by her country customer at the Island House. Rascals like Chūbei never come to a good end. They either get involved in a love suicide or else they wind up stealing some prostitute's clothes. They're sure to bring disgrace on their friends by being exposed in the stocks at the Main Gate with one sidelock shaven.[29] That's what is meant by being outside the pale of human society. If you care for Chūbei, don't let him in here again.

NARRATOR: Umegawa, hearing his words, is torn by mingled grief and pity and a feeling of helplessness. Silent tears rack her breast.

UMEGAWA: I wish I had a knife or even a pair of scissors so I could cut out my tongue and die.

NARRATOR: The women downstairs can guess the agony she undergoes.

PROSTITUTE: Umegawa must be miserable. What an unlucky girl! Poor Umegawa, I feel sorriest for her!

NARRATOR: The servants, the cooks, and even the young maids wring their sleeves for the tears.

Chūbei, always hot-tempered, is unable to endure more. He bursts into the room and plops himself down almost in Hachiemon's lap.

CHŪBEI: Well, Mr. Hachiemon of the Tamba-ya. Just as eloquent as ever, I see. Ah, there's a man for you, a prince! A gathering of three is a public meeting, they say—how kind of you to make an inventory of my possessions before this assemblage!—Look here! This jar was an understanding between friends. I handed it to you only after first asking indirectly if you'd accept it in order to reassure my mother. You agreed. But are you so worried now you might lose the fifty ryō you lent me that you must blab it all over the Quarter and ruin my reputation? Or have you taken a bribe from that customer at the Island House to win over Umegawa and deliver her to him? I've had enough of your nonsense! You've nothing to worry about. Chūbei's not a man to cause a friend to lose fifty or a hundred ryō. My esteemed Mr. Hachiemon—damn you, Hachiemon! Here's your money! Give me back the pledge!

[28] Shōtoku Taishi, one of the chief figures in the establishment of Buddhism in Japan (573–621?).
[29] A punishment imposed by the authorities of the Quarter on customers who transgressed its regulations.

NARRATOR: He pulls out the money and is about to untie the packet when Hachiemon stops him.

HACHIEMON: Chūbei—wait! Don't let your foolishness get the better of you. I know your character well enough to realize you'd never listen to any advice from me. I hoped that if I could persuade the people of the Quarter to keep you at a distance, you might pull yourself together and become a normal human being again. I acted out of kindness to a friend and for no other reason. If I had been afraid for my fifty *ryō,* I'd have said so before your mother. Why, I even wrote out a crazy receipt to humor your mother, though she can't read. And have I still not been considerate enough?—That packet you've got there looks like 300 *ryō.* I don't suppose it belongs to you. No doubt it's money you'll have to account for. If you tamper with it, you won't find another Hachiemon to settle for a pomade jar! But perhaps you intend to give your head in exchange? I suggest that instead of flying off the handle you deliver the money to its owner. You unsettled lunatic!

NARRATOR: He roundly upbraids Chūbei, point for point.

CHŪBEI: Stop trying to act the part of the disinterested friend! What makes you so sure that this money belongs to somebody else? Do you think I haven't three hundred *ryō* of my own? Now that you've called my fortune into question before all these women, my honor demands all the more that I return your money.

NARRATOR: Unfastening the packet, he scoops out ten, twenty, thirty, forty, and then—the final step to disaster—fifty *ryō.* He quickly wraps the coins in paper.

CHŪBEI: Here's proof that nobody loses any money on account of Chūbei of the Kame-ya! Take your money!

NARRATOR: He flings it down.

HACHIEMON: What kind of insult is this? Say "thank you" politely and offer it again.

NARRATOR: He throws back the money.

CHŪBEI: What thanks do I owe you?

NARRATOR: Again he throws the money at Hachiemon, who throws it back. They roll up their sleeves and grapple. Umegawa, overcome by tears, runs downstairs.

UMEGAWA: I've heard everything. Hachiemon is entirely right. Hachiemon, please forgive Chūbei, for my sake.

NARRATOR: She raises her voice and weeps.

UMEGAWA: Shame on you, Chūbei! How can you lose your head that way? Men who come to the Quarter, even millionaires, are frequently pressed for money. A disgrace here is no disgrace at all. What do you hope to achieve by breaking the seal on someone else's money and scattering it around? Would you like to get arrested and dragged off to prison with a rope around you? Would you prefer such a disgrace to your present trouble? It wouldn't be only a matter of disgrace for you—what would happen to me? Calm yourself at once and apologize to Hachiemon. Then wrap up the money and deliver it as quickly as you can to its owner. I know you don't want to give me up to another man. I feel the same. I have plans all worked out in my mind if I should have to sacrifice myself. My contract still has two years to run. Then, even if I have to sell myself to some country brothel—Miyajima, who knows?—or become a streetwalker on the Osaka docks, I'll look after you. I'll never let my man suffer. So calm yourself. You're acting shamefully.—But whose fault is it? Mine. And knowing it's entirely my fault, I feel grateful and sorry for you at the same time. Try to imagine what I am going through.

NARRATOR: She pleads with him, and her tears, falling on the pieces of gold, are like the dew settling on the primroses of Idé.

Chūbei, utterly carried away, has recourse to a desperate last resort; he remembers the money he brought with him as an adopted son.

CHŪBEI: Be quiet! Do you take me for such a fool? Don't worry about the money. Hachiemon himself knows that I brought it from Yamato when I came here as an adopted son. It was left in someone's keeping, but I've claimed it now in order to ransom you. Madam, come here!

NARRATOR: He summons her.

CHŪBEI: The other day I gave you a deposit of fifty *ryō*. Here are 110 *ryō* more. That makes a total of 160 *ryō*, the money needed to ransom Umegawa. These forty-five *ryō* are what I owe you on account —you worked it out the other day. Five *ryō* are for the Chaser.[30] I believe that Umegawa's fees since October come to about fifteen *ryō* altogether, but I can't be bothered with petty calculations. Here're twenty *ryō*, and now please clear my account. These ten *ryō* are a present for you, by way of thanks for your trouble. One *ryō* each goes to Rin, Tama, and Gohei. Come get it!

[30] A teahouse employee who served as both a procuress and a guardian of the courtesans.

NARRATOR: He showers gold and silver in the momentary glory of the dream of Kantan.[31]

CHŪBEI: Please arrange the ransom at once so that Umegawa can leave this evening.

NARRATOR: His words stir the proprietress into sudden animation.

KIYO: It's a strange thing with money—when you haven't got it, you haven't got it, but when it comes, it comes in a flood. There's nothing more to worry about. I hope you're happy, Umegawa. I'll take this precious money to the owner. Rin and Tama—come along.

NARRATOR: They hurry out together. Hachiemon looks unconvinced.

HACHIEMON (*to himself*): I don't believe he's telling the truth, but it's money he owes me anyway, and it'd be foolish reticence to refuse. (*To Chūbei.*) Yes, I acknowledge receipt of the fifty *ryō*. Here's your note!

NARRATOR: He throws it at Chūbei.

HACHIEMON: Umegawa, you're lucky to have such a fine man. Enjoy yourselves, girls.

NARRATOR: He departs, stuffing the money into his wallet.

PROSTITUTES: We should be going too. Congratulations, Umegawa.

NARRATOR: They leave for their respective houses. Chūbei is impatient.

CHŪBEI: Why is the madam taking so long? Gohei, go tell her to hurry.

NARRATOR: He urges the man frantically.

GOHEI: I'm sorry, sir, but when a woman is ransomed the owner's permission is necessary. Then the elders of the Quarter cancel the seals on her contract. Finally the manager of the Quarter for the current month has to issue a pass or she can't go out the Main Gate. It'll take a bit longer.

CHŪBEI: Here, this is to speed them.

NARRATOR: He throws another gold piece.

GOHEI: Leave it to me, sir!

NARRATOR: He races off nimbly: a piece of gold is more effective in building strong legs than a moxa cure.[32]

---

[31] Reference to the Nō play *Kantan* (originally based on a Chinese legend) which tells of Rosei, a man who slept on a magic pillow in Kantan, and dreamed a lifetime of glory. He awoke to discover that scarcely an hour had passed since he went to sleep.

[32] The burning of the herb *mogusa* (moxa) at various places on the skin is still believed to strengthen different parts of the body.

CHŪBEI (*to Umegawa*): You get ready in the meanwhile. You look a mess. Here, tighten your sash.

NARRATOR: He speaks with desperate urgency.

UMEGAWA: Why are you so excited? This is the most wonderful occasion of my life. I'd like to offer the other girls a drink and say good-by properly. Please give me more time before I leave.

NARRATOR: Her face is flushed with innocent high spirits. Chūbei bursts into tears.

CHŪBEI: My poor dear! Didn't you realize that something was wrong? That money was an urgent remittance for a samurai residence in Dōjima. I knew that once I touched the money my life was ended. I tried very hard to restrain myself, but I could tell how mortified you were to see your lover humiliated before your friends. I wanted so badly to cheer you that my hand went unconsciously to the money. Once a man goes that far, he can't back away. Please try to think of our troubles as the workings of fate.—Hachiemon is on his way now to tell my mother—it was written all over his face. People will be here any moment from the eighteen courier houses to question me. We are now one foot over the brink of hell. Run away with me!

NARRATOR: He clings to her and weeps. Umegawa moans and begins to tremble. Her voice shakes into tears.

UMEGAWA: There—isn't this what I've always predicted? Why should we cling any longer to life? To die together is all we can ask. I would gladly die this very moment. Calm yourself, please, and think.

CHŪBEI: Could I have committed such a terrible crime if I had planned to go on living? But let us stay alive and together as long as we can, though we are resolved that sooner or later we must kill ourselves.

UMEGAWA: Yes, we'll stay together in this world as long as it's possible. But someone may come at any moment. Hide here.

NARRATOR: She pushes him behind a screen.

UMEGAWA: Oh, I left my good-luck amulet in the chest of drawers in my room. I wish I had it.

CHŪBEI: How could we escape punishment for our crime, no matter how powerful your amulet may be? Make up your mind to it—we are doomed to die. I will offer prayers for your repose. Please offer them for mine.

NARRATOR: He raises his head above the screen.

UMEGAWA: Ugh—how horrible! Please don't do that—you look too much like something I can't bear.[33]

NARRATOR: She throws her arms around the screen and chokes with tears.

The proprietress of the Echigo House and her servants return.

KIYO: Everything's been settled. I've had your pass sent round to the West Gate. That's the shortest way for you.

NARRATOR: She speaks words of good cheer, but the husband and wife are trembling, and their voices shake as they repeat, "Good-by, good-by."

KIYO: You sound as if you're cold. How about a drink?

CHŪBEI: The saké wouldn't get down my throat.

KIYO: I don't know whether to congratulate you or to tell you how sorry I am to see you go. I could chatter on a thousand days and still not run out of things to say.

CHŪBEI: I wish you hadn't mentioned "Thousand Days."[34]

NARRATOR: They take their farewells as the cock is crowing. His extravagance has been with others' money; now all is scattered like sand. They pass Sand Bank,[35] and let their feet guide them, come fields or come mountains, along the road to Yamato.

ACT THREE

Scene One: The road to Ninokuchi Village in Yamato.
Time: The next day and the following three weeks.

NARRATOR:
  The green curtains, the crimson bedding,
  The chamber where once, under familiar coverlets,
  They ranged pillows all night through
  And heard the drum sound the Gate's closing—
  All has now vanished, comes not again even in dreams.

[33] His head appearing over the screen looks like the severed head of a criminal exposed on a wall.
[34] Sennichi (Thousand Days) was an execution ground in Osaka.
[35] Sunaba (Sand Bank) was just outside the West Gate of the Quarter.

UMEGAWA:

> Yes, though my lover promised without fail
> He'd ransom me before autumn, I waited in vain.[36]
> I trusted the fickle world, I trusted people,
> But now my ties with the world and people are broken.
> Though once we shared midnight trysts at the Gate,
> Now we are kept apart by the barrier of men's eyes.
> His hair is uncombed since yesterday;
> When I take my comb to smooth his twisted locks,
> My fingers are frozen with tears.
> We press our chilled limbs to each other's thighs,
> Making a double *kotatsu.*
> The bearers pause, a moment's breathing spell—
> How strange that we still breathe, that our lives go on!

NARRATOR:

> They weep at Spillway Gate.[37]
> There's still a while before the dawn, they think,
> And lift the blinds of their palanquin.
> Their knees remain entwined; they remember
> Meetings at night in her little room—so alike,
> But when did charcoal ashes turn to morning frost?
> When summoned by the night winds,
> Only the maid-pines [38] of the fields resepond,
> Recalling nights gone by, a source of tears.

CHŪBEI: Why are you so distraught? This is our foretaste of rebirth on one lotus.[39]

NARRATOR: He comforts Umegawa and takes comfort himself in smoking a double pipe with her.[40] The thin smoke and the morning fog melt and clear; the wind blows wild through the wheat sprouts. Ashamed to be seen by the early-rising farmers or by some field watchman who might ask them for a light, they stop their palanquin

---

[36] Most of the above description is taken almost word for word from the Nō play *Hanjo,* though the phrases acquire a somewhat different meaning in this context.

[37] Kobore-guchi, the gate leading to Hirano.

[38] *Kaburomatsu* are low, thick-growing pines. *Kaburo* (or *kamuro*) is the name of a courtesan's maid; here the contrast is made between the gay quarters where *kaburo* answered when summoned, and the windswept fields where only the *kaburomatsu* reply.

[39] In Pure Land Buddhism, saved souls are reborn on lotuses in the Western Paradise. Lovers hope to be reunited on the same lotus, in the manner that Chūbei and Umegawa now share one palanquin.

[40] A pipe with two stems leading to a single bowl, smoked by lovers.

and dismiss the bearers. They do not begrudge the bearers' fees, nor even their uncertain lives, much less the hardship of walking barefoot. All that they begrudge is their remembrance of this world.

Never before has she worn an old woman's wadded hat.

UMEGAWA: Here, please warm yourself with this. It's more important than that I hide my face.

NARRATOR: She offers her purple kerchief to protect him from the wind, but for them purple passion is a thing of the past; today they are truly husband and wife.

They worship at the Kōshin Shrine [41] where prayers are answered. They turn back and see some boy actors praying for popularity before the Aizen of the Shōman Temple amid offerings from the Dōtombori players and the women of the familiar houses of the Quarter. Among the lanterns marked with crests she knows, she notices one—oh, painful memories!—from the Tsuchi-ya, her own house.

UMEGAWA: Look, here is your crest, the muskmelon, and next to it mine, the double pine cone. When we offered this lantern, we prayed for the pine's thousand years, but our vows were ill-fated.

CHŪBEI: Tonight, as the lanterns of our existence flicker out, let us consider the crested robes we wear are our mourning shrouds, and journey hand in hand to hell.

UMEGAWA: Yes, I will be led by you.

NARRATOR: Again they take each other's hands; the tears they shed glaze the ice on their sleeves.

Though no one bars their way, they advance but slowly, asking directions at every turn. Umegawa is still in this morning's attire; [42] her frozen sandals stick to her bare feet. A bank of clouds in the sky threatens sleet, and leaves flutter in a wind mixed with hail. They have reached Hirano. [43]

CHŪBEI: Many people know me here. Come this way.

NARRATOR: They cover their faces with their sleeves and twist their way through the back streets of the town and over rice field paths till they reach Wisteria Well Temple. [44]

[41] A shrine south of the South Gate of the Tennō-ji. Shōman Temple is northwest of the same group of buildings. The Guardian King Aizen was popular with courtesans, boy actors, and others who depended on *ai* (love).

[42] She wears a courtesan's robes, conspicuous outside the quarter. Courtesans do not wear *tabi* (linen socks).

[43] About five miles south of Osaka; today part of the city.

[44] *Fujii-dera.* Twisting streets are associated with the twisting of a wisteria (*fuji*) vine.

CHŪBEI: Look—you see, even the remotest village belongs to the world of love!

NARRATOR: A girl of seventeen or so, picking vegetables behind her house, is singing:

"You, standing by the gate,
Are you my secret lover?
The field winds will do you harm,
Please come inside the house."

They envy others' words of tenderness.

CHŪBEI: Do you remember? When was it—that morning of the first snow when the early customers were arriving and you walked back with me, still in your night clothes, through the thin snow by the Great Gate? The snow today is no different, but our hopes have entirely changed. You poor dear—it was because of me that you were first made to suffer, step by step the white cloth was dyed deeper, from blue to indigo. If divine punishment should strike for the vows we wrote, the Hachiman of Konda as our witness, may it spare you!

NARRATOR: He weeps.

Though for a while I may escape
The prying eyes of men. . . .

UMEGAWA: I'm as much to blame as you!

NARRATOR: Her words dissolve in endless tears that soak her folded handkerchiefs. Her skirts are torn by the dun-colored weeds. In the frost-withered fields the wind crackles through desolate stretches of pampas grass.

CHŪBEI: Was that rustling the sound of people coming after us?

NARRATOR: He stands over Umegawa, concealing her, but when he glances up, he realizes that the sounds were not of men.

CHŪBEI: For what crime are we being punished that we should be frightened by the flapping of pheasants' wings?

NARRATOR: Flocks of crows over the forest of Tonda harshly scold, weeping—or laughing?—to see the lovers attempt to comfort each other, unwilling to allow them even one untroubled night. At Takama Mountain—shades of the god of Katsuragi—[45] they hesitate to travel by daylight on their fugitive road, their road of love, their road through a world made narrow by themselves. At Within-the-Bamboos Pass their sleeves are soaked. Next they journey the stony road called

[45] The god of Katsuragi was so ashamed of his ugliness that he appeared only at night.

Cavern Crossing. They struggle on, across fields, mountains, and villages, all for love.

The laws of a well-governed land are strict; pursuers have been despatched to the home provinces in search of the guilty pair. Yamato especially, as Chūbei's birthplace, is canvassed by men from the seventeen courier houses, some disguised as pilgrims, others as dealers in old clothes or itinerant performers. They peep into the houses and with peep shows and sweets beguile the children into furnishing clues. Umegawa and Chūbei are like birds in a snare or fish in a weir: they are doomed not to escape. Unfortunate Chūbei!—it is hard enough to conceal himself alone, but impossible to keep Umegawa's appearance from attracting attention. They spend days in hired sedan chairs, five nights at an inn in Nara, and three nights at a teahouse in Miwa. In a little over twenty days they have spent forty *ryō,* and only half a *ryō* remains of the money. They pass by without stopping at Hatsuse Mountain—how misty the sound of its bell!—and finally reach Ninokuchi Village, his father's home.

Scene Two: Ninokuchi Village, outside the hut of Chūzaburō.
Time: The end of the twelfth moon.

CHŪBEI: O-ume,[46] this is the town where I was born and grew up. I spent my first twenty years here, but I can never remember having seen so many beggars and peddlers of every description at the end of the year, nor even at New Year, for that matter. Look—do you see those men standing there? There were a couple of others at the edge of the fields. I'm beginning to feel nervous. Another four or five hundred yards farther on and we'll be at my real father's—Magoemon's —house, but I daren't go there. I haven't heard from my father since I went away and, besides, there's my stepmother. This thatch-covered hut belongs to Chūzaburō, a tenant farmer with an allotment from my family. He's been a close friend ever since I was a boy, and I know I can trust him. Let's call on him.

NARRATOR: He leads her inside the hut.

CHŪBEI: Chūzaburō, are you at home? I haven't seen you in ages.

NARRATOR: He goes boldly in. A woman, apparently Chūzaburō's wife, meets him.

---

[46] Umegawa's real name, presumably. Umegawa was her name as a courtesan.

WIFE: Who is it, please? My husband's been at the headman's house since this morning, and he's still not come back.

CHŪBEI: Chūzaburō never used to have a wife. Who might you be, please?

WIFE: I came here as his bride three years ago, and I don't know any of my husband's old friends. Excuse me, but I wonder if you folks wouldn't happen to be from Osaka? People have been talking about our landlord Magoemon's stepson [47]—Chūbei's his name. He went to Osaka as an adopted son and took up with a prostitute. They say he stole some money and ran off with her. The magistrate's investigating now. Magoemon disowned his son long ago, and he says that whatever may happen to Chūbei is no concern of his, but all the same, they're father and son, and it must be hard on a man of his age. My husband's an old friend of Chūbei, and he has the idea that Chūbei may be wandering in this neighborhood. He'd be sorry to see him get caught, and he's been keeping watch everywhere. Today the village headman sent for my husband. What with meetings and papers to seal, the whole village is in an uproar—now, at the end of the year!— all on account of that prostitute. She's certainly causing a lot of trouble.

NARRATOR: The woman babbles unrestrainedly. Chūbei is stunned.

CHŪBEI: Yes, rumors about Chūbei are going around Osaka too. My wife and I are on our way to Ise for an end of the year retreat at the shrine. I stopped by for old times' sake, happening to be in the neighborhood. Would you please ask Chūzaburō to come here a moment? I'd like to see him before I leave, even if there isn't time to sit down. But please don't tell him we've come from Osaka.

WIFE: Are you in such a big hurry? I'll go fetch him at once. But you know, there's a priest from Kyoto who's been giving sermons every day at the temple in Kamada Village. My husband may have gone there directly from the headman's house. Please keep the fire going under the soup while I'm away.

NARRATOR: She rolls up her sleeves and runs out. Umegawa shuts the back gate and fastens the latch.

UMEGAWA: We're really in the midst of the enemy here. Do you think we'll be all right?

CHŪBEI: Chūzaburō has an unusually chivalrous nature for a farmer. I'll ask him to put us up for the night. If I'm to die, it's best that it be

---

[47] Possibly called "stepson" because he is not the child of Magoemon's present wife.

here, where my body will become the earth of my native soil. I'd like to be buried in the same grave with my real mother so that in the future world I can present to her my bride.

NARRATOR: His eyes grow heavy with tears.

UMEGAWA: How happy that would make me! My own mother lives at Rokujō in Kyoto. I'm sure that the authorities have gone to question her during these past days. She's always suffered from dizzy spells, and I wonder how she's taken the news. I'd like to go to Kyoto and see my mother again before I die.

CHŪBEI: I'm sure you would. I'd like to meet your mother too, and tell her I'm her son.

NARRATOR: They embrace, for no one can see. The rain of tears is too much for their sleeves to hold; a driving shower beats against the windows.

CHŪBEI: It seems to have started raining.

NARRATOR: He opens the patched paper *shōji* a crack. Through the lattice window facing west, he looks out on a windswept road across the fields. Worshipers are hurrying towards the temple, their umbrellas tilted to protect them from the rain slanting from behind.

CHŪBEI: I know them all—they're people of the village. The man in front is Sukezaburō from Taruibata, a leading man in the village. And that old woman is Den's mother, Den the humpbacked porter. What a tea drinker she is! That man over there with his head almost completely shaved used to be the poorest man in town. He had so much trouble paying his taxes that he sold his daughter to Shimabara Quarter in Kyoto. A rich paper merchant ransomed her and made her his wife. Now, thanks to his son-in-law, the old man is a property holder—five *chō* of ricelands and storehouses in two places. I've ransomed a courtesan too, just as the paper merchant did, but it breaks my heart to think of the unhappiness I've brought your mother.—That old man is Tōjibei the Leveler.[48] At eighty-eight he ate a quart and a half of rice and didn't leave a grain. This year he's turned ninety-five. That priest coming up after him is Dōan the needle-doctor.[49] He killed my mother with his needle. He's my mother's enemy, now that I think of it.

[48] Tōjibei was asked, in deference to his auspicious old age, to make leveling rods for rice measures. The eighty-eighth birthday is called the "rice anniversary" (*beiju*) because of the calligraphic pun on the character 米.

[49] Acupuncture is still a branch of traditional Japanese medicine.

NARRATOR: His bitterness comes from grief.

CHŪBEI: Look! That's my father! You can see him now.

UMEGAWA: The man in the hemp jacket? [50] Yes, his eyes are just like yours.

CHŪBEI: To think that a father and son who look so much alike cannot even exchange a few words! This must be my father's punishment!—He's grown old. How unsteady his legs are! Farewell, father, for this life!

NARRATOR: He joins his hands in prayer.

UMEGAWA: I see you for the first and last time. I am your son's wife. My husband and I are doomed not to know even our next moments, but I hope that when you have passed your hundred years we shall meet again in the future life.

NARRATOR: She murmurs the words to herself. The two join hands and, in voices choked with tears, lament.

Magoemon passes by their door, pausing again and again to rest his aged limbs. He slips on the ice of the ditch at the edge of the fields and, when he checks himself, the thong of his high *geta* snaps. He falls heavily on his side into the muddy field. Chūbei cries out in dismay. He writhes in anguish and alarm but, fugitive that he is, he dares not leave the house.

Umegawa rushes out. She lifts the old man in her arms, and wrings the muddy water from the skirt of his kimono.

UMEGAWA: You haven't hurt yourself anywhere, have you? What a dreadful thing to happen to an old gentleman! I'll wash your feet and mend the thong. Please don't feel the least embarrassed with me.

NARRATOR: She comforts him, massaging his back and knees. Magoemon raises himself.

MAGOEMON: Thank you, whoever you are. No, I haven't hurt myself. What a kind young lady! You've shown me a solicitude not even a daughter-in-law could match, merely because of my years. Some people go to the temple for the sermons, but if they are cruel here, in their hearts, they might just as well not go. Your kindness is an act of true piety. Please wash your hands now. Luckily there's some straw here. I'll use it to mend the thong myself.

NARRATOR: He takes some coarse paper from his wallet.

[50] A sleeveless jacket worn by believers in Pure Land Buddhism when they went to worship.

UMEGAWA: I have some good paper. I'll twist it into a cord for you.

NARRATOR: Magoemon is surprised to see how skillfully she tears the soft paper into strips.

MAGOEMON: You know, I don't recall ever having seen you before in this neighborhood. Who are you, and why are you so kind to me?

NARRATOR: He closely examines her face. Umegawa's breast feels all the more constricted.

UMEGAWA: I'm traveling through. I have a father-in-law just your age, and he looks exactly like you. I don't feel in the least as if I'm helping a stranger. It's a daughter-in-law's duty, after all, to serve and comfort her aged father when he is stricken. You can't imagine how happy it makes me to be of help! I'm sure that, if he could, my husband would all but fly to your side, taking you for his father. Please give me your paper in exchange for mine. I'll ask my husband to keep it next to his skin as a keepsake of an old gentleman who looks like his father.

NARRATOR: She tucks the coarse paper in her sleeve. Hide the tears as she will, her emotion betrays itself in her face.

Magoemon guesses everything from one word and another, and he cannot suppress his fatherly love. His aged eyes are blinded with tears.

MAGOEMON: You say you show me such devotion because I look like your father-in-law? That makes me happy and furious at the same time. I have a grown son with whom I broke off relations for certain reasons. I sent him to Osaka as an adopted son, but some devil got into him, and he laid his hands on a good deal of money belonging to other people. The upshot was that he ran away, and now the search for him has extended to this village. If you want to know who's to blame, it's all my daughter-in-law's fault. It's a foolish thing, I know, but just as in the old proverb this is a case of not hating the son who steals but resenting instead the people who involved him in the crime. Now that I've broken with him, I suppose I should feel utterly indifferent whether he comes to good or ill. But you can imagine how happy it used to make me, even when people said Magoemon was a fool, an idiot, to have disinherited a son so clever, intelligent and well-behaved that he'd made a fortune since going to Osaka as an adopted son. Now, when he is hunted and soon to be dragged off a prisoner, you can imagine my grief even when people praise my foresight and good luck in having disinherited him in good time. I shudder to think what will happen. I'm on my way now to worship before Amida and the Founder,[51] and to pray that I may die at least one day ahead of my son. I do not lie to the Buddha.

NARRATOR: He falls prostrate on the ground and weeps aloud. Umegawa sobs and Chūbei holds his hands out through the *shōji,* bowing in worship before his father. His body is shaken by grief.

Magoemon again brushes away the tears.

MAGOEMON: There's no disputing blood. A child, even one disinherited for all eternity, is always dearer to his parent than the closest friend.—Why didn't he take me into his confidence before he embarked on his stealing and swindling? If he had sent me word privately that he was in love with such and such a courtesan and needed money, for whatever purpose it was, I would, of course, have come to his help. Trouble brings a family together, they say, and we are father and son. And he's a motherless son at that. I'd have sold the fields I've saved to support me in my old age to keep him from the jailer's rope. Instead, he has become notorious. He's brought hardship to Myōkan, his foster mother, and caused others losses and suffering. Could I still say, "You're Magoemon's son," and harbor him? Could I even offer him shelter for a single night?

It's all his own doing. He's suffering now, and society is too small to hold him. He's brought misery on his wife, and he must slink through the wide world hiding from his dearest friends, his acquaintances, and even his kin. I didn't bring him into the world so that he might die a disgraceful death! He's a scoundrel, I know, but I love him.

NARRATOR: He falls into uncontrollable weeping. How hard it is for those who share the same blood! Still weeping, he takes a piece of silver from his purse.

MAGOEMON: I happen to have this coin with me. I had intended to offer it for the building fund of the Naniwa Temple. I do not give you this money because I take you for my daughter-in-law, but by way of thanks for your kindness a while ago.—But if you wander about this neighborhood, people will notice your resemblance to the fugitive woman. They'll arrest you, and they'll certainly arrest your husband. Use this money for your journey. Take the Gosé Road

[51] Shinran Shōnin (1173–1262), founder of the Shin Sect of Pure Land Buddhism.

and leave this place as fast as you can. I'd like a glimpse of your husband's face. No—that would be shirking my duty to society. Send me good news soon, that you're safe.

NARRATOR: He takes two or three steps, then turns back.

MAGOEMON: What do you think? Would there be any harm in my seeing him?

UMEGAWA: Who will ever know? Please go to him.

MAGOEMON: No, I won't neglect my duty to his family in Osaka.[52] —Urge him, I beg you, not to violate nature by making a father mourn his son.

NARRATOR: He chokes with emotion. They part at last, turning back again and again. Then the husband and wife collapse in tears and, forgetting that others might see, they abandon themselves to their grief. How pathetic the ties between this father and son! Chūzaburō's wife returns, drenched with rain.

WIFE: I'm sorry to have kept you waiting. My husband went straight from the headman's house to the temple, and I couldn't get to see him. The rain is beginning to let up. I'm sure he'll be coming back soon.

NARRATOR: At that moment Chūzaburō runs up, all out of breath.

CHŪZABURŌ: Chūbei—your father's told me everything. Police agents have come to the village from Osaka to arrest you, and the magistrate is conducting a search. Your luck has run out. You're surrounded by swords in broad daylight. Somebody must've recognized you. They've suddenly started a top to bottom, house to house search. They're at your father's place now, and my house will be next. Your poor father— he was out of his mind with grief. He begged me to help you to get away quickly. You're in the jaws of the crocodile now. Hurry, make your escape. Take the road back of the house to the Gosé Highway and head for the mountains.

NARRATOR: Chūbei and Umegawa are at their wits' ends. Chūzaburō's wife does not realize what is going on.

WIFE: Shall I run away with them?

CHŪZABURŌ: Don't be a fool.

NARRATOR: Pushing her aside, he helps Chūbei and Umegawa into old straw raincoats and rainhats. Their hearts and footsteps are agitated like reeds in a driving rain, but this kindness will not be forgotten even though they die; profoundly touched, they secretly creep out.

---

[52] See Introduction, p. 33.

Hardly has Chūzaburō breathed a sigh of relief than two parties of raiding constables from the magistrate's office, led by the headman and a village official, simultaneously break into Chūzaburō's house from front and back gates. They roll up the mats, break through the flooring, turn over cabinets, rice chests, and dustbins in their search. The hut is so small that there is nowhere for anyone to hide.

OFFICER: This house is all right. Search the roads through the fields.

NARRATOR: The men hunt for the couple among the tea bushes in the field. Magoemon rushes up, barefooted.

MAGOEMON: What's happened, Chūzaburō? Tell me—they're all right, aren't they?

CHŪZABURŌ: They're all right. There's nothing to worry about. They've both managed to escape.

MAGOEMON: Thank you. I'm grateful to you. I owe this to Amida's grace. I must go to the temple again immediately and offer my thanks to the Founder. How happy and grateful I am!

NARRATOR: The two start off together.

VOICE: Chūbei of the Kame-ya and Umegawa of the Tsuchi-ya have been apprehended!

NARRATOR: A crowd mills north of the village. Soon the constables lead in the husband and wife, tightly bound. Magoemon loses consciousness and seems about to expire. Umegawa, seeing Magoemon, weeps till her eyes dim over, to think that she and her husband, bound prisoners, are powerless to help. Chūbei shouts.

CHŪBEI: I am guilty of the crime and I am ready for my punishment! I know that I cannot escape death. I humbly request you to pray for my repose. But the sight of my father's anguish will prove an obstacle to my salvation. Please, as a kindness, cover my face.

NARRATOR: An officer takes the towel at Chūbei's waist and tightly binds his eyes, as though for blindman's buff. Umegawa weeps, a sanderling by a river whose flow is uncertain as human fate.

They leave behind in Naniwa the name of two who gave their lives for love.

THE BATTLES
OF COXINGA

First performed on November 26, 1715. "The Battles of Coxinga" was Chikamatsu's most popular work. Its first run lasted seventeen months, and it was frequently revived thereafter. The popularity of the play has been attributed to the appeal it exerted on the Japanese during the period of Tokugawa seclusion, when they were prohibited by law from going abroad. The Chinese scenes undoubtedly had an exotic interest for the audience, but the quality of the writing was in the end responsible for the play's great success. It is Chikamatsu's finest history play (*jidaimono*), and the only one represented in this collection. Unlike his domestic tragedies, "The Battles of Coxinga" is filled with heroics and even bombast. The incessant surprises and shifts of mood may also bewilder some readers, but this variety, which exploits to the full the possibilities of the puppet stage, has delighted audiences for over two hundred years.

Cast of Characters

WATŌNAI, later known as Coxinga
IKKAN, also called Tei Shiryū Rōikkan, his father
EMPEROR of China
CROWN PRINCE, later Emperor Eiryaku
GO SANKEI, loyal minister of the emperor
KANKI, ally of Coxinga
KING of Tartary
BAIROKU, a Tartar prince
RI TŌTEN, Chinese confederate of the Tartars
RI KAIHŌ, his brother
AN TAIJIN, captain under Ri Tōten
GŌDATSU, his henchman
SARYŌKO, URYŌKO, Tartar generals

FIRST OLD MAN, ghost of first Ming emperor
SECOND OLD MAN, ghost of Liu Po-wen
BOY, god of Sumiyoshi
SOLDIERS, BEATERS
EMPRESS of China
SENDAN, a Chinese princess
RYŪKAKUN, wife of Go Sankei
KINSHŌJO, wife of Kanki, half sister of Coxinga
KOMUTSU, wife of Coxinga
MOTHER of Coxinga
LADIES, MAIDS

ACT ONE

*Scene One: The court of the Emperor Shisōretsu in Nanking.
Time: May, 1644.*

NARRATOR:
Blossoms scatter and butterflies take fright
At spring's departure, but men are not grieved:
In the Water Pavilion and Gallery of Clouds
Another spring has been created.
From dawn a thousand ladies in gay attire
Dazzle the eye with glossy brows and crimson lips.
The ground itself seems rich with plum flower scent;
The peach and cherry blossom eternally
In glorious Nanking where brilliance reigns.

Now, he who is styled the Emperor Shisōretsu, the seventeenth
sovereign of the great Ming, is the second son of the Emperor Kōsō.
The thread of succession has passed unbroken from generation to
generation; the lands to the four directions, bowing in submission like
a green willow in the wind, offer rich treasures in tribute. The emperor delights in song, dancing, and revels, and within his lovely palace
he keeps three consorts, nine spouses of the second rank, twenty-seven of
the third rank, and eighty-one concubines. Some three thousand maids
of honor delight him with their beauty. His ministers and nobles, vying
for his favors, present him with rare and precious gifts: in dead of
winter he is offered summer melons. Such is the luxury of his court.

Now, the Lady Kasei, most beloved by the emperor of his three thousand women, conceived in the autumn of last year, and in this month an imperial birth is expected. Great is the pleasure of the emperor and the joy of his subjects, for although he has reached his fortieth year there is no crown prince to carry on the succession. The previous prayers to Heaven and Earth have this time been granted. When the forthcoming birth of a royal child was confirmed, the lying-in chamber was decked with pearls and jade. Swaddling clothes have been sewn of Etsu silks and Shoku brocades, and everything is ready for the birth which may occur at any moment.

Among those at court Ryūkakun, the wife of Go Sankei, the president of the council of war, was safely delivered recently of her first child and, especially because her milk is for a boy, she has been designated as the wet nurse for the imperial child. Other wet nurses, serving maids, and palace ladies of every rank attend Kasei, and carefully watch over her, as though she were a precious jewel in their hands.

Early in May of the seventeenth year of Sōtei,[1] the Great King Junji, lord of Tartary, has sent an envoy to offer presents to the emperor—tiger skins, leopard skins, cloth from the South Seas washed in fire, horse-liver stones from Ceylon,[2] treasures from remote kingdoms and islands. The envoy, Prince Bairoku, respectfully addresses the throne.

BAIROKU: Tartary and China have vied for supremacy from ancient days. We have quarreled over territory, mobilized troops, fought with our weapons, and formed lasting enmities—a violation of the friendship expected of neighboring nations and a source of affliction to our peoples. Tartary is a big country and, I may say, we are not wanting in the Seven Precious Things[3] or the Ten Thousand Treasures, but our women are not as beautiful as those of other lands. Our great king, hearing that there is a peerless beauty named Lady Kasei at the court of the emperor of China, has become enamoured and deeply desires her. He asks that the emperor send the Lady Kasei to him so that he may honor her as the consort of the great king and thereby establish future relations like those of parent and child between China and Tartary. He has sent these tributary offerings in order to promote lasting peace. I,

[1] 1644. For a further explanation of the historical personages of this scene, see Keene, *The Battles of Coxinga*, p. 179.

[2] One of the magical properties of this stone was that it would turn white hairs black.

[3] Gold, silver, lapis lazuli, crystal, coral, agate, and pearls, according to one classification.

Prince Bairoku, though a person of no account, have come to this court to welcome our new queen.

NARRATOR: The emperor and the nobles great and small are astonished by this unprecedented and unreasonable Tartar demand, and the emperor wonders uneasily if it may lead to war. At this moment the general of the right Ri Tōten, first of his vassals, steps forward and reports to the throne.

RI TŌTEN: I have until now kept concealed what I felt was this country's shame. Several years ago, in the Year of the Serpent,[4] the five grains did not ripen at Peking. When the people were reduced to starvation I secretly requested Tartary to aid us with some ten million bushels of rice and millet. I thereby saved the people. I solemnly swore in return that if ever the Tartars desired anything of us it would be granted them on one occasion, no matter what their wish might be. You, my lord, possess the Land within the Four Seas and rule the people because of the generosity of Tartary at that time. He who knows not gratitude is no better than a brute beast. It is natural that you feel regret, but you would do well to send the Lady Kasei away as soon as possible.

NARRATOR: Go Sankei, the president of the council of war, has been listening attentively in an antechamber. He leaps up the stairs and over the balustrade and seats himself abruptly beside Ri Tōten.

GO SANKEI: Alas! When did you become the slave of those animals? In China the three emperors and the five rulers[5] invented the rites and music; Confucius and Mencius transmitted their teachings; and since then the way of the five constant virtues and five relationships has flourished as it does today. In India the Buddha taught the doctrine of cause and effect, and the way of renouncing evil and cultivating virtue is practiced. In Japan there is the way of the eternal gods enjoining honesty. In Tartary though they eat their fill and wear warm clothes,[6] there is neither a way nor laws. The strong stand on top and the weak are pushed below. They make no distinction between good and evil nor between wise and foolish. These northern barbarians are no differ-

[4] 1641.
[5] Three emperors: Fu Hsi, Shên Nung, and Huang Ti. Five rulers: Shao Hao, Chuan Hsü, Ti K'u, Yao, and Shun.
[6] A quotation from Mencius: "But men possess a moral nature; and if they are well fed, warmly clad, and comfortably lodged, without being taught at the same time, they become almost like the beast" (Legge, *Chinese Classics*, I, 251).

ent from beasts, and their country is therefore commonly spoken of as a beast-land.

It is most suspicious, however much you may have requested their aid, that the Tartars should have been willing to save this country by providing ten million bushels of grain. But why were the people reduced to the point of starvation? It was because you encouraged senseless extravagance at the court, expended the treasury in feasting, and exacted cruel levies from the people. If you had ceased these expenditures with which you indulged your taste for luxury, a great country like ours would not have lacked the strength to nourish its people for five or even ten years of lean harvests. Now, disregarding the wishes of the emperor, and without even consulting the nobles, you wish without further ado to deliver our empress, who is with child, into the hands of the barbarians. I do not in the least comprehend your intent.

The agreement was between you and the Tartars. The emperor was no party to it. The tribute offerings of a beast-land are a defilement to the palace. Officers! Take these objects and throw them away!

NARRATOR: His contempt for the northern barbarians and proud display of his country's might recall Kuan Chung who nine times summoned the feudal lords.[7] The Tartar envoy Prince Bairoku is enraged.

BAIROKU: Any country, whether large or small, which does not appreciate help it has received to feed its people and which breaks solemn promises should be termed a beast-land beneath human contempt. China has proved herself to be without a way and without laws. You have only to count the days until we attack with our troops, capture your emperor and empress both, and make them the shoe bearers to our great king!

NARRATOR: He kicks aside his seat and rises to depart, when Ri Tōten stays him.

RI TŌTEN: Just a moment! Just a moment! Your indignation is well merited. I acted as a loyal minister should when I accepted your country's help a few years ago and saved my country, without taking a grain of rice for myself. But now men would break promises, incite armed disturbance, trouble the emperor, and afflict the people, and worst of all, cause it to be said that China is a beast-land which knows no gratitude. This would be a disgrace to the dynasty and a disgrace to the country. It is now the task of a loyal minister to sacrifice himself, to

[7] Kuan Chung was the famous counselor of Duke Huan of Ch'i (d. 643 B.C.).

reassure the emperor, and to wipe out our country's shame. Behold what I do!

NARRATOR: Grasping his dagger with the point downwards, he thrusts it into his left eye, then turns it round along his eyelids. He draws out the crimsoned eyeball.

RI TŌTEN: Excellency! A man's eyes are his sun and moon. The left eye belonging to the yang principle is his sun.[8] I have become deformed without that eye. I offer it to the king of Tartary. This is the conduct expected of a loyal minister of the emperor of China, a man who preserves his integrity by respecting the way.

NARRATOR: He places his gouged-out eye on a ceremonial baton and offers it to Prince Bairoku, who reverently accepts it.

BAIROKU: What noble devotion! Go Sankei's words a moment ago all but plunged our countries against our wills into a contest of strength and even into warfare. But you have settled the issue by sacrificing yourself on behalf of your country. Magnificent! Words fail me when I realize what a loyal and wise minister you have proved. I feel as though I had already received the empress as my master's bride. The great king will be moved, and I who have served as his envoy could know no greater honor. I shall take my leave now.

NARRATOR: The Emperor is highly pleased.

EMPEROR: The way Ri Tōten gouged out his eye reminds me of Wu Tzu-hsü, and Go Sankei's far-reaching plans suggest those of Fan Li.[9] With these two ministers correcting our rule the country will endure unchanged for a thousand generations, for ten thousand generations. Let the Tartar envoy return to his country.

NARRATOR: With these words he goes into the banqueting hall. Indeed, wicked and loyal ministers look much alike on the surface and may easily be mistaken. The lord of Nanking, who cannot distinguish good from evil, devotes himself to a prodigality without example.

[8] The yang (male, positive, bright, left) principle and the yin (female, negative, dark, right) principle are elemental in Chinese conceptions of the universe.
[9] Wu Tzu-hsü was a counselor of the king of Wu. When the king of Wu defeated the king of Yüeh at Kuai-chi Mountain, and then made peace, Wu Tzu-hsü criticized him, declaring that he should instead crush Yüeh. Wu Tzu-hsü's plan was rejected by the king of Wu, who gave him a sword with which to commit suicide. Wu, in despair over the king's stupidity, gouged out his own eyes and placed them on the eastern gate, where they would see the Yüeh troops advancing on Wu. Fan Li was the counselor of the king of Yüeh at this time. His wisdom brought about the final victory of Yüeh.

Scene Two: *The apartments of the Princess Sendan.*

NARRATOR: The Princess Sendan, younger sister of the emperor, is a maiden barely sixteen, of such jewellike beauty that one might take her for the offspring of some dweller of the moon, fallen to earth with the dew. She excels at music, each word of her poems excites wide praise. In Japan they say that poetry makes sweet the ties between men and women.[10] Here in China too poetry serves as a go-between in love.

The princess, older than her years, shows her disapproval of the extravagance of her brother, the emperor, by conducting herself with the utmost decorum. Sometimes she summons her attendant ladies and they talk of love, but only in whispers. Her ears yearn for such tales, though her eyes reprove them. Her heart is versant in love, and her days are spent in smouldering dreams.

From the Pavilion of Long Life comes the cry, "His majesty the emperor!" and he enters, accompanied by two hundred ladies, none more than twenty years of age. They bear aloft artificial branches of plum and cherry, a hundred of each.

EMPEROR: My lady sister. Ever since first I ascended the throne the general of the right Ri Tōten has been the most faithful of my many subjects in obeying my commands. When I learned that this first of my loyal ministers, a man who brings me comfort day and night, had fallen in love with you, I was delighted to think that I might make him my sister's husband, but you have to this day refused absolutely to hear him. Today Tartary made us an outrageous proposal, and when it seemed that we had already reached the point of war and national calamity, Go Sankei, with the smug air of a loyal minister, reasoned with his tongue, as anyone might. But Ri Tōten gouged out his left eye and appeased the envoy, who at once returned to his country. For the sake of his country, for the sake of his emperor, he sacrificed himself and became deformed. This minister whose loyalty stands unrivaled throughout the ages must be rewarded. I promised him that I would without fail make him my sister's husband and yield to him the capital

---

[10] A reference to the preface of the *Kokinshū* (A.D. 905), written by Ki no Tsurayuki (883–946): "Poetry makes sweet the ties between men and women and comforts the heart of the brave warrior."

at Peking. Knowing, however, that you were unlikely to agree, I have ordered a tournament of flowers. The plum blossoms will be your side—they suggest your airs of the learned lady and your unfeeling heart.[11] My side will be the cherry blossoms. I shall ask the ladies to join in battle. If the cherry blossoms scatter and the plum triumphs, you may have your way, but if the cherry wins and the plum blossoms fall, your defeat is decided, and you will become Ri Tōten's wife. Let the marriage be determined as Heaven wills it! Whoever wins, whoever loses, we shall have a battle of elegance! Lay on! Lay on!

NARRATOR: The plum and cherry branches, obedient to his command, divide into two ranks and stand ready. The princess, powerless to resist the imperial edict, has no choice but to oppose a match that goes against her heart. Her flowering branch and her person are to the fore.

SENDAN: I shall be the general in the contest to decide the marriage of the Princess Sendan, younger sister to the emperor.

NARRATOR: Hardly has she proclaimed herself than the bough of plum she bears aloft brushes someone's sleeve, and a fluttering as from the wings of a cluster of song thrushes scatters the blossoms. The air is heavy with the fragrance of plum. They do battle, thrusting and parrying. The princess gives commands.

SENDAN: You can tell that there must be a wind underneath the willow whose leaves are twisted round. Against their weak branches lean your budding twigs. Against their strong branches make the blossoms of your achievements burst into bloom! Change your faded boughs for fresh ones, and join your efforts with the others!

NARRATOR: They attack with a cry of battle, obeying her flower-wise commands. Some regret the blossoms trampled underfoot, but they charge boldly forward, branches held horizontally over their heads, scattering blossoms like snow in February. Blossoms tumble pell-mell from the branches; the battle sends the flowers flying.

The court ladies, however, deliberately allow the plum blossom side to be vanquished, acting in accord with the previous commands of the emperor. The branches and blossoms are broken and strewn, and the ladies fall back in confusion. The cherry blossoms, victory on their faces, cry, "The marriage between the princess and Ri Tōten is now decided!" They raise cries of triumph, and their voices ring through

[11] Plum blossoms, because they come out early in the spring, are associated with coldness and chastity. They are also known as the scholar's flower.

Watōnai vanquishes the tiger in the bamboo grove.
(WATŌNAI: *Ichikawa Ennosuke II*)

the palace like the notes of a thousand song thrushes or a hundred plovers twittering together.

Go Sankei, the president of the council of war, bursts in on their gathering without a word of apology. He is splendidly attired in armor and helmet. Waving his crescent-topped spear, he furiously slashes down plum and cherry blossoms, then bows before the emperor.

GO SANKEI: A moment ago word came that there was fighting by the throne, and war cries echoed through the halls. I came running here, buckling on my armor, alarmed by so extraordinary a disturbance in the palace. But what senselessness do I find! In all the pages of history since the world was created, you will find no such foolish example as this battle of flowers to decide the marriage of your sister and Ri Tōten. Does your majesty not know that if the One Family is loving, the entire state will become loving, but if the One Man is covetous the state will be in disorder?[12] It is customary for the people to follow the preferences of their superiors. When word of this incident spreads, there will be flower tournaments at this place and that, wherever a woodcutter or farmer is planning a marriage for his son or daughter, and these tournaments will develop into quarrels and feuds. It is clear as looking into a mirror that once the blossoms scatter there will be recourse to swords, and real battles will follow the contests of flowers. If now a treacherous subject were to attack the palace, people would suppose, even if his war cries were heard, that it was merely another battle of flowers, and no one would rush to your aid. Then if your august person were cruelly put to the sword by this treacherous subject, the deed would be impious and ignoble, but what would it avail to regret your past folly?

The treacherous subject, the false minister of whom I speak is Ri Tōten. Has your majesty forgotten? When you were young a man named Tei Shiryū[13] incurred your displeasure by urging you to expel the false courtiers. Tei Shiryū was driven into exile as a result. I hear that he now lives at Hirado of Hizen Province in Japan, where he goes by the name of Rōikkan. If Tei Shiryū were to hear of what has happened today, would he not reveal China's shame to the Japanese? A few years ago, when China was suffering from famine, Ri

[12] From the Confucian classic *The Great Learning* (tr. Legge, *Chinese Classics,* I, 376). The One Family is the imperial family, as the One Man is the emperor.
[13] Chêng Chih-lung (1604–61), the father of Coxinga. See Keene, *The Battles of Coxinga,* pp. 45–48.

Tōten used his wiles to steal rice from the granaries of the different provinces. He spread word that he was obliged to accept aid from Tartary because your majesty had no love for your people. He claimed to have saved them himself. He scattered his largesse throughout the country, ingratiating himself with the masses and strengthening the axis of sedition. How foolish of you to be unaware of what has happened!

Ri Tōten gouged out his left eye as a signal to his Tartar confederates. Look at the plaque hanging in this hall of state—*ta ming*, it says, meaning "great" and "bright." The character *ming* is written by placing the symbols for sun and moon side by side.[14] This great Ming is a land of the south and of the yang principle; it is a country of the sun. Tartary is a northern yin country, linked with the moon. Ri Tōten gouged out his left eye, which belongs to yang and corresponds to the sun, as a warrant to his allies that he would deliver this great bright land of the sun into the hands of the Tartars. The envoy understood the meaning at once, and returned joyfully to Tartary. Unless this treacherous subject, guilty of accumulated wickedness and villainy, is at once subjected to the five punishments,[15] this land which has given birth to the sages will soon fall under the yoke of Mongolia,[16] and we shall become their slaves, differing from animals only in that we do not wag tails or have bodies covered with fur. Heaven will be wroth, the gods of our ancestral halls will curse us, and the fault will be attributed to the emperor. Doubt rather that I should miss the earth when striking at it with my fist, than these words of Go Sankei are mistaken. How deplorable your attitude has been!

NARRATOR: The emperor is exceedingly displeased.

EMPEROR: Enough of your lectures on ideographs with that smug look! Such logic could prove that snow was actually black! Everything you say comes from your jealousy of Ri Tōten. You, who for no reason whatsoever have approached my presence in your helmet and armor, are the treacherous subject!

NARRATOR: Rising, he kicks Go Sankei's forehead when, strange to

[14] The character 明 (*ming*) combines 日 (sun) and 月 (moon).

[15] Branding, cutting off of the nose, cutting off of the feet, castration, and death.

[16] The Manchus, the actual conquerors of China, are usually called "Tartars" in this play, but occasionally "Mongols." Their country is called Mongolia here.

relate, there is a repeated rumbling in the palace, and the plaque written in the imperial hand begins to shake. The golden-sword stroke in "great" [17] and the symbol for "sun" in "bright" crumble into powder, a fearsome augury from Heaven. Go Sankei, still unconcerned for his own safety, cries out.

GO SANKEI: Alas! Are your eyes blinded? Have your ears gone deaf? The ideograph for "great" is written by combining "one" and "man". The One Man refers to the Sun of Heaven, the emperor. When a stroke is taken from the One Man, the emperor becomes only half a man. When the symbol for sun is removed from the ideograph for "bright," the country, deprived of the light of the sun, becomes a land of eternal darkness. That plaque was inscribed by the brush of your ancestor, the first emperor of the Ming, as he meditated on the eternal prosperity of his line. Reflect how terrible will be the wrath of the gods of your ancestral temples! Mend your ways, correct your injustices, and preserve your dynasty! Then, though Go Sankei, whose life lies before you, be trampled or kicked to death, he will not complain. I shall not violate the way of a true subject though my body turn to earth, though it turn to ashes!

NARRATOR: He clings to the emperor's robe and cries aloud. Weeping, he remonstrates. Here is a model for all the ages.

At this moment the noise of men and horses echoes from all directions. Horns and gongs are sounded, drums beaten, and war cries shake the earth, loud enough to tilt Heaven itself. Go Sankei, who has expected this disaster, races up to a vantage point and looks out. The mountains and towns swarm with the Tartar hordes. With waving banners and bows and muskets they surround and storm the palace, irresistible as the onrushing tide. Prince Bairoku, commander of the invading host, rides into the palace garden and utters a great shout.

BAIROKU: Hear my words! I lied when I said that the lord of our land, the Great King Junji, had become enamoured of the empress of this country, the Lady Kasei. Our scheme was to cut off the seed of the emperor by capturing his pregnant consort. When Ri Tōten demonstrated his allegiance to our cause by gouging out his eye, we decided to attack without delay. You are no match for us, Go Sankei!

---

[17] The third stroke ＼ in *ta* 大 . The character is further analyzed by Go Sankei into a combination of ー and 人 .

We will seize the emperor and the empress and compel them to bow before us. They will squat in the kitchens of the king of Tartary and prolong their lives by drinking the water we use to wash our rice!

GO SANKEI: What nonsense! For you to attack the Ming court, where not even plants or trees have stirred for 180 years,[18] is as futile as an ant stalking a whale whose bulk bestrides the ocean! Drive them back! Drive them back!

NARRATOR: He races about giving orders to his men, but they amount to no more than a hundred foot soldiers. Not one of the nobles or military lords joins him in his struggle. As he stands in dismay, fists clenched, his wife Ryūkakun leads on the empress with one hand, clutching her baby to her breast with the other.

RYŪKAKUN: Alas! The imperial fortunes are at an end. Everyone, from the highest noble and minister of state down to the lowliest menial sides with Ri Tōten. We are the only friends to the imperial cause. Most mortifying of days!

NARRATOR: She gnashes her teeth in woe.

GO SANKEI: Cease your lamenting. It serves no purpose. The empress is the most precious person, for she lodges in her womb the emperor's seed. I shall cut open an avenue of escape and escort the emperor and the empress to safety. Leave our child with me too. For the present you are to look after the Princess Sendan. Make your way from here to the harbor Kaidō.[19]

RYŪKAKUN: As you command.

NARRATOR: With this brave reply she leads the Princess Sendan by the hand, and together they slip out through the Golden Stream Gate along a narrow path.

GO SANKEI: Now I shall engage the enemy at the main gate and disperse them so that I may lead your majesties to safety. Please do not leave this spot.

NARRATOR: He rushes off with this final injunction. He proclaims himself, "President of the Council of War Go Sankei, first of the subjects of the Ming court," and with his force of less than a hundred men drives into the millions of Mongol troops. As they slash forward reck-

---

[18] The figure 277 years would be more accurate. The phrase about plants and trees means that the dynasty is so stable that nothing in the country is ever disturbed.

[19] Probably an imaginary place name, invented by Chikamatsu.

lessly, the Tartar hordes cry, "Kill them all!" and the fighting rages amidst incessant volleys of bullets and stones from their muskets and catapults.

Ri Tōten and his brother Ri Kaihō profit by the confusion to burst wantonly into the imperial presence. They seize the emperor from both sides. The empress, wondering if this is not some nightmare, clings to them.

EMPRESS: Impious villains! Have you forgotten your obligations to the emperor and the divinity that protects him?

RI TŌTEN: You won't escape either!

NARRATOR: He thrusts her aside and touches his icy blade to the emperor's chest. The emperor's face is wet with tears of wrath.

EMPEROR: It is true, as they say, that the rust on a blade grows from the blade itself. The fire in the cypress forest rises from the cypresses and consumes them. Now I know that the hatred or love a man receives comes from himself. I did not heed the advice of Tei Shiryū or Go Sankei, but was duped by your flattery. I have lost my empire and now I am about to lose my life and leave behind an odious name for all time to come. How foolish I was not to have realized that food sweet to the taste proves harmful in the stomach!

You are no doubt aware that my wife bears in her womb my child, now in its ninth month. Her delivery cannot be long off. I pray you, the one kindness I ask, that you let this child see the light of the sun and moon.

NARRATOR: These are his only words before he is overwhelmed by tears.

RI TŌTEN: No, never! Why did I gouge out my precious eye? Not because of loyalty or duty. It was to throw you off your guard and to demonstrate my allegiance to Tartary. My eye has won me a fief—your head will fetch me a kingdom!

NARRATOR: He pulls the emperor to him and slashes off his head.

RI TŌTEN: Ri Kaihō—I must send this head to the king of Tartary. Bind the empress and bring her with you.

NARRATOR: He rushes off to the invaders' camp. Go Sankei, having slaughtered many of the enemy, has easily opened a path of escape. He returns to the spot where he left the emperor, intending to rescue him, when to his horror he beholds the headless corpse lying on the ground, bathed in crimson, and Ri Kaihō about to lead off the captive empress.

GO SANKEI: I find you in the nick of time! In my battle of vengeance for my sovereign I have arrived too late for the main meal, and will have to content myself with an afternoon snack! [20]

NARRATOR: He flies at Ri Kaihō and splits his skull in two. He cuts the ropes binding the empress and tearfully lifts the emperor's body. Next to the skin he finds the sash and seal, the symbol of enthronement handed down from generation to generation of rulers.

GO SANKEI: Good! As long as the prince about to be born has this, he need not worry about succeeding to the throne.

NARRATOR: He thrusts them into his armor next to the skin.

GO SANKEI: Should I escort the empress to safety first? Or should I first hide the emperor's body?

NARRATOR: His problem is twofold, but he has only one body. As he stands perplexed, the enemy hordes charge at him in wild tumult.

GO SANKEI: I'm ready for you!

NARRATOR: He slashes into their ranks. When they attack he strikes, topples, throws down, and routs the enemy. He runs back to the empress.

GO SANKEI: That will take care of them for the moment. We must hurry. Nothing can be done about the emperor's body. The most important thing is his successor.

NARRATOR: He takes the empress's hand and starts to lead her, when his own child, longing for its mother's breast, begins to howl.

GO SANKEI: Confounded nuisance! But you are my heir.

NARRATOR: He lifts the baby and fastens him to the shaft of his lance.

GO SANKEI: If your father is killed you must grow up and become his successor as a loyal minister to the young prince. You are the last of our line.

NARRATOR: He lifts the infant to his shoulder, then hurries with the empress towards safety. The enemy soldiers press forward to halt the fugitives, but Go Sankei stands his ground and engages them. He slashes and pounds, beating a path of escape. At last they reach the harbor of Kaidō as the tide is receding.

[20] *Toki* (main meal) and *hiji* (afternoon snack) are Buddhist terms. Here Go Sankei means that he has come too late to kill Ri Tōten and must content himself with Ri Kaihō.

Scene Three: The coast at Kaidō.

NARRATOR: Go Sankei has planned to cross to Taisufu[21] from Kaidō, but not a single boat is to be seen by the shore. They start to follow along the coast when suddenly musket fire sweeps down on them like a driving rain from the surrounding woods and mountains. Go Sankei shields the empress, taking bullet after bullet on his stoutly fashioned armor, but—has her destiny run out?—a shot strikes her breast. The jeweled thread of her life is snapped and she breathes her last. Go Sankei stands in dismay, at a loss what to do.

GO SANKEI: Nothing can help the empress mother now, but there is no reason why the imperial seed should perish darkly within her womb.

NARRATOR: He unsheathes his sword and cuts open the empress's robes to the skin. He presses the blade into her abdomen, and makes a cross-shaped incision. A baby's first cry from within the rush of blood comes from a jewellike prince. The occasion is at once joyous and sad. Go Sankei, overcome by helpless tears, rips off the empress's sleeve and uses it to wrap the prince. He lifts the baby in his arms.

GO SANKEI: But wait! If the enemy surrounding us should discover the empress's dead body, they would know that the prince had been spirited away, and they would search till they found him. I would have no chance to rear him to manhood.

NARRATOR: He pauses a moment in earnest thought, then draws his own child to him. He removes the infant's clothes and puts them on the prince. Again he takes up his sword, this time to plunge it through his baby's chest. He pushes the dead child into the empress's abdomen.

GO SANKEI: Noble child! You have been blessed by fortune. You were lucky enough to have been born at a time when you could die in place of a prince destined to be our emperor. You have done well. Do not grieve for the parents you leave behind in this world of delusion. Your parents will not grieve to be parted from you.

NARRATOR: Despite his words, his heart is filled with sorrow. He chokes in tears he conceals with the sleeve of armor in which he cradles the baby prince. How pitiful he seems as he leaves his own son behind!

[21] T'ai-chou-fu, the modern Lin-hai-hsien in Chekiang Province.

Ryūkakun, knowing nothing of this, has guided the Princess Sendan to the harbor mouth. The enemy swarms around them.

RYŪKAKUN: Let us try to go as far as we can.

NARRATOR: They push aside the thickly growing reeds and hide themselves behind them. An Taijin, a captain serving under Ri Tōten, bursts on the scene with a party of soldiers.

AN TAIJIN: I'm sure that our last volley of musket fire struck either the empress or Go Sankei.

NARRATOR: They search the vicinity.

AN TAIJIN: Look! Our shot has killed the empress! Her belly's been ripped open, and we've killed the prince in her womb. Go Sankei, for all his show of loyalty, has deserted his sovereign and destroyed his own reputation. Was he afraid for his life? The villain is dishonored now. Our only task remaining is to search for Go Sankei's wife Ryūkakun and the Princess Sendan. Keep your eyes peeled and win a name for yourselves!

NARRATOR: They spread out in all directions. Among the soldiers is a ruffian called Gōdatsu.

GŌDATSU: I'll capture the Princess Sendan and take all the glory for myself!

NARRATOR: He throws a straw raincoat over his armor and poles a little fishing boat from inlet to inlet.

GŌDATSU: There's something suspicious about these reeds.

NARRATOR: He uses the tip of his oar to spread apart the reeds. Ryūkakun firmly grasps it and pushes back with all her strength. Gōdatsu loses his balance and tumbles head first overboard. He sinks with a splash, and when he struggles to the surface, Ryūkakun strikes him again and again, hard enough to break the oar. When she strikes he sinks, and when he rises she strikes again. She allows him not a moment's breathing space; he is like a snapping turtle swimming in the mud. Finally he dives and makes his escape.

RYŪKAKUN: Your stolen march has done you no good, and it has brought us a boat! This is a case of finding a boat at a crossing! [22]

NARRATOR: She takes up the sword Gōdatsu left lying in the boat, and fastens it by her side. Next she helps the Princess Sendan aboard the boat and is about to climb in herself when Gōdatsu crawls up from somewhere, his armor dripping wet. He leads in pursuit twenty men armed with spears, determined not to let the women escape.

[22] A proverb for finding something when one needs it.

RYŪKAKUN: I certainly have my hands full! Look! Our enemies are coming after us! There's fury in their faces! Please hide in the bottom of the boat while I stave them off.

NARRATOR: She awaits their onslaught brandishing a sword in each hand, the sword she found and the one she had all the time. Gōdatsu soon rushes up.

GŌDATSU: Loathsome woman! I'll pay you back for hitting me with the oar!

NARRATOR: He lunges at her with his long-handled spear.

RYŪKAKUN: And I will pay you back for the sword you left me!

NARRATOR: She slashes right and left, one woman surrounded by over twenty swords. Some men, seagulls of the reeds bewildered on shore, are struck down, no match for her, before they can even flap their wings; others escape with severe wounds. Ryūkakun and Gōdatsu are both badly wounded and covered with blood. They charge back and forth into a clump of reeds, blood streaming into the eyes of both. They strike blindly, uncertain where they aim; their swords strike sparks from the edge of the rocks, sparks as brief as their lives, a frightening spectacle.

Gōdatsu's spear is broken. He hobbles forward and attempts to wrest the sword from Ryūkakun's grasp. In the struggle he loses his footing and falls on his back. At once she pounces on him, driving the blade in, and slices off his head. Ryūkakun smiles, her heart filled with incomparable joy.

RYŪKAKUN: Your highness, are you all right? Is the boat still there?

NARRATOR: She staggers closer.

RYŪKAKUN: I cannot join you in this frightful condition, nor can I withstand the enemy if they attack again. Let the tide take your boat from here wherever it will. I shall stand by on land until you reach the open sea. Tens of thousands of the enemy may attack, but I shall fight on as long as life is left me, as long as my strength stays with me. We shall meet again only if fate wills and we remain alive. May you be safe. I pray to the Buddhas of all the heavens, and especially to the eight great dragon gods,[23] that they will protect the boat of the imperial princess!

NARRATOR: She grasps the crossbar and shoves off the boat. An ebb tide is flowing and carries the boat from shore. Sendan, powerless to control her grief over parting, yields to tears in the salt breeze. Her

[23] Gods of the sea who controlled the rain and the waves.

boat, caught by a wind from the offing vouchsafed by the gods, drifts far out to sea.

RYŪKAKUN: What a relief! And what a joy! Now if I prolong my life I shall be alone, and if I die none will journey with me, not even the companion birds.[24] I would escape the sea of life and death, but worry over my husband, my child, my sovereign, remains with me. It is hard to surmount the waves of attachment to this mortal world. But however difficult the sea to cross, the swift boat of my devotion will not break in the breaking waves, though the oars of love and integrity and the rudder of courage be snapped.[25] But do I hear war cries approaching?

NARRATOR: She clutches her swords and staggers about painfully. A storm blowing down from the mountain through the pines on the beach combs her disheveled locks. She stands glaring fiercely about her. Her story has been written down and transmitted as a model for women in Japan and China.

ACT TWO

Scene One: The beach at Hirado, an island off the west coast of Kyushu.
Time: Late autumn of the same year.

NARRATOR: The twittering yellow thrush rests on the corner of the mound. If a man fails to rest in the place meant for him, does it mean that he is inferior to this bird? [26]

There lives in the town of Hirado, in the county of Matsura of Hizen Province in Japan, a young man named Watōnai Sankan [27] who earns his living by casting his line and drawing his nets. His wife follows the same fisher's trade and, like the creature *warekara* [28] that lives

---

[24] Here, as elsewhere in the work, a desire for a play on words leads Chikamatsu into an irrelevant phrase. *Tare wo tomo* (taking whom as a friend) leads into *tomo-chidori* (companion plovers).

[25] This sentence is formed by a series of *engo* (related words) on ships.

[26] From *The Great Learning* (tr. Legge, p. 362). The meaning here would seem to be that Watōnai and Ikkan are admirable in that, like the yellow bird, they know their proper tasks.

[27] This name was invented by Chikamatsu. For more historical information on Coxinga, see Keene, *The Battles of Coxinga*, pp. 44–75.

[28] *Warekara* is at once the name of a sea creature, *Caprella* and a word meaning "of oneself".

in the seaweed, she has of herself, without asking a go-between, joined her pillow to a man's. She is blessed with the name Komutsu—"Little Friend"—and lives on friendly terms with the world.

Now the father of this Watōnai was originally not a Japanese. He served as a loyal subject to the great Ming court, where he was known as the Grand Tutor Tei Shiryū. He admonished in vain the foolish emperor and, threatened with banishment, fled instead to the Bay of Tsukushi in the Land of the Rising Sun, where he changed his name to Rōikkan. Marrying a woman who lived by the bay, he begot this son to whom he gave the name of Watōnai, with Wa standing for Japan, his mother's birthplace, and Tō for his father's old home.[29]

Twenty and more springs have elapsed since the boy was born, and autumn is now passing, but November is warm as a second July.[30] Husband and wife go out together in the evening calm, fishing baskets hung from their rakes, to dig clams for their livelihood. They look out over the beach and see the seagulls imprinting their seals in the sand, and the bay plovers clustering on the offshore islets. Watōnai rakes the beach dried by the receding tide, and Komutsu, treading on clams, gathers shells of every kind, indifferent to the water that soaks her skirts. What are the shells that they gather?

Hermit crabs, periwinkles, carpet clams . . . When the bamboo blind-shell is raised by the salt-blowing-shell, I catch a glimpse of a princess-shell and fall in love at first sight. I would like to take my brush and send a letter on a flat-shell. When her red lips-shells part and she smiles-shell, my heart-goes-to-her-shell—ah, what pain-shell! "You draw me to you and I would cling-shell to you, but my love is one-sided as the abalone shell. Oh, cruel one! I could give you a taste of my fist-shell in your monkey-face-shell. Plum blossom-shells, cherry blossom-shells . . ."[31] "Sleeplessly I all alone spend-the-night shell. For whom do I wait-shell? I forget-shell that people-may-see-shell, and only dream of how, when lying together in bed-shell, the joys of marriage will sink-shell into our hearts, and we will celebrate-shell with a triumphant peal-shell the happy beginning of our wedded bliss-shell."

These were the shells that they gather. Among the shells is one, a

---

[29] *Wa* is an ancient name for Japan. *Tō* (T'ang in Chinese), the name of a dynasty, was frequently used for China. *Nai* means "between".

[30] Literally "little sixth moon", meaning Indian summer.

[31] The catalogue of shells is so arranged as to yield a mildly erotic story when the names of the shells are taken into account. The first statement "You draw me . . ." is presumably by the man, and the second "Sleeplessly . . ." by the woman.

huge clam, with its mouth open to the sun. Unaware that someone stands nearby, ready to capture him, the clam is blowing foamy brine.

WATŌNAI: Yes, they say that clams sometimes spew out vapor to form castles.[32] This must be an example.

NARRATOR: As he gazes on in fascination, a snipe flying across the seaweed in quest of food swoops down with a curious flapping of the wings. It spots the clam and approaches with angry beak, intent on snapping up the clam with one swift peck. Horrid master snipe! Don't you who chant the sutras realize that you break the command against taking life? And see how the clam immodestly gapes, in flagrant violation of the Buddha's injunction! [33]

The snipe flies at the clam and pecks furiously, but suddenly the shells clamp on the snipe's bill and hold it fast. The pleasure drains all at once from the snipe's face. It tugs frantically with its bill. With a flap of the wings, it shakes its head and edges over to the base of a rock, hoping in its bird wisdom to smash the clam. But the clam digs back into the sand, struggling to drag down into a puddle of sea water its prize. The snipe, straining its feathers, flies up a dozen feet, only to fall with the clam's weight. It rises quickly again, to fall just as abruptly. The snipe struggles desperately, beating its wings a hundred times, standing its feathers on end.

Watōnai, absorbed, throws down his rake.

WATŌNAI: Extraordinary! I understand now why the priest discovered his true nature in the snow that broke the bamboos—and how, by cutting off his arm he learned the meaning of the teachings brought by the Master from the West.[34] I have studied at my father's command the Chinese texts of military strategy, and examined the principles underlying the success or failure in battle of the great Japanese generals

---

[32] One variety of *hamaguri* (clam) was said to be a kind of dragon which could emit a vaporous castle. See Hozumi Ikan *Naniwa Miyage* (in *Jōruri Kenkyū Bunken Shūsei*), p. 182.

[33] The chirps of the snipe were said to resemble the chanting of Buddhist sutras. The clam was violating the command against keeping one's mouth open—i.e., looseness of speech.

[34] A reference to the story of Hui-k'o (d. 593). When Hui-k'o went to see the great Zen teacher Bodhidharma to ask for instruction, the teacher would not see him. Hui-k'o continued to wait in his garden even though it snowed so heavily that the bamboos broke under the weight of the snow. Bodhidharma, moved to pity, asked what he wanted. Hui-k'o asked for instruction, but was refused. He thereupon cut off his arm and placed it before the master to prove his sincerity. Chikamatsu has misused this story as an example of sudden enlightenment.

of ancient and modern times. I have devoted my attention to problems in tactics. But only now have I gained sudden enlightenment into the profoundest secret of the science, thanks to this battle between a snipe and a clam.

The clam, secure in the hardness of its shells, did not realize that a snipe would attack. The snipe, proud of its sharp beak, did not foresee that the clam would snap shut its mouth. The shells will not let go, and the snipe, straining all its energies to free itself, has no time to look behind. Nothing could be simpler than for me to seize both of them in one swoop. The hardness of the clam's shells will be of no avail, and the snipe's sharp beak will not frighten me. This is the secret of military tactics: to provoke a quarrel between two adversaries, and then catch both when they least expect it. This was in China the strategy behind the vertical and horizontal alliances the first emperor of the Ch'in used to swallow up the Six Kingdoms.[35] When we read the *Taiheiki*[36] of Japan, it tells how the Emperor Godaigo ruled the country laxly, like the clam with its shells open. A snipe named the Lay Priest of Sagami beat his wings in Kamakura; his arrogant beak was sharp. He attacked at Yoshino and Chihaya and forced the clam to blow salt water, only for his beak to be caught in an attack by the two shells called Kusunoki Masashige and Nitta Yoshisada.[37] Takauji, a master of martial strategy, struck at snipe and clam, profiting by their preoccupation, and seized empty shells and clam together.[38]

I have heard that in the land of my father Ikkan's birth a battle is now raging between China and Tartary, exactly like that between snipe and clam. If I were to go to China and attack, applying what I have now learned to the present struggle, I am sure that I could swallow up China and Tartary both in one gulp!

NARRATOR: He racks his brains with schemes of conquest, not taking his eyes from the snipe and the clam. The determination which stirs in this warrior promises splendid deeds. What could be more natural than that this man should cross to China, conquer China and Tartary,

[35] The stratagem was advocated by Chang I, a counselor of the state of Ch'in, and succeeded in winning all China for the ruler of Ch'in.

[36] A chronicle written about 1360; translated by H. C. McCullough.

[37] Kusunoki Masashige (1294–1336) and Nitta Yoshisada (1301–38) were loyal generals of the Emperor Godaigo. They defeated Hōjō Takatoki ("the Lay Priest of Sagami"), but were ultimately vanquished by Ashikaga Takauji (1305–58).

[38] Not an exact parallel—if the shells are Kusunoki and Nitta, the snipe (Takatoki) is no longer around to be captured by Takauji.

and gain glory abroad and at home? This young man is no other than the future Coxinga, prince of Empei.[39]

KOMUTSU: Look! The tide is already coming in. What are you staring at?

NARRATOR: She runs up.

KOMUTSU: Well! The snipe and the clam are kissing! This is the first I knew they were married. Shame on them—in broad daylight, like dogs! I'll separate them somehow.

NARRATOR: She pulls out a hairpin and prizes the shell apart. The snipe, delighted, heads for the reeds, while the clam buries itself in the sand as the tide flows in.

WATŌNAI: It looks like rain. Let's go back.

NARRATOR: He happens to glance out at the end of the sand bar, and sees a rudderless boat of curious construction drifting towards them.

WATŌNAI: That's not a whaling boat. I wonder if it's a Chinese tea boat? [40]

KOMUTSU: I have no idea.

NARRATOR: They examine the boat and discover inside a high-born lady of sixteen or more years, who looks like a Chinese. Her face is a lotus blossom, her eyebrows willow leaves. Her sleeves are wet with a tide of tears, and the sea winds have washed the rouge and powder from her face that is pale and drawn. She is touchingly lovely, like the first flowers of spring wilted by the rain.[41] Komutsu speaks in a whisper.

KOMUTSU: She must be a Chinese empress, the kind they draw in pictures, who's had a love affair and been exiled.

WATŌNAI: Yes, that's a good guess. I made the mistake of thinking that she might be the ghost of Yang Kuei-fei,[42] and it frightened me. Anyway, she's certainly a lovely girl, isn't she?

KOMUTSU: You horrid man! Do Chinese women attract you? If your father'd stayed all along in China, you'd have been born there too, and you'd be sleeping with a woman like that in your arms. But unluckily for you, you were born in Japan, and you're saddled with a wife like me. I feel sorry for you!

[39] Empei is Yen-p'ing in Chinese. I have used Japanese pronunciations of the Chinese names which figure in the play, but retained Chinese pronunciations for historical names.
[40] A "tea boat" was a kind of sampan.
[41] I have omitted the phrase, not intended by Chikamatsu to be comic, "with a nose and mouth attached."
[42] A celebrated Chinese beauty (718–756). See below, p. 255.

WATŌNAI: Don't be silly! No matter how pretty a Chinese woman may be, her clothes and the way she does her hair make me think I'm looking at Benzaiten! [43] I could never get to sleep with one—I'd feel much too on edge!

NARRATOR: He laughs. As they talk the lady steps on shore and beckons them.

SENDAN: Japanese! Japanese! *Na mu kya ra chon nō to ra ya a ya!* [44]

NARRATOR: Komutsu bursts out laughing.

KOMUTSU: What sutra is *that?*

NARRATOR: She holds her sides with amusement.

WATŌNAI: You mustn't laugh! She said, "Japanese, come here. I have something to request of you."

NARRATOR: He brushes Komutsu aside and goes to the lady, who is blinded with tears.

SENDAN: Great Ming *chin shin nyō ro.* Sir, *ken ku ru mei ta ka rin kan kyū, sai mō su ga sun hei su ru,* on the other hand, *kon ta ka rin ton na, a ri shi te ken san hai ro. To ra ya a ya, to ra ya a ya.*

NARRATOR: These are her only words before she melts in tears again. Komutsu plops down on the beach, convulsed with laughter, unable to endure more. Watōnai, who learned his father's tongue, touches his hands to the ground and bows his head.

WATŌNAI: *U su u su u sa su ha mō, sa ki ga chin bu ri ka ku san kin nai ro. Kin nyō, kin nyō.*

NARRATOR: He claps his hands, then takes the lady's hands in his, most intimately. His tears of sympathy suggest that they are old friends. Komutsu, enraged, catches the breast of his kimono.

KOMUTSU: See here, you! I don't want to hear any more of your Chinese talk. For all your flirtations, when did you manage to get in touch with her in China? You've extended your operations too far afield! And as for you, with your *to ra ya a ya,* how dare you go *kinnyō-kinnyō*-ing to my precious husband? I won't give you the chance to taste what a Japanese man is like. Try a taste of this instead!

NARRATOR: She brandishes her rake, but Watōnai snatches it away.

WATŌNAI: Open your eyes before you start being jealous! This is the Princess Sendan, the younger sister of the emperor of China, my fa-

[43] A Buddhist goddess of beauty, known in Sanskrit as Sarasvatī.
[44] The words, as used here, have no meaning, and merely represent what Chinese sounds like to a Japanese. For the derivation see Keene, *The Battles of Coxinga,* p. 184.

ther's former master he has so often told us about. The storms of a revolution have blown her here. We cannot abandon her in this pitiful condition. But if we take her directly home, we'll have to bother with the village headman's permission, and the governor's office is sure to investigate. The best plan is to ask my father's advice. Go home and bring Father here at once. Quickly, before people see!

NARRATOR: Komutsu claps her hands.

KOMUTSU: The poor dear! I've heard how ladies of noble birth have met with stormy winds even in Japan. How much worse it must be for a princess from China to be brought to such a sorry state! Some deep connection between master and retainer must have guided her boat ashore here, out of all the many harbors. I'll call Father at once. You poor thing, *to ra ya a ya, kin nyō, kin nyō.*

NARRATOR: Her eyes fill with tears as she leaves on the road home.

Ikkan and his wife, unaware of what has happened, are walking along the beach on their return from the Sumiyoshi shrine of Matsura where they have worshiped following a strange and wonderful dream. Watōnai calls them to him.

WATŌNAI: The Princess Sendan has fled the disorders in China, and her boat has been stranded here. See what a piteous state she is in!

NARRATOR: Before he has finished speaking, Ikkan and his wife bow their heads to the ground.

IKKAN: I believe that your highness may have heard of me. I was formerly known as Tei Shiryū. My present wife and my son are Japanese, but I should not be acting as a loyal subject if I failed to repay old obligations. I am bent with years, but my son is well versed in martial matters and, as you can see, he is of a naturally powerful build. He is bold and invincible, a hero who will restore the dynasty of the great Ming and bring peace to the late emperor in the other world. Please be of good cheer.

NARRATOR: He speaks reassuringly. The princess is moved to tears.

SENDAN: Are you indeed the Tei Shiryū of whom I have heard so much? Ri Tōten treacherously allied himself with Tartary. He killed my brother, the emperor, and usurped the country. I too would have been killed had it not been for the loyal protection of Go Sankei and his wife. Their efforts have preserved to this day a life which I would not begrudge. I put myself in your hands, helpless and uncertain as the dew.

NARRATOR: These are her only words before she melts again in tears. Only because of some lasting connection are these reiterated words of regret over the past exchanged between strangers. Watōnai's mother can hardly wring out her sleeve for the tears.

MOTHER: I see now it must have been as a sign that we would hear such tidings that my husband and I had the same revelation in dreams this morning. It plainly foretold that a battle would be waged two thousand leagues from here,[45] followed by a victory in the west. Watōnai, you must interpret this dream and bear it in mind as you strive in loyal service for the success of the imperial cause. What do you say?

NARRATOR: Watōnai answers respectfully.

WATŌNAI: A few moments ago on this beach I witnessed an extraordinary encounter between a snipe and a clam. It has enlightened me about the profoundest secret of military strategy. The prophecy that victory would come in the west a thousand leagues from here must refer to China, a country situated a thousand leagues over the rough waves to the west of Japan. The ideograph for strategy is written with the symbol for "water" and the symbol for "to leave".[46] This was clearly a divine message enjoining me to entrust myself to the waters of the rising tide and leave Japanese soil at once. My fortune is the "hexagram of the general." "The general" stands for an army. The hexagram is arranged with the trigram for earth above and that for water below. One yang controls many yin,[47] it says, meaning that I alone shall be general commanding tens of thousands of troops. I shall leave Japan immediately, on the rising tide indicated by the symbol for water, and push on to Nanking and Peking. I shall join counsel with Go Sankei, if he still survives in this mortal world, and crush the traitorous followers of Ri Tōten. Gathering an army round me, I shall counterattack Tartary and twist the Tartars by the pigtails on their

---

[45] The distance between Japan and China is variously estimated at one, two, and three thousand *ri*. To keep the meaning vague, I have translated *ri* as "league".

[46] The symbols are 氵 (water) and 去 (to leave). Combined they form 法 (strategy).

[47] The seventh hexagram in *I-ching* (Book of changes). Legge says of it (*Yi King*, p. 72), "The conduct of military expeditions in a feudal kingdom, and we may say, generally, is denoted by the hexagram Sze." The hexagram has one yang (unbroken) line and five yin (divided) lines.

shaven pates.[48] I'll behead them all! I'll drive them back, cut them down, and then raise a hymn of victory for the long prosperity of the Ming! These are the plans that fill my soul. They say that "opportunities of time vouchsafed by Heaven are not equal to advantages of situation afforded by the Earth, and advantages of situation afforded by the Earth are not equal to the union arising from the accord of Men."[49] And again, "Good or bad fortune depends on man and not on the stars." I shall set sail without further delay, and persuade the barbarians of islands along the way to join my forces. Then I shall do battle in the manner I have planned. To the front!

NARRATOR: In his bold figure they seem to behold the Empress Jingū standing fiercely at the helm as she set off to conquer Korea.[50]

His father is greatly impressed.

IKKAN: What noble and promising sentiments! Indeed, the text is true which says that a single flower seed does not rot in the ground, but grows at last into a thousand blossoms.[51] You are truly a son of Ikkan! Your mother and I should offer to accompany the princess in the same boat, but if we are too many we shall attract attention, and there is the danger that we may be arrested at one of the points of shipping control. We shall therefore sail secretly instead from the Bay of Fujitsu.[52] You depart from here and leave the princess at some convenient island on the way. Then change course and catch up with us. They say that the gods dwell in honest heads; a divine wind will surely guide over the sea so loyal a father and son. Let us meet at the Bamboo Forest of a Thousand Leagues, famous throughout China. Wait for us there. Now hasten on your way!

NARRATOR: Husband and wife take leave of the princess and set off on their distant journey. Watōnai takes the princess by the hand and leads her aboard the Chinese boat. He is about to push off when his wife runs up, all out of breath. She seizes the hawser.

KOMUTSU: Your father and mother weren't home. I thought something funny was up, and I see I was right. You and your father planned

---

[48] The Tartars shaved their heads except for a tuft at the top which hung behind as a pigtail.

[49] From *The Book of Mencius*, translated by Legge (*Chinese Classics*, I, 208).

[50] The conquest of Korea by Jingū (also called Jingō) apparently occurred in the fourth century A.D.

[51] From the Nō play *Semimaru*. See Sanari, *Yōkyoku Taikan*, iii, 1680.

[52] The coast of Fujitsu-gun in the present Saga Prefecture.

this long ago. You sent for a wife from his country, and now the four of you are going off to China with all our property, leaving me behind! This is too brutal of you, too heartless! What did I do to displease you? We promised each other we'd go together not merely to China or Korea, but to India or to the ends of the clouds. We were joined by pledges and oaths locked in our hearts, and not by go-betweens or formalities. For the love you once bore me, however weary of me you may have become, take me aboard the boat with you. I won't complain though you throw me into the waves five or ten leagues from shore and I become food for sharks. Please let me die at my husband's hands, Tōnai.

NARRATOR: She beats on the prow, she weeps, she pleads with him, and gives no sign of releasing the hawser.

WATŌNAI: Your bawling face will bring me bad luck, just when we're starting on an important mission. Be off—or I'll teach you a lesson!

NARRATOR: He menaces her with an oar. The princess, alarmed, clings to him, but he brushes aside her restraining hand and beats the side of the boat hard enough to break the oar. Komutsu thrusts herself under the blows intended only as a threat.

KOMUTSU: Beat me to death—that's all I ask!

NARRATOR: She falls on the beach and rolls over in anguish, wailing at the top of her lungs.

KOMUTSU: And I still can't die! Very well! My trouble all along has been that I'm too good-natured. I'll throw myself to the bottom of the sea, and my fury will turn into a serpent of jealousy. The love I once bore you will today become hatred. I'll have my revenge!

NARRATOR: She picks up some stones and drops them into her hanging sleeves. She starts to climb a cliff over the sea, when Watōnai rushes up after her and takes her in his arms.

WATŌNAI: Don't act so rashly! I'm sure now that I can depend on you. I shall leave the princess in your care until the warfare in China ends and peace is restored. It was my intention to leave her here in Japan, but I had to test you, a woman of low birth, to see if you were worthy. That is why I deliberately acted so cruelly. Now I entrust you with the princess, the equal in importance of all 400 districts of China— that should prove that your husband's heart has not changed. It will be a hundred times more exacting to serve the princess than to serve your father-in-law or your husband. I ask this most seriously—it is a matter of life and death. When peace is restored in China I will send a ship for the princess, and I want you to escort her.

NARRATOR: Komutsu listens obediently to his soothing words.

KOMUTSU: Don't worry about anything here. May all go well with you!

NARRATOR: She speaks bravely, but her woman's heart weakens.

KOMUTSU: Not even one night together before you leave? What a nightmare separation this is!

NARRATOR: She clings to her husband's sleeve and weeps aloud, inconsolable. Watōnai too is choked with emotion, and his eyes cloud over in sympathy. For a moment both are torn by conflicting emotions.

WATŌNAI: We can't keep saying good-by indefinitely. I must leave you. Farewell!

NARRATOR: He takes his leave. Sendan is also in tears.

SENDAN: I will await your boat.[53] Then I shall return to my country with your wife. I hope it will come soon.

NARRATOR: Watōnai bows in assent; then, still weeping, he pushes off the boat. Komutsu again catches the hawser.

KOMUTSU: I have something else to tell you. Wait just a moment.

NARRATOR: She stops him.

WATŌNAI: Unreasonable woman!

NARRATOR: He cuts the rope and rows the boat out to the deep. She follows him helplessly, till her body is soaked in the waves. She can only raise her hand and call to the boat, though by now it is too distant for her cries to be heard. She runs back on shore and climbs a stony crag. She watches on tiptoes as the boat moves ever farther out to sea.

KOMUTSU: I feel now like the women for whom they named the Watching Wife Mountain of China and the Scarf-waving Mountain of Japan.[54] I shall not move. I shall not leave this spot, though I turn to stone, though I become a part of the mountain.

NARRATOR: She assures him of her love, weeping with unstinted tears. They call to each other, but the salt spray hides their figures, and the waves of the open sea interrupt their voices. The sea gulls and beach plovers hovering offshore join their cries of sorrow over parting.

[53] Literally, "I shall await the welcoming palanquin."

[54] A legend tells of a woman who climbed a mountain in Anhwei Province in China to watch for her husband's return. She remained there so long that she eventually turned to stone. The "Scarf-waving Mountain" relates to the wife of Ōtomo no Sadehiko, a fifth-century courtier, who waved to her husband's ship when it left for Korea.

Scene Two: The Bamboo Forest of a Thousand Leagues.

NARRATOR: Father and son part, bound for their uncertain destination. Their boats, leaving behind Tsukushi of burning sea fire[55]
hidden in clouds, meet with a divine wind that carries them through
the myriad waves to arrive on the shores of Cathay at one and the same
hour. Tei Shiryū Ikkan, in honor of his homecoming, changes to a
costume of Chinese brocades. He turns to his wife and son.

IKKAN: This is my native land, but the times have changed, and
the dynasty is no longer the same. The entire country, thanks to Ri
Tōten's machinations, has been enslaved by the Tartar barbarians.
Who of all the friends and family I once knew is left? There is no
way to tell. How can I raise a standard for loyal troops to follow when
I am not sure where Go Sankei may be, or even if he is still alive?
Where shall I find a castle in which to entrench our forces? I know
of none.

Yet, when I departed this country in the fifth year of Tenkei[56] and
crossed the seas to Japan, I left behind in her nurse's sleeve a daughter
barely two years old. Her mother died in childbirth, and I, her father,
have been separated from her by the broad barrier of the sea. The girl
has never known father or mother, and she has grown as plants and
trees grow, by the grace of the rain and dew. Heaven and Earth have
been her parents and her succor. Traveling merchants have told me
that she has reached womanhood and become the wife of the lord of
a castle, a prince named Gojōgun Kanki. I have no one else to turn
to. If only my daughter is willing to help us, out of love for her father,
I'm sure that it will be simple to ask Kanki's cooperation. His castle
is 180 leagues from here. People will suspect us if we travel together,
so I shall journey alone, by a different road. Watōnai, take your mother.
Use your intelligence: if you tell people that you've been shipwrecked
from a Japanese fishing vessel, they'll let you stay in their houses. You
can catch up later if you fall behind. Ahead of us lies the famous
Bamboo Forest of a Thousand Leagues, the haunt of tigers. Beyond
this huge forest is the Jinyō River where monkeys live. Next you'll see

[55] *Shiranuhi* (sea fire) is used both as an epithet for Tsukushi (Kyushu) and as a
pivot-word, where it means "unknown" (destination).
[56] 1625.

a tall mountain of majestic aspect called the Red Cliff. That was where Su Tung-p'o was exiled in days of old.[57] Wait for me at the Red Cliff, where we will make our future plans.

NARRATOR: Not knowing which direction to follow, they take the sun shining through the white clouds for their guide and part to east and west. Watōnai, in obedience to his father's instructions, keeps an eye open for houses where he may hide. He steadfastly trudges forward, his mother on his back. He jumps and leaps over unscalable rocks and boulders, the roots of massy trees, and swift currents but, though he speeds ahead swift as a bird in flight, China is a land of immense distances, and he wanders into the vast bamboo forest, far from the habitations of men. Watōnai is baffled and bewildered.

WATŌNAI: Mother, I can tell by the strain in my legs that we must have come forty or fifty leagues, but we have met neither man nor monkey. The farther we go, the deeper we get in the forest. Ah, I have it! This must be the work of Chinese foxes. They see that we Japanese don't know the way, and they're playing tricks on us. If they want to bewitch us, let them! We have no other inn on our journey—we'll stay wherever they take us, and we'll be glad to share in a dish of rice and red beans! [58]

NARRATOR: He pushes and tramples through the underbrush and tall bamboos, penetrating ever deeper into the forest when—strange to tell—thousands of voices suddenly echo, together with a noise of hand drums and bass drums, bugles and trumpets, coming closer as if in attack.

WATŌNAI: Good heavens! Have they discovered us? Are those the advancing drums of an enemy surrounding us? Or is it the work of foxes?

NARRATOR: He stands perplexed when a gale all at once arises, blowing fiercely enough to scoop holes in the ground and curl back the bamboo leaves. The bamboo stalks broken by the wind are like swords, and the scene horrifying beyond description. Watōnai is not in the least perturbed.

WATŌNAI: I know what this is—a Chinese tiger hunt. Those gongs and drums were the beaters. These are the hunting grounds of the

[57] *The Red Cliff* is a prose poem in two parts by Su Tung-p'o (1036–1101). He was exiled to various places, but the Red Cliff (in modern Hupei Province) was not one of them.

[58] Rice boiled with red beans was believed to be a favorite dish of foxes. In children's stories one finds accounts of people bewitched by foxes who are treated to this dish.

Thousand Leagues. They say that when a tiger roars a wind rises. I'm sure that this storm must be the work of some wild beast. Yang Hsiang, one of the twenty-four examples of filial piety, escaped danger from a ferocious tiger because of his devotion to his parents. I am not his equal in piety, but my courage is braced by my loyalty. This will be the first test of my strength since my coming to China. But it would be unmanly to face a tiger with my sword, knowing that the blade is imbued with the strength of the Japanese gods. I can crush with one blow of my fist an elephant or a demon, let alone a tiger!

NARRATOR: He tucks up his skirts from behind and readies himself. As he stands guard over his mother, he is a sight to inspire terror even in the Indian lion, the king of beasts.

Exactly as he predicted, a raging tiger appears on the heels of the storm. It rubs its muzzle against the base of a ringed bamboo, and sharpens its claws on a jutting rock, glaring at the strangers all the while. The tiger snaps its jaws angrily, but Watōnai remains unimpressed. He strikes the tiger with his left hand, and fends it off with his right. Watōnai dodges as the tiger attacks with a twisting motion. The tiger falters and Watōnai nimbly leaps on its back. Now up, now down, they engage in a life-and-death struggle, a test of endurance. Watōnai shouts under the effort, and the tiger, his fur bristling, roars in fury, a noise as of mountains crumbling.

Watōnai's hair is disheveled, and half the tiger's fur has been pulled out. Both are out of breath. When Watōnai clambers on a boulder to catch his breath, the tiger, exhausted, hangs its head among the rocks. Its heavy panting echoes like some powerful bellows. Watōnai's mother rushes up from her shelter in the bamboo grove.

MOTHER: Watōnai! You were born in the Land of the Gods and you mustn't harm the body, hair, and skin you received from them in a contest with a brute beast. Japan is far away, but the gods dwell in your body. Why shouldn't this sacred charm from the Great Shrine by the Isuzu River [59] be effective now?

NARRATOR: She offers him the charm she wears next to her skin.

WATŌNAI: Indeed, it is as you say.

NARRATOR: He accepts the charm reverently and points it at the tiger. He lifts the charm, when—what is the mysterious power of the Land of the Gods!—the tiger, the very embodiment of ferocity, suddenly droops its tail, hangs its ears, and draws in its legs timidly. It

[59] The Great Shrine at Ise stands by this river.

creeps into a cave in the rocks, trembling with fear. Watōnai, seizing
the tiger by the base of its tail, flings it backwards, forces it down.
When it recoils, he leaps on it and presses it beneath his feet, showing
the divine strength of the god Susanoo when he flayed the piebald
colt of Heaven.[60] How awe-inspiring is the majestic power of the
goddess Amaterasu!

At this moment a swarm of beaters rushes up. One of them, obviously the chief, shouts.

AN TAIJIN: Where have *you* come from? Vagabond! How dare you
deny me my glory? This tiger is one we've been hunting so that we
might offer it to the king of Tartary as a present from our exalted
master, the general of the right Ri Tōten. Surrender it at once! If you
refuse, you're a dead man! Ho, officers!

NARRATOR: Watōnai smiles with pleasure at mention of Ri Tōten.

WATŌNAI: They say that even a devil counts as a human being! You
certainly talk the part of a bold man! I was born in great Japan, and
you've said one word too many in calling me a vagabond. If you want
the tiger so badly, ask your master Ri Tōten or Tokoroten,[61] or whatever his name is, to come and beg for it! I've business with him and
must see him personally. Otherwise you'll never get your tiger.

NARRATOR: He glares at the man.

AN TAIJIN: Don't let him say another word! Kill him!

NARRATOR: The men all draw their swords.

WATŌNAI: I'm ready for you!

NARRATOR: He places the charm on the tiger's head and stations the
beast beside his mother. The tiger lies motionless, as though rooted
to the spot.

WATŌNAI: Now I have nothing to worry about!

NARRATOR: He lifts his broadsword and, charging into the throng,
slashes his way irresistibly in every direction, rolling the men back. An
Taijin, the chief of the beaters, counterattacks, leading his officers.

AN TAIJIN: Kill the old hag too!

NARRATOR: They make a beeline for her with flailing swords, but—
a further sign of divine protection—the gods lend their strength to
the tiger. It springs up and, quivering, bares its teeth. It leaps with a

---

[60] A reference to the story in the first book of the *Kojiki* telling of how the god Susanoo,
to spite his sister Amaterasu, flayed a piebald colt backwards and threw it into her halls.
[61] Watōnai is making fun of Ri Tōten's name. *Tokoroten* is a kind of jellied noodle
served cold in summertime.

fierce roar at the enemy. An Taijin and the beaters cry, "We're no match for him!" They fling at the tiger their hunting spears, rough lances, and whatever else comes to hand, and slash with their swords. The tiger, possessed of divine strength, leaps about at will, snatching their swords in mid-air with his jaws and dashing them to splinters against the rocks. The glint of the blades scatters like a hail of jewels or slivers of ice.

The officers, with no more weapons to wield, are clearly beaten, and they flee in confusion. Watōnai appears behind them. With a shout of "I won't let you go!" he grips An Taijin's neck and lifts him high in the air. He whirls him round and round, then flings him like a ripe persimmon against a rock. An Taijin's body is shattered and he perishes. Now if the officers attempt to retreat they are confronted by the jaws of the ferocious tiger, and if they go forward Watōnai, bold as a guardian king, menaces them.

OFFICERS: Forgive us, please. We crave your pardon.

NARRATOR: They join their hands in supplication and weep bitterly, their faces pressed to the ground. Watōnai strokes the tiger's head.

WATŌNAI: Vile creatures! You who despise the Japanese for coming from a small country—have you learned now the meaning of Japanese prowess, before which even tigers tremble? I am the son of Tei Shiryū, of whom you have no doubt heard. I am the Watōnai who grew up at Hirado in Kyushu. I met there by chance the Princess Sendan, the sister of the late emperor, and I returned to my father's country hoping to restore order and thereby repay the debt of three lifetimes.[62] Join me, if you value your lives. Refuse, and you become food for the tiger! Will it be yes or no?

NARRATOR: He presses them for an answer.

OFFICERS: Why should we say no? We served the king of Tartary and Ri Tōten only because we feared for our lives. From now on we shall be your followers. We beg your indulgence.

NARRATOR: They bow till their noses scrape the ground.

WATŌNAI: Hurrah! But if you're to be my men, you'll have to shave your foreheads in the Japanese manner. Once you've had your coming of age ceremony, change your names. Then you can serve me.

NARRATOR: He orders them to remove their short swords—even these

[62] A familiar saying had it that the relations between parent and child lasted one lifetime, those between husband and wife two lifetimes, and those between ruler and subject three lifetimes.

can be used in an emergency for razors. His mother helps collect the blades. Together they shave at a breakneck pace the heads lined up before them, not troubling to sprinkle or massage the scalps. The razors slash away with abandon, sometimes going so far they leave only a fringe of hair on the sides or the crown. The shaving is completed in the flash of an eye, and the victims, despite a couple of desperate strokes of the comb, are left with only an unkempt tangle of hair. Their heads are Japanese, their beards Tartar, and their bodies Chinese. They exchange looks of consternation. Then the shaven heads feel the wind, and soon they have caught cold. They sneeze again and again, with running noses and tears like driving rain. Mother and son burst out laughing.

WATŌNAI: My followers are all matched now! Take new names in the Japanese style, on the order of something-*zaemon* or something-*bei*, or using numbers, from *tarō* and *jirō* all the way to *jūrō*.[63] Put the place you come from at the head of your name. Then form two ranks and start moving.

NARRATOR: "Yes, sir" is the reply. The first to set out are Chang-chowzaemon, Cambodiaemon, Luzonbei, Tonkinbei, Siamtarō, Champajirō, Chaulshirō, Borneogorō, Unsunrokurō, Sunkichikurō, Moghulzaemon, Jakartabei, Santomehachirō, and Englandbei.[64] His new followers to the fore, the rear of Watōnai's train is brought up by draft horses and his mother's striped steed. He helps his mother onto the tiger's back and wins a name for filial piety, as soon he will win the country. His fame spreads to both China and Japan, as his legs in the saddle and stirrups when he jumps on the tiger's back; he displays his might to the world for a thousand leagues round.

ACT THREE

Scene One: The Castle of Lions. Outside the Great Gate.
Time: Early spring, 1645.

NARRATOR:

Even the benevolent ruler cannot support a worthless minister;

---

[63] Familiar suffixes to Japanese personal names. The eldest son often had a name ending in *tarō* (first son), and subsequent sons might be given names ending in *jirō*, *saburō*, *shirō*, etc., standing for second, third, or fourth sons. *Jūrō* would be the tenth son.
[64] There is disagreement about some of the place names here given. Unsun was a game of cards introduced by the Dutch. Sunkichi is unknown.

Even the kindest father cannot love a good-for-nothing child.[65]

Though the ways of Japan and China differ in many respects, in essence they are one: father and son, hastening on divergent roads, do not wander astray, for they follow the true path.[66]

The parents and son, after meeting as planned at the foot of the Red Cliff, travel together to the Castle of Lions, the seat of Gojōgun Kanki, about whom all they know is that he is Ikkan's son-in-law. The castle exceeds their expectations: the stone walls towering on high are crowned by roof tiles, sparkling with the frost of the still-cold spring night, and at the crest dolphins wave their fins in the sky. The indigo water of the moat coils into the distant Yellow River like an enormous rope. The castle gate is tightly bolted, and from within the walls a night watchman's gong noisily rings out. Every loophole in the wall is provided with a crossbow, and catapults installed here and there are ready to be fired in time of danger. This is a fortress unmatched for strength by any in Japan. Ikkan is dismayed.

IKKAN: In these troubled times, when the castle is so strictly defended, I doubt that anyone will believe my words even if I knock boldly at the gate in the middle of the night and announce that Kanki's father-in-law, a man unknown to anyone, has arrived from Japan. Even if my daughter should hear me, it will be no easy matter to gain admittance to the castle, no matter how many proofs I may offer that I am her father, separated from her when she was two years old, her father who went to Japan. What shall I do?

NARRATOR: He murmurs unhappily. Watōnai cries out at once.

WATŌNAI: It's too late now to be surprised! Ever since leaving Japan I have been resigned to having no allies except myself. Rather than make friendly overtures—"I am your long-lost father-in-law!" "My dear son-in-law" and the like—only to suffer some humiliation, we ought to make a direct proposal: "Can we rely on you or can't we?" If he says "No," he becomes our enemy on the spot. His wife—the daughter you left when she was two—is my half sister, it's true, but if she had any affection for her father you'd think that she'd have wanted to know what was happening to him in Japan and would

---

[65] From a poem by Ts'ao Chih (192–232). Here, as in the poem that opens the second act, the case of Watōnai and Ikkan is the opposite to that given: Watōnai is a dutiful son and Ikkan is a valuable minister.

[66] Two meanings are compressed here: the ways of Japan and China are different, but in essence their teaching are the same; and the roads that father and son follow are different, but they reach the same destination.

have sent letters. But there weren't any. We can't depend on her. I'll stage a series of attacks with the barbarians I conquered in the bamboo forest as the nucleus of my force. In no time at all I'll pick up another fifty or a hundred thousand men. There's no use in asking favors. I'll kick down the castle gate and twist off the head of my unfilial sister. Then I'll have a fight to the finish with your son-in-law Kanki!

NARRATOR: He jumps up, ready for action, but his mother restrains him by clinging to him.

MOTHER: I don't know what's in the girl's heart, but it is customary for women to obey their husbands and not to do as they please. She is your father's daughter and of the same seed as yourself. I am the only stranger. Though we have always been separated by thousands of leagues of ocean and mountains, I cannot escape being called her stepmother.[67] It's inconceivable that the girl should not long in her heart for her father and her brother. But if you force your way into the castle, people will say that it was because the girl's Japanese stepmother envied her. It will be a disgrace not only to me but to Japan.

You have conceived the noble plan of destroying the powerful Tartar enemy and restoring the Ming dynasty, though only a commoner yourself. You should forget about personal disgrace and endure the resentment you feel. Try to win others to your side. I have heard that the essence of military strategy is to gain as your ally even a single private from the enemy camp. How much truer is this of Kanki, the lord of a castle and commanding general of a whole region! Do you think it will be easy to persuade him to join us? Control your emotions and ask him to admit you to the castle!

NARRATOR: She cautions him. Watōnai stands outside the gate and shouts.

WATŌNAI: I have something to discuss privately with General Kanki. Open the gate!

NARRATOR: He beats on the gate and the sound echoes within the castle walls.

The soldiers on guard shout variously.

SOLDIERS: Our master, General Kanki, left yesterday by command of the great king. We have no information when he'll return. You'd like

[67] In Japan (as elsewhere) the stepmother is generally depicted as an envious, disagreeable woman.

to meet him personally? What impudence, whoever you are, to make such a request in the middle of the night, when he's away! Speak up, if you've something to say. We'll tell him when he gets back.

NARRATOR: Ikkan answers in a low voice.

IKKAN: My message may not be relayed. If Lord Kanki is absent, I should like to meet his wife and address myself to her. She will surely understand if you inform her that I have come from Japan.

NARRATOR: Hardly has he spoken than the castle resounds with angry cries.

SOLDIERS: What effrontery! The rogue wants to see our general's lady! We've never even seen her ourselves—and he's a Japanese! Beware!

NARRATOR: They wave their long-handled lanterns, and beat gongs and cymbals. The crowd of soldiers on the wall all train their muskets on the visitors.

SOLDIERS: Release the catapults! Crush the intruders! Fuses! Bullets!

NARRATOR: They mill around in tumult. Kanki's wife in her apartments must have heard their disturbance. She rushes to the gate.

KINSHŌJO: Stop this commotion! I shall listen to what they have to say, and until I give the command to fire, you are not to shoot. Do nothing rash!

You outside the gates! I am Kinshōjo, the wife of General Kanki. The entire country bows before the great king of Tartary. My husband, in keeping with the times, has joined the staff of the great king, and has been entrusted with this castle. I do not understand why you wish to see me when my husband is away and the strictest precautions are observed. But anyone from Japan is dear to me. Tell me who you are. I long to hear.

NARRATOR: Even as she speaks she wonders, "Can it be my father? Why should he have come?" She feels anxious and frightened, but nostalgic memories are uppermost in her mind.

KINSHŌJO: Soldiers! Do nothing rash! Don't fire your muskets accidentally!

NARRATOR: Her fears are understandable. Ikkan's first glimpse of his daughter's face under the misty spring moon is clouded by tears. He raises his thickened voice.

IKKAN: Forgive me for speaking so abruptly, but was not your father Tei Shiryū of the Ming? Your mother died in childbirth, and your

father, incurring the emperor's wrath, fled to Japan. At the time you
were but two years old, and could not understand the sorrow of parting
from your father, but you must have heard what happened from your
nurse's gossip. I am your father, Tei Shiryū. I have spent long years
at the Bay of Hirado in Hizen, a province of Japan, and my name is
now Rōikkan. This man is your younger brother, born in Japan, and
this is your new mother. I have something to tell and to ask of you
in private. That is why I have come, not concealing the shame of my
reduced circumstances. Would you please have the gate opened?

NARRATOR: His words of earnest persuasion strike home. Kinshōjo
wonders, "Is it indeed my father?" She would like to run down to
him, cling to him, gaze into his face. Her heart is torn a thousand ways,
but she remains every inch the wife of Kanki, the lord of a castle.
She holds back her tears lest the soldiers see.

KINSHŌJO: I remember everything as you describe it, but your arguments are unconvincing without some proofs. I should like to learn
what proofs you may have that you are my father.

NARRATOR: The soldiers at once cry out.

SOLDIER A: Proof! Furnish proof!

SOLDIER B: His only proof is to say that he's her father!

SOLDIER C: He's a villain!

NARRATOR: They all point the barrels of their matchlocks at Tei
Shiryū. Watōnai runs between his father and the soldiers.

WATŌNAI: If you even pretend to shoot your damned guns, I'll
slaughter you!

SOLDIERS: Don't let him escape either!

NARRATOR: They lift the caps of their matchlocks and cover the
party from all sides. With rising intensity they press Ikkan for proofs,
and the situation seems perilous, when Ikkan raises his hands.

IKKAN: I have it! The proof must be in your possession! When I was
about to leave China I had my portrait painted, thinking that it would
serve as a memento of me when you were grown. I left this picture
with your nurse. Old age has changed me, but some vestiges of my
former appearance must remain. Compare the picture and my face,
and remove your doubts!

KINSHŌJO: Those words are already proof!

NARRATOR: Standing by the high railing, she unfolds the portrait which has never left her person, and takes out her mirror. She reflects in the mirror her father's face illuminated by the moonlight, and closely compares and matches it with the portrait. In the picture the face has its former luster and glossy sidelocks; in the mirror is the present gaunt old age. The head is now covered with snow, but left unchanged, just as once they were, are the eyes and mouth, which closely resemble her own features. The mole on her forehead inherited from her father is indisputable proof that they are father and daughter.

KINSHŌJO: Are you truly my father? How I have longed for you! How dear you are! I was told only that my mother lay under the sod in the other world, and that my father was in Japan. I sought word, but I had no one to help me. I knew that Japan was at the eastern end of the world, and so I worshiped the rising sun at dawn as my father. At dusk I would spread out a map of the world, and say to myself, "This is China, and here is Japan. My father is here!" On a map Japan seems so close, but it is more than three thousand leagues from here, they say. I had given up all thought of seeing you in this world and, hoping we might meet in the world of the dead, I awaited the future life even before I died. I passed my days in sighs and my nights in tears. The days and nights of twenty years have been hard to bear. How grateful I am that you have kindly stayed alive, and that I can behold my father!

NARRATOR: She weeps for joy, not caring who might hear. Ikkan, choking with tears, clings to the gate tower. He looks up and she looks down, their hearts too full for speech. Only their tears have no end. Watōnai, for all his impetuous martial spirit, is overcome like his mother by emotion, and even the unfeeling Tartar soldiers dampen the rope matches of their guns with overflowing tears. After a while Ikkan speaks.

IKKAN: We have come to make an important and secret request of Kanki. First I should like to discuss it with you. Please have the gate opened and admit us to the castle.

KINSHŌJO: Normally I should of course invite you in, without a word from you, but the country is still in the midst of a war, and by order of the king of Tartary it is strictly forbidden to allow foreigners—even close relatives—within the castles. But this is surely a special case. Soldiers! What do you say?

NARRATOR: The obdurate Chinese cry out.

SOLDIERS: No! Impossible! Never! Leave at once! *Bin ḳan ta satsu bu on bu on!* [68]

NARRATOR: They aim their muskets again. The visitors, not expecting such treatment, are in despair, but Watōnai's mother comes forward.

MOTHER: You are right—an order from the great king may not be disobeyed. But you need not worry about an old woman like myself. All I ask is a word with the lady. Please admit me alone. This will truly be the kindness of a lifetime.

NARRATOR: She joins her hands in supplication, but the soldiers will not listen.

SOLDIERS: No! Nothing exempted women from the order. . . . But we will be reasonable. You must be bound like a criminal all the while you are within the castle walls. If we admit you under this condition, our general will have an excuse to offer and we ourselves will be absolved if the king of Tartary should hear of it. Hurry—tie on the ropes! If you refuse, leave at once! *Bin ḳan ta satsu bu on bu on!*

NARRATOR: Watōnai's eyes flash fire.

WATŌNAI: Dirty Chinese! Where are your ears? Are you all deaf? This is the wife of Tei Shiryū Ikkan—my mother, and the same as a mother to your lady too. How dare you suggest binding her with ropes like a dog or cat on a leash? No Japanese will tolerate such nonsense. It makes no great difference even if you won't let us inside this bothersome place. Let's go!

NARRATOR: He starts to lead his mother away, but she shakes off his hand.

MOTHER: Have you forgotten what I told you a few moments ago? A person who has an important service to ask of others must expect to be subjected to unpleasant experiences of every kind and even to humiliation. As long as our request is granted, I shall not mind being fettered hand and foot, much less bound with ropes—it will be like getting gold in return for broken tiles.[69] Japan is a small country, but her men and women do not abandon a just cause. Please put the ropes on me, Ikkan.

[68] Nonsense language, intended to sound like menacing Chinese.
[69] A proverb. The ends of Japanese tiles were round and had markings on them like those on a coin; this may have been the origin of the expression.

NARRATOR: Watōnai, shamed, has no choice but to take out the rope he keeps by his waist for an emergency. He binds his mother at elbows and wrists. Mother and son exchange glances and force a smile—a sign of the gallant training of a Japanese. It is hard for Kinshōjo to bear the sight, but she hides her grief.

KINSHŌJO: Everything is governed by the times, and the laws of a country may not be disobeyed. Have no fear about your mother while she is in my care. I do not know what her request may be, but I shall hear it through, and I shall transmit her words to my husband Kanki with the prayer that he grant your wishes.

The water in the moat around this castle has its source in a conduit in the garden by my dressing chamber, and flows eventually into the Yellow River. If my husband Kanki hears me and grants your request, I shall dissolve some powder in the conduit. The river water flowing white will tell you that all has gone well. In that case, enter the castle in good cheer. But if he does not grant your request, I shall dissolve some rouge in the water. The river water flowing red will tell you of failure. Go then to the gate and escort your mother from here. Watch the river water and you will see by the white damask or Chinese crimson whether good or ill fortune is your lot. Farewell!

NARRATOR: The moonlit gate is opened and the mother is led inside. She stands at the threshold of life and death, but instead of the Gate of Enlightenment, she is at the Gate of Delusion of this world.[70] The bolt drops with an ominous thud.

Kinshōjo's eyes grow dim: weakness is the way of the Chinese woman. Neither Watōnai nor Ikkan weeps: this is the way of the Japanese warrior. The opening and closing of the great gate resound like the firing of a catapult, the way of Tartary. The single echo makes them feel a huge distance separates them.

Scene Two: Inside Kanki's Residence.

NARRATOR: Only on journeying to distant China, a country she had never visited even in dreams, does the mother first learn what it means to have a daughter. They are joined by bonds of affection so strong

[70] Buddhist terms; instead of passing into the realm of enlightenment the mother is about to go to a place where she will suffer.

that the mother submits to criminal fetters, a rare instance even in foreign countries. Rare too, as the plum blossoms first opening in the snow, is their meeting; no interpreter is needed for the voices of the song thrushes, alike in note whether in China or Japan. Kinshōjo, deeply attentive to her mother, leads her to a room in her apartments. She arranges double layers of cushions and triple layers of quilts, politely offers delicacies from the mountains and sea and famous wines; her courtesy would do honor to heaven itself. But the bonds at elbows and wrists make the mother look like a criminal guilty of the Ten Villainies and the Five Inhuman Acts,[71] a sight too pitiful to behold. Kinshōjo waits on her devotedly, gentle as to her own mother, admirable in her solicitude.

Her maidservants gather round.

FIRST MAID: Have you ever seen a Japanese woman before? Her eyes and nose are like ours, but what a funny way she does her hair! See how peculiarly her clothes are sewn! I suppose the young women must dress the same. Her skirts and hem billow all the way out. Why, at the first gust of wind you could see all the way up to her thighs! Isn't it shameful?

SECOND MAID: I don't agree. If I have to be born as a woman again, I want to be a Japanese. I'll tell you why. Japan is called the Land of Great Gentleness.[72] Wouldn't a country where everyone is gentle be wonderful for a woman?

THIRD MAID: Yes, it certainly sounds so.

NARRATOR: They narrow their eyes enviously and nod. Kinshōjo approaches.

KINSHŌJO: Now what are you gossiping about with such pleasure?— Filial affection and duty both make me feel greater obligation to this mother who did not bear me than to my real mother. But, alas, I am forced by the laws of the country to bind her like a criminal. And I am worried lest my husband be blamed if the king of Tartary hears that we admitted her. Torn between fears for both, my role is the hardest to play. I ask you all to assist me.

[71] The Ten Villainies were the killing of living beings, theft, adultery, lying, the use of obscene language, cursing, being double-tongued, covetousness, anger, and foolishness. The Five Inhuman Acts were patricide, matricide, wounding Buddha's person, killing his immediate disciple, and murdering a Buddhist priest.

[72] The name Yamato is written with characters which mean literally "great gentleness".

I'm told that Japanese food is quite unlike our own. Ask my mother what she would like, and prepare it for her.

MAID: If it please you, my lady, we prepared a meal most carefully —rice cooked with longans, soup made with duck and fried beancurd, pork in sweet sauce, steamed lamb, and beef-paste cakes. We offered these dishes to her ladyship, but she only said, "How disagreeable! I don't like such food at all. I can't manage it with my hands tied. Please make something simple—*musubi* will do." I had no idea what kind of food *musubi* might be. I gathered everyone and asked their opinion. Somebody said that in Japan they call a *sumō* wrestler a *musubi*.[73] I searched everywhere for one, but it's a poor season for wrestlers, and I couldn't find a one to suit her taste.

NARRATOR: A carriage rumbles outside and the shout goes up, "His excellency has returned!" Chests of clothes are borne ahead of the carriage, and a splendid silken parasol shades Kanki—a dignified procession worthy of his high name. Kinshōjo goes out to meet him.

KINSHŌJO: You've returned earlier than I expected. What happened at court?

KANKI: The great king of Tartary was highly pleased with my achievements, and he granted a promotion in excess of my deserts. I have been appointed banner leader of one hundred thousand horsemen, with the rank of general of cavalry. He bestowed on me the headgear and court costume of a prince, and commanded me to perform important services. No higher honor could come to our house.

KINSHŌJO: I congratulate you. Good fortune has come twice to our house today. I have often told you how much I miss my father and long for him. Today he came to our gate with my Japanese mother and brother. He said that he had a request to make of you, but I told him that you were away. My father and brother, in deference to the strict laws of the country, have departed, but I have kept my mother with me. I feared, however, that the government might hear of this, and she was therefore bound with ropes before she entered the castle. I have offered her entertainment in the women's pavilion, but you can imagine how sad it makes me to see in criminal bonds my mother —though I am not of her flesh and blood.

KANKI: You were wise to have her bound. Now I have an excuse

---

[73] *Musubi* are cold rice balls; one class of wrestler is today called *ko-musubi*.

to offer if the government should learn of this. Treat her with the utmost kindness. But I should like to meet her myself. Please lead me to her.

NARRATOR: His voice must have carried: the mother cries out from the double doors.

MOTHER: Kinshōjo, has Lord Kanki returned? He does me too great an honor. It is for me to go to him.

NARRATOR: Her figure as she comes forward suggests an ancient pine twisted and bound with wisteria vine. Kanki's eyes are filled with pity as he watches her struggle painfully towards him.

KANKI: It is true—a mother will journey ten thousand leagues over mountains and rivers because she has a child somewhere in the world. But, alas, we are compelled by the laws of our times to bind you in this fashion. Wife, make sure that the ropes do not hurt your mother. I mean not the least disrespect towards so rare a guest. I promise that I shall grant whatever you may request, providing that it is within my competence. Tell me—there is no need to hesitate.

NARRATOR: His manner is extremely gentle. The old mother's expression relaxes.

MOTHER: Thank you. I feel I can trust you. Why should I hesitate, now that I have your assurance? I should like to tell you privately our important request. Please come closer.

NARRATOR: Her voice drops to a whisper.

MOTHER: Longing for our daughter has not been our only reason for coming to China. Early last winter the Princess Sendan, the younger sister of the Ming emperor, was blown ashore in a small boat at a place called the Beach of Matsura in Hizen Province. She told us that China had been seized by the Tartars. Your father was formerly a minister at the Ming court, and my son Watōnai, though he follows a humble fisherman's calling, has studied the texts of military science of both China and Japan. As soon as they heard the princess's story, they decided to overthrow the great king of Tartary and restore the former dynasty with the princess on the throne. We left the princess for the time being in Japan, and came ourselves to China. But, alas, how distressing it is to find that everything, even the plants and trees, sways before the Tartars. No one wishes to join the adherents of the Ming. Only one man can we trust to be Watōnai's right arm—you, Kanki. I implore you, sir—lend us your strength. I bow before you.

NARRATOR: She forces her forehead down to her knees; she seems possessed of but a single determination. Kanki is greatly surprised.

KANKI: So this Watōnai of Japan I've been hearing about is Kinshōjo's brother and the son of Tei Shiryū Ikkan! Even in China we're impressed by his bravery. His plan is promising and the obvious course. My forefathers were all vassals of the Ming, but after the death of the emperor there was no sovereign I could serve. I had no choice but to accept the rewards of Tartary. I was resigned to spending my days in this fashion, but your request now exactly fulfills my hopes. I should like to declare myself your ally on the spot, but the matter requires some further consideration, and I am not at liberty to assent immediately. I shall seriously consider your proposal and then make my reply.

NARRATOR: The mother interrupts.

MOTHER: How cowardly of you! You contradict yourself! Once so important a matter is mentioned, it becomes common knowledge. Supposing word leaks out while you are deliberating our proposal —no amount of regret will restore our cause if such a slip leads to defeat. We will bear you no grievance if you refuse, but whether your answer is yes or no, make it at once!

NARRATOR: She presses him for a reply.

KANKI: If you insist on an immediate answer, it is quite simple. Kanki most assuredly will be Watōnai's ally.

NARRATOR: Hardly has he finished these words than he catches Kinshōjo by the front of her kimono and pulls her to him. He draws his sword and presses it to her throat. The old mother rushes over in alarm and forces herself between them. She kicks away Kanki's hand that holds her daughter, then with her back pushes Kinshōjo down and lies over her in protection. She cries out in a loud voice.

MOTHER: Monster! What does this mean? Does Chinese custom compel you to stab your wife when you are asked a favor? Or is this rage directed at your wife because you were obliged by her relative to hear an offensive request? Or is it madness? Wicked man—you would kill your wife before her mother's eyes, the very first time I come to see her! I can imagine how you must behave on ordinary days! If you don't wish to join us, don't! My precious daughter, you have a mother now. You have nothing to fear any more. Hold tight to your mother!

NARRATOR: She sacrifices herself to become an intervening wall protecting her daughter. Kinshōjo cannot understand her husband's motives, but she is grateful for her mother's love.

KINSHŌJO: Don't hurt yourself!

NARRATOR: These are her only words; the two choke with tears. Kanki jumps back.

KANKI: Your doubts are natural, but I assure you that I am neither a villain nor mad. Yesterday the king of Tartary summoned me. He said, "An insignificant wretch named Watōnai has recently come here from Japan intending to overthrow the king of Tartary and restore the dynasty of the Ming. He is resourceful and well versed in military strategy, though a man of low birth and base demeanor. Who will punish this villain?"

Finally he chose me from among all the nobles present, and appointed me general of cavalry with a command of one hundred thousand men. I of course never dreamt that Watōnai was my wife's brother. I answered boldly, "Watōnai may know as much about military strategy as Kusunoki, or whatever that Japanese general's name was, and he may be bold as Asahina or Benkei, but I have mastered the essence of Chu-ko Liang's strategy.[74] I shall borrow the secrets of Fan K'uai and Hsiang Yü to pursue and rout him in a single engagement. I shall return with Watōnai's shaven head borne aloft on a pike."

If, after boasting in this manner, I should calmly become your son's ally without having crossed swords or shot a single arrow, I am sure that the Tartars would say—knowing Kanki is not a man to be frightened by tales of Japanese martial prowess—that I lost my courage and forgot my duties as a soldier because I was tied to my wife's apron strings and influenced by her relatives. If such is their gossip, my sons, grandsons, and even my remote descendants will be unable to escape disgrace. I would kill my dearly beloved wife in order to be able to join Watōnai cleanly—not influenced by his relation to my wife, and revering still the principles of justice and fidelity.

Kinshōjo—your mother's words when she stopped me were filled with compassion. The point of your husband's sword was tempered by a sense of loyalty. Give up your life, for your mother's love and for loyalty!

[74] Kusunoki Masashige, Asahina Yoshihide, and Musashibō Benkei were all Japanese military heroes. Chu-ko Liang and the two men mentioned in the next sentence were famous Chinese strategists.

NARRATOR: These are the unadorned words of a soldier.

KINSHŌJO: I understand. I am capable of such loyalty. I do not regret sacrificing for the sake of filial piety this body I have received from my parents.

NARRATOR: She pushes her mother aside and steps forward. She opens the front of her kimono, and draws to her the icy blade so terrible to behold.

MOTHER: Alas!

NARRATOR: She rushes up and tries to separate husband and wife, but in vain; she cannot use her hands to intervene. She catches her daughter's sleeve with her teeth and pulls her back, only for Kanki to come closer. She takes the husband's sleeve in her mouth, but the daughter approaches again, determined to die. Frantic as a mother cat carrying her kittens to a new nest, her eyes dim with the strain, and she falls with a cry. The mother seems oblivious to what happens around her. Kinshōjo clings to her.

KINSHŌJO: I never knew my mother before, and when I met her at last, I failed to perform a single act of daughterly affection. How shall I repay her for all her kindness? Please let me die instead, Mother.

NARRATOR: She pleads, laments, and bursts into tears.

MOTHER: What a sad thing to say! You have three parents, two in this world and one in the world of the dead. To your other two parents you owe the great debt of having been brought into this world. I am the only one who has failed to show you kindness or generosity. I shall not be able to rid myself of the name of a stepmother, however I try. If I allow you to die now, people will say that your Japanese stepmother hated her Chinese stepdaughter so much—though they were separated by three thousand leagues—that she had her put to death before her eyes. Such a report would disgrace not only me but Japan, for people would say, judging the country by my acts, that the Japanese were cruel-hearted. The sun that shines on China and the sun that shines on Japan are not two different lights, but the Land of the Rising Sun is its origin, and there you will find humanity, justice, and the other constant virtues. Could I, having been born in the Land of the Gods, where mercy is honored above all virtues, look on as my daughter is killed and then still go on living? I pray that these ropes that bind me will reveal themselves as the sacred ropes of the Japanese gods and strangle me on the spot. Then, though my corpse be exposed in a foreign country, may the ropes lead my soul to Japan!

NARRATOR: She raises her voice in tearful pleading, a voice filled with understanding, love, and pathos. Kinshōjo clings to her, and the mother's sleeve is wetted by the tears that both shed. Kanki too is persuaded by the mother's reasoning, and yields to helpless tears. After a while he strikes his chair impatiently.

KANKI: It can't be helped, then. I can do nothing to change matters. Your mother has refused to accept my plan. From this day forth Watōnai and I are enemies. But I do not wish it to be supposed that I detain our mother here as a hostage. Prepare a palanquin for her, and send her wherever she wishes to go.

KINSHŌJO: No, it won't be necessary to send her anywhere. I promised my brother that if I had good news I would drop white powder in this conduit flowing to the Yellow River, or, if his wish was not granted, that I would color the water with rouge. I shall dissolve some rouge in the water, and her companions will come to fetch her when they see the water flowing red.

NARRATOR: She goes into her chamber. Watōnai's mother is lost in thought, as she wonders what to tell her husband and son when she returns, now that everything has gone contrary to their hopes; her helpless tears of blood make a scarlet brocade, even before the rouge is set flowing. Kinshōjo in the meanwhile is dissolving rouge in an agate bowl.

KINSHŌJO: Thus the brocade bridge is cut before the father and daughter could cross.[75] Now is the moment of farewells.

NARRATOR: The rouge slips into the moonlit waters of the spring and rushes like the crimson leaves of autumn through the turbulent waters, telling the sad news. The bubbles in the garden stream, dyed the same hue, flow crimson through the conduit to the waters of the Yellow River. Watōnai sits on the bank, his straw raincoat thrown over him, watching the surface of the river to see if the water flows red or white.

WATŌNAI: Great heavens! The rouge is flowing! He's refused my request! I can't trust my mother to that villain Kanki who won't join me!

[75] Reference to poem 283 in the *Kokinshū:* "In Tatsuta River the red leaves seem to flow by in confused patterns. If I should cross, the brocade would be cut through the center."

NARRATOR: His feet rush forward furiously up the rapids of the river. When he reaches the moat at his destination, he leaps across, climbs the inner wall, tramples down wattled fences and lattice railings, and finally arrives at the spring within the garden of the women's apartments of Kanki's castle.

WATŌNAI: What a relief—Mother's safe!

NARRATOR: He flies to her and cuts the ropes that bind her. He plants himself squarely before Kanki.

WATŌNAI: So you're that bearded Chinese of a Kanki! I tied up my mother, the only one I'll ever have in heaven or on earth, because I honored you for what I thought you were, and because I wanted you for my ally. But the respect I paid you seems to have gone to your head. Is it because of my inadequacy as a general that you refuse to be my ally? I expected you to follow me, if only because your wife is my sister. I, Watōnai, peerless in all Japan, now make my request directly—answer me!

NARRATOR: He lays his hand on his sword hilt and draws himself up.

KANKI: You are all the less likely to succeed if you mention your relationship to my wife. You may be without peer in Japan, but I am the unique Kanki of China. I am not the kind of general who makes alliances because of his wife's influence, but I have no ground for divorcing her. Nor am I disposed to wait patiently for her to die. Take advantage of the favorable breeze and leave at once. Or would you prefer to give me your head as a memento?

WATŌNAI: No! I'll take yours back to Japan as a souvenir of my visit!

NARRATOR: Both are about to draw their swords when Kinshōjo cries out.

KINSHŌJO: See! You won't have to wait for me to die! Here is the source of the crimson water!

NARRATOR: She opens the front of her robe to reveal that she has stabbed herself, slashing diagonally with her dagger from under her breast to her liver. The mother cries out and swoons at the sight of the wound bathed in crimson. Watōnai is also dumbfounded, and even Kinshōjo's husband, who had been ready to kill her, is stunned. Kinshōjo speaks painfully.

KINSHŌJO: Mother would not let me be killed for fear of the disgrace it might bring to Japan. But if I begrudge my life and fail to help my parents and my brother, it will be a disgrace to China. (*To Kanki.*) Now that I have stabbed myself, no one will slander you by saying that you were under your wife's influence. Kanki, please join my father and brother and become a source of strength to them. Tell my father of this too.—Please say no more. Oh, I am in pain!

NARRATOR: These are her only words before she loses consciousness. Kanki hides his tears.

KANKI: Nobly done! I promise that your suicide will not have been in vain.

NARRATOR: He bows his head before Watōnai.

KANKI: My ancestors were vassals of the Ming, and I should gladly have joined you, but I feared that people might say I had been led astray by a relative of my wife. She has killed herself in order to encourage me on the path of justice. I can now become your ally honorably. I look up to you as my commanding general, and I shall offer you a new name, one fit for a supreme prince. I give you the name Coxinga, lord of the imperial surname, Tei Seikō, prince of Empei.[76] Pray wear the robes of your office.

NARRATOR: Kanki draws forth from a Chinese chest, that opens as Coxinga's fortunes have opened, a scarlet court robe of double-thickness brocade, the sleeves óf gauzy and figured silks, a ceremonial hat, shoes with floral patterns, a belt set with coral and amber, and a sword of polished gold. A silken parasol is lifted above Coxinga's head, and a hundred thousand or more troops line up before him, armored sleeve against sleeve, bearing imperial flags with pendant streamers, conical ensigns, shields, spears, bows, and muskets: it seems as though the king of Yüeh had come a second time to Kuai-chi Mountain.[77]

Coxinga's mother cries out joyfully.

MOTHER: What a glorious day! My hopes have been realized! See, Kinshōjo—because of your sacrifice the prayers of my husband and son have been granted. But these prayers are not ours alone—they are shared by the whole world. This dagger is a mere nine and a half inches long, but your suicide has determined the destiny of all China. For me to prolong my life now would render false my first words, and bring further shame on Japan.

[76] For the historical circumstances behind Coxinga's names, see Keene, *The Battles of Coxinga*, p. 46.
[77] See n. 9, above.

NARRATOR: She seizes her daughter's dagger and plunges it into her own throat. Everyone exclaims in horror, but she calls out.

MOTHER: Don't come any closer!

NARRATOR: She glares fiercely about her.

MOTHER: Kanki, Coxinga. Under no circumstances must you lament or grieve over the death of your mother and her daughter. Consider the king of Tartary as the enemy of us both, and you will be strengthened in your vengeance. Do not forget these last words of a mother whose kindness consisted in not allowing your determination to relent. (*To Watōnai.*) Your father Ikkan is still alive, and you will not want for a parent. Your mother exhorts you by dying; your father, living on, will continue to instruct you. With such guidance you should become a great general with perfect accomplishments.—My thoughts of this fleeting world go no farther.

NARRATOR: She thrusts the dagger in again and twists it, severing the bundle of her liver.[78]

MOTHER: Kinshōjo, do you feel no regret at leaving this world?

KINSHŌJO: What regret should I feel?

NARRATOR: Her words are brave, but regret lingers for the husband she leaves behind. Mother and daughter take each other's hands and nestle together. They look up and down Coxinga's robes of office, then expire at the same moment, the happy smiles on their faces a memento for this world.

Coxinga, so bold that he might be mistaken for a devil, and Kanki, courageous as a dragon or tiger, are overwhelmed by tears. But Coxinga is determined not to disobey his mother's injunctions, and Kanki not to violate his wife's noble purpose. Coxinga is ashamed to weep before Kanki, and Kanki before Coxinga; they hide their downcast faces.

Along the road over which the sad remains are borne to the grave, the army sets out for battle. The quick and the dead take the same road. For Coxinga his mother's last words were like a sermon to Buddha;[79] his father's instructions will be an iron bar in a devil's hands. When he fights he will triumph; when he attacks he will conquer all before him. Here is a warrior endowed with wisdom and love, a marvel of the ages.

[78] It was believed in Japan that the liver had seven lobes joined together at the top.

[79] A proverbial expression of unnecessary instruction: Coxinga is determined to restore the Ming even without his mother's admonition. The iron bar in the devil's hands is another proverbial phrase, meaning to make stronger what is already strong.

The banks of a pool which holds a jewel cannot be broken;
The pond where a dragon lives will never run dry.[80]

The country which has produced such a hero is a well-ordered country, and its prince is a true prince. Here is the prodigy of Japan, a man who illuminates a foreign land with the brilliance of his martial talents.

ACT FOUR

Scene One: Before the Shrine of Sumiyoshi in Matsura.
Time: Autumn of the same year.

NARRATOR: The days and nights at Komutsu's house by the Beach of Matsura have been spent in anxious waiting for news from China. The Chinese princess living with Komutsu has become the subject of the neighbors' gossip; they suspect that she may be a countryless wanderer from the isles where the waves of China and Japan come together.[81]

When Komutsu learned that her husband had changed his name to Coxinga, lord of the imperial surname, and become the commanding general of many tens of thousands of troops, her heart leapt with excitement, and she at once assumed male attire. Her sidelocks are now combed back to form a thick queue, and her glossy backlocks hang loosely behind: she might be the son of a Shinto priest or an ointment seller,[82] but hardly a woman. She wears light blue breeches and a cloak, and carries a wooden sword in a vermilion scabbard with a scarlet sword knot. Her rouged lips are like a flower, her face white with snowy powder. Her wicker hat is pulled deep over her face, but her skirts are lifted high as she steps lightly as a plover along the beach on her daily visit of prayers to the Sumiyoshi shrine of Matsura.

She arrives before the shrine and joins her hands in fervent prayer:

[80] This passage, quoted from the Chinese classic *Hsün-tzu*, means here that a country which has produced a hero like Coxinga is invincible, just as a pond which holds a dragon can never run dry.

[81] *Chikura* designated the region between Japan and China, and is sometimes identified with the island of Tsushima.

[82] The reference is not clear, but it has been suggested that a Shinto priest would be especially well groomed. Ointment sellers (particularly those of Seikenji) were young men whose full head of hair and dandified appearance attracted customers. See Statler, *Japanese Inn*, pp. 158–59.

"May my vows be fulfilled!" The next instant, still kneeling, she has whipped out her sword, a feat of dexterity. She jumps up and, wooden sword held high, assaults with bold shouts her opponent, a sacred pine. Swift as summer lightning or the lion in his leap, her hands and feet move nimbly as she wields her broadsword, now high, now low, skillfully feinting and dodging. She charges in and fells with a stroke of her wooden blade a branch from the ancient tree. Here indeed is a latter-day Ushiwaka.[83]

The Princess Sendan—how long has she been watching Komutsu here?—runs up from the forest shadows.

SENDAN: Komutsu—every day at the same hour you leave the house in that strange costume. Today at last I have followed you and discovered where you went. Who taught you to use a sword? I marvel at your skill.

KOMUTSU: I've never had a teacher. I merely imitate what I've observed of my husband's sword practice.

We don't know when word may be coming from China, but I intend, even if no ship is sent for us, to accompany you over the seas. I have been praying to the god here for a sign whether we would be successful or fail, and look! I cut a branch from the pine with a wooden sword, exactly as if I had used a steel blade! It must be a sign that the god has granted my prayers! A merchant ship happens to be sailing today for China—let's take passage aboard her!

SENDAN: With great pleasure. I am sure that all will go well. Please take me back to China as soon as possible.

NARRATOR: She is overjoyed.

KOMUTSU: Have no fears. Sumiyoshi, the god of this shrine, is the protecting divinity of the sea lanes. When the Empress Jingū embarked on her conquest of Korea, he used his ebb-tide pearl and flood-tide pearl[84] to guard her ship. That is why they call him also the god of ships. Many years ago a man from China named Haku Rakuten[85] crossed to the Islands of the Dragonfly,[86] thinking to test the wisdom of Japan. As soon as he saw the scenery before his eyes he wrote a poem:

---

[83] The youthful name of Minamoto Yoshitsune (1159–89).

[84] These treasures are enshrined at the Matsura shrine of Sumiyoshi today.

[85] The Japanese pronunciation of Po Lo-t'ien (or Po Chü-i). For this legend, see Waley, *The Nō Plays of Japan*, pp. 205–13. The two poems in fact have nothing to do with Po Chü-i.

[86] A poetic name for Japan.

Green moss donned like a cloak
Lies on the shoulders of the rocks.
White clouds like a sash
Girdle the mountain's waist.

The great god Sumiyoshi, appearing in the guise of a humble old fisherman, recited a poem in reply:

Strange, that the rocks have no sash,
Though they wear a cloak of moss,
And that the cloakless mountain
Should have to wear a girdle! [87]

Rakuten, at a loss to match this poem, returned at once to his country, they say. My traveling robe will be the moss cloak the god sang of in his poem, the god who protects our country. Let us be on our way!

NARRATOR: They set off together. Their path across the water stretches distantly before them.

Scene Two: The journey of the Princess Sendan from Hirado to China.

NARRATOR:

In a Chinese hairdo, a Satsuma comb,
In a Shimada hairdo, a Chinese comb:
Yamato and Cathay are blended here.[88]
How uncertainly they face the journey ahead!
On their way by boat and by land
They must keep with them their bamboo hats
And pillows folded inside their kimonos
On which the dreams of many nights will unfold,
Resolved to voyage a thousand leagues:
A woman's courage is roused by love for a man.

KOMUTSU:

I leave on a journey that takes me from home,
Yours is a journey back to your land.
How different our lots, but yours is the brighter!

[87] The poem is a satirical rejoiner based on the conceit that "cloaks" and "sashes" should go together.
[88] Sendan wears a Japanese comb in her hair and Komutsu wears a Chinese comb in hers; in this way the two countries are united.

NARRATOR:

> Sendan is strengthened by Komutsu's reproach,
> And plucks up courage for the voyage to China.
> How distant her thoughts now range!

SENDAN:

> Why should she, with a husband and parents, grieve?
> The daybreak moon itself will be the same,
> But she will remember with many regrets
> The moon they shared in their marriage chamber.

NARRATOR:

> At Ōmura Bay the beach wind brings a shower
> That splashes but to clear, as tears do not,
> Tears they conceal and with trailing sleeves wipe
> At Mirror Shrine, where they leave their reflections.
> Will people see at Seaweed Bay that they weep not?
> They stare westward at the course of the moon,
> The distant sky of their destination.

KOMUTSU:

> When shall we return? Heaven-flying geese,
> Tempt him, tempt my husband back to me.
> Twenty-five the years that we've been pledged,[89]
> Twenty-five, like the strings of my lute.
> I'll play, and when in Hakozaki's pines
> I hear he pines for me, I'll hurry forward.

NARRATOR:

> Along the beach the children of fisherfolk
> Who gather drifting seaweed are clustered,
> Playing jacks and marbles, odd or even,
> Counting three, four, five—happy, childish games.
> Even the water plays at hide-and-seek
> On its way to the Pool of Seven Rapids,[90]
> Hiding the reflections of old-time lovers.
> The children sing, "Before the devil comes!" [91]
> —The women's sleeves are wet with tears that do not dry.
> They wait at Matsura River for the China boat;

[89] Perhaps meaning that Watōnai and Komutsu were destined from birth to be married.
[90] A series of numbers runs through the lines, from three to seven. The pool adjoins the Matsura River.
[91] "The devil" is the "it" in a game of hide-and-seek.

The harbor is swept by winds from Nearby Bay.
The princess glances at the harbor shore:
In Kuriya River, where nets are hauled from the bank,
Aboard a fishing boat rocked by the waves,
A boy with parted hair [92] is fast asleep,
His net not lowered, a string dangling from his pole.

SENDAN: Say there, my lad! We are travelers bound for China. Please take us part of the way aboard your boat.

BOY: That's simple enough! One of you, I see, is Chinese, and the other from Tsukushi. There must be someone you love in China for you ladies to be traveling there! I'm sure you're yearning for lovers two thousand leagues away.[93] This is not the night of the full moon, but now, while no one can see, come quickly aboard my boat. It will sail like the moon through the sky.

NARRATOR: He punts his boat closer with his water-wise pole.

BOTH WOMEN: What strange chance is this?

NARRATOR: They board his boat, and at once he rows out towards their unknown destination. The white waves calm, and their boat glides over the smooth surface of the sea.

SENDAN: What are all those islands we can see? Would you please tell a stranger as a memento of this journey?

NARRATOR: The boy steps up to the prow and points in the distance over the broad expanse of sea.

BOY: Listen well, travelers! First, stretching off out there, are the twelve islands of Kikai, one group of five and the other of seven. That one, where flocks of white birds are poised, is Whitestone Island, and there, where the smoke rises, is Sulphur Island. The tall island to the south hung with mist is Chido. And that island is called Two Gods because in ancient times two gods sported there, the goddess Amaterasu dancing to Sumiyoshi's flute. What say you to that, my Chinese lady?

NARRATOR: Even as he speaks they have left Japan behind, and the islands ahead, or what seem to be islands, are peaks of clouds; what seem to be mountains rise in the sky and not in the sea. No wind stirs, but the little skiff races ahead as once the bird boat and rock

[92] In ancient times, as we may gather from works of art, boys wore their hair parted in the middle and tied at the ears. This style, completely out of fashion in Chikamatsu's day, suggests that the boy in the boat has something supernatural about him.

[93] Allusion to lines by Po Chü-i: "When on the night of the fifteenth moonlight bathes anew the sky, I think of old friends two thousand leagues away."

boat of Heaven [94] flew through the sky. Mountains appear to the west, where no mountains had been. Faster than the moon, apace with the sun, they reach the habor of Sung-chiang [95] where men are still fishing for sea bass in an autumn wind exactly like the wind that blew when they left the Land of the Rising Sun. They step ashore from the boat.

SENDAN: Our passage has been smooth as if we sat in our parlor, truly thanks to you, my lad. Who might you be who have carried us in an instant across the high seas?

BOY: You talk as if I were a mortal man! I am without a name, but people call me the Boy of the Sea from Sumiyoshi because I have dwelled from ancient times in the Land of the Rising Sun.[96] I say good-by to you now and go back to Sumiyoshi, where I shall await your return to Japan.

NARRATOR: He rows his skiff back from the shore with the evening waves, and favored by the breeze he moves out to the open sea, far out to the open sea.

Scene Three: The Mountain of the Nine Immortals.

NARRATOR: It is related how T'ao-chu Kung served Kou Chien. He shut himself up at Kuai-chi Mountain where he plotted various stratagems, finally crushing the king of Wu and satisfying Kou Chien's dreams of revenge.[97]

In ancient days, in times far removed from the present, there was such an example; today this is Go Sankei's fate. He wanders from mountain to cloud-covered mountain, hiding his identity and rearing the prince. With the reversal of his fortunes, he has learned to sleep on moss for his mattress; the willows in front of the palace and the blossoms before the royal halls have given way to withered trees on mountain peaks. When the evening mists settle, Go Sankei makes a blanket of his body to warm the infant prince; and for the prince to ride in, he fashions a handcart of ivy vines in place of a brocaded

---

[94] Boats used by the Japanese gods in the old legends.

[95] Sung-chiang was famous for its sea bass. Chikamatsu undoubtedly learned this fact from Su Tung-p'o's poem *The Red Cliff*.

[96] The name Sumiyoshi contains the word *sumi* (dwelled).

[97] T'ao-chu Kung was another name for Fan Li. His loyal service to the king of Yüeh. Kou Chien, is described in n. 9, above.

palanquin. When the morning dews lie thick, the prince rides on the shoulders of the valley monkeys. Two years have passed, quickly as yesterday turning to today. Their nights are spent in mountains, their days are passed in mountains. Go Sankei in his journeys hides his own name and the prince's face from the eyes of men. The rainbow bridge to the world has been broken by clouds; the cries of the crows and night birds deep in the mountains, and even the voices of the parrots [98] screeching at the tops of the trees suggest nothing of the past.

Go Sankei has been pushing his way through bamboo underbrush, and through thickets of black pine and cypress, far from any water, deep in the mountains. He wearily struggles up a steep mountain road towards the towering summit of the Mountain of Nine Immortals in Hsing-hua-fu, known to him only by name. As he pauses a while he notices two old men with shaggy eyebrows and white hair, seemingly in perfect harmony with the pine breeze, as friends who have lived together long years. They have put a go [99] board on a rock before them, and are utterly absorbed in their game, watching the black and white stones form scattered pockets or diagonal lines like flights of geese over the 361 intersections. Their thoughts move freely, like a spider's thread in the air, and their bodies have become empty cocoons on a withered branch. This is the art of conversing by hand, far removed from the usages of the world.

GO SANKEI: Can this be the pure world of Brahma? [100]

NARRATOR: He transfers the prince to a ledge in the rocks and, leaning his chin on a withered stump, gazes in fascination on the game, purified of the dust of worldly concern. Carried away, he cries out.

GO SANKEI: Old gentlemen, I should like a word with you. I am interested to see you play the game of go. Is there some special pleasure to be found in this contest played without the help of the Three Friends—music, poetry, and wine?

NARRATOR: One old man, not seeming to answer, speaks.

OLD MAN: If it looks like a go board to you, it is a go board, and for

[98] The parrot was an exotic bird, and Chikamatsu therefore places it for local color in the Chinese mountains.

[99] A game played with black and white stones on a board. Proficiency in the game is believed to be akin to a mastery of military tactics.

[100] A stage of enlightenment at which one transcends all earthly desires, reached in this case by absorption in the game of go.

the eye that sees *go* stones, they are merely *go* stones. But there is a text which likens the world to a *go* board. For those who see with their minds, the center of the universe is here. From this vantage point, what will cloud our view of the mountains, rivers, grasses, or trees of all China? The ninety intersections in each quarter of the board represent the ninety days of each of the four seasons. Together they come to 360.[101] How foolish of you not to realize that we spend one day on each intersection!

GO SANKEI: Extraordinary! But why should you two oppose each other as your sole pleasure in heaven and earth?

OLD MAN: If there were not both yin and yang there would be no order in creation.

GO SANKEI: And the result of your contest?

OLD MAN: Does not the good or bad fortune of mankind depend on the chance of the moment?

GO SANKEI: And the black and the white?

OLD MAN: The night and the day.

GO SANKEI: What are the rules of the game?

OLD MAN: The stratagems of war.

GO SANKEI: Breaking up formations, checking, opening offensives . . .

NARRATOR: In *go* as in war the sparks are set flying. The black and the white may be likened to crows in restless flight or to clusters of snowy herons. How natural that before this spectacle a king of old lost track of the days and the nights, and his axe handle rotted before he knew it!

The old man speaks again.

OLD MAN: A heroic general named Coxinga has crossed here from Japan and taken up the Ming cause. He is now in the midst of a battle. The scene of the fighting is far from here, but the power of vision that comes from concentration on *go* will permit you to see how the battle progresses, plainly before your eyes.

NARRATOR: His voice and the mountain wind echo in the sound of the *go* stones. Go Sankei suddenly realizes where he is.

GO SANKEI: This must be the Mountain of the Nine Immortals that commands a view of all China!

[101] There are actually 361 intersections, ninety in each quarter plus one in the middle, but Chikamatsu says 360 here because he wishes to make a parallel with the 360 days in a year of the lunar calendar.

NARRATOR: He gazes at a distant peak, faintly visible—or is it a cloud? The veil of mist descends to the foot of the mountain, where it is blown away by a spring breeze, to reveal a mid-April sky.[102] He can clearly see a castle swathed in the brocade of mingled willow shoots and cherry blossoms. What man of what country has fortified himself here? The gates are high and the moat is deep. Shielding walls have been erected around the encampment, and an imposing tower rises boldly at the heart of the fortress. The soaring larks and the wild geese returning, mistaking the many-colored pennants for flowers, might approach to rest their wings. In the gentle sunlight of a spring morning, flags marked with the sun and the moon display the fair name of Japan to the world. It hardly need be said that this is Shih-t'ou Castle, captured by Coxinga, prince of Empei.

Here are white sandalwood bows, muskets, Korean spears, lances, and halberds; flags large and small incline to one another; conical ensigns, shrine banners, and the general's standard flap in the wind. They tint the heavens in every hue, as if the wisteria, azaleas and primroses of the season are reflected skywards. But even as Go Sankei watches the flowers blossom and fall, the days of spring are piling up like stones on a *go* board.

The young leaves have grown out and turned a deep green, and through a rift in the clearing clouds appears the Cloud Gate Pass to Nanking. Cuckoos fly singing from the gate and verbena hedges grow tall as tents. It is mid-summer of the year.

GO SANKEI: For thirty leagues around felled trees have been laid, points towards the enemy. The generals of the pass Saryōko and Uryōko guard it with three thousand troops.

OLD MAN: The stars on their helmets shine.

GO SANKEI: They beat their drums wildly.

OLD MAN: Even if one could i-

GO SANKEI: -mi-

BOTH OLD MEN: -tate the crowing of the cocks, one could never get through such a stronghold.[103] Swords are thick as pampas grass in a summer meadow, and rope matches glow like fire-

[102] The battles to be narrated occur in the four seasons, beginning with spring, with appropriate descriptions for each.

[103] From a poem (*Goshūishū*, no. 940) by Sei Shōnagon: "The dawn has not come; even though you imitate the crowing of the cock, you won't be able to get through Ōsaka Pass where we might meet." The allusion is to the story of a nobleman who

flies in a marsh. Not even a bird could slip through the gate of this imposing barrier.

NARRATOR: Coxinga was reared in Japan, and it would be easier for him to smash through this barrier, even if it were fortified with iron and stone, than for a child to break a single thickness of paper window. But drawing to mind the catalpa bow of Musashibō Benkei who, long ago in the Bunji era [104] of his country, tricked the barrier keeper at Ataka, a glorious martial exploit, he winks a signal to his men and cries.

COXINGA: Hear ye! Hear ye! This is the foot of Mount Li, the site of the grave of Yang Kuei-fei.[105] We are itinerant priests gathering funds wherewith to build again the T'ai-chen Palace. Listen to our Book of Gifts and pray subscribe, O gatekeeper.

NARRATOR: He produces an attendance roll of his troops and, praying in his heart for the success of his forces and the downfall of the enemy, he reads aloud.

COXINGA: The autumn moon of enlightment lies hidden by pitiless clouds from the Tartars and rebels, but none can yet raise them from their long uncertain dream of life and death. Here in days gone by lived an emperor whose name was Hsüan Tsung. When he lost the beautiful princess he dearly loved, he could not master his longing, and tears, like strings of pearls, flowed from his eyes. Then, turning his thoughts to her repose in the world of the dead, he built in her memory the T'ai-chen Palace. I, a descendant of the magician from Lin-ch'iung, grieving that so holy a place should come to ruin, am soliciting funds throughout the land. Those who fight on the enemy's side even in a single battle will have their heads transfixed by our spears; those who fight for us will raise shouts of triumph after the victory. I bow my head in devotion and respect.

NARRATOR: He reads, loud enough to make the heavens resound. Saryōko and Uryōko, the guardians of the barrier, cry out.

---

actually succeeded in getting through the barrier at night by imitating a cock's crows so skillfully that the barrier keeper opened the gate, thinking it was dawn. The effect of divided speech here was achieved by several chanters performing the different parts.
[104] The Bunji era was 1185–89. The following passage is based on a scene in the Nō play *Ataka*. The Kabuki version in *Kanjinchō* is well known.
[105] Coxinga changes the names in the passage from *Ataka* to suitable Chinese ones, substituting Yang Kuei-fei for the consort of the Emperor Shōmu and the T'ai-chen Palace for the Tōdaiji.

SARYŌKO AND URYŌKO: Look! Coxinga has flown like a summer moth into the flames!

NARRATOR: They attack, humming like cicadas in a treetop. Coxinga smiles at their folly.

COXINGA: Fan K'uai's style was not so remarkable—see how Asahina of Japan used to break down gates!

NARRATOR: He rips through the gate bar and the tangle of felled trees. He knocks down those who oppose him and, catching those who flee, tosses them like pebbles. He slays Saryōko and Uryōko and easily passes the barrier. The months and days too are passing on the *go* board, and an autumn wind can be heard blowing from the barrier. The mists clear over the mountain castle where the Tartar general Prince Kairi is entrenched. Before the castle is a precipice, and behind it is the sea. Coxinga, noting the carelessness that reliance on the fortress breeds, stages an attack this autumn night. As he rides his horse the bit tinkles clearly, like the cry of an insect awaiting the moon. His troops stealthily advance to the castle moat. Suddenly, as one man, they raise thousands of paper lanterns on poles. It is like seeing the thousand suns and moons of a thousand worlds in one instant, and the soldiers of the castle, dumfounded, scurry about in wild consternation. They buckle their helmets around their knees, don their armor upside down, carry their horses on their backs. Shouting hysterically, they throw open the front gate of the castle, and pour out, waving their swords. The attackers raise war cries to the accompaniment of horns and gongs. Coxinga signals his men with his commander's fan.

The Japanese style of battle command includes Yoshitsune's method of attacking and crushing the enemy, and Kusunoki's of catching the enemy off guard and then striking.

Here, as at the rout of Kurikara, the downhill charge at Ichinotani, or the battle on the beach at Yashima, the attackers are irresistible, and the enemy, cut to pieces, withdraws towards the castle. "Now is our chance!" cries Coxinga, and in the evening darkness his men light hand grenades, the secret Japanese weapon, which they hurl at the enemy. The roar of the explosion is loud enough to make one think Mount Shumi [106] is crumbling. From the battlements and tower pour smoke thick as from the shore where fishermen burn salt or from a charcoal kiln. The flames suggest masses of crimson leaves in autumn,

[106] Sumeru, the central mountain of the Buddhist universe.

or the Hsien-yang Palace reduced to ashes by the torch of the man from Ch'u.[107]

Coxinga, raising a shout of victory, pulls back his horse's reins, and rides round and round in triumph; and, as the months and days roll around, faithful in their course, the early winter rains have begun to fall. The rains lift to reveal a high-gated citadel by a hill. This is Ch'ang-lo Castle in Foochow, captured by Coxinga. The glittering tiles at the eaves give the color of jewels to the first hail, falling and piling. A night storm mingled with sleet blows. How wonderful to see the walls and towers buried in the snow!

Coxinga has captured thirty-eight other strongholds in Min, Ken, and other provinces.[108] In anticipation of the future visit of the crown prince, he has erected outworks at different places, and provided them with military stores and garrisons. His might may be sensed in the air itself.

These sights are so clearly visible to Go Sankei that he feels he can almost touch them. In his excess of joy he forgets himself and the others with him, and clasping the crown prince in his arms, rushes off towards the castled mountain. The two old men stay him.

FIRST OLD MAN: How foolish of you! All you have witnessed, though it seemed to take place directly before your eyes, has in fact occurred hundreds of leagues away. You may think that but a moment has passed since you came to this mountain, but you have spent here the springs and autumns of five whole years. You do not suspect, do you, that these battles you have watched were fought during the four seasons of four different years. Even as I speak, the months and the days are passing. See how the prince has grown, and look well at your own face reflected in the water. The water is pure, and the reflection will be true. I, who stand reflected in the mirror of your loyal and faithful heart, am the first sovereign of the Ming.

SECOND OLD MAN: And I am Liu Po-wen of Ch'ing-t'ien.[109]

BOTH OLD MEN: Our home is the moon, where the leaves of the laurel, blown over,

---

[107] The Hsien-yang Palace was the residence of Ch'in Shih-huang, the first emperor of China. It was burnt by Hsiang Yü, "the man from Ch'u" (233–202 B.C.).

[108] Either Min or Ken might refer to Fukien Province; probably Chikamatsu was none too sure of his Chinese geography.

[109] Usually known as Liu Chi (1311–75), one of the most celebrated among the counselors of the founder of the Ming dynasty.

SECOND OLD MAN: Appear to the eyes that see true the waxing

FIRST OLD MAN: And the waning, but

SECOND OLD MAN: The ordinary man, confused of mind, takes it for a mere contest between *go* stones.[110]

FIRST OLD MAN: The fish swimming in the water

SECOND OLD MAN: Mistakes it for a fishhook.

FIRST OLD MAN: The bird soaring above the clouds

SECOND OLD MAN: Is frightened, thinking it a bow.

FIRST OLD MAN: The moon does not descend,

SECOND OLD MAN: Nor do the waters rise.

BOTH OLD MEN: Behold the abiding moon whose light waxes but to wane, and wanes but to wax again. Though hidden a while in clouds, in the end it will be free and illumine the world.[111] The day will soon dawn when the crown prince assumes his office, with the help of the divine strength of Japan, the Land of the Rising Sun.

NARRATOR: Their voices blend with the wind through the pines. For a moment their images linger on, but they too presently vanish in the wind from the peak of the pine-clad mountain.

Go Sankei, dazed, wonders if he has dreamed, but he has not been sleeping. And, a sign that five years have indeed elapsed, a long beard has grown on his face. The prince's appearance has changed in the wink of an eye: he has the height and bearing of a seven-year-old. His voice calling, "Go Sankei, Go Sankei!" is grave beyond his years, and recalls to Go Sankei the first cries of the song thrush heard deep in snow-covered mountains. He bows his head in response, then worships Heaven and Earth, so overjoyed that his legs are unsteady, and he feels again that he may be dreaming.

He brings his hands together reverently before the prince.

GO SANKEI: I have heard reports that Coxinga, the only son of the former minister Tei Shiryū, has come from Japan and raised a loyal army in our cause. His military exploits during the past five years have been brilliant, and he has already retaken half the empire of the great Ming. I should like to communicate with Coxinga, and inform him that your highness is here.

[110] The dark side of the leaves of the laurel creates the impression of the waning moon; the ignorant man, not realizing this, imagines that he sees black *go* stones triumphing over white *go* stones when the moon wanes.

[111] The moon here stands for the Ming power.

NARRATOR: Scarcely has he spoken than from the other side of the valley a voice calls.

IKKAN: Is that not Go Sankei, president of the council of war, across the valley? Go Sankei! Go Sankei!

NARRATOR: Go Sankei gazes in the direction of the voice.

GO SANKEI: Are you Tei Shiryū, the former minister?

IKKAN: Go Sankei! What a miracle that we should both be alive and able to meet here! My son Coxinga's wife has escorted the Princess Sendan to China from Japan.

NARRATOR: He beckons, and the princess comes forward.

SENDAN: Dear Go Sankei! I escaped in a drifting boat thanks to your wife Ryūkakun's self-sacrificing devotion, and I was carried by the wind over a sea of griefs to Japan. Now, the kindness of Ikkan and his family has brought us the blessing of this extraordinary reunion! Where is Ryūkakun? What has become of your baby? I should like to see them as soon as possible. Please take me to them.

NARRATOR: Her longing is natural.

GO SANKEI: Alas, my wife perished from the severe wounds she received at the time. The empress also lost her life to the enemy guns, and I cut open her womb to deliver her child. Later I killed my own son to throw the enemy off the track. Since then I have been rearing the prince safely in these mountains. He is already seven years old. He is with me now.

NARRATOR: The princess utters a cry of dismay at the news, and falls to the ground where she weeps, heedless of the others' eyes; her grief stirs them to pity.

Ikkan turns back to the foot of the mountain.

IKKAN: Look! That villain Prince Bairoku has discovered the princess, and he has come now in pursuit with thousands of men. I shall summon up the strength left in these old bones, stand my ground, and defend her to the death!

NARRATOR: His words are brave, but the princess's life is in danger.

IKKAN: If only I could escape with her to the other side of the valley! But I don't know my way in these mountains. Is there no way across?

GO SANKEI: No, it is sixty leagues around the mountains, and the gorge is bottomless. I cannot lead you here, nor can I cross the valley to you. What shall we do? What is there to do?

NARRATOR: He bows to the empty air.

GO SANKAI: First Emperor of the Ming and Liu Po-wen of Ch'ing-t'ien who showed yourselves but a moment ago in a miraculous revelation! Vouchsafe your wondrous, immortal strength and rescue us from this grave peril!

NARRATOR: The crown prince prays by his side in single-hearted devotion. The princess and Komutsu also join their hands in prayer.

SENDAN *and* KOMUTSU: Hail to the great god Sumiyoshi of Japan, gatherer of happiness boundless as the sea!

NARRATOR: They earnestly pray with undivided hearts. Heaven is moved and Earth hears their prayers: from a crevice in the mountains a stream of cloud issues forth and trails idly across the gorge to form a bridge in the sky. Is this the bridge the magpies built with their wings for the lovers to cross? [112] It spans the abyss like the stone bridge of Kume, built by the god of Katsuragi, though night has not fallen.[113] They climb to the peak on the other side of the valley as in a dream, with no sensation of crossing the bridge or even of moving. Their legs tremble under them.

Soon afterwards the rebel soldiers surge up in swarms.

SOLDIERS: Look—the crown prince and Go Sankei too! What an unexpected haul! We've cast our nets for sardines and come up with a whale! They're fair targets for us! Get your bows and muskets ready! Shoot them down! Kill them!

NARRATOR: They jostle together in wild excitement. Prince Bairoku shouts his commands.

BAIROKU: Wait! They have plenty of room behind them to escape. Bows and muskets can't take care of them. Look—a cloud bridge! That's something I've never seen before. No doubt Coxinga's brought it from Japan, this abacus bridge or folding bridge or whatever it is. What a clumsy piece of strategy—providing his enemy with a weapon! Follow me, men! Over the bridge!

NARRATOR: More than five hundred soldiers storm eagerly onto the bridge, shouting and pushing to be first across. When they are about at the mid-point, a mountain wind and a valley wind spring up and

---

[112] A famous Chinese legend tells how on one night of the year the magpies build a bridge with their wings over which the Herd Boy and the Weaving Girl (two stars) cross to meet.

[113] Because the god of Katsuragi was so ugly that he was ashamed to be seen by day, he built his bridge at night.

blow to shreds the bridge of clouds. The general and his men plummet one after the other to the bottom of the gorge, where heads are split and skulls are crushed. Groaning and shrieking, they pile ever higher.

Go Sankei and Tei Shiryū cry, "Victory! Hurrah! Wonderful!" They seize rocks, logs, whatever comes to hand, and fling them at the Tartars until not a man is left alive. In a moment's time the enemy horde is converted to mincemeat. Only the general, Prince Bairoku, has managed to escape, climbing up a vine that grows along the base of the cliff. Go Sankei lifts the *go* board of the immortals and shouts.

GO SANKEI: This *go* board has been kneaded of taro root, and is harder than stone. It's bitter, and I daresay it won't suit your taste, but how about a bite? You've only one *go* stone left to play, and you're not much of an opponent now! See what a strong game is like!

NARRATOR: When Bairoku shows his head, Go Sankei smacks it squarely; when he shows his face, Go Sankei strikes it smartly. He belabors Bairoku with repeated blows, till brains and skull are smashed to bits, and he perishes.

IKKAN: You've fulfilled my hopes! There's a similar example in Japanese history too, Tadanobu and his *go* board at Yoshino.[114] Tadanobu's board was of *kaya* wood,[115] this of taro root from the Mountain of Nine Immortals.

The time has come for our side to take the offensive. Let us surround, infiltrate, cut off, and corner them, arrest and pursue.[116] When sure that victory is ours in our struggle, we will pick up the enemy pieces. We will restore the country and the dynasty, the reward for our labors. The path of loyalty lies this way, the way is before us.

NARRATOR: Together they enter the Castle of Foochow.

[114] Tadanobu figures in various old *jōruri* plays. In one, he is caught by his enemies at the house of a Kyoto lady and defends himself with a *go* board.
[115] *Torreya* wood.
[116] "Surround", "infiltrate", and the rest are technical terms of *go*.

ACT FIVE

Scene One: Coxinga's camp in Dragon-horse Fields, Kiangsi Province.

NARRATOR: No man can take Mount T'ai under his arm and leap over the north sea, but it is not impossible for a king to act like a king.[117]

Coxinga, the prince of Empei, uses his troops masterfully, as though he turned them in the palm of his hand. He has reduced over fifty cities, and his military strength grows day by day. His wife has brought the Princess Sendan from Japan, and Go Sankei has accompanied the crown prince in his progress from the Mountain of the Nine Immortals. Coxinga has offered the prince the imperial sash and seal, and proclaimed him the Emperor Eiryaku.[118] He has raised a wooden encampment half a mile square in the Dragon-horse Fields, and encircled it with camp curtains, outer tents, and brocade hangings. Sacred wands with paper streamers from the two shrines of Ise in Japan fly over the camp, inviting the divine presence. Coxinga has installed the crown prince in a palace of his own.

Now Coxinga sits on a camp stool in the center of the fort. To his left and right sit President of the Council of War Go Sankei and the General of Cavalry Kanki. They have been exchanging views on the decisive struggle between Tartary and the Ming. Go Sankei takes up his military fan.

GO SANKEI: The best plans are those which arrive at great results from insignificant beginnings.

NARRATOR: He holds up a bamboo tube.

GO SANKEI: I have stuffed this tube with honey and a great number of hornets. We should prepare thousands of tubes like this, and give them to our front-line troops to carry. They will advance, pretending to do battle, only to retreat and abandon the tubes on contact with the enemy. The Tartar hordes, with their usual gluttony, will suppose that the tubes contain food, and will undoubtedly retrieve them. As soon as they remove the stoppers, tens of thousands of hornets will swarm out

[117] An allusion to *The Book of Mencius* (tr. Legge, *Chinese Classics*, I, 142): "In such a thing as taking the T'ai mountain under your arm and leaping over the north sea with it, if you say to people, 'I am not able to do it,' that is a real case of not being able."
[118] Chinese pronunciation: Yung Li. For an account of this pretender, see Keene, *The Battles of Coxinga*, p. 53.

and sting the rebels viciously. While they are staggering about in confusion, our troops should return and attack from all directions. Look!

NARRATOR: He removes the stopper and a great many hornets fly out, buzzing their wings.

GO SANKEI: The rebel soldiers, once they realize what has happened, will make fun of the tubes. They will say, "What a childish trick to deceive us! Let's burn the lot and make them ashamed of themselves!" They will pile up the tubes and set them on fire. In an instant the gunpowder prepared at the bottom of the tubes will explode with a roar. There won't be a soldier left for half a league around.

NARRATOR: He touches a rope match to the tube. At once it sputters forth flames that suggest his device will indeed work.

Kanki brings forward a basket filled with fruit.

KANKI: I am impressed by Go Sankei's unusual plan, but I also have a suggestion. We should make two or three thousand baskets of this kind, and fill them with poisoned sweetmeats, rice balls, and appetizers. We should dispose these baskets at various places inside the camp, and lure the enemy close to our lines. Then we should retreat about ten leagues, pretending to have been defeated in battle. The Tartars, flushed with victory, will enter the camp after one of their usual long marches. When their eyes light on the food, the officers and men will imagine that they have come to a mountain of treasures, and they will surely struggle to see who will be first to grab the food and swallow it. As soon as it touches their lips, one after another they will vomit up poisoned blood. We will slaughter them without staining our swords.

NARRATOR: Both have taxed their ingenuity in military stratagems. The plans they offer differ considerably. Coxinga nods.

COXINGA: Your suggestions both have merit. Indeed, they are beyond criticism. However, my mother's last words have penetrated my soul, and I cannot forget them. "Consider the king of Tartary as your mother's enemy, Coxinga, and your wife's enemy, Kanki, and carry out your great plan! We have died so that you would not relent in your determination." Her words have soaked into my bones and permeate my entire being. I have never forgotten them for an instant. What need have we of elaborate stratagems? I shall attack boldly, challenge both the king of Tartary and Ri Tōten at close quarters, then cut them to shreds. If I fail to kill them in this fashion, I shall be guilty of unfilial conduct towards my mother, though I perform a million other martial feats, though I prove myself loyal to my sovereign and just to my fellow men.

NARRATOR: Tears pour from his mirror-clear eyes. All present, from Go Sankei and Kanki downwards, wet their sleeves with tears.

COXINGA: My mother, though a woman, did not forget her native land. She thought to her last breath of the honor of Japan, revering the country of her birth. I too was born in Japan, and I shall not abandon my country. Behold! I humbly beg the great goddess Amaterasu to vouchsafe her protection. The divine strength of Japan has enabled me to rise from the common people, capture many cities, and to become now a prince of the Chinese empire, honored by all. That is why I insisted that the barbarians I subdued in the bamboo forest must have their heads shaved in the Japanese style. I shall put them in the van of my forces and give out that they are reinforcements from Japan. The Tartar barbarians will be frightened at the news, for they know that the Japanese excel in the use of bow and arrow, and are peerlessly trained in all the martial arts. While the Tartars hesitate, intimidated, we shall launch a massive attack and seize the city. This is the plan my wife and I have devised together. (*To Komutsu.*) Minamoto no Ushiwaka! [119] Lead your soldiers here!

NARRATOR: He lifts his commander's fan, and Komutsu shouts a word of assent. She comes forward, her hair tied with a paper cord. Her troops, their heads blue from a close shaving in the Japanese manner, present a colorful sight in their Chinese brocades.

The princess rushes forth from the curtains of the temporary palace.

SENDAN: Coxinga, this is your father's ensign, and here is a note in his writing—a most upsetting message.

NARRATOR: Coxinga kneels to receive the letter, and reads aloud.

COXINGA (*reads*): "I returned to China, foolishly imagining that I might repay my debt to the emperor of the Ming, but I have achieved nothing, have won no glory. What pleasure may I expect from the years of old age left me? Tonight I shall go to the walls of Nanking and, dying in battle, shall leave a fair name in Japan and China. I shall die in my seventy-third year. Tei Shiryū Ikkan."

NARRATOR: Even before he has finished reading, Coxinga springs to his feet.

[119] Komutsu is called Ushiwaka because of her masculine garb. See n. 83, above.

COXINGA: My hatred for the enemy is complete. My mother's enemy is now my father's enemy too. I need no stratagems. What will military tactics avail me? Whatever you may choose to do, I, Coxinga, can wait no longer. Alone I shall ride into the city of Nanking and twist off the heads of the king of Tartary and Ri Tōten. I shall die fighting where my father falls, and journey with my parents to the world of the dead. Farewell for this life!

NARRATOR: He starts off precipitously, but the two generals catch him by the sleeves.

KANKI: How inconsiderate of you! The Tartars are the enemies of my wife and my father-in-law.

GO SANKEI: And the enemies of my wife and baby.

COXINGA: You're right. They are enemies to all of us equally. We three will take on the enemies of the whole world! Come on!

NARRATOR: They rush off together. The most powerful demon or god of ill fortune would not have dared face the points of their swords.

Scene Two: The Tartar camp.

NARRATOR: Tei Shiryū Rōikkan bravely sets out, attired for the dark mists of evening in armor braided of black leather. He creeps up to the outer walls of Nanking and raps on the great wooden gate.

IKKAN: I am Coxinga's father, Ikkan. I am old and my knees buckle under me. I cannot fight like a man in his prime, yet when the young men talk of battle I cannot listen idly. I have ventured here in the hope I might find a quick death and end my life as I had always planned. Grant me the favor, Ri Tōten, of showing yourself, and taking this white-haired head! This is all I ask before I die.

NARRATOR: In answer to his shout, a strapping fellow six feet tall calls from the castle.

MAN: Nobly said, Ikkan. I'll take you on!

NARRATOR: He pushes open the gate and emerges swinging his sword.

IKKAN: I'm ready!

NARRATOR: They exchange two or three blows of the sword, when Ikkan suddenly closes and lops off his opponent's head. Much displeased, he shouts loudly.

IKKAN: I am old, but I will not yield my head to a common soldier of his kind! Ri Tōten, come out and fight! I'll deal with anyone else as I did with this man.

NARRATOR: He stands glaring at the wall. The great king of Tartary shows himself on the tower of the Shou-yang Gate.

KING: That villain is Rōikkan, Coxinga's father. I have many things to ask him. Don't kill him, but capture him and bring him to me.

NARRATOR: Forty or fifty men shout assent. They surround Ikkan with their clubs and beat him mercilessly, without allowing him the chance to defend himself. They twist him to the ground, tie him, and drag him off into the castle. Ikkan is chagrined beyond words.

Soon afterwards Kanki and Go Sankei with Coxinga at the fore race up to the front gate of the city. Behind them sixty thousand and more troops led by Komutsu, the general of the rear guard, press eagerly forward, resolved that today they will fight to the finish. Coxinga issues his commands.

COXINGA: We still do not know whether my father is dead or alive. We must be extremely careful. There are twelve major gates and thirty-six smaller ones around the walls of Nanking, and if we leave even one unguarded, the enemy is sure to escape through it. Keep a sharp lookout on all sides, then let's attack!

NARRATOR: At a signal they fall into position, strike their quivers, and raise war cries loud enough to overturn Heaven itself.

Komutsu advances to the fore, wielding a short sword in the Ushi-waka style with the skill born of constant practice.

KOMUTSU: I will take on any opponent, whoever he may be, when or where he may choose, providing he is willing to die!

NARRATOR: Proclaiming herself boldly, she charges into the enemy ranks and furiously does battle.

Many of the rebel soldiers are slain, but the city of Nanking, in which seven hundred thousand troops are entrenched, shows no sign of capitulating. Coxinga, hoping to discover somehow whether his father is dead or alive, races around the walls, but without success. He advances to the front ranks and shouts.

COXINGA: Never in the five years since coming to China, in all my numerous battles, have I fought without swords. Today, for a change, I shall not lay my hand on my sword hilt. You Tartars who are such masters of horsemanship and pride yourselves on your skill with your swords, come out and fight!

NARRATOR: Such is his challenge.

TARTARS: Kill the loathsome braggart!

NARRATOR: They rush out at him, howling as they attack. Coxinga pulls his assailants to him. He wrenches away their swords, beats and crushes them. He wrests away lances, spears, and halberds, twisting, bending, and snapping the blades. If the onrushing villains touch his legs, he tramples them to death; if they touch his hands, he twists and strangles them, spurning their bodies like pebbles before him. Mounted warriors he catches horse and all, and toys with them a moment before tossing the horses like jackstones. He mixes human jackstones, horse jackstones, and stone jackstones in a display of strength that does not seem human. The Tartars, for all their vaunted prowess, are forced to retreat, and the fall of the city seems imminent when Ri Tōten shows himself, the king of Tartary before him, and with them Ikkan, bound to the face of a shield.

RI TŌTEN: Coxinga, you crawled forth from your insignificant country of Japan and ravaged all China. Not content with capturing cities at various places, you've dared approach the seat of the great king. Your outrageous insolence has compelled us to bind your father in this fashion. Shall we cut his belly in the Japanese manner? Or will you and your father agree to return to Japan immediately? If you agree, we'll spare Ikkan's life. Otherwise, we'll slit him open now before your eyes. Make your answer, one way or the other!

NARRATOR: He shouts the demand. Coxinga until this moment has been in high spirits, but suddenly his head spins, his strength ebbs, and he seems utterly dejected. His troops are disheartened, and the camp becomes utterly still. Ikkan gnashes his teeth.

IKKAN: Coxinga! Do you hesitate? Have you lost your courage? What use would it be for me, a man over seventy, to prolong his life? Have you forgotten how you praised your mother's dying words? You will be disgraced for all ages to come if it is said that, having virtually achieved your great goal, you allowed worry over the life of a wrinkled old man to bring you to failure. And think of the name you will give your country! Will it not be a disgrace to Japan if Japanese acquire abroad the unfortunate reputation of being so weak emotionally that they abide by no principles? Your mother, though she was a woman, respected her country, and gave up her life sooner than bring disgrace to Japan. Have you forgotten? Now that you have reached this critical moment, you must not flicker an eye, not even if your father is hacked to bits before you. You must charge the enemy, carry out your plan, and restore the dynasty of the Ming! Where have you lost your resolution? Ahhh—you are a weakling, you are contemptible!

NARRATOR: He stamps in fury, rebuking his son. Coxinga, stung by his father's words, plucks up his courage and makes a rush at the great king. Ri Tōten at once presses his sword against Ikkan. Coxinga's senses fail him. He stands stockstill, unable to move, his legs trembling under him. Even had Mount Shumi crumbled over his head, at this moment he would not have noticed. Coxinga seems utterly beside himself. Kanki and Go Sankei, exchanging glances, rush up and prostrate themselves before the king of Tartary.

KANKI *and* GO SANKEI: Great king, we have been successful until this moment, but your fortunes are the stronger. Coxinga's luck ran out when his father was captured, and we can hope for nothing more from such a general. If you will but spare our lives, we will take Coxinga's head and offer it to you. Grant us your answer, backed with your oath.

NARRATOR: The king of Tartary at once replies.

KING: Splendid! Splendid!

NARRATOR: They spring on him even as he speaks and, kicking him to the ground, grasp him by the throat. Coxinga the next instant leaps forward and twists off his father's bonds. He seizes Ri Tōten and, pushing him onto the shield where his father had been tied, he binds Ri Tōten in the same manner, at elbows and wrists. The three heroes look at one another and raise a shout of joy that echoes through the entire country. The soldiers, once more in high spirits, escort the crown prince and the Princess Sendan to the spot.

COXINGA: I shall punish these rogues in your presence. This one is the king of Tartary. Though his is a land of barbarians, I shall send him back to his country alive, after first tying him to a stake and whipping him.

NARRATOR: His men divide to left and right, with 500 whips for each side. When they have thrashed the king until he is half dead, they let him escape.

COXINGA: And now we come to Ri Tōten, the cause of all our griefs, a monster guilty of the Eight Grave Crimes,[120] the Five Inhuman Acts,

[120] The Eight Great Crimes were crimes of treason and great atrocity as defined by the Taihō penal code of A.D. 701. For the Ten Villainies and the Five Inhuman Acts, see n. 71, above.

the Ten Villainies. I myself shall cut off his head, so that there will be no resentment among us. Kanki, Go Sankei—cut off his arms!

NARRATOR: Standing on three sides of Ri Tōten, they raise their swords with a great shout, and in one motion slice off his head and arms.

They wish the Emperor Eiryaku a reign of ten thousand years, and offer prayers for the peace and safety of the country. This joy they owe to the divine, the martial, and the saintly virtues of the emperor of Great Japan, a land endowed with these perpetual blessings, which will prosper forever as her people prosper. All pray that by this benefaction the five grains will continue to ripen in abundance, and that the emperor's reign will endure a hundred million years.

GONZA THE LANCER

First performed on September 26, 1717. Chikamatsu modeled this play on events which occurred about six weeks before the first performance. He changed the names of the characters and removed the scene of the final action from the Kōrai Bridge in Osaka to the Capital Bridge in Fushimi. He further called the chief character Gonza, the hero of a half-century-old ballad, perhaps in deference to the feelings of those connected with the tragedy. The play is otherwise contemporary, and the audience undoubtedly saw through the thin disguise.

The play has a subtitle, "The Double Hempen Kimonos," suggesting that the action takes place in summer, when hempen kimonos are worn, and hinting at Osai's double love life.

Cast of Characters

SASANO GONZA, aged 25, a samurai
ASAKA ICHINOSHIN, aged 49, a tea master
KAWAZURA BANNOJŌ, a samurai, brother of Oyuki
IWAKI CHŪTABEI, aged 68, father of Osai
IWAKI JIMBEI, younger brother of Osai
TORAJIRŌ, aged 10, son of Ichinoshin and Osai
KAKUSUKE, NAMISUKE, servants
BOATMAN, BYSTANDERS, SERVANTS, GROOMS
OSAI, aged 37, wife of Ichinoshin
OYUKI, aged 18, betrothed of Gonza
GOVERNESS of Oyuki, aged 60
MOTHER of Osai
OKIKU, aged 13, daughter of Ichinoshin and Osai
OSUTE, aged 9, daughter of Ichinoshin and Osai
MAN, SUGI, servants in Osai's household
DANCERS

ACT ONE

Scene One: The Japan Sea coast north of Matsue. The scene depicts a Shinto shrine with pines and a riding ground.
Time: Summer, 1717.

NARRATOR: The nation rejoices in a reign of eternal peace. In Izumo, a well-ordered province, though the daimyo is absent,[1] his men devote themselves to archery and the chase, twanging their bows as they gallop over the castle riding course and out into the countryside. Here, at the mounted archery range along the road that leads to the Shrine-on-the-Beach, a wind whistles through the avenue of trees, and the waves crash wildly on the shore. But Sasano Gonza, foremost of all the young samurai attending his lordship, rides so well it seems he can hurdle even the breakers. He is the pride of the martial profession, and so good-looking people acclaim him in song—"Gonza the Lancer's a gallant lad, yes, Gonza is truly handsome";[2] he's a man who's loved alike by girls and boys.

Gonza rides a well-fed, cream-colored horse, a mettlesome steed that prances along, perfect in all its quarters, a white froth flecking its mouth as though it munched on snow. Its tail swings like a green willow branch as it proudly struts ahead. Gonza sits in the saddle in the Ōtsubo style and, with the skill born of constant practice, draws in the bright-colored reins. When the moment is ripe he shouts, "Heigh!" and the grooms holding the horse from either side release the reins with a twirl of their mustaches, and off it bounds. The wind billows the ends of Gonza's trousers and sends ripples through the horse's mane. Gonza gallops back, turns, and rides out once again, pine boughs brushing his sleeve. The pine is a maiden-pine[3] and a maiden of eighteen waits beside it, her trailing sleeves dyed in the Kyoto fashion, her face shielded by a wide wicker hat. From what great family has such a girl come? A woman, apparently her governess, stands nearby, a small parcel in her hand.

---

[1] In Edo, observing the "alternate attendance" required of daimyos.

[2] The refrain of a popular ballad, quoted several times in slightly different versions during the course of the play. The ballad considerably antedates the other material in the play.

[3] A red pine. A calligraphic wordplay divides the character 松 (pine) into the elements 十 (ten), 八 (eight), and 公 (princess), to give the meaning of "a young lady of eighteen years".

The girl follows Gonza with amorous eyes, pretending to duck out of sight each time his horse flashes by, but only getting in the way. He recognizes her, and his wild pony furiously cavorts, excited by her bright-colored robe. Gonza shouts to the horse and, as if too absorbed with its movements to notice the girl, he applies the whip again and again. The horse, unfortunate victim, runs faster and faster, till its bit tinkles, the saddle flaps flap, and a beating wind rustles the bamboos in front of the grounds. The horse flies over the field again and again, its hooves barely touching the ground as it races the 250 yards of the course without pausing for breath.

For an hour or so Gonza shows his skill in training the horse, till saddle and stirrups are drenched with sweat. When at last he halts, his servants and grooms rush up.

SERVANTS: Have you finished, sir?

GONZA: I'm in more of a sweat than usual, boys. Run back to the house and fetch a change of clothes. The grooms in the meanwhile can rest themselves in the shrine.

NARRATOR: "Yes," cry his men and rush off, eager for a rest. As soon as they leave, Oyuki glides up and firmly catches Gonza's toes in the stirrup.

OYUKI: It's been a long time, Gonza. I'm glad to see that you're looking well.—You needn't pretend you haven't noticed me. Was it necessary to give your poor horse a week's workout in one day? I wonder why, if you dislike me so much, you haven't trampled me to death under your horse instead of avoiding me all this time? You're a samurai, but when I think of the barefaced lies you told me!

NARRATOR: Her eyes, even as they glare at him, mist over—how weak women are with their tears!

GONZA: Oyuki—I'm trying to treat you as your position demands. Could I lie to Kawazura Bannojō's sister and amuse myself at her expense, as I might with some common strumpet? My feelings haven't changed in the least, but I had to do something to throw my servants off the track. I was so frantic that they might see you here that I hardly even remembered I was on a horse. Look, see how I've sweated! (*To governess.*) I must say, nurse, you haven't shown much discretion. How could you have come all this way with a young lady? You didn't discourage her, though you knew that people might see! Sup-

posing some unfortunate rumor started in his lordship's household [4]
—I couldn't remain in service another day. I give you my word, I
won't break the vows we exchanged. Now, go back home, both of
you, quickly, quickly!

NARRATOR: He starts to ride off, but the governess catches the horse's
bit and stays him.

GOVERNESS: You say that I lack discretion! What an irresponsible
charge! Gonza, I'm sure you can't have forgotten—when I brought
you and Oyuki together last winter at my house, did you stipulate
that it would be for that once only? Oyuki's not a girl to be sold for
a single night's pleasure. How lucky you were! But since then you
haven't deigned a word or a gesture. Every time I've taken you a letter,
you've promised to answer, but have you ever sent a reply? Oyuki's
parents are both dead. I am supposed to be her chaperon, but I've always agreed to her wishes. One word from you to Bannojō and the
marriage would soon be arranged. Tell me, do you intend to make her
your wife or don't you? If you don't, say so plainly, and I'll see what
I can do. It's not merely that I'm proud of her because I reared her
myself, but I've never let any man lay a finger on her. She's eighteen,
at the height of her sweet charms, a delectable mouthful in her tenderness. Can I let her be poked and picked over? No, that won't do.
You'll regret it!

NARRATOR: Her voice rises to a piercing shriek.

GONZA: I'm not surprised that you, a woman, are angry with me. I
was wrong not to answer, but I hesitated to write for fear that the
letter might go astray. Bannojō and I both study the tea ceremony
under Asaka Ichinoshin, the steward of the fief, and we are good
friends, but—forgive me for saying so—something strange about his
disposition makes it hard to talk to him freely. It embarrasses a young
man like myself to ask a friend for his sister. I wish you'd find a suitable
go-between and get him to make overtures to both parties. I am willing, and once Bannojō gives his consent, I'll take the matter to the
fief supervisors. [5] From then on it's in the hands of the gods. If ever
I am untrue to what I say, may I fall that instant headfirst from my

---

[4] The household of the daimyo who rules over the fief.

[5] Second-rank officers in charge of accounts and other important matters in a daimyo's
household.

horse and be trampled to death! My feelings for you, Oyuki, will never change—I swear it.

NARRATOR: Oyuki's face brightens into a smile. She opens the parcel her nurse carries.

OYUKI: Do you see the crests embroidered on this sash? Three bars in a circle—that's yours. And here is mine, a reverse chrysanthemum. I know it's not very handsome, but I made the sash myself. I took special pains so that the padding would hold your swords in place, but I'm afraid that you may not like the stitching. Anyway, I sewed it especially long, hoping you'd wear it a long time. Please find a go-between—the formal proposal should come from you. This sash will be our private token of engagement until then. Keep me close to you always like the sash, never letting me from your side—I'm sure you will.

NARRATOR: Gonza takes the hand she places on the saddlebow and squeezes it.

GONZA: I'm so happy, words fail me. I swear to Hachiman that my heart will never change. Look, the horse is listening too. I'd be more ashamed to lie before a beast than a human being. You be my witness, horse! Have you heard what I've said?

NARRATOR: But how could the horse understand? Gonza's words go in one ear and out the other, and the horse merely neighs in the wind. Gonza folds the sash and puts it inside his kimono.

GONZA: Look! A chestnut horse is riding this way from the shore. It's your brother Bannojō!

OYUKI: Yes, that's right! Nurse, look, my brother's coming!

GOVERNESS: The master? How dreadful! It'll ruin all our plans if he finds you here. Come this way, quickly.

NARRATOR: They hurry off to the shrine buildings. Presently Bannojō rides up.

BANNOJŌ: Gonza—have you been riding in the country too? That cream-colored colt of yours has improved enormously in the past year or so, thanks to your hard work and your skill with horses. I suggest you sell the horse if you can find a buyer. You'll make a profit of five or even seven *ryō*. With the money you can then buy another cheap horse, train it, and sell that one too. You'll be rich in no time. You're lucky to have learned such a useful art.

NARRATOR: Sneering at others is his habitual manner of speech. Gonza is well acquainted with his disposition.

GONZA: The horse of a low-ranking samurai never gets decent attention or feeding. It's all right for show, but of no use when you really need it. But a high-ranking samurai like yourself can afford any number of grooms for your horse and you give it the proper nourishment. When the moment comes for action, your horse is on his mettle and it's sure to win. You should treasure it.

BANNOJŌ: I suppose you're alluding to the fact that my horse was beaten by yours the other day on the castle riding course. Come on, let's race our horses once around and see which is the better. Get on your horse and let's go.

NARRATOR: He urges Gonza.

GONZA: I'd like to accept, but I've just finished giving the horse a workout and, as you can see, we're both exhausted. I'm on my way home now. Let's make it another time. Come, grooms.

NARRATOR: Bannojō refuses to listen.

BANNOJŌ: You say you're exhausted, but that's just an excuse in case you get beaten. I won't let you leave without a race.

NARRATOR: He gathers the reins and starts off. Gonza can no longer refuse. He has rested the horse and he himself has stopped perspiring. He gives his moon-colored horse the whip in the Cherry Blossom Hunt style,[6] now gathering, now loosening the reins in the secret tradition. He wheels his horse clockwise before the starting point and Bannojō makes a circle in the opposite direction. Each man, determined not to let the other get a headstart, circles the starting point two or three times. Finally, Gonza loosens the reins, presses his spurs, and gives a shout: at once his horse, a prize racer, streaks out onto the course. Bannojō's chestnut stallion cringes under the whip, and beat, rein, or spur it as he may, the horse only paws the ground and loudly neighs. Bannojō cannot keep in the saddle with all the bucking and rearing, and tumbles off backwards like a collapsing screen. He lands on his seat at the base of a tree. His servants roar with laughter at his shrieks of pain, oblivious to the disgrace of their master.

Gonza jumps from his horse in alarm and rushes to Bannojō.

GONZA: Are you hurt?

[6] A method of applying the whip in time with the horse's breathing.

BANNOJŌ: Gonza, that horse of yours is my enemy. Give it to me. I'm going to kill it. Owww! Massage my back, you servants, or your heads'll be in danger!

NARRATOR: He glowers at Gonza, furious with him, though for no reason. As Gonza stands there, holding down his anger at this unprovoked hostility, Iwaki Chūtabei, the officer in charge of presentations,[7] appears. He is robust by nature, though a man of sixty-eight, and his shaven head gleams like copper.

IWAKI: So you're here! I was about to call at your houses. I'm lucky I've found you. A letter has come from the senior counselor in Edo. He says that all members of the daimyo's family from nearby provinces are to be invited to a banquet here at the end of the month to celebrate the marriage of the young master. A True Table[8] tea ceremony is to be performed for the occasion. My son-in-law Asaka Ichinoshin is in Edo, and the counselor therefore commands that one of Ichinoshin's pupils who has learned the formal ceremony should perform it in the Hall of Audience with full paraphernalia. I don't know who has learned this ceremony, and that's why I'm asking your help, gentlemen. Any assistance you can give will be a service to his lordship, and at the same time redound to your credit. It will also bring great satisfaction to Ichinoshin. What do you say, gentlemen? If either of you has picked up a knowledge of the ceremony and would like to make a name for yourself, now is your chance.

NARRATOR: Bannojō speaks with headstrong arrogance.

BANNOJŌ: The True Table ceremony is no problem. I've never received a formal initiation, it's true, but secret traditions when you get to know them always turn out to be as close to your eyes as your lashes. I know a good deal about the tea ceremony already. My only reason for studying it all these years has been to be of service to his lordship on such an occasion. I'll perform it. You have nothing to worry about.

IWAKI: That's splendid. What about you, Gonza? Don't you know the ceremony?

GONZA: I can't say that I do or I don't. The True Table is the most secret mystery of the tea ceremony. Many traditions are preserved

---

[7] An officer in a daimyo's household charged with receiving and offering presents.

[8] The *shin no daisu* tea ceremony. The *daisu* is a kind of cabinet in which the implements of the ceremony are displayed. Of the three styles of decorating the cabinet (named after the three styles of calligraphy), the *shin* or "true" is the most formal.

in the different schools, but Ichinoshin's are in the direct line of the Shogun Yoshimasa.[9] These are precious teachings, transmitted only from father to son. There's no chance for the likes of Gonza to be initiated. I have, however, heard something of the principles from my teacher, and I can probably perform it well enough to escape criticism.

NARRATOR: Bannojō interrupts.

BANNOJŌ: Do you think a makeshift will do on such an important occasion? I alone will perform the ceremony. Please consider the matter settled, Chūtabei.

IWAKI: It's nothing I can decide myself. My daughter, as you know, is Ichinoshin's wife, and she must be consulted. Any mistakes made about initiation into the formal ceremony will disgrace his lordship. Our best plan is to talk over matters together before making a decision. Well, gentlemen, are you returning? May I accompany you?

BANNOJŌ: If you insist . . .

NARRATOR: He limps painfully. Chūtabei is irritated.

IWAKI: Are you limping, sir? Do you suffer perhaps from rheumatism?

BANNOJŌ: I'm a champion horseman, but even the best horse sometimes stumbles. I fell from my horse. I was disequitated, you might say.

NARRATOR: Chūtabei, amused by his incoherent and repetitious words, decides to tease him.

IWAKI: You've fallen from your horse and been disequitated! What a very elaborate way to be thrown! No wonder it hurts! Disequitation is quite prevalent these days. I've heard of a certain samurai, Wildhorse the Warrior, whose ague was completely disequitated by one dose of a miraculous drug. Just this morning I went to somebody's house and before I knew it, I disequitated an important fast. In times like these when disequitation is so rampant you can't be too careful what you say. Your head might get disequitated! [10]

NARRATOR: He speaks astringently, no doubt because he has a tea master for his son-in-law.

[9] Ashikaga Yoshimasa (1436–90), the eighth Ashikaga shogun, was a great patron of the tea ceremony.
[10] The facetious use of the word "disequitation" (*rakuba*) is intended as a thrust at Bannojō for having used so pompous a word to describe his mishap. In each case the simple word *ochiru* would be normal.

Scene Two: Asaka Ichinoshin's house.
Time: Later the same day.

NARRATOR: Yesterday seems today the beginning of long ago. The finest tea, called "Long Ago," comes from Uji, but in people, they say, breeding is more important than birth.[11]

Osai watches over Asaka Ichinoshin's house during his absence. Elegant and gay, as a tea master's wife should be, her slender and delicate build gives her a grace and charm that belie her thirty-seven years, though she is the mother of three children. She sweeps and dusts the tea room, never letting a maid inside, so devoted to tidiness that her broom seldom leaves her hand. Today she scatters pine needles along the path of stepping-stones to the teahouse.[12] The stone lanterns are encrusted with moss, and the water basin formed of a single boulder.[13] She rakes the fallen leaves under the thick stand of trees, praying that she and her husband will grow old together like this garden, and that her children will flourish like the Takasago pine.[14]

Her son Torajirō, the middle child of three, runs into the teahouse garden, a bamboo pole held aslant. With him is the apprentice Kakusuke, who brandishes a stick.

TORAJIRŌ (*sings*): "Kagekiyo laughs to see their presumption. Flashing his sword in the light of the setting sun, he falls upon his enemies. They cannot withstand his blade, but scatter in all directions."[15]

NARRATOR: The two boys trade blows accompanied by fierce shouts.

OSAI: Fie, fie! A little of that mischief goes a long way. (*To Kakusuke.*) You foolish boy. You're big enough to count as a man, but you're so silly the others won't even take you to Edo. Instead you pick on a small child you might easily hurt. Supposing you damaged the

---

[11] *Hatsumukashi* means "early long ago". It is also the name of a famous tea. Uji is the town where the best tea is grown; it is a homophone for a word meaning "family lineage". The meaning of the whole is, roughly, that the best tea comes from Uji, but in people breeding is more important than *uji*.

[12] Scattering pine needles on the garden path is considered an elegant preparation for the tea ceremony. It suggests that the hut is in rustic surroundings.

[13] The passage contains overtones of the famous *Kimi ga yo* poem, which says that the emperor's reign will last until pebbles turn into boulders and are covered with moss.

[14] A quotation from the Nō play *Takasago*, about a long-lived pine, is imbedded in the text here.

[15] From the Nō play *Kagekiyo*. See Waley, *The Nō Plays of Japan*, p. 98.

wall of the teahouse, what would you do then? And you, Torajirō, why do you make friends with that simpleton? I'm writing down every naughty thing you do in my notebook, and when Father comes back you can be sure I'm going to tell him.

TORAJIRŌ: No, Mother, I'm not being naughty. I'm a samurai, and I'm practicing how to use a lance.

OSAI: For shame. You're ten years old, a big boy, and you still don't understand the simplest things! Of course you're a samurai, but look at your father. He's enjoyed his lordship's favor and his stipend has been increased, not because he's handy with weapons—there's nothing remarkable about *that* in a samurai—but because he performs the tea ceremony so well. That's why his services are in demand and he is treated with such consideration. Now, while you're still young, you should learn how to hold the tea ladle and how to fold the napkins. I'll get a terrible reputation if people start saying that you children are being brought up badly while your father's away in Edo. I'll be disgraced. Yes, I can see why they say that a boy should be trained by a man. Go to your grandfather's and study the *Great Learning*.[16] As for you, idiot, escort him there and bring him back before dark.

NARRATOR: She must give attention to everything inside and outside the house: it is a strain for a wife when her husband's absent.

Okiku is exactly as an eldest daughter should be.

OKIKU: Mother, you have so much on your mind. Please rest a little while.

NARRATOR: She offers powdered tea in a cup of Otowa ware. Osai notices how grown-up her manner has become.

OSAI: You're a good daughter, and that was very thoughtful of you. What a fine little lady you've become! Where is your sister Osute? Out playing somewhere with the nurse, isn't she? Have you had your bath? Who braided your hair for you? This looks like Man's handiwork. The bun hangs a little low in back, and the bangs are too severe. It doesn't become you at all. The way a girl's back hair falls and her sidelocks are brushed makes her hair-do seem pretty or ugly. And don't forget, a girl's eyebrows are just as important as her features. I can't leave your front lock this way either. Let Mother rearrange your hair.

NARRATOR: She opens the comb box and looking glass stand. More than a mirror, man in this world is the mirror for man. The conduct

---

[16] *Daigaku* (or *Ta Hsüeh*), a Confucian classic widely used in teaching the young.

of others serves as our guide to the good and bad in our own behavior.
The artist's brush tells us of the fair women of Kyoto and Osaka, and
with our mind's eye we can visualize the cherry blossoms of Yoshino
and Hatsuse: so Osai imagines her daughter as a married woman.
"Never let anyone see your hair in morning slumber, your face when
you come from the bath, your hair after washing. You must be careful
when your hair is untidy or disheveled by sleep, and even on your
pillow your face should be composed. Beauty is granted at birth, but
as it says in the *Essays in Idleness,* well-groomed black hair can make
any woman seem lovely; [17] it is her most precious possession." Osai
unravels the secrets of ladylike appearance and conduct as she strokes
her daughter's hair with the fine teeth of the comb. Under her loving
hands the girl's hair takes on an unrecognizably handsome sheen.

OSAI: There—see what an unusually pretty young lady you've become. If you think I'm not telling the truth, look in the mirror for
yourself. But they say a parent's eyes are prejudiced. We need an outsider's judgment. Come here, Man! Sugi, the cook, come quickly!
I want you both to look at Okiku's hair.

NARRATOR: The maids come running with cries of "Yes, ma'am!"

MAN: My, my, how clever you are, madam! The way you've fixed
her bangs and the rest make her naturally pretty face all the prettier.
She puts even a girl in a dither. I'd like to hold her naked body tight
in my arms and sleep with her.

NARRATOR: Such are Man's praises. Sugi claps her hands.

SUGI: So that's it! I've always wondered about something and now
at last I understand. Every time I look at my face in the mirror I
think how strange it is that no man's ever fallen for a girl with such
good features. Now I see I'm such a wallflower, poor thing, only because of the way I do my hair. Excuse me for saying so, but if madam
would arrange my hair for two or three days, I'm sure every man in
the county would fall for me like pampas grass before the autumn
wind.

NARRATOR: Her voice is boisterous.

OSAI: It's unbecoming for a mother to praise her own child, but I
should hate to give a daughter like this to any ordinary man. I've
long thought quite seriously that if we choose a husband for her
among the samurai of this fief, I would like it to be Sasano Gonza.

[17] See G. B. Sansom, "The *Tsuredzuregusa* of Yoshida no Kaneyoshi," p. 14.

He's the best-looking man in the province, a master of the military arts, and none of my husband's other pupils in the tea ceremony can approach him. Besides, he has such a pleasant disposition that nobody can dislike him. He's a real man among men.

NARRATOR: Okiku answers in a childish voice.

OKIKU: But Mother, Gonza's a grown-up. He's old enough to be my uncle. I don't want to marry him.

NARRATOR: She shakes her head.

OSAI: You're talking foolishness. Mother is thirty-seven. I was born in the Year of the Bird, just like Father, who's forty-nine, born in the previous Year of the Bird.[18] We're twelve years apart, but what wonderful children we've had! Gonza was born in the Year of the Bird after mine, which makes him twenty-five, and you in the next Year of the Bird. That's twelve years apart too—just the right combination. In a couple of years' time you'll be using make-up and wearing fitted clothes.[19] You and Gonza will make a perfect pair. Isn't it strange—all four of us born in the Year of the Bird. No more silly talk now —accept him for your husband! If you refuse him, Mother will take him instead! Really, if I didn't have a husband named Ichinoshin, I'd never give up Gonza to anybody else!

NARRATOR: Such imprudence is the jest of the moment, uttered out of love for her child, but it has an unpleasant ring, bespeaking some evil connection from a past existence.

OSAI: Come, put on fresh clothes now, and let's see how you look in a party dress.

NARRATOR: She takes her daughter's hand and leads her to the inner room.

A voice is heard at the front entrance. Man calls from the sitting room, "Who is it?" and goes to greet the guest. It is Sasano Gonza. He carries a small keg of saké.

GONZA: Is Iwaki Chūtabei here?

MAN: He comes every day for a visit, but he hasn't appeared yet to-day.

---

[18] The Bird is the tenth of the twelve celestial signs used in the Chinese-Japanese astrology. The prototypes of Gonza, Osai, and Ichinoshin were in fact born in the Year of the Dog, the following sign. Chikamatsu altered their ages because 1717, the year of the play's composition, was a year of the Bird. Okiku's prototype was born under the Bird.
[19] It was customary when a girl reached marriageable age for her kimonos to be taken in under the sleeves closer to her body.

GONZA: In that case I'd like to leave a message for your mistress. I'm sorry I've been out of touch with her lately, but I trust that everything has been going smoothly during her husband's absence. I have a small matter I'd like to discuss with her. I'll give Chūta the details. This is a keg of Kamigata sweet saké. I brought it for the children as a souvenir of my visit today. Please inform your mistress when you have the chance.

NARRATOR: He prepares to depart.

MAN: Wait just a moment, please!

NARRATOR: She runs inside. Osai has eavesdropped on the conversation.

OSAI: I've heard everything. How odd that I should have just mentioned him. Tell him it's quite all right, he should please come in.

NARRATOR: She puts away the comb box and looking glass stand. The two feathers of the duster show the depths of the sinister bond between them: they suggest paired birds which fly on one wing each.[20]

Sasano Gonza hesitantly enters her private apartments.

OSAI: It's kind of you to have come. Thank you for your visit and for the wonderful present you've brought for the children. You've called so often before, but I've never invited you beyond the front door. What brings you here today? Please tell me for yourself. There's no need to approach me through my father.

NARRATOR: She greets him in open and courteous terms. Gonza bows before her.

GONZA: I am grateful for your kindness. I had intended to ask either Chūtabei or your brother Jimbei to speak to you on my behalf. I have a most presumptuous favor to ask. A formal tea ceremony is to be held as part of the entertainments celebrating his lordship's marriage, and it has been commanded that the ceremony be performed by one of Ichinoshin's pupils. I have often heard Ichinoshin speak of this ceremony, and I have acquired a general knowledge of the procedure. Unfortunately, I have never seen the scroll of instruction,[21] nor have I received any certificate of initiation into the traditions. I can't claim publicly to have mastered the ceremony. In this age of lasting peace,

[20] A Chinese fable tells of a pair of birds so devoted to each other that each has only one wing of its own, and must remain with its mate in order to fly. The two feathers of the duster suggest that Osai and Gonza will be united like the fabulous birds.

[21] Drawing which shows the placing of the implements and the manner of performing the ceremony.

it is hard for a samurai to make a name for himself unless he is proficient in one of the arts. Please let me see the scroll. For years I have had this great ambition, and it is particularly important to me now. I shall be indebted to you through all the lives and worlds to come.

NARRATOR: He bows his head to the matting with all the courtesy expected of a disciple.

OSAI: I admire your zeal and your unusual devotion. As you know, however, the secret teachings are transmitted within a family, and may be revealed only by the master to his son. In unavoidable cases a pupil may be shown the scroll, but only after a contract of marriage has been arranged with the master's daughter. In that connection—it's extremely awkward of me to bring it up now and I can't imagine what you will think—it'll come as a surprise to you, a bolt from the blue—there's something I've been mulling over for a long time, wishing for an opportunity to discuss it with you. I'll tell you now. I have hoped for years to give you my daughter Okiku as your bride. I was talking about it just before you came. It sounds when I mention it this way as if I am offering to give you instruction in the formal ceremony in return for your marrying my daughter. That would reflect on her dignity and destroy the value of secret traditions. So let us consider the two matters quite separately. If I give Okiku to you, you will, as my son-in-law, be no less entitled than a son to receive the teachings. I am sure that Ichinoshin will be satisfied when he hears of this arrangement, and, best of all, you are the son-in-law of my heart. If I were trying to advertise Okiku, I could go on talking forever about her good qualities as a wife. Let me say simply that her features are regular, and she is our dearest joy. There is no other man but you I'd like to see as her husband. The question is, are you willing?

NARRATOR: He looks down bashfully without answering.

OSAI: What do you say? Why are you so embarrassed? Does that mean that you don't like my daughter? Hmmm. Judging from the way you shake your head, you don't dislike her. Ah, I have it. You're already engaged to somebody else. That must be it. Well, there's no helping it when a flower already has an owner. What a pity—to have my affection cooled for a man I was so fond of!

NARRATOR: She starts to go.

GONZA: You really embarrass me now. I'm not engaged to anybody. I'm a young man, not made of wood or stone, and naturally I've had my share of temporary sweethearts, but that is another matter. I assure you that I've made no promises to anyone. It would be an honor to become my teacher's son-in-law. Yes, I shall certainly take your daughter Okiku as my wife.

OSAI: Thank you. I'm so happy! My wish has come true. I know it may seem odd to take precautions when once a samurai's given his word, but this marriage has been arranged without a matchmaker. Would you please say a few words by way of an oath to reassure me?

GONZA: It's natural that you take every precaution.—If I should violate this oath, may I never again wear armor on my back, may I be slashed to bits by Ichinoshin's sword, and may my dead body be exposed on the public highway!

NARRATOR: Osai interrupts.

OSAI: That's enough, more than enough. Today is marked auspicious in the calendar. Tonight I'll give you the book of initiation into the True Table ceremony and the scroll of authorization. You should send back your servants in the meantime. I won't introduce you to my daughter just yet. If she's like me, she's sure to be very jealous. Please, I beg you, give her your whole heart. Don't look for amusement elsewhere—I'll encourage my daughter's jealousy if you commit indiscretions! Put your hand on this keg of saké you brought us, and I'll put mine there too. Now it is exactly as if we'd exchanged pledges with a cup of saké. They say that you can't make a crossing without a bridge. The True Table ceremony has been our bridge for the marriage, and your keg is another.

NARRATOR: She celebrates the forthcoming marriage in which she serves as a bridge—an omen that, like the magpies who formed the Bridge of Heaven, her body will soon be stained with crimson, and the bridge occasion the gossip of the world.[22]

An old woman's voice is heard at the front door.

GOVERNESS: Excuse me, maids, but I have a little favor to ask. I'm the governess of Kawazura Bannojō's sister, Oyuki. I've never had

[22] Reference to the Chinese legend which relates how every seventh night of the seventh moon the magpies form with their wings a bridge over which the Herd Boy star and the Weaving Girl star pass to meet. One version has it that the magpies were stained with the "tears of blood" shed by the girl. The bridges in this passage are the instruction in the ceremony, the keg of saké, and finally Osai herself, who is to join Gonza and Okiku. It is predicted that she may therefore be spattered with blood like the magpies. Chikamatsu here foreshadows the scene on Capital Bridge in which the lovers are slain.

the pleasure of meeting your mistress. Please say that I've come un-invited as a messenger from Oyuki.

NARRATOR: Gonza suddenly changes color.

GONZA (*aside*): Bothersome old creature! I never expected her here. What could have brought her? She's the worse thing that could happen to me. If she finds me here, I'm ruined. I must slip out of here some-how.

NARRATOR: He looks around him in consternation.

OSAI: Bannojō, that beast among samurai! And now his sister's governess has come. What business can she have with me?

Do you know why I call him a beast among samurai? He's become infatuated with me—a married woman—and he keeps sending love letters. Think of it—a man so immoral that he insults a woman with a husband! I've thought of complaining to the fief officials and dis-gracing him. But that would destroy Bannojō's career as a samurai, and force Ichinoshin, when he returns, to choose between life or death for him. I dismissed the maid who acted as Bannojō's go-between, but now it seems that the sister's governess has come as the messenger for the brother's improper advances! I couldn't endure to meet her face to face. I'll send word that I'm not at home, and eavesdrop from inside on the conversation. Receive her, Man, hear whatever she has to say, and send her away. Lead the gentleman out very quietly so the old crone doesn't see him. (*To Gonza.*) Please be sure to come back to-night when the place has quieted down. I'll let you have the scroll of the secret traditions.

NARRATOR: She disappears into the back room. Man is a quick-witted, intelligent girl. She nods with a wink, and leads Gonza to the en-trance, screening him with her sleeve.

MAN: Oh, there you are, governess, if that's what you're called. What a long way for an old lady on a hot day like this! Here, let me wipe away the perspiration.

NARRATOR: She presses her crinkled-silk handkerchief against the wrinkled face and energetically rubs away. Gonza safely slips out, profiting by the old woman's confusion.

MAN: Have I wiped too hard? Does your face hurt? I'm sorry to tell you, after you've made this special trip, but the madam went this morning to visit her family, and she's likely to stay quite a while. Please tell me any message you may have.

GOVERNESS: Well, then, I'll address myself to you. Oyuki, the young lady I've brought up, is secretly engaged to Sasano Gonza, but their marriage has been delayed because they haven't a go-between. As a matter of fact, at my instigation they spent one night together, and Gonza sent me a pair of leather-soled sandals and a *ryō* of silver to show his appreciation. That proves they're really engaged. It's a serious matter when a samurai deflowers another samurai's sister, and he can't back out of it. I've privately settled everything with Gonza, and the lady of the house has only to add her voice for the marriage to be smoothly arranged.

Your lady has children, and I'm sure she offers priests money to pray for them. But a good deed performed for another becomes a prayer for which you don't have to pay a priest. Of course, there will be a suitable present for your mistress after the wedding is over, and you won't be asked to exert yourself either without thanks. Please ask her for me to act as a go-between—it will be in name only. . . . Dear me, this is the first time I've ever talked so much. Ho-ho-ho! I'm ashamed of myself.

MAN: Yes, indeed. If it has seemed like a long speech even to you, imagine how much longer it seemed to me! My mistress is not the kind to take presents for acting as a go-between. She particularly dislikes flighty women who twitter away, no doubt because she was born in the Year of the Bird. Please leave at once.

NARRATOR: The old woman is disconcerted by her unpleasant tone.

GOVERNESS: I was born in the Year of the Dog. That makes me just sixty. I'll go before I get hit with a stick for barking too much.[23]

NARRATOR: She leaves with this parting yelp.

Osai, inside the house, gives vent to a fit of pure jealousy. Her wrath breaks its moorings and cannot be tamed.[24] At that moment a young servant appears to announce the arrival of her father Iwaki Chūtabei. The household, intimidated, falls silent. Osai, though far from amused, greets her father with a charming smile.

IWAKI: I'm delighted that you're in such good spirits even with Ichinoshin away. Tora and Sute, the little devils, have been playing

---

[23] Prolonged barking by a dog was considered an unlucky omen.

[24] Puns here include *ikari* (anchor) and its homonym "wrath"; *shizume-kanetaru* (hard to subdue) and its homonym "hard to sink".

at my house. They missed their naps and they're sleepy. They said they wanted to go home and get to sleep, so I brought them back. The nights are short these days, but the best prescription for any child is still early to bed and early to rise, with plenty of exercise in between. Are you keeping Okiku inside? It's best for a girl when she gets to be twelve or thirteen not to come too close to the front door. Okiku and Sute take after you, but Tora is the living image of Ichinoshin. Look, here comes Ichinoshin back from Edo! (*To Torajirō*.) Go to Mother now.

NARRATOR: He jokes out of love for his grandson.

OSAI: You've played a long time today. I'm sure you've been making a terrible racket for your grandparents. Go inside and rest beside your sister. Nurse! See to it they don't catch a chill while they're sleeping. Kakusuke, why haven't you lit the lamps in the garden now that you're back? Can't you see that it's become dark? Man, please offer grandfather a little of the saké we received today. I think he'll like it.

IWAKI: No, the teahouse garden gives me more pleasure than saké or anything else. I never get tired of looking at it, though I see it every day. It shows what elegant taste Ichinoshin has, and it makes me feel completely relaxed. By the way, has Sasano Gonza—I've already told you my private hopes for him—[25] come to ask about the True Table ceremony?

OSAI: Yes, he begged my help so fervently that I finally promised to show him the scroll.

IWAKI: Excellent, excellent. He's an unusual young rascal. He shows a promising aptitude in all the arts. Remember, if he performs the ceremony badly, it will be blamed on Ichinoshin, and reflect unfortunately on his lordship. Let him learn all of the secret traditions. But you must not breathe a word of this even to the servants—not that they'd understand—it's much too important for our family. Mum's the word. Well, I'll be leaving before it gets late. Lanterns, somebody! Light some lanterns for me! (*To Osai*.) See that everybody gets to bed early, but tell the servants they must keep one eye open at night while their master's away. I'll come to see you again tomorrow. (*Calls*.) Kakusuke! You're the only man here. Keep an eye on the front gate and the back of the house. Not that you're likely

[25] Presumably Chūtabei all along has wanted Gonza to perform the True Table ceremony.

to stay awake at night, Kakusuke who snores cock-a-doodle-do even at noon! [26]

NARRATOR: With an old man's pleasantry he goes off in the evening gloom. They bolt the gate behind him.

The garden's elegance is typical of a tea master: the row of trees in fresh leaf has a hoary look, the dew on the bamboo grass, glittering in the flickering light of dim lanterns along the path, might be taken for fireflies. A noisy croaking of frogs visits the eaves of the reed-thatched hut; a flowing stream murmurs in the deepening stillness of the night.

Osai stands by the edge of the verandah, immersed in thought. The rest of the household is asleep. No one will criticize her in her own house, and she lets her tears fall as they may.

OSAI: The more I think about it, the more jealous I feel. Must I give my beloved daughter to some utterly undistinguished man? I searched and searched, as if I were getting married myself, till finally I found the truly unusual man I had set my heart on as a husband for my precious daughter. But how can I keep from being jealous now? This afternoon that old witch blurted out that Oyuki and Gonza were secretly engaged. Oh, I'm seething with jealousy! I don't care if people call me a jealous woman, jealous over somebody else's love affair. Secret traditions, indeed! They're nothing more to me than empty husks. The tea table, the kettle, and the rest mean less than discarded peel. How hateful! How infuriating!

NARRATOR: She throws herself down on the verandah. Overflowing tears soak her sleeve, and she wrings it like a tea cloth.

OSAI: I wonder, is my jealousy decreed by fate, or is it some kind of sickness? How could a woman as jealous as I have allowed her husband to slip out of her hands and go to Edo, mountains and oceans away? I must have been afraid of his lordship. Yes, I see how my jealousy comes entirely from my willfulness. A mother's jealousy over her daughter's husband is the first seed of a bad reputation. I will put it from my mind completely.

NARRATOR: She tries to shake off these thoughts, but her breast still burns with emotion. Her tears flow now out of habit.

Sasano Gonza, as he promised, comes alone. He softly knocks at the gate. Osai silently hurries to him. "Who is it?" she asks. "Sasano"

[26] The pun in the original is on *ibiki kaku* (to snore) and *Kaku*suke.

is his only reply. She opens the door, only to shut it the instant he enters.

OSAI: Come at once to the teahouse.

NARRATOR: In one hand she holds a candlestand and in the other the box with the scrolls. Their furtive figures would surely arouse suspicions, but of this they seem unaware. Sliding open the single thickness of the *shōji,* they enter the teahouse.

OSAI: This is the illustrated scroll. Here, you see the tables used at weddings, manhood ceremonies, and departures for the front. This is a picture of a tea ceremony behind a screen of state. And this is the True Table ceremony, performed on the occasion of an imperial visit. The three hanging scrolls, the three utensils,[27] the placing of the decorative tea caddies—everything is explained in these scrolls of authorization. Once you've read them you won't need any oral instruction. Please compose yourself and read carefully.

NARRATOR: Gonza accepts the scrolls reverently and peruses them. The world outside grows still, and the voices of the frogs tell that the night has deepened. Meanwhile Kawazura Bannojō nervously wanders outside the wall of Ichinoshin's house. His servant carries an empty fifteen-gallon barrel. Bannojō strains to catch any sounds. He speaks softly.

BANNOJŌ: Namisuke! Everybody inside is fast asleep. I'll creep into Osai's bedroom and make love to her. I'm sure that with my gifts of persuasion I can satisfy my pent-up longings and at the same time wheedle her out of the scrolls for the True Table ceremony. I'll put that Gonza in his place. In case anyone wakens and tries to interfere, remember, there are only women and children. Stuff their mouths with sand and keep them from making any noise. Here, knock the ends from this barrel.

NAMISUKE: Yes, sir.

NARRATOR: He stamps on the barrel, and the bottom and top fly off. Bannojō pushes the cask into the hedge, and though the leaves and branches grow thick, the barrel makes a path untouched by thorns.

BANNOJŌ: Keep watch in all directions. Follow me later.

NARRATOR: Bannojō stealthily crawls in. He emerges in the garden and sees, reflected on the *shōji* by the lamp inside the teahouse, the shadows of a man and a woman meeting in secret. They nod their

[27] An incense burner in the center, flanked by a flower vase and a candle stand.

heads in nocturnal whisperings, face close to face in lovers' intimacy—
the prelude to going to bed or the fond recollections thereof? Now
is the moment of sweetest delight! Bannojō, dizzy at the sight, does
not notice how his trousers are disarranged. He had thought to profit
by Ichinoshin's absence, only to have another man carry the fort.[28]
He stands with trembling knees like a defeated warrior, his throat
parched with envy. Gonza's voice is heard.

GONZA: Somebody seems to be in the garden.

OSAI: Nobody ever comes even by day. Who would come so late
at night?

GONZA: Listen—the frogs were croaking a minute ago, but now
they've stopped altogether.

OSAI: Even frogs have to rest sometime. Don't be so nervous. Read
the rest of the scrolls. There—you see—the frogs are croaking again.

NARRATOR: As she speaks Namisuke is crawling through the barrel
into the garden. Bannojō and his servant stand silently together.

GONZA: They've stopped again. I'm sure somebody must be there.
I'll have a look.

NARRATOR: He picks up his sword and starts out.

OSAI: No, don't. There's a high wall on three sides and on the north
a thorn hedge that not even a dog or a cat can crawl through. Nobody
can get in. You seem so nervous to be alone with me. Are you afraid
that some woman, jealous of our being together, might come and
raise trouble?

GONZA: What a foolish thing to say! The thought never entered
my head.

OSAI: No? I'm sure it has. I know that you've made secret plans
for a wedding and you're only waiting for a go-between to say the
word. Ahhh—women are certainly brainless! They're so dazzled by a
man's appearance that they never learn what is going on inside him.

NARRATOR: She bursts into tears of rage.

OSAI: All evening long I've been keeping down my burning indignation, masking my face in smiles for fear that people might whisper
about my jealousy over my future son-in-law, but my endurance has
reached the breaking point. How dare you flaunt that sash with your
crest and a reverse chrysanthemum joined in a lovers' knot? Who

---

[28] The original contains a reference to the contest between the warriors Sasaki and
Kajiwara as to who would be first across the Uji River.

sewed it for you? Who gave it to you? I'll rip it apart with my teeth!

NARRATOR: She flies at him fiercely.

GONZA: I have a reason for wearing this sash.

OSAI: I know there's a reason, and that's what makes me jealous.

NARRATOR: They struggle with each other, weeping and striking by turns. She tears open his sash, and as it unwinds, she beats him with it again and again.

OSAI: Ugh—how repulsive! My hands are contaminated!

NARRATOR: She bunches up the sash and flings it into the garden, all but inviting an accuser to retrieve it. There is no helping it when passion beclouds the senses. Their shadows on the *shōji* show that their hair is disarrayed.

GONZA: What a predicament you've put me in! I can't do without my sash.

NARRATOR: He is about to jump down into the garden, but Osai stops him.

OSAI: Are you so devoted to that sash? Here, I know you won't like it, but wear my sash instead. It will become a vengeful snake, wrap itself around your waist, and never let you go.

NARRATOR: She unties her own sash and throws it at him. Gonza is furious.

GONZA: I've never worn a woman's sash and I never will.

NARRATOR: He throws her sash into the garden after his. Bannojō instantly picks up both sashes and shouts.

BANNOJŌ: Ichinoshin's wife and Sasano Gonza have committed adultery! They've been sleeping together in the teahouse! I have their sashes as proof! I'm going to tell Iwaki Chūtabei!

NARRATOR: He makes his escape through the barrel.

GONZA: Damnation! Bannojō, I swear to Hachiman, god of bow and arrow, that you won't get away!

NARRATOR: Drawing his sword, he kicks aside the *shōji* and jumps into the garden. As he gropes for Bannojō in the faint light from the stone lanterns, he bumps into Namisuke, wandering in confusion. Gonza seizes him.

GONZA: What has happened to Bannojō?

NAMISUKE: He got out and left me here.

GONZA: Did he? Well, you at least are going to accompany me to hell!

NARRATOR: He thrusts his sword into the man's entrails and violently twists the blade. Namisuke emits a horrible shriek and expires with the second blow. Immediately Gonza turns the point towards himself and prepares to drive it into his side, when Osai clutches his arm.

OSAI: What are you doing? Bannojō is the criminal. Your reputation is spotless. What fault have you committed? Why should you kill yourself?

GONZA: Don't be foolish! He's taken our sashes as proof we've been sleeping together. The disheveled state of our hair confirms it. What excuse could we offer? My reputation as a samurai is ruined, and you are now a brute beast. Ah, it breaks my heart!

NARRATOR: He weeps.

OSAI: Then you and I have become animals outside the pale of human society?

GONZA: What punishment of Buddha is this? Our share of his blessings is exhausted.

OSAI: Are we now despicable in the eyes of the world? Ahhh—

NARRATOR: She collapses with a cry and moans till it seems she must expire.

OSAI: Nothing can restore matters now. We are ruined, whether we live or die. And once people in Edo point at Ichinoshin and whisper about his stolen wife, he won't be able to look them in the face, much less continue in service. We are doomed, but at least let us give Ichinoshin the chance to regain his reputation. Let us become lovers, adulterers, and then let him kill us. I would be most grateful.

NARRATOR: She sinks in tears again.

GONZA: No, we needn't stoop to adultery. It's enough for Ichinoshin's reputation if he kills us, even without justification. After we are dead, we will be cleared of this infamy, and our own reputations will also be vindicated. It would degrade me to become your lover.

OSAI: Yes, I understand your reluctance, of course. But if our names are later cleared, Ichinoshin will be humiliated a second time, this time for having killed a man who was actually not his wife's lover. I know how the thought repels you, but please call me here and now your wife, and I will call you my husband. Believe me, I pity you that you must lose your reputation and even your life because of this unpredictable disaster, and I am fond of you. But of course you can never take the place of a man I've lived with twenty years, the father of my three children.

NARRATOR: She wails in her grief. Gonza, seeing her falter, weeps a man's tears of humiliation.

GONZA: To call another man's wife my own is a torture a hundred times, a thousand times, more painful than having to vomit out my entrails or swallow molten iron. My luck as a samurai has run out —else I should never have sunk to this. There's no helping it now. You are Gonza's wife.

OSAI: And you my husband.

GONZA: Ahhh—we are accursed!

NARRATOR: They cling to each other, but can only weep.

GONZA: Let us leave quickly before the others waken. The night is short.

NARRATOR: He lifts her to her feet.

OSAI: My poor little children. They must be sleeping peacefully, dreaming, never suspecting that their mother would run away from this house where she has lived so long. I'll take one last look at their sleeping faces.

GONZA: No weakness now. What more can you ask of the world than to be killed by Ichinoshin?

NARRATOR: He is about to open the front gate when lanterns flash outside and they hear the sound of running feet. A knocking resounds at the gate.

IWAKI: It's Iwaki Jimbei. I want to see Sasano Gonza. Is everybody fast asleep? Open up! Open up!

OSAI: This is dreadful. It's my brother Jimbei. We can't leave by the front gate. There's no back gate, and the walls are so high.

NARRATOR: As they rush back and forth aimlessly, the household awakens. The pounding at the gate continues. They look around in desperation until the thorn hedge catches their eyes.

GONZA: Look, the villain made a hole through the hedge. It's a godsend for us.

NARRATOR: Hand in hand, they wander the crossroad between life and death. They crawl into the barrel, their avenue of life, but their burden of sin is greater than the barrel's capacity: they get stuck midway and can move neither forward nor back. In their struggles they turn head over heels with the barrel and roll over and over out of the hedge.[29] It is dawn, just past four in the morning. Two heads, four legs, and the saké barrel for a trunk—they roll like a man besotted along the darkness of the road to hell. Did they pledge themselves to grow old and share the same grave? They are now within the hoops of one barrel and everything indicates that they will be buried in the same hole.[30]

ACT TWO

Scene One: The journey of Gonza and Osai from Matsue to Fushimi.

NARRATOR:

> Gonza the Lancer's a splendid lad,
> Smooth as if you poured him from a cask of oil.
> You can't resist him, he's so full of charm.
> Gonza's handsome, you won't deny,
> A flower fallen from a branch in bloom.
> You can't resist him, he's so full of charm,
> A man that every woman must adore.

Even before she was released by the first of the two bows she loved,[31] the bowstring snapped, and she was sped in a direction she never meant to go. In her lonely bed when her husband was away, her eyes remained wide open, and her mind gave itself to the tortured, pointless jealousy that finally became the seed of her undoing and the slander of the world. The water of Asaka trickled away from this rootless plant, to mingle confusedly with the dew of bamboo fields.[32]

---

[29] The passage is replete with wordplays between terms connected with saké and with Buddhism.

[30] For a man and wife to be buried in one grave was considered felicitous, for it meant that they were together in death as in life, but here the tragic deaths of Gonza and Osai are hinted at.

[31] The two bows suggest Osai's two husbands. Before Ichinoshin had lost interest in her, she was sent into Gonza's arms.

[32] A complicated set of wordplays devolves around Asaka, the surname of Osai's husband and also the name of a marsh; "bamboo field", the literal meaning of Sasano, Gonza's surname; the word "dew" used both because of association with marshes and bamboo and because it suggests love-making; and the verb *oku* which means "to settle" of the dew, but is the homophone of a word meaning "to get up" after making love.

Awake or in dreams or in aimless wandering, they weep, unable to forget the homes they have left. Tears gush forth hot as the springs at Izushi Mountain, but they cannot cure the sickness called love.[33]

OSAI: The bathing pools of Tajima,[34] count them—five and seven make twelve, the years that separate us two. How much older than you I look in the moonlight! People might well take me for your older sister. When we sleep together, stones for our pillow, I am ashamed to be seen even by the grasses of the field.

GONZA: You are another man's woman. To call you "wife" makes me flush with shame, tinged like the autumn leaves with the colors of guilt through no choice of my own, my name tossed about wildly like the trembling mimosa.

NARRATOR: To weep for such a cause is pitiful indeed. Above their heads rises Ōe Mountain, where Minamoto vanquished the demons.[35] The peak is swathed in fresh green leaves, the valleys and crests thickly grown with trees, but even the mountain's loveliness holds no charm for them. They come to a village, gloomy in the shadow of the pines, in the shade of bamboos. Look at the women hulling wheat—do you see the girl from next door? Thirty years old, and her teeth are stained black, but she wears a girl's trailing sleeves,[36] and she sings of love:

> I hate the blacksmith
> Worse than the carpenter
> For the blacksmith makes the lock,
> The lock of my bedroom door.
> Yes, the blacksmith makes the lock,
> He makes the lock for my bedroom door.

OSAI: Whose fault was it I first unfastened the lock, the chain across the barrier, and my heart began to wander? The fault has been mine that this young lord now looks so wretched! Of the two swords he wore, one disappeared to pay for our journey, the other is left, an

[33] A reference to the hot springs at Kinosaki, famous for their curative powers. Each of the places mentioned directly or suggested is on the route followed by Gonza and Osai from Matsue to Fushimi.

[34] Another reference to Kinosaki, but mention of the bathing pools comes from a song about hot springs in Shikoku.

[35] Minamoto no Raikō (948–1021) is said to have conquered a demon known as Shuten Dōji at this mountain in Tamba Province.

[36] Married women formerly stained their teeth, but the wearing of trailing sleeves (*furisode*) was confined to unmarried women. This woman, perhaps a widow, shows an unseemly reluctance to give up youthful pursuits.

unharvested stalk of grain; his waist wears the mournful look of autumn's end. How lonely, how sad, how desolate!

NARRATOR: Embracing, they can only weep. At home she has parents and children, in the East a husband. Her thoughts are torn a hundred ways, a thousand ways. Her tears stream like hemp from a reel. The world will say that she had a secret lover, and she cannot dam the rumors with her hands; in the river water by Harima Beach the hempen robes are stretched. After nights of fitful sleep, her eyes are dull and listless, her hair is dusty, and her appearance, worse than that of a fisherwoman burning salt on the beach, suggests a scarecrow on a mountain farm.

> The scarecrows, the scarecrows,
> For quails in the millet,
> For cranes in the marsh;
> The songbirds, they warble,
> The mandarin duck lives alone in the pond.[37]

The mandarin duck, like her husband, watches over an empty house, the lonely life of a widower. Even a bird's fate makes Osai grieve, is the source of more tears. Behind them gathering clouds threaten showers and sharp gusts come blowing. The noise of the wind, and even the trembling of the reeds on the moor, make them wonder if pursuers are on their track.

> Through dewy fields of bamboo,
> Running together, they force their way:
> Once when he chased plovers on the shore
> And, grasping his lance's metal tip,
> Reared back with his arm,
> The smallest bird could not escape
> The lance's leaflike point.

Now even the wind aroused by the wings of birds frightens him. Afraid to board a ship, because of the eyes of the other passengers, they hurry along on foot, but they do not go far. For such as they, who have no friends at hand, Sumiyoshi is pleasant to live in only by name,[38] in reality drear. Bowed by their sorrows they reach Mount

[37] Mandarin ducks in Japan (as in China) were symbols of conjugal fidelity. The sight of a lone mandarin duck without its mate suggests Ichinoshin.

[38] The name Sumiyoshi is taken here to mean *sumi* (living) and *yoshi* (good)—that is, a good place to live. I have omitted a pun on the place name Naniwa, the modern Osaka.

Fushimi of doleful name.[39] Though their clothes are not dyed black, the will to leave the world has inked their hearts; they spend their days hiding in this town of priests.

Scene Two: Iwaki Chūtabei's house.
Time: Some weeks later.

NARRATOR:
Once, long ago,
I looked to the future
With hope, but now
I know that growing old
Is life's worst misery.[40]

Iwaki Chūtabei has learned from bitter experience the truth of this old poem. Before his door are piled chests of kimonos, lacquered traveling boxes, wicker baskets, trunks—a complete set of bride's furnishings, all returned by Asaka Ichinoshin. His messengers dropped the lot at Chūtabei's door with a parting shout, "Take back what belongs to the adulteress!"

Osai's mother has long suffered from dizzy spells, but since the day that Osai disappeared she has been oppressed by nervous cramps in the chest, and it is harder than ever for her to leave her bed.

MOTHER: What's that? Her belongings have come back? Are our relations with Ichinoshin and our grandchildren broken? How dreadful!

NARRATOR: She staggers to her feet and goes outside.

MOTHER: Everything I see and hear breaks my heart.

NARRATOR: She throws her arms around a wicker basket and falls, seemingly at her last gasp.

MOTHER: What demon could have possessed her? She never showed the least depravity, nothing which would make her do such a thing. She was a straightforward, obedient daughter, and she brought up her own children admirably. I can hear her voice saying, "Mother dear, with so many daughters I won't throw away a single article of my bridal presents. I'll keep everything for their dowries. My husband's in-

---

[39] A play on the words *ukifushi* (wretched things) and *Fushimi*.

[40] A modified version of the poem (no. 1719) by the priest Dōen in the collection *Shoku-Kokinshū*, compiled in 1266.

come is limited, and I don't want to cause him financial strain."

She lived up to her word. These belongings are twenty years old, but she's kept them so well they don't show their age. How could such a thoughtful person be capable of such wickedness? Was she bewitched? Or was she paying for the sins of a former life?

NARRATOR: Fresh tears come as she rehearses her griefs.

MOTHER: I can understand Ichinoshin's resentment, but this is too unkind. He should have given Osai's possessions to the children instead of piling them here in this unseemly manner. Doesn't he realize the disgrace he is causing the children? Servants! Maids! Hurry, bring everything inside before too many people notice.

NARRATOR: She weeps with anguish.

IWAKI: Now, now, Grandmother. I've listened to your complaints, but I can't see that they serve any purpose. Ichinoshin is entirely correct. Supposing he kept these belongings of a woman he must some day kill with her paramour—what could he do with them? She's outside the pale of human society, her furnishings are contaminated. They would pollute a samurai's house. Servants! Break up all these boxes and burn them!

SERVANTS: Yes, sir.

NARRATOR: With clubs, mallets, spades, hoes, axes, and whatever else they can find, they set to work smashing Osai's possessions. Her mother, unable to bear the sight, holds out her arms.

MOTHER: Wait, wait! Grandfather, I don't begrudge losing these things, but I'll never again see Osai's face in this world or the next. I'd like to keep something touched by her hands, if only one small object, as a memento for my old age. One can never forget a child, even if she runs away from home, even if she's in China or Korea. It breaks my heart too when I remember how much she wanted to leave her belongings to her children. Please let me take one thing for each of the children.

NARRATOR: She pulls a wicker basket to her, clings to the clothes chest, weeping the while in agony.

IWAKI: If you think that what has happened now is sad, remember that you and I will have even sadder tidings to hear.[41] What shall we do then? When you grow old, hearing unhappy news becomes your

[41] That is, the death of Osai.

"*Osai unravels the secrets of ladylike appearance and conduct as she strokes her daughter's hair with the fine teeth of the comb.*"

Ichinoshin slashes the disarmed Gonza on the bridge. "If only I had a bamboo pole! Even with one hand I could leave the world some remembrance of how I acquired the name Gonza the Lancer!"
(ICHINOSHIN: *Yoshida Tōtarō, operator;* GONZA: *.Yoshida Tamao, operator*)

part in life. Resign yourself and swallow your tears. I too will endure the worst.

NARRATOR: This country samurai speaks severely, but his throat is choked by tears.

IWAKI: There's no escaping it. What will our friends think, what will people in other provinces say if we accept Osai's possessions? (*To the servants.*) Don't let the smoke rise too high.[42] Burn each piece separately.

NARRATOR: The servants are reluctant, but they cannot disobey their master's orders. They drag out the baskets, chests, and lacquered trunks, and break them. Lonely flames rise as from a fisherman's fire: the mother is the more distraught not to see a face in the smoke.[43]

MOTHER: When Osai left our house to be married we burnt a fire at this very gate,[44] and we prayed for her future happiness. The presents we gave her then will turn to ashes in the flames of a later gate fire. Why don't you cremate my body with this firewood?

NARRATOR: Seeing her lament makes the maids and servants, even the lowly apprentices, wring the tears from their sleeves.

IWAKI: All that remains is that oblong chest. Break it up and burn it too.

NARRATOR: But when they open the lid, they find inside the two little girls weeping and clinging to each other. The grandparents can hardly believe their eyes.

IWAKI: That was a narrow escape! You children are certainly lucky. What would have happened if the chest had been set on fire? Why didn't you say something? Did your strict father forbid you? What well-behaved children! How could your mother have abandoned such children, lovely as the cherry blossoms or the maple leaves?

NARRATOR: The old people caress the children's hair. Osute says innocently:

OSUTE: I want to see Mother. Please call her.

[42] Or people will notice it.
[43] When the incense known in Japan as *hangonkō* was burnt by the Emperor Wu of the Han Dynasty, he saw in the smoke the face of his beloved Li Fu-jen. But this is the smoke not of *hangonkō* but of burning furniture.
[44] It was customary to light a fire at the gate when a girl left home to be married. She was thereby enjoined to remain with her new husband for the rest of her life and never to return to her parents' home.

NARRATOR: She weeps. Her older sister Okiku is mature beyond her years.

OKIKU: Father says he's going to kill Mother. Grandfather, Grandmother, I beg you both. Please apologize to Father. Ask him to spare Mother's life and take mine instead.

NARRATOR: She throws herself down, leaning her head against their knees by turn.

IWAKI: Noble child! I'm sure that your mother doesn't give as much thought to you!

Why wasn't Torajirō sent with you? It's the custom in divorces to give the daughters to the mother, but we don't distinguish among our grandchildren. It would distract us from our griefs to see the three of you all day long. Osute, Grandmother gave you your name "Rejected One"[45] because you were two years old when your father was forty-two. Now your father, mother, brother, and sister are all rejected by the world.

NARRATOR: He crumples with grief as he recounts these memories. His old man's face, sere as a withered tree, is unrecognizable for the tears.

IWAKI: Don't cry, don't cry. There's nothing to fret over. Your mother may have abandoned you, but your grandparents love you, and you have your Uncle Jimbei. Come into the house.

NARRATOR: He takes them by the hand, and weeping they go inside.

Asaka Ichinoshin wears his hair in the tea-whisk style.[46] He has but a wisp of an income, but he has practiced the martial arts, and his heart boils like a kettle for revenge; the success of his mission will rest with fate. Hardly had he returned from Edo than he was obliged to set out for revenge, and with this in mind he disposed of his children. He breathed easier then, but while in his province he is ashamed to be seen.

He approaches his father-in-law's gate with hat pulled over his face. This time, unlike previous visits, it is impolite to enter without an-

---

[45] "Forty-two" (*shini*), the homophone of the word for "death", is unlucky. "Forty-four" (*shi-shi*), the combination of the ages of father and daughter, also suggested death. The name Osute was given to ward off the bad luck: *sute* means "abandon", and it was customary to abandon an ill-starred child, then later to accept him as a foundling when a stranger, by request, rescued the child.

[46] The passage contains various images drawn from the tea ceremony, in keeping with Ichinoshin's profession. The tea-whisk style of coiffure was favored by samurai, particularly when traveling.

nouncing himself, yet to request admission would be too stiff. As he stands looking into the entrance, wishing that there were some way to say good-by, his father-in-law Chūtabei dashes out of the house, his skirts tucked high over his thin shanks. A vermilion scabbard, warped enough to use as a pothook, dangles by his side. Ichinoshin calls out and catches Chūtabei's sleeve. He removes his wicker hat and throws it aside.

IWAKI: Ichinoshin! This morning we received that vile creature's belongings together with our two granddaughters. I presume you've come to say good-by before you set out on your journey. Thank you for taking the trouble. I trust that I shall have good news soon.[47]

NARRATOR: With these words he hurries off again.

ICHINOSHIN: No, just a moment! You have such a strange look, it worries me. Forgive me, but I shan't let you go till I learn your intentions.

IWAKI: I was humiliated, Ichinoshin, that when you returned from Edo, I could not show you the severed head of my accursed daughter. My son Jimbei has been searching for the guilty couple ever since the day of the crime. I am an old man, but not too weak to stand on my feet, and I cannot sleep peacefully until I wet my sword with blood. My rage is too great to keep within myself. I wished for an adversary, when I recalled that Kawazura Bannojō was the first to produce proofs of her immorality, and spread the report to us and then to the whole province. I have decided to kill the villain, a final remembrance for my old age. Now let me go.

ICHINOSHIN: I understand your feelings, but you may be killed by Bannojō—you're an old man, after all. I'd be obliged to put aside vengeance on my wife's seducer in order to kill my father-in-law's enemy. With two such obligations coming together, I don't know what I'd do. Please, I beg you, give up your plan. I ask it as a favor.

NARRATOR: He bows his head.

IWAKI: Do you mean, Ichinoshin, that if I were killed you would avenge me, the father of such a depraved wife?

ICHINOSHIN: Your question surprises me. My wife may have become a brute beast, but that does not alter the fact that you are my father-in-law. How could I fail to avenge you if you had an enemy? You need not have asked such a question.

---

[47] The death of Osai is meant.

IWAKI: Ichinoshin, your goodness is more than I deserve. I am overcome.

NARRATOR: He bends his aged limbs on the ground and weeps tears of gratitude. Ichinoshin's eyes darken with tears though he cannot extend his hand. Here are two men who act as warriors should.

IWAKI: Please drink a parting cup with Grandmother. I'm sure you'd also like to see your daughters once again. I won't ask that you go inside, when you're all dressed for your journey. (*Calls.*) Ichinoshin is here! Come, everybody!

ICHINOSHIN: I told the little imps they mustn't, but I suppose that they cried anyway.

IWAKI: No, they acted like angels. You needn't have worried.

NARRATOR: They sit at the entrance. The old woman comes out with her two grandchildren, leading one with each hand, and soon food and saké appear. The family is gathered as for a holiday feast, or to celebrate the children's birthdays. The place is the same as ever; only the number present is changed. They exchange glances and silently nod. Their faces holding back the tears are more pathetic than if contorted with weeping. Even the serving maids wet their sleeves, though no saké is spilled. The grandmother, unable longer to restrain her tears, bursts into wails.

MOTHER: Poor dear children—are you still obeying your father's instructions? When I look at you, so grown up though the tears shine in your eyes, I wonder how such wonderful children could have issued from that sinful, bestial, monstrous mother. If only she possessed a normal disposition, our family would be complete, and the world would have praised Chūtabei and his wife for their children and grandchildren.

Why have you kept Tora with you? Did you send back only the girls because you think that daughters belong to the mother? Will you treat the Iwaki family as strangers and break your connections with us? What a heartless man you are! You make me hate you!

NARRATOR: She raises her voice and pours into her last phrase all her pent-up tears.

ICHINOSHIN: Your resentment is misplaced. I have not the least intention of breaking with you. His lordship has released me from my post, and I now am without duties. Yet I cannot abandon the tea ceremony taught me by my father, my greatest pleasure to this day. I have sent

Torajirō to study the ceremony with Sen no Kyūsai. Please overcome your resentment and drink a parting cup with me.

MOTHER: Of course. I should have known.

NARRATOR: Her anger melts, and they exchange cups without reserve. Their only words are, "May all go well!" and "Rest assured—I shall be successful soon!" What trick of fate, what fault of the times, what evil connection from the past makes them anticipate with joy the accomplishment of his vow—killing his children's mother, his own wife? The thought so oppresses Ichinoshin that his heart, strong as iron or stone, is thrown into confusion; before he knows it, he is choking in tears.

Osai's brother Jimbei returns, worn out from a journey with nights spent in the fields. He is accompanied by a servant. Chūtabei stands to greet him.

IWAKI: Jimbei, what happened? Ichinoshin is about to leave. Tell us everything.

NARRATOR: The others rise to their feet, straining for news.

JIMBEI: Ichinoshin—what a calamity in your absence—and so unforeseen! Father urged me to kill the adulterers and have their heads ready to show you before you returned. I set out immediately on the morning of their elopement. I traveled with food at my side, investigating every inn, relay station, and harbor along the coastal road. I at first searched even the remote villages on the other side of the mountains, but I realized that a man traveling with a woman, a poor walker at best, and himself frightened and confused, was unlikely to choose a distant hiding place. I searched the Hōki Road, but without success. I was planning to continue the hunt, but I remembered that I left with only a hasty excuse to my fellow officers on duty, and without the senior officer's permission. It was clearly improper to be absent so many days without leave, so I turned back. I returned a short while ago and at once notified the authorities. Everything is settled now and I've stopped by for a moment to see my parents. How fortunate to have found you! A few moments earlier or later for either of us and we should never have met. How tragic that would have been! I'm sure our lucky meeting is a sign that we shall succeed in our undertaking. Let's leave together.

NARRATOR: His voice rings with excitement. Ichinoshin claps his hands admiringly.

ICHINOSHIN: Many thanks for your trouble and efforts. Your kindness and your father's move me more than I can say. But you need not accompany me. I shall travel alone. I have nothing to ask of anyone. Rest yourself, please, Jimbei.

JIMBEI: You needn't stand on ceremony with me. I know how courageous you are, but the best plans misfire when there aren't enough men to execute them. That's why such a calamity struck while you sat calmly in Edo, never dreaming that anything could happen.

Gonza must have relatives and friends in the other provinces. There's no telling what steps he may take. Something unexpected might happen while you're on the road for three or four days at a time, and you'll be glad for a helping sword. I urge you most earnestly, take me along.

ICHINOSHIN: I know I can depend on you, but could I say that I had carried through my revenge if I asked my wife's brother to help kill her lover?

JIMBEI: I can help you anyway, even if I don't use my sword.

NARRATOR: His voice rises angrily. Ichinoshin loses his good humor.

ICHINOSHIN: You seem to think that because I'm a tea master I only know how to take the lid from a kettle and don't know how to take a man's head. I swear by Hachiman, god of bow and arrow, that although I am only of humble standing and my armor is broken, my weapons are ready, and when the moment comes, I can hold my own against the great saber-rattlers.

NARRATOR: Jimbei bursts out laughing.

JIMBEI: You make me laugh. Why, if you're such a great warrior, haven't you killed the seducer in your own back yard?

ICHINOSHIN: The seducer in my own back yard? You mean Kawazura Bannojō?

JIMBEI: Yes. If you can remember his name so quickly, why haven't you killed him?

NARRATOR: Ichinoshin is taken aback.

ICHINOSHIN: It's true, I found several improper letters from him in my wife's writing box. I intended to use my sword on him, but I couldn't take care of everything at once. I decided to leave him for a later day.

JIMBEI: There you are! You can't handle two enemies at once, even when one is right under your nose. I don't know how you decided which enemy to dispose of immediately and which in the future, but though you refused my help, Ichinoshin, one of your enemies has already been accounted for by Iwaki Jimbei's sword. Look!

NARRATOR: He rips off the end of the provision kit at his side: it contains the newly washed head of Bannojō. Ichinoshin cries out, amazed. The two old people are highly pleased.

IWAKI: "An enemy so hateful you'd search for him to the bottom of hell." The phrase describes that villain exactly. But he is a retainer of this fief. What excuse have you made to your superiors?

JIMBEI: None is necessary. He knew that he'd soon have to answer for his crime, and he ran away without asking permission. I caught him at the border of Inaba Province and satisfied my grievance.

IWAKI: Splendid! I'm proud of you. Ichinoshin, what more promising sign could there be at the outset of your revenge mission? Take Jimbei with you—it is my command. I need hardly tell you, Jimbei, that you are not to blemish Ichinoshin's reputation by depriving him of the satisfaction of personally killing his enemies.

ICHINOSHIN: I obey your command, sir. I take my leave.

NARRATOR: He is about to depart when he catches sight of a boy in traveling attire furtively peeping into the house from his hiding place behind a gatepost. Ichinoshin, puzzled, runs to the spot and discovers his son Torajirō, a manly figure in traveling garb.

ICHINOSHIN: Where do you intend to go dressed up that way? Bothersome child!

NARRATOR: He catches the boy by the wrists and drags him from hiding.

TORAJIRŌ: I am going with you, Father. Okiku and Osute are girls. I'm a man. I wouldn't be a samurai if I let you go off alone to kill your enemies.

NARRATOR: He starts to run ahead, but Ichinoshin stops him.

ICHINOSHIN: Do you intend to kill your own mother?

TORAJIRŌ: Why should I kill Mother? I'm going to kill that wicked Gonza who took Mother away. You can't stop me.

NARRATOR: He insists on his way.

ICHINOSHIN: That's a poor plan. Your uncle and your father are going. That will leave only old people and girls at home. I intend to station you here as a safeguard to kill Gonza in case he returns. I want you to study the tea ceremony with Kyūsai very diligently. You should call here once in a while to make sure that everything is all right. Be a good boy to your grandparents and look after your sisters. If Gonza comes, cut him down on the spot. Of course, if you're afraid to be left alone, we'll take you with us.

NARRATOR: He cajoles the boy with soothing words.

TORAJIRŌ: I'll be glad to stay here alone. Don't worry about us after you've gone, but be sure to be successful.

NARRATOR: A sensible answer from a clever lad. The old people's eyes are clouded.

MOTHER: What wonderful children! A mother who wouldn't wish to see such children grow up must be a monster! I don't feel sorry for her. Slash her or stab her, whatever you please, but finish your mission quickly.

NARRATOR: This is a farewell in tears. The three children cry out in their different voices.

CHILDREN: "Kill that bad man Gonza." "Please bring Mother back safely." "Good-by, Father."

NARRATOR: But when their father attempts to pronounce even the word "good-by," his eyes mist over and his heart is clouded with thoughts numerous as the clouds over his native town.[48]

Scene Three: The Capital Bridge at Fushimi.

NARRATOR: "Who is that in the moonlight? Come, sleep with me, come lie in my boat." In Fushimi,[49] the town that owes its name to the boats where one lies and looks at the moon, if you come in the evening to Capital Bridge,[50] the wind strikes cool against the sleeve as it blows over Uji River, here one stream with Kamo waters, borne down from the capital.

Gonza and Osai have stayed three days in Fushimi, but they cannot bear to remain long in the same place. By the Ink-Dyed Cherry Tree,[51]

[48] Izumo, the province in which Matsue is situated, is written with characters which mean "emerging clouds."

[49] The name Fushimi is here interpreted as meaning *fushi* (lying down) and *mi* (to look at). Fushimi, a river port, is now part of the city of Kyoto.

[50] A calligraphic wordplay. If the left side of the character 涼, meaning "cool", is removed, we have 京, meaning "capital".

[51] A landmark of Fushimi. Mention of the cherry blossoms is suggested by the inability of the lovers to remain three days, the life span of cherry blossoms.

withered in autumn, they hear the evening bell. It seems to sound their last day of life; they wonder if they will hear tomorrow's. Ignoring the warning, they decide to travel on to Osaka. They furtively board a passenger boat, and once aboard nod their heads in pretended sleep. Refreshment boats are rowed alongside, selling noodles and buckwheat vermicelli, bean curd, Nara congee, and tea. The waters of Uji River flow into this stream and Osai, woman that she is, recalls the past with sorrow in her breast.[52]

Ichinoshin is at Gokō Shrine, Jimbei in Misu Village. Every day each informs the other of his whereabouts. Today Jimbei, alone in the sunset shadows beneath Capital Bridge, surveys the boats.

JIMBEI (*to boatman*): I'd like passage if one of you is leaving soon.

NARRATOR: He examines the boatman.

BOATMAN: This is your boat, if you want one leaving soon. I'm shoving off at the first bell.[53]

JIMBEI: The boat looks terribly crowded.

BOATMAN: It's not crowded. Stoop down and take a place behind the partition next to the young gentleman and his missus. There's plenty of room there. Please step aboard.

JIMBEI: I'm not fussy about where I sit—anywhere will do. But the first bell is too late. I'll take the day boat tomorrow.

BOATMAN: Have it your own way. The boat is mine, but it's your privilege to come aboard or not. I won't force you.

NARRATOR: While the man speaks Jimbei is carefully noting the boat's interior.

JIMBEI (*to himself*): I can't see their faces, but I'm absolutely certain it's they.

NARRATOR: He jumps for joy, but afraid that he might be observed from behind the partition, he slowly, deliberately steps back onto the bridge, and saunters back and forth a couple of times, as if out for the evening cool. He prays for luck, and something in his heart says he has drawn the winning lot. He rushes to Ichinoshin's lodgings as fast as his feet will carry him.

Gonza pushes aside the partition.

GONZA: I've forgotten something extremely important. Boatman, please let us go ashore.

[52] Mention of tea suggests Uji, and this in turn makes Osai think of her husband, the tea master.

[53] About 8 P.M.

osai: Yes, somebody asked us to make an important purchase. We've even accepted the money. But we were in such a hurry to get aboard that we forgot all about it. Please put us ashore.

boatman: How far must you go to make this purchase of yours?

gonza: Let me see. What was that street called again? Oh, yes. It was just beyond Wisteria Grove on the other side of Bellhammer Street.

boatman: You've really bit off more than you can chew! Have you any idea how far that is from here? It's about four miles! By the time you get back, the ship will have left. No, I can't let you go ashore.

narrator: His voice is unemotional; he takes no further notice of them.

gonza: If we're late, shove off and don't worry about us. I'll pay two fares before we go ashore. Please, I beg you.

narrator: He does not take his eyes from the area between the bridge and the shops to the north and south.

boatman: Sir, you're so carried away you don't realize what silly things you're saying. I'd lose my reputation if I took your money and then didn't take you anywhere. Stay where you are, please.

gonza: Show a little kindness, boatman. It'll become very crowded aboard if more passengers show up like that man a moment ago. Please put us ashore.

boatman: Don't worry about the boat being crowded. I promise to deliver you in Osaka tomorrow morning to your entire satisfaction. If we really get crowded tonight, I'll cut your missus in two and slice you in pieces, the better to stow you both away! But don't pay any attention to my jokes—stretch yourself out and repose in peace.[54]

narrator: His words add one more burden to their hearts. Osai is much agitated.

osai: Excuse me, Mr. Boatman, but there's such a thing as consideration for other people's feelings. You say that if you accept our money without taking us anywhere, your reputation as a boatman will suffer. But what will happen to our reputation if, after we've been entrusted with people's money, we fail to deliver the purchases? I entreat you, please put us ashore.

narrator: She exhausts every argument at her command, and at last he listens.

boatman: In that case, you'd best go ashore at once.

[54] The boatman's jokes all foreshadow the manner of death of the lovers.

GONZA: Thank you, thank you so much.

NARRATOR: The two rush off hand in hand. The boatman notices their hurrying feet.

BOATMAN: You're going to hurt yourselves that way. Take care not to stumble on the gangway or the lady will get a gash on top of the big one she already has!

NARRATOR: His usual boatman's joke today has an unpleasant ring. They hide behind the waiting room.

GONZA: Jimbei's here and it's certain that Ichinoshin's also in the area. Well, our wish has been granted. Prepare yourself now for the end.

OSAI: I've long been prepared. Ever since the night we ran away from home, my life has been for my husband to take. I shall not begrudge it. But to die at my brother Jimbei's hands would be mortifying, a dog's death. I'm sure we're both agreed that, if we see it's Jimbei, our duty to Ichinoshin obliges us to escape as best we can. But we can't remain here. Where shall we spend tonight?

GONZA: What about Misu Point? Or Aburakake? We might gradually make our way to Kyoto.

NARRATOR: The evening sky is already darkening. Cutwork lanterns lit at the eaves here and there are decorated with floral designs and picture puzzles.[55] In the shops people fan themselves as they chat about the theater. Dancing girls, twelve or thirteen years old, and some as young as eight, are charming figures in their black coats tucked in at their waists and dark purple coifs. They dance together, a graceful sight.

DANCERS:

> *Soré, soré, soré, soré, yattosé.*
> I vowed to love forever
> After one night spent among Naniwae reeds,
> But the gate of love is barred.
> I think it best I give him up,
> But I swore I'd never leave him,
> And I fear the wrath of Heaven.
> My parents may disown me,
> But I'll never take another man.
> Soon we'll meet again,

---

[55] Ornamental lanterns were decorated with thinly cut strips of wood and paper fashioned in various designs including rebuses.

Though I have to travel a thousand leagues
Across a dreadful forest.
Danda, furé, furé.
And that's the end! [56]

NARRATOR: How nostalgic the dancing figures make Osai!

OASI: Those dancers—my daughters at home are the same age! I wonder if they're alive or dead or sick? Poor dears—they won't be dancing this year. I'm cut off completely from my children now, and my death, wherever it occurs, will be degrading. No child will offer water at my last rites. And who will wash my body and arrange it for the funeral? I wish I could die now and, with these lanterns as my light through the darkness of the realm of Six Ways,[57] dispel my delusions. At least in the world to come I want to be saved.

NARRATOR: She murmurs these words as they trudge along. Gonza's heart is overcast and—despite the drought this year, has someone prayed for relief?—knowledge of his fate brings an endless rain upon his sleeves.

Ichinoshin is armed with his favorite blade, a Bizen Kunimatsu. "Luck is with me now," he thinks. The ties with his wife are now as faint as the tan dye of the hempen robe twisted around his loins. He and Jimbei move apart like sunset clouds, now one ahead, now the other. The time is the latter part of the Hour of the Bird,[58] harbinger of hell. Luck is indeed with him: at the northern end of the bridge he runs into the guilty pair.

ICHINOSHIN: Sasano Gonza! Seducer of my wife! Do you remember me?

NARRATOR: Even before he finishes these words his sword is flashing.

GONZA: I have been expecting you.

NARRATOR: He holds up his left arm. Ichinoshin instantly lops his hand off at the wrist. Gonza springs back.

GONZA: I must as a samurai at least go through the motions of defending myself.

[56] Their song is filled with puns on the names of famous poets represented in the *Hyakunin Isshu. Yamabe,* for example, is used for *yamen* (give him up) and Sarumaru for *saru* (to leave).
[57] After death, according to Buddhist belief, the soul spends forty-nine days wandering in the dark before it arrives at its destination, one of the Six Ways. Osai would like to illumine the darkness with one of the lanterns.
[58] About 7 P.M.

NARRATOR: He unsheathes his dirk and points it at Ichinoshin.

BYSTANDERS: A wild man! He's stabbed him! He's stabbed him! It's a fight! Bring me a stick! Don't let the dancing girls get hurt!

VOICE: Okichi-sama!

VOICE: Osen-sama!

VOICE: Hambei!

VOICE: Gonsuke!

NARRATOR: What with people calling one another and fleeing from the scene, the eight or nine streets all around are in an uproar, as if the Ten Man Massacre were being reenacted tonight.[59] Osai catches a glimpse of Jimbei.

OSAI: I want to be killed by my husband's sword. It would be a dog's death to be killed by my brother.

NARRATOR: She hides a while in the shadow of the bridge.

Gonza lunges forward with his dirk and, missing Ichinoshin, the point sinks into the bridge railing so deeply he cannot dislodge it.

GONZA: If only I had a bamboo pole! Even with one hand I could leave the world some remembrance of how I acquired the name Gonza the Lancer! Never mind, I'll give them a show with my feet!

NARRATOR: His movements as he ducks under his enemy's blade, himself swordless, are incredible in a wounded man and worthy of a master. Ichinoshin throws all his strength into the greatest effort of his life. He slashes Gonza aslant from the right shoulder to the chest, but Gonza does not flinch, despite this staggering blow: his final actions are worthy. The bridge is flecked as if with crimson autumn leaves. In this rare encounter of enemy and enemy, Ichinoshin charges again and again, until Gonza, wounded five times, at last tumbles over backwards. His is the corpse of a true samurai—not a single wound says he has turned his back.

Ichinoshin has lost track of the woman. In consternation, he runs north, then back south again, wondering where she has vanished. His eyes as he searches from corner to corner flash like a cat's prowling for a mouse. On the bridge Gonza's body still writhes in anguish. It is the middle of the seventh moon, and his blood streaming into the moonlit water makes Fushimi River look like Tatsuta River in maple time.[60]

[59] A reference to the night attack by the Soga brothers against the camp of Minamoto Yoritomo in 1193. They slew ten men.

[60] The autumn scenery of Tatsuta River, when crimson leaves floated in blue waters, was a hackneyed subject of poetry.

Jimbei appears, dragging his sister.

osai: It would be humiliating to be killed by you, his second. Please let me die at my husband's hands.

jimbei: What need would a splendid swordsman like Ichinoshin have for a second?

narrator: He pushes her onto the middle of the bridge.

osai: My dear husband!

narrator: She approaches Ichinoshin. With one hand he slashes her from hip to hip, and she topples on her face with a shriek. He grips her by the sash and lifts up her face. A look at her brings pity for his children; his breast floods with tears of wrath at this hateful, hateful woman. He shakes off the thought and, driving his sword into her again, he pushes back her body. He stamps on her breast and thrusts his sword point deep into her vitals. Such is his fury that he slashes his own right foot from heel to sole without realizing it. He turns at once to Gonza. Stamping on his chest, he deals the final thrust.

Gonza the Lancer's lance is an old one, his wounds are old, the tale is old, and the song about Gonza goes back many years, but this story of his life will linger in the valleys of bamboo, in the gossip of the world, long as the handle of his lance.

THE UPROOTED PINE

First performed on the day after New Year of the third year of Kyōhō (February 1, 1718). The title of the play in Japanese, *Nebiki no kadomatsu*, contains an elaborate play on words. It may mean a pine tree, uprooted entirely to symbolize longevity and hung at gates at New Year; it may also refer to a "Pine," the highest rank of courtesan, who is "uprooted" or ransomed from service in a brothel. The title and probably also the ending may be explained in terms of the New Year festivities which accompanied the first performance of the play.

Cast of Characters

YOJIBEI of Yamazaki

JŌKAN, his father, a rich merchant

JIBUEMON, his father-in-law, a samurai

YOHEI, a poor young man

HIKOSUKE, a tobacco merchant

KUROZAEMON, host at the Izutzu House, a teahouse

KAN'EMON, owner of Azuma's contract

SHINSUKE, a boy

AZUMA, a courtesan of the highest rank

OKIKU, Yojibei's wife

OKAYA, a "Chaser"

OLD WOMAN, Yohei's mother

COURTESANS' MAIDS, "LAUNCHES," "TOWBOATS," "DEBUTANTES," and other prostitutes of different ranks

ACT ONE

*Scene One: A street in the Shimmachi Licensed Quarter of
Osaka.*
Time: New Year, 1718.

NARRATOR:
>   Like the white jewels of the waterfall
>   Tumbling from the peak of Mount Tsukuba,[1]
>   The shuttlecock goes bounding back and forth,
>   One, two, three, four, five, six, seven, eight,
>   Nine-house Street[2] is where the mated battledores[3]
>   Polish the shuttlecock to its full luster
>   As the courtesans' maids, now sprouting first leaves,
>   Will be polished by love.

They send the shuttlecock back and forth lazily three, four, five
times, young pines with enlacing branches, and their drawling tones[4]
are familiar to the New Year pines, to those kept Pines who pine for
their customers; in Shimmachi on the first Day of the Rat[5] of this
year the green deepens in the Pines so numerous that the uprooting of
Pines on this day will never cease, though a thousand generations pass.[6]

MAID: Shinsuke! You insist on batting the shuttlecock even when I
tell you I don't want you to. Now look what you've done! You've
knocked it into the pine tree. Bring it down again!

NARRATOR: She clings to his sleeve.

SHINSUKE: Let go of my sleeve! You should've known in the first
place that it'd get knocked up if you let a man at it. What's so strange?

NARRATOR: He shakes his sleeve free and claps his hands.

[1] The name Tsukuba suggests the words *tsuku* (to strike) and *ha* (feather), words related
to "shuttlecock" which follows.

[2] Name of a section of the Shimmachi Licensed Quarter.

[3] At New Year people played at battledore and shuttlecock. The battledores were paired,
one decorated with the picture of a prince, and the other with that of a princess.

[4] Courtesans' maids (*kamuro*) prolonged the last syllable of their words; the text has
mi-i and *yo-o* for *mi* (three) and *yo* (four).

[5] On the first Day of the Rat (*hatsune*) people formerly went out into the fields to
uproot young pines as part of the New Year festivities. *Hatsune*, written with different
characters, also means "first sleep [day]," when courtesans met their customers for the
first time in the year.

[6] When uprooting pines it was customary to pray for a thousand generations of happiness. The sentence otherwise contains puns on the pine tree, the Pine (the highest rank
of courtesan) and the verb "to pine for".

SHINSUKE: Ha-ha! That's none of my concern! The red of my eye
to you!

NARRATOR: He runs inside the house.

MAIDS: Don't let him escape! Catch him!

NARRATOR: They fly after him in a manner befitting a quarrel that
started over a shuttlecock.

Beautiful enough to entice the first sprouts of love through the
valley snows white as their feet, wearing sleeves of mist fragrant with
rare incense and sashes bright as rainbows, cloaks of clouds draped on
their shoulders, the Launches and Debutantes sally forth in full glory.

> Indigo and saffron, pale hues, light blues,
> Woven silks, embroidered silks,
> Every kind of dyeing in figured patterns,
> Triple-dyed and double-dyed,
> Dappled silk of azure and dappled silk of green,
> Purple silks dappled with snows of passing years
> And griefs that crimson silks, like poppies, make us forget.⁷

A procession in dazzling colors moves along Echigo Street. The
three thoroughfares are bright with a triple flush of spring, the season
when the Pines put forth Young Shoots and the Plum begins to flower.⁸
The Chasers' new aprons glow sunrise scarlet under an intoxicated
sky, and men get drunk on this year's first cups of saké. The courtesans toast the New Year at their houses, then set out together on calls
of thanks: the clatter of their sandals strikes up a tune of spring. Among
them no flower is the peer of Azuma, the famous Pine of the Wisteria
House, who rules the Quarter as purple rules the colors.⁹ Her eyes flash
love and wisdom, her whole appearance as she promenades so brims
with tenderness that passers in the street must stop to gaze, and even
the wild geese, deserting the spring blossoms for the north, turn back
to the Quarter for one last glimpse.

An old woman of seventy, unashamed of either her station or her
age, an old cotton bonnet pulled around her face, and wrapped, in

---

⁷ A pun on *keshi* (the poppy) and *keshi* (to obliterate [the griefs of past years]). Purple
was the color worn by senior courtesans (here, Azuma). The passage contains numerous
other plays on words and allusions.

⁸ "Young shoots" were *kamuro* expected to become future "Pines"; the second rank
of courtesans were known as "Plum trees".

⁹ Purple from ancient times was considered the most noble color. It is associated here
with the name "Wisteria House".

honor of the spring no doubt, in a wadded cloak of greenish-brown,[10] redeemed from the depths of a pawnshop, rubs her sleeve against Azuma and trails on her heels. Okaya, the Chaser, calls in a loud voice.

OKAYA: Look here, old woman! Why, when you have a great, broad street to walk on must you go creeping after the lady, as if you were the old dame in *Takasago*[11] and you'd been separated from your husband? You're an eyesore and a nuisance. And who is that young man sneaking behind you? I don't suppose he carries your palanquin. Is he your accomplice? Out of the way, both of you, at once!

NARRATOR: She pushes her aside, but the old woman is not provoked.

OLD WOMAN: Ah, you may well say that. Please pardon me. I know it's presumptuous of me, but I have something to discuss privately with the great Azuma. I've been wandering all over the Quarter looking for her. Please grant me this kindness. It will help me even in the world to come. Oh, I feel so ashamed! I'm sure that the exalted lady must think a wrinkled old crone like myself is nothing but a curiosity-seeker.

OKAYA: You're quite a clever talker, but it's an old, old trick to watch for a courtesan going by in her full finery and then to announce that you're her aunt or her grandmother. But that's what a Chaser is for. My eyes are quite sharp—watch out!

OLD WOMAN: Please don't say such dreadful things. Do I look as if I'm trying to trick her?—Ah, it's a curse to be poor. My husband was Yozaemon of the Naniwa-ya, a man well known in Semba, with a thousand *kamme* at his beck and call. But he fell behind in payments on the exchange and he was forced to shut up his shop in Osaka and move to Yawata, where he died. The old woman before you was his wife, and this young man with his face covered is his only son. The boy was brought up in a household where he was warmed by the steam from a cauldron of a thousand *kamme,* but now he hasn't as much as a string of copper coins to his name. Yohei, Hard-luck Yohei,[12] they call him, and he's a day laborer earning just enough to see him through each day.—Yes, I can see why you might think I was up to some trickery.

[10] Literally, "*uguisu*-brown". The *uguisu* is a bird of greenish-brown hue which sings in the springtime.

[11] A Nō play about a faithful old couple, translated in *Japanese Noh Drama*, published by Nippon Gakujutsu Shinkōkai.

[12] He should be called Naniwaya Yohei, after the name of his father's shop, but the name Naniwa is shortened to *nan,* meaning "hard luck".

NARRATOR: Tears shine in her eyes as she rambles on, an old woman's wont. Even as she tells this story no one has asked to hear, she seems lost in old memories. The "Towboats" and courtesans' maids answer boldly.

MAIDS: Oh, is it about you, granny, that they sing in the dance tunes— "Yah, yah, Yamazaki, Yamazaki, Yohei's ma from Yamazaki. Some money, please, she says, I truly need the money."—Come again the day before yesterday!

NARRATOR: They laugh, but Azuma meanwhile has been weeping in sympathy.

AZUMA: What are you all laughing about? When someone's down on his luck, it doesn't matter whether or not it's because of love, we in the profession never turn our backs. Dear, sweet old lady! I'm touched that you should have put your trust in me. I swear by the providence of courtesans that I will hear you. But it's so crowded here. (*To Towboat.*) Shigeyama, please hire a place in one of those little shops on the side street off Ageya Lane. We can talk there. Come with me.

NARRATOR: She takes her hand; the old woman weeps.

OLD WOMAN: Thank you, thank you very much. I'm sure you must be wondering what request an old woman of my years could make of you. Yohei—he's a rascal, but he's the moon and stars of my life—was sent here to Shimmachi by his employer to deliver a letter. He saw you then, Azuma, and he fell in love at first sight. (*She laughs uneasily.*) It's embarrassing for a mother to talk about such a thing, but the boy is sick from love. I've scolded him time and again, I've told him that the landlord and the neighbors would hear of it and that it was a sure sign that he'd be holding out a beggar's bowl before long. I thought of chasing him from the house for once and for all. But then I recalled that if we had our former fortunes the young man would be in the midst of affairs with all kinds of kept women and mistresses. Forgive me for saying so, but we could have bought him the exclusive favors of even the highest rank of courtesan for a year or two at a time without feeling any financial strain. That's the style of living he was brought up in. I love him and I wish I could do something to help, but my own feeble struggles and my son's hopes have been overpowered by the enemy called Money. I seemed to have no choice but to look on helplessly as my son's life wasted away. Finally I told him, "Don't worry, love is Azuma's business. I'll beg her to drink a cup of saké with you. And with that you must break off your attachment." I've brought him with me, and I've trailed after you, all out of love for my son. If a mother's life were worth the price of a courtesan for a single night, I would cheerfully kill myself here and now. I don't mean to force you, but won't you please drink a little saké from this cup?

NARRATOR: She produces from her sleeve a small saké bottle filled to overflowing with maternal love, and a chipped saké cup painted in lacquer with a design of monkeys. The others smile, but their laughter soon turns to tears; even the Chaser, who does not know what weeping means, is so moved she looks the other way.

The more she hears, the more Azuma droops her head.

AZUMA: You're a very knowing old lady. Words quite fail me. Where has Yohei gone? I'd like to see his face. Ask him to come here.

NARRATOR: The old woman feels as though in one instant her life has been prolonged a thousand years, like the New Year pine in whose shadow Hard-luck Yohei has been hiding. Called to, he creeps out embarrassedly, his finger in his mouth. Azuma takes his sleeve and pulls him towards her.

AZUMA: It's an honor for a woman of my profession when even some casual customer says, "I've fallen for you," though it's only an empty phrase. I am happy to have stirred pangs of love in a man built like Kimpira himself.[13] Thank you. I should like to have you as my lover always, and to offer you my body and soul, but I am so deeply pledged to another man that I am not free to exchange even so much as a few words of love with anyone else. His name is Yojibei of Yamazaki. From my first night in this profession we have exhausted love's pleasures and sorrows together. I am a courtesan in name only. You might more properly call us husband and wife, for we are so close that no one can come between us. But now that I've heard your mother's earnest request and know your feelings, I wouldn't be content merely to exchange a cup of saké with you here, standing up, and have done with it. Shigeyama—bring me the packet I left with you.

NARRATOR: The Towboat with a word of assent takes from her sleeve an object wrapped in silk. Even without her saying so they know it contains ten or more pieces of gold.

AZUMA: This money has a special meaning for my dear Yojibei and

[13] Kimpira was the name of the hero of a kind of roughhouse Kabuki and puppet play, very popular in the seventeenth century in Edo.

myself, but I offer it to you, madam. Please use it to buy whatever clothes Yohei needs to cut a splendid figure in this Quarter. (*To Yohei.*) Selling her body to even the most casual customers means nothing to a prostitute. We two have never shared pillows, it is true, but let us drink one cup of saké together and with it wash away your months and years of unhappy memories.

NARRATOR: Yohei takes the money Azuma offers and throws it at her feet.

YOHEI: How heartless of you! How utterly devoid of understanding! I'm not in love with your money. Do you despise me because I'm poor and think you can shut my mouth with your gold? We live in a house so small—seven and a half mats, including the kitchen—that you might take it for the temporary quarters of the God of Poverty, and I wear the same thin clothes even in the dead of winter. But could I dare show my face anywhere if people said that I took money from a prostitute to visit the brothels? You've misjudged me badly, Azuma, if you think I was pretending to be in love so that I could take your money. I'm ashamed to have exposed my mother, a woman over seventy, to the contemptuous stares of all these people. Please forgive me, Mother.

NARRATOR: He stifles his sobs.

YOHEI: But come to think of it, how foolish I am to be so bitter! You'll soon be ransomed by Yojibei and become his wife. Supposing some day I go to your house as a day laborer—it will be very awkward for you if I gossip with the servants. You were wise to consider carefully such possibilities. But don't worry. I'm quite resigned. And here's proof that when I say I love you, they're not just shallow words.

NARRATOR: He unsheathes the dirk at his waist and is about to cut off his little finger when Azuma clutches his arm.

AZUMA: Stop, please! It was my mistake.

NARRATOR: She at last restrains him.

AZUMA: I was wrong to offer you money, but it was not because I am so ignoble as to think of my future convenience or reputation. Yojibei has a proper wife, his childhood sweetheart, and his father is a notoriously uncompromising old gentleman. I can't describe the domestic troubles that I have occasioned. Between his wife's jealousy and his father's complaints, ever since the twentieth of last month when I met Yojibei for a minute I've had nothing but the letters saying he couldn't meet me which he sent through the palanquin bearers and teahouse people. I've been obliged to take care of their gifts and to offer Yojibei's New Year presents to me! My contract still has some time to run, but I've extended it in order to raise some money. The more I try to hide his failings, the more acutely I feel the torments of never being able to extricate myself from this place. Pity Azuma, who is fated to become an old woman in the Quarter.

NARRATOR: She discloses her shame and her grief. The tears she inadvertently sheds ill accord with the New Year, but on her face they do not seem ugly. She removes her thin outer kimono, the sleeves so soaked with tears she must wring them out, and unties her sash, revealing a jet-black crested robe thick enough to keep the warmth of her lover's bed the night they met from cooling till they meet again.

AZUMA: This underrobe belongs to Yojibei. I have never taken it from my person for even a moment. My whole heart goes with it—wear the robe and consider yourself my acknowledged customer.

NARRATOR: She removes the underrobe and gives it to Yohei.

YOHEI: This is true kindness. My love has been fulfilled.

NARRATOR: He presses the robe to his forehead and can only weep. His mother has been listening in bewilderment.

OLD WOMAN: What a complicated business it is coming to terms with a courtesan!

NARRATOR: How lovable she seems as she strains to catch their words! Yohei wipes away his tears.

YOHEI: Only since we met have I have learned what real tears are. Yojibei is a lucky man to have your love. He won't find another woman like you, not if he wears out a pair of iron sandals in the search. I'll return the kimono and accept instead the money you kindly offered.

NARRATOR: But his mother sharply slaps his hand as he reached for the coins.

OLD WOMAN: How unmanly of you! That's not what you were saying before! Are you trying to blemish the reputation of the house of Naniwa? You mean villain!

NARRATOR: Yohei shakes his head at her words of reproach.

YOHEI: No, I'm not acting out of greed. It would dishonor me if I abandoned Azuma and Yojibei, now that I know how much they mean to each other. This money, unless I accept it, will end up as presents for the teahouse and become worthless as dust. These may look like gold coins, but actually they are the oil wrung from Azuma's body.[14] I accept responsibility for the money, and with the oil of my body I'll start an oil business. I'll leave at once for Edo, a place where you can make or lose a fortune in no time. I'll turn these ten gold coins into a hundred, a hundred into two hundred, two hundred into five hundred—once the profits start rolling in, I'll turn my fortune into a thousand pieces of gold quick as shooting an arrow. The Kantō trade and its tricks have always been a specialty of our family. I'll never live down the disgrace unless I can repay the affection shown me today by ransoming Azuma and seeing her joyfully united to Yojibei. I have so often thought, "If only I had the money I would buy here and sell there"—my head is full of ideas. Half a gold piece will more than cover my expenses to Edo. Mother, if I can leave you with your brother-in-law in Yokobori, it'll ease my mind. I'll send money from Edo before long. My success will mean Azuma's deliverance and Yojibei's dreams come true.

NARRATOR: Here is a man of uncommon ability: in one leap he covers a thousand miles.

AZUMA: The more I hear, the more confidence you inspire. To think —you love me yourself, but you're going to leave now for Edo so that you may join me forever to Yojibei! You are the god who will bring us together! Let me drink a parting cup with you and tell you my thanks most warmly. We'll go to the Izutsu House. Would your mother like to join us?

OLD WOMAN: No, if Yohei has what he wants, I ask nothing more. I feel as if I've attained Buddhahood while still alive. Lady Courtesan, good-by. I hope that you'll always be kind to Yohei.

NARRATOR: She taps Yohei's back.

OLD WOMAN: You're a lucky boy. Are you happy? Are you happy, son?

NARRATOR: With lighthearted words she eases his tension; the mother plays jester to her son's great patron. Here is a guest who enjoys more affection from Azuma than the most lavish spender. As the mother hurries back home through the bustling, lively street, long chests filled with courtesans' belongings jostle by on their way to the teahouses.

CHASER: Look, Azuma, that bothersome man is coming this way.

[14] The images are drawn from the pressing of oil from rapeseed.

TOWBOAT: You're right. It's that loud Hikosuke, and he's walking so unsteadily he must be dead drunk. If he sees us we'll be in for his usual abuse.

Scene Two: The Izutsu House, a teahouse in Shimmachi.

NARRATOR: They pull Azuma into the Izutsu House, drawn by its protection, and whisper to the proprietress what has happened. The latter answers merely, "I understand," and Yohei, in Yojibei's borrowed robe, becomes a patron for the nonce. He plunges into the unfamiliar hurly-burly of the teahouse; trembling with love, he cuts a pitiful figure.

Hikosuke's gait is unsteady with drink, but his eyes are still sharp. He takes up the whole street as he reels along, *hakama* and jacket askew, and stumbles unceremoniously into the Izutsu House. Azuma clenches her teeth on her pipe, and silently stares in the opposite direction. Yohei, hoping to escape notice, buries his head in the quilts of the foot warmer. He is engulfed in layer upon layer of damask, but even more numerous are the thoughts that beset him. Hikosuke pulls the hostess aside.

HIKOSUKE: Most esteemed procuress, kindly listen carefully to what I say. I beg to inform you of my best wishes for the New Year season.[15] That's what they all say—but me, I'm so drunk on New Year's saké that I'm going to beg to inform you instead of all of my grievances. You don't want to hear? They're very interesting, I promise. You— that Chaser over there—you listen too, attentively. Yes, you can call her my lady Azuma, the great courtesan, all you please, but when you come down to it, she's just a high-priced whore—right? No, you can't deny it. Well, on top of that, she sells herself to Yojibei of Yamazaki. Why doesn't she sell herself to me, Hikosuke the tobacco merchant? I've never asked her to come down on her price, no, not a penny, not a fraction of a penny. Who does she think I am? I proudly claim the honor to be an unrelated descendant of the Emperor Kammu,[16] Hikosuke the tobacco merchant, a native of Hattori in the province of Settsu, and I've got a shop with a thirty-foot frontage in

[15] Hikosuke gives the stereotyped New Year's greeting, then twists it.

[16] *Mutai* (unrelated descendant) is a play on *kutai* (ninth-generation descendant), found in the Nō play *Funa-Benkei* in the line, "I am the ghost of Tomomori, a ninth-generation descendant of the Emperor Kammu." Hikosuke is being humorous.

Osaka. Doesn't she realize what a rich man I am? No, it's impossible for her not to know, if I must say so myself. I spent a fortune on Takahashi from Shimabara in Kyoto, and got her to send me a lock of her hair. And I gave a pile of money to Takao from Fushimi,[17] who cut her nails to the quick to prove how much she loved me. Why, girls have been glad to slice pieces from their ears and noses for me—that's how big a patron I am. But to have Yojibei get the better of me and be refused three, no, four times by Azuma of the Wisteria House—that doesn't leave my pride a leg to stand on. Not half a leg. Well, I've grabbed her now, and I'm going to keep her for three days, starting this minute. This'll be my first purchase of that high-priced whore, but I'm willing to bet that if I scatter around enough pieces of gold and silver, Azuma will come round to my tune. Anyway, I'm buying her.

NARRATOR: He leans suggestively against Azuma. She slaps his cheeks smartly to disabuse him of the notion.

AZUMA: I don't want to hear any more of your empty boasting. I suppose that your Takahashi and Takao, or whatever their names are, really do cut their hair and pull out their fingernails even for a fool like you, providing you give them the money. I don't know about Kyoto or Fushimi, but a Shimmachi courtesan is of a different breed. I'm sure that no matter what happens—even if I have to spend the rest of my life paying house fees for the privilege of not answering your call—I'm not the kind of prostitute to be manipulated by a rotten scoundrel like you with the lever of your money. If you're as bold as you talk, see how far you get at winning over Azuma.

NARRATOR: She stands abruptly.

HIKOSUKE: Your pride makes me fall for you all the more. I'll show you how Hikosuke wins you over. You'll turn to my tune, yes, you will. That Chaser's face is turning round and round, the room is turning round, round and round like the old woman of the mountains who went round and round from mountain to mountain. This is fun. Yes, by hook or by crook, I'll take you to a back room, Azuma.

NARRATOR: He drags her with the violence that drunkenness and his native brute strength supply. The Towboat cries out in dismay and tugs him back, but Hikosuke blows a frontal gale at her, pushes the

[17] Takahashi was the name of a courtesan from the Shimabara Licensed Quarter in Kyoto. Takao is from the Fushimi Licensed Quarter.

hostess off to one side, and tosses the Chaser before him, sending all scattering in confusion like falling plum blossoms.

Hard-luck Yohei has always been quick-tempered, and though he grits his teeth, he can now endure no more. He thrusts his arms out of the quilts and firmly gripping Hikosuke's ankle, twists it powerfully.

HIKOSUKE: Ow, wow! My ankle is coming off!

NARRATOR: His brows contract in pain, but still he babbles on.

HIKOSUKE: There must be a wolf in the foot warmer.

NARRATOR: He tries to kick his foot free, but Yohei knocks him over. Sweeping aside the quilting, he leaps out and stands there, legs astride, his lemon-sour face thrust before the nose of Hikosuke, who stinks like an overripe persimmon.

HIKOSUKE: Who's this blackguard?

YOHEI: Open your eyes, if you can, and you'll see. I'm a human being, a man. Take a good look at what a real man looks like. And who are you, swine?

HIKOSUKE: A man called Hikosuke the tobacco merchant. Take a good look.

YOHEI: How dare you call yourself a man? Stop pretending! What kind of man plucks his brows[18] and then torments these poor prostitutes? If you're so sure you're a man, have it out with me! Are you afraid? I'll teach you what a fight among real men is like.

NARRATOR: He throws himself on Hikosuke, jerks him up by the wrists and, lifting him over his shoulder, sends him spinning head over heels, to land with a thud on his belly. Yohei follows this with seven or eight kicks in the small of Hikosuke's back, after which he stands humming to himself, his arms folded in satisfaction. Azuma and the others suppress smiles of amusement which come to their lips, then look dismayed, thinking of possible consequences. Hikosuke finally struggles to his feet.

HIKOSUKE: I understand. You're one of Yojibei's spies. That's why you've trampled on me. Yojibei of Yamazaki, remember this! I've been trampled on, but seven tenths of the victory belongs to me—my person and fortune have been stamped out, so early in the New Year. Besides, this is the Year of the Dog, and dogs lie on the ground—

[18] A man who plucked his brows daily was considered to be unusually well-groomed and dashing.

I've been doing exactly what the divination signs decree.[19] South-southeast be my lucky direction!

NARRATOR: Squaring his elbows, he boldly strides off.

CHASER: If he talks that big even after he's been licked, what must he be like when he's trampled on somebody else?

NARRATOR: The sound of laughter grows boisterous, and the tea-house begins to bustle with the excitement of the first buying of prostitutes of the New Year. Samisens sound in the kitchen under the decorations, and behind the stairs is a grab bag. The man of the year[20] scatters beans for good luck and cries, "A woman who sleeps with Daikoku of the hammer head[21] for her lover will have luck through the year. Paste Ebisu charms in the kitchen,[22] hang dried bream, kumquats, citrons, and oranges, and all will be well. Here are lucky products from everywhere—zebra grass from Yoshino, dried chestnuts, sea lentils (the genuine article), lacquered trays of sweet-meats." He offers saké in unglazed cups, but the others say, "Just a moment. First let us pray that this year will be more prosperous than last, and that the hostess will be younger than ever!" The first water of the New Year bubbles forth with joyous abandon at the Izutsu House.[23]

Yojibei of Yamazaki, who has crossed the mountain of love[24] and attained the ultimate refinement in courtship, enters the Quarter from the West Gate, hurrying his palanquin. The bearers lustily shout, "The great patron has come!" At once the people of the house, barefoot as they are, rush out with cries of welcome, all the way to the gate, to give him the reception due a god of good fortune. They lead Yojibei

---

[19] In order to "avoid calamities" it was necessary to observe the astrological information in the old calendars; this included lucky and unlucky directions and appropriate conduct for the year.

[20] A man designated to perform the rites at *setsubun* (the beginning of spring) on behalf of the entire family. He scatters beans and cries, "Out with devils and in with good luck!"

[21] Daikoku, a god of good luck, carries a mallet and stands on a sack of rice. There is a pun on *ine* (rice) and *ne* (sleep).

[22] Ebisu is another god of good luck, and the items enumerated all have felicitous associations.

[23] The name Izutsu-ya means literally "Well Curb House". Here the association is made between "first water" and "well".

[24] The place name Yamazaki contains the word *yama* (mountain). "Mountain of love" refers to someone with a great deal of experience in love.

in with joyous shouts, and take him to a back room where a heater is ready. The master brings the lacquered tray, the mistress a jug of saké, and the daughter of the house an unglazed cup.

KUROZAEMON: Look—even an old creature like myself is celebrating today, and Azuma is in full glory. We've managed to pay our year-end bills very comfortably, thank you. How about some of this spiced tea to start things off? Azuma has an unusual story to tell you.

NARRATOR: Azuma introduces Yohei to Yojibei and relates all that has happened.

YOJIBEI: I've had my troubles with Hikosuke in the past, and I was wondering what I ought to do about him. Thank you, Yohei, for helping me out. I hope that we'll always be good friends. But please don't bow to me that way—relax!

NARRATOR: Such is his greeting. Yohei is embarrassed by the unfamiliar surroundings and by a way of speech which he is unaccustomed to use or to hear. But most of all he is afflicted by numbness in his legs from sitting too long in one posture, and all he can utter is moans.

YOJIBEI: Your strength is a great asset, and your plan of going to Edo a fine one. Don't worry about Azuma. Concentrate instead on making a respectable fortune for yourself. Come back to Osaka when you're successful. In honor of your departure we'll spend tonight (*sings*) "in drinking and in song—who knows what the morrow will bring?"

YOHEI: It'll be pitch dark before we know it, and I know my mother worries when it gets so late. I'm much obliged for your kindness. Yojibei, Azuma, and all you other people, I'm sorry to have caused so much trouble. I'll be leaving now.

NARRATOR: He stands.

YOJIBEI: Why are you in such a big hurry? Surely there's no harm in relaxing this one night.

YOHEI: No, if I give myself an inch I'll take a mile. Carelessness is the enemy of success.

NARRATOR: He unfastens his sash and prepares to return Yojibei's kimono, but Azuma stops him.

AZUMA: You mustn't stand on ceremony in this cold weather. Keep the kimono, just as it is.—On your way to Edo there's the River Ōikawa. They say it's a dangerous place. Do be careful. We'll be waiting for the good news that you've arrived safely. And we'll see you again very soon.

NARRATOR: These are her parting words. Yojibei also sees him off.

YOJIBEI: Yohei, please consider that you have a brother in Yamazaki, and that you can depend on me.

YOHEI: Excuse my presumption, but I wish you'd also consider you have a brother in Edo. Let us write each other so we'll know that we're both all right.

NARRATOR: After they have parted, the doors and *shōji* are shut. The moon lies fast asleep in a pool of clouds, and storm winds snore in the pines. The closing drum has sounded by the time that Yohei takes two or three slow steps along Nine House Street; the Quarter is still. Hikosuke, the tobacco merchant, is lying in wait. He imagines that he recognizes Yojibei from the crest on the kimono, and darting up from behind stabs at Yohei, who nimbly leaps aside.

YOHEI: Here's the clown of the evening! Were you hoping for a return match?

NARRATOR: He charges and, knocking Hikosuke to the ground, slashes at him, the point of his dagger held downwards. Hikosuke, struck between the eyes, writhes in anguish on the ground and screams, "Murder!"

YOHEI: If they find me I'll never make my fortune.

NARRATOR: Yohei, who normally would never turn his back on an enemy, makes his escape, swift as the wind. The Quarter suddenly erupts in a tumult, with frantic shouts of "Get a stick!" "A rake!" "Lanterns, somebody!" "Shut the gates!" Hikosuke shrieks confusedly.

HIKOSUKE: Yojibei of Yamazaki stabbed me! He's at the Izutsu House.

NARRATOR: Yojibei, hearing the cry, realizes at once what has happened. He steps forward.

YOJIBEI: Here I am, if anybody wants Yojibei.

NARRATOR: Hikosuke, guided by the voice, grabs Yojibei from behind and holds him tightly.

HIKOSUKE: I've caught my assailant. I've got him pinned. (*To Yojibei.*) Don't try to start anything now.

NARRATOR: Azuma, the Towboat, and the Chaser rush out frantically, and try to calm Hikosuke, but he only grips Yojibei more firmly. The women burst into tears, but to no avail; Yojibei's fate stands in doubt.

ACT TWO

Scene: Jōkan's house in Yamazaki.
Time: Some weeks later.

NARRATOR: What strange curiosity stirred in that man of old the desire to behold "the moon of exile" though guilty of no crime? [25] So wonders Yojibei, confined by order of the magistrate to quarters unvisited even by the sun, for the quarrel in Nine House Street in which Hikosuke was wounded. Once the assailant was identified as Yojibei of Yamazaki, his sense of honor kept him from revealing Yohei's guilt, and he took the punishment on himself. Yojibei has been left in the custody of his father Jōkan, and life or death depends on whether his accuser's wounds heal or he dies. Uncertain as the pools and shoals of Asuka River, Yojibei helplessly awaits what the morrow will bring. Of all the household his wife Okiku is the most distraught.

OKIKU: He's never known a single day of hardship. I'm afraid this confinement will bring on some sickness. If only I could comfort him in some way!

NARRATOR: She toasts rice cakes for him, and they burn like the flames of longing in her breast. She follows along the garden path to Yojibei's quarters and opens the *shōji*. Yojibei, his face pale, stares blankly at the floor in utter dejection.

OKIKU: You haven't eaten for two or three days. If anything hurts you, you should take some medicine.—You see what a constant source of worry your short temper has been. If by some chance I had been unfaithful, it would have been normal for you to strike down the other man or even kill him. But after all, a prostitute is an article for sale, and Azuma has to sell herself to any number of men. This trouble has all started from your foolish jealousy. Or is it because you consider Azuma no less precious than myself? If I had suspected that was the case, I'd never have let you set foot out of the house. I'm only sorry now that I wasn't more jealous.

NARRATOR: Bitterness is mixed in her tears of indignation.

[25] Refers to an anecdote about Minamoto no Akimoto (1000–47) related in *Tsuredzuregusa* by Yoshida Kenkō (Sansom translation, p. 12). Akimoto, having read many poems written by men in exile bewailing their fates, thought he too would like to know what it felt like to be exiled.

YOJIBEI: Please don't say such things. I feel more ashamed before you than before all the rest of the world. But, as the Hachiman Temple at Iwashimizu is my witness, it wasn't I who stabbed Hikosuke. He deliberately started the fight, determined that I wouldn't escape—the result is the same as if I actually stabbed him. Besides, the real assailant is a man I'm under obligation to, and I intend to go on saying, even if I drop into hell, that I stabbed Hikosuke. If he dies, I'll be killed—I'm resigned to that. And yet, you know, his wounds are not so serious. It's clear as a mirror that this is a trick to extort money from me. My life obviously can be bought, but it seems that no money will be forthcoming from the coffers here. The day I was confined was the anniversary of my mother's death, a sure sign that this has all been a punishment for my having been such a bad son.

NARRATOR: He bows his head, a piteous sight.

OKIKU: Yes, my father has said the same thing. "I don't understand Jōkan. A man can't be miserly all the time. It may cost him a thousand or even two thousand pieces of gold, but is that too much to pay for the life of his only son? If he'd put aside his greed, the matter could be settled quickly. It's a great shame. If only I weren't a former samurai myself—" He's so upset that he keeps rambling on in that strain. He'll probably be coming again today. I'll speak to him privately and urge him to make your father feel ashamed of himself. I'm sure he'll yield then, no matter how stingy he is. Oh, I hear my father's voice now. I'll have good news soon.

YOJIBEI: Are you going already? Come back to see me later. My poor dear! I know how lonely you must be.

NARRATOR: Their faces are downcast, but he shuts the *shōji* to stop the tears. The light from the opened *shōji* made his heart all the darker.

Kajita Jibuemon comes on the ferry over the River Yodo to visit Yojibei every day. Because of his daughter he thinks about his son-in-law, worries his old heart for him, but Yojibei's own father Jōkan seems unconcerned.

JŌKAN: I'm glad to see you, Jibu. Let's get back to our game of chess, the one we began yesterday. Please come in.

JIBUEMON: Really, Jōkan, this is too much. I drag my aged limbs here every day because I'm worried about Yojibei, not to play chess. What does it matter who wins the game? Put it away, please.

JŌKAN: No, that fool must be left to his own fate.—The pieces are all just where they were yesterday. Come, play the game.

JIBUEMON: Well, this will be the last one, whoever wins. I'm under a handicap playing against an opponent who's had all last night to stare at the board. Is it your move? Go ahead.

JŌKAN: First I'll move this pawn in front of my rook.

JIBUEMON: Are you after my queen? I'll move it over here.

NARRATOR: Jōkan raps his head.

JŌKAN: Blast it! My knight's trapped.

> "When I galloped my horse
> Down into the deep paddy-fields,
> Though I drew the reins
> He wouldn't get up,
> Though I whipped him,
> He wouldn't go on;
> Even his head disappeared." [26]

What a predicament!

NARRATOR: He ponders the situation. Okiku comes up beside the board.

OKIKU: Father, don't you see that if the other side gets beaten, your side is beaten too? You'll never settle the contest as long as you remain at odds. Only one piece is in trouble, and Jōkan has plenty of gold and silver in reserve.[27] If he would forget his greed and merely disburse a little of his treasure, his knight would be saved. Please, I beg you, try to think of some way of dislodging his gold and silver. Do you understand me?

NARRATOR: She tugs at his sleeve. Jibuemon nods.

JIBUEMON: Ah-ha! Thank you for the advice. I'll do as you say.

NARRATOR: But Jōkan ignores this exchange.

JŌKAN: You mustn't help him just because he's your father. I'll put this pawn here for protection.

JIBUEMON: What have you in reserve?

JŌKAN: Three gold, three silver, and some pawns. If I make good

---

[26] A quotation from the Nō play Kanehira. The general Kiso no Yoshinaka, attempting to escape his enemies, rides into a quagmire and is trapped. Here suggested by the predicament of Jōkan's knight, literally a "horse". See Sanari, Yōkyoku Taikan, I, 728.

[27] In shōgi, a game rather similar to chess, one unusual feature is that captured enemy pieces may be held in reserve and then used as the occasion arises to help one's own side. "Gold" and "silver" are the names of two pieces in shōgi.

Okiku watches as Jibuemon and Jōkan play chess. "A samurai's child is reared by samurai parents and becomes a samurai himself because they teach him the warrior's code."
(OKIKU: *Nakamura Fukusuke VII;* JIBUEMON: *Onoe Koisaburō III;* JŌKAN: *Ichikawa Sadanji III*)

use of the pawns, I'm sure my gold and silver will multiply. Aren't you jealous of such a rich man?

JIBUEMON: Before you start bragging of your riches—my bishop is threatening you. If I move it here, you'll have to lay down some gold and silver.

JŌKAN: No, I won't part with any. I'd rather lose my knight.

NARRATOR: Jibuemon is at the end of his patience.

JIBUEMON: What a miser you are! What will you do with all the gold and silver you're clutching there? Do you plan to take it to the next world? Look here. If I pull back this rook so, your king, the one and only you have, will be cornered, confined to his quarters, you might say, and in no time he'll be lost. Don't you want to protect him by laying down some gold and silver?

JŌKAN: I'm perfectly well aware that I'm stingy. But I don't care whether the king is driven into a corner or trapped in the middle of the board—I'm not letting any gold or silver out of my hands. I'll show you how much trouble I can create with my pawns!

JIBUEMON: Wouldn't you be sorry if, while you're busy with your pawns, your king in turn were beheaded by a pawn? [28]

JŌKAN: It wouldn't matter. But first I'd try to escape.

JIBUEMON: In the meanwhile your king may be transfixed by a spear.[29] Would you still refuse to part with your treasure?

JŌKAN: It wouldn't be worth it. Even if my king is run through, even if his head is exposed on a prison gate, I won't give up my gold and silver.

NARRATOR: His greed is drawn taut like pieces marshaled in strongest array. Okiku watches in distress. She covers her tears with her hand, like a player unwilling to divulge his reserves: it seems as though Yojibei's life has been checkmated.

Jibuemon, wrath written on his face, snatches up the pieces on the board and throws them squarely at Jōkan's forehead. Okiku is astonished, but Jōkan does not move a muscle. Jibuemon edges up to him.

JIBUEMON: For shame, Jōkan! Fathers-in-law are essentially strangers, and it's a waste of breath, I know, to talk with a man so indifferent

---

[28] Refers to an old expression describing the humiliation of a warrior who is killed in battle by a common soldier—here meaning Hikosuke.

[29] A "spear" is a *shōgi* piece which advances in straight lines forward—here the word probably refers to some official judgment against Yojibei.

to shame that he doesn't object even when chess pieces are thrown in
his face. But I have been trying to tell you indirectly, under pretext of
talking about the chess game, that you should use your money to
reach a settlement with Hikosuke and save Yojibei's life. I can't believe that you failed to understand me. How can you refuse to part
with your money, even if it means that his head will be taken by a
menial or he'll be stabbed! Do you find it so interesting or amusing
to infuriate me? You have an only son and I an only daughter. No
one can take the place of either. I love my son-in-law as my own child.
Don't you think of his wife as your daughter too? You don't care at
all, do you, that if Yojibei is beheaded my poor Okiku will be brokenhearted? Ah, you make me seethe with rage!

My wife tried to stop the marriage when they were first engaged.
She insisted that Okiku would do better to marry a samurai, even a
poor one, and that if she married a businessman, no matter how rich
he might be, they would never get along together. I argued with her.
I told her that Jōkan of Yamazaki was a well-known man, accepted
even in samurai circles. I had my way, but of late my wife has been
reproaching me. Thanks to your stinginess and your cruelty, I have
quarreled with my wife after we have spent fifty years together. But
I don't suppose that a man who refuses to part with his money to
save his own son's life would care even if his relatives were dying of
starvation. I'm no longer a samurai myself, but members of my family
are still full-fledged samurai. What an unspeakable thing to have
besmirched our family name by joining it in marriage to that of such
an obstinate fool!

NARRATOR: He sobs and weeps. Jōkan blinks his eyes for the tears.

JŌKAN: A samurai's child is reared by samurai parents and becomes
a samurai himself because they teach him the warrior's code. A merchant's child is reared by merchant parents and becomes a merchant
because they teach him the ways of commerce. A samurai seeks a fair
name in disregard of profit, but a merchant, with no thought to his
reputation, gathers profits and amasses a fortune. This is the way of
life proper for each. With sicknesses too, each one, no matter how
grave or difficult to cure, has an appropriate treatment. If a man's life
is in danger because he has broken the law, it won't help to douse
him in ginseng infusions, but he can be saved by money. This trouble

would never have arisen if only Yojibei had realized that money is so precious a treasure that it can even buy human lives. I am well aware that however much I begrudge spending my money, however much I hoard it, all that will be left me when I am dead is a single hempen shroud. But until I die I am bound to respect my gold and silver like the gods or Buddha himself—that is the way prescribed by Heaven for merchants. Supposing I gave still more money to that rogue, lavished it on him, even after he's been punished for his wicked extravagance. What dreadful punishment, what disasters would he then encounter! The more affectionately I think of him, the harder I find it to give him the money. I have the reputation of being a miser. Money is not the only thing I prize. I am loath to part even with dust and ashes. How could I not be reluctant to lose the life of my only son?

NARRATOR: He leans his shaven head over the chessboard and weeps.

JŌKAN: I realize, Jibu, that your affection for Yojibei has made you bitter. But if you are so fond of him, why didn't you invite him to see you regularly and give him your advice? This sort of thing would never have happened.—But here I am forgetting that the foolishness was my son's, not yours. Next I may be saying something quite uncalled for. I'm going inside, Jibu.—Ah, my wife is lucky to be dead!

NARRATOR: He rises, choking with tears, and Jibuemon, unable to speak a word of reproach, goes outside weeping. Okiku, left behind, stands there helplessly, wondering what to do with the chessboard or herself.

OKIKU: There's something in what Jōkan says, but the fact remains that without money Yojibei's life is doomed. What good are money boxes in the safe if they're not put to use? They're worthless as these chess pieces here. What a heartless father to have!

NARRATOR: Her eyes dim with tears at this realization of the uncertainty of the world; a sense of the impermanence of things steals over her as the evening bell tolls its doleful message and the darkness spreads.

Under a misty moon across whose face the flying geese might be counted, helpless, like a lone rook seeking its nest, Azuma of the Wisteria House hurries to the country, her palanquin freighted with her agitation, her life unstable as the flow of the River Yodo. She follows mist-enshrouded paths through the rice fields "to Yamazaki, going or returning, still in Yamazaki." [30] Seeing the log bridge over the river—frightening to eyes unaccustomed to the sight—she stops her palanquin and descends. She wears the plain robes of a townsman's wife, and the unfeeling midnight winds calling to one another through the pines snap at the hems of her skirts. She asks a passerby for Yamazaki where her lover lives. "Over there, just ahead," he tells her, pointing at a house unusually imposing for the countryside. A glance at the rear gate and walls tells her intuitively that this is his prison.

AZUMA: Bearers, this is where Yojibei lives. That room you can see over the wall must be his. The poor man—I'm sure that's where he's confined. I'll go to him. It may take a little time before I return, but wait for me without fail. I depend on you to take me back. If you're out of tobacco I'll give you some, may I? I'll come back very soon.

NARRATOR: She lifts her kimono and steps lightly towards the wall, but the closer she gets, the higher it seems. She stands on tiptoes, she stretches high as she can, but the house is so carefully guarded that not even a chink of light escapes. A harsh wind rattles the garden door, and her heart dances with expectation as she pounds on it. She presses her ear to the wall and listens, but all is silence.

AZUMA: I might stand here forever, and there'd still be no assurance that he'd discover me. I'll call out that Azuma has come.

NARRATOR: She hesitates, her feet cold as nails or ice, her body chilled by the bitter cold. Okiku, worrying whether Yojibei is asleep or still lies awake in his prison room, which lacks even a foot warmer, goes to visit him. At the sound of her sandals echoing along the steppingstones in the garden, Azuma all but jumps for joy. She thinks, "It is he!"

AZUMA: Yoji, is that you? It's Azuma. I've come to see you. I couldn't stand waiting any longer.

NARRATOR: Okiku is startled by the words.

OKIKU (*to herself*): The brazen hussy! What has she come here for? I'll test her.

NARRATOR: She taps on the wall from inside, gently and somehow affectionately.

AZUMA: He's heard me! (*Calls out.*) I was so sure that the doors

[30] A quotation from a seventeenth-century song about Yamazaki.

would all be locked and I wouldn't be let inside that I wrote everything I've been thinking in this letter. Please read it carefully and send an answer in your own hand. This is the greatest favor I ask in this life.

NARRATOR: She throws the letter over the wall.

OKIKU (*to herself*): Such impudence! At the house of a married man, not knowing who might retrieve it!

NARRATOR: She opens the letter. It is in a woman's hand she well knows—even by the pale light of the moon there is no mistaking Azuma's writing. The letter has an impressive, formal look. Okiku reads, "This razor is a blade sharpened by my love. Should the necessity arise, I beg you not to allow yourself to die at some base executioner's hands, but to end your life honorably. The hour may differ, but I shall die that same day and, though apart in death, in the next world we shall share an everlasting bond on the same lotus. May all be well."

OKIKU: Imagine putting a razor in a letter! Yojibei's life is so precious to us that my father and I have been weeping ourselves sick. We've even quarreled with Yojibei's father. But she, under pretense of kindness, sends this letter, ordering him in this superior way to die! What does she mean ending it "May all be well"? Shall I order my servants to beat her from the door? No, if I do that it'll be all the worse for my husband's reputation. I'll meet her. I'll put her in her place.

NARRATOR: She opens the garden door and comes out.

AZUMA: Is that you, Yojibei? I've missed you so.

NARRATOR: Okiku firmly seizes the groping hands.

OKIKU: So you're the Azuma I've heard so much about! I've seen your letter just now. I am Yojibei's wife, Kiku. It was good of you to come such a distance. I am sure that you would like to see my husband, but he has been confined to his quarters for reasons of which you are no doubt aware, and I do not intend to bring you together. No, I shall not let you meet.

I ought really to have called on you long ago, Azuma, to express my gratitude. Thanks to you my husband has neglected the family business and has shown himself completely indifferent to what happens at home. Day and night he spends in visits to the Quarter, to the displeasure of his father and the evil gossip of the world. Now, with his present troubles, people are mocking him more than ever. "Have you ever seen the like?" they ask. Do you suppose that I, as his wife, can help being furious? I've always restrained myself lest people call me a bad wife and a disgrace to my husband, and people have said, "Okiku's an admirable woman, a model wife who's never jealous." I have been flattered into submission. And you, Azuma, have made a fool of me. I thought of you merely as a prostitute, but I wonder now if you're actually not a fiend or some diabolical spirit. What did you mean by sending this razor to another woman's husband with the command that he kill himself? If you think that death is so desirable, you should die by yourself. Whose fault it is that my precious husband's body has been wasted and the secrets of his heart ferreted out, that he's slandered in the public gossip, and now is reduced to such straits that he doesn't know if he'll live or die? It's all because of you, my lady courtesan.—Cursed strumpet! Shameless creature!

NARRATOR: Yojibei, hearing her voice rise with pent-up rage, softly slides open the *shōji*. Each woman has her claims; he alone has no excuse. His heart goes out to both and, though his face is flushed as from a burning brand, cold sweat flows. His only wish is to vanish altogether.

AZUMA: Now that we've met, I have no excuses to offer, however bitterly you may abuse me. Even a prostitute, for all her many customers, knows like another woman what jealousy and envy are. I can well understand that a lady who's had your strict upbringing would consider me a faithless strumpet, a deceiver and betrayer of men, an utterly hateful person. But when I've been with Yojibei neither of us has ever suggested that I become his wife, his kept woman, or even his mistress. At first we met merely on a professional basis but, as we became more intimate, our love grew from one night to the next. Madam, you have a fine husband, a man whose looks make every woman fall in love with him, and you are now the only one who can look after him.

Yojibei's present troubles began when he gallantly accepted blame for another man's crime, but the source of his difficulties goes back much farther, to me. Tonight I heard the other women saying that Hikosuke is on the point of death. I was the only one upset by the news. I sneaked from the Quarter because I wanted to tell Yojibei and to prepare him. I knew that if I were caught outside I'd be punished as a warning to other women. I brought my razors so that if Hikosuke died Yojibei could kill himself and I might join him. My desire was to save your husband from disgrace, and to kill myself afterwards in gratitude for his love. I had no intention of interfering in his relations with you. Please let me see his face just once again. I will then shut my eyes for the last time. Have pity on me.

NARRATOR: She takes out a razor kept hidden at her bosom, and presses it against her throat. Before a grief too intense to yield to tears of regret at leaving this world of dust, Okiku at last feels her heart relent. She stays Azuma's arm.

OKIKU: Azuma! Anyone willing to give up her life, even if it is only a gesture to society, cannot be lying. I am touched by your sincerity. My husband, I am sure, will want to see you. I'll take you to him secretly.

AZUMA: Thank you. How understanding you are, Okiku! Forgive me, please, for having so often held your beloved husband in my arms and slept with him.

OKIKU: You can't change what has happened. Consider you've had that much good fortune.

NARRATOR: As the two of them stand in the lane, their reserve melted, they hear Jōkan's voice calling Okiku. Soon he approaches, a mousetrap in his hand.

JŌKAN (*offstage*): Where is my daughter-in-law?

OKIKU: My father's come. At the worst moment. Wait here a few minutes.

NARRATOR: She hides Azuma in the shadow of the wall.

OKIKU: Haven't you retired yet, Father? What brings you here so late at night?

JŌKAN: Nothing in particular. Look at this, Okiku. It's a mousetrap that the young servants have laid. I heard the noise of the trap springing, and I opened it, but it seems that the mouse has escaped. The trap is empty. This little incident has given me a sudden understanding of the world. If a mouse's greed for the bait makes him careless, he'll fall into the trap and be killed at once. If, however, he resolutely renounces the bait and makes his escape, not only will his own life be saved, but the whole family of mice—there must be a father mouse, a father-in-law mouse, and a wife mouse, too—will all

rejoice. You can imagine the special relief and joy of the old father
mouse. Perhaps the young mouse imagines in his thoughtlessness
that after his escape the father mouse may fall into the same trap. He
may entertain foolish notions of that kind, but the father mouse has
the cunning of the old. He will never allow himself to be caught in
the trap. I'm sure there must be an uncle mouse, too. As long as the
young mouse hides in the uncle mouse's nest and does not show himself
here, not a sound will be heard from the mousetrap, and everything
will quickly blow over. If only his present experience in the mousetrap chastens the young mouse into forsaking his running along the
rafters every night, his scampering through the cupboards, chewing
on the cups, sneaking off with his father's gold pieces, and all his
other wildnesses! Can you imagine how much joy it would bring the
father mouse to see his son one day enjoy the prosperity of the white
mouse? [31] Of late I've been unable to sleep at night, wondering how
that foolish, irresolute mouse can fail to understand what he must do.

NARRATOR: His voice blurs with tears.

OKIKU: Of course, I see now. How kind of you to make such elaborate calculations on behalf of the mouse. I shall certainly persuade
him to escape.

JŌKAN: I'm satisfied. I have nothing more to ask. A heavy weight
has been lifted from my heart. Lately I have been so obsessed with this
worry that even when I stood before the altar I could not see the
Buddha's face. I feel infinitely relieved. Tonight I will be able to read
the sutras with a mind at peace.

NARRATOR: As she watches him depart, strengthened by his belief in
the power of prayer, Okiku is assailed by unshakable melancholy.

Yojibei rushes out and looks in the direction from which his father's
voice came. Tears of gratitude start to his eyes. Okiku lifts in her hands
the earth trodden by her father-in-law's feet.

OKIKU: Yojibei—did you hear those words of mercy? The sooner
you leave, the greater will be your father's relief, and the better son
you will show yourself. I shall remain to look after Jōkan. I promise to
take better care of him than ever. Don't worry, I beg you, about what
may happen once you leave. I wish I could send someone with you.
What shall I do?

[31] This passage of course describes in thinly veiled terms Jōkan's hope that Yojibei will
make his escape. A "white mouse" was considered to be a harbinger of good luck, and
a house where white mice dwelt would surely prosper.

NARRATOR: She reflects a moment.

AZUMA: Okiku! I am here. Azuma is here, for just that purpose. I left the Quarter at the risk of my life, and I have no desire to return. I shall be most grateful if you will consent and say, "Go with him." I will never return to the Quarter.

NARRATOR: Okiku catches the note of urgency in her words.

OKIKU: Then everything is arranged. Hurry, before it gets too late.

NARRATOR: She tugs at Yojibei's sleeve, urging him on, but he shakes his arm free.

YOJIBEI: No, that's impossible. They say that a man's highest duty as a father is to show compassion for his child, and as a child to serve his father.[32] I am in my father's custody now. If I escape and Hikosuke dies, they will immediately arrest my father in my place and behead him as the culprit. Even if Hikosuke recovers, my father will be guilty of having allowed his charge to escape, and they will punish him accordingly. My father has fulfilled his duty as a parent by showing a compassion indifferent to danger. But I have disobeyed my father's wishes in everything, to this very day. If I were to crown my sins by running away and saving my life at the expense of his, I could never mingle in human society again, not if I lived a hundred or a thousand years. Life in this world would be intolerable. I don't wish to disobey him again—causing him grief gives me no pleasure—but I ask you to let me die as I am. I would like, by giving up my life, to discharge the filial duties of a lifetime.

NARRATOR: He raises his voice and weeps.

OKIKU *and* AZUMA: Yes, what you say is reasonable too.

NARRATOR: The two women cannot shake his resolve; they can only weep.

Jōkan calls from inside.

JŌKAN: Okiku, Okiku! Do I hear aright? Is that disobedient scoundrel saying that he won't escape? Heartless, inhuman wretch!—I haven't told anyone for fear that people might say that old Jōkan at the age of seventy allowed himself to be blackmailed, but I secretly sent a man to Hikosuke. I tried to settle things privately by offering up to two hundred pieces of gold. Hikosuke took advantage of my position, and said he was unwilling, even for a thousand pieces. I've heard that his wounds are superficial, but he's mortal, after all, and there's no telling when he might die. Can you imagine the agonies

[32] A paraphrase of a passage in the Confucian classic *The Great Learning*.

I've gone through as a father? I have tried to distract myself with chess, only to be harassed. The more I have been reminded of Yojibei's plight, the more painful it has been. All evening long I have racked my mind thinking up that plan of escape from the trap. Try to understand the immeasurable fatherly love that went into it. (*To Yojibei.*) You can't remain a child all your life. Some day you'll be a father yourself. If only I could make you realize how a father feels for his son! Tell me at once—will you or won't you escape?

NARRATOR: His voice is harsh, but the tears on his face may be surmised even by those outside the wall. Yojibei, weeping, prostrates himself.

YOJIBEI: My gratitude makes it all the more impossible to run away. Forgive me, I implore you.

NARRATOR: He bows his head in tears.

JŌKAN: Very well. A man normally hopes to survive an aged father, even by a single day, and he tries to remain in good health so that on the anniversaries of his father's death he may offer prayers for his happiness in the other world. Would you prefer to be mourned by your father and make him suffer? Very well, stay here if you like, but first I will thrust this dagger into my wrinkled belly! *Namu Amida Butsu.*

YOJIBEI: Father! I'll go away! Wait!

NARRATOR: He collapses in tears.

JŌKAN: Do you swear it?

YOJIBEI: How could I lie to you?

JŌKAN: I'm happy. My mind is at rest. I forgive you all your disobedience of the past. I accept this one act as the equivalent of thirty years of dutiful service as a son. Your dead mother must also be rejoicing. Okiku has a father, and I have Okiku. Don't worry about us here.—I see that you'll have a lady to go with you. Madam, please make sure that Yojibei takes moxa treatment[33] however much he objects, and don't let him drink any saké. Always travel in a sedan chair, even if it's expensive—people may recognize you on horseback. Please do as I ask.

NARRATOR: His words are brief, but his agitated heart is torn in ways numberless as the stripes of the purse he tosses to Yojibei. "Farewell" is his only word; the rest is choked by tears.

[33] In this treatment, still practiced today, pellets of medicinal herbs are burned at various places on the patient's skin. It is believed to be effective for many ailments.

Yojibei, overwhelmed by his father's kindness and his wife's love, seems numbed by the grief of parting. He staggers forward as in a trance, unaware of what happens.

AZUMA: I'm Azuma—don't you recognize me? And that is your wife, Okiku. At least say good-by to her. How fainthearted you are!

NARRATOR: She tries to lend him strength, but tonight she too must hide.

AZUMA: Come, let us climb into this sedan chair for two. No one can see us there.

NARRATOR: She whispers to him and, brushing away the spring frost that lies on her sleeve, she calls to her bearers.

Okiku's voice is hoarse with tears.

OKIKU: When you find a haven, wherever it may be, write me that you are safe. I'll be waiting for your letter. Please be careful not to catch a chill on cold mornings and evenings at the inns where you stay. I have so many things to tell you, but they're in my heart and don't come to my lips. All I can say is, keep safe and well.

NARRATOR: These are her only words—the rest is tears.

OKIKU (*to herself*): I should be the one going off with my husband —that's the proper way. Why has such a thing happened to me? Here I am sending him off in a chair for two with that woman I've envied and detested so. I feel only jealousy and utter misery.

NARRATOR: Many are the reasons for her tears, but all are joined in the single thread of love for her husband. As she watches the chair disappear into the distance, the late night bell tolls, drowning the voices calling last farewells. The clouds seem to retreat across the sky, but the palanquin hurries relentlessly forward, not pausing even to give the bearers a momentary rest. To the heavy burden of love borne in the chair is added the sorrow of father and son at parting as Yojibei leaves, bound for no one knows where.

ACT THREE

Scene One: The journey of Azuma and Yojibei from Yamazaki to Nara.

NARRATOR:

The butterfly that tempts the cherry to blossom
Will not know the taste of the rapeseed;

The butterfly dancing over the rapeseed,
Though hatched the same spring,
Will not have known the cherry blossoms.
Each unknown to the other,
Each unaware the other exists,
They will never know love's first delights,
Nor the madness of passion.

What a sad contrast to Yojibei! Azuma draws closer to him.

AZUMA: I am so happy! Do you feel calmer now? Look—see how even butterflies, the swallowtails, fly close to their mates! We two are together, a couple well-versed in love, yet how timorous you are!

NARRATOR: She tries to encourage him.

YOJIBEI (*sings*):
Ransom Azuma, Yojibei!
Ransom her, ransom her, Yojibei!
When was it the pangs of love were first assuaged,
Loosened with the strings of your lady's underclothes?
Now when you think of the past,
How sad, how bitter it seems!
How sad, how bitter, the past you remember,
How sad and how bitter!

AZUMA: Alas, who might you be if not Yojibei of Yamazaki, a man never outdone by others, who never had a hair out of place? But now your senses are disordered. You have even forgotten Azuma's face, you have lost your mind.

NARRATOR: She places a staying hand on him.

YOJIBEI: Are you Azuma of the Wisteria House? You've been cruelly treated by Yojibei—how poor your coloring is, unhappy woman! I thought I would surely ransom you soon and enable you to live in comfort. We would have a house and a child and, when we proudly walked together through the streets of Yamazaki, a nurse would carry our child on her shoulders, and her husband would hold a parasol. But I have rejected the kindness of my father in Yamazaki, and now I am dependent on you, in appearance no longer the man I was. From Otokoyama we go to Akishino.[34] Now I have wearied of people. O pines of Toyama, I would ask you something—which is more painful, to wait or to part? The wife my father bestowed on me, so that

---

[34] Places between Kyoto and Nara; the name Akishino contains the word *aki,* meaning "weariness [of people]".

I would have neither to wait nor to part, I thought of with respect and affection, but in vain, for we could not remain together. I am now an untethered steed roaming the ends of the moors. Yesterday I carried my love to Azuma;[35] today as I weep in longing I am drawn to my home. I am an autumn leaf careening madly of itself, too unsettled to alight; for me there is no waking and no sleeping; only tears of waiting wet my sleeve. "Even if by chance you're waited for, never become the one who waits," they say. The mountains between my father and me block all news from Yamazaki, where my wife must be distraught with waiting, her disheveled hair unbound. Her last words to me will be my strength.

AZUMA: My love, a threefold sash,[36] has bound you close during the long nights we have slept together. I felt no jealousy nor envy, but one is half owner of an object given in trust, they say.[37] Have you forgotten our last moon-viewing at the Izutsu House? In the moonlight that filled every corner, completely given to each other that night, we danced till the dawn. How wonderful it was! I shan't forget it, not if I live to be a hundred years.

YOJIBEI: It's something I'll never forget. I couldn't get my fill of you as you walked along, your toes pointed out,[38] lovely enough to kill a man with a glance, to steal his senses away. A courtesan's basin is her faithful companion, her wife, and she may herself seem desirable enough for you to make her your wife, but once you ransom her the bottom of the basin drops away, it holds no more moonlight.[39] After spending the night with you, I weep for the father I have lost, I long for my wife. My heart is one but torn in two, like the notes of the cuckoo which passes us now, telling its name.[40] "You resemble your

[35] Azuma means at once his sweetheart and the direction East; the eastern part of Japan is sometimes called Azuma.

[36] The phrase possibly suggests that Azuma is so wasted with love that her sash, which normally goes twice around the body, can be wrapped three times around her.

[37] A proverb, which here refers to Yojibei's being left by Okiku in Azuma's care.

[38] Japanese women normally walk with toes pointed inwards; in this more seductive walk the toes are first pointed outwards, then turned in.

[39] This line may also mean that the bottom fell out of Yojibei's plans to ransom Azuma. The effect of the whole (rather obscure) passage is to show that running away with the great courtesan, Yojibei's dream for so long, does not actually bring him happiness; he needs his wife and father too.

[40] The cuckoo's call is in two notes. The following line alludes to the cuckoo's habit of leaving its eggs in another bird's nest.

father, but your song's not like his." The son's first song brought him fame in the gay quarters. . . . I wore no cap of office, but they called me "minister of state." [41] I passed through the gate where the procuresses examine the customers; I saw the Chasers slap the dozing harlots' maids. All was a world within a dream and, when I awoke, elegance and vulgarity seemed much the same. These things I knew, but when I was caught like a tangle of willow branches in a sudden mountain wind, how my father's harsh words of reproof, my wife's single word of farewell filled me with longing and love!

NARRATOR: They take each other's hands and weep, giving voice to their grief.

The setting sun approaches the mountain crest. In the northwest a wind rises, and the feet of the clouds scurry to the southeast sky. The bough tips and the branches rustle; water murmurs in a little stream; clouds spread their feather sleeves, inclining them now this way, now that, round and round as they circle. The moon follows its appointed course, but Yojibei's suffering has no limits. His father's wrath has struck him now, and he rushes ahead, oblivious to his fate. He runs; his reflection in the stream runs too. He stops; it stops. Azuma's sleeves were unruffled, but now they are twisted too, and her mind seems about to snap—a courtesan's fate is beyond her control. They search in their misery for a humble farmer's cottage, a place to pause for a while in their flight through the world.

Scene Two: The Izutsu House in Shimmachi.
Time: Late summer of the same year.

NARRATOR: The shores of Naniwa Bay are famous for Plum blossoms; the Pines grow thick, and even by day the Maple leaves form a bright brocade.[42] Nocturnal brothels have recently been permitted,[43] and men eagerly throng to the Quarter to see Shimmachi at night. Lanterns gleam like stars deep under the eaves along the four streets, more brilliant than the face of the full Moon.[44] The swelling Tides, the

[41] *Daijin*, meaning "a minister of state", is the homophone of *daijin*, meaning "a great patron [of the gay quarter]".
[42] "Maple leaves" were courtesans of the third rank.
[43] The brothels had formerly been allowed to operate only during the day, but in 1675 nocturnal visits were permitted. It is not clear why Chikamatsu says "recently."
[44] The Shimmachi Quarter had four streets. Moons, Tides, Reflections, and Half-prices

shining Reflections, the experienced Half-prices, all bespeak good service to customers: the towels in the chambers have no time to dry. No one has beaten the drum, but at the Great Gate resounds a horse's loud neighing; the guest riding up to the Izutsu House is Hard-luck Yohei of Yawata. He leaps from his mount, high-spirited and handsome, to be greeted by the master of the house with exaggerated bows.

YOHEI: You needn't get so excited, Kurozaemon. Have you forgotten me? I'm Yohei. Last New Year I was hospitably received here, and you were personally very kind. Then I was a minister without portfolio or money, but I come to you today a minister of the treasury, with ready cash in my wallet and something to discuss in private. I'll go in now.

NARRATOR: He steps confidently inside.

KUROZAEMON: Yes, indeed, I remember now. What a surprise to see you again! But first, please have a cup of tea and a smoke.

NARRATOR: He speaks in obsequious tones. The oil lamp is immediately replaced with candles:[45] life in this Quarter is dedicated to pleasure.

YOHEI: Come closer, Kuroza. As you know, I accepted money from Azuma of the Wisteria House at the New Year. I took it to Edo, where it soon began to sprout, and I made a quick fortune without harming anyone. My backbreaking toil was worth it—I've come back now with a well-laden horse. I learned on the road that Azuma's escaped and that she's being sought on charges of having illegally left the Quarter. I'd be disgraced as a man if I abandoned her now, after having accepted her generosity and sworn I would help her. I will ransom Azuma and enable her to go where she pleases. I'm sure that you have the documents for her contract. I want them. Please arrange everything so that I can redeem them for cash and settle matters this evening. I'm counting on you, Kuroza.

KUROZAEMON: Splendid! My congratulations! I need say no more about Azuma since you have already heard the rumors. But the most curious thing has happened. This evening a rustic-looking old samurai appeared. He wishes to buy up the contract even though Azuma

---

were ranks of courtesans, named (in the first three instances) after a passage in the Nō play *Matsukaze*: "The moon is one, the reflections two, the three-fold tide swelling in . . ." (Sanari, *Yōkyoku Taikan,* v, 2829). Thus, a prostitute who received a one-*momme* fee was called a "Moon", etc.

[45] Candles were more extravagant than oil lamps and were therefore put out for customers.

herself is not here. He hasn't any money, but he will offer in exchange a two-foot broadsword authenticated as a genuine Kuniyuki. The old gentleman is waiting inside. I haven't informed the owner of the contract yet, but I'll go at once and report on both the offers.

NARRATOR: He starts to leave. A clamor at the gate announces Hikosuke.

KUROZAEMON: You're quite a stranger, sir.

HIKOSUKE: How's business these days? You're a lucky fellow, Kuroza —if you're trying to make money, I'm your man. This is a casual visit, merely to discuss a ransom.—Impressed with me, aren't you? Early this spring, as you remember, I had my hair trimmed a bit by that scoundrel Yojibei of Yamazaki. I complained to the police, absolutely determined, as the god Hachiman is my witness, that I would not endure such an affront. Yojibei was left in his father's custody. Ever since then Jōkan has secretly been sending people with apologies. I told him that I wouldn't call off the suit, not for a million pieces of gold—that's the kind of man I am. However, as you can see, my wounds are completely healed, and though I detest that villain Yojibei, I feel sorry for his father, and I've forgiven him. Jōkan, as a token of his thanks, sent me a pittance to buy myself some drinks. They say it brings bad luck if you return saké when it's offered as a present, so I decided to accept. Then Azuma, at Yojibei's instigation, ran away from the Quarter, and Yojibei broke his confinement to escape with her. Jōkan has paid for this. All his possessions have been impounded, and he himself has been placed under house arrest until Azuma and Yojibei are discovered. I'm told that Yojibei dropped dead on the road somewhere. Lucky for him, isn't it, considering that he was sure to be beheaded the moment he showed himself. But to get back to our business. I came to talk about Azuma. She's guilty of having left the Quarter illegally, and there's not much chance of saving her life. But I was born with a heart warm as Buddha's—it's my great weakness—and I'd like to rescue her. I'll redeem Azuma's contract first and look for her later, at my leisure. When I find her I'll use her as my cook or my washerwoman, or perhaps I'll let her massage my hands and feet. I'm resolved to kill her with kindness for the rest of her life. Only a man of my stature would make such a proposal. Discuss it with the owner and reach a settlement. Here's the ready cash.

NARRATOR: He throws a bag of fifty pieces of gold before the master.

Yohei, who has heard everything, slides open the partition with an "Excuse me."

YOHEI: Master! My request to redeem Azuma came first! Here is the money.

NARRATOR: He sets down a plain wooden stand laden with a packet of a thousand pieces of gold. A voice calls from the next room.

JIBUEMON: If you are disputing who came first, I claim that honor!

NARRATOR: A samurai enters.

JIBUEMON: I offer as the price of the ransom this sword with an attested value of three thousand *kan*.

NARRATOR: He throws down sword and certificate both. Yohei does not recognize the sword, but he is certain from the man's appearance that this must be the Jibuemon of whom Yojibei had spoken. He gazes at the man in silence. Kuroza is at a loss to decide among the three contenders.

KUROZAEMON: In any case, it's up to the owner to decide. Shall I send for him? No, I'll go myself. Alas for poor Kuroza!

NARRATOR: He rushes off talking to himself. The three men left behind glance at one another. Hikosuke is ill at ease before Yohei, recalling his terrible beating. His nerves are on edge, but true son of Hattori that he is, he looks strong as the local tobacco;[46] pulling over the tobacco tray, he begins with a sour expression to smoke. His pipe is a good distraction, and he keeps knocking out the ashes as he waits for an answer.

The owner of Azuma's contract, Kan'emon, enters accompanied by the master of the house.

KAN'EMON: I've gathered what's happened from Kuroza's description. Ransoming Azuma under these circumstances would be quite unprecedented in the Quarter. It's difficult for me to answer one way or the other. If I surrender her contract—it doesn't matter to whom— word of this will get around. People will form the unfortunate impression that they can get away with anything, even absconding with a woman from the Quarter, provided they give enough money. The Quarter will be in an uproar with elopements and runaways on all sides and constant violations of our code. This represents a difficult problem for owners of contracts. It is pointless to discuss the matter further. I'll do what I can when once I've seen Azuma.

[46] Hattori was a famous tobacco-growing region.

NARRATOR: Hikosuke interrupts.

HIKOSUKE: I see. I don't know what anybody else plans to do, but I'm going at once to search for Azuma. Ransoming her will be my privilege—I've sworn as much. I'm leaving.

NARRATOR: He springs to his feet.

YOHEI: I won't let you!

NARRATOR: Yohei grabs Hikosuke's wrist and, raising him over his shoulder, flings him violently to the floor. He firmly straddles Hikosuke's back.

YOHEI: You're a born racer—a fast man on your feet when it comes to running from me. If you make a move, I'll smash your head in. Do you understand? (*To owner.*) I find your arguments entirely reasonable, sir. Are you quite certain that you will allow Azuma to be ransomed on the spot, providing you see her face?

KAN'EMON: Why should I lie to you? Azuma's contract hasn't much longer to run, and she's made a good deal of money for me in the past. I certainly wouldn't deceive you.

YOHEI: Excellent! And I take it that there'll be no trouble with the police?

KAN'EMON: I'm sure that everything will be settled quite simply if I ask them to withdraw the complaint.

YOHEI: Splendid! Servants, bring those two leather trunks over here. Master, would you open them, please?

NARRATOR: The master quickly unfastens the straps and from inside the trunks emerge Azuma and Yojibei, restored to his senses. Hikosuke is astonished, and the owner and master look dumfounded. Jibuemon, overjoyed, can no longer conceal his identity.

JIBUEMON: Yojibei! It's Jibu! I'm delighted that you're safe.

NARRATOR: The rest is speechless tears of joy. Yojibei bows his head.

YOJIBEI: Please forgive me for everything and offer my apologies to my father.

JIBUEMON: There is no need to ask that. He's told me his feelings and I know that he understands. Azuma, you've had a harrowing ordeal. Here, Kan'emon, please take this sword in exchange for the contract and surrender Azuma to me.

NARRATOR: He bows humbly.

AZUMA (*to master*): I've been away a long time, Kuroza. Please offer the owner my apologies.

NARRATOR: She weeps. Yohei vigorously jerks Hikosuke to his feet.

YOHEI: Listen carefully. My reason for going to Edo was to raise money so that I could ransom Azuma and rescue her from the hardships of the Quarter. I was so determined to succeed that I easily managed to make close to 500 *kamme* in one transaction. On my way back I met Yojibei, and learned from him the exact situation. I, Yohei, was the man who stabbed you. You falsely accused Yojibei and extorted a great deal of money, didn't you? I could thrash you all day and still not feel satisfied. But since this is a festive occasion—leave at once!

NARRATOR: He pushes him away.

HIKOSUKE: Thank you. At New Year you threw me to the floor of this very room, and later you stabbed me. Today I rather expected to get killed, and I'm grateful to be spared. The third time is the lucky time for me.

NARRATOR: As Hikosuke makes his escape Jibuemon twists his arm and wrenches him down.

JIBUEMON: I won't let you leave. You must inform the police of Jōkan's innocence, and secure his release from confinement.

NARRATOR: He quickly ties Hikosuke.

JIBUEMON: Is the ransom completed, Yohei?

YOHEI: No, not yet. Here are one thousand pieces of gold. I offer them in exchange for the contract.

NARRATOR: Yohei places the money before the owner. Kan'emon shakes his head.

KAN'EMON: Azuma's term expires next March. She'll become a free woman. What would people think if I accepted your thousand pieces of gold? I'd be disgraced. I'd prefer not to take any money at all, but I'm sure you wouldn't agree. I'll accept three hundred pieces for the six months remaining in her contact. The rest I don't need.

NARRATOR: He pushes the money away. Yohei, by nature a lighthearted fellow, shouts:

YOHEI: It's all over! I've got the contract. He's taken the money. Azuma's ransom's completed!

Here are the three hundred pieces to ransom her, clap hands on that.[47]

NARRATOR: Clap, clap, once again, clap, clap.

[47] The 300-*ryō* ransom paid by one Sakanoue Yojiemon for the courtesan Azuma about 1670 occasioned a famous ballad, and probably was one of the origins of this play.

YOHEI: Clap hands once again. Master, I put aside these thousand pieces of gold for the ransom. I won't feel right if even one copper coin remains. Three hundred pieces are my present for you.

KUROZAEMON: I'm deeply obliged.

YOHEI: Put them together and they make six hundred. Clap hands once again! Clap, clap! Four hundred pieces still remain, four hundred pieces weigh on my brain. Come close and celebrate.

NARRATOR: He scatters pieces of gold all over the floor, till you can't see its color any more. Men and maidservants, each for himself, jostle and shove to pick up the pelf.

YOHEI: Have you taken them all? Hurrah, hurrah! Celebrate with three rounds more. Clap, clap!

NARRATOR: With a clapping of hands and a rhythmical song, to a joyous beat they drink three and three and nine times long. They pledge that through a thousand years, ten thousand years of life, they'll remain to the end a loving husband and wife.[48]

[48] Apparently Yojibei and Azuma will be joined happily; it is not clear what will happen to Okiku.

THE GIRL FROM HAKATA,
OR LOVE AT SEA

First performed on January 10, 1719. Chikamatsu's inspiration for this play was furnished by an event of the previous month. A band of smugglers was arrested in Osaka. Its ringleaders were executed, and the other men were either mutilated or severely fined. Some prostitutes were arrested with the smugglers, but were later released. Chikamatsu borrowed or slightly adapted the names of some historical personages (Ogura Zen'emon, for example, became Oguraya Den'emon), but the central love story is apparently fictional.

Cast of Characters

KOMACHIYA SŌSHICHI, a Kyoto merchant

KEZORI KUEMON, leader of the smugglers

KOMACHIYA SŌZAEMON, aged 78, Sōshichi's father

HISHIYA KAEMON, owner of Sōshichi's house

OGURAYA DEN'EMON, YAHEIJI, NANIWAYA NIZA, HEIZAEMON, ICHIGORŌ, SANZŌ, smugglers, henchmen of Kezori

SHIROZAEMON, master of the Okuda House

YOKUICHI, a blind musician

OFFICER

SUPERINTENDENT

SERVANTS, POLICE, BEARERS, WATCHMAN, SAILORS

KOJORŌ, a courtesan at the Okuda House

SHIGENOJŌ, her maid

EGUCHI, KATSUYAMA, USUGUMO, MISAO, ŌGURA, OTHER COURTESANS

OLD WOMAN

SERVANTS, MAIDS, PROSTITUTES

ACT ONE

Scene One: Aboard a ship anchored off the port of Moji in Kyushu.

Time: Autumn, 1718.

NARRATOR:

> If you're putting your boat out to sea,
> Put it out by dead of night;
> If I should glimpse its sail,
> How it would weigh on my heart!

Autumn dusk in Nagato [1]—at Moji famed in song and at Shimono-seki, the greatest harbors of the West Country. To the north, the sea of Pusan in Korea; to the west, Nagasaki and Satsuma Beach. From morning to night wares from China and Holland are traded here; a thousand ships depart each day, a thousand others enter port, laden with a thousand *kamme,* ten thousand *kamme.* Pieces of gold race about, and silver flies through the air: such indeed must be the world of paradise.

Offshore, a large, ocean-going ship [2] that hoists a fifty-foot sail waits—but for what? Aboard her the captain and crew loll in their bunks in quilted kimonos, but on deck four or five passengers are staring intently at the sea, alert to every splash of the waves, to every ship-like object. Their faces are strained, their cheeks sunken, and their eyes are as sharp as a lice-picking monkey's. Their leader, Kezori Kuemon, speaks the dialect of his native Nagasaki.

KEZORI: Well, you rogues. No sign yet of the ship with Ichigorō and Sanzō? I'm worried, I tell you. Last night I was so on edge I heard every noise. I couldn't sleep a wink. If all goes according to plan, we'll head the ship straight for Hakata, ransom some tarts in Willow Lane, [3] and take them to Osaka.—The front cabin's been hired by a stranger from Kyoto, an old friend of the captain's. It seems we'll have to give

---

[1] The western end of Honshū, the main island of Japan, where it comes closest to the island of Kyūshū. Shimonoseki is in Honshū; Moji lies on the Kyūshū side of the strait. A tunnel now joins the two ports.

[2] Japanese were at the time forbidden to travel abroad. The size of the ship marks it as suspicious. The original text further describes the ship as possessing a "cypress wood fence," meaning elaborate railings on both sides, another sign of its unusual size.

[3] The licensed quarter is Hakata (Yanagi Machi).

him passage as far as Hakata. But, of course, the ship won't be sailing to Hakata at all if our plans misfire. I wish that we had some sign that everything was all right. Call the passenger in the front cabin. The time'll pass quicker if we've someone to talk to.

NARRATOR: "Aye, aye!" responds Heizaemon, going below to summon the passenger. The others, men fierce enough to battle devils, bring up grass mats and spread them on deck. They throw a pinch of China tea in a pot. The tea is pale as they pour it, but the respect they offer their chief makes it fragrant: courtesy is the flower of any company.

The passenger in the front cabin, Komachiya Sōshichi, is capital-bred and by nature polite. He appears on deck when sent for and sits formally, his knees apart.

SŌSHICHI: I've taken advantage of my friendship with the captain to ask passage aboard. I should have come earlier, even without your invitation, to express my compliments. Please forgive the discourtesy.

KEZORI: No need to be so formal! Living on the same ship and eating food cooked in the same pot makes us all like one family. Come, lift your hands—no more bowing, please. These five men are my pals. We tell each other everything—no secrets among us. Come closer and join the conversation. But let me introduce myself. My name's Kuemon. I'm from Nagasaki and I'm in the China trade, though only on a small scale. This fellow here is Yaheiji, a Nagasaki man like myself. The next two are Oguraya Den'e and Naniwaya Niza, both from Osaka. The man I sent to call you was Heizaemon from Tokushima in Awa. He can shave your forehead and dress your hair—not a professional job, but passable enough aboard ship. Feel free to call on him at any time. And now, may I ask your name and where you come from?

SŌSHICHI: Nagasaki is my home town too, but I moved away with my parents when I was still a boy, and I live now in Kyoto. My father's name is Komachiya Sōzaemon, and mine is Sōshichi. I travel every year on business between Kyoto and Hakata. I hope, gentlemen, that you will forgive any lapses on my part while aboard ship. I'm delighted to have such pleasant companions.

NARRATOR: When these polite formalities are over, he sits less stiffly, and as he warms to the conversation, he soon is soon stretched on his belly, relaxed as with friends of a thousand years' standing. His reserve melts away like the morning frost. Kuemon's face also softens.

KEZORI: There's nothing like a good story to while away the lonely hours aboard ship. Listen to the true-life story of how when I was twenty-seven I had a fight with a Satsuma man.

The seventh and ninth days of the ninth moon are the festival of the Suwa Shrine in Nagasaki. There's Kabuki dancing and Chinese dancing—it's a marvelous sight. Well, there was this Satsuma samurai—just a brat, but a stout enough fellow. He'd been drinking at a place called Motokōsen Street, and a couple of mugs of straight saké had gone to his head. I was on my way to see the dancing at Suwa, and as he passed coming from the other direction, he poked me in the side with the damned point of his rusty old scabbard. That was all I needed. I grabbed the end of the scabbard and threw him over backwards, hard enough to squash him against the wall. That was something to see! The Satsuma man knew that if he returned home alive they'd kill him for letting himself get knocked down by a man from another province. He thought that he might as well die on the spot, and drew his sword. "Don't try to be funny," I said, and lifting him over my shoulder, I threw him again. His skull was smashed against the jagged rocks along the ditch. Oh—it's bad luck aboard ship to use the word "smashed" [4]—his skull was dashed, the blood raced, and his tears ran. He was carried off to his inn on a servant's back, his head in his hands. I see now that I acted much too impetuously. There was no need to get so excited. People in Kyoto, your part of the country, are known for their gentle dispositions. I'm sure you'd never behave that way.

NARRATOR: His words, delivered in a loud voice, are punctuated by gestures. Everyone listens absorbed.

KEZORI: Now let's have a story from our guest from the capital. I'll ask the rest of you for stories by-and-by. Kyoto's a city of romance, and I'm sure you've had your share. Tell us about your love life.

NARRATOR: The others join in coaxing, and Sōshichi falls into their trap.

SŌSHICHI: Very well, then.—My father keeps me under strict surveillance, and while I'm in Kyoto or Osaka I can't spend a penny as if it were my own. But my annual visits to Hakata have permitted me to meet Kojorō in Willow Lane. We fell madly in love from the start. This year I am determined to ransom her. I've made her my promise, and she's willing to become my wife.

[4] The word "smashed" (yabureta) was taboo because it suggested a shipwreck.

NARRATOR: Kuemon interrupts.

KEZORI: You needn't say another word—the rest I can guess. We're also on our way to Hakata, and the five of us will serve as go-betweens when you ransom Kojorō. Remember us generously, your worship!

NARRATOR: Kuemon rises respectfully, and the others chorus:

A: Hail to the Patron and Ransomer!

B: Excuse me, but whose Great Patron might this be?

C: The Lady Kojorō's!

NARRATOR: They surround Sōshichi with their taunts. Sōshichi is angered by their excessive merriment.

SŌSHICHI: Are you making fun of me? Or do you really despise me?

NARRATOR: He presses his hands on his chest to restrain his rising fury, and this sets off a fit of coughing.

SŌSHICHI: I've caught a cold this morning and I have a headache. I'll continue my story later. Please don't let me break up your party.

NARRATOR: He offers these parting words, but in his great agitation he has trouble rising, and only with effort manages to crawl off below.

KEZORI: His purse must be warmly lined if he's got enough money to ransom a girl—why should he have caught cold? I wonder what's wrong with him?

NARRATOR: As he spews forth slander and abuse, from Kokura a fast skiff slides through the waves, rowed unwaveringly along a straight path to their ship. Kuemon and the others raise a shout of welcome.

KEZORI: Sanzō! Ichigorō! How did the business go?

SANZŌ: The best we've done in years. We collected the goods and paid for them. The other party was pleased and we were lucky. We'll deliver the merchandise as soon as we check it against the bill of lading.

NARRATOR: Kuemon is delighted at the news.

KEZORI: Captain, on deck! All hands, report here! Bring the goods aboard!

SAILORS: Aye, aye.

NARRATOR: In high spirits they unload 105 tigers skins, a stirring sight.[5] Next come five boxes of shrimp-tailed ginseng weighing thirty pounds, some seven chests of heavy damask, two hundred bolts in all, and finally they transfer from the skiff forty pods of the finest musk.

[5] The wares unloaded are all highly exotic. Tiger skins were presumably for decoration only, but ginseng was an expensive and highly prized medicine. I have omitted two irrelevant phrases about success as the best medicine, and heavy-handedness as the cause of failure; these are induced by mention of the medicine ginseng and the heavy damask.

KEZORI: Are you sure the harbor guards didn't notice you?

ICHIGORŌ: Don't worry. There was no sign of them. Here are fifteen boxes of striped silk gauze and twelve rolls of the best five-gauge satin. And here's seven pails of finely worked lacquer and—I was lucky with this—the night before last, with the moon shining bright, I acquired a hundred pounds of lustrous tortoise shell. Well, that's the haul, and I'm proud of it. Oh, I forgot—here are eighty coral beads as radiant as the morning star, a gift from heaven. Now I've delivered everything listed in the bill of lading. This tally is your identification for next summer's ship. They said you should send out a boat to meet theirs.

NARRATOR: He hands the pass to Kuemon, who lifts it respectfully to his forehead.

KEZORI: Well done! A splendid job! You deserve a rest. (*To men.*) Break out the saké for both of them!

SANZŌ: Congratulations to you, chief!

ICHIGORŌ: We hope you'll reward us liberally. Thanks for the saké—we'll drink in honor of your success.

NARRATOR: The men climb from the skiff to the main ship. Kuemon summons his gang and speaks in a low voice.

KEZORI: Did the rest of you notice? While we were loading the goods that damned passenger from Kyoto stuck his head out over the railing. He was watching us with a suspicious look on his face. If we let him get away alive, he's sure to blab and cause us trouble later on. I wouldn't want to use our swords on him—the sight of blood is bad luck at the start of an important mission. Let's strangle him and dump the body into the sea. Be careful. I think he has a servant with him.

A: Right! Leave it to us!

B: On your toes, everybody!

C: We're with you!

NARRATOR: They knot handkerchiefs around their heads, tuck up their sleeves and kimonos, and flex their muscles, readying themselves for a test of strength. They watch for the right moment, shielding themselves behind the bulkhead. Then, with a cry of, "Let's go!" they stealthily descend the hatch. The ship is far from shore, and all aboard are in the plot. Save for the salt wind, none will see, none will hear, none will ever know—or so they suppose. But events prove that they are mistaken: the servant suddenly shrieks, "Come, get us!" and makes a desperate leap for the deck. Yaheiji and Den'emon pursue and trap him. They lift the servant overhead and with a "Yo-heave-ho" fling him into the foaming waves. Alas for the servant, doomed to become debris at the bottom of the sea!

A: That takes care of one of them. But where's Sōshichi? Let's search for him! No—there he is by the gangway!

NARRATOR: At the cry Sōshichi snatches up an oar and flies at them like a madman.

SŌSHICHI: You dirty smugglers! I've seen everything! You may kill me, but I won't die alone!

NARRATOR: He brandishes the oar furiously. Ichigorō sneaks up from behind and, watching for an opening, grabs Sōshichi, only to be hurled to the deck. But in falling Ichigorō seizes Sōshichi's ankle, and pulls him down, heels over head. The gang falls on Sōshichi, its movements muffled by the pounding waves, and sends him plummeting head first into the boundless sea. The men roar with laughter.

MEN: That's that! Hurrah!

NARRATOR: When Sōshichi revives, he discovers that he is lying inside the skiff. He unfastens the hawser and plies the oars softly, aware that any noise would be disastrous. Fleeing this spot, harder to escape than a shark's or serpent's jaws, he rows some distance, then cries:

SŌSHICHI: Sorry to have caused so much trouble, gentlemen! I offer you my thanks from here, and I promise to repay you soon.

NARRATOR: In his eagerness to escape he pulls for dear life on the oars—his luck lies with Heaven and his boat!

Scene Two: The Okuda House in Hakata.
Time: About a week later.

NARRATOR:

Iiki nite nite
Suicha encha
Suwa hisu fui chō
Hii tara kowa imi sai hanya
Sanso uwa uwa u.[6]

FIRST MAID: Stop it! Stop it! Yokuichi, I can't dance to that rhythm.

---

[6] A Chinese song, sung in this approximation of current Chinese pronunciation.

If you don't know how to accompany the Drum Dance,[7] you should say so from the beginning. I suppose you think you're the Izaemon of Nagasaki[8] and enjoy special privileges. No, I won't dance any more.

YOKUICHI: You think your dancing will improve that way? Keep dancing till I stop playing the samisen.

SECOND MAID: Say what you please, I won't dance. You'd do better to stop grinding out those tunes and grind flour in a mill or grind your teeth![9]

YOKUICHI: Grind my teeth! Don't try to make fun of me because I'm blind. You've got two eyes, but I can still show you a thing or two!

NARRATOR: Waving his samisen, he chases the girls round the room, guided by the sound of their voices. The master of the house, Okudaya Shirozaemon, steps in from the kitchen.

SHIROZAEMON: What's going on here? Yokuichi—behave yourself. You're acting like a child. If you maids persist in making such a commotion, I'll tell the Chaser about you and see to it that she gives you a scolding. (*To one of maids.*) Shigenojō! Today's the thirteenth anniversary of the death of Kojorō's mother. She's taken the day off at her own expense to offer prayers for her mother's repose. Can't you hear her reciting the sutras in the back room? It never seems to have occurred to you to offer incense for the mother of the courtesan you serve. Instead, you tease a blind man. What does this mean?

SHIGENOJŌ: I wasn't teasing him. The two of us were practicing the Drum Dance, and Yokuichi was interfering with his samisen.

SHIROZAEMON: The Drum Dance! That makes it all the worse. You could have chosen a more appropriate time to practice that dance! Go back and see if Kojorō needs you. Both of you, at once! And as for you, Yokuichi, the rich Mr. Gen from Dazaifu is in the front room upstairs. Have you welcomed him yet?

YOKUICHI: I'm on my way! He's my chance to make a gold piece.

NARRATOR: Counting on another man's wallet, he counts his chickens before they are hatched;[10] he goes off to collect largess from the guest.

---

[7] A Chinese dance (*zenidaiko*) accompanied by samisens and small drums.

[8] Izaemon, the hero of Chikamatsu's play *Yūgiri Awa no Naruto*, was the prototype of the great spender in the gay quarters.

[9] In the original there are three plays on the word *hiku*, meaning to "play" an instrument, to "turn" a stone mill, and to "limp". I have attempted to approximate these uses with the word "grind".

[10] Literally, he tightens his pursestrings before receiving any money.

Though a hundred years have yet to pass, Komachiya[11] Sōshichi
feels decrepitude upon him. He barely escaped with his life from grave
danger at Shimonoseki and, though love has directed his oars to Hakata,
his only assets now are his hands and feet. He is too ashamed of his
appearance to call on or write his acquaintances, but he cannot forget
Kojorō's love. Though he has come to Willow Lane caressed by the
breezes of love, his poverty humiliates him, and he is naturally timid.
He peeps in at the gate of the Okuda House, shrinks back, only to look
again. As he stands there hesitantly, someone inside, taking him for a
beggar, harshly cries:

VOICE: We've already given our leftovers away. Move on!

SŌSHICHI: I must look like a beggar. I've sunk to the depths of
degradation! They'll never listen to me if I show myself in this condition and ask to see Kojorō. Even if they let me in, I'd only be a disgrace to Kojorō. I'll give up the idea. I won't see her.

NARRATOR: As he leaves a voice behind him—Shigenojō's—calls.

SHIGENOJŌ: Wait a moment, please! You're lucky—the great courtesan happens to be offering prayers today. Here's a penny in alms for
you.

NARRATOR: She holds out the coin, then exclaims:

SHIGENOJŌ: My goodness! This beggar is wearing silk!

NARRATOR: She peeps under the hat at the face.

SHIGENOJŌ: Why, you're Mr. Sōshichi from Kyoto. Madam, Mr.
Sōshichi's become a beggar!

NARRATOR: Sōshichi shakes his head and starts away.

SHIGENOJŌ: Don't go! Wait, please!

NARRATOR: She stays him, clinging to his sash. In the meanwhile
people pour from the house in alarm. Kojorō rushes to the gate and
snatches off Sōshichi's hat.

KOJORŌ: Yes, it's really you. I'm so happy you've come! But why are
you dressed this way?

NARRATOR: Her tears fall even before she has heard his story.

KOJORŌ: Shiroza. I would like to talk privately with Sōshichi in the
back room.

SHIROZAEMON: Of course. I understand. Sōshichi's an old customer.
Please let me know, sir, if you need anything.

[11] A reference to Komachi, a famous beauty who eventually became a hundred-year-old
hag.

NARRATOR: Encouraged by the master's kindness, they are in each other's arms even before they go inside.

KOJORŌ: Lovers as close as we are don't need to say, "I love you," "How I've missed you!" or the rest. But why are you dressed so shabbily? Have you been disinherited by your father? I'm sure there's some good reason. Why haven't you told me? Is it because you still consider me merely a prostitute? My body must remain in the Quarter, but in my heart I've long since been your wife. I'll never break the promises we've exchanged, not even if we're reduced to rags and must go hand in hand to people's doors to beg their charity. This is the thirteenth anniversary of my mother's death. I'm sure my parents must have stretched forth their hands from the world of the dead to bring us together today. Can't you pronounce the simple words, "Have you been well, my wife?"

NARRATOR: Her sincerity shines in the jewels of her tears. The man also weeps, and his voice trembles.

SŌSHICHI: Kojorō—how have you been? I wish, after a year's absence, I could appear before you in splendid clothes and tell you of wonderful triumphs. Listen to what has happened instead. I was on my way here with a stock of merchandise for my annual visit. At Shimonoseki I happened to take passage aboard a smugglers' ship and, as a result, my servant was thrown into the sea before my eyes, and only by good fortune was I able to escape with my life. I had to abandon everything aboard ship—my baggage with the merchandise and all my clothes. I hadn't a penny on me, and I was forced to sell both my under kimonos, one after the other. That was the only way I could prolong my life as long as I have. I made you the solemn vow that when I came to Hakata this time I would ransom and marry you, but the money I saved for the purpose is in other men's hands. Imagine how miserable it makes me to break my word and fail in my promise! But what worried me most was the thought that you might be angry with me. I felt so sorry that I decided to come here, exposing my wretched appearance to the eyes of the world, in order to offer my apologies and see your face again. What a humiliation it has been for me!

NARRATOR: His voice is blurred by tears.

KOJORŌ: Thank you for telling me. Don't worry—your fortunes will improve when you least expect it. I'm happy just to know that you're still alive. I'm sure I can manage somehow to support you. You poor dear—you must be freezing in those clothes. And your face has become so thin.

NARRATOR: She takes him under her outer robe, and embracing, they stand weeping. At the gate a servant's lusty voice rings out.

SERVANT: The Great Patron has arrived!

KOJORŌ: Someone has come. This way!

NARRATOR: She takes Sōshichi's hand and, nestling together, they go into a back room.

The guests, the smugglers of a while before, are led by Kezori Kuemon. Yaheiji, Den'e, Niza, Heiza, Ichigo, and Sanzō file in behind him. "Welcome!" cries the host, ushering them in, and the guests shuffle up on metal-shod sandals, luxuriously attired on top and underneath in imported cloths: serge, *stamijn, karsaai, laken,* satin, and velvet.[12] The heads are Japanese, but the bodies foreign; the boundary line is their collars. These artful imposters of uncertain origins are expert in gaining overnight wealth. They charge into the Okuda House in their unwonted finery, and seat themselves in a row. Kezori, in complete control, wears the pompous expression of the director-general.

KEZORI: Well, mine host, I imagine you have but faint recollection of us. Until yesterday we were forced to crisscross the Quarter in search of the cheapest whores, but we've become millionaires overnight, as you can see. From this day on, our sport is with the great courtesans. On my way here I glanced in on Eguchi of the Figure One House, Katsuyama and Usugumo of the Round House, Misao of the Oil House, Ōgura of the Izumi House, and Ōiso of the Carriage House, and I decided to ransom the six of them as companions for my men here. I can't wait till tomorrow. I want you to complete the arrangements today.

SHIROZAEMON: That's a difficult request.

NARRATOR: Shirozaemon starts for the door.

KEZORI: Wait. It's boring when the host's not here. Why don't you send someone instead?

[12] *Stamijn* (a Dutch word) was a fabric woven of wool and hemp. *Karsaai* (Dutch, from English kersey) and *laken* (a Dutch word) both denoted a kind of wool cloth. Mention of these cloths is intended to create an impression of exoticism and luxury.

SHIROZAEMON: I will, sir.

NARRATOR: He takes brush and paper and, dashing off a note, sends a messenger dashing off for the courtesans.

SHIROZAEMON (*to messenger*): Hurry back. (*To maids.*) Bring some carp soup. Open the two big rooms into one. See that the children don't cry, and tell my wife to take her medicine.

KEZORI: What's that? The madam's sick? (*To servant.*) Bring me my traveling box. (*To host.*) You can't neglect an illness. She should take ginseng—it's the best remedy. I happen to have brought some. Allow me the pleasure.

NARRATOR: He opens the box and takes out a bundle from which he extracts over a pound of first-quality large ginseng.

KEZORI: Shiroza, how many children have you?

SHIROZAEMON: One girl and two boys.

KEZORI: A fine family. Give these coral beads to your sons.[13] They're small, but they make a pair and weigh eight *momme*. And use these three rolls of damask and five of satin—they're what I have here— to make kimonos for your daughter. The crimson crepe will do nicely for the lining.

NARRATOR: He even adds money for the silk padding, throwing out presents on presents till the host's arms ache from lifting them to his forehead. Shirozaemon is dazzled.

SHIROZAEMON: I'm overwhelmed. I don't know how to thank you. May I ask when you acquired such immense wealth?

NARRATOR: Kuemon, pressed for an answer, speaks the first thing that enters his head.

KEZORI: It wasn't easy, I can tell you that. Business with Edo was slow, so I struck the Hell's Bell at Sayo no Nakayama,[14] and struck it rich. But I had to practice strict austerities before I even struck the bell. The particulars are described in the scripture known as the Millionaire's Gospel preserved in the temple. Shall I relate the contents?

NARRATOR: He laughs, and the host claps his hands in wonder.

SHIROZAEMON: The blessed scriptures! Please instruct me in this holy work. I would like to be favored by a little of your good fortune.

NARRATOR: He earnestly begs Kuemon.

[13] Presumably to be used for *netsuke,* the ornamental fastenings on tobacco pouches.
[14] It was believed that anyone who struck this bell, formerly at the Kwannon Temple in Sayo no Nakayama (the modern Shizuoka Prefecture), would enjoy great wealth in this world, but would suffer for it in hell (*mugen*) after death.

*Sōshichi watches from the porthole below as the smugglers load
their goods aboard ship. Kezori, on deck, notices him.*
(SŌSHICHI: *Nakamura Kanzaburō XVII;* KEZORI: *Matsumoto
Kōshirō VIII*)

KEZORI: Very well, then. Listen carefully.

NARRATOR: He ostentatiously produces a notebook of uncertain contents, and reads at the top of his lungs wild fabrications on the theme of avarice, styling them the Millionaire's Gospel.

The origins of the Hell's Bell may be traced to a rich man of India named Gakkai,[15] a remarkably stingy millionaire. The Buddha used to visit this man every morning in the hopes of bringing him enlightenment. When he pounded his begging bowl, Gakkai, pretending not to hear, would not so much as grunt in recognition. Then the Buddha, as a last resort, exuded from his body a saffron halo, exactly like gold, and the miser, at sight of the precious metal, was led by greed to put an offering in Buddha's hand, hoping to peel the gold leaf away. Thus he was caught in Buddha's toils and—alas, alack, and hail Amida Buddha!—against his will Gakkai offered money to cast this sacred bell.

The miserly millionaire's heart still lingers in this latter-day world, for when you strike the bell early in the evening, it echoes not only the impermanence of all things,[16] but his regret over the donation. When you strike the bell late at night, it echoes the truth that fortunes are born only to perish. The bell at dawn echoes mortally high costs; it is the voice of annihilating waste and of the 108 sufferings of the penny-wise and pound-foolish. He who hears the sound of this bell will in this world become a millionaire, but he is doomed in the after life to roast in hell. So wondrous a bell is not lightly to be struck.

Now, as to the discipline to be observed. Never wear silk or pongee. Cotton quilts should seem the height of luxury. Make a habit of sleeping under straw matting. Remember, tastes are a matter of habit. Nara tea-gruel makes excellent fare; animal food and vegetables are unnecessary. Eat no more than twice a day, morning and night. Twice a year at festival time [17] tuck up your kimono and hurry through the streets, in one and out the other: something is bound to have been dropped—don't leave it there! Always pick up something when you fall, even a handful of dirt. Rise in the morning at four. Never lend

---

[15] In Buddhist texts Gakkai figures as a devout believer in Buddha who generously gave of his wealth; here his character is distorted for comic effect.

[16] A suggestion of the opening lines of *The Tale of the Heike:* "The sound of the bell of the Gion Temple echoes the impermanence of all things."

[17] New Year and the Bon Festival, the most important holidays of the Japanese year. Here the thrifty man is enjoined to keep his eyes open for objects dropped by celebrants.

money without security. It's money saved when you don't buy what you want. It's money lost not to do nightwork when the moon is bright. Poverty never overtakes a diligent man. Split your firewood into mustard-seed lengths, and then a thousand times more before you burn it, and never discard the ashes.[18] Nothing should ever be thrown away. Use the soot around a pot to paint false eyebrows. Bits of rice stalk make an infallible remedy for pins and needles. A dried-up well is useful for storing ladders, and even a rat's tail makes a gimlet sheath. Dry your umbrella immediately after use and never lend it. Each time you lend a stick of dried cuttlefish, a pestle, an earthen mortar, a whetstone, a stone mill, or a medicine chopper, it invariably comes back a little thinner, though you may not detect the difference.

Moreover, be affable to customers, thrifty and saving, and stick to your studies and your abacus. Remember, there will be no limit to your desires if you look at the scale of living of people better off than yourself, but as long as you observe these rules, taking people below you for your models, little grains of dust will build into a mighty mountain.

The golden rules of the millionaire are infallible. Hell's Bell is merely a name, but he who does not disobey these admonitions will prosper in the present and future worlds: such is the true source of happiness and prosperity. Hearken ye!

SHIROZAEMON: I can't say yes or no to that. If everybody conducted himself in the way you prescribe, the Okuda House would go out of business.

NARRATOR: He laughs. Only a single thickness of *shōji* separates this room from Kojorō's, and the men's uproar strikes home to her heart.

KOJORŌ: Those with money have more than they need! You'd think that money was dirt to hear him talk about ransoming five or six great courtesans, doing this and doing that. I've never before had the least craving for more money than I could earn, not even when I saw my parents living in poverty, but today I feel so jealous of those women about to be ransomed that I want money desperately. It's wrong, I know, to envy people who are lucky, but I want to see what such a rich man looks like.

NARRATOR: She peeps through a crack in the *shōji*.

KOJORŌ: Why, he's a friend of mine! He assured me that if ever I was in trouble I could depend on him. I'll ask him for some money.

---

[18] Ashes in a brazier help to preserve the fire.

NARRATOR: Sōshichi restrains her as she starts into the adjoining room.

SŌSHICHI: Your old friendship is a secret between the two of you, and others will be listening now. Don't you think it would seem disgraceful if a courtesan asked a guest to lend her money?

KOJORŌ: There are times for concealing one's shame and times when that's impossible. Wasn't I telling you just a few moments ago that my customer from Chikugo has privately arranged with the Sado House at the Quarter entrance to ransom me next month? That's why I've been waiting so impatiently for you. I can't go on living if I'm to be handed over to another man. It's no disgrace to borrow money, providing I return it. Let me do things my way.

NARRATOR: She shakes herself free. Sōshichi weeps to let her go. Kojorō too is in tears that she hides as she slips into the next room. She sits beside Kezori. The perfume from her robe pervades the room. The rough men around her exchange glances and hastily straighten their crested cloaks, with the embarrassment of devils at a flower-viewing party.

KOJORŌ: I'm glad to see you again, Kezori. I have a favor to ask of you. Some serious trouble has come up, and I must ask a certain man to ransom me immediately. Unfortunately, he hasn't got the indispensable thing—money. You once said you would help me. I'm asking you now please to lend me until I can scrape it together the money needed for my ransom. This is the favor I ask.

KEZORI: How hard it must be for you, the most elegant woman in Japan, to pronounce the words "lend me the money"! You won't have to ask a second time. Anything you need, whether it's a thousand pieces of gold or ten thousand, you'll have. Host! I'll ransom Kojorō along with the other girls. Afterwards she can go wherever she wishes. The money is my responsibility. And now, while we're waiting for the other girls, I'll borrow Kojorō. Drink up, everybody, and sing!

NARRATOR: He shouts boisterously.

KOJORŌ: Wait just a moment, please. The man I mentioned before— my dearest lover—is in the next room. I'd like to bring him here and let him express his thanks too. Please don't go back on your promise, Kezori.

KEZORI: I swear by my good fortune as a man and a merchant that I never lie. Bring in your friend!

NARRATOR: With this reassurance she hurries back joyfully to her lover.

The cry goes up, "The great ladies have come!" From the gate, to the accompaniment of shouts loud as waves pounding on a beach,[19] enter Katsuyama, Eguchi, and Ōiso, the flower of the fair.

KATSUYAMA: Usugumo, Misao, and Ōgura will join us later.

YAHEIJI: I see my soul mate!

NARRATOR: The atmosphere grows sultry as Kezori's infatuated companions gaze in rapture at the courtesans. Kezori calls out:

KEZORI: Host! I have a little business to conduct. Have the girls wait in the room by the entrance. When the other "great ladies" appear, I don't want them brought here.

SHIROZAEMON: Very well, sir. (*To courtesans.*) Come this way.

NARRATOR: They meekly depart with the host; in the country even the courtesans are obedient.

Sōshichi hesitates, uncertain whether or not to show himself, but yielding to Kojorō, he slides open the *shōji* and steps inside. He and Kezori, brought face to face, exchange astonished glances.

KEZORI: So you're Kojorō's sweetheart! I remember you now!

SŌSHICHI: I was hoping I might meet you all again. (*Calls.*) Isn't anybody here? These rascals are from Shimonoseki and they're—

NARRATOR: Kezori's companions raise a great tumult, and prevent Sōshichi from finishing his sentence.

SMUGGLERS: Don't let him say another word! Kill him!

NARRATOR: They spring to their feet, upsetting the saké cups and warming pots. Saké spills over the *tatami*.

SERVANT: It looks like a fight over a woman. I hope nothing serious happens.

NARRATOR: The parlormaids and menservants, pale with alarm, feel more dead than alive. Kezori does not budge an inch.

KEZORI: Don't make such an uproar! I have an idea. Yaheiji and the rest of you—join the girls. Leave everything to me.

YAHEIJI: We can't do that. Let us deal with him. We'd be worried to leave you here alone, chief.

KEZORI: Do you think anyone's likely to get the better of Kezori? You men would only get in the way if you were here. Leave, and be quick about it.

NARRATOR: He glowers at them.

YAHEIJI: All right, then, we'll go. You do things your way, chief.

NARRATOR: They go together to the front room.

[19] Mention of waves on a beach is induced by the name Ōiso, literally "great shore".

Kojorō, at a loss to understand what is happening, sits by Sōshichi, watching the eyes of the two men.

KEZORI: Well, young man, Mr. Sōshichi. One word about what you saw the other day and it will be your last. I suggest that you keep quiet. I need not explain our trade. You saw it with your own eyes. I further suggest, in the interest of your health, that you put up with the treatment you received aboard ship. If you raise a fuss, it will lead to serious consequences. I urge you—show forbearance. Think how unhappy it would make Kojorō if your promises to ransom her proved worthless. The poor girl, she is thinking of you all the time. Why, she loves you so much that she risked her reputation as a courtesan to beg me for money. You'd be heartless to bring all her efforts to nothing. Take my advice—please join us. I'll make Kojorō your wife, and I'll advance you fifty or even a hundred *kamme*. I promise, moreover, to lend a generous hand if your father cuts off his support.

The bigger our number, the less advantageous it is for us, but our business depends on luck, and if luck's against us, we're done for. Anybody who can survive the treatment you received the other day must be blessed by the gods with amazing luck. I'm sure you can help us. That's why I'm asking you most humbly—please join us.

NARRATOR: His words are humble, but his sword is ready; his expression plainly reveals that if refused he will attack. Sōshichi is driven to the wall for an answer. If he joins the smugglers he will bring disaster on his family and invite execution. If he refuses he must yield Kojorō to another man, and his life will be taken besides. His fate is death, whichever he chooses. Should he respect the laws of the land? Or should he choose marriage with Kojorō? His mind is torn two ways at once, but he has only one body. He wavers, unable to decide.

KOJORŌ: Excuse me, Sōshichi. I don't know what this gentleman's business is but, as they say, some ride in sedan chairs and others carry them. People differ in their stations, but the road they travel is the same. How kind of him to advance the money and to do everything to help you! If his offer won't hurt you, why don't you say "yes" and join him so that we can soon be living together? But if for any reason joining him would do you harm, give him a definite refusal. Remember, I won't go on living unless I can be with you. Your "yes" or "no" will decide whether you make me your wife or kill me. Think carefully before you answer.

NARRATOR: She slips her hand into the fold of his kimono.

KOJORŌ: How you're perspiring!

NARRATOR: She uses all her paper handkerchiefs to wipe away the sweat; they tear with moisture as a man's heart with love, the road it is hardest to turn back on. Sōshichi nods resolutely.

SŌSHICHI (*to Kezori*): I accept your offer wholeheartedly. I am with you from now on and I will not disobey your orders. I hear that in Nagasaki you seal agreements by drinking blood mixed in saké. Here—to prove my sincerity, to prove that I'm not deceiving you, I'll cut my arm and swear in my blood.

NARRATOR: He bares his arm.

KEZORI: I believe you. I can tell an honest man when I see one. Why should you deceive me? Let's have another round of drinks. (*Calls.*) Come here, everybody!

NARRATOR: He summons the others.

KEZORI: I'm sure you're happy, Kojorō. (*To host.*) How much does the total cost of the ransom come to?

SHIROZAEMON: Here's the bill, sir.

NARRATOR: Kezori takes the bill and runs his eye over it.

KEZORI: So, the ransom for the seven girls including Kojorō amounts to 1,450 pieces of gold, does it? I don't want to bother with change— I'll give you the extra fifty pieces. Here, take the whole 1,500 pieces of gold.

NARRATOR: He lays down 750 *ryō* each in pieces of one and two *ryō*, to both parties' delight.

KEZORI: Splendid. Sōshichi is now one of us. We must all be closer than brothers. And now, a song, a song.

> The village I come from
> Lies deep in the mountains,
> The chestnuts fall from the tree.
> I sleep with my head
> On the roots of the tree,
> The chestnut tree.
> My sweetheart is mountain-born
> She loves making love with me,
> *Namaidabutsu*.[20]

[20] The invocation of Buddha's name was often used as the burden of popular songs. (See also "The Love Suicides at Amijima," p. 390.) The song has been interpreted as meaning that Kojorō will slip from her sash as a chestnut from its outer burr.

Untie your sash and come, my dear,
I'll take you in my arms,
And we'll lie down straight away—
This is the life for me!

NARRATOR: They make merry. The night watchman of the Quarter bursts in excitedly.

WATCHMAN: A criminal—a murderer—is at large in the Quarter. The authorities have ordered all guests to be checked. Nobody's allowed to leave. The raiding constables will be here soon.

NARRATOR: He dashes out, taking the proprietor with him. The six or seven smugglers from Kezori on down, though they pride themselves on their imperturbability, go limp with fear, and their faces suddenly wilt like boiled turnips.

KEZORI: This is intolerable. Isn't there some alley we can take back to the ship? Never mind how much it costs—I can't very well burrow into the ground—I wonder if there isn't some ladder I can climb into the sky? I wish I had a hat or cape to make me invisible!

NARRATOR: They stand trembling, each man at a loss how to dispose of himself. Sōshichi takes Kojorō's hand. As they wait in breathless suspense, watching the door, a clattering is heard—this house or the next? The shout is heard, "We arrest you!" The others, petrified, groan in dismay; not a man retains control of his senses. The host Shiroza returns.

SHIROZAEMON: Nothing to worry about! They've caught some poor devil in the teahouse next door. He killed a courier at Tonomachi here in Hakata, and stole his money. They've taken him to the police station. It doesn't concern anybody here.

NARRATOR: They exchange glances.

A: What a relief!

B: Thank heavens! I had my heart in my mouth.

NARRATOR: They breathe sighs of relief, life coming back into their ugly faces, like the second hot douche in a case of malignant smallpox.[21]

KEZORI: There's no point in staying any longer. Sōshichi, let's be on our way to Kyoto. We're leaving, everybody. The girls will go to the wharf in palanquins.

[21] In cases where smallpox did not follow an established pattern of symptoms, it was described as "malignant" and as many as three hot douches were given to restore the "natural" order.

NARRATOR: Eight voices say in unison, "Good-by, host!" as they leave.

SHIROZAEMON: What a prodigious patron! Ransoming seven great courtesans at the same time! I've never heard the like before. I'd like to make out tags listing the price of each lady and string them up.[22]

KEZORI: String them up! You make my hair stand on end! Don't do that!

SHIROZAEMON: But your exploits would be publicized.

KEZORI: The last thing I want is to be publicized! Say no more.

NARRATOR: He leaves: manly pride shows in their seven haughtily lifted noses!

ACT TWO

Scene: Shinsei Street in Kyoto; a large house (Sōshichi's) next to which is a small building serving as the neighborhood meeting place.
Time: Some months later.

NARRATOR: An auction is in progress and household effects and furnishings are being knocked down to bidders one after the other at sacrificial prices, without regard to cost. Cupboards, chests of drawers, lacquered chests, candlesticks, dishware, soup bowls, chopping boards, a Buddhist altar and—what's this?—three pairs of hanging scrolls in the Kanō style, the mounting alone worth one hundred *kan,* knocked down for the price of a wicker hat. Lanterns, fine Nanking dishes go for eight to nine *momme,* a medium-length dagger with a finely wrought guard for the same price. Pots, pans, and sooty kettles, mats taken up from the floor, the floor boards themselves, household tools, bamboo utensils—every last object down to the sweepings and ashes is up for auction. "What am I offered for the cat?" The price jumps by five *fun* at a time, soaring like a skylark. Next the guardian deity of the house, a hanging inkstand, and a pot for tooth blackening

[22] The pun in Japanese is on *haritsuke* (affixing [a notice]) and *haritsuke* (crucifixion), the punishment for smuggling. In the following exchange *arawareru* (to be revealed) is used three times: Kezori's exploit is "made known", he does not wish to be "found out", and the men's pride is "revealed".

are held up—did they suppose *that* would bring in money?—and from mouth to mouth the rival bids fly. The neighborhood echoes with the din of the auction place.

The owner of the house, Hishiya Kaemon, rushes up, astonishment on his face.

HISHIYA: What an outrage! What does this mean? This is my house, and I let it to Komachiya Sōshichi, a merchant from the west. He and his wife have gone to Osaka for ten days, leaving only an old woman in charge here. He asked me to keep an eye on the house during their absence, and I expect them back today or tomorrow. As for you, old woman—why do you suppose they asked you to take care of the house? (*To Sōzaemon.*) And who, may I ask, are you? Is it possible that at your age you are still unaware of the customs of this city? You force yourself into this house when the occupants are away, without a word of explanation to the neighborhood office, and proceed to sell off the contents, down to the mats on the floor. How do you propose to make up for this? Do you imagine that, as an elder in charge of public order in Shinsei Street and a property owner, I can disregard this outrage? I intend to take action against you and the old woman both. The house next door is the neighborhood meeting office. Come along with me, and quickly.

NARRATOR: His tone is sharp. The old woman, in tears, turns her head away, but Sōshichi's father, Sōzaemon, touches his hands to the ground in a polite bow.

SŌZAEMON: As the owner of this house and a district elder you are quite justified, sir, in your complaints. Permit me to introduce myself. I am Sōshichi's father, Komachiya Sōzaemon by name. I am a native of Nagasaki, but I've lived in this part of the country for twenty years. Never having had enough capital to run a successful business, I've been living in reduced circumstances near Yamashina. Sōshichi has taken business trips every year to the west, using my old connections there. This time he sent me no word of any unusual success, but while I was waiting anxiously for news one way or the other, I heard bits of gossip from people here and there of how Sōshichi had made a great fortune, how he'd ransomed a Hakata courtesan, and how he'd established himself in a splendid shop in Shinsei Street. They said that, though outwardly Sōshichi seemed to be living very quietly with a minimum of servants, he was actually leading a millionaire's life of luxury. The more rumors I heard, the less I could understand. Last night for the first time I came to call. I was astonished at the appointments and the merchandise in the shop—they were exactly as the rumors had described. I questioned the old woman, but she told me she knew little about the occupants. You are a merchant and I myself have earned my living in business for seventy-eight years. We know, surely, that even if a man keeps doubling his original investment, there's a limit to the profit he can make. Sōshichi was always an honest and devoted son. Even when his profits were no more than ten or fifteen *ryō,* he would proudly inform me, to make me happy. I can't believe, when he hides such wealth from his father, that his money was honestly earned. He's sure to go from bad to worse, and bring disaster on the whole neighborhood, particularly on you, sir. He'll never die a natural death.

I acted as I have out of fatherly love. I wanted to make the lesson sink into his flesh and bones that ill-gotten money does not stick. I hoped that this painful experience would teach him that he must observe honest business practices. I was suddenly obliged to run around to the secondhand dealers and hunt up scrap merchants, and in the confusion I neglected to report to the neighborhood office. I humbly beg your pardon, sir, for not having informed you in advance. Please accept my profound apologies. Now, kindly give me the lease papers. I intend to vacate the house.

NARRATOR: He bows his bald head.

HISHIYA: I accept your apologies. However, Sōshichi let this house through an agent, and for his future reference I'd like you to make a declaration and have it countersigned by the caretaker woman. Please come with me to the neighborhood office.

NARRATOR: He shuts the gate behind him. This is not the stone door of heaven,[23] but here too is a sign: "House to Let." Not a stick of furniture remains: the house is empty.

Kojorō of Hakata, wearing with assurance a city matron's attire, returns with her husband. For Sōshichi, accustomed now to voyages hundreds of anxious leagues over the waves, even to Tsukushi of

[23] A pun on *kami* (god) and *kami* (paper). "Although this is not the stone door (or cave) of heaven, here too is a *god*"; "a *paper* sign proclaims a house to let." The stone cave of heaven is known from the episode in the *Kojiki* in which the goddess Amaterasu hides there.

mysterious fires,[24] in quest of dangerous wealth, Kyoto and Osaka are neighboring towns.

They arrive at their gate to discover that the shop curtains have been removed, and on the barred door hangs a notice in bold, black characters: "House to Let."

SŌSHICHI: What does this mean?

NARRATOR: He can find no words for his distress. He forces open the side door and enters. Not a kettle is left in which they might make tea, and even the mats have been ripped from the floor. The house is so deserted that wild birds might sing here undisturbed. Sōshichi can only stand in his tracks, unable even to weep, his mouth gaping in blank dismay. With the smart of a guilty conscience, he sits heavily on the bamboo flooring. Kojorō speaks impatiently.

KOJORŌ: This is no time to rest!—The owner of the house has always been so kind, and I've been on friendly terms with his wife. Just the other day, when we went to Osaka, she asked me to bring back a pair of Miyoshi geta[25] as a souvenir. What an incredible way to treat us, when we've been so close! I intend to discover what's at the bottom of this.

NARRATOR: She hurries to the door.

SŌSHICHI: Wait! A woman's intervention won't settle anything. This house belongs to Hishiya in name only. The place was an utter wreck when I took over, and I myself paid for all the repairs. I've never been in arrears with the rent—in fact, I've always paid two or three months in advance. And now my belongings have been taken, and even the caretaker woman has disappeared. The authorities must be behind this. I wonder if they became suspicious about the money and merchandise I've left with various people? Whatever it was, our lives are at stake. We can't remain here another night. It couldn't be helped —my luck has run out. (*To servants, who appear from the back.*) You servants can see what has happened to me. I haven't the strength to fight back. Our ties as master and servant have come to an end. The only money left after my expenses in Osaka is one *bu* and some small change. The three of you can divide it. I dismiss you. Good-by.

NARRATOR: He throws them a purse of cloth worked with gold.

[24] "Mysterious fires" (*shiranuhi*) was an epithet for Tsukushi, the northern part of Kyūshū.

[25] Apparently a popular brand of *geta* (Japanese clogs)—an advertisement?

SERVANTS: We don't know what to say, except that we're sorry. We accept your gift gratefully. It would be rude to refuse. We hope we may serve you again.

NARRATOR: They wring out the words; when they wring the purse, out pop eight or nine *ryō* in gold pieces. They are astonished but, coldhearted like all contract-servants,[26] they rush out together without looking back.

The noise of their arrival is heard next door. The old woman slips out of the neighborhood office and enters.

OLD WOMAN: What a dreadful business—dreadful! Last night your father came, and he told me the strangest things. He said, "My son has been driven by greed to join a gang of smugglers. He seems to think that money, however wickedly gained, is a blessing, but he'll end up strung to a tree [27] any day now. I always told him that an honest profit, even three coppers from peddling green vegetables and turnips, stays with you—but he spurned my advice. How did he acquire all these furnishings and merchandise? They are my son's enemies!" The poor man—he called for the secondhand dealers even while he was still brushing away the tears, and he disposed of everything for a mere song. Once he vacated the house he went next door to the office. He's been making his apologies before the officials. All his suffering has been on account of you.

NARRATOR: She bursts into tears and Sōshichi joins her.

SŌSHICHI: I left an important document in my hanging inkstand. It would be a disaster if that got included in the sale. Did it go to some dealer along with the stand?

OLD WOMAN: No, the inkstand was sold, but your father removed the document, and put it away in his wallet.—But you'd do better, instead of worrying about such things, if you left the neighborhood at once. Listen—that sounds as if they're calling me from the office next door. I must be going. We may meet again if I'm still alive and fate wills it. I pray that you'll both be safe.

NARRATOR: She leaves—a parting which occasions grief. Sōshichi sits in a daze.

SŌSHICHI: Now that my father knows our secret, you can be sure that everybody else knows it. I have a friend at Yokkaichi in Ise

---

[26] Servants hired for six months or a year, instead of the usual indefinite period.

[27] Meaning here "crucified", the punishment for smuggling.

Province. Let's try to make our escape in that direction and travel as far as we can. It's already four o'clock. Get ready.

NARRATOR: As he speaks a voice is heard.

KEZORI: Sōshichi, are you at home? You've certainly closed your gate early!

NARRATOR: Kezori Kuemon enters, bursting through the side door. Sōshichi is flustered.

SŌSHICHI: An unexpected pleasure! What brings you here? Please come in. (*To Kojorō.*) The tobacco tray, and some tea!

NARRATOR: The more casual he tries to appear, the more suspicious Kezori's expression becomes.

KEZORI: Enough of your chatter, Sōshichi. I told you when I saw you in Osaka four or five days ago that I'd be going to Kyoto soon. We agreed to meet here. What's this now? You seem to be moving house. What's the occasion? Where are you going? You worry me.

SŌSHICHI: It's nothing to worry about. We've just this moment arrived back in Kyoto, and we haven't had time even to wash our feet after the journey. We've decided that it was foolish for us to be living away from my aged father when we could be much cosier together. We're in the midst of confusion what with moving the furniture and the rest. Where are you staying? I'll call on you as soon as we're settled. But rest a while before you go.

NARRATOR: He starts for the door.

KEZORI: Wait a moment. There's something peculiar about the way you two are acting. Our business season will be starting soon. I leave for Nagasaki tomorrow. I've come to collect the identification pass we need for the islands. The gang left it with you. Let me have the document before you go.

SŌSHICHI: Of course. I've been taking extremely good care of it. I put the pass in a box, sealed it, and left it with my father. I'll send it to you shortly.

NARRATOR: Kezori colors at the words.

KEZORI: You left our pass with your father! That pass is the heart of our operations all around the world! Don't try to deceive me! What did you do with it? It's my guess that you're trying to break from the gang and take the profits for yourself. Yes, that's why you suddenly moved without telling anyone—it all adds up. I'm sure you've got the pass on you. I'll show you how I get what I want.

NARRATOR: He snaps the latches shut and bolts the main and side doors. He advances menacingly on Sōshichi; Kojorō is alarmed.

KOJORŌ: Come now, Kezori, you and Sōshichi are as close as fish and water—why should he lie to you? I promise to deliver the pass myself without fail in the next two or three days. Please leave now.

NARRATOR: She tries to push him out, but he grabs her wrist and hurls her violently to the floor.

KEZORI: Damned nuisance!

SŌSHICHI: Coward! If you've something on your mind, tell me, but don't hurt this woman!

NARRATOR: He lays his hand on his dagger.

KEZORI: Do you think your sword can intimidate me into letting you go without first getting the pass?

NARRATOR: He draws his own sword. Sōshichi springs back and engages him. Both men have steady arms, but the bamboo of the flooring is rotten in places, and there are weak knots in the webbing. They barely manage to keep their feet from breaking through the boards. Each thrust to the right sends their feet sliding to the left, each slash to the left makes them slip through the flooring to the right. Kojorō forces her way beween the clashing sword points at the risk of her life, treading a floor unsure as ice melting on a spring day. Metal broom in hand, she struggles from a distance to knock the sword from Kezori's grip. She catches the hem of her kimono on a floor board and tumbles over, while the swords flash dangerously overhead. The noise reaches the people of the neighborhood but, too terrified to intervene, they pretend to hear nothing. Sōzaemon, however, is unable to endure more; love for his son cannot be denied.

SŌZAEMON: I'll give you the pass! Don't get hurt!

NARRATOR: He goes to the front gate and pushes and pounds on the door, but it does not yield. He peeps through the hole in the door bolt—the sight fills him with dismay and alarm. He runs around to the back gate, writhing with anxiety.

Inside, Kojorō has unhinged a *shōji* and uses it as a shield to separate the men. She attempts to batter down Kezori's sword, watching for every opening to strike, now stepping forward to block him, now dodging back. But she loses her footing and tumbles over, the *shōji* on top of her. Kezori, not wasting a moment, stamps on the *shōji*, but his foot crashes through the frame, and he falls on top of Kojorō. He tries to stab her through the *shōji*.

sōshichi: If you hurt her, I'll finish you with one stroke!

narrator: The point of Sōshichi's sword glitters above him; this is the most perilous of perilous moments.

Sōshichi's father, in an agony of fear, hacks at the wall until he opens a hole big enough to admit his hand. He pushes the pass into the room; the father's waving hand seems to address them. Sōshichi instantly notices it.

sōshichi: Kezori, calm yourself! I'll give you the pass. There's nothing more to fight about. I'm putting my sword back in the scabbard. Put yours away too.

narrator: He sheathes his sword, grateful for his father's love which so unexpectedly has saved his life. He takes the pass and reverently lifts to his forehead the hand that holds it.

sōshichi: Here—take your pass.

narrator: Kezori quickly examines the document.

kezori: It seems to be all right. Yes, I accept it. In our business, Sōshichi, it's one man's life against another. It's our rule to keep each other on our mettle. But as soon as we stop fighting we're friends again. My bitterness is gone.—You look worried and tired. Remember —you can't survive in this business unless you can keep calm even when mountains are crumbling on top of you. Come to Nagasaki at the usual time. I'll see you there.

narrator: He sets out with this farewell, a bold figure. Sōshichi lifts Kojorō to her feet.

sōshichi: Did you see that? What an inspiring thing a father's love is! Bow your head to this break in the wall, if to nothing else.

kojorō: How grateful I am for his goodness! But must this thickness of wall prevent me from seeing the face of a father-in-law who has favored me with such loving kindness?—Ahhhh, I am out of breath. I can't say more. Some tea, please, or even cold water.

narrator: She is in pain, but there is not a cup or dipper in the house.

sōshichi: My poor dear! What am I to do?

narrator: His voice is heard next door. A loving father's hand passes through the wall a teacup filled with warm water. The couple burst into tears of reverence and gratitude at his gesture. They hold the cup, then cling to the hand.

sōshichi: Could a precious wine cup, an elixir, a sacred potion from the gods be more precious than this?

narrator: By turns they lift the cup and drink.

kojorō: I have touched your hand, sir, but I have never seen your face. I am your son's wife, though without your permission. Please forgive Sōshichi and talk to him. And please, it may be for the first and last time in this life, let me see your face.

narrator: She presses her father-in-law's hand to her face and weeps. His grief also betrays itself in the piteous trembling of his arm. He frees his hand, wet by unquenchable tears, and throws in a purse of money. The hand points to the gate, all but saying, "Hurry and go," and then is withdrawn.

kojorō: Is our last remaining tie with Father broken?

narrator: She seems about to swoon with weeping.

sōshichi: Such fatherly love for me, the arch-example of an unfilial son! To refuse his kindness, when he offers money for our journey, would make me the more unfilial.

narrator: Husband and wife by turns lift the purse reverently to their foreheads.

sōshichi: It's dark enough so that people won't recognize us. This is really good-by now.

narrator: Each tucks up the other's kimono in preparation for the journey. They go weeping through the gate, but Sōshichi turns back for a look inside the neighboring fence. He calls in a low voice.

sōshichi: Old lady—please let Kojorō have a glimpse of my father. I'd also like to thank him myself for the money.

narrator: The old woman hears, and goes towards him, but Sōzaemon calls.

sōzaemon: Why are you hovering by the gate, old woman? That money was the proceeds from the sale of the furniture next door. I merely threw it back where it came from. There is no occasion for thanks.—I raised my child on decent business practice, and I have no son who's a smuggler. How contemptible of him—and how pitiful! Doesn't he realize that a man is punished not by heaven, the moon, and the sun, nor by the gods and Buddha, but because he himself seeks out punishment? Heaven supplies sustenance for each living creature. When a man comes into the world, his mother's breast offers heaven-sent nurture. If he bestirs himself at an honest trade, heaven itself will offer milk from its breast, in keeping with his station. How many men, though seeming to enjoy lives of luxury from dishonest gain, have been cut off from the breast of heaven, rejected by the entire world, and finally driven to sordid deaths! A cat dozes all day on the hearth, but a dog must scour the ground for his food. The dog, knowing what is proper for him, does not imitate the idle cat. When I think what the end must be for a man who lacks the in-telligence even of a brute beast in discovering his appointed way of life, my pity for him makes me furious.

NARRATOR: He cannot hide the tears.

SŌZAEMON: Sōshichi! If you wish to be considered my son, live honestly, though it entails menial labor. Don't cut your life short by a contemptible death. Let me die before you, and at my funeral ac-company me in white mourning garb. Then you will be truly my son, and I will rejoice in my coffin.—But now you must leave quickly.

NARRATOR: With these words he bursts into tears. His weeping voice lingering in their ears, a final memento, father and children part.

ACT THREE

Scene: The journey of Sōshichi and Kojorō from Kyoto to Yokkaichi.

NARRATOR: Love and clothes have the same design: the closer the fit to the body, the better the sleeping or wearing.

Sōshichi and Kojorō, though perfectly matched as lovers, have been rejected by the world and driven from their house. Anxious lest neighbors see their faces, they steal out while houses and shops are shut, and the stars before dawning still shine in the late night sky. Their hearts have been greatly lightened by the repeated kindnesses of his father, but on their journey this morning the clothes are thin on their skins, and their bodies ache with fear. Their fates are their own doing, it is true, but how forlorn they feel! In the streets of Kyoto, so dear and familiar, they hesitate by the Little Bridge of Sanjō, afraid they might meet someone they know. Is this the way to Awata?[28] Their hearts race forward to Seki Temple[29]—how shameful the fall from splendor of the present Komachiya Sōshichi, brought to this fate by love for Kojorō of Hakata!—memories of her are always stretched on the frame of his heart.

SŌSHICHI: Now that I have been disinherited by my father, I can never again see Kyoto. This is our final glimpse.

NARRATOR: At his words they both weep.

KOJORŌ: It does no good to complain about your unbroken string of griefs. You are by no means at the end of your tether.[30] Do not speak with such despair.

When I asked a boy who passed us on the way, he said he was making a secret pilgrimage—"secret" had an unpleasant ring![31] O gods, protect us!

NARRATOR: She bows again in prayer, joining her sleeves in the sacred dances at Belling Deer Mountain; they are moistened at Eighty Shoal River.[32]

SŌSHICHI: When you and I first fell in love, we promised our hearts would not change in two lives nor three. Here is the resolution of our madness—Down-the-Hill.[33] It would have been better, knowing that we might tumble, if our love had not been so strong. How sad to see your thin face, pale as a faded cloth from your singlehearted love!

NARRATOR: The dew of tears wrung from their sleeves brings color to the grass and leaves of the field. "Weep, give yourselves to grief," they seem to say.

KOJORŌ: I have no comfort but you. Yet if Kojorō of Hakata had not existed, the happiness of your home would not have been shattered, you would never have sunk to such misery. We are husband and

[28] A play on words between *awan* (might meet) and *Awata*. There was an execution ground at Awata.

[29] A play on *seki* (hurry forward) and the name of the temple. Seki Temple in the province of Ōmi was associated with the poetess Komachi, who also fell from glory.

[30] The passage abounds in wordplays on the names of different kinds of cloth and related words.

[31] "Secret" suggests secret trade, or smuggling.

[32] Belling Deer Mountain (Suzukayama) was a well-known landmark on the Tōkaidō route to Ise. Eighty Shoal River is apparently a general name for the many rivers at the foot of the mountain.

[33] Down-the-Hill (Sakanoshita) was one of the 53 stages of the Tōkaidō. Used here to suggest the downfall of their hopes.

wife in this world of dreams and illusions, and through the worlds
and worlds to come.

NARRATOR: She clings to him, weeping.

KOJORŌ: They say, "The Jizō of Seki is kinder than a father," [34] but
I can't believe that my father-in-law is inferior even to you, Jizō—
please restore his good spirits.

NARRATOR: She prays, and at once palanquins come to their rescue.
The bearers step up, pleased to help.

BEARERS: We'll take you by chair.

SŌSHICHI: We are bound for Owari. How much does it cost to go
to the next station?

BEARER A: That's at Stone Buddha, two leagues up the road. We
charge *korori.*[35]

SŌSHICHI: What do you mean by *korori?*

BEARER B: You don't know? That means one hundred *mon.*

SŌSHICHI: That's high.

BEARER A: We'll come down on our price.

SŌSHICHI: Make it seventy.

BEARER B: Very well, sir. Seventy it is.

NARRATOR: They lower their chairs for the passengers. The road is
one, the palanquins two; who would have guessed that the lovers'
cares would make the chairs so heavy on the bearers' shoulders?

BEARER A: Look out for the stream!

BEARER: Watch it!

BEARER A: Change shoulders!

BEARER B: Right!

NARRATOR: They pass Walking Stick Hill, Little Valley, and Big
Valley—endless days on an endless journey to an unknown destination. It seems only yesterday or even today that they left the capital,
but four days [36] have passed. They have reached Oiwake near Yokkaichi.

Sōshichi prays in his heart that all will go well, but the bearer's
word *korori* has filled him with foreboding; he can all but feel the
prison ropes binding him.

[34] Quoted from a popular ballad which said that Jizō was kinder than a father because
he would bring about even marriages forbidden by the parents.

[35] Argot of the palanquin bearers, meaning 100 *mon.* The word suggests to Sōshichi
korori, onomatopoetic for the sound of a head being lopped off.

[36] *Yokka* (four days), used in order to introduce the place name Yokkaichi.

The passengers coming from the opposite direction have descended from their chairs, but Sōshichi, shrinking with apprehension, cannot bring himself to get down.[37]

sōshichi: Kojorō—you change to the other chair first and go on ahead.

kojorō: If that is your wish, I will.

sōshichi: Wait for me at Yokkaichi, if that's what the place is called.

kojorō: Bearers, take the gentleman quickly!

narrator: Kojorō changes palanquins at Kawai Village, unaware that anything is amiss; guided by the bearers she goes to the relay chair.

The bearers of a chair coming from Stone Buddha shout.

bearer c: Is that the chair with the lady's companion? We're the relay for him. The price has already been settled.

sōshichi's bearer: That's fine. (*To companion.*) Put down the chair. (*To Sōshichi.*) Sir, this is where you change. Please step down.

narrator: He raises the blinds of the palanquin. The passenger coming from the other direction, already out of his palanquin, carries a bundle in his hand. He is lightly clad in a lined kimono with breeches; his leggings fastened with clasps show he is ready for action. Sōshichi notices that the man carries at his waist a rope for binding criminals —a chilling sight. Sōshichi averts and muffles his face so that he will not be recognized. With scarcely a word of thanks to the bearers, he bolts into the relay chair. Once inside, he pulls down the blinds.

sōshichi: I'm in a great hurry. I'll give you extra. Let's go.

narrator: They can hear how his voice is shaking.

officer: Komachiya Sōshichi—I arrest you!

narrator: He throws a fine hempen net over the palanquin. Sō-shichi, trapped inside, writhes in anguish but, lacking wings, he cannot fly. A bird in a cage,[38] he can only weep helplessly. At a signal, menials brandishing iron clubs surround the palanquin.

officer: I'm sure you know the crime with which you're charged. We have received orders to arrest you and your eight confederates on

[37] Passengers at a transfer point exchanged palanquins with travelers coming from the opposite direction.

[38] A pun on *kago* (cage) and *kago* (palanquin).

indisputable evidence. Will you permit us to arrest you quietly or must we tie you up by force?

NARRATOR: There is no reply save for a voice repeating the *nembutsu*.

OFFICER: We can't deal with him here, in between towns. Take him as he is to the next post station, where we'll tie him and send him back to Kyoto. Move on, bearers.

BEARER C: Yes, sir. But he shouldn't be left untied. There's no escaping death for such a man.

NARRATOR: They return, grumbling, to the palanquin. When they raise it, blood trickling from inside spreads on the earth like a scarlet carpet. The occupant groans in pain.

BEARERS: He's killed himself inside the palanquin! Come, everybody!

NARRATOR: They drop the palanquin and recoil in terror. The officer and his men approach, and removing the net, lift the blinds. What horror is this—Sōshichi's dagger is buried to the hilt, and the point protrudes from his left side! His breathing is faint and his eyes fixed in a stare. Even the officer stands in helpless dismay. Kojorō is led to the spot, bound as a criminal. But grief over her own misfortune is forgotten before her grief at this sight. In her distraction she steps in the pool of Sōshichi's blood. She thrusts her head inside the palanquin.

KOJORŌ: I've come. Kojorō is here. They've put ropes on me. I'm tied up now too. Only last night we were sleeping on the same pillow. We swore we would always stay together, but have you deserted me now? Do you wish me to go on living alone in misery?—But you must be in pain. Does it hurt terribly?

NARRATOR: She is overcome by tears. Unaware what she does, she weeps. Sōshichi painfully opens his eyes.

SŌSHICHI: Kojorō—have they tied you too? I've been a vile criminal, a man who broke his country's laws and defied his father. The wide world has shrunk around me. I have behaved so disgracefully that I have no longer even my own home to live in. I have wandered here without hope of refuge, without destination. I am caught in the net of heaven,[39] bound by the ropes of earth. If I allowed myself to be dragged home and executed there, I would shed blood on the name

---

[39] A metaphor, derived ultimately from *Tao Tê Ching*, meaning that nothing slips through the fine meshes of heaven's net.

of my whole family—the finishing touch to a lifetime of unfilial behavior. I decided to kill myself instead. I've worn satins and silks ever
since I joined Kezori's smugglers, and I've dressed you in damask and
brocade. But I must pay for it now. My last garment will be of coarse
matting.[40] My crimes have caused them to bind you, insult you,
torment you—wives are customarily treated according to their husbands' deserts. If not for me, you would never have met with these
indignities. How you must be suffering! We have been together only
a short while, but you may have to die for it. Forgive me, please,
Kojorō.

NARRATOR: His breath, even as he speaks, comes painfully. Scant hope
for him remains. Even the stern-looking officers show an unwonted
leniency.

OFFICER: You won't see each other again once we deliver you to
the prison. Man must help man, they say—take your last looks now.

NARRATOR: Each word Sōshichi spoke has made Kojorō the sadder.

KOJORŌ: Who is to blame for all our troubles? I am. You were so
anxious to keep me from falling into some other man's hands that
you took me as your wife, though it meant giving up your father,
giving up even your life. Do you love me so much? I'm deeply be-
holden to you. I know it's more than I deserve. I'm sure there are no
words even in China or India, much less Japan, to express the thanks
I feel. If only my hands were not tied, I would bow humbly before
you, and then kill myself.

NARRATOR: She presses her face in her husband's lap, so choked with
tears that she seems about to swoon or die.

SŌSHICHI: These are our last moments together in this world, but
in the world to come we shall still be husband and wife. *Namu Amida
Butsu, Mida Butsu.*

NARRATOR: His voice grows faint. He starts to pull the sword from
his side, but his breathing has ceased. Kojorō utters a wail of despair.

KOJORŌ: Wait—I want to go with you! Sooner or later I'm sure to
be executed—please, all of you, in the name of mercy, kill me now,
kill me!

NARRATOR: She runs from person to person, trembling like one de-
mented.

At this moment police, led by a superintendent, bring in the smug-

[40] A criminal's body was wrapped in matting after he was executed.

glers arrested at various places together with their whores, all bound in ropes. The superintendent unfolds a document.

SUPERINTENDENT: Listen with gratitude, you criminals, to what I am about to read. You are guilty of the serious crime of violating the law of the land by seeking out communications with foreign ships anchored off the coast. You have dived through the waves and sneaked over the bottom of the sea to contact these ships, and you have trafficked in their merchandise. Your crime is punishable by death, but the emperor, in honor of his accession,[41] has remitted by one degree all sentences of death.

NARRATOR: Even before they have heard the whole proclamation, the prisoners immediately brighten, feeling as though life has been restored them. The superintendent addresses the courtesans separately.

SUPERINTENDENT: You women are birds of passage, and you have stayed with these rogues because such is the nature of your profession. You are guilty of no crime. You are free to go where you please. (*To his men.*) Untie them!

NARRATOR: His underlings bow in assent, and unfasten the ropes. The women rub and blow the marks left by the ropes.

COURTESAN: What solicitude the emperor has shown us! Now that my hands are free, I feel as if I've really left the Quarter behind me.

NARRATOR: She laughs, but amidst the rejoicing of the other women Kojorō continues to weep bitterly, unable to stanch her tears. She lifts her head.

KOJORŌ: My husband Sōshichi did not live long enough to enjoy this act of mercy. He left me in this world to fly alone to the other one. The bird that soars on conjugal love has lost a wing.[42] Kojorō of Hakata can fly no more. I still live, but to no purpose. Have mercy— kill me, I beg you.

NARRATOR: She weeps, not holding back her voice.

SUPERINTENDENT: I understand. Your husband Sōshichi was a smuggler, like the others, but his youthful spirits, his infatuation for you, led him to it. His offense was clearly not so grave as the others'. How unfortunate that he should have killed himself! Now you must take your husband's place in serving your father Sōzaemon with perfect

---

[41] A false clue—no emperor ascended the throne at the time.
[42] A fabulous bird. Male and female each had one wing; they could therefore fly only together.

devotion, and you should pray for Sōshichi's repose. (*To men.*) Get rid of these rascals in the manner prescribed in the imperial edict.

NARRATOR: The officers make sure that the smugglers will do no more mischief. They brand and tattoo the faces, cutting off the ears of some culprits and the noses of others, and drive them away covered with blood.

Countless people in provinces near and far relate the tale of Kojorō of Hakata, and wherever heard it will remain a topic of gossip for many years to come.

THE LOVE SUICIDES AT AMIJIMA

First performed on January 3, 1721. No source for this play, often acclaimed as Chikamatsu's masterpiece, has been determined, but traditional (though unreliable) accounts state that the suicides at Amijima occurred on November 13, 1720, one day earlier than in the drama. Takano Masami, a recent Japanese critic, has suggested that *The Love Suicides at Amijima* was a reworking of *The Love Suicides at Umeda* (1706) by Chikamatsu's rival, Ki no Kaion. There are striking points of resemblance between the two plays, and it may be that Chikamatsu, when shaping into dramatic form the events which took place at Amijima, borrowed from the earlier work. Chikamatsu's play has in turn been many times revised. The version most commonly performed today dates from the early nineteenth century.

Cast of Characters

KAMIYA JIHEI, aged 28, a paper merchant
KONAYA MAGOEMON, his brother, a flour merchant
GOZAEMON, Jihei's father-in-law
TAHEI, a rival for Koharu
DEMBEI, proprietor of the Yamato House
SANGORŌ, Jihei's servant
KANTARŌ, aged 6, Jihei's son
A MINSTREL PRIEST
PORTERS, FISHERMEN, PERSONS OF THE QUARTER
KOHARU, aged 19, a courtesan at the Kinokuni House in Sonezaki
OSAN, Jihei's wife
OSAN'S MOTHER (who is also Jihei's aunt), aged 56
OSUE, aged 4, Jihei's daughter
PROPRIETRESS at Kawachi House
KIYO, a receptionist
TAMA, Osan's servant
SUGI, Koharu's maid
MAIDS, PROSTITUTES, SERVANTS

ACT ONE

Scene One: A street in Sonezaki New Quarter, Osaka.
Time: November 4, 1720.

NARRATOR:

Sanjō bakkara fungoro nokkoro
Chokkoro fungoro de
Mate tokkoro wakkara yukkuru
Wakkara yukkuru ta ga
Kasa wo wanga ranga ra su
Sora ga kunguru kunguru mo
Renge rengere bakkara fungoro.[1]

The love of a prostitute is deep beyond measure; it's a bottomless sea
of affection that cannot be emptied or dried. By Shell River,[2] love songs
in every mood fill the air, and hearts stop short at the barrier [3] of doorway lanterns. Men roam the streets in high spirits, humming snatches
of puppet plays, mimicking the actors, or singing bawdy ballads as
they pass; others are drawn into the houses by samisens played in upstairs rooms. But here is a visitor who hides his face, avoiding the gift
day.[4] See how he creeps along, afraid to be forced into spending too
much!

Kiyo, the receptionist, notices him.[5]

KIYO: Who's this trying to avoid me?

NARRATOR: She snatches again and again at his hood-flap; he dodges

[1] Japanese scholars have puzzled over these curious syllables for years, and many explanations of them have been offered. Their meaning, if any, is less important than the
lively rhythm, which evokes the atmosphere of the Sonezaki Quarter.

[2] Shijimi River, frequently mentioned in the course of the play, flowed along the border
of the Sonezaki Quarter. Its name *shijimi* means the *corbicula,* a small mollusc related
to the clam. There is a play on words here: the sea cannot be emptied by ladling it
with tiny clam shells.

[3] A play on words: *moji ga seki* (the barrier of Chinese characters) suggests that customers stop short when they read on doorway lanterns the names in characters of their
favorite teahouses; *Moji ga seki* (the Barrier of Moji) refers to the Straits of Shimonoseki.

[4] Festive days in the gay quarter on which customers were required to make presents
to the teahouses. For a detailed description, see Shively, *The Love Suicide at Amijima,*
p. 100.

[5] The following few lines are based on a passage in the Nō play *Kagekiyo.* See Waley,
The Nō Plays of Japan, p. 98. The maid's name Kiyo suggests that of Kagekiyo, and
the effect is one of burlesque.

her twice or thrice, but this is a valuable customer, and she refuses to let him escape. At last she pounces on him with the cry:

KIYO: No more of your nonsense! Come along!

NARRATOR: And the customer, caught flap and cap, is trapped into folly by this female Kagekiyo.

Among the flowers on display—even the bridges are called Plum and Cherry Blossom—[6] here is Koharu of the Kinokuni House, now graduated from the smock of a bath attendant in the South [7] to the garments of love in the New Quarter. Is her name "Second Spring" [8] a sign that she is fated to leave behind a fleeting name in November?

"Who has sent for me tonight?" she wonders, uncertain as a dove in the uncertain light of a standing lantern. A prostitute passes her, then turns back.

PROSTITUTE: Is that you, Koharu? Where have you been keeping yourself? We don't get invited to the same parties any more, and I never see you or hear a word from you. Have you been sick? Your face looks thinner. Somebody was telling me that the master at your place now gives all your customers a thorough examination and hardly lets you out of the house, all on account of your Kamiji.[9] But I've also heard that you're to be ransomed by Tahei and go live with him in the country—in Itami, was it? Is it true?

KOHARU: I'd be much obliged if you'd please stop talking about Itami! The relations between Jihei and myself, I'm sorry to say, are not as close as people suppose. It's that loud-mouthed Tahei who's started the rumors and spread them everywhere, until every last customer has deserted me. The master blames Kamiya Jihei, and he's done everything to keep us from meeting. Why, I'm not even allowed to receive letters from Jihei. Tonight, strangely enough, I've been sent to Kawashō.[10] My customer's a samurai, I'm told. But I keep worrying that I might meet that dreadful Tahei on the way. I feel exactly as if I had some mortal enemy. Do you suppose he might be over there?

[6] References to Umeda Bridge and Sakura Bridge over the Shijimi River.

[7] The "south" refers to the Shimanouchi Quarter, a section of low-class brothels which originally had been bathhouses. Sonezaki Quarter was north of this section.

[8] The name Koharu, literally "little spring", means Indian summer.

[9] A familiar contraction for Kamiya Jihei.

[10] A contraction of Kawachi House and the owner's name, which began with the syllable "Shō".

PROSTITUTE: If you feel that way about Tahei, you'd better hide quickly. Look—coming out of the first block—there's one of those street minstrels, singing his nonsense hymns.[11] I can see in the crowd round him a dissolute-looking fellow with his hair tricked up in some funny style—the stuck-up swell! I'm sure it's Tahei. Oh—they're heading this way!

NARRATOR: A moment later the defrocked priest, in a flat cap and ink-black robes with the sleeves tucked back, comes bumbling along, surrounded by a crowd of idlers. He bangs at random on his bell, mixing his nonsense with the burden of a hymn.

MINSTREL:

"Fan Kuai's style was no great shakes—
See how Asahina of Japan used to break down gates!"
He rips through the gate bars and tangle of felled trees,
Slays Uryōko and Saryōko and passes the barrier,
As time passes by.[12]
Namamida Namaida Namamida Namaida.
Ei Ei Ei Ei Ei.
"Though I wander all over,
The sad world holds no one
Who looks like my dear Matsuyama!" [13]
—He weeps, he howls, only to burst into laughs.
"How wretched that I must end my life in madness!"
He falls prostrate, the grass for his pallet,
A sight too sad for the eyes to behold.
Namamida Namaida Namamida Namaida.
Ei Ei Ei Ei Ei.
Tokubei of the dyer's shop,
Since he first fell in love with Fusa,
Has yielded to passion that absorbs his fortune,
A love stained so deep lye itself cannot cleanse it.[14]
Namamida Namaida Namamida Namaida
Namamida Namaida.

SUGI: Excuse me, priest.

[11] Sections from popular puppet dramas with a quasi-religious refrain.
[12] Adapted from *The Battles of Coxinga*. See above, p. 256.
[13] From the play *Wankyū Sue no Matsuyama* (1707). See Shively, p. 104.
[14] From the festive epilogue to *Yosaku from Tamba*. See above, p. 91, and also Shively, pp. 104–5.

MINSTREL: What is it?

SUGI: It's bad luck to sing those songs, just when stories about love suicides in the Quarter have at last quieted down. Why don't you give us instead a *nembutsu* song on the journey from *The Battles of Coxinga?*

NARRATOR: Sugi offers him some coins from her sleeve.

MINSTREL:

> For a mere one or two coppers
> You can't expect to travel all the way,
> Three thousand leagues to the Land of Great Ming!
> It doesn't pay, it doesn't pray Amida Buddha.

NARRATOR: Grumbling in this strain, he moves on.

Scene Two: The Kawachi House, a Sonezaki teahouse.

NARRATOR: Koharu slips away, under cover of the crowd, and hurries into the Kawachi House.

PROPRIETRESS: Well, well, I hadn't expected you so soon.—It's been ages even since I've heard your name mentioned. What a rare visitor you are, Koharu! And what a long time it's been!

NARRATOR: The proprietress greets Koharu cheerfully.

KOHARU: Oh—you can be heard as far as the gate. Please don't call me Koharu in such a loud voice. That horrible Ri Tōten [15] is out there. I beg you, keep your voice down.

NARRATOR: Were her words overheard? In bursts a party of three men.

TAHEI: I must thank you first of all, dear Koharu, for bestowing a new name on me, Ri Tōten. I never was called *that* before. Well, friends, this is the Koharu I've confided to you about—the good-hearted, good-natured, good-in-bed Koharu. Step up and meet the whore who's started all the rivalry! Will I soon be the lucky man and get Koharu for my wife? Or will Kamiya Jihei ransom her?

NARRATOR: He swaggers up.

KOHARU: I don't want to hear another word. If you think it's such an achievement to start unfounded rumors about someone you don't even know, throw yourself into it, say what you please. But I don't want to hear.

NARRATOR: She steps away suddenly, but he sidles up again.

[15] The villain of the play *The Battles of Coxinga.* See above, pp. 198 ff.

TAHEI: You may not want to hear me, but the clink of my gold coins will make you listen! What a lucky girl you are! Just think—of all the many men in Temma and the rest of Osaka, you chose Jihei the paper dealer, the father of two children, with his cousin for his wife and his uncle for his father-in-law! A man whose business is so tight he's at his wits' ends every sixty days merely to pay the wholesalers' bills! Do you think he'll be able to fork over nearly ten *kamme* [16] to ransom you? That reminds me of the mantis who picked a fight with an on-coming vehicle! [17] But look at me—I haven't a wife, a father-in-law, a father, or even an uncle, for that matter. Tahei the Lone Wolf—that's the name I'm known by. I admit that I'm no match for Jihei when it comes to bragging about myself in the Quarter, but when it comes to money, I'm an easy winner. If I pushed with all the strength of my money, who knows what I might conquer?—How about it, men?—Your customer tonight, I'm sure, is none other than Jihei, but I'm taking over. The Lone Wolf's taking over. Hostess! Bring on the saké! On with the saké!

PROPRIETRESS: What are you saying? Her customer tonight is a samurai, and he'll be here any moment. Please amuse yourself else-where.

NARRATOR: But Tahei's look is playful.

TAHEI: A customer's a customer, whether he's a samurai or a towns-man. The only difference is that one wears swords and the other doesn't. But even if this samurai wears his swords he won't have five or six—there'll only be two, the broadsword and dirk. I'll take care of the samurai and borrow Koharu afterwards. (*To Koharu.*) You may try to avoid me all you please, but some special connection from a former life must have brought us together. I owe everything to that ballad-singing priest—what a wonderful thing the power of prayer is! I think I'll recite a prayer of my own. Here, this ashtray will be my bell, and my pipe the hammer. This is fun.

Chan Chan Cha Chan Chan.
Ei Ei Ei Ei Ei.
Jihei the paper dealer—
Too much love for Koharu

---

[16] This would amount to over $5,000 in current purchasing power. The price is un-usually high; no doubt Tahei is exaggerating.

[17] A simile, derived ultimately from ancient Chinese texts, for someone who does not know his own limitations. See Shively, p. 107.

Has made him a foolscap,
He wastepapers sheets of gold
Till his fortune's shredded to confetti
And Jihei himself is like scrap paper
You can't even blow your nose on!
Hail, Hail Amida Buddha!
Namaida Namaida Namaida.

NARRATOR: As he prances wildly, roaring his song, a man appears at the gate, so anxious not to be recognized that he wears, even at night, a wicker hat.[18]

TAHEI:Well, Toilet paper's showed up! That's quite a disguise! Why don't you come in, Toilet paper? If my prayer's frightened you, say a Hail Amida![19] Here, I'll take off your hat!

NARRATOR: He drags the man in and examines him: it is the genuine article, a two-sworded samurai, somber in dress and expression, who glares at Tahei through his woven hat, his eyeballs round as gongs. Tahei, unable to utter either a Hail or an Amida, gasps "Haaa!" in dismay, but his face is unflinching.

TAHEI: Koharu, I'm a townsman. I've never worn a sword, but I've lots of New Silver[20] at my place, and I think that the glint could twist a mere couple of swords out of joint. Imagine that wretch from the toilet paper shop, with a capital as thin as tissue, trying to compete with the Lone Wolf! That's the height of impertinence! I'll wander down now from Sakura Bridge to Middle Street, and if I meet that Wastepaper along the way, I'll trample him under foot. Come on, men.

NARRATOR: Their gestures, at least, have a cavalier assurance as they swagger off, taking up the whole street.

The samurai customer patiently endures the fool, indifferent to his remarks because of the surroundings, but every word of gossip about Jihei, whether for good or ill, affects Koharu. She is so depressed that she stands there blankly, unable even to greet her guest. Sugi, the maid from the Kinokuni House, runs up from home, looking annoyed.

[18] Customers visiting the Quarter by day wear these deep wicker hats (which virtually conceal the face) in order to preserve the secrecy of their visits; but this customer wears a hat even at night, when the darkness normally is sufficient protection.
[19] A play on words devolving on the syllables *ami*, part of the name Amida and on *amigasa*, meaning "woven hat".
[20] Good-quality coinage of about 1720. It was necessary to specify the kind of silver one meant because devaluations and revaluations altered the value of coins of nominally the same denomination.

SUGI: When I left you here a while ago, Miss Koharu, your guest hadn't appeared yet, and they gave me a terrible scolding when I got back for not having checked on him. I'm very sorry, sir, but please excuse me a minute.

NARRATOR: She lifts the woven hat and examines the face.

SUGI: Oh—it's not him! There's nothing to worry about, Koharu. Ask your guest to keep you for the whole night, and show him how sweet you can be. Give him a barrelful of nectar![21] Good-by, madam, I'll see you later, honey.

NARRATOR: She takes her leave with a cloying stream of puns. The extremely hard-baked[22] samurai is furious.

SAMURAI: What's the meaning of this? You'd think from the way she appraised my face that I was a tea canister or a porcelain cup! I didn't come here to be trifled with. It's difficult enough for me to leave the Residence even by day, and in order to spend the night away I had to ask the senior officer's permission and sign the register. You can see how complicated the regulations make things. But I'm in love, miss, just from hearing about you, and I wanted very badly to spend a night with you. I came here a while ago without an escort and made the arrangements with the teahouse. I had been looking forward to your kind reception, a memory to last me a lifetime, but you haven't so much as smiled at me or said a word of greeting. You keep your head down, as if you were counting money in your lap. Aren't you afraid of getting a stiff neck? Madam—I've never heard the like. Here I come to a teahouse, and I must play the part of night nurse in a maternity room!

PROPRIETRESS: You're quite right, sir. Your surprise is entirely justified, considering that you don't know the reasons. This girl is deeply in love with a customer named Kamiji. It's been Kamiji today and Kamiji tomorrow, with nobody else allowed a chance at her. Her other customers have scattered in every direction, like leaves in a storm. When two people get so carried away with each other, it often leads to trouble, for both the customer and the girl. In the first place, it inteferes with business, and the owner, whoever he may be, is bound to prevent it. That's why all her guests are examined. Koharu is nat-

---

[21] I have altered the imagery used by the maid from puns on saltiness (soy sauce, green vegetables, etc.) to puns on sweetness, somewhat easier to manage in English.

[22] A technical term of pottery making, meaning "hard-fired". Here used to introduce the mention of "tea canister" and "porcelain cup".

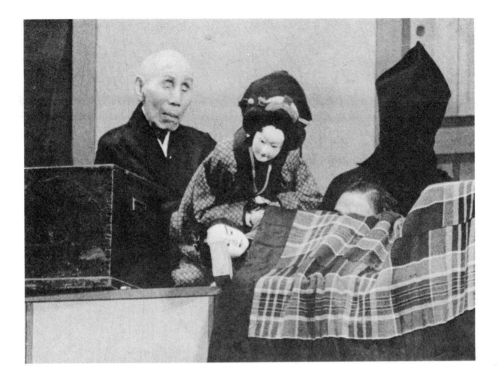

Osan rouses Jihei lying in the kotatsu. *"Please get up. Mother and Magoemon are coming. They'll be upset again if you let them see you, a businessman, sleeping in the afternoon."*
(OSAN: *Yoshida Bungorō IV* [*Naniwa-no-jō*], *operator;* JIHEI: *Yoshida Eiza II, operator*)

urally depressed—it's only to be expected. You are annoyed, which is equally to be expected. But, speaking as the proprietress here, it seems to me that the essential thing is for you to meet each other halfway and cheer up. Come, have a drink.—Act a little more lively, Koharu.

NARRATOR: Koharu, without answering, lifts her tear-stained face.

KOHARU: Tell me, samurai, they say that, if you're going to kill yourself anyway, people who die during the Ten Nights²³ are sure to become Buddhas. Is that really true?

SAMURAI: How should I know? Ask the priest at your family temple.

KOHARU: Yes, that's right. But there's something I'd like to ask a samurai. If you're committing suicide, it'd be a lot more painful, wouldn't it, to cut your throat rather than hang yourself?

SAMURAI: I've never tried cutting my throat to see whether or not it hurt. Please ask more sensible questions.—What an unpleasant girl!

NARRATOR: Samurai though he is, he looks nonplussed.

PROPRIETRESS: Koharu, that's a shocking way to treat a guest the first time you meet him. I'll go and get my husband. We'll have some saké together. That ought to liven things a bit.

NARRATOR: The gate she leaves is illumined by the evening moon low in the sky; the clouds and the passers in the street have thinned.

For long years there has lived in Temma, the seat of the mighty god,²⁴ though not a god himself, Kamiji,²⁵ a name often bruited by the gongs of worldly gossip, so deeply, hopelessly, is he tied to Koharu by the ropes²⁶ of an ill-starred love. Now is the tenth moon, the month when no gods will unite them;²⁷ they are thwarted in their love, unable to meet. They swore in the last letters they exchanged that if only they could meet, that day would be their last. Night after night Jihei, ready for death, trudges to the Quarter, distractedly, as though his soul had left a body consumed by the fires of love.

²³ A period from the sixth to the sixteenth nights of the tenth moon when special Buddhist services were conducted in temples of the Pure Land (Jōdo) Sect. It was believed that persons who died during this period immediately became Buddhas.

²⁴ Temma, one of the principal districts of Osaka, was the site of the Tenjin Shrine, to the memory of the deified Sugawara no Michizane (845–903).

²⁵ The word *kami* for "paper" is the homophone of *kami*, "god". We have thus "Kami who is not a *kami*"—the paper dealer who is not a god.

²⁶ The sacred ropes (*mishimenawa*) at a Shinto shrine. Here mentioned (like the gongs) as a word related to the imagery of Shinto.

²⁷ The tenth month, called *kannazuki* (literally "month of no gods") was a time when the gods were believed to gather at Izumo; they were thus absent from the rest of Japan.

At a roadside eating stand he hears people gossiping about Koharu. "She's at Kawashō with a samurai customer," someone says, and immediately Jihei decides, "It will be tonight!"

He peers through the latticework window and sees a guest in the inside room, his face obscured by a hood. Only the moving chin is visible, and Jihei cannot hear what is said.

JIHEI: Poor Koharu! How thin her face is! She keeps it averted from the lamp. In her heart she's thinking only of me. I'll signal her that I'm here, and we'll run off together. Then which will it be— Umeda or Kitano? [28] Oh—I want to tell her I'm here. I want to call her.

NARRATOR: He beckons with his heart, his spirit flies to her, but his body, like a cicada's cast-off shell, clings to the latticework. He weeps with impatience.

The guest in the inside room gives a great yawn.

SAMURAI: What a bore, playing nursemaid to a prostitute with worries on her mind!—The street seems quiet now. Let's go to the end room. We can at least distract ourselves by looking at the lanterns. Come with me.

NARRATOR: They go together to the outer room. Jihei, alarmed, squeezes into the patch of shadow under the lattice window. Inside they do not realize that anyone eavesdrops.

SAMURAI: I've been noticing your behavior and the little things you've said this evening. It's plain to me that you intend a love suicide with Kamiji, or whatever his name is—the man the hostess mentioned. I'm sure I'm right. I realize that no amount of advice or reasoning is likely to penetrate the ears of somebody bewitched by the god of death, but I must say that you're exceedingly foolish. The boy's family won't blame him for his recklessness, but they will blame and hate you. You'll be shamed by the public exposure of your body. Your parents may be dead, for all I know, but if they're alive, you'll be punished in hell as a wicked daughter. Do you suppose that you'll become a Buddha? You and your lover won't even be able to fall smoothly into hell together! What a pity—and what a tragedy! This is only our first meeting but, as a samurai, I can't let you die without trying to save you. No doubt money's the problem. I'd like to help, if five or ten ryō would be of service. I swear by the god Hachiman

[28] Both places had well-known cemeteries.

and by my good fortune as a samurai that I will never reveal to anyone what you tell me. Open your heart without fear.

NARRATOR: He whispers these words. She joins her hands and bows.

KOHARU: I'm extremely grateful. Thank you for your kind words and for swearing an oath to me, someone you've never had for a lover or even a friend. I'm so grateful that I'm crying.—Yes, it's as they say, when you've something on your mind it shows on your face. You were right. I have promised Kamiji to die with him. But we've been completely prevented from meeting by my master, and Jihei, for various reasons, can't ransom me at once. My contracts with my former master [29] and my present one still have five years to run. If somebody else claimed me during that time, it would be a blow to me, of course, but a worse disgrace to Jihei's honor. He suggested that it would be better if we killed ourselves, and I agreed. I was caught by obligations from which I could not withdraw, and I promised him before I knew what I was doing. I said, "We'll watch for a chance, and I'll slip out when you give the signal." "Yes," he said, "slip out somehow." Ever since then I've been leading a life of uncertainty, never knowing from one day to the next when my last hour will come.

I have a mother living in a back alley south of here. She has no one but me to depend on, and she does piecework to eke out a living. I keep thinking that after I'm dead she'll become a beggar or an outcast, and maybe she'll die of starvation. That's the only sad part about dying. I have just this one life. I'm ashamed that you may think me a coldhearted woman, but I must endure the shame. The most important thing is that I don't want to die. I beg you, please help me to stay alive.

NARRATOR: As she speaks the samurai nods thoughtfully. Jihei, crouching outside, hears her words with astonishment; they are so unexpected to his manly heart that he feels like a monkey who has tumbled from a tree. He is frantic with agitation.

JIHEI (*to himself*): Then was everything a lie? Ahhh—I'm furious! For two whole years I've been bewitched by that rotten she-fox! Shall I break in and kill her with one blow of my sword? Or shall I satisfy my anger by shaming her to her face?

NARRATOR: He gnashes his teeth and weeps in chagrin. Inside the house Koharu speaks through her tears.

[29] The master at the bathhouse where Koharu formerly worked.

KOHARU: It's a curious thing to ask, but would you please show the kindness of a samurai and become my customer for the rest of this year and into next spring? Whenever Jihei comes, intent on death, please interfere and force him to postpone and postpone his plan. In this way our relations can be broken quite naturally. He won't have to kill himself, and my life will also be saved.—What evil connection from a former existence made us promise to die? How I regret it now!

NARRATOR: She weeps, leaning on the samurai's knee.

SAMURAI: Very well, I'll do as you ask. I think I can help you.—But there's a draft blowing. Somebody may be watching.

NARRATOR: He slams shut the latticework *shōji*. Jihei, listening outside, is in a frenzy.

JIHEI: Exactly what you'd expect from a whore, a cheap whore! I misjudged her foul nature. She robbed the soul from my body, the thieving harlot! Shall I slash her down or run her through? What am I to do?

NARRATOR: The shadows of two profiles fall on the *shōji*.

JIHEI: I'd like to give her a taste of my fist and trample her.—What are they chattering about? See how they nod to each other! Now she's bowing to him, whispering and sniveling. I've tried to control myself —I've pressed my chest, I've stroked it—but I can't stand any more. This is too much to endure!

NARRATOR: His heart pounds wildly as he unsheathes his dirk, a Magoroku of Seki. "Koharu's side must be here," he judges, and stabs through an opening in the latticework. But Koharu is too far away for his thrust, and though she cries out in terror, she remains unharmed. Her guest instantly leaps at Jihei, grabs his hands, and jerks them through the latticework. With his sword knot he quickly and securely fastens Jihei's hands to the window upright.

SAMURAI: Don't make any outcry, Koharu. You are not to look at him.

NARRATOR: At this moment the proprietor and his wife return. They exclaim in alarm.

SAMURAI: This needn't concern you. Some ruffian ran his sword through the *shōji,* and I've tied his arms to the latticework. I have my own way of dealing with him. Don't untie the cord. If you attract a crowd, the place is sure to be thrown in an uproar. Let's all go inside. Come with me, Koharu. We'll go to bed.

NARRATOR: Koharu answers, "Yes," but she recognizes the handle of the dirk, and the memory—if not the blade—transfixes her breast.

KOHARU: There're always people doing crazy things in the Quarter when they've had too much to drink. Why don't you let him go without making any trouble? I think that's best, don't you, Kawashō?

SAMURAI: Out of the question. Do as I say—inside, all of you. Koharu, come along.

NARRATOR: Jihei can still see their shadows even after they enter the inner room, but he is bound to the spot, his hands held in fetters which grip him the tighter as he struggles, his body beset by suffering as he tastes a living shame worse than a dog's.[30] More determined than ever to die, he sheds tears of blood, a pitiful sight.

Tahei the Lone Wolf returns from his carousing.

TAHEI: That's Jihei standing by Kawashō's window. I'll give him a tossing.

NARRATOR: He catches Jihei by the collar and starts to lift him over his back.

JIHEI: Owww!

TAHEI: Owww? What kind of weakling are you? Oh, I see—you're tied here. You must've been pulling off a robbery. You dirty pickpocket! You rotten pickpocket!

NARRATOR: He drubs Jihei mercilessly.

TAHEI: You burglar! You convict!

NARRATOR: He kicks him wildly.

TAHEI: Kamiya Jihei's been caught burgling, and they've tied him up!

NARRATOR: Passersby and people of the neighborhood, attracted by his shouts, quickly gather. The samurai rushes from the house.

SAMURAI: Who's calling him a burglar? You? Tell what Jihei's stolen! Out with it!

NARRATOR: He seizes Tahei and forces him into the dirt. Tahei rises to his feet only for the samurai to kick him down again and again. He grips Tahei.

SAMURAI: Jihei! Trample him to your heart's content!

NARRATOR: He pushes Tahei under Jihei's feet. Bound though he is, Jihei stamps furiously over Tahei's face. Tahei, thoroughly trampled and covered with mire, gets to his feet and glares around him.

[30] A proverb of Buddhist origin, "Suffering follows one like a dog," is imbedded in the text.

TAHEI (*to bystander*): How could you fools stand there calmly and let him step on me? I've memorized every one of your faces, and I intend to pay you back. Remember that!

NARRATOR: He makes his escape, still determined to have the last word. The spectators burst out laughing.

VOICES: Listen to him brag, even after he's been trampled on! Let's throw him from the bridge and give him a drink of water! Don't let him get away!

NARRATOR: They chase after him. When the crowd has dispersed, the samurai approaches Jihei and unfastens the knots. He shows his face with his hood removed.

JIHEI: Magoemon! My brother! How shaming!

NARRATOR: He sinks to the ground and weeps, prostrating himself in the dirt.

KOHARU: Are you his brother, sir?

NARRATOR: Koharu runs to them. Jihei, catching her by the front of the kimono, forces her to the ground.

JIHEI: Beast! She-fox! I'd sooner trample on you than on Tahei!

NARRATOR: He raises his foot, but Magoemon calls out.

MAGOEMON: That's the kind of foolishness responsible for all your trouble. A prostitute's business is to deceive men. Have you just now waked up to that? I've seen to the bottom of her heart the very first time I met her, but you're so scatter-brained that in over two years of intimacy with the woman you never discovered what she was thinking. Instead of stamping on Koharu, why don't you use your feet on your own misguided disposition?—It's deplorable. You're my younger brother, but you're almost thirty, and you've got a six-year-old boy and a four-year-old girl, Kantarō and Osue. You run a shop with a thirty-six foot frontage,[31] but you don't seem to realize that your whole fortune's collapsing. You shouldn't have to be lectured to by your brother. Your father-in-law is your aunt's husband, and your mother-in-law is your aunt. They've always been like real parents to you. Your wife Osan is my cousin too. The ties of marriage are multiplied by those of blood. But when the family has a reunion the only subject of discussion is our mortification over your incessant visits to Sonezaki. I feel sorry for our poor aunt. You know what a stiff-necked gentleman of

[31] It was customary to refer to the size of shops by giving their frontage on the street.

the old school her husband Gozaemon is. He's forever flying into a rage and saying, "We've been tricked by your nephew. He's deserted our daughter. I'll take Osan back and ruin Jihei's reputation throughout Temma." Our aunt, with all the heartache to bear herself, sometimes sides with him and sometimes with you. She's worried herself sick. What an ingrate, not to appreciate how she's defended you in your shame! This one offense is enough to make you the target for Heaven's future punishment!

I realized that your marriage couldn't last much longer at this rate. I decided, in the hopes of relieving our aunt's worries, that I'd see with my own eyes what kind of woman Koharu was, and work out some sort of solution afterwards. I consulted the proprietor here, then came myself to investigate the cause of your sickness. I see now how natural it was that you should desert your wife and children. What a faithful prostitute you discovered! I congratulate you!

And here I am, Magoemon the Miller,[32] known far and wide for my paragon of a brother, dressed up like a masquerader at a festival or maybe a lunatic! I put on swords for the first time in my life, and announced myself, like a bit player in a costume piece, as an officer at a residence. I feel like an absolute idiot with these swords, but there's nowhere I can dispose of them now.—It's so infuriating—and ridiculous—that it's given me a pain in the chest.

NARRATOR: He gnashes his teeth and grimaces, attempting to hide his tears. Koharu, choking the while with emotion, can only say:

KOHARU: Yes, you're entirely right.

NARRATOR: The rest is lost in tears. Jihei pounds the earth with his fist.

JIHEI: I was wrong. Forgive me, Magoemon. For three years I've been possessed by that witch. I've neglected my parents, relatives—even my wife and children—and wrecked my fortune, all because I was deceived by Koharu, that sneak thief! I'm utterly mortified. But I'm through with her now, and I'll never set foot here again. Weasel! Vixen! Sneak thief! Here's proof that I've broken with her!

NARRATOR: He pulls out the amulet bag which has rested next to his skin.

[32] Magoemon is a dealer in flour (for noodles). His shop name Konaya—"the flour merchant"—is used almost as a surname, in the manner that Jihei is known as Kamiya Jihei.

JIHEI: Here are the written oaths we've exchanged, one at the beginning of each month, twenty-nine in all. I return them. This means our love and affection are over. Take them.

NARRATOR: He flings the notes at her.

JIHEI: Magoemon, collect from her my pledges. Please make sure you get them all. Then burn them with your own hands. (*To Koharu.*) Hand them to my brother.

KOHARU: As you wish.

NARRATOR: In tears, she surrenders the amulet bag. Magoemon opens it.

MAGOEMON: One, two, three, four . . . ten . . . twenty-nine. They're all here. There's also a letter from a woman. What's this?

NARRATOR: He starts to unfold it.

KOHARU: That's an important letter. I can't let you see it.

NARRATOR: She clings to Magoemon's arm, but he pushes her away. He holds the letter to the lamplight and examines the address, "To Miss Koharu from Kamiya Osan." As soon as he reads the words, he casually thrusts the letter into his kimono.

MAGOEMON: Koharu. A while ago I swore by my good fortune as a samurai, but now Magoemon the Miller swears by his good fortune as a businessman that he will show this letter to no one, not even his wife. I alone will read it, then burn it with the oaths. You can trust me. I will not break this oath.

KOHARU: Thank you. You save my honor.

NARRATOR: She bursts into tears again.

JIHEI (*laughs contemptuously*): Save your honor! You talk like a human being! (*To Magoemon.*) I don't want to see her cursed face another minute. Let's go. No—I can't hold so much resentment and bitterness! I'll kick her one in the face, a memory to treasure for the rest of my life. Excuse me, please.

NARRATOR: He strides up to Koharu and stamps on the ground.

JIHEI: For three years I've loved you, delighted in you, longed for you, adored you, but today my foot will say my only farewells.

NARRATOR: He kicks her sharply on the forehead and bursts into tears. The brothers leave, forlorn figures. Koharu, unhappy woman, raises her voice in lament as she watches them go. Is she faithful or unfaithful? Her true feelings are hidden in the words penned by Jihei's wife, a letter no one has seen. Jihei goes his separate way without learning the truth.[33]

ACT TWO

Scene: The house and shop of Kamiya Jihei.
Time: Ten days later.

NARRATOR: The busy street that runs straight to Tenjin Bridge[34] named for the god of Temma, bringer of good fortune, is known as the Street Before the Kami,[35] and here a paper shop does business under the name Kamiya Jihei. The paper is honestly sold, the shop well situated; it is a long-established firm, and customers come thick as raindrops.

Outside crowds pass in the street, on their way to the Ten Nights service, while inside the husband dozes in the *kotatsu,*[36] shielded from draughts by a screen at his pillow. His wife Osan keeps solitary, anxious watch over shop and house.

OSAN: The days are so short—it's dinnertime already, but Tama still hasn't returned from her errand to Ichinokawa.[37] I wonder what can be keeping her. That scamp Sangorō isn't back either. The wind is freezing. I'm sure the children will both be cold. He doesn't even realize that it's time for Osue to be nursed. Heaven preserve me from ever becoming such a fool! What an infuriating creature!

NARRATOR: She speaks to herself.

KANTARŌ: Mama, I've come back all by myself.

NARRATOR: Her son, the older child, runs up to the house.

OSAN: Kantarō—is that you? What's happened to Osue and Sangorō?

KANTARŌ: They're playing by the shrine. Osue wanted her milk and she was bawling her head off.

[33] An extremely complicated set of word plays runs through the last two sentences. See Shively, p. 113.
[34] The reference is to Temma Tenjin, the name as a deity of Sugawara no Michizane.
[35] Again a play on the words *kami* (god) and *kami* (paper).
[36] A source of heat in which a charcoal burner is placed under a low, quilt-covered table.
[37] Ichinokawa was the site of a large vegetable market near the north end of Tenjin Bridge.

OSAN: I was sure she would. Oh—your hands and feet are frozen stiff as nails! Go and warm yourself at the *kotatsu.* Your father's sleeping there.—What am I to do with that idiot?

NARRATOR: She runs out impatiently to the shop just as Sangorō shuffles back, alone.

OSAN: Come here, you fool! Where have you left Osue?

SANGORŌ: You know, I must've lost her somewhere. Maybe somebody's picked her up. Should I go back for her?

OSAN: How could you? If any harm has come to my precious child, I'll beat you to death!

NARRATOR: But even as she screams at him, the maid Tama returns with Osue on her back.

TAMA: The poor child—I found her in tears at the corner. Sangorō, when you're supposed to look after the child, do it properly.

OSAN: You poor dear. You must want your milk.

NARRATOR: She joins the others by the *kotatsu* and suckles the child.

OSAN: Tama—give that fool a taste of something that he'll remember! [38]

NARRATOR: Sangorō shakes his head.

SANGORŌ: No, thanks. I gave each of the children two tangerines just a while ago at the shrine, and I tasted five myself.

NARRATOR: Fool though he is, bad puns come from him nimbly enough, and the others can only smile despite themselves.

TAMA: Oh—I've become so involved with this half-wit that I almost forgot to tell you, ma'am, that Mr. Magoemon and his aunt [39] are on their way here from the west.

OSAN: Oh dear! I'll have to wake Jihei in that case. (*To Jihei.*) Please get up. Mother and Magoemon are coming. They'll be upset again if you let them see you, a businessman, sleeping in the afternoon, with the day so short as it is.

JIHEI: All right.

NARRATOR: He struggles to a sitting position and, with his abacus in one hand, pulls his account book to him with the other.

JIHEI: Two into ten goes five, three into nine goes three, three into six goes two, seven times eight is fifty-six.

NARRATOR: His fifty-six-year old aunt enters with Magoemon.

---

[38] A pun on the two meanings of *kurawasu:* "to cause to eat" and "to beat".

[39] Magoemon's (and Jihei's) aunt, but Osan's mother.

JIHEI: Magoemon, aunt. How good of you. Please come in. I was in the midst of some urgent calculations. Four nines makes thirty-six *momme*. Three sixes make eighteen *fun*. That's two *momme* less two *fun*.[40] Kantarō! Osue! Granny and Uncle have come! Bring the tobacco tray! One times three makes three. Osan, serve the tea! [41]

NARRATOR: He jabbers away.

AUNT: We haven't come for tea or tobacco. Osan, you're young I know, but you're the mother of two children, and your excessive forbearance does you no credit. A man's dissipation can always be traced to his wife's carelessness. Remember, it's not only the man who's disgraced when he goes bankrupt and his marriage breaks up. You'd do well to take notice of what's going on and assert yourself a bit more.

MAGOEMON: It's foolish to hope for any results, aunt. The scoundrel even deceives me, his elder brother. Why should he take to heart criticism from his wife? Jihei—you played me for a fool. After showing me how you returned Koharu's pledges, here you are, not ten days later, redeeming her! What does this mean? I suppose your urgent calculations are of Koharu's debts! I've had enough!

NARRATOR: He snatches away the abacus and flings it clattering into the hallway.

JIHEI: You're making an enormous fuss without any cause. I haven't crossed the threshold since the last time I saw you except to go twice to the wholesalers in Imabashi and once to the Tenjin Shrine. I haven't even thought of Koharu, much less redeemed her.

AUNT: None of your evasions! Last evening at the Ten Nights service I heard the people in the congregation gossiping. Everybody was talking about the great patron from Temma who'd fallen in love with a prostitute named Koharu from the Kinokuni House in Sonezaki. They said he'd driven away her other guests and was going to ransom her in the next couple of days. There was all kinds of gossip about the abundance of money and fools even in these days of high prices.

My husband Gozaemon has been hearing about Koharu constantly, and he's sure that her great patron from Temma must be you, Jihei. He told me, "He's your nephew, but for me he's a stranger, and my daughter's happiness is my chief concern. Once he ransoms the prosti-

[40] Meaningless calculations. Twenty *fun* made two *momme*.
[41] The name Osan echoes the word *san* (three).

tute he'll no doubt sell his wife to a brothel. I intend to take her back before he starts selling her clothes."

He was halfway out of the house before I could restrain him. "Don't get so excited. We can settle this calmly. First we must make sure whether or not the rumors are true."

That's why Magoemon and I are here now. He was telling me a while ago that the Jihei of today was not the Jihei of yesterday—that you'd broken all connections with Sonezaki and completely reformed. But now I hear that you've had a relapse. What disease can this be?

Your father was my brother. When the poor man was on his death-bed, he lifted his head from the pillow and begged me to look after you, as my son-in-law and nephew. I've never forgotten those last words, but your perversity has made a mockery of his request!

NARRATOR: She collapses in tears of resentment. Jihei claps his hands in sudden recognition.

JIHEI: I have it! The Koharu everybody's gossiping about is the same Koharu, but the great patron who's to redeem her is a different man. The other day, as my brother can tell you, Tahei—they call him the Lone Wolf because he hasn't any family or relations—started a fight and was trampled on. He gets all the money he needs from his home town, and he's been trying for a long time to redeem Koharu. I've always prevented him, but I'm sure he's decided that now is his chance. I have nothing to do with it.

NARRATOR: Osan brightens at his words.

OSAN: No matter how forbearing I might be—even if I were an angel —you don't suppose I'd encourage my husband to redeem a prostitute! In this instance at any rate there's not a word of untruth in what my husband has said. I'll be a witness to that, Mother.

NARRATOR: Husband's and wife's words tally perfectly.

AUNT: Then it's true?

NARRATOR: The aunt and nephew clap their hands with relief.

MAGOEMON: Well, I'm happy it's over, anyway. To make us feel doubly reassured, will you write an affidavit which will dispel any doubts your stubborn uncle may have?

JIHEI: Certainly. I'll write a thousand if you like.

MAGOEMON: Splendid! I happen to have bought this on the way here.

NARRATOR: Magoemon takes from the fold of his kimono a sheet of oath-paper from Kumano, the sacred characters formed by flocks of crows.[42] Instead of vows of eternal love, Jihei now signs under penalty of Heaven's wrath an oath that he will sever all ties and affections with Koharu. "If I should lie, may Bonten and Taishaku above, and the Four Great Kings below afflict me!"[43] So the text runs, and to it is appended the names of many Buddhas and gods. He signs his name, Kamiya Jihei, in bold characters, imprints the oath with a seal of blood, and proffers it.

OSAN: It's a great relief to me too. Mother, I have you and Magoemon to thank. Jihei and I have had two children, but this is his firmest pledge of affection. I hope you share my joy.

AUNT: Indeed we do. I'm sure that Jihei will settle down and his business will improve, now that he's in this frame of mind. It's been entirely for his sake and for love of the grandchildren that we've intervened. Come, Magoemon, let's be on our way. I'm anxious to set my husband's mind at ease.—It's become chilly here. See that the children don't catch cold.—This too we owe to the Buddha of the Ten Nights. I'll say a prayer of thanks before I go. Hail, Amida Buddha!

NARRATOR: She leaves, her heart innocent as Buddha's. Jihei is perfunctory even about seeing them to the door. Hardly have they crossed the threshold than he slumps down again at the *kotatsu*. He pulls the checked quilting over his head.

OSAN: You still haven't forgotten Sonezaki, have you?

NARRATOR: She goes up to him in disgust and tears away the quilting. He is weeping; a waterfall of tears streams along the pillow, deep enough to bear him afloat. She tugs him upright and props his body against the *kotatsu* frame. She stares into his face.

OSAN: You're acting outrageously, Jihei. You shouldn't have signed that oath if you felt so reluctant to leave her. The year before last, on the middle day of the Boar of the tenth moon,[44] we lit the first fire in the *kotatsu* and celebrated by sleeping here together, pillow to pillow. Ever since then—did some demon or snake creep into my

---

[42] The charms issued by the Shinto shrine at Kumano were printed on the face with six Chinese characters, the strokes of which were in the shape of crows. The reverse side of these charms was used for writing oaths. See Shively, p. 116, for a fuller description.

[43] A formal oath. Bonten (Brahma) and Taishaku (Sakra), though Hindu gods, were considered to be protective deities of the Buddhist law. The four Deva kings served under Sakra and were also protectors of Buddhism.

[44] It was customary to light the first fire of the winter on this day, which would generally be towards the end of November in the Western calendar.

bosom that night?—for two whole years I've been condemned to keep watch over an empty nest. I thought that tonight at least, thanks to Mother and Magoemon, we'd share sweet words in bed as husbands and wives do, but my pleasure didn't last long. How cruel of you, how utterly heartless! Go ahead, cry your eyes out, if you're so attached to her. Your tears will flow into Shijimi River and Koharu, no doubt, will ladle them out and drink them! You're ignoble, inhuman.

NARRATOR: She embraces his knees and throws herself over him, moaning in supplication. Jihei wipes his eyes.

JIHEI: If tears of grief flowed from the eyes and tears of anger from the ears, I could show my heart without saying a word. But my tears all pour in the same way from my eyes, and there's no difference in their color. It's not surprising that you can't tell what's in my heart. I have not a shred of attachment left for that vampire in human skin, but I bear a grudge against Tahei. He has all the money he wants, no wife or children. He's schemed again and again to redeem her, but Koharu refused to give in, at least until I broke with her. She told me time and again, "You have nothing to worry about. I'll never let myself be redeemed by Tahei, not even if my ties with you are ended and I can no longer stay by your side. If my master is induced by Tahei's money to deliver me to him, I'll kill myself in a way that'll do you credit!" But think—not ten days have passed since I broke with her, and she's to be redeemed by Tahei! That rotten whore! That animal! No, I haven't a trace of affection left for her, but I can just hear how Tahei will be boasting. He'll spread the word around Osaka that my business has come to a standstill and I'm hard pressed for money. I'll meet with contemptuous stares from the wholesalers. I'll be dishonored. My heart is broken and my body burns with shame. What a disgrace! How maddening! I've passed the stage of shedding hot tears, tears of blood, sticky tears—my tears now are of molten iron!

NARRATOR: He collapses with weeping. Osan pales with alarm.

OSAN: If that's the situation, poor Koharu will surely kill herself.

JIHEI: You're too well bred, despite your intelligence, to understand her likes! What makes you suppose that faithless creature would kill herself? Far from it—she's probably taking moxa treatments and medicine to prolong her life!

OSAN: No, that's not true. I was determined never to tell you so long as I lived, but I'm afraid of the crime I'd be committing if I concealed the facts and let her die with my knowledge. I will reveal my great secret. There is not a grain of deceit in Koharu. It was I who schemed to end the relations between you. I could see signs that you were drifting towards suicide. I felt so unhappy that I wrote a letter, begging her as one woman to another to break with you, though I knew how painful it would be. I asked her to save your life. The letter must have moved her. She answered that she would give you up, though you were more precious than life itself, because she could not shirk her duty to me. I've kept her letter with me ever since—it's been like a protective charm. Could such a noble-hearted woman violate her promise and brazenly marry Tahei? When a woman—I no less than another—has given herself completely to a man, she does not change. I'm sure she'll kill herself. I'm sure of it. Ahhh—what a dreadful thing to have happened! Save her, please.

NARRATOR: Her voice rises in agitation. Her husband is thrown into a turmoil.

JIHEI: There was a letter in an unknown woman's hand among the written oaths she surrendered to my brother. It must have been from you. If that's the case, Koharu will surely commit suicide.

OSAN: Alas! I'd be failing in the obligations I owe her as another woman if I allowed her to die. Please go to her at once. Don't let her kill herself.

NARRATOR: Clinging to her husband, she melts in tears.

JIHEI: But what can I possibly do? It'd take half the amount of her ransom in earnest money merely to keep her out of Tahei's clutches. I can't save Koharu's life without administering a dose of 750 *momme* in New Silver.[45] How could I raise that much money in my present financial straits? Even if I crush my body to powder, where will the money come from?

OSAN: Don't exaggerate the difficulties. If that's all you need, it's simple enough.

NARRATOR: She goes to the wardrobe, and opening a small drawer takes out a bag fastened with cords of twisted silk. She unhesitantly tears it open and throws down a packet which Jihei retrieves.

JIHEI: What's this? Money? Four hundred *momme* in New Silver? How in the world—

NARRATOR: He stares astonished at this money he never put there.

[45] The medical images are occasioned by considering Koharu's plight as a sickness. If 750 *me* is half the sum needed to redeem Koharu, the total of 1,500 *me* (or 6,000 *me* in Old Silver) is considerably less than the 10 *kamme*, or 10,000 *me* in Old Silver, mentioned by Tahei. See above, p. 392.

OSAN: I'll tell you later where this money came from. I've scraped it together to pay the bill for Iwakuni paper that falls due the day after tomorrow. We'll have to ask Magoemon to help us keep the business from betraying its insolvency. But Koharu comes first. The packet contains 400 *momme*. That leaves 350 *momme* to raise.

NARRATOR: She unlocks a large drawer. From the wardrobe lightly fly kite-colored Hachijō silks;[46] a Kyoto crepe kimono lined in pale brown, insubstantial as her husband's life which flickers today and may vanish tomorrow; a padded kimono of Osue's, a flaming scarlet inside and out—Osan flushes with pain to part with it; Kantarō's sleeveless, unlined jacket—if she pawns this, he'll be cold this winter. Next comes a garment of striped Gunnai silk lined in pale blue and never worn, and then her best formal costume—heavy black silk dyed with her family crest, an ivy leaf in a ring. They say that those joined by marriage ties can even go naked at home, though outside the house clothes make the man: she snatches up even her husband's finery, a silken cloak, making fifteen articles in all.

OSAN: The very least the pawnshop can offer is 350 *momme* in New Silver.

NARRATOR: Her face glows as though she already held the money she needs; she hides in the one bundle her husband's shame and her own obligation, and puts her love in besides.

OSAN: It doesn't matter if the children and I have nothing to wear. My husband's reputation concerns me more. Ransom Koharu. Save her. Assert your honor before Tahei.

NARRATOR: But Jihei's eyes remain downcast all the while, and he is silently weeping.

JIHEI: Yes, I can pay the earnest money and keep her out of Tahei's hands. But once I've redeemed her, I'll either have to maintain her in a separate establishment or bring her here. Then what will become of you?

NARRATOR: Osan is at a loss to answer.

OSAN: Yes, what shall I do? Shall I become your children's nurse or the cook? Or perhaps the retired mistress of the house?

NARRATOR: She falls to the floor with a cry of woe.

JIHEI: That would be too selfish. I'd be afraid to accept such gen-

---

[46] Hachijō silks were woven with a warp of brown and a woof of yellow thread to give a color like that of the bird called the kite. "Kite" also suggests that the material flies out of the cupboard.

erosity. Even if the punishment for my crimes against my parents, against Heaven, against the gods and the Buddhas fails to strike me, the punishment for my crimes against my wife alone will be sufficient to destroy all hope for the future life. Forgive me, I beg you.

NARRATOR: He joins his hands in tearful entreaty.

OSAN: Why should you bow before me? I don't deserve it. I'd be glad to rip the nails from my fingers and toes, to do anything which might serve my husband. I've been pawning my clothes for some time in order to scrape together the money for the paper wholesalers' bills. My wardrobe is empty, but I don't regret it in the least. But it's too late now to talk of such things. Hurry, change your cloak and go to her with a smile.

NARRATOR: He puts on an under kimono of Gunnai silk, a robe of heavy black silk, and a striped cloak. His sash of figured damask holds a dirk of middle length worked in gold: Buddha surely knows that tonight it will be stained with Koharu's blood.

JIHEI: Sangorō! Come here!

NARRATOR: Jihei loads the bundle on the servant's back, intending to take him along. Then he firmly thrusts the wallet next to his skin and starts towards the gate.

VOICE: Is Jihei at home?

NARRATOR: A man enters, removing his fur cap. They see—good heavens!—that it is Gozaemon.

OSAN *and* JIHEI: Ahhh—how fortunate that you should come at this moment!

NARRATOR: Husband and wife are upset and confused. Gozaemon snatches away Sangorō's bundle and sits heavily. His voice is sharp.

GOZAEMON: Stay where you are, harlot!—My esteemed son-in-law, what a rare pleasure to see you dressed in your finest attire, with a dirk and a silken cloak! Ahhh—that's how a gentleman of means spends his money! No one would take you for a paper dealer. Are you perchance on your way to the New Quarter? What commendable perseverance! You have no need for your wife, I take it.—Give her a divorce. I've come to take her home with me.

NARRATOR: He speaks needles and his voice is bitter. Jihei has not a word to reply.

OSAN: How kind of you, Father, to walk here on such a cold day. Do have a cup of tea.

NARRATOR: Offering the teacup serves as an excuse for edging closer.

OSAN: Mother and Magoemon came here a while ago, and they told my husband how much they disapproved of his visits to the New Quarter. Jihei was in tears and he wrote out an oath swearing he had reformed. He gave it to Mother. Haven't you seen it yet?

GOZAEMON: His written oath? Do you mean this?

NARRATOR: He takes the paper from his kimono.

GOZAEMON: Libertines scatter vows and oaths wherever they go, as if they were monthly statements of accounts. I thought there was something peculiar about this oath, and now that I am here I can see I was right. Do you still swear to Bonten and Taishaku? Instead of such nonsense, write out a bill of divorcement!

NARRATOR: He rips the oath to shreds and throws down the pieces. Husband and wife exchange looks of alarm, stunned into silence. Jihei touches his hands to the floor and bows his head.

JIHEI: Your anger is justified. If I were still my former self, I would try to offer explanations, but today I appeal entirely to your generosity. Please let me stay with Osan. I promise that even if I become a beggar or an outcast and must sustain life with the scraps that fall from other people's chopsticks, I will hold Osan in high honor and protect her from every harsh and bitter experience. I feel so deeply indebted to Osan that I cannot divorce her. You will understand that this is true as time passes and I show you how I apply myself to my work and restore my fortune. Until then please shut your eyes and allow us to remain together.

NARRATOR: Tears of blood stream from his eyes and his face is pressed to the matting in contrition.

GOZAEMON: The wife of an outcast! That's all the worse. Write the bill of divorcement at once! I will verify and seal the furniture and clothes Osan brought in her dowry.

NARRATOR: He goes to the wardrobe. Osan is alarmed.

OSAN: My clothes are all here. There's no need to examine them.

NARRATOR: She runs up to forestall him, but Gozaemon pushes her aside and jerks open a drawer.

GOZAEMON: What does this mean?

NARRATOR: He opens another drawer: it too is empty. He pulls out every last drawer, but not so much as a foot of patchwork cloth is to be seen. He tears open the wicker hampers, long boxes, and clothes chests.

GOZAEMON: Stripped bare, are they?

NARRATOR: His eyes set in fury. Jihei and Osan huddle under the striped *kotatsu* quilts, ready to sink into the fire with humiliation.[47]

GOZAEMON: This bundle looks suspicious.

NARRATOR: He unties the knots and dumps out the contents.

GOZAEMON: As I thought! You were sending these to the pawnshop, I take it. Jihei—you'd strip the skin from your wife's and your children's bodies to squander the money on your whore! Dirty thief! You're my wife's nephew, but an utter stranger to me, and I'm under no obligation to suffer for your sake. I'll explain to Magoemon what has happened and ask him to make good whatever inroads you've already made on Osan's belongings. But first, the bill of divorcement!

NARRATOR: Even if Jihei could escape through seven padlocked doors, eight thicknesses of chains, and a hundred girdling walls, he could not evade so stringent a demand.

JIHEI: I won't use a brush to write the bill of divorcement. Here's what I'll do instead! Good-by, Osan.

NARRATOR: He lays his hand on his dirk, but Osan clings to him.

OSAN: Father—Jihei admits that he's done wrong and he's apologized in every way. You press your advantage too hard. Jihei may be a stranger, but his children are your grandchildren. Have you no affection for them? I will not accept a bill of divorcement.

NARRATOR: She embraces her husband and raises her voice in tears.

GOZAEMON: Very well. I won't insist on it. Come with me, woman.

NARRATOR: He pulls her to her feet.

OSAN: No, I won't go. What bitterness makes you expose to such shame a man and wife who still love each other? I will not suffer it.

NARRATOR: She pleads with him, weeping, but he pays her no heed.

GOZAEMON: Is there some greater shame? I'll shout it through the town!

NARRATOR: He pulls her up, but she shakes free. Caught by the wrist she totters forward when—alas!—her toes brush against her sleeping children. They open their eyes.

CHILDREN: Mother dear, why is Grandfather, the bad man, taking you away? Whom will we sleep beside now?

NARRATOR: They call out after her.

OSAN: My poor dears! You've never spent a night away from Mother's

[47] I have omitted here an irrelevant allusion to Urashima Tarō. See Shively, p. 85.

side since you were born. Sleep tonight beside your father. (*To Jihei.*) Please don't forget to give the children their tonic before breakfast. —Oh, my heart is broken!

NARRATOR: These are her parting words. She leaves her children behind, abandoned as in the woods; the twin-trunked bamboo of conjugal love is sundered forever.

ACT THREE

Scene One: Sonezaki New Quarter, in front of the Yamato House.
Time: That night.

NARRATOR: This is Shijimi River, the haunt of love and affection. Its flowing water and the feet of passersby are stilled now at two in the morning, and the full moon shines clear in the sky. Here in the street a dim doorway lantern is marked "Yamatoya Dembei" in a single scrawl. The night watchman's clappers take on a sleepy cadence as he totters by on uncertain legs. The very thickness of his voice crying, "Beware of fire! Beware of fire!" tells how far advanced the night is. A serving woman from the upper town comes along, followed by a palanquin. "It's terribly late," she remarks to the bearers as she clatters open the side door of the Yamato House and steps inside.

SERVANT: I've come to take back Koharu of the Kinokuni House.

NARRATOR: Her voice is faintly heard outside. A few moments later, after hardly time enough to exchange three or four words of greeting, she emerges.

SERVANT: Koharu is spending the night. Bearers, you may leave now and get some rest. (*To proprietress, inside the doorway.*) Oh, I forgot to tell you, madam. Please keep an eye on Koharu. Now that the ransom to Tahei has been arranged and the money's been accepted, we're merely her custodians. Please don't let her drink too much saké.

NARRATOR: She leaves, having scattered at the doorway the seeds that before morning will turn Jihei and Koharu to dust.

At night between two and four even the teahouse kettle rests; the flame flickering in the low candle stand narrows; and the frost spreads in the cold river-wind of the deepening night. The master's voice breaks the stillness.

DEMBEI (*to Jihei*): It's still the middle of the night. I'll send somebody with you. (*To servants.*) Mr. Jihei is leaving. Wake Koharu. Call her here.

NARRATOR: Jihei slides open the side door.

JIHEI: No, Dembei, not a word to Koharu. I'll be trapped here till dawn if she hears I'm leaving. That's why I'm letting her sleep and slipping off this way. Wake her up after sunrise and send her back then. I'm returning home now and will leave for Kyoto immediately on business. I have so many engagements that I may not be able to return in time for the interim payment.[48] Please use the money I gave you earlier this evening to clear my account. I'd like you also to send 150 *me* of Old Silver to Kawashō for the moon-viewing party last month. Please get a receipt. Give Saietsubō[49] from Fukushima one piece of silver as a contribution to the Buddhist altar he's bought, and tell him to use it for a memorial service. Wasn't there something else? Oh yes—give Isoichi a tip of four silver coins. That's the lot. Now you can close up and get to bed. Good-by. I'll see you when I return from Kyoto.

NARRATOR: Hardly has he taken two or three steps than he turns back.

JIHEI: I forgot my dirk. Fetch it for me, won't you?—Yes, Dembei, this is one respect in which it's easier being a townsman. If I were a samurai and forgot my sword, I'd probably commit suicide on the spot!

DEMBEI: I completely forgot that I was keeping it for you. Yes, here's the knife with it.

NARRATOR: He gives the dirk to Jihei, who fastens it firmly into his sash.

JIHEI: I feel secure as long as I have this. Good night!

NARRATOR: He goes off.

DEMBEI: Please come back to Osaka soon! Thank you for your patronage!

NARRATOR: With this hasty farewell Dembei rattles the door bolt shut; then not another sound is heard as the silence deepens. Jihei pretends to leave, only to creep back again with stealthy steps. He

[48] On the last day of the tenth moon (November 29, 1720). This day was one of the times established during the course of the year for making payments.

[49] The name of a male entertainer in the Quarter. Fukushima was west of Sonezaki.

clings to the door of the Yamato House. As he peeps within he is startled by shadows moving towards him. He takes cover at the house across the way until the figures pass.

Magoemon the Miller, his heart pulverized with anxiety over his younger brother, comes first, followed by the apprentice Sangorō with Jihei's son Kantarō on his back. They hurry along until they spy the lantern of the Yamato House. Magoemon pounds on the door.

MAGOEMON: Excuse me. Kamiya Jihei's here, isn't he? I'd like to see him a moment.

NARRATOR: Jihei thinks, "It's my brother!" but dares not stir from his place of concealment. From inside a man's sleep-laden voice is heard.

DEMBEI: Jihei left a while ago saying he was going up to Kyoto. He's not here.

NARRATOR: Not another sound is heard. Magoemon's tears fall unchecked.

MAGOEMON (*to himself*): I ought to have met him on the way if he'd been going home. I can't understand what takes him to Kyoto. Ahhh—I'm trembling all over with worry. I wonder if he didn't take Koharu with him.

NARRATOR: The thought pierces his heart; unable to bear the pain, he pounds again on the door.

DEMBEI: Who is it, so late at night? We've gone to bed.

MAGOEMON: I'm sorry to disturb you, but I'd like to ask one more thing. Has Koharu of the Kinokuni House left? I was wondering if she mightn't have gone with Jihei.

DEMBEI: What's that? Koharu's upstairs, fast asleep.

MAGOEMON: That's a relief, anyway. There's no fear of a lovers' suicide. But where is he hiding himself causing me all this anxiety? He can't imagine the agony of suspense that the whole family is going through on his account. I'm afraid that bitterness towards his father-in-law may make him forget himself and do something rash. I brought Kantarō along, hoping he would help to dissuade Jihei, but the gesture was in vain. I wonder why I failed to meet him?

NARRATOR: He murmurs to himself, his eyes moist with tears. Jihei's hiding place is close enough for him to hear every word. He chokes with emotion, but can only swallow his tears.

MAGOEMON: Sangorō! Where does the fool go night after night? Don't you know anywhere else?

NARRATOR: Sangorō imagines that he himself is the fool referred to.

SANGORŌ: I know a couple of places, but I'm too embarrassed to mention them.

MAGOEMON: You know them? Where are they? Tell me.

SANGORŌ: Please don't scold me when you've heard. Every night I wander down below the warehouses by the market.

MAGOEMON: Imbecile! Who's asking about that? Come on, let's search the back streets. Don't let Kantarō catch a chill. The poor kid's having a cold time of it, thanks to that useless father of his. Still, if the worst the boy experiences is the cold I won't complain. I'm afraid that Jihei may cause him much greater pain. The scoundrel!

NARRATOR: But beneath the rancor in his heart of hearts is profound pity.

MAGOEMON: Let's look at the back street!

NARRATOR: They pass on. As soon as their figures have gone off a distance Jihei runs from his hiding place. Standing on tiptoes he gazes with yearning after them and cries out in his heart.

JIHEI: He cannot leave me to my death, though I am the worst of sinners! I remain to the last a burden to him! I'm unworthy of such kindness!

NARRATOR: He joins his hands and kneels in prayer.

JIHEI: If I may make one further request of your mercy, look after my children!

NARRATOR: These are his only words; for a while he chokes with tears.

JIHEI: At any rate, our decision's been made. Koharu must be waiting.

NARRATOR: He peers through a crack in the side door of the Yamato House and glimpses a figure.

JIHEI: That's Koharu, isn't it? I'll let her know I'm here.

NARRATOR: He clears his throat, their signal. "Ahem, ahem"—the sound blends with the clack of wooden clappers as the watchman comes from the upper street, coughing in the night wind. He hurries on his round of fire warning, "Take care! Beware!" Even this cry has a dismal sound to one in hiding. Jihei, concealing himself like the god of Katsuragi,⁵⁰ lets the watchman pass. He sees his chance and rushes to the side door, which softly opens from within.

⁵⁰ The god was so ashamed of his ugliness that he ventured forth only at night.

JIHEI: Koharu?

KOHARU: Were you waiting? Jihei—I want to leave quickly.

NARRATOR: She is all impatience, but the more hastily they open the door, the more likely people will be to hear the casters turning. They lift the door; it gives a moaning that thunders in their ears and in their hearts. Jihei lends a hand from the outside, but his fingertips tremble with the trembling of his heart. The door opens a quarter of an inch, a half, an inch—an inch ahead are the tortures of hell, but more than hell itself they fear the guardian-demon's eyes. At last the door opens, and with the joy of New Year's morn [51] Koharu slips out. They catch each other's hands. Shall they go north or south, west or east? Their pounding hearts urge them on, though they know not to what destination: turning their backs on the moon reflected in Shijimi River, they hurry eastward as fast as their legs will carry them.

Scene Two: The farewell journey of many bridges.

NARRATOR:

    The running hand in texts of Nō is always Konoe style;
    An actor in a woman's part is sure to wear a purple hat.[52]
    Does some teaching of the Buddha as rigidly decree
    That men who spend their days in evil haunts must end like
        this?

Poor creatures, though they would discover today their destiny in the Sutra of Cause and Effect,[53] tomorrow the gossip of the world will scatter like blossoms the scandal of Kamiya Jihei's love suicide, and, carved in cherry wood,[54] his story to the last detail will be printed in illustrated sheets.

Jihei, led on by the spirit of death—if such there be among the

---

[51] Mention of New Year is connected with Koharu's name, in which *haru* means "spring."

[52] The Konoe style of calligraphy, originated by Konoe Nobutada (1565–1614), was invariably used in books of Nō texts. Custom also decreed that young actors playing the parts of women cover their foreheads with a square of purple cloth to disguise the fact that they were shaven.

[53] A sacred text of Buddhism (Karma Sūtra); Chikamatsu here alludes to the line from that text: "If you wish to know the past cause, look at the present effect; if you wish to know the future effect, look at the present cause." See Shively, p. 125.

[54] The blocks from which illustrated books were printed were frequently of cherry wood. The illustrated sheets mentioned here featured current scandals, such as lovers' suicides.

gods—is resigned to this punishment for neglect of his trade. But at times—who could blame him?—his heart is drawn to those he has left behind, and it is hard to keep walking on. Even in the full moon's light, this fifteenth night of the tenth moon,[55] he cannot see his way ahead—a sign perhaps of the darkness in his heart? The frost now falling will melt by dawn but, even more quickly than this symbol of human frailty, the lovers themselves will melt away. What will become of the fragrance that lingered when he held her tenderly at night in their bedchamber?

This bridge, Tenjin Bridge, he has crossed every day, morning and night, gazing at Shijimi River to the west. Long ago, when Tenjin, then called Michizane,[56] was exiled to Tsukushi, his plum tree, following its master, flew in one bound to Dazaifu, and here is Plum-field Bridge.[57] Green Bridge recalls the aged pine that followed later, and Cherry Bridge the tree that withered away in grief over parting. Such are the tales still told, bespeaking the power of a single poem.[58]

JIHEI: Though born the parishioner of so holy and mighty a god, I shall kill you and then myself. If you ask the cause, it was that I lacked even the wisdom that might fill a tiny Shell Bridge.[59] Our stay in this world has been short as an autumn day. This evening will be the last of your nineteen, of my twenty-eight years. The time has come to cast away our lives. We promised we'd remain together faithfully, till you were an old woman and I an old man, but before we knew each other three full years, we have met this disaster. Look,

[55] November 14, 1720. In the lunar calendar the full moon occurs on the fifteenth of the month.

[56] Sugawara no Michizane, unfairly abused at court, was exiled to Dazaifu in Kyushu. When he was about to depart he composed a poem of farewell to his favorite plum tree. The tree, moved by this honor, flew after him to Kyushu. The cherry tree in his garden withered away in grief. Only the pine seemed indifferent, as Michizane complained in another poem. The pine thereupon also flew to Kyushu. See also n. 24, above.

[57] Umeda Bridge. "Green Bridge" is Midori-bashi.

[58] The poem by Michizane bewailing the inconstancy of his pine tree.

[59] Shijimi Bridge. Twelve bridges are mentioned in the michiyuki. The lovers' journey takes them along the north bank of Shijimi River to Shijimi Bridge, where they cross to Dōjima. At Little Naniwa Bridge they cross back again to Sonezaki. Continuing eastward, they cross Horikawa, then cross the Temma Bridge over the Ōkawa. At "Eight Houses" (Hakkenya) they journey eastward along the south bank of the river as far as Kyō Bridge. They cross this bridge to the tip of land at Katamachi, and then take the Onari Bridge to Amijima.

there is Ōe Bridge. We follow the river from Little Naniwa Bridge to Funairi Bridge. The farther we journey, the closer we approach the road to death.

NARRATOR: He laments. She clings to him.

KOHARU: Is this already the road to death?

NARRATOR: Falling tears obscure from each the other's face and threaten to immerse even the Horikawa bridges.

JIHEI: A few steps north and I could glimpse my house, but I will not turn back. I will bury in my breast all thoughts of my children's future, all pity for my wife. We cross southward over the river. Why did they call a place with as many buildings as a bridge has piers "Eight Houses"? Hurry, we want to arrive before the down-river boat from Fushimi comes—with what happy couples sleeping aboard!

Next is Temma Bridge, a frightening name [60] for us about to depart this world. Here the two streams Yodo and Yamato join in one great river, as fish with water, and as Koharu and I, dying on one blade will cross together the River of Three Fords.[61] I would like this water for our tomb offering!

KOHARU: What have we to grieve about? Though in this world we could not stay together, in the next and through each successive world to come until the end of time we shall be husband and wife. Every summer for my devotions [62] I have copied the All Compassionate and All Merciful Chapter of the Lotus Sutra, in the hope that we may be reborn on one lotus.

NARRATOR: They cross over Kyō Bridge and reach the opposite shore.[63]

KOHARU: If I can save living creatures at will when once I mount a lotus calyx in Paradise and become a Buddha, I want to protect women of my profession, so that never again will there be love suicides.

NARRATOR: This unattainable prayer stems from worldly attachment, but it touchingly reveals her heart.

[60] The characters used for Temma mean literally "demon".

[61] A river in the Buddhist underworld which had to be crossed to reach the world of the dead. Mention here is induced arithmetically: one blade plus two people equal three fords.

[62] It was customary for Buddhist monks and some of the laity in Japan to observe a summer retreat from the sixteenth day of the fourth moon to the fifteenth day of the seventh moon, a period of ninety days. During this time they practiced various austerities and copied out the holy books or wrote the Buddha's name over and over.

[63] "Opposite shore" suggests the Buddhist term *higan* (nirvana).

They cross Onari Bridge.[64] The waters of Noda Creek are shrouded with morning haze; the mountain tips show faintly white.

JIHEI: Listen—the voices of the temple bells begin to boom. How much farther can we go on this way? We are not fated to live any longer—let us make an end quickly. Come this way.

NARRATOR: Tears are strung with the 108 beads of the rosaries in their hands. They have come now to Amijima, to the Daichō Temple; the overflowing sluice gate of a little stream beside a bamboo thicket will be their place of death.

Scene Three: Amijima.

JIHEI: No matter how far we walk, there'll never be a spot marked "For Suicides." Let us kill ourselves here.

NARRATOR: He takes her hand and sits on the ground.

KOHARU: Yes, that's true. One place is as good as another to die. But I've been thinking on the way that if they find our dead bodies together people will say that Koharu and Jihei committed a lovers' suicide. Osan will think then that I treated as mere scrap paper the letter I sent promising her, when she asked me not to kill you, that I would not, and vowing to break all relations. She will be sure that I lured her precious husband into a lovers' suicide. She will despise me as a one-night prostitute, a false woman with no sense of decency. I fear her contempt more than the slander of a thousand or ten thousand strangers. I can imagine how she will resent and envy me. That is the greatest obstacle to my salvation. Kill me here, then choose another spot, far away, for yourself.

NARRATOR: She leans against him. Jihei joins in her tears of pleading.

JIHEI: What foolish worries! Osan has been taken back by my father-in-law. I've divorced her. She and I are strangers now. Why should you feel obliged to a divorced woman? You were saying on the way that you and I will be husband and wife through each successive world until the end of time. Who can criticize us, who can be jealous if we die side by side?

KOHARU: But who is responsible for your divorce? You're even less reasonable than I. Do you suppose that our bodies will accompany

[64] The name Onari is used here for the bridge more properly called Bizenjima because of a play on words meaning "to become a Buddha".

us to the afterworld? We may die in different places, our bodies may be pecked by kites and crows, but what does it matter as long as our souls are twined together? Take me with you to heaven or to hell!

NARRATOR: She sinks again in tears.

JIHEI: You're right. Our bodies are made of earth, water, fire, and wind, and when we die they revert to emptiness. But our souls will not decay, no matter how often reborn. And here's a guarantee that our souls will be married and never part!

NARRATOR: He whips out his dirk and slashes off his black locks at the base of the top knot.

JIHEI: Look, Koharu. As long as I had this hair I was Kamiya Jihei, Osan's husband, but cutting it has made me a monk. I have fled the burning house of the three worlds of delusion; I am a priest, unencumbered by wife, children, or worldly possessions. Now that I no longer have a wife named Osan, you owe her no obligations either.

NARRATOR: In tears he flings away the hair.

KOHARU: I am happy.

NARRATOR: Koharu takes up the dirk and ruthlessly, unhesitatingly, slices through her flowing Shimada coiffure. She casts aside the tresses she has so often washed and combed and stroked. How heartbreaking to see their locks tangled with the weeds and midnight frost of this desolate field!

JIHEI: We have escaped the inconstant world, a nun and a priest. Our duties as husband and wife belong to our profane past. It would be best to choose quite separate places for our deaths, a mountain for one, the river for the other. We will pretend that the ground above this sluice gate is a mountain. You will die there. I shall hang myself by this stream. The time of our deaths will be the same, but the method and place will differ. In this way we can honor to the end our duty to Osan. Give me your under sash.

NARRATOR: Its fresh violet color and fragrance will be lost in the winds of impermanence; the crinkled silk long enough to wind twice round her body will bind two worlds, this and the next. He firmly fastens one end to the crosspiece of the sluice, then twists the other into a noose for his neck. He will hang for love of his wife like the "pheasant in the hunting grounds." [65]

[65] A reference to a poem by Ōtomo no Yakamochi (718–85): "The pheasant foraging in the fields of spring reveals his whereabouts to man as he cries for his mate" (*Shūishū*, no. 21).

Koharu watches Jihei prepare for his death. Her eyes swim with tears, her mind is distraught.

KOHARU: Is that how you're going to kill yourself?—If we are to die apart, I have only a little while longer by your side. Come near me.

NARRATOR: They take each other's hands.

KOHARU: It's over in a moment with a sword, but I'm sure you'll suffer. My poor darling!

NARRATOR: She cannot stop the silent tears.

JIHEI: Can suicide ever be pleasant, whether by hanging or cutting the throat? You mustn't let worries over trifles disturb the prayers of your last moments. Keep your eyes on the westward-moving moon, and worship it as Amida himself.[66] Concentrate your thoughts on the Western Paradise. If you have any regrets about leaving the world, tell me now, then die.

KOHARU: I have none at all, none at all. But I'm sure you must be worried about your children.

JIHEI: You make me cry all over again by mentioning them. I can almost see their faces, sleeping peacefully, unaware, poor dears, that their father is about to kill himself. They're the one thing I can't forget.

NARRATOR: He droops to the ground with weeping. The voices of the crows leaving their nests at dawn rival his sobs. Are the crows mourning his fate? The thought brings more tears.

JIHEI: Listen to them. The crows have come to guide us to the world of the dead. There's an old saying that every time somebody writes an oath on the back of a Kumano charm, three crows of Kumano die on the holy mountain. The first words we've written each New Year have been vows of love, and how often we've inscribed oaths at the beginning of the month! If each oath has killed three crows, what a multitude must have perished! Their cries have always sounded like "beloved, beloved," but hatred for our crime of taking life makes their voices ring tonight "revenge, revenge!" [67] Whose fault is it they demand revenge? Because of me you will die a painful death. Forgive me!

[66] Amida's paradise lies in the west. The moon is also frequently used as a symbol of Buddhist enlightenment.

[67] The cries have always sounded like *kawai, kawai*, but now they sound like *mukui, mukui*. These Japanese sounds seem more within the range of a crow's articulatory powers than "beloved" and "revenge".

NARRATOR: He takes her in his arms.

KOHARU: No, it's my fault!

NARRATOR: They cling to each other, face pressed to face; their side-locks, drenched with tears, freeze in the winds blowing over the fields. Behind them echoes the voice of the Daichō Temple.

JIHEI: Even the long winter night seems short as our lives.

NARRATOR: Dawn is already breaking, and matins can be heard. He draws her to him.

JIHEI: The moment has come for our glorious end. Let there be no tears on your face when they find you later.

KOHARU: There won't be any.

NARRATOR: She smiles. His hands, numbed by the frost, tremble before the pale vision of her face, and his eyes are first to cloud. He is weeping so profusely that he cannot control the blade.

KOHARU: Compose yourself—but be quick!

NARRATOR: Her encouragement lends him strength; the invocations to Amida carried by the wind urge a final prayer. *Namu Amida Butsu.* He thrusts in the saving sword.[68] Stabbed, she falls backwards, despite his staying hand, and struggles in terrible pain. The point of the blade has missed her windpipe, and these are the final tortures before she can die. He writhes with her in agony, then painfully summons his strength again. He draws her to him, and plunges his dirk to the hilt. He twists the blade in the wound, and her life fades away like an unfinished dream at dawning.

He arranges her corpse head to the north, face to the west, lying on her right side,[69] and throws his cloak over her. He turns away at last, unable to exhaust with tears his grief over parting. He pulls the sash to him and fastens the noose around his neck. The service in the temple has reached the closing section, the prayers for the dead. "Believers and unbelievers will equally share in the divine grace," the voices proclaim, and at the final words Jihei jumps from the sluice gate.

JIHEI: May we be reborn on one lotus! Hail Amida Buddha!

NARRATOR: For a few moments he writhes like a gourd swinging in the wind, but gradually the passage of his breath is blocked as the

[68] The invocation of Amida's name freed one from spiritual obstacles, just as a sword freed one from physical obstacles. Here the two images are blended.

[69] The dead were arranged in this manner because Shakyamuni Buddha chose this position when he died.

stream is dammed by the sluice gate, where his ties with this life are snapped.

Fishermen out for the morning catch find the body in their net.[70]

FISHERMEN: A dead man! Look, a dead man! Come here, everybody!

NARRATOR: The tale is spread from mouth to mouth. People say that they who were caught in the net of Buddha's vow immediately gained salvation and deliverance, and all who hear the tale of the Love Suicides at Amijima are moved to tears.

[70] "Net" (*ami*) is mentioned because of the connection with fishermen. It is echoed a few lines later in the mention of the name *Ami*jima. The vow of the Buddha to save all living creatures is likened to a net which catches people in its meshes. For a further explanation of this image (and of the title of the play), see Shively, p. 41.

THE WOMAN-KILLER

AND THE HELL OF OIL

First performed on August 9, 1721. The murder which inspired this work occurred, as in Chikamatsu's dramatization, on the night before the Boys' Festival in 1721. Little is known of the events surrounding the crime, but Chikamatsu's version may have been influenced by a slightly earlier Kabuki play on the same theme. Chikamatsu attempted to relieve the gloomy atmosphere with lighter touches (apparently borrowed from Saikaku), but the play was not well received, and its present high reputation dates only from the end of the nineteenth century.

Cast of Characters

YOHEI, aged 23, an oil merchant
TOKUBEI, his father, owner of the Kawachi-ya
TAHEI, aged 26, Yohei's brother
SHICHIZAEMON, an oil merchant, owner of the Teshima-ya
YAMAMOTO MORIEMON, a samurai, uncle of Yohei
OGURI HACHIYA, Moriemon's master
WHITE FOX, a mountain priest (*yamabushi*)
YAGORŌ THE BRUSH, henchman of Yohei
REDFACE ZEMBEI, another henchman of Yohei
KOHEI of the Cotton Shop, a moneylender
GOROKURŌ, a paper merchant
"WAXY" of Aizu, a rich customer of Kogiku
MASTER OF A TEAHOUSE
LEADER OF PILGRIMS
PILGRIMS, POLICEMEN, MOURNERS, TEAHOUSE EMPLOYES
OKICHI, aged 27, wife of Shichizaemon
OKIKU, aged 9, daughter of Okichi

Yohei struggles with the wounded Okichi. "In the darkness enveloping the room and his heart, Yohei slips and slides in the spilled oil and flowing blood."
(YOHEI: *Jitsukawa Enjirō II;* OKICHI: *Onoe Kikujirō IV*)

OKIYO, aged 6, daughter of Okichi
ODEN, aged 2, daughter of Okichi
KOGIKU, a courtesan of the Flower House
MATSUKAZE, a courtesan of Shimmachi Quarter
OKAMÉ, a widow, owner of the Flower House
OSAWA, wife of Tokubei
OKACHI, aged 15, daughter of Tokubei and Osawa
MAIDS, GIRLS

ACT ONE

*Scene: A journey on boat and on foot to the Temple of Kanzeon
in Nozaki.*
Time: May 6, 1721.

NARRATOR:

When it comes to boats,
A new one rides best.[1]
You and me, me and you,
Riding high, here we come.
With a splash of oars,
With a plash of oars,
Pillows close on the waves.
Where's the wine cup?
I like to drink from your cup,
Big as the moon of Musashi Plain:
While the moon shines, let's enjoy
This long night together.

Rowdy merrymaking to the beat of the oars. The Flower House in
the North New Quarter[2] has lost its master, but his widow Okamé
keeps the business blooming. The current customer—Waxy's the name
he uses here—was born in Aizu,[3] and his spending is measured to
keep his reputation from melting away. It wasn't long ago that he
first came to this quarter of Osaka, and now he's so madly in love

[1] *Shinzō*, meaning literally "newly built", was a term used of young women, particularly
of one just launched on a career as a prostitute.
[2] The Sonezaki licensed quarter.
[3] Aizu in northern Japan (modern Fukushima Prefecture) was known for its production
of wax; hence, the customer's nickname and other allusions.

with Kogiku of the Tennōji House, so anxious to be loved by her, that he's slithering over Catfish Creek on a pleasure boat bound for Nozaki. It's the middle of May, time for the first summer heat, but a leap month [4] will follow later this year; they brave with saké in riotous revels a river wind still cold to the touch.

The Buddha who of old taught the Lotus at Ryōzen [5] now is called Amida in the Western Paradise; he has manifested himself in this world of dust as Kanzeon. Through three existences—past, present, and future—he brings divine favors, and for three years running there have been celebrations. The year before last, in the spring of the Year of the Boar, [6] even souls living in ignorance and sin in squalid tenements, hoarding their scant coppers at the bottom of needle boxes or rosary bags, unseen by the eye of day, offered their pittances to Buddha, who seized their coins in his thousand hands and glistened at once with a skin of purest gold: this was the display of the Kanzeon image at Nachi. Last year at the Hōryūji in Yamato, they celebrated the one thousand one hundredth anniversary of Prince Shōtoku, another incarnation of the mercy of Kanzeon, the Buddha of salvation. And this year we have the revelation of the image at Nozaki.

Mountain villages are deserted when the cherry blossoms have fallen, but here the flower of men and women, young and old, are in blossom; no wind racing through the sky will scatter these lovely, elegant pilgrims lightly stepping on their way. Do you hear the song that grownups and children are singing?

"Some are going, some returning,
Some have come again."

A passenger launch, boarded by a friend's kindness, carries them to Tokuan Embankment—so much cheaper than hiring a boat! Stem to stern the boats are rowed along, so close they make one craft. The customer from Aizu, beaming with self-satisfaction, seems ready for amorous play. Catering to men's desires is Kogiku's livelihood, but she is ashamed and embarrassed now before the others. She lightly jumps ashore. A hood pulled deep over her face conceals her brows,

---

[4] Months were sometimes inserted in the lunar calendar to make it correspond with the season. Here the calendar has slipped behind; although it is the middle of the fourth moon (normally, late May) the weather is still cold.

[5] This passage is derived from a Buddhist poem by the Chinese monk Hui-ssu describing the identity of the Buddhas of past, present, and future worlds.

[6] 1719.

but her high-waisted Nagoya sash reveals that this is no townsman's wife.[7] At sight of her, men are helpless as the dew on the bamboo; all prudence, calculation, and parsimony go astray. Idlers follow Kogiku and brush against her, addressing remarks as tedious as they are unwelcome, unpleasant, and exasperating. She beckons to the boat accompanying her. Someone sings.

"Behold above Atago Mountain
Three lines of incense smoke rising,
Three lines, three lines are rising."

But four are the lines the roads take: southeast to Nara, the Kyoto Road to the northeast, the road southwest to Tamatsukuri, and to the west the road they've taken here from Kyōbashi. Beyond Noda Town are Yamato River and Okayama, known for its Pine of Longevity, the Hidden Oka of the poets.[8] They disembark at Sarara and cross the log bridge before the Kanzeon of Nozaki, whose saving strength is boundless as the sea; Kanzeon, bringer of measureless joy, who watches all creatures with merciful eyes; Kanzeon, who swore to save those who invoke his name. All who ask or tell of his miracles, all who travel here whether on foot or by boat, will be freed of delusion; with open fans[9] the worshipers tell their beads at his altar.

Here comes a lovely woman. She's from Hontemma-chō, a street narrow as her willowy waist, and her tresses are glossy as willow leaves. Her husband Teshimaya Shichizaemon is a merchant of seed oil, sweet-scented oil, fine-grained oil, sesame oil. She has brought her three daughters, the oldest one nine, for the showing of the image of the Buddha in Nozaki. A child clutches at her skirts, another is held in her arms, but passersby turn back to look: no one would guess that this woman in the bloom of youth was the mother of three. Her name is Okichi.[10] Her middle daughter, Okiyo, is six.

OKIYO: Mama, I'd like a cup of tea.

NARRATOR: They happen to be passing an outdoor tea stall.

[7] It was the custom at the time for women to shave their eyebrows when they married. Kogiku hides her eyebrows with her hood, but her dress gives away the fact that she is not a married woman.

[8] "Hidden Oka" (*Shinobi no Oka*) is a name found in various old poems.

[9] It was the custom when worshiping to open one's fan, place it on the ground before one, and then bow to the gods or Buddha.

[10] I have left out a phrase: "Who took the character *yoshi* from the name Yoshino and called her O-kichi?" The same character may be pronounced *yoshi* or *kichi;* some scholars therefore argue that the name should be read Oyoshi, but Okichi is normal.

OKICHI: Let's sit down here.

NARRATOR: As they are resting, along comes Yohei of the Kawachi-ya, a young man of twenty-three who lives in his parents' house, diagonally across the street from Okichi. He has come on a pilgrimage to Nozaki with Yagorō the Brush and Redface Zembei, oil merchants like him, his companions in pleasure. They drink the time away as if life were all a dream, but awakened now they amble along, carrying by turns a picnic box and a three-gallon cask.

YOHEI: Kogiku and her customer will probably come staggering back along this street on their way from the temple.

NARRATOR: A voice calls from inside the teahouse.

OKICHI: Hello there, Yohei! Do come here.

YOHEI: Okichi—a pilgrimage with your children, is it? If I had known I could have accompanied you. Did Shichizaemon stay behind to look after the shop?

OKICHI: No, we came together, but he had some errands along the way. He ought to be here any moment. Ask your friends in too. Please.

NARRATOR: She urges him politely.

YOHEI: Well then, I'll have a smoke, if you don't mind.

NARRATOR: He plumps himself down with the assurance of the rake.

OKICHI: Have you ever seen such a crowd of pilgrims, Yohei? So many well-to-do young ladies and married women of good families. Oh—do you see that woman in the purple coat shading to lavender, the one with the striped satin sash? She's a professional, no doubt about that.

YOHEI: Just look at the dappled sash over the striped crepe kimono! It's the Shimmachi style, I'm sure. That girl's the most stunning of the lot.

OKICHI: Yes, it doesn't surprise me that on such an occasion a young man would want to bring some glorious creature and squander his money. I'm sure you'd like to be with one. Which would you choose for today, Kogiku from the Tennōji House in Sonezaki or Matsukaze from the Bizen House in Shimmachi? You see how well I know! Why didn't you come with one of them?

NARRATOR: Yohei falls into the trap she lays.

YOHEI: It's a crying shame. I'd been planning for weeks how I'd impress everybody by appearing with a really marvelous girl today. But Matsukaze had the gall to inform me that she had a previous engagement and couldn't be borrowed from her customer. Then Kogiku told me that Nozaki was an unlucky direction for her, and she wouldn't attend, no matter who asked. But listen to this. Kogiku was engaged by her Aizu customer today, and they came early this morning by pleasure boat. I'll never live it down if some country bumpkin gets the better of me. I'm waiting for Kogiku to return so I can have it out with her.

NARRATOR: As he speaks his two companions are hand-wrestling and showing off their strength. Each seems capable of tackling a devil.

OKICHI: There! The proverb is right—a man'll let slip what he won't tell when he's asked! I detect the truth under all your clever talk—is this what you'd call a pious pilgrimage to Kanzeon? It's more like an outing of professional bullies! Your parents know only too well the courtesans and prostitutes you've been buying—which girl from which house. I feel sorry for them. They've come to my husband and me imploring us to intervene. "Yohei is constantly at your house, whenever he has a moment. Please give him some good advice." I'm sure my husband's already spoken to you, and it must annoy you to have a young woman like myself lecturing you here in a public place, a roadside tea stall, instead of keeping her mind on her brood of children. But if you act so outrageously, pushing and shoving your way through these crowds, people will point at you and say, "That's the second son of Tokubei the oil merchant from Hontemma-chō. He can't even settle his accounts at the teahouses, but just look at him now!" That would be most unfortunate. You should be more reliable, like your brother. Remember, a true merchant never wastes a penny, but builds his fortune bit by bit, as the swallow makes its nest. Resolve to work harder and help your parents. It's for your own dignity, and for no one else's sake. You don't answer—I see you dislike what I'm saying.— Come, children, let's hurry to the temple.—If you happen to meet my husband on the way, please tell him that we'll be waiting at the main hall.—Thank you for the tea, proprietor.

NARRATOR: She takes eight or nine coppers from her sleeve and leaves them for the tea, then steps lightly on her way to the temple.

Redface Zembei is Yohei's abettor in mischief.

ZEMBEI: Isn't that the woman who lives across the street from you, Yohei? She's got a pretty face and a seductive way of talking, but what a hardheaded woman!

YOHEI: Yes. She's only twenty-seven, and she hasn't lost her looks, but she's already spawned a slew of kids. She's a model housewife, the picture of domestic simplicity—it's her worst fault. She's a piece of wax fruit [11]—pretty to look at, but not much to taste!

NARRATOR: Yohei laughs. At this moment, quite unaware of the trap awaiting her, Kogiku approaches, escorted by her customer, a rustic unversed in the world of pleasure. Their party includes the widow who owns the Flower House. The customer sings a ditty in his dialect, supplying a vocal accompaniment.

WAXY: For a romantic lead there's Jinzaemon, for a thoughtful type take Kōzaemon, Shiroza's best for the tearful scenes,[12] *chintsu, chintsu, chinchiri, tsute, tsute* . . .

VOICES: The best singer in Japan! Bravo!

NARRATOR: Their praise is directed less at his song than at his money, the key to success in any art!

VOICES: Look who's coming now!

NARRATOR: The three men wait, expectancy written on their faces. Kogiku, recognizing them from the distance, is alarmed.

KOGIKU: Okamé, it's boring to go back over the same road. I'd prefer the boat we came on.

NARRATOR: She lifts her kimono hem and hesitates. Ahead of her stands Yohei, unwavering as a mast, and behind him his two cronies like sentinels.

ZEMBEI *and* YAGORŌ: Don't get flustered, Yohei. Have it out with the whore. Show her you're a man. If that waxy Aizu candle flares up, we'll trim his wick and stamp him out.

NARRATOR: They thrust their sandals in their belts and fold their arms, ready for action. The customer is startled; Okamé and the maids in utter distraction surround Kogiku, who trembles with fear.

YOHEI: I'm borrowing Kogiku, and once an old customer like Yohei borrows her, she won't get away.

[11] Literally, "a bird made of bean paste". Formerly street vendors used to model hollow birds of paste by blowing air through a straw into a lump of the clay-like material.
[12] Yamatoyama Jinzaemon (1677–1721), Takeshima Kōzaemon II, and Sakurayama Shirozaburō II were popular actors of the day.

NARRATOR: He pulls her to a bench outside the teahouse, and forces her to sit.

YOHEI: You harlot! You cheap prostitute! You told me that the direction of Nozaki was unlucky, that you wouldn't go there with anybody, no matter who. You lied because you didn't want to go with me. As long as you're with a customer you like, I suppose that the direction doesn't matter? Make your excuses now.

NARRATOR: He argues with her, his eyes fierce as any devil's. Kogiku reproves him gently.

KOGIKU: Come, Yohei, you mustn't be so uncouth. Everybody knows how intimate we are. If my name is mentioned once, yours is sure to be mentioned three times. It's only because I'm so fond of you that I didn't come with you today. Why do you allow yourself to be provoked by other people? I swear I love you, and here's the proof.

NARRATOR: She clings tightly to him and murmurs sweet words into his ear. Yohei, though he makes no show of affection, is inwardly delighted. An expression of relief and gratitude crosses his face. Kogiku's customer, unable to bear more, brusquely sits beside them.

WAXY: I don't understand you, Kogiku. What possessed you to tell me that nobody in Osaka was as dear as your Aizu gentleman? I thought of the reputation I'd get back home and how lucky I was, and I've been spending my precious money like water on this river outing. But I haven't come to be made a fool of. Unless you repeat to me now, in the presence of this man, what you told me last night, I'm returning home, and I'll never come back to this maddening place. Well, what do you say?

NARRATOR: He presses her for an answer. Yohei's two companions at a signal march boldly up to the man.

ZEMBEI: You clod! We'll take care of the slut. Leave her and go. Or would you like some river mud in your face as a souvenir to take back east?

NARRATOR: They converge on him from both sides, prepared to fling mud. The eastern rustic stands his ground firmly.

WAXY: What's this? Vermin! I've heard about your kind—tattooing your arms to intimidate people, snatching their wallets under pretext of a quarrel. You may be so broke that your legs are shaking under you, but you go on whoring till your knees give way. I'll give you something better than Osaka mud—an easterner's muddy feet!

NARRATOR: He closes and lashes out with his ankle. The Brush's chin is knocked out of joint by the kick, and he is sent tumbling over and over till he lands with a splash in the river. Redface catches the easterner with a shout, only to be kicked in the groin. He doubles up in pain.

ZEMBEI: Damn it!

NARRATOR: He crawls off, staring dazedly at the sky as if watching a bird in flight, and makes his escape.

YOHEI: I'm not going to stand by while my friends are being flung around. I'll plant you upside down!

NARRATOR: He grabs the Aizu man, who shakes him off.

WAXY: Insolent whippersnapper! I'll smash your jawbone!

NARRATOR: But Yohei, dodging his fist, pounds the man in return. Back and forth they grapple and clash.

KOGIKU: Stop that rowdy behavior, both of you!

NARRATOR: She rushes in between to block them.

OKAMÉ: Don't get hurt, my precious one!

NARRATOR: The hostess shields Kogiku, and the maids pull her away. The bystanders start shouting, "Fight! Fight!" and the teahouse shuts its doors. The two men battle desperately, their feet trampling the edges of the embankment, till finally they crash one after the other into the river. Now they fling weeds, mud, and sand from the broken bank, tangling and flailing, a battle of wills in which none can intervene.

At this moment Oguri Hachiya, a samurai risen from page to counselor of the lord of Takatsuki, happens to be passing by. He wears formal dress and is visiting the temple in his master's name. His escorts, young foot soldiers, wear matching cloaks of orange-brown with crests of nine-fold circles. The leader of the procession cries, "Make way! Make way!" but Yohei, heedless of the shouts, continues slinging mud. Unfortunately for him, some spatters over the cloak of the mounted samurai, and splashes his horse's trappings. The chestnut-colored steed is transformed to a motley brown, and the saddle shivers on the rearing back. Yohei is frightened, and the foot soldiers swarm around him with shouts of, "Don't let him escape!" The Aizu man crosses to the opposite bank of the river, while Kogiku and the hostess quickly lose themselves in the crowd of worshipers. The leader of the foot soldiers, Yamamoto Moriemon, tackles Yohei and pitches him face downwards onto the ground. His knees press into Yohei's spine.

YOHEI: Sir samurai! It was a dreadful mistake! I beg you, pardon me! Have mercy, sir, mercy!

NARRATOR: His face is contorted with blubbering.

MORIEMON: Ruffian! After throwing mud all over his excellency's cloak and his horse's trappings, it's not enough to say that it was a mistake. Show me your face!

NARRATOR: He twists Yohei's head around.

YOHEI: Uncle Moriemon!

MORIEMON: You—Yohei!

NARRATOR: They stare at each other in astonishment.

MORIEMON: You're only a commoner. No disgrace will harm your reputation. But I receive a stipend from my lord and boast a samurai's name. I can't spare a ruffian just because he's my nephew. I'm going to cut off your head. Get up!

NARRATOR: Seizing Yohei's wrists, he drags him to his feet. Oguri Hachiya, still mounted, calls out.

OGURI: Moriemon! Your swords look rather loose in their scabbards. If one should slip out and wound somebody, the sight of blood would make it impossible for me to continue this pilgrimage. We would have no choice but to return. Be extremely careful with your swords until the return journey. Come here by me, Moriemon.

NARRATOR: Moriemon respectfully obeys.

MORIEMON: As for you, I'll cut off your head on the way back. You've been reprieved for a while.

NARRATOR: He pushes Yohei aside. He wants to say, "Take care not to let me see you," but samurai that he is, he can only gesture dumbly, a fledgling thrush in summer, as the escorts in the van again clear the way. The envoy, true to the samurai code, is indifferent to petty annoyances, and the horse too bounds forward at a quickened pace.

Yohei's mind is a blank. As one in a drunken stupor, he wonders whether he saw a dream or reality.

YOHEI: Great heavens! I'm to be cut down by my uncle on his return! If he cuts me down, I'll die. And if I die, what'll become of me?

NARRATOR: His heart sinks, his spirits are up in the air. He starts to run, hoping to escape.

YOHEI: Wait—if I go this way I'll end up in Nozaki. Which way to Osaka? I can't tell the direction. This must be the way to Kyoto. But is that mountain Kuragari? Or is it Hiei? Which way shall I escape?

NARRATOR: He stands bewildered, his eyes rolling helplessly, wondering what to do, when he catches sight of Okichi, a sight welcome as Jizō [13] to a sinner in hell.

YOHEI: Okichi! On your way back? I'm in danger now. I may be killed. Help me, please. Take me with you to Osaka. I beg you on bended knees.

NARRATOR: In tears, he prostrates himself.

OKICHI: Oh, but I'm not going back home yet. I managed to go seven or eight hundred yards towards the temple, but there was such a crowd that I turned back. I'm waiting here for my husband. But you look dreadful. You're covered with mud from head to toe. Have you lost your senses, Yohei?

YOHEI: I don't blame you for thinking so. I had a fight and was trading fistfuls of mud with another man when some splashed a samurai on a horse. When he returns from the temple I'm to be killed. Help me, I beg you.

NARRATOR: He will not leave her.

OKICHI: I'm shocked. Your poor parents—they'll be sick when they hear of this. But I can't remain indifferent to a neighbor from across the street. I'll hire a room in this teahouse and help you get rid of that mud. As soon as you're clean, hurry back to Osaka, and try to behave yourself in the future. (*To innkeeper.*) I'd like to hire a room again.—Okiyo, when father comes, let me know.

NARRATOR: The two of them go through the reed blinds to the back of the house, and the long day advances towards noon. Teshimaya Shichizaemon, sure that his wife and daughters are waiting impatiently, hurries along, not pausing for a cup of tea though his throat is parched, carrying his lunch box in one hand and leading his oldest daughter with the other. His middle daughter Okiyo, watching for him in front of the teahouse, runs up with a cry of "Father!"

SHICHIZAEMON: Have you been waiting long? Where's Mother?

OKIYO: Mother's inside the teahouse with Yohei from the Kawachi-ya. They've taken off their sashes and kimonos.

[13] Jizō, a bodhisattva much beloved in Japan, is honored by roadside shrines everywhere; one of his functions was to rescue sinners from hell.

SHICHIZAEMON: What's that? She and Yohei have taken off their sashes and are naked? This is intolerable! I've been shamefully deceived! What happened afterwards? What did they do?

OKIYO: Then she wiped him with tissues and washed him.

NARRATOR: Shichizaemon colors. His eyes glaze over with wrath. He stands menacingly at the door and shouts.

SHICHIZAEMON: Okichi and Yohei, come out! If you don't come out, I'm going in after you!

OKICHI: Is that you, husband? Where have you been? And how could you have forgotten the children's lunch time so?

NARRATOR: She emerges, followed by Yohei.

YOHEI: Shichizaemon. I'm ashamed to appear before you looking this way. I accidentally got involved in a fight, and I fell in the mud. Your wife has kindly helped me to get myself clean. It's thanks to you, I know, and I'd like to express my gratitude.

NARRATOR: His head is spattered with mud from sidelocks to crown, and his body resembles a wet rat. Shichizaemon, uncertain whether to be angry or amused, does not acknowledge his greetings.

SHICHIZAEMON: It's all very well, Okichi, to be kind to others, but there are degrees. It's highly indecent for a young woman to untie a young man's sash and wipe him with paper. People are sure to suspect the worst. Let others take care of themselves, and let us go visit the temple. It's getting late.

OKICHI: I've been waiting to go. I'll tell you everything on the way.

NARRATOR: She takes the eldest daughter by the hand and lifts the youngest in her arms. The middle one rides on her father's shoulders. They've come to hear the teachings of the Law, but they intend to enjoy the excursion too; they hurry gaily off through the crowd. Yohei, alone, lingers dispiritedly in the teahouse. The master of the house and five or six others of the neighborhood gather around him.

MASTER: You've been here for quite a while. Are you on your way to or from the temple? I can't imagine why you should loiter in this one place. It's time you were leaving.

NARRATOR: He hurries Yohei out just as cries of "Make way! Make way!" are heard, and with them the rustle of a horse's reins. Oguri Hachiya is returning on foot from the temple. Yohei is so confused that he bungles his escape and plunges into the van of the escort. Unluckily, he is noticed by his uncle, who catches Yohei and twists him to the ground.

MORIEMON: I spared your life before because we were on our way to the temple, but now that we've completed our worship, forbearance is no longer necessary. I'm going to slash you to bits.

NARRATOR: He lays his hand on his sword hilt.

OGURI: Wait, Moriemon. What reason have you to kill him?

MORIEMON: This is the scoundrel who bothered us before. I'd be inclined to be somewhat more lenient if he were a stranger—I might even beg you to pardon him—but this ruffian's mother is my sister. I cannot spare my own nephew.

NARRATOR: Oguri Hachiya interrupts.

OGURI: Then, what is his crime?

MORIEMON: You need hardly ask, sir. He threw mud on your excellency's clothes and defiled your person. That is his crime.

OGURI: I don't understand why you say he defiled my person. Where on my clothes do you see a trace of mud?

MORIEMON: The mud was on the cloak you were wearing before you changed.

OGURI: Well, then, now that I've changed my clothes isn't it exactly as if no mud had touched them?

MORIEMON: It's generous of you to say so, sir, but your horse's saddle and the stirrups were so badly spattered that you've been obliged to return on foot. His lordship has been insulted, and here is the guilty man.

OGURI: Be silent. It is precisely because it was foreseen that a horse's trappings might get soiled that mudguards[14] were invented. What would there be to guard against if mud never fell on a horse? There's been no disgrace, offense, or crime. The only disgrace a samurai knows is when even a single drop of muddy water falls on his fair name. That will not come out in washing, nor can it be rinsed away. Base villains like this man are in my eyes so much muddy water, and I am the lotus undefiled by the mud through which it rises. My reputation is untarnished. Spare the man.

NARRATOR: "Yes, sir," Moriemon says and, obedient to his master's welcome command, he swings his hand as a signal, and the men fall in line as they start the homeward journey.

---

[14] Devices made of leather or fur which protected a horse's flanks from mud.

ACT TWO

Scene: The Kawachi-ya, an oil shop in Osaka.
Time: May 27, 1721—three days before the Boys' Festival.

PILGRIMS: Deliver us, deliver us, deliver us from suffering, deliver us all, deliver us all. Sendari and Matōgi, save us. Hail, Master of the Five Elements! [15]

NARRATOR: This is the mountain pilgrimage of the oil merchants' guild. Though a lay organization, some of its young leaders have been granted priests' names for having made the pilgrimage so often; others are along for the first time. The group saved twelve months to make the journey; now they approach blowing conch shells, gallantly swinging their pilgrims' staffs. Fur tassels hang at their waists, rosaries circle their necks, and at their hips are water bottles in place of wallets.[16] They stop before the Kawachi-ya, owned by Tokubei.

LEADER: Hello there, Yohei. Are you home? Everything went smoothly, and we had a wonderful pilgrimage up the mountain. Our friends must've known that we'd be back today—they kindly came all the way to Kuwatsu to welcome us. You were the only one who didn't show up. Weren't you feeling well? We saw the most marvelous miracle. I'll tell you about it now, just to give you an idea of our pilgrimage. There was a boy of twelve or thirteen, blind in both eyes—they said he was from the west—who climbed the mountain praying all the way. While he was worshiping En the Ascetic, suddenly both his eyes opened and he could see. He ran down Ozasa Hill without even using a stick. We decided, on thinking it over, that this must be a sign from the gods that conditions will improve this autumn. Do you see? A blind boy is *ko-mekura:* this means that the rice granaries, *kome-kura,* will be opened and prices will fall as easily as the boy ran downhill. If you're free, come over tonight. We've lots of stories to tell about our trip. That's one way to get rid of our fatigue. "Deliver us, deliver us . . ."

NARRATOR: They start off boisterously. Tokubei, Yohei's father, rushes out.

TOKUBEI: Young men, are you coming from the mountain? What

[15] These sacred spells, in obscure language are derived from various sutras.
[16] The costume described is that of the *yamabushi,* men who perform various ascetic rites and work magical cures through the use of spells.

splendid devotion! This year I've given that worthless scamp of mine four *kan* and 600 *mon* for mountain pilgrimages, journeys to worship En the Ascetic, and heaven knows what else, and he's had four *kan* from his brother Tahei in Junkei Street. He's taken nearly ten *kan* in all, but he's never gone anywhere. He didn't even go to welcome you back. He leads such a dissolute life, never giving a thought to the punishment the gods and Buddhas have in store for him. I wish you'd show your friendship by giving him a good talking to.

NARRATOR: Yohei's mother, Osawa, appears from the back of the house with teacups in her hands.

OSAWA: I congratulate you on your safe return. Here, please have a cup. . . . I suppose it may be a punishment for Yohei's having lied about going to the mountain, but his sister Okachi has been sick with a cold for over a week, and hasn't left her bed. We've changed doctors three times, but her fever still hasn't gone down. The holidays will soon be here. We've made all the arrangements for her wedding, and the boy's family is impatient.[17] There's always something for my husband and me to worry about. It's all a curse that comes from that good-for-nothing Yohei's having lied to En the Ascetic. Young men, I beg you please to pray that he will be forgiven.

NARRATOR: Her voice is earnest. The leader of the pilgrims answers.

LEADER: I'm sure that's not the cause of your daughter's illness. If it were a curse from the mountain, the sickness should have fallen on Yohei. How could the Buddha known as En the Ascetic be so incompetent as to work his punishment on any but the guilty? Your daughter's illness must have some other cause. You won't need medicine or a doctor for that. There's a mountain priest they call the White Fox—(*To the other men.*) you all know about him, don't you?—who works the most amazing cures. He's very popular now. I'm sure Yohei's heard about him too. You ask this mountain priest to help you. I'm positive that it'll take only one prayer to effect a complete cure. Go to him at once and ask his help. He won't refuse.

NARRATOR: She rejoices at his words.

OSAWA: I'm so grateful. I'm sure this must be a sign from the Ascetic. I'll go immediately to the doctor. Please rest here as long as you like.

[17] The husband for Okachi was to be taken into Tokubei's household as his heir; hence Yohei's opposition.

LEADER: No, thank you. We're all anxious to see our parents, our wives and children, and tell them of our safe return.

NARRATOR: Joyfully blowing their conch shells and intoning the sacred spells that vanquish devils, they go their separate ways, chanting, "Deliver us, deliver us."

Tahei of Junkei Street, a man quite unlike his perverse younger brother, comes along, a gloomy, preoccupied look on his face.

TOKUBEI: Is that you, Tahei? Have you come to visit Okachi? You needn't have bothered now, when you're so busy with your accounts.[18]

NARRATOR: Tahei comes up beside him.

TAHEI: I met Mother in the street and I told her the whole story as we stood there, but the fact is, I've just received by messenger a letter with surprising news from Uncle Moriemon. Listen to this.

(*He reads.*) "Last month when I accompanied my master on a pilgrimage to Nozaki, that dissolute wretch Yohei was also at the temple. He became involved in a quarrel with his friends, during the course of which he offered extraordinary insults to my master. I determined to kill Yohei on the spot and commit suicide afterwards, but the matter was peacefully settled, thanks to my master's kind intercession. Since our return, however, the incident has become the sole topic of conversation, not only among the retainers, but even among the townspeople. I cannot continue serving my master, brazenly disregarding the disgrace to my name. I plan to go to Osaka in four or five days. It is impossible to wear my swords any longer unless I can discover a way to restore my honor as a samurai."

That's what his letter says.

NARRATOR: Tokubei strikes his knee.

TOKUBEI: Exactly as I expected. I've known all along that one day he'd commit some serious offense, and I was right. And on top of everything else, there's Okachi's sickness and his uncle's difficulties. There's no telling what mischief the scoundrel may still commit.

NARRATOR: He scratches his head.

TAHEI: Put an end to your worries. Throw him out, once and for all. You've always been too lenient, too timid with both of us, just because we're not your own children. I've thought of you, ever since you mar-

---

[18] On the night before the Boys' Festival (the fifth day of the fifth moon) bills were computed and collected.

ried Mother, as my real father. You still beat Okachi, though she's
big enough to be married, but you've never laid a hand on that idiot.
You've let him do whatever he pleased. Your hesitation about everything has been the worst thing for him. Beat him and drive him from
the house. Send him to me. I'll put him in the service of some harsh
master who'll mend his faults.

TOKUBEI: It's heartbreaking. Yes, I see now that even a stepfather is
after all a father, and that he mustn't hesitate to punish his child. But
you were my master's children. When he passed away you were seven
and that rogue was four. I'm sure he can still remember how I used to
address you both as "young master," and how you would say, "Tokubei, do this. Tokubei, do that." At first, you know, I called your mother
"Ma'am" or "My lady." The marriage was your uncle Moriemon's
idea. He said that if I didn't look after the family my master's widow
and children would be begging in the streets. He urged me to do as he
requested. That's how it happened that my master's lady and I became
man and wife. I've brought up my master's children as my own, and
I've been rewarded by seeing you become independent and successful.
I did everything I could to establish Yohei in business. I gave him
assistants, slaved to build a storehouse for him, but it was like stuffing
money into a pocket with a hole [19] or trying to ladle water with a sieve
—everything trickled away. It's his nature to spend a hundred pieces of
silver for every one he earns. But if I venture to utter one word of
reproach, he pays me back with a thousand. Ah, it all stems from the
fact that the children were a master's, but their stepfather was a servant.
My efforts were bound to be as futile as driving a nail into rotten
wood. My position is hopeless.

NARRATOR: He bites his lips.

TAHEI: That good-for-nothing has taken advantage of your honesty
and trampled you to his heart's content. But thanks to you, Father, the
three of us were never forced to sleep under bridges or stand begging
at people's gates. Mother has told me again and again that the debt
we owe you for having taken care of our family is no less than what
we owe our real father. Your deference to Yohei worries her. She
wonders if it hasn't even made you feel constrained before her, as
Yohei's mother. She told me, "I've had all I can stand of Yohei, that

[19] Literally, a string of copper coins without a knot at the end to keep the coins from
slipping off.

shameless failure. Tahei, I beg you, send him to Edo or Nagasaki. If he dies there, let him die. I never want to see his face again. I haven't a grain of affection left for him." She swore to Buddha that she meant it. Why should you hesitate? Disinherit him.

NARRATOR: Okachi is awakened by the arguing voices.

OKACHI: Ahhh, I have the most terrible pain! Mama, Mama! Isn't Mama back yet?

NARRATOR: Okachi, hidden by a screen, calls out in anguish. At the door a voice is heard.

PRIEST: Excuse me. Is this the house of Tokubei of the Kawachi-ya? I am the priest of the fox-god. I am calling at the request of the mountain brotherhood.

TAHEI: Is he going to pray for Okachi? That's splendid. I must dash off a reply to Uncle Moriemon. I'll be leaving now.

NARRATOR: He goes to the gate.

TAHEI: Tokubei is at home. We most appreciate your having come so soon. Please come in.

NARRATOR: As Tahei leaves, the mountain priest enters the room at the end of the house.

Yohei, the oil merchant, slides through life in slipshod fashion; he squanders on fleshly pleasures whatever money he collects. Now he is squeezed dry—principal, interest, and even the dregs drained from the oil cask he shoulders heavily. His sweat is from summer heat: the cask he carries home is empty and cool as autumn.

YOHEI: What a rare visitor—a mountain priest! I recognize you, you're the White Fox. Have you come to pray for my sister's recovery? I'll lay my head on it that your prayers won't drive out whatever possesses her. (*To Tokubei.*) Mother's gone out for medicine, has she? Okachi's sickness is mortal—the best doctor couldn't cure it. You're all wasting a lot of effort for nothing. Father, there's a more important matter than Okachi's sickness. I told Mother as soon as I heard, but it's slipped my mind ever since. Today I happened to remember, and I stopped work at the shop to come and tell you. Last month I ran into Uncle Moriemon at Nozaki. "It's lucky I met you," he said, "I was about to send a special messenger. I've embezzled over three *kamme* of silver, and if I don't return the money by the holidays I'll be obliged to commit suicide or else be beheaded as a common thief. Tell them I'm asking the favor of a lifetime. I hope that they can scrape the money together without telling Tahei. That scoundrel knows nothing about duty or principles. Let them send the money with you."

That was his message. He was in deadly earnest. It'll reflect on your reputation if you let Uncle commit hara-kiri for a mere two or three *kamme*. You'll never be able to hold your head up again. Today's the twenty-seventh.[20] You have only tomorrow and the day after left. Put everything else aside. Please collect the three *kamme* today and hand them over to me. If I leave the first thing in the morning, I can get to Takatsuki and back by noon.

NARRATOR: He speaks the reverse of the message in his uncle's hand of a few minutes before. Tokubei is both annoyed and amused.

TOKUBEI: He may be your uncle, but any samurai who embezzles his master's money is better off if he commits hara-kiri. Three *kamme* —that's a lot of money. I haven't three coppers to spare. What about your business? You haven't shown us a penny since last year, but if you reckon up your assets, you ought to have three or four *kamme* left. Give him that, if you're so anxious to help. I haven't the time to engage in foolish discussions when my precious daughter has fallen sick, on the eve of her marriage. Priest of the Mountain, I'm sorry to have kept you waiting. Please be so kind as to examine Okachi.

NARRATOR: He changes the subject and takes no further notice of Yohei.

YOHEI: Do you think you'll succeed in marrying her? Go ahead and try. I'll watch.

NARRATOR: He sprawls in front of his father, an abacus for his pillow; he seems to have made a serious miscalculation.

The priest carefully examines Okachi's wasted face as her father gently lifts the girl in his arms.

PRIEST: How old is she?

TOKUBEI: Fifteen.

PRIEST: When did she take sick?

TOKUBEI: On the twelfth of last month.

PRIEST: Hmmm. The feast day of Yakushi Buddha. Fifteen is Amida's number.

NARRATOR: He takes a volume from his kimono, and spreads it open. After some calculations on his fingers, he declaims in portentous tones.

PRIEST: It is written in the play *The Priest of the Treasury of the*

[20] The second day of the fifth moon; bills fall due on the fourth day.

Laws [21] that Amida and Yakushi were once husband and wife, and so forth and so forth. That is to say, Okachi's malady is a melancholy arising from the desire to get married at the earliest possible moment. Some other possession—a minor one—is also involved.

NARRATOR: Tokubei looks convinced, and the priest, pleased with himself, continues.

PRIEST: The teachings of the White Fox, the messenger of the Great God Inari, do not deviate from the truth by so much as a hair's breadth. His prayers and incantations are the same as medicine. Each god and Buddha has his particular function. For the cooling of fevers there are the twenty-one shrines of Mount Hiei,[22] and for the warming of chills, the god of Atsuta.[23] For maladies of the head there is the bodhisattva Atago,[24] for maladies of the feet Ashiku Buddha.[25] Fudō's iron noose keeps absconders and thieves from escaping.[26] The Shrine of the Wind [27] is the place to pray when you have a cough. The White-Whiskered God [28] takes care of the infirmities of age, the all-merciful bodhisattva Jizō of the special malady of fair youths.[29] The god Azabu and Shakyamuni Buddha bring pictures at cards.[30] If you're the banker in a gambling hell, pray for luck to the god of the four, three, five, Six Shrines, the Eight Sermons, and the Seven Sacred Halls.[31] My own specialty is the market in copper and gold coins and rice. I can command the prices to rise or fall at will. I pray on behalf of commodity-

[21] Title of a puppet play (*jōruri*) in six acts (date and author unknown); citation of a popular play instead of a sacred book as authority for a theological point is, of course, intended to be humorous.

[22] The twenty-one shrines of the Hiyoshi Jinja. The name Hiei suggests the word *hie*, meaning "chill".

[23] The name Atsuta contains the word *atsu* (hot).

[24] The name Atago suggests *atama* (head).

[25] The name Ashiku contains *ashi* (foot).

[26] The Guardian King Fudō holds in his left hand a noose with which he catches malefactors. It is called "iron" because no man can untie it.

[27] A small shrine inside the precincts of the Ise Shrine.

[28] Shirahige Myōjin, whose shrine stands on the west shore of Lake Biwa. I have omitted here Shiraga Yakushi, "the White-haired Yakushi," a fictitious deity.

[29] There is a pun on Jizō, which contains the word *ji* (piles).

[30] Playing cards, originally introduced into Japan by the Dutch, had honors called *aza* and *shaka*, here worked into the names of divinities.

[31] Four-three and five-six were recognized combinations in Japanese dice games; here worked into the Six Shrines (Ise, Iwashimizu, Kamo, Matsuo, Inari, and Kasuga). The Eight Sermons were offered at the Jūhō Temple on Mount Hira. The Seven Shrines are the above six plus Hirano.

holders to the eight million gods on the High Plain of Heaven for rising prices and a seller's market. For people short of supplies who want prices to fall, there's the Buddha of Saga and the god of Cheapside.[32] When I pray simultaneously for sellers and buyers, the Great God of High-low [33] in Kawachi Province finds a middle course between cheap and dear. It's as plain as taking something down from a shelf that prayer works miracles. The fee is generally thirty pieces of gold, payable at any time. And now for the prayer.

NARRATOR: He shakes his metal staff and fingers the flat beads of his rosary. Before he can make his magical gestures, the sick girl lifts her heavy head.

OKACHI (*she speaks as in a trance*): I don't want your prayers, and I hate your spells. The way to cure Okachi's sickness is to call off the wedding arrangements. Yohei is tortured by his debts, which are merely the result of youthful indiscretion. His pains bring me agony in the afterworld and will cause me torments in hell. Redeem the woman Yohei loves and to whom he is pledged, though she be a lowly prostitute. Let her be his bride, and give him this household as his own. If you insist on bringing in a husband for Okachi, her life is no more. Have you understood? Take heed!

NARRATOR: She stares wildly around her.

OKACHI: Ohhh—this pain is unbearable!

NARRATOR: She groans in agony and babbles meaninglessly. Her father pales with fright, but the priest is undaunted.

PRIEST: Demon, whence dost thou come? Hie thee hence at once! Hie thee hence! Thinkst thou that the powers of En the Ascetic are defeated by such as thee?

NARRATOR: He brandishes his metal staff and rings his bell, exorcising the spirit with a final "Do as I command!"

Yohei springs to his feet.

YOHEI: What are you talking about? The devil take you and your "Hie thee hence!" Damn you, priest! Not another word from you!

NARRATOR: He pushes the priest from the room.[34]

PRIEST: Are you unaware of the powers of a mountain priest? Do you imagine I shall leave before I have worked a cure?

[32] Saga suggests *sagaru* (to come down [in price]). "Cheapside" is a free rendition of Yasuda, in which *yasu* means "cheap".
[33] Takayasu (dear-cheap) was the site of a shrine.
[34] Literally, to a part of the room on a lower level.

NARRATOR: He rushes into the room and rings his bell, ting-a-ling, ting-a-ling. Every time Yohei drags him out, the priest runs back. Finally, the priest is ejected, amidst grunts and groans suggesting Fudō's sacred spells. He staggers off, his bell a mere tinkle, his life a mere tinkle.

NARRATOR: Yohei, rolling up his kimono, strides to his father.

YOHEI: Did you hear, Father, what Okachi was saying in her delirium? Will you still refuse to let me marry the woman I love, and to give me a place to live, though it means torturing a dead man and sending him into hell? Won't you relent?

TOKUBEI: Don't make such a row. We have neighbors, you know. I've had enough of your impertinence. I was capable, I assure you, of maintaining a family of five or six quite comfortably, even if I had never succeeded to your father's estate. As a matter of fact, I assumed his name in order that I might pray for him on his anniversary, and spare him suffering and the torments of hell. I have been paying for it ever since. Supposing I redeem that prostitute you're so fond of and make her your wife—within six months you'll destroy our fortunes. I won't even be able to pray for your father's repose. I can't permit that.

YOHEI: Then you're absolutely determined to adopt a husband for my sister and give her the household?

TOKUBEI: Yes, that's my intention.

YOHEI: You dare say that! You obstinate fool!

NARRATOR: He rises and kicks Tokubei down on his face, then stamps on his shoulders and spine.

OKACHI: Oh, how dreadful! How depraved of you, Yohei!

NARRATOR: She clings to him.

TOKUBEI: Don't interfere, Okachi. Let him trample me to his heart's content.

NARRATOR: The father lies motionless, making no attempt to escape. His daughter can endure no more.

OKACHI: It's too wicked of you. I didn't know what I was doing. You told me to pretend that I was possessed by a ghost, and dictated every word I was to say. You swore that in the future you'd devote all your energies to your business, and that you'd be a model son and never disobey our parents. I believed you. I was so happy that I agreed. I pretended to be delirious. You made me lie and perform that horrible imitation of a dead man. Now you've kicked and stamped on Father.

Is that your way of being a good son? Father's an old man. He might easily lose consciousness. I won't stand for it.

YOHEI: Damned little strumpet! You swore you wouldn't tell, no matter what happened. You swore up and down, and now you've blabbed, curse your lying face! I'll teach you that you can expect more pain from a living spirit named Yohei than from any dead one!

NARRATOR: He kicks her down, as he kicked his father.

TOKUBEI: Your sister's weak from her sickness. You'll kill her. Monster!

NARRATOR: Yohei kicks aside his father's clutching hand.

YOHEI: You told me to trample you to my heart's content. This is how I content my heart!

NARRATOR: He stamps furiously, not caring whether his feet land on their heads or faces. His mother returns at the height of his frenzy, and, dropping with a cry of dismay the medicine in her hand, she seizes Yohei's hair and topples him to the floor. She falls on him, and her fists pound his face mercilessly.

OSAWA: Shame on you! Villain! [35] The meanest servant, the vilest lackey, would not treat another human being that way. Do you know who Tokubei is? He's your father! Don't you realize that the feet you've kicked him with will soon rot and fall off? You'll be punished. Heartless monster! Some people are born blind or crippled, but their souls at least are human. What did I fail to give your body when I brought you into the world? Why haven't you a human disposition? I've worried about your every gesture, for fear people might say that my second marriage had warped my nature and the change in me had implanted evil thoughts in you. You've sliced years from my life with the sword of your heart. The other day you had the effrontery to deceive your own mother by telling me that your uncle from Takatsuki had embezzled his master's money. But I've just met your brother Tahei, and he showed me your uncle's letter. Your outrageous behavior at Nozaki disgraced him as a samurai, and he's had to resign his post and go down to Osaka. Your deception is exposed. If I had thoughtlessly passed on to Father your lies when you first told them and then the truth had come out, he would have suspected us of acting in collusion. I would have proved utterly wanting in my duties to my husband.

[35] Osawa calls Yohei by the name Daiba, the Japanese version of Devadatta—a villainous, treacherous disciple of Buddha.

Wherever I go, in the neighborhood or the town, I hear gossip about you, and never a good word. Accursed child—with each new outrage you are chopping the flesh from your mother's body bit by bit! You won't remain an hour longer in this house! Get out! You're disinherited!

NARRATOR: She strikes him, she pummels him, but one hand wipes away the tears.

YOHEI: I have nowhere else to go.

OSAWA: Go to that harlot of yours. Stay with her.

NARRATOR: She catches his wrist and pushes him out.

OKACHI: I don't want to inherit the property if Yohei's sent away. Forgive him, please!

OSAWA: What do you know about it? Out of my way. Tokubei, why do you stand there doing nothing? Whom are you afraid of? Oh, it's infuriating! I'll drive him from the house!

NARRATOR: She snatches up a balance pole and brandishes it, but Yohei, adroitly dodging, tears it from her hands.

YOHEI: I'll give you a taste of this pole!

NARRATOR: He furiously belabors her. Tokubei flies at him, and wrenches away the pole. He deals Yohei seven or eight rapid blows, not giving him the chance to catch his breath. His eyes glare with rage, but they hold tears.

TOKUBEI: Even a doll carved of wood or molded from clay would have human feelings if you put a soul in it—but you! Listen to me carefully, if you've still got ears. I'm your father, but I still think of you as my master's child. That's why I let you trample me to your heart's content, without lifting a finger against you. But when you struck your own mother in that unspeakable way, my eyes were too outraged to watch any longer. My body trembled all over. It wasn't I who beat you, but your own father, stretching his arms from the grave. Don't you see that? I can tell you now—the story that I was adopting a husband for Okachi was utterly untrue. Alas! It was a ruse I tried, hoping that if you thought I had chosen your sister to inherit the property you would be shamed into changing your disposition. Don't worry. I intend to give her away as a bride. Her husband won't come here.

Some deep connection from a former life must have made strangers like ourselves into father and child, and you have been twice as dear as a child of my own flesh. When you had smallpox I gave up my ancestors' faith in Amida and temporarily joined the Lotus Sect so that I might pray Nisshin for your recovery.[36] I watched over you in everything you did. I shouldered heavy loads myself without hiring an assistant, because I wanted some day to make you the master of a great establishment. But the more I slaved the more you squandered. If you were a real merchant you'd throw yourself into your work while you're still in your prime, in the hope of becoming the owner of a shop with a thirty or forty foot frontage. But you'd be happy with a six-foot or three-foot frontage! [37] You strike your mother and kick your father. You lie and cheat wherever you go. If you continue in these ways, it's inconceivable that you'll ever be master of a shop. You're more likely to end up the possessor of a prison gibbet.[38] This is the worst grief a father can know.

NARRATOR: He wails uncontrollably.

OSAWA: You exasperate me, Tokubei. Talking to him is like asking riddles of a stone. Do you think he'll listen? (*To Yohei.*) Get out! Get out, I say! I'll call the neighborhood elders [39] if you delay another moment! They'll chase you out!

NARRATOR: She snatches up the pole again and prods Yohei with the point. Brazen and unruly though he is, mention of the elders frightens Yohei. He stands there, consternation on his face.

OKACHI: I won't stay here either if you drive out Yohei.

NARRATOR: Okachi tries to catch her mother's arm, but she pushes the girl back.

OSAWA: Get away at once! Haven't you tasted this pole enough?

NARRATOR: She lifts the pole and pokes Yohei roughly, pushing him outside. As he crosses the narrow groove of the threshold it becomes a river of tears shed at the parting of parents and child. Tokubei intently watches Yohei's figure disappear down the street. He sobs aloud.

TOKUBEI: The older he grows, the more he becomes the living image of the late master—his face, his posture. When I see him standing

---

[36] Nisshin (1407–88) was a celebrated priest of the Nichiren sect. Persons of other sects sometimes became converts for a hundred days in order to pray to Nisshin for a miraculous cure.

[37] The size and importance of shops were calculated by their frontage.

[38] Literally, to become the owner of a prison post (on which heads of decapitated prisoners are exposed).

[39] The elders were groups of five men responsible for the maintenance of order within a ward. In cases of disinheritance the group was informed.

there by the crossroads, I feel as if I'm driving away not Yohei, but my master himself. It's sinful, it's heartbreaking.

NARRATOR: He sinks to the floor and weeps aloud, not caring that others can see. Yohei's mother, though she called him a villain, can no longer restrain the tears. She stands on tiptoes and strains to catch a glimpse of his face, though he is now too far away. He has disappeared, hidden by the neighbors' holiday banners.[40]

ACT THREE

Scene One: The Teshima-ya, the oil shop owned by Shichizae-mon.
Time: May 29, 1721, the evening of the Boys' Festival.

NARRATOR: The Boys' Festival is at hand. Today, as for long years past, every roof is festooned with southernwood and iris, and banners flapping noisily tell which families have boys. At the Teshima-ya, where there are only girls, the master is out collecting bills, and the mistress is busy minding the house, paying the tradesmen's accounts, selling oil, and watching over her three daughters. "I'll start with the oldest," she says, opening her comb box. She rubs some fragrant plum oil into a rough-toothed comb.

> More important than her hair,
> More important than her figure,
> Is the comb that cleanses the dust
> From the heart of a girl.
> The house she goes to when she's married
> Is her husband's house;
> The house she lived in as a girl
> Is her parents' house;
> Apart from the house of her mirror,
> She has no house she can call her own.
> In what age did they first allow us
> On this one night only, the Boys' Festival,
> To speak of a house as a woman's? [41]

[40] During the Boys' Festival, banners (today often paper carp) are displayed outside the houses of families in which there are sons.
[41] Women are in charge of the house because the men and boys are all out celebrating the festival.

She smooths the child's hair with a prayer that nothing will happen to mar this festive month, this festive day. But as she draws the comb through the girl's locks, a tooth snaps. Okichi lets out a doleful cry, and in her dismay throws down the comb, an act abhorred as an omen of separation.[42] She says no word, but her heart is heavy. Does this little comb of boxwood portend something?

Shichizaemon, seven tenths[43] of his bill collecting quickly accomplished, returns home before starting out again.

OKICHI: You've finished earlier than I expected. I've been busy too. I've cleaned up all the household accounts. I've had orders for three quarts of lamp oil and one pint of plum blossom oil from the money-changer in Brokers Lane, and for two quarts of lamp oil on account from the paper shop at Imabashi. I've entered everything in the current ledger. Wash up and get to bed soon. Tomorrow you'll have to get up early to make your holiday calls.

SHICHIZAEMON: No, I can't go to bed yet. I must make a call in Ikeda Street in Temma.

OKICHI: That's a shame. Haven't you done enough for one day? Ikeda Street is at the northern end of town. As long as you've collected the accounts in the neighborhood, you can leave that one for after the holiday.

SHICHIZAEMON: What are you saying? If money's not collected before the holiday it'll never be collected later on. They promised to pay the money after dusk today. I've got to hurry now. Here—this money belt contains 580 me of New Silver. Lock it up in the cupboard with the money in my wallet. I'll be back soon.

NARRATOR: He rises to leave.

OKICHI: In that case, have some saké before you go. Okiku, warm some saké for your father.

NARRATOR: Okiku goes to the cupboard and starts to pour saké from a bottle into a pan.

SHICHIZAEMON: Don't bother to warm it. I won't need anything to

---

[42] Superstitions which may be traced to the episode of the *Kojiki* (Vol. I, sect. ix) in which Izanagi (the male deity) visits Izanami (the female deity) in the world of the dead. At one point he breaks off a tooth of his comb. Later, he is pursued by a demon and escapes by throwing down his comb (which instantly turns into bamboo sprouts). The section ends with his eternal separation from Izanami.

[43] The name Shichizaemon contains the word *shichi* (seven).

eat, or even a cup. Just serve the saké in the lid of a rice bowl. The
night is short and I'm in a hurry. Pour it directly from the bottle.

NARRATOR: Okiku answers "Yes," but she cannot reach his cup if
she remains seated. She stands. Okichi notices that both server and
recipient are standing.

OKICHI: What are you doing? That's bad luck. You should surely
know, even if the child doesn't, that if you drink saké standing up
you'll see somebody to the grave. It sends chills through me.

NARRATOR: Her husband quickly sits. He lifts his cup again.

SHICHIZAEMON: I was about to drink a standing toast to unpaid bills
before I went out collecting. (*Lifts cup.*) Farewell, all unpaid bills!
I'll see you in the grave! You won't be long in this world! [44]

NARRATOR: The more cheerful he tries to make his words, the more
ominous they sound; his departure seems a last farewell. Okiku, a
dutiful daughter, begins to spread out bedding for the night, singing,
"Here are the mats and here the pillows." The mosquito net has long
loops, but she cannot reach them on legs short as summer nights.

OKIKU: I've put Oden to bed and she's comfortable. Mama, you rest
a while too, please.

OKICHI: You're a good girl. Papa probably won't be returning till
late. I'll keep an eye on the front gate from inside the mosquito netting.
You go to sleep now.

OKIKU: No, Mama. I'm not sleepy.

NARRATOR: But even as she speaks she is nodding off, the gentle child.
Try as he may, Yohei of the Kawachi-ya cannot survive the holiday
reckoning: his plans have all been thwarted. Long only in ambitions,
he wears an old kimono with sleeves too short for him and carries a
three-quart oil jug. Tonight, though never before, a dagger is concealed
at his waist—a last resort in his dilemma. He peeps in at the familiar
gate of the Teshima-ya. Behind him a voice calls out.

KOHEI: Is that you, Yohei?

YOHEI: Yes, I'm Yohei. Who are you?

NARRATOR: He turns around and recognizes the moneylender Kohei
from the Cotton Shop in Uemachi.

KOHEI: I've been looking for you. I went to your brother's place in

---

[44] Puns in the text refer at once to the successful collection of bills and to death. The
translation is approximate.

Junkei Street and I was told to try at your parents'. I went there, only to discover they'd kicked you out. But even if you weren't around, your father's seal was still on the note. I decided that unless I got back my *kamme* in New Silver tonight, I'd denounce him to the authorities tomorrow.

YOHEI: You're trying to be nasty. The figure on the face of the note is one *kamme,* it's true, but I actually received only 200 *me.*[45] You promised, didn't you, that if I returned the 200 *me* in the course of the night you wouldn't make any trouble?

KOHEI: Yes, if you return the money by six tomorrow morning, you owe me 200 *me,* but at the crack of dawn tomorrow the debt becomes one *kamme.* I suppose you think it's to my advantage if I get back one *kamme* for my 200 *me,* but I feel sorry for your father, making him pay all that money for a debt he never made. I'm pushing you this way only because I have your interests at heart. Pay me tonight without fail.

YOHEI: You don't have to remind me. I'm a man of my word. I know where I can get the money, and I'll bring it to you before cockcrow. Do me a favor and wait up, even if you get sleepy.

KOHEI: If you still need money after you pay back your debt, I'll lend it to you the first thing tomorrow. That's my business, after all. I'm always glad to lend you a *kamme* or two. I know you're a man of your word.

NARRATOR: With words soft as cotton batting, Kohei of the Cotton Shop closes the vise around Yohei's neck. He departs. Yohei, though he has grandly given his word to pay, has not a penny he can call his own. He managed to avoid paying the teahouse debts, but he cannot escape these 200 *me.*

YOHEI: There must be money somewhere. With all the people in the world, you'd think somebody'd drop a couple of hundred *me* on the street.

NARRATOR: He turns at a noise behind him, and sees a small lantern.

YOHEI: It has "Kawa" written on it. It must be my father's. Damn it!

NARRATOR: He conceals himself, flattening his body like a spider

[45] One *kamme* in New Silver was worth about $1,000. Two hundred *me* was one fifth of that sum.

against the closed doors of the shop. Tokubei does not notice him. He softly opens the side door of the Teshima-ya and steps inside.

TOKUBEI: Shichizaemon—have you finished with your calls?

OKICHI: Tokubei, what a surprise! My husband hasn't finished yet. He's gone off to the outskirts of Temma.—I've been so distracted lately that I haven't had the chance to visit Okachi. It's good of you to come. You must have your hands full with Yohei on top of the holiday reckoning.

NARRATOR: She emerges from the mosquito netting.

TOKUBEI: That's certainly true. You have your little daughters to worry about; we have a full-grown man to give us headaches. But it's a father's job to worry over his children, and I don't consider it any special hardship. It's a great comfort as long as you have your children living with you, but when you disinherit a reprobate like Yohei, there's no telling what he may do. He may get desperate and throw himself in the fire tomorrow.[46] Or he may use a forged or stolen seal on a promissory note for ten *kamme* in order to raise one *kamme,* and suffer the rest of his life for it. I can think of so many grim possibilities. But when his own mother drove him from the house, I was so timid I dared not interfere. I'm only his stepfather, after all. I gather that he's staying with his brother in Junkei Street. If he should happen to wander this way, would you and Shichizaemon tell him that his father has decided to forgive him. Urge him to apologize sincerely to his mother and to return home with a changed disposition.

My wife Osawa's family were all samurai, and that's why, I suppose, it's her way not to go back on any decision she's made. But that libertine doesn't inherit her strict sense of duty. His real father, my master, was a perfect gentleman, a man who understood duty and human feelings too. All my efforts on behalf of his two children were by way of service to my late master. Now I've driven out Yohei. His father, who never in his life used a harsh word, will hate me from the grave. What a misfortune—and I bear it alone! Imagine what this means to me, Okichi.

NARRATOR: He chokes with tears, but pretends, naturally enough, that smoke from his pipe is in his eyes.

OKICHI: I can well imagine. My husband will be back before long. Please wait and talk with him.

[46] Meaning, perhaps, that he will be executed and cremated.

TOKUBEI: No, I know how busy he must be tonight. I'd only be in the way. Look, I have here 300 *mon*. I slipped them in my wallet when my wife wasn't looking, and crept out with them. If Yohei comes, please tell him to use the money to buy a summer kimono. It'll soon be warm. But under no circumstances mention my name. Say that it's a present from Shichizaemon, or anything you think of. I'll be most grateful.

NARRATOR: He offers the money. At the back gate a voice is heard.

OSAWA: Okichi, have you shut up shop for the night?

NARRATOR: The visitor is Osawa. Tokubei is astonished.

TOKUBEI: I don't want her to see me. I must hide. Excuse me, please.

NARRATOR: Osawa glimpses his back as he disappears within the mosquito netting.

OSAWA: Tokubei—why are you hiding from your wife?

NARRATOR: Her husband is thrown into confusion, and Okichi, disconcerted, fails to greet Osawa. Outside, Yohei mutters.

YOHEI: My cantankerous old mother's shown up! What's she got to say, I wonder.

NARRATOR: He presses his ear to the door bar and listens intently. Osawa sits on the step.

OSAWA: Well, Tokubei, what brings you here? What business is so urgent with neighbors from across the street you can meet any time? You rushed through your work at home to come here tonight when we're all so busy and Shichizaemon is away. What can it be? You're past the age for mischief. Have you come to complain about Yohei? You take your obligations as a stepfather much too seriously. His own mother chased him out—it won't give you a bad reputation. Do you intend to give these 300 *mon* to that ruffian? After you've always begrudged every penny spent on yourself—it's like throwing money down a well. Your pampering has been his poison. That's not the way I do things. Once I pronounce the word "disinherited", it's final. If he falls into the river in paper clothes or catches fire when his body is smeared with oil, let him, for all I care. You allow that criminal to steal all of your attention. Doesn't it matter what happens to your wife and daughter? Please go home now, ahead of me.

NARRATOR: He shakes off her hand tugging at his sleeve.

TOKUBEI: That's cruel of you, Osawa, and you're wrong. Nobody can act like a parent as soon as he's born. It takes years for a child to become a parent, and every parent was once a child. A child grows up by his parents' love. A parent, in turn, rises through his child's devotion. I haven't been very lucky myself. I had always thought that, even though I've never been able to afford servants during my lifetime, at least at my funeral, whenever I died, I would have two sons to bear my coffin, one in front and one behind. I thought how much more glorious a death that would be than if a hundred strangers saw my coffin to the grave. I have sons, it is true, but they do me no good. Rather than have my coffin carried by people who are nothing to me, I'd sooner drop on the road and be shunted on a board to a pauper's grave.

NARRATOR: He chokes again with tears, a pitiful sight.

OSAWA: Yohei's not your only child. There's Tahei and—she's a girl, of course, but isn't Okachi your child? Come, hurry back home.

TOKUBEI: If I'm to leave, let's go together. Come with me.

NARRATOR: He pulls Osawa's sleeve. Something falls from the fold of her kimono and drops heavily on the board floor. What was that? A *chimaki*[47] and 500 *mon*.

OSAWA: Oh, dear! How embarrassing!

NARRATOR: She throws herself over the money, hiding it. Her voice rises in grief.

OSAWA: Tokubei, forgive me, I beg you! This money was taken from the collection of our accounts, 500 *mon* I stole to give to Yohei. After twenty years of married life! It'd break my heart if you thought something had come between us. How could I, his mother, hate that wicked creature, even if he were like those people they tell of in sermons, the idiot Shurihandoku or the fiendish Prince Ajase?[48] Some evil deed of mine, some evil connection from a past existence, must account for such a child's having come from my womb. My guilt makes me feel twice the pity and love a father could have for him. But I was afraid that if I showed my pity too openly, you, being only his stepfather, might have thought me a doting mother. I was sure that you'd hate me for shielding Yohei excessively, and making it the harder for him to mend his ways. So I deliberately acted unkind. I beat him cruelly. I demanded that you chase him out of the house and

[47] A kind of sweet wrapped in bamboo leaves, eaten especially at the time of the Boys' Festival.
[48] Shurihandoku (Kṣudrapanthaka) was the most foolish of Buddha's disciples. Prince Ajase (Ajāśatru) killed his father and imprisoned his mother.

disinherit him. I treated him harshly because I wanted you to feel sorry for him. It was a woman's foolish trick. Forgive me please, Tokubei. I scolded you bitterly for leaving that money without telling me, but in my heart I thanked you three times over. I'll tell you why I stole for him. The rogue has always been something of a dandy, and I was sure he'd want to mix in society, smartly groomed and barbered, especially during this festive season. He's received presents at every Boys' Festival since he was born, and I wanted to give him something this time at least, if never again. That's why I exposed myself to shame in such an ignominious fashion. I planned to ask Okichi to send him this money. And I would do more. If some doctor prescribed as a cure for Yohei's evil disposition a medicine infused from his mother's liver, torn from her living body, I would gladly be hacked into eight pieces. I stand revealed before you, a wife who never in her life made a penny's mistake with her husband's money, but was led by love of her child into darkness.[49] I have stolen, and I am ashamed.

NARRATOR: She bursts into wails. Her husband sighs in understanding, and Okichi, who has children of her own, weeps sympathetically as she thinks of their future. The mournful droning of mosquitoes makes them weep all the more.

TOKUBEI: This senseless weeping and wailing doesn't suit the holiday season. Leave your money with Okichi. Ask her to give it to Yohei. Let us excuse ourselves now.

NARRATOR: His wife is overwhelmed by tears.

OSAWA: How can you give him this stolen money? You've already provided for him amply, out of the goodness of your heart.

TOKUBEI: It doesn't matter. Let him have it by all means.

OSAWA: No, I can't. Please forgive me.

NARRATOR: Husband and wife are deadlocked by their sense of duty to each other. Okichi is scarcely able to restrain her tears.

OKICHI: I understand your feelings, Osawa. Of course it's difficult for you to give Yohei the money. Let it stay on the floor where it fell. When some suitable person comes along, I'll ask him to retrieve it.

OSAWA: Thank you. And, if I may ask one more favor, please feed this *chimaki* to a suitable dog.

[49] Allusion to the poem (no. 1103 in *Gosenshū*) by Fujiwara no Kanesuke (877–933): "Though a parent's heart is not in darkness, it will wander for love of a child."

NARRATOR: Again the parents burst into tears. Their hearts were never divided, but the bar dropped between them by their son's misconduct is lifted now. Through the open door husband and wife leave together.

Yohei, seeing his parents depart, nods to himself. Unsheathing the dagger at his side, he slips it into the fold of his kimono. He deftly opens the bolted side door. Once inside, he fastens the door again and pauses a moment to steady his nerves.

YOHEI: Where's Shichizaemon gone? His accounts've all been collected, I'm sure.

NARRATOR: He calls Okichi from a distance, sounding her out.

OKICHI: Is that you, Yohei? I was wondering who it was. What a lucky fellow you are! You've come at the right moment, not a minute too late or too soon. Look—800 *mon* and a *chimaki* have dropped down from heaven with the command that I give them to you! Please take them. They say, you know, that even a disinherited son's luck improves with money he gets at the Boys' Festival.

NARRATOR: Yohei shows not the least surprise.

YOHEI: Is this some charity from my parents?

OKICHI: That's a hasty conclusion. Why should your parents give you money after chasing you from the house?

YOHEI: There's no point in pretending. I was listening at the door all the while, though the mosquitoes were devouring me. I wept through the whole sad story.

OKICHI: You heard everything? Did you understand what your parents have gone through? I'm only an outsider, but my eyes are swollen with weeping. You mustn't waste a penny of this money. Use it carefully and honestly in your business. Make sure that your parents are carried in state at their funerals. Otherwise, you don't count as a man or anything else. If you disobey your parents, Heaven will punish you, Buddha will punish you, and the gods of Japan will wreak their terrible punishment.[50] No good can come to you in the future. But now, accept the money.

YOHEI: I do understand perfectly. I understand that from now on I must become a good son and devote my strength to serving my parents. However, this precious money, this gift of their love, is not enough. I have certain obligations which I can't reveal even to my parents or

[50] Punishment is promised from Confucian, Buddhist, and Shinto sources.

my brother. I'm sure you have in the shop some cash on hand or money collected from accounts. I beg you, lend me 200 *me* of New Silver, that's all, until my parents call off my disinheritance.

OKICHI: Ah, your words betray you! In what way have you reformed? Your sense of decency should keep you from asking me for money, even as a joke. I suppose you intend, though it violates all propriety, to borrow money to pay your debts in the houses of ill fame so that you can start frequenting them again. Yes, it's true, we have 500 *me* of New Silver in the inner safe, and other money besides, but how could I possibly lend a single copper when my husband's away? The day of the pilgrimage to Nozaki I merely helped wash your clothes, and I was suspected of improper conduct. It took days to explain it away. No, the thought is odious. Please take that money and go. Don't come back till my husband returns.

NARRATOR: He edges up as she speaks.

YOHEI: Commit an improper act, then. Please lend me what I ask.

OKICHI: After I've told you that I wouldn't! You really are trying.

YOHEI: I won't be trying any more. Please lend me the money.

OKICHI: If you think you can make sport of me because I'm a woman, I'll scream.

YOHEI: I'm human too. My parents' words have sunk deep into my heart. I'm miserable. Could I at such a time think of making sport of you? I won't hide anything. On the fifteenth of the month I forged my father's seal and borrowed 200 *me* of New Silver, payable tonight. (*Okichi starts to interrupt.*)—No, please listen to the rest. The promissory note reads one *kamme* in New Silver, though I borrowed only 200 *me*. I promised that if I failed to return the money tonight I would pay one *kamme* tomorrow, as it says on the note. What upsets me most is that the moneylender is sure to denounce me not only to my father and brother but to the elders and five-man associations of their wards. Things have reached a point where neither tears nor laughter will help me raise the money. I've decided to kill myself and make an end to it. I left the house with this dagger hidden in my kimono. But when I heard my parents grieving and worrying over me, I thought how heavily the debt would weigh on them if I killed myself. My crowning act of wickedness would be to bring about their financial ruin. The more I considered it, the less I could commit suicide. I'm begging you, trusting to your goodness. If you hadn't the money, it couldn't be helped, but since the money is here, all I'm asking for is just 200 *me,* an act of mercy to save my life. I'll never forget your kindness, not even if I sink into the pit of hell. Okichi, please, I beg you. Lend me the money.

NARRATOR: The look in his eyes seems so genuine that Okichi thinks he may be telling the truth, but on reflection she decides, in view of his previous lies, that he must be up to another trick.

OKICHI: Such lies and told with such an honest expression! Go ahead, invent whatever stories you please, but when I said that I wouldn't give you the money, I meant it definitely.

YOHEI: You won't give it, even after I've sworn on my honor as a man? What am I to do?—Very well. I won't ask to borrow from you.

NARRATOR: As he speaks a plan is forming in his mind.

YOHEI: In that case, please fill this cask with three quarts of oil on credit.

OKICHI: That means business for both of us. There'd never be any business if there weren't lending and borrowing. Yes, I'll certainly fill it.

NARRATOR: She goes to the shop and, never suspecting that the lamp of her life will flicker out in the brief moments she measures out the oil, she takes up her measuring box and ladle. She does not see, she does not know that behind her, his merciless dagger drawn, Yohei is waiting.

OKICHI: Spend the holiday in good cheer. I shouldn't be surprised if, after you've had a heart-to-heart talk with my husband, he decides to help you, providing of course he can spare the money. Please don't bear me any grudge for refusing you. Even among couples who've been married for fifty or sixty years, the wife is not accustomed to act as she pleases.

NARRATOR: Okichi is startled as she speaks by the glint of his blade reflected in the lamp oil.

OKICHI: What was that just now, Yohei?

YOHEI: It wasn't anything.

NARRATOR: He hides the dagger behind him.

OKICHI: Why do you stare at me with that terrible expression? Show me what you have in your right hand.

NARRATOR: He shifts the dagger to his other hand.

YOHEI: See—there's nothing in it, nothing at all.

NARRATOR: Okichi is trembling, despite his reassurance.

OKICHI: There's something terrifying about you. Don't come any closer.

NARRATOR: She steps backwards towards the entrance, and tries to unfasten the door behind her to escape.

YOHEI: Why are you looking so scared?

NARRATOR: He follows her from place to place.

OKICHI: Help, somebody!

NARRATOR: She emits this one shriek and Yohei, not waiting for another, flies at her. He seizes her in his grip.

YOHEI: I'll teach you to raise your voice, hussy!

NARRATOR: He plunges his dagger into her throat. Her arms and legs flail out in agony.

OKICHI: I won't raise my voice again. If I die, my three little children will be left to wander the streets. Those poor children! I don't want to die. Take all the money you want, but spare my life please, Yohei.

YOHEI: I'm sure you don't want to die. That's natural. But I feel just as sorry for my father who loves me as you feel for your daughters. I must pay the money and reestablish my reputation. Resign yourself —die quietly. People might hear if I prayed aloud, but I'll invoke Amida's name in my heart for you. *Namu Amida. Namu Amida Butsu.*

NARRATOR: He pulls her to him and slashes from right to left, down to her waist, hacking and slicing with the blade. A night wind from the world of the dead welcomes Okichi, noisily fluttering the banners at the gate, and the light in the shop is extinguished by the swirling gust. In the darkness enveloping the room and his heart, Yohei slips and slides on the spilled oil and flowing blood. His blood-smeared body, his reddened face belong to a demon in hell. Shaking the horns of evil that sprout from his head, he rends Okichi's body. She climbs the Mountain of Swords, and before her eyes are the torments of the Hell of Oil.[51] People hang irises at the eaves on this festive day to ward off a thousand sicknesses, but there is no escape from the sickness of the sins of a past existence. Brief-lived as the dew on an iris blade, the spirit departs, her breathing has ceased.

Yohei looks at the dead face, formerly so high-spirited, and a shudder

---

[51] The Mountain of Swords is a region of hell. Commentators have suggested that the Hell of Oil, from which this play derives its subtitle, was a variation by Chikamatsu on the familiar Lake of Blood, oil being especially suited to the professions of the characters.

goes through him. His courage fails, his knees shake, and he struggles
to steady his heaving breast. He tears from Okichi the key she carries
and, darting a glance inside the mosquito netting, trembles again as
he imagines that the faces of the children, peacefully sleeping, glare
at him. He turns the key in the lock. The grating noise strikes him
with terror, like a sudden clap of thunder overhead. He presses his
body against the safe, and pulls out the money belt. It holds 580 *me*
of New Silver, just as Okichi had led him to expect. He stuffs it hastily
into the front of his kimono. It weighs him down and his steps are
heavy. He walks as though over thin ice or flames.

YOHEI: I'll throw the dagger into the river from Sandalwood
Bridge.[52] As it sinks, so I will one day sink in hell. But that is for the
future to decide. My luck in this world is just beginning.

NARRATOR: He slips out of the house and runs away, as fast as his
legs will carry him.

Scene Two: The Shimmachi Licensed Quarter.
Time: July 11, 1721.

NARRATOR: The spring in Osaka yields to that of Kyoto, but Kyoto
is no match for Osaka during the Summer Music of the Waterless
Moon.[53] The four streets of the Shimmachi Quarter are filled with flowers that know no fading through the four seasons; the brilliant costumes
of the throngs of courtesans, the splendor of the teahouses, make this a
mountain of love, the most glorious scenery in Japan, unrivaled even by
Fuji. The brothel-keepers complain that a year of 360 days is three gift
days short,[54] but the more the gift days, the more the courtesans impose
on their guests, and some are forced to break their engagements. Others
—the patrons of the grand establishments—can be depended on to
offer their presents with good grace; they arrive on gift days, more
imposing than ever, borne in their flying palanquins. The customers
of the lesser teahouses sneak in, faces hidden behind fans. Large parties,
a courtesan for each customer, are common enough these days. Men

---

[52] A bridge (Sendanoki) connecting Kitahama and Nakanoshima in Osaka.

[53] The Waterless Moon (*minazuki*) was a poetic name for the sixth moon. The Summer
Music (*natsukagura*) was performed at two Shinto shrines in Osaka.

[54] Gift days (*mombi*) were days on which customers were obliged to offer presents to
the brothels they patronized. There were thirty-three such days a year, averaging about
three a month. But this year (1721) there was a leap month, and the proprietors felt
cheated of three days.

who swagger through the quarter are merely window-shopping, and those who ask about courtesans' ranks are clearly country bumpkins. The regular customers are chatting in bed, and the courtesans' invited guests [55] smugly whisper, "The curfew drum has sounded already." Some have parents or masters to pay for their pleasures; others destroy their own fortunes; and bankrupts mingle among them. Passersby in in the streets, ashamed, it would seem, to keep silent a moment, imitate the gestures and voices of Kabuki actors, sing songs or snatches from puppet plays, bandy jokes back and forth from West Gate to East Gate, as they come and go at their pleasure: the great crowds each evening tell how prosperous are the times.

Yamamoto Moriemon, amazed at reports of Yohei's actions, has taken temporary leave of his master and journeyed to Osaka. Nobody knows for sure that Yohei murdered the woman and stole the money, but his loose conduct has aroused general suspicion. Moriemon, wondering if the rumors are true, decides to investigate, but Yohei is never at home. Moriemon searches from place to place and comes at last to the quarter. He inquires at the East Gate, and they tell him that Yohei should be at such and such a place. But all the houses are of the same construction and he hesitates, uncertain which is the Bizen House, the Bizen House they told him about. A courtesan's maid trips by from the West Gate, a bulky letter in her hand.

MORIEMON: Excuse me, please. Could you tell me which of these brothels is the Bizen House? And kindly inform me if you know where I can find a courtesan named Matsukaze of that house. I'm a stranger in this neighborhood, and I would appreciate your help.

NARRATOR: He speaks stiffly.

GIRL: What a solemn way you have of talking! This is the Bizen House here. The room at the west end with the door shut is Matsukaze's.[56] She must be entertaining a guest. There, samurai! Lift your left leg. That's right! Now lift your right leg. Very well lifted! I'm terribly obliged!

NARRATOR: She prances off, mocking him.

MORIEMON: Very familiar with people! It's what you'd expect in such a place. Impudent little baggage!

[55] The paramours of the courtesans, who sometimes lived off the courtesans' earnings.
[56] Lower-class brothels in Osaka were built in rows of small rooms, each with direct access to the street.

NARRATOR: He laughs. He goes to the room the girl indicated but, though he can see a light burning inside, the door is firmly bolted.

MORIEMON: The customer is surely Yohei. I'll grab him when he comes out.

NARRATOR: He has not long to wait. The door opens, and a man wearing a wicker hat emerges. Moriemon pinions the man at once. The prostitute follows them out in alarm.

MATSUKAZE: Who are you? Don't start any trouble.

NARRATOR: She pulls them apart.

MORIEMON: Don't worry. I'm not starting any trouble. Yohei, you scoundrel! Did you think I wouldn't find you if you hid?

NARRATOR: He rips off the hat and looks the man in the face.

MORIEMON: Good heavens! You're not Yohei! I've made a mistake. Please forgive me. I'm thoroughly ashamed.

NARRATOR: He bows deeply and rubs his hands in apology. The other man—he must be indulging in a secret amour—merely nods and, hiding his face, runs off towards the East Gate.

MORIEMON: Matsukaze, I've heard that you and Yohei are on intimate terms. Hasn't he been here in the last day or two? I have some business with him—nothing for you to worry about—and that's why I've come. It'll do him no good if you hide the truth. Please tell me.

MATSUKAZE: He was here a little while ago, but he went off saying something about an urgent call in Sonezaki.

MORIEMON: He's gone to Sonezaki? Damn it. I've come too late. I'll have to go after him. But while I'm at it, I have one more question to ask. Has Yohei at any time from around the Boys' Festival to the present—today's the eleventh of July already—paid his debts or spent a great deal of money here? Don't hide anything from me.

MATSUKAZE: He may have. I don't know about money matters. You should ask the Chaser.

NARRATOR: She breaks off the conversation and abruptly returns to her room.

MORIEMON: I blundered that time. Well, in that case, the way to find out is to confront Yohei himself. It's just a jump and a step to Sonezaki. I know the way.

NARRATOR: Tucking up his kimono around his waist, he rushes off impatiently.

Scene Three: The Licensed Quarter in Sonezaki.

NARRATOR:

> Nights when I wait for you, wait for you,
> I hate the West, I hate the East,
> I hate the South.
> Nights when I wait for you,
> The North is best.[57]

Kogiku too waits for Yohei, and he in his infatuation visits her so often that even the street dogs know him by sight. So eager is he to see Kogiku that he deserts the flowers of Shimmachi like the north-ward-flying geese [58] to make his way to the Flower House by Shijimi River. The widow Okamé comes out to greet him.

OKAMÉ: It's customary to welcome guests who come only once in a while by saying, "We're honored by your visit," but in your case, Yohei, this is your house. Shall I be a little original and say instead, "Welcome home!" (*To maid.*) Call Kogiku.—We're full up this evening, upstairs and downstairs, every last room. Why don't you sit here on a bench by the river and have a drink outside? [59] Oh, Kogiku —come sit here. (*To maid.*) Put some oil in the lamps. Speaking of oil, I hear that Kōzaemon's done a play on the murder of the oil merchant's wife, except he's changed it to a saké merchant.[60] Bunzō takes the part of the murderer. They say he's positively loathsome. Haven't you seen it yet, Yohei? Do go, and take Kogiku along. Oh, there aren't any cups! (*To maid.*) Bring the cups!

NARRATOR: She carries on a lively monologue.

YOHEI: Widow, control yourself and let someone else say a word. I've never in my life drunk saké on such a filthy bench, but I forgive you this time. You should rent the premises to the east and build a special wing for my use. I'll honor you by paying all the expenses— lumber, carpentry, and the rest. How's that for a promise?—What disgustingly thin slices of fish-paste you serve!

---

[57] A pun on *kita* (north) and *kita* (you have come): nights when you have come are best.
[58] An untranslatable pun, plus a reference to Sonezaki's location north of Shimmachi. Wild geese, of course, fly north in the spring.
[59] Literally, a carpenter's drink—a pun on *nomi* (a chisel) and *nomi* (a drink).
[60] A Kabuki play on this theme opened on the seventh day of the seventh moon of 1721, eight days before Chikamatsu's play was performed.

NARRATOR: He boasts of extravagances beyond his means, furiously guzzling saké all the while.

YAGORŌ: Yohei—so this is where you've been, is it? I've got something to tell you.

NARRATOR: Yagorō the Brush sits on the bench.

YAGORŌ: A samurai is looking for you.

YOHEI: A samurai! What kind of samurai?

NARRATOR: The lump of evil deeds concealed in his heart sends chills of foreboding through his breast. Sudden agitation sweeps him, and he stares wildly around him.

YAGORŌ: There's nothing to get upset about. It's that samurai who's been staying since yesterday at your brother's place.

NARRATOR: Yohei thinks, "What a relief! It's my uncle Moriemon from Takatsuki. I certainly don't want to meet him, and he may come looking for me here. The best thing would be to leave quickly and avoid him." But he cannot suddenly run away. He searches for some pretext.

YOHEI: Oh, I've just remembered. I forgot my wallet in Shimmachi. It was stuffed so full of money it was positively groaning. I'll run over and be back before you know it. Brush, you come with me.

NARRATOR: He rises, but Kogiku stays him.

KOGIKU: Why are you so excited? As long as you know where the wallet is, you can pick it up tomorrow.

YOHEI: No, I can't. It's no fun being here unless I've got enough money on me.

NARRATOR: He shakes loose his sleeve, and the two men hurry off in search of a wallet which has never been forgotten, boasting of imaginary riches. In less time than it takes to drink four or five cups of hot tea, Moriemon appears at the gate of the Flower House, guided by its lantern.

MORIEMON: I want to see the madam. Tell her to come here.

NARRATOR: He summons her.

MORIEMON: I'm looking for Yohei of the Kawachi-ya. Is he upstairs or downstairs? I'm going in.

NARRATOR: He marches boldly inside.

OKAMÉ: Wait, wait, please. He left a moment ago saying he'd forgotten his wallet in Sonezaki.

MORIEMON: What—he's gone!

OKAMÉ: He can't have gone much farther than Umeda Bridge.

MORIEMON: Too late again. Give Yohei something to drink as soon as he returns, even if it isn't till tomorrow, and keep him here. Don't forget to send word to Tokubei of the Kawachi-ya.

I stopped off on my way here at Sakurai House—Gembei's—and they told me that Yohei paid them three *ryō* in gold and 800 *mon* the night before the Boys' Festival. How much did he pay you? It won't do him any good if you conceal the facts. Tell me the truth.

OKAMÉ: He came here the same night and paid us three *ryō* in gold and one thousand coppers.

MORIEMON: What was he wearing that night?

OKAMÉ: A lined cotton kimono with wide sleeves. I'm almost certain it was light blue, but I couldn't swear to it.

MORIEMON: Very well. You can go back inside now.

NARRATOR: With these parting words he takes the road by which he has come, back to Shimmachi.

Scene Four: Shichizaemon's House.
Time: The thirty-fifth night after the murder of Okichi.

NARRATOR: "He prayed that women would be reborn as men, and vowed that they would gain Buddhahood.[61] May he in his charity grant to all creatures equal enlightenment, and cause them to dwell in the land of peace and happiness."

Fellow-worshipers have gathered on the thirty-fifth night to mourn the death of Myōi, the disciple of Buddha.[62] The service has already concluded. The oldest mourner is Gorokurō, the ledger paper merchant.

GOROKURŌ: It seems like only yesterday that Okichi died, but it is already the thirty-fifth night. She was a mere twenty-seven years of age when she met this unexpected, tragic end, but in her everyday goodness of disposition she excelled others, and her heart was filled with profound gratitude to Saint Shinran for his blessings. In this world indeed she suffered the pain of a sword, but in the life to come

---

[61] In the Amida sects, of which this is a text, women could not gain Buddhahood directly, but had first to be reborn as men.

[62] Okichi's posthumous name.

she will be spared all grief from former sins, and there can be no doubt but that she will go to the Pure Land promised us in the Original Vow.[63] Let your hearts awaken to this summons to the faith, and perform the Invocation of the Name with the more fervor and joy. Shichizaemon, do not, I implore you, give yourself to lamentations. The murderer will soon be discovered. Your most important task now is to look after your daughters. That will bring the greatest happiness to the departed one.

NARRATOR: Shichizaemon melts in tears at these words of comfort.

SHICHIZAEMON: Yes, I am sure that is so. I shall forget about Okichi and redouble my faith, rejoicing in the Buddha's mercy. Awake or asleep I shall not neglect to invoke the holy name. And yet, I cannot help worrying about the children. The youngest, Oden, is only two years old. My heart went out to the poor child deprived of her mother's milk. I sent her to a nurse the day after Okichi's death, with some money for her care. I explained to the oldest girl what had happened, and she understood. Now she spends all her time by the altar, making sure there are always flowers and incense. But the middle daughter howls morning, noon, and night for her mother. I am at my wits' end.

NARRATOR: He turns quickly towards the wall behind them and silently sobs. The other worshipers murmur, "Yes, you must be," and there is not a dry sleeve among them. At this moment a rat races over the beams and rafters of the living room, kicking up a great quantity of soot and dust. It dislodges a scrap of paper before its rampage subsides.

MOURNER: Something's fallen down, Shichizaemon.

SHICHIZAEMON: Yes, what can it be?

NARRATOR: He picks up a piece of paper and examines it. On a half sheet is written the single item "Ten *momme,* one *bu,* five *rin.*[64] Share of expenses at Nozaki. May 28th." There is no indication of an address or sender, but here and there, though the color has changed, the bill is stained with blood. The paper is passed from hand to hand with expressions of amazement.

MOURNER A: I've seen this handwriting before, whosever it is.

[63] Amida Buddha vowed that all who invoked his name would go after death to the Pure Land.

[64] *Momme, bu,* and *rin* were silver coins; the total value was about $10.00.

MOURNER B: I'm sure I've seen it too.

SHICHIZAEMON: It's Yohei's, Yohei of the Kawachi-ya.

MOURNERS: Yes, yes, that's right.

NARRATOR: When four or five mourners determine that the hand is Yohei's, Shichizaemon speaks.

SHICHIZAEMON: Yes, I remember now the dead person telling me that on the sixth of May, the day we worshiped at Nozaki, Redface Zembei, Yagorō the Brush, and Yohei visited the temple together. This bill must be for somebody's share of the expenses. It gives us a clue to the murderer of Okichi. I'm sure that the rat knocked down the paper tonight, the thirty-fifth night of mourning, as a sign from the dead person. This too I owe to Buddha's mercy. *Namu Amida Butsu.*

NARRATOR: He makes an obeisance and his heart rejoices.

Yohei has been paying occasional condolence calls, despite the unpleasant feelings they arouse, in the hope that they will prevent people from realizing that he committed the murder. He enters now, announcing himself, twice as arrogant as ever but wearing an expression of innocence.

YOHEI: It's already the thirty-fifth night, and the murderer is still at large. A shocking business. But I'm sure he'll be found soon.

NARRATOR: From his mouth comes the oracle the others await. Shichizaemon, hitching up his kimono, seizes a stick.

SHICHIZAEMON: Yohei! You killed my wife, didn't you? Have you come here so we could arrest you? You won't escape!

NARRATOR: He lifts his stick menacingly.

YOHEI: Don't lose your head, Shichizaemon. What proof have you I killed her?

SHICHIZAEMON: Hold your tongue. Here's a note, unquestionably in your hand, demanding a share of the expenses of the visit to Nozaki. It's spattered with blood. What further proof is needed? Catch him, friends!

NARRATOR: Yohei sees that he stands revealed and will soon be caught, but he controls the emotions surging in his breast and forces a smile.

YOHEI: Is it inconceivable that in this wide world several people might have similar handwritings? I paid all the expenses for the visit to Nozaki, and I know nothing about sharing a bill. At your age it doesn't become you to talk like a fool. And what do you people mean by making such a row?

SHICHIZAEMON: The first thing we'll do is this!

NARRATOR: He clutches at Yohei, who fends him off. When he approaches, Yohei kicks him down and stamps on him, making the greatest display of strength of his life. He twists away Shichizaemon's stick and, waving it once in the air, runs off with a shout. He looks for an avenue of escape, but the mourners surround him with cries of "You won't get away!" While they battle to and fro in the little garden, Yohei at last sees his chance. Flinging open the side gate, he rushes outside. Several men have been waiting at the gate, and they pounce on him with shouts of "We've got him!" They twist him to the ground. These are the chief of police and other officers. Moriemon, coming up behind them, calls to Yohei.

MORIEMON: These gentlemen have been standing by the gate since you arrived. They've heard every word spoken inside. Don't attempt to make any cowardly excuses.—Yes, it was inevitable, I suppose. Nine out of every ten people I heard gossiping named you as the murderer. Imagine how I felt each time I heard such talk. I thought I'd send you off to some distant province before the truth was brought to light, or else urge you to commit suicide and hide your shame. But I missed you everywhere I visited in Shimmachi and Sonezaki. That was your misfortune. Tahei, bring Yohei's kimono here. This is the kimono you wore on the eve of the Boys' Festival. It's stained in places and stiff. The suspicions of the police have been aroused, and they are investigating to discover whether or not this kimono is positive proof of your guilt. Your fate is hovering between life and death. Bring me saké, somebody.

NARRATOR: Several men bring flasks and a pan to warm the saké. Moriemon pours the gurgling saké onto the kimono. Moriemon and Tahei, brokenhearted, weep to have such a nephew, such a brother: before their eyes the saké turns blood red wherever it strikes the stains on the kimono. Moriemon and Tahei exchange glances, unable to utter more than sighs of dismay.

Yohei speaks at last in tones of resignation.

YOHEI: All my life I've been a bad son and a profligate, but I never stole so much as a sheet of paper or a copper coin. I could have been six months or even a year late in paying my bills at the teahouses and brothels without running into any trouble. But I borrowed money on a promissory note calling for one *kamme* of silver, and if I failed to pay that bill before the night was over, it would have ruined my father. All I could think of was how wicked it would be to compound my crimes of unfilial behavior. I did not consider the consequences, the grief and suffering I would bring to others by this murder. Twenty years an an unfilial son and the evil karma from my lawlessness turned me into a devil and blinded my mind's eye. I, Yohei, killed Okichi and stole her money. Amida Buddha, I call on thee. Have mercy on the murdered woman and on her murderer!

NARRATOR: The men seize him before he can finish, and bind him with thick ropes. His arms are pinned behind him, and his head pressed down. By now the people of the neighborhood have rushed to the scene. They drag him at once to his final destination, the execution grounds at Sennichi.[65] In a thousand days a thousand people hear of the crime, and when ten thousand hear, the numbers soon swell to a hundred thousand. Yohei's fate will serve as a lesson to everyone; the evil reputation he leaves will long be remembered, even in these glorious times.

[65] Sennichi was the site of the execution grounds in Osaka. The word *sennichi* means "a thousand days", and both senses are intended here.

APPENDIX I

A NOTE ON PROSTITUTION
IN CHIKAMATSU'S PLAYS

Most of Chikamatsu's domestic plays are directly connected with the activities of the gay quarters, and scenes or whole acts of some of the history plays are also set in this world. The prominence of prostitution in the plays of course reflects conditions in society. In the major cities of Chikamatsu's day the licensed quarters were a center of urban life. It was no disgrace for townsmen to visit the quarters, and their affairs with prostitutes were matters of common gossip. Samurai also frequently visited the quarters, though they might feel obliged to conceal their faces beneath broad wicker hats.

Townsmen and samurai alike went to the quarters for an escape from the tensions and obligations of the feudalistic society in which they lived. They were also likely to be bored with married life. The long-suffering, obedient Japanese wife, for all her virtues, was not an especially interesting partner in conversation, and married men (as well as young blades) found female companionship in the quarters.

In 1679 there were over one hundred licensed quarters in Japan.[1] The courtesans were divided into two classes, the *age-jorō* and the *mise-jorō*. The *age-jorō* was often women of considerable culture whose skill in the arts or conversation won them renown. Though prostitutes, they were privileged to refuse would-be customers. Azuma in *The Uprooted Pine* is a *tayū*, the highest rank of *age-jorō*, and she is represented as refusing her favors to all men except her sweetheart Yojibei. The *mise-jorō*, on the other hand, were common prostitutes, obliged to sleep with any man who paid their fees. Most of the courtesans in Chikamatsu's plays are of this class. He is frequently at pains

[1] See the illuminating article by Ivan Morris, "Hierarchy of Lust in 17th Century Japan" (*Today's Japan*, August, 1960).

to show that, although these women are reputed to be cold-hearted and calculating, they actually possess the deepest affections. Ohatsu in *The Love Suicides at Sonezaki* and Koharu in *The Love Suicides at Amijima* are among the *mise-joro* who join the men they love in death.

Both *age-joro* and *mise-joro* were ranked in an elaborate hierarchy. The three top classes of *age-joro* were the *tayū, tenjin,* and *kakoi,* known also as Pines, Plum-blossoms, and Maple-leaves because of complicated literary allusions. Below these lofty ranks came the Tides, Reflections, and Moons, names derived from a passage in the Nō play *Matsukaze,* "The moon is one, the reflections two, the swelling tides. . .". "Swelling" is the homonym for "three" (*mitsu*), and the passage, as applied to courtesans, came to mean that a Tide received three pieces of silver for her services, a Reflection two pieces, and a Moon only one piece. There were even poorer paid *mise-joro* in houses (*mise*), as well as streetwalkers. The prices for courtesans ranged from about $350 for a single night with a *tayū* down to about fifty cents for a night with a common *mise-joro*. Only a "great spender" (*daijin,* a homonym for a word meaning "minister of state") could afford the pleasures of a *tayū*'s company. One reason why her services came so high was that she was invariably accompanied by a Towboat (*hikifune*) of the *kakoi* rank and a courtesan's maid (*kamuro*), both of whom had to be paid for, though they did not sleep with the customer. A steady patron of a courtesan also had to reckon on innumerable tips to her house. On gift days (*mombi*) throughout the year, and especially at the New Year, costly presents had to be offered persons at the courtesan's house, including the proprietress (*kasha*) and the Chaser (*yarite*). The latter apparently served both as a procuress and guardian of the courtesans, but in Chikamatsu's plays she usually figures in the latter function, warding off unwanted guests.

Courtesans of the *mise-joro* class were generally driven into prostitution by poverty. In many of the plays a *mise-joro* is portrayed as supporting indigent parents or even working to keep her father out of a debtor's prison. The *age-joro,* on the other hand, was normally a woman long trained for her calling. At first she served as a *kamuro,* waiting on some great courtesan. Later she graduated to Launch (*shinzō*), or fledgling courtesan, and finally took her place in the hierarchy. An *age-joro* who had not previously served as a *kamuro* was known as a Debutante (*tsukidashi*).

The pleasures of the quarter frequently ruined the guests. The worst danger to a man's finances was that he might fall deeply in love with a prostitute and decide to buy her freedom. Ransom (*miuke*) involved negotiations with the proprietor of the courtesan's house and then with the owner of her contract. It was an unbelievably expensive process, judging by the figures given in the plays, for it entailed numerous tips and presents. Chūbei (in *The Courier for Hell*) scatters close to ten thousand dollars in gold (using a rough approximation of what the money would buy today) when ransoming Umegawa, a courtesan of low rank. Chikamatsu undoubtedly exaggerated the ransom for theatrical effect, but the cost by any standards was enormous.

APPENDIX II

PUPPET PERFORMANCES OF
CHIKAMATSU'S PLAYS

Chikamatsu's major works were written for the puppet theater. Many later came to be performed also by Kabuki actors, but puppet performances are still considered more authentic than those by actors. Yet the puppet theater itself has changed considerably over the years, and contemporary performances are thus only relatively more faithful than Kabuki to the works as presented in Chikamatsu's day.

The puppet theater was an invention of the late sixteenth century. At this time the three main elements were joined—the puppets (known at least five centuries earlier in Japan), the texts of the plays (derived from historical romances and other narratives), and the musical accompaniment (the samisen, a three-stringed musical instrument introduced from the Ryukyu Islands about 1570). Puppet performances in the seventeenth century, judging from surviving accounts and drawings, were extremely crude. The theaters were at first small, unroofed areas fenced in only by rough bamboo stockades, and without even a rudimentary flooring. Not until 1670 or thereabouts were performances on rainy days made possible by overhead protection. The stage was about thirty feet across, and equipped with both a curtain and a backdrop. The operators in the seventeenth century (as now) stood in trenches several feet below the level of the stage as they moved the puppets.

The puppets in use during Chikamatsu's lifetime were large hand puppets, about two and one half feet tall, operated by one man who held the puppet over his head by inserting both arms inside the skirts of the figure. The operators were at first concealed from the spectators, but the opaque curtain shielding them gave way to one of a gauzy material in 1699, and in 1703, for the final scene of *The Love Suicides at Sonezaki,* the curtain was removed altogether, permitting the operators to be seen plainly.[1]

The chanters, who sang and recited both the narration and the parts of the different characters, until the end of the seventeenth century remained out of the sight of the audience, seated behind the playing stage. But from the time of *The Love Suicides at Sonezaki,* the chanter at times appeared before the public, sitting to stage left with the samisen player who accompanied him. In 1728 the Takemoto Theater installed as a regular part of the theater a dais to stage left for the chanter and musician, and this has remained their place.

Thus, the Japanese puppet theater which originally (like Western counterparts) sought to achieve an illusion of reality by concealing both operator and narrator, in order that the audience might imagine that the puppets moved independently and spoke their lines, gradually turned its back on such realism. This may explain why the puppet theater in Japan attained a higher artistic level than similar entertainments elsewhere.

By renouncing the illusion of reality, the puppet theater was able to develop many refinements. The three-man puppet, the most notable feature of performances today, was evolved after experiments with several different types of puppets. String-operated marionettes were known in the seventeenth century, but were superseded by the puppets most common in Chikamatsu's day (operated from below, in the manner already described). Puppets which could be operated with one arm (and were thus more mobile than the two-arm variety) were tried in the early eighteenth century in an attempt to enhance the spectacular effects. A start was made on three-man puppets in 1728, and they came into general use in 1734.[2] The chief operator of the three men moves the head, body, and right arm; the second operator moves the left arm; and the third operator the feet. Coordination of the movements is extremely difficult, but the three-man puppet is capable of extraordinary subtlety of portrayal. Indeed, the puppets at times surpass actors in ther ability to suggest states of emotional agitation or exaltation; in some plays even today the Kabuki actors deliberately imitate the movements of puppets. The obvious presence of the three

---

[1] See Mori Shū, *Chikamatsu Monzaemon,* pp. 64–66.
[2] Utsumi Shigetarō, *Ningyō Jōruri to Bunraku,* p. 340.

operators, the chief of them attired in formal costume and unmasked [3] (the two assistants usually wear black hoods), never permits the reverse to happen—an attempt by the puppets to imitate Kabuki actors. Despite the demands made on the audience to blot out mentally the presence of the human intruders in the world of the puppets, a powerful dramatic effect is obtained, and the spectators enjoy seeing their favorite operators lovingly follow the puppets around the stage.

Of the three elements which make up puppet performances—the puppets, the texts, and the music—the texts are traditionally considered to be of the greatest importance. The chanters lift the texts reverently before a performance, to express their intent of interpreting them faithfully. The chanter's part is the hardest: he must be expert in speaking with the voices of men and women, old and young, often in rapid succession. The gruff muttering of a warrior is followed by a woman's gentle protestations, and then by a child's plaintive piping, all delivered with intense conviction. The chanter must also possess the vocal beauty necessary for such lyrical passages as the *michiyuki*. Sometimes several chanters divide the parts of a single scene, a young chanter taking the part of the child, an old chanter the part of an old woman, and so on, but more commonly one chanter takes all the parts of a given scene. Each chanter generally works in partnership with his favorite samisen player. In a few plays an accompaniment on an instrument other than the samisen is required, including the *koto* (a zither-like instrument) and the *kokyū* (a doleful-sounding instrument played with a bow).

For most spectators, however, the *jōruri* is above all a theater of puppets. The puppets today stand about three and one half to four feet tall (male puppets are larger and have feet). The costuming is colorful, and the sets, stylized representations of familiar scenes, are at once attractive and designed to permit maximum freedom of movement for the puppet operators. The puppets must be manipulated in

---

[3] Sometimes, as in the plate facing p. 298, all operators are hooded, either because the work is a modern adaptation or because the operators are not of the first rank. However, in the case of a great master like Bungorō (shown in plate facing p. 394) the audience derives almost as much pleasure from watching his face as it does from the puppets' movements. Another point to be noticed in the plate facing p. 298 is the operator's insertion of his own hands through the puppet's sleeves in order to hold the comb and mirror.

exact time with the chanter's words, and he in turn is guided by the samisen.

Chikamatsu's puppet plays have no stage directions in the texts, but various traditions (some perhaps dating back to the eighteenth century) are observed in the stage business (*kata*). The following passage from *Yosaku from Tamba* illustrates how the puppet for the character Shigenoi is operated by Kiritake Monjūrō, an outstanding contemporary performer.

SHIGENOI: Now here you are. You're only a child, I know, but you're the heir of a disgraced father, and I'm worried what may happen if they find you out. (*She strokes Sankichi's right shoulder.*) Never tell anyone that you're Yosaku's child. (*Her voice suggests that she is whispering the words into Sankichi's ear; all the while, however, she is looking from right to left, from one end of the stage to the other, as if to make sure that no one can hear them. She looks into Sankichi's face. Suddenly her emotions overpower her, and she draws him to her lap. She weeps, only to push him away and rise.*) Hurry outside now. (*Sankichi remains crouching helplessly on the floor in tears. She takes his hands and lifts him in her arms, only again to reject him, this time resolutely. She stands and moves stage left.*) Ahhh— (*she glances towards the rear, the quarters of her mistress*) what did I ever do to deserve such a fate? (*She turns stage right towards her child.*) To have my own child (*points with her left hand at Sankichi*) become a horse driver, and not to know where my husband is. (*Points into the distance.*) What use is it to wear fine clothes (*lifts her right and then her left sleeve, and looks at each; then she rearranges the hanging part of the sleeves, as if to assert her dignity*), to be addressed respectfully as madam governess, milady in waiting (*moves her head by degrees from stage left to stage right*), or to ride in a splendid palanquin? (*She swings her sleeves from right to left in irritation; but, suddenly remembering that the robe was a present from her ladyship and should not be treated so roughly, she lifts the right sleeve of the garment reverently over her head for a moment, only to lower it. Fearful that the sound of her weeping may be overheard, she stuffs the sleeve into her mouth and lowers her gaze in grief.*) [4]

This climactic moment, when Shigenoi bites her sleeve to stifle her sobs, is heightened by the prolonged notes of the chanter's voice and the sharp accents of the samisen. The elaborate stage business sug-

[4] These stage directions are derived from the article by Yoshinaga Takao, "Ningyō no Enshutsu ni tsuite," in *Kaishaku to Kanshō*, XXII (no. 1), 45.

gests how much is lost when we read, rather than see, Chikamatsu's plays. We can only hope that the puppet theater, faced by public indifference and financial problems, will somehow survive, so that one of the world's great dramatists may continue to be seen under the circumstances which do him the most justice.

BIBLIOGRAPHY

I have appended brief comments to the Japanese books listed, in the hope that they may be helpful to Western scholars intending to consult them.

TEXTS

Fujii Otoo. *Chikamatsu Zenshū.* 12 vols. 1925–28. A great piece of scholarship and the standard text of Chikamatsu's complete works, but of limited use to Western readers because of the paucity of notes.

Higuchi Yoshichiyo. *Kessaku Jōruri Shū: Chikamatsu Jidai* (in *Hyōshaku Edo Bungaku Sōsho* series). 1935. Helpful and fairly detailed comments on twelve plays given in full or in part.

Itō Masao. *Shinjū Ten no Amijima Shōkai.* 1935. The best commentary and modern Japanese translation of a single play by Chikamatsu.

Kawatake Shigetoshi. *Gendaigoyaku Chikamatsu Meisaku Shū.* 2 vols. 1938. Translations into modern Japanese of fourteen plays. Often helpful, but the *michiyuki* and other complex passages are not translated.

Kuroba Hideo. *Chikamatsu Meisaku Shinkō.* 1957. Detailed commentaries and translations into modern Japanese of five plays. The translations are sometimes mistaken and often misleading.

Shigetomo Ki. *Chikamatsu Jōruri Shū,* I (in *Nihon Koten Bungaku Taikei* series). 1958. Admirable texts and good (though somewhat skimpy) notes on fourteen domestic plays. Now the standard texts for the plays included.

Shuzui Kenji, and Ōkubo Tadakuni. *Chikamatsu Jōruri Shū,* II (in *Nihon Koten Bungaku Taikei* series). 1959. Admirable texts but inadequate notes on six history plays and the preface to *Naniwa Miyage.*

————, and Urayama Masao. *Chikamatsu Meisaku Hyōkai.* 1949. Useful notes and translations into modern Japanese of *Sonezaki Shinjū* and *Nebiki no Kadomatsu.*

Tadami Keizō. *Chikamatsu Jōruri Shū* (in *Yūhōdō Bunko* series). 3 vols. 1926. Texts are punctuated and the speakers indicated, but the notes on these forty-two plays are grossly inadequate. Useful now mainly for plays not found in editions with commentaries.

Takano Masami. *Chikamatsu Monzaemon Shū* (in *Nihon Koten Zensho* series). 3 vols. 1950–52. Texts of nineteen plays with fairly detailed notes.

—— *Chikamatsu Monzaemon Shū* (in *Koten Nihon Bungaku Zenshū* series). 1959. Translations into modern Japanese of thirteen plays. The translations are generally free.

Wakatsuki Yasuji. *Zen'yaku Chikamatsu Kessaku Shū.* 3 vols. 1928–30. Extremely helpful and honest translations into modern Japanese plus useful notes on twenty-four domestic plays. Still indispensable, despite more recent commentaries.

SECONDARY WORKS

Barth, Johannes. "Kagekiyo. Eine Betrachtung zum japanischen historischen Schauspiel." Deutschen Gesellschaft für Natur- und Völkerkunde Ostasiens, *Jubiläumsband,* I (1933), 299–329.

Brenan, Gerald. *The Literature of the Spanish People.* New York, Meridian Books, 1957.

Chikamatsu Kenkyūkai, ed. *Chikamatsu Monzaemon.* 1956. Essays, mainly introductory, plus some bibliographical information.

Engeki Kenkyūkai, ed. *Chikamatsu no Kenkyū to Shiryō.* 1959. A small but valuable collection of essays and source materials.

Fergusson, Francis. *The Idea of a Theater.* Garden City, N.Y., Doubleday, 1949.

Harvey, Paul, ed. *The Oxford Companion to English Literature,* Oxford, Clarendon Press, 1946.

Hibbett, Howard. *The Floating World in Japanese Fiction.* New York, Oxford University Press, 1959.

Higuchi Yoshichiyo. *Chikamatsu Kō.* 1955. Themes in Chikamatsu's writings illustrated by excerpts from the plays. Somewhat old-fashioned in approach, but unquestionably the product of a profound knowledge of the texts.

Hirosue Tamotsu. *Chikamatsu Josetsu.* 1957. A stimulating but sometimes doctrinaire left-wing approach.

Katō Junzō. *Chikamatsu Shishō no Kenkyū.* 1926. Still the best work on Chikamatsu's style.

Kawatake Shigetoshi. *Chikamatsu Monzaemon.* 1958. A popular introduction to Chikamatsu's life and views.

———— *Nihon Engeki Zenshi.* 1959. A mine of information on all aspects of the Japanese theater.

Keene, Donald, ed. *Anthology of Japanese Literature.* New York, Grove Press, 1955.

———— *The Battles of Coxinga.* London, Taylor's Foreign Press, 1951.

Kitani Hōgin. *Chikamatsu no Tennō Geki.* 1947. Chikamatsu's "emperor plays" classified and described; a product of the postwar "humanization."

Kuroki Kanzō. *Chikamatsu Monzaemon.* 1942. Mainly devoted to summaries of the chief plays, but contains some valuable essays.

McCullough, H. C., trans. *The Taiheiki.* New York, Columbia University Press, 1959.

Maejima Shunzō. *Chikamatsu Kenkyū no Johen.* 1925. Advanced for its time, but now largely superseded.

Mashimo Saburō. "Chikamatsu no Sakuhin ni mirareru Joseigo," *Kokugo to Kokubungaku,* October, 1959. An important study of women's language in Chikamatsu.

Minamoto Ryōen. "Chikamatsu ni okeru Ai to Shi," *Kokoro,* June, 1960. A student of philosophy examines themes in Chikamatsu.

Miyamori, Asataro. *Masterpieces of Chikamatsu.* London, Kegan Paul, 1926.

Mori Shū. *Chikamatsu Monzaemon.* 1959. The best book on Chikamatsu; unqualifiedly recommended.

Morris, Ivan. "Hierarchy of Lust in 17th Century Japan," *Today's Japan,* August, 1960.

Nakada Yasunao. "Chikamatsu to Chōnin no Sekai," *Kokugo to Kokubungaku,* January, 1955. An interesting study of the background of the plays.

Nakamura Kichizō. *Nihon Gikyoku Gikō Ron.* 1942. Analysis by a student of Western drama of the structures and techniques of plays by Chikamatsu and later men.

Ōkubo Tadakuni. *Chikamatsu* (in *Nihon Koten Kanshō Kōza* series). 1957. Extracts with notes from six plays, plus a number of good essays.

Sanari Kentarō. *Yōkyoku Taikan.* 7 vols. 1931. The standard work.

Sansom, G. B. "The *Tsuredzuregusa* of Yoshida no Kaneyoshi," Asiatic Society of Japan, *Transactions,* XXXIX, 1911.

Seo Fukiko. "Chikamatsu ni okeru Nōminteki naru mono," *Bungaku,* July, 1951. Stiffly written but well documented study of the "peasant mentality" in Chikamatsu's plays.

Sheldon, Charles David. *Rise of the Merchant Class in Tokugawa Japan.* Locust Valley, N.Y., J. J. Augustin, 1958.

Shigetomo Ki, ed. *Chikamatsu no Hitobito.* 1950. Essays of uneven interest, the best being one by Tanabe Yukio on the character of Chūbei.

Shinoda Jun'ichi. "Shusse Kagekiyo no Seiritsu ni tsuite," *Kokugo Kokubun,* June, 1959. Brilliant analysis of the background and structure of Chikamatsu's important early play.

Shively, Donald H. "Chikamatsu's Satire on the Dog Shogun," *Harvard Journal of Asiatic Studies,* XXVIII (1955), 159–80.

—— *The Love Suicide at Amijima.* Cambridge, Harvard University Press, 1953.

Shuzui Kenji. *Chikamatsu Monzaemon.* 1949. A general introduction.

—— *Giri.* 1941. An interesting essay on the manner in which *giri* is treated by Chikamatsu and later playwrights.

Statler, Oliver. *Japanese Inn.* New York, Random House, 1961.

Takano Masami. "Chikamatsu Sakuhin no Bunruihō," *Kokugo to Kokubungaku,* March, 1948. A useful guide to the classification of Chikamatsu's plays.

Takano Tatsuyuki. *Nihon Engeki no Kenkyū.* 1921. Valuable essays by a great scholar.

—— *Nihon Engeki Shi,* III. 1949. Unexciting but thorough.

Tanamachi Tomomi. "Chikamatsu Kenkyū Bunken Mokuroku," *Kaishaku to Kanshō,* January, 1957. The best bibliography of Chikamatsu studies. Particularly useful because of its evaluations.

Tjikamats, Monzâemon. *Dramatische Verhalen,* translated into Dutch by S. van Praag. Santpoort, C. A. Mees, 1927.

Tsunoda, Ryusaku, *et al. Sources of the Japanese Tradition.* New York, Columbia University Press, 1958.

Ueda Mannen, and Higuchi Yoshichiyo. *Chikamatsu Go-i.* 1930. Universally praised but maddening work. One loses so much time consulting it that the information gained seldom seems worth the trouble. Mercifully now largely superseded.

Utsumi Shigetarō. *Ningyō Jōruri to Bunraku.* 1958. Emphasizes the importance of puppets in *jōruri.* Long and diffuse.

—— *Ningyō Shibai to Chikamatsu no Jōruri.* 1940. Much in the same vein as the preceding, but more engrossing.

Wakatsuki Yasuji. *Chikamatsu Ningyō Jōruri no Kenkyū.* 1936. A massive study, full of useful information.

—— *Ningyō Jōruri Shi Kenkyū.* 1942. Probably the best history of the *jōruri.*

Waley, Arthur. *The Nō Plays of Japan.* New York, Knopf, 1922.

Watsuji Tetsurō. *Nihon Geijutsu Shi Kenkyū,* I. 1955. A scholarly work by an outstanding authority.

Yokoyama Tadashi. "Chikamatsu Michiyuki Zakkō," *Kokugo Kokubun*, September, 1940. This and the following three articles are careful studies of specific features of Chikamatsu's writings.

────── "Chikamatsu no Maruhon," *Kaishaku to Kanshō*, January, 1957.

────── "Chikamatsu Shinjū Jōruri no Tenkai," *Kokugo to Kokubungaku*, May, 1958.

────── "Chikamatsu Shoki Shinjū Jōruri ni okeru Bōto Hyōgen," *Kokugo to Kokubungaku*, October, 1958.

Yoshinaga Takao. "Ningyō no Enshutsu ni tsuite," *Kaishaku to Kanshō*, January, 1957. Valuable especially for the detailed account of a present-day production of a scene from *Tamba Yosaku*.

Yuda Yoshio. "Chikamatsu Nempyō," *Kaishaku to Kanshō*, January, 1957. The best chronology of Chikamatsu.

────── "Sonezaki Shinjū no Kabukiteki Kiban" (in Kansai Daigaku Kokubungakkai: *Shimada Kyōju Koki Kinen Kokubungaku Ronshū*, ed. by Iida Shōichi and others, 1960). Excellent account of Kabuki precedents for Chikamatsu's famous play.